目录

文章

004　无法呈现的呈现 | 夏季风
006　工作坊：策展人是如何工作的——兼为《艺术与投资》创刊四周年而写 | 左靖
010　做艺术是我的工作 | 卢迎华
012　工作中的艺术家 | 董冰峰
014　艺术家是如何工作的？ | 苏文祥

图版（艺术家、作品、问卷）

030　董文胜
038　何云昌
048　蒋志
058　金石
068　李超
076　李景湖
084　李明
092　梁硕
104　李郁/刘波
114　卢征远
124　马秋莎
132　邱黯雄
140　石青
148　苏文祥
156　孙建春
164　汤艺
172　屠宏涛
180　王光乐
188　王宁德
196　邬建安
204　吴俊勇
212　吴小军
220　杨俊
228　张耿豪华
236　章清
244　赵要
252　赵赵
260　周啸虎

艺术家简历

CONTENTS

ARTICLE

016   A Presentation of the Unpresentable | Xia Jifeng

018   Work in Progress: How Do Curators Work? - On the 4th Anniversary of *Art and Investment* | Zuo Jing

022   Art Making Is My Profession | Carol Yinghua Lu

024   Artist at Work | Dong Bingfeng

026   In What Way Does the Artist Work? | Su Wenxiang

PLATES (Artists, Works and Questionaires)

031   Dong Wensheng

039   He Yunchang

054   Jiang Zhi

064   Jin Shi

069   Li Chao

078   Li Jinghu

086   Li Ming

096   Liang Shuo

109   Li Yu & Liu Bo

117   Lu Zhengyuan

128   Ma Qiusha

134   Qiu Anxiong

143   Shi Qing

150   Su Wenxiang

158   Sun Jianchun

166   Tang Yi

174   Tu Hongtao

185   Wang Guangle

192   Wang Ningde

197   Wu Jian'an

207   Wu Junyong

214   Wu Xiaojun

223   Jun Yang

230   Chang Kenghau&Chang Genghwa

239   Zhang Qing

246   Zhao Yao

253   Zhao Zhao

262   Zhou Xiaohu

BIOGRAPHY

无法呈现的呈现

夏季风

艺术家是如何工作的？在我看来，这是一个挑逗他人窥探欲望同时在实践中无法解决的命题：在艺术家的作品中，工作过程的每一步总是不断地会被作品的前进所背叛，作品本身的最终完成，实际上意味着对之前创作过程的覆盖和抹灭。即便艺术家有意留下工作札记或创作手稿，甚至于身边放置一台摄像机，忠实而完整地记录下整个工作过程，也终究对业已完成的作品说明不了什么问题。这么说的意思是，作品的完成仅靠可见的工作行为来证明是难以成立的，艺术家和作品之间的关系，就像是巫术中的通灵，彼此心性的转移，隐秘而难以言说。从理论上来讲，似乎没有一种途径能有效地解决艺术家工作中的秘密。

但是，艺术家工作中的秘密是不是存在着某种可能触及的"边界"？我认为是可以探究和值得一试的。正如《当代艺术与投资》三年来所做的，杂志邀请了近30位极具实验性和创作力的年轻艺术家，在"工作坊"栏目中，对看起来无法呈现的工作秘密做了有意思的呈现——至少艺术家个体在观念思考、创作实验以及艺术生产过程中的种种可能性，最大限度地作了表现。至于对秘密"边界"企及的深浅程度，则另当别论。尽管如此，但问题依然接踵而来，作于一本杂志或者说杂志中的一个栏目，到底能为艺术家如何工作的过程，提供多大程度的揭密平台？杂志自身的局限性，会不会又成为艺术家呈现工作秘密的另一种"边界"？

因此，对这个有趣的、自我相悖的命题，作深入的调查和研究显得非常有必要。另一方面，也出于对过去杂志中纸本"工作坊"栏目的延伸与回应，我们决定继续邀请栏目中的艺术家，参与到"工作坊：艺术家是如何工作的"展览中来。或许，从杂志纸面的、扁平化的形式到立体空间式的呈现，尤其是随着艺术家工作观念形态与物质特性的改变，我们可能会发现他们的工作秘密进一步被拓展了边界。

我们知道，这同样是一次无法呈现的呈现。陶渊明说"弱女虽非男，慰情聊胜无"，梁启超又说"用自鞭策，得寸得尺，聊胜于无"，仿佛都能成为这个不可能休止的命题的最好注脚。

2009-11-18

工作坊：策展人是如何工作的
兼为《艺术与投资》创刊四周年而写

左靖

"工作坊：艺术家是如何工作的"，这个展览真正的缘起，是在2006年底的杭州，受我的好友，也是《艺术与投资》杂志的总编夏季风之命，我和卢迎华开始编辑一本名为《当代艺术与投资》的杂志（作为前者的副刊）。为了便于大家理解一本杂志的诞生和我们最初的想法，这里不妨引用我在"发刊词"《一年前和半个月》中的一段话：

"对于我们这些从1980年代走过来的人，往往喜欢把结社和办杂志当作自己的最大梦想。今天看来，办杂志，特别是办艺术杂志，这种向可能的公众传达有关艺术的各种想法的古老方式，在我们这个时代遭遇到了自身和外在的巨大压力——比如，因为探讨一些小众话题而造成的自我的边缘化，因为其他传媒的成本低廉、信息快捷而失去原有优势所引发的生存危机，或者因为投资方的兴趣转移而面临朝不保夕的尴尬处境。在过去的日子里，我们看到了太多太多这样的艺术杂志的生生灭灭。"

很显然，这本杂志是我们1980年代的杂志梦在现实中的达成，也就是说，它带有很强烈的同仁色彩(时至今日，我们羞于使用"理想"这个词)。当然，我们并没有放弃构建一个所谓纸本的"当代艺术生态链"的想法。在最初的栏目设置中，"注目"，作为杂志最重要的专题栏目，我们关注的是艺术界（很少美术界）最新的动向，我们选择的依据是趣味；"个案"栏目[1]关注的是重要艺术家不同时期的作品,并试图清理出它们在历时性创作过程中的上下文关系；"工作坊"栏目着重介绍年轻艺术家的创作，呈现其创作思路和作品；"概念"栏目则是出示艺术家的手稿、笔记、草图、方案，也就是说，一切尚在概念之中——这是一种对所期待之物的提前探视；"策展"栏目是为策展人开辟的空间，计划是每期详细介绍一个策划人的策展理念，有时会包括策展手记（日记）、与艺术家的交流记录、实施展览过程中可能出现的问题，或者干脆就是在纸上虚拟一个展览；"空间"栏目每期选取一个独立艺术空间，叙述其主要活动、学术方向和运作模式；"小组"栏目则着重推介一个独立艺术组织，介绍其主要人物和活动内容；"影像"栏目主要表明我们对中国独立电影的特别关注等等。

另外，我们有一个特邀编委会。三年来，特邀编委中的绝大多数同仁为杂志做了很多实际的工作，而不是仅仅只是挂一个名字。值得一提的是，他们来自美术、设计、建筑、电影、音乐、舞蹈、哲学、文学等不同领域，美术圈中的人极少，从中大家不难发现我们对当代艺术"话语生产"的理解。我们一直认为，这种生产必须建立在一个跨领域，或者说是一种越界的"知识共同体"的氛围之中。当然，时代在更迭，我们没有天真到把办刊的实际行动还停留在1980年代的状态中。我们相信，围绕着它所构建的不断变化着的生态链必然会有着太多的可能发生——能量始终在一点点积聚，总会有引发它们的机缘。

2007年3月，由卢迎华建议，姚嘉善策划的"假的！"展览开始盯上了这本杂志。把一本杂志做成展览通常都会有的"画册"替代品并不是件新鲜的事情。关键在于，"假的！"这个展览探讨的是"当代艺术中复制、造假和伪造的问题"。那么，一切开始变得有意思起来：能否把一期杂志变成"虚构"的杂志？姚嘉善和她的参展艺术家们展开了讨论，并把讨论付诸了实施——用各种文章探讨有关真实和虚构的艺术/哲学问题，也就是说，把真假杂陈的内容编辑到这本杂志中并让这些内容进行文本上的"自我指涉"或者相互指涉，进而揭示所谓的"真相"。于是，2007年第4期杂志上就有了"假的"文章（讨论一个完全虚构的问题）、假的广告（洪浩、徐震经常使用的方式）、假的展览(发生在北京的一个并不存在的酒店里)、假的消息(李青受委托赴英国为女王造像)……在这里，杂志成了一个与艺术家、批评家的创作进行互文的实验性空间。这是《当代艺术与投资》迄今为止最有意思和最不寻常的一期。

2008年4月，伊比利亚当代艺术中心成立，于是有了由杂志"个案"栏目所派生的第一个展览"趣味的共同体——伊比利亚当代艺术中心开幕展"，在同名的文章中，在提到这个展览与杂志的关系之后，我写道：

"在杂志的'编辑思想'里，我们试图说明，这本杂志展示的是作为'现在时'的实验性的、跨界性的当代艺术生产。在我们奢侈的愿望中，杂志应该努力挣脱传统所赋予它的定义，使它的'本质'游离而成为一个开放性的能动主体。也就是说，它不仅仅是一本冷冰冰的仅供人翻检的纸媒体，而应该是一种通过展览、活动、出版，以及建立在其上的各种可能的建构。因此，我们不妨把这个展览称之为一次'杂志-策展实践'。"[②]

由此可见，这次的"工作坊"展览是又一次的"杂志-策展实践"（2010年的"纸上美术馆"展览将成为第三次"杂志-策展实践"）。与"趣味的共同体"不同的是，后者被我称之为在学术性展览和商业性展览之外的"第三种展览"模式，正如有人后来具体指陈的那样，"（趣味共同体的）主展、独立影像单元和西班牙艺术家单元不是很恰当的组合在一起，但又可以分别说明伊比利亚当代艺术中心的影响力、学术追求和机构背景。"坦率地说，我非常希望能把"工作坊"展览做成一个学术性展览。作为"当代艺术生态链"的重要一环，相比"个案"中出现的重要艺术家所代表的"现在"，"工作坊"里的艺术家年轻而更富于锐气，无限的可能性已经在他们面前展开，事实上，他们代表了中国当代艺术的"未来"。但是，如果把杂志三年来介绍的30位艺术家的作品凑合起来的话，这个展览显然又会成为一个让人提不起来胃口的大杂烩。这些天来，像一个不太负责任的策展人通常所做的那样，我花了几个小时浏览了三年来"工作坊"栏目中出现的艺术家作品和文字介绍，随手记下了我的碎片式的第一观感，"邱黯雄——对涉及东西方文化问题的思考，追溯古代文献；周啸虎——临时雕塑，对公众以及对社会的干涉，自动写作（摄影）；章清——个人历险和社会干预，"中立"角度；刘波、李郁——搬演，带有个人趣味的社会关注；蒋志——暴力与控制，光的隐喻，有意的"事件纪念"；何云昌——个人历险，时间与忍耐；石青——历史想象和对宏大叙事的思考，从古代文献出发；吴俊勇——马戏团，幽默，性与政治；李永斌——时间；马秋莎——身体；李明——日常经验；杨俊——对想象的研究；董文胜——江南美学；苏文祥——对机器"主体性"的强迫性研究；孙建春——个人趣味与社会学采样；汤艺——语言自虐狂和科学迷；王光乐——作为玄学的绘画；李景湖——从平凡之物开始（无意义）/权力思考（有意义）；邬建安——造型与材料，民间造型语言的运用；梁硕——艺术本体／有意义无意义之辩；张耿豪华——互动；李超——视角主义的视觉实践；金石——艺术语言+底层政治；吴小军——事件性……"

然后，难道我们就像往常那样，按部就班，把上述的内容分析、归纳，提炼出主题，分解成不同单元？——显然，这不是我们所想要的。那么，如果从艺术家的创作思路、创作方法以及创作过程这个角度出发呢？——把最后呈现的作品放在一个相对次要的位置，着重展示一件作品的实现过程——精神的（通过物质材料实现）、物质的；或者是一位艺术家历时性创作的上下文关系的呈现，即通过一系列的作品来展示创作的方法与观念的内在演进过程，包括一贯性的，或断裂的过程；再或者是，像巫鸿先生所做的"张洹工作室"个案研究那样，从对艺术家"工作坊"的整体结构的功能性研究出发，进而呈现艺术家在创作中的多种机制和模式，并通过这种呈现来讨论艺术家与艺术品的关系……于是就有了展览的副标题"艺术家是如何工作的"，展览的可能性也开始变得越来越丰富。但是，我们马上遇到了新的问题——如何完成一个"艺术家是如何工作的"的视觉展示？就像爱森斯坦当年声称要把《资本论》拍成电影，如何拍摄？我明白，我们选择了去完成一件不可能完成的任务。

创作手记？创作流程？失败之作？废稿？草图？方案？照片？访谈？那么，又必须通过什么方式把它们串联成一条可供辨识的整体线索？或者，展示经过选择后的作品系列，并提示它们之间的逻辑关系？我们的目的，是完成研究资料的汇集，还是研究成果的呈现（这次可能吗）？会不会形式大于内容？是不是"去视觉化"了？又一个"文献展"？如何编辑图录？如何布展？我们呈现了一个怎样的"当代艺术的未来"？我们会在何种程度上接受因为时间仓促等原因而把一个如此具有开创性的展览推向失败深渊的结果？或者，我们终于愿意放低姿态，开始研习修辞术来与别人展开辩论？——这些命中注定会出现的问题，以及艺术家的个人性和私密性、艺术创作过程中的多变性和不可预见性都使得这个展览看起来怎么都像是一场无法预知结果的挑战和冒险。以上的种种考虑，既有学术的，又有政治的。我们只有等待这个时刻的到来，并希望最终会有人来清理这个战场，得到大家所期待的认识的东西。

最后，我想说明的是，之所以在文章的前半部分回顾了一些跟"工作坊"展览无关的杂志二三事，一方面是想告诉大家，这本杂志在完成自身的任务之外，还有哪些可能性存在；另一方面，值此杂志创刊四周年（《当代艺术与投资》杂志创刊三周年）之际，有关杂志也好，有关展览也罢，我愿意做一篇小小的自供状。

2009-11-15

---

① 2009年第1期开始由新任执行主编董冰峰将之更名为"纸上美术馆"，内容也开始改为每位艺术家由一位策展人策划的体例，着重介绍艺术家的最新进行的项目与其创作思考的重要线索，并着力呈现文本和图像的视觉立体关系。

②文中我还提到了"杂志-出版实践"，在《当代艺术与投资》创刊三周年之际，由杂志析出的若干栏目的内容，经过编辑计有近10本，以"伊比利亚系列图书"为名将由新星出版社于明年春节前出版。

做艺术是我的工作

卢迎华

在一次闲聊之中，作家韩东的出版人楚尘描述了韩东的工作方法，他说韩东写小说总是先写完第一稿，打印出一份纸稿，然后把电子文档从电脑中删掉，对照着打印的文稿在电脑上重新写一次，再打印出一份书稿，再删除第二个电子文稿，再重写，如此反复三至四遍，才能最终定稿。一篇将近三十万字的小说也要按照此法重复书写三次。·如此把自己逼到绝境，不留任何退路，才得到如此凝练的文字。了解这个创作上的细节对于体会他的作品非常重要，虽然诸多对于韩东的小说的关注和赞赏聚焦在其小说的内容之上，但实际上作者最富于创造性和魅力的地方在于其小说的结构和情节的设计以及被反复推敲后高度简洁准确而充满质感的语言。无独有偶，美国观念大师John Baldessari曾经亲手将他所有"成功的作品"摧毁掉，重新再来。归零，再开始。居住在瑞典马尔默的美国艺术家Alison Gerber展开了一项历时三年的社会调查，运用经典的社会学研究方法来开发一套介定艺术家的"劳动"的评估系统，并出版了一本手册，帮助人们了解在艺术家的工作之中"创造性"和"事务性"的"劳动"之间的区分和组合。

这里涉及到对艺术家这一职业的认识的问题。虽然是从事一项带有创造性的工作，但"做艺术"既不是一种姿态，也不是一种身份，它包含了"至高的目标和基本的要求"。这个基本的要求包括了艺术家各方面的职业素质：知识、技法、智力、方法论、态度、嗅觉、恒心、勤奋和正直的品德。艺术作为一个至高的目标同时也建立在整个艺术系统里各个角色细致入微和专业的工作，包括很多基础性的工作，从画廊的助手，美术馆的门卫到运输公司和博览会的组织者，不可或缺。在任何时候，艺术家的作品都是主角，但往往主角的出场和传播又离不开艺术系统中各种关系和力量的支持。必须意识到的是艺术家这一职业所需要和占用的社会资源是巨大的。

了解艺术家是怎样工作的是一个"去神话"的过程，这似乎和某些艺术家力求树立的公共形象和工作的动机背道而驰。曾经有一位知名的艺术家这样比喻艺术家的工作，他从地面捡起一块普普通通的石子，直言道艺术就是将这个石子用金箔一层一层地包裹起来，直到人们不再能够辨别其石子的本质，而以为它是一块金子为止。这个信念也成为该艺术家工作的主旨和核心，不惜代价地围绕着树立其"大师"的地位和传播"神话"而工作。这也构成了一种艺术家工作的类型，为自己的艺术身份和创作塑造语境，争取主动性。分析艺术家的工作要求认识艺术创作的多样性以及辨别艺术家创作的类型，这个艺术家的艺术是以什么为支撑和驱动的：是他的制作水准和媒介还是他的观念和理论？是他对于艺术系统的认识和分析还是他对于艺术家身份的不断叩问？是对社会现实的关怀和反思还是对自身存在与日常的检验和游戏？是他长期的实践还是一些物化的标志？是迎合艺术创作的规则还是挑衅艺术行业的规则？艺术家如何描述他的工作？透露多少细节？揭示多少秘密？对于这些界限的斟酌和把握也是艺术家如何看待他的工作和如何工作的一种揭示。

不仅仅看到艺术家最终呈现出来的"成品",而是试图与艺术家一起共同讨论和分析其工作的方式方法和方向不是抵消或轻视艺术家的身份和工作,而是建立起认识艺术家创作的多元化桥梁和框架,取消对于艺术创作悬念的迷恋和对于结果的过度强调,也是提倡对于"过程"的重视和对多种类型的创作的甄别和开拓不同的了解和描述创作的方法。有的艺术家的创作恰恰在过程之中显现其意义的,有的艺术家的创作需要通过一个相当长的时间段的沉淀和发酵和积累了一定的数量才得以发挥作用。将艺术家的创作作为一项工作来讨论和呈现使了解艺术家的创作有了除去解读意义和直观的视觉感受之外的可能性。思考、技法、技术含量、理论基础、规范和职业感等等也可以被纳入讨论和思考的范围。

对于在艺术领域中工作的所有人,包括艺术家和策展人或批评家而言,认识到艺术作为一项工作这个务实的态度是必备的。它帮助也要求我们在面对艺术家的作品的时候,能够通过多个途径来形成一个全面的认识,也不局限于借助单一的标准来作出判断和衡量。了解一个艺术家是如何工作的:他日常的工作方法、工作习惯、他的工作场所、他的教育背景、他所接受的家庭影响和启蒙影响、他阅读的广度和深度、他的旅行、他的性格和兴趣、他的交往、他的消费习惯、他对自己艺术家身份的认识和塑造、具体到他的素材的来源、他的美学修养、他的创作过程、他使用的器材、他所关注的问题、他的思考的惯性、艺术生产的方式、销售的渠道、展览的场所、他在权力榜上的排名、他合作的画廊、他的收藏记录、他的公众形象等等,都构成了他的创作的丰富的语境和他者进入他的思考的渠道和与之对话的可能。

当然,艺术既然是一项专业的工作,它就需要专业的标准和同行的衡量。但目前中国的艺术行业里却面临着一个尴尬的现状:艺术行业里缺乏独立的、专业人士的衡量,而充斥的是混淆了标准的,处于各种勾结关系之中的相互吹捧。这种专门从事吹捧的专业人士是不可靠的,他所建立起来的标准也是很值得质疑的,往往本末倒置。另一个被赋予了不恰当甚至是有危害性的普遍标准是市场和销售的成果,有没有广泛的购买群体本不是衡量艺术创作的标准。但在这里,很多时候,艺术思考的质量和艺术家的重要性却与艺术家的市场普及度混为一谈,而实际上仅仅依赖这个标准的艺术创作和活动是单一而且无益的。建立一个健康的、多元的、允许独立声音的、民主化的、以学术为重而不是以销售和权力为重的艺术生态成为确保艺术家能够独立和深入地展开工作的一个关键的前提。艺术的专业化不仅是对于艺术家的挑战,也是批评家和艺术系统所共同承担的责任。

---

① 《这种文学》,韩东,2009-05-18,"韩东博客" http://blog.sina.com.cn/s/blog_4fe548220100cx0s.html~type=v5_one&label=rela_prevarticle

工作中的艺术家

董冰峰

今天，艺术家仍然在"工作"吗？

这是一个看起来非常含混、而且充满悖论的问题。当然，我们讨论的范围仍然是局限在"当代艺术"的概念。即便这个概念在今天变得非常陈旧、官腔十足和极具保守意味，但也没更合适的词汇来取代它了。

对于那些越来越迅速成长的中国年轻一代艺术家而言，坚决拥护与思考日常生活和大众文化：一个时刻处在动态过程中的背景；或干脆停止"工作"，取消艺术与现实之间的关联，这就随时可保持思考的敏锐与新鲜度。这些举措听起来非常遥远且乌托邦，但远比当代艺术在中国落地早期所承负的"前卫"和"实验"理想的那一代所显示出宏大的社会责任，或"地下艺术"这样浓厚意识形态色彩的样式来的轻易、简单而真实。事实上，年轻一代艺术家所信奉的是自由、新的身份与无障碍的交流。

与真实的现实相似，中国每日都会涌现出新的艺术观点及不同的创作形态，既非全然拿来西方、也非传统中国理念的简单现代版延伸，而是一种试图超越现存的博物馆规则、逆转市场的狭隘定义及固有批评范畴所无法容纳的"新艺术"，呈现出一种奇妙的混合性。布莱顿·泰勒在《当代艺术》中指出，这种迹象出现的年代按照全球艺术发展态势可以廓划为1999至2004年，但在中国，实际发生的时间要更晚些，部分缘由则是：90年代个体艺术家的鲜明反叛特征被急促赶至的高度消费市场时代所飞速消解、取代；与此同时，更具讽刺意味的是，更多的被市场机遇影响的艺术家纷纷创立了规模化的"工作室"；仅以北京为例，保守估算，不计算每年几千名处在不断流动中的、独立的艺术家工作室约有上万个。全球日益成长对中国当代艺术的浓厚兴趣，在过去几年中经济衰退并未明显时，曾经达到一个狂热的高潮。

这在某些方面确实阻碍了"严肃的思考艺术"的步伐继续前行，以至于每一严肃的展事或作品的产生，都不得不主动迎合流行文化的主体特征或消费潮流的惯用语汇，使其更容易被广泛的受众所理解和接受，不至成为"空中楼阁"。

今天，当代艺术在中国的概念也从未这样丰富、混淆与令人费解，在脱离了可能承载的人文、精神性诉求后，变得完全娱乐化，倾注在无休止的"制造景观"中，从而组成中国高速发展的社会符号中的某一类角色。几乎完全分野的官方协会、艺术院校、全球资本构造的商业画廊或绝对意义上的边缘群落，都宣称自己拥有纯粹的"当代艺术"观点和判断。同时，期待看到"当代艺术"成为文化产业政策中的重要链条或彰显开放的全球信号（除去必要保持的题材禁区外）的政府，成为强力的推动者；对于普通公众来说，近年中"中国当代艺术"所引发的市场狂潮，那些成百倍、千倍上涨或跳跃的数字使人眼花缭乱，谁会严肃考虑其表现的真正内涵所在？ 一切看起来在所难免。

在今天，艺术家如何开始工作？
这似乎是个好问题。

2009-11-15

那些成百倍、千倍上涨或跳跃的数字使人眼花缭乱，谁会严肃考虑其表现的真正内涵所在？ 一切看起来在所难免。

在今天，艺术家如何开始工作？
这似乎是个好问题。

艺术家是如何工作的？

苏文祥

艺术家是如何工作的？这是艺术研究者们都会共同关注的话题，甚至于还有更普通的对艺术抱有兴趣的人群。不光艺术史家们的著书立说，艺术家的自传自述等出版物，各个美术馆画廊等艺术机构也都通过它们的教育与推广活动极力的向人们推荐行销——它们所选择的艺术家是如何创造性的工作并生存。不管它们各自怀着何种目的，人们几乎都在做着殊途同归的事情。因为对于艺术这样看起来神秘的未知事物，人们报有强烈的好奇心，包括对从事它的艺术家们。其实，与其说人们对于艺术家的工作如何抱有兴趣，毋宁说人们对某种物品在这些特殊的人的手里如何成为艺术品有着强烈地探究的心愿。

我们都知道如果一直用单一的目光关注世界，那肯定会造成缺憾。如果一直用一种方式关注艺术，势必也会同样如此。然而，在人们既有的理解艺术的概念和经验中，特别是参观展览的时候。人们只拥有对某一个艺术创作的结果进行考察和探究的权利，展览图录——其实那更像是一本成果汇报书。因而很难知其所以然。

艺术家究竟是如何工作的？我们不能不说，现有的展览体制并不能很好的反映和揭示这一问题，相反有时甚至是阻隔和屏蔽了人们对于艺术家工作的理解。因为更多的展览展出的只是一个艺术家某项工作的结果，对于艺术家是如何产生这一结果依然是一无所知。一段时间内业内人士甚至形成一个共识，了解一个艺术家的最好的方式也许是去参观他的个展。而群展的可看性则大打折扣，因为在那里看到的是真正的切片，或者叫片断。这当然与当代艺术所衍生出的策展行业的滞后有关。现在的群展更多的时候像是博览会，而那些口碑稍好的展览无非是相对专——些的主题性的挑选，更多的是杂烩与拼盘。其他的原因包括文化针对性、主动性的缺失，或者经济消费主义的影响等等，这里不再展开。

回到艺术家，浅显地说，对于一个艺术家的思想和观念的缘起形成、发展、以至于最后产生一件艺术作品；以及上一个作品和下一件作品之间的观念延续甚至断裂，就我的理解，这是本次展览所十分注重的。这很像一种历史分析法，得出某个预定的结果并不是首要的，首要的是寻找更多的佐证，最后将它们并置的时候，自然有一些不证自明的东西会显现出来，这样甚至会超越最初的判断。当我们做出一个最后的决定，通常并不是一蹴而就的，在决定形成过程中的细枝末节也是不得不重视的，这期间曾经发生过的某个细小的念头也许都会最终影响未来的判断。现在的决定无非是最适合当时的一个选择，或者是偶然。所以人们经常会说历史是必然的，又是偶然的。这样的分析在艺术家的传记，或是美术史专题研究中并不缺少重视。我们在展览会上对一个艺术家的了解，还建立在对他以往的某些作品甚至人格的印象，从而最终影响甚至左右我们对眼前所见到的这一作品的理解。

不过需要清楚的指出，这个展览并非和当下流行的过程性的观念艺术创作那样：找到和确定一个概念，然后将搜寻其过程中的证据——保留，这样就可以称之为完成了一件作品。重要的问题是希望通过展览和出版物弄清楚连续性是通过什么样的方式得以维持并对艺术家众多不同或连续的思想观念起作用并构成现有的局面。

众所周知我们正在经历一场"危机"，我想它适度警醒了一些沉睡的人们，不仅要关注艺术曾经如何与消费、商业成功的协作，也应该关注一下，在这个联合体中的一些其他重要部分如艺术家，他们是如何工作、以及是如何将它们努力继续下去的。也许大家都在试图改变现时乏味单一的局面。同作为一个创作者，我尤其期待这样的事物。

2009-11-14

A Presentation of the Unpresentable

Xia Jifeng

How do artists work? From my point of view, this is a question that entices voyeuristic cravings while being practically impossible to answer. The work of an artist, each step of the working process is constantly revised as the work itself progresses. The completion of a work, in fact, simultaneously signifies the concealment and erasure of the previous creative efforts. Even if the artist intentionally preserves his/her notes or drafts, or better yet, employs a camcorder to faithfully record this working process, it does very little to explain the completed work. In other words, the visible portion of art-making alone is far from enough to account for the final work. The relationship between the artist and his/her work can be similar to telepathy: it is an invisible, inexplicable process that depends on a mutual exchange of thoughts. Theoretically there seems to be no effective solution to understanding the mystery that surrounds the artist's process.

Still, is there a possibility to graze the borders of the secret to the artist's work? I believe this to be worthy of attempts and investigations. And as to how far this "border" reaches? That is another story. For example, *Contemporary Art and Investment* magazine, has been investing in such attempts for the past three years. By inviting nearly 30 young artists – all experimental and full of creative energy – to participate in its Project column, the magazine has put together intriguing presentations of the seemingly un-presentable secret of the artist's work. At the very least, it presented to the best of its ability, a variety of possibilities produced by an individual artist in the conception, experimentation and production of his/her works. Even so, the questions do not stop there: as a magazine, or a column within a magazine, how much can this platform provide for working artists to reveal their secrets? Will the limitations of the magazine medium itself become another "border" that restricts the presentation of the secrets of an artist's work?

Then a thorough investigation becomes necessary for this fascinating paradox comparable to M. C. Escher's works. As an extension of and response to the past editions of the Project column, we decided to invite the artists involved to the exhibition: Work in Progress: How Do Artists Work?. However, perhaps with the transition of presentation from a two-dimensional print medium to a three-dimensional space, and especially accompanied by the consequential changes of the physical characteristics and the artists' working concepts, we could still further push the limits to reveal the secrets of their works.

We understand that this exhibition cannot escape its fate as another presentation of the un-presentable. Tao Yuanming, a poet from the Jin Dynasty once wrote:

"a little gift for comfort is better than nothing". And from the Qing Dynasty reformist Liang Qichao: "...for self-motivation, better to have an inch or a foot (of improvement) than none at all". Perhaps these phrases would serve as the best footnote to our never-ending proposition.

2009-11-18

*Work in Progress: How Do Curators Work?
- On the 4th Anniversary of "Art and
Investment "*

Zuo Jing

At the end of 2006, in Hang Zhou, Xia Jifeng (a close friend and the editor-in-chief of *Art and Investment*), invited me and Carol Yinghua Lu to start a new magazine called"Contemporary Art and Investment"(a sub-edition for *Art and Investment*). This is where the idea for the exhibition"The Work in Progress: How Do Artists Work" came from. In order to make our audiences understand the launch of a magazine, as well as our original concerns, I would like to quote from my forward in the magazine, entitled *One Year and a Half Month*:

For people like us, who have been through the 8os', to set up associations and start a magazine is often our biggest dream. From today's perspective starting a magazine, especially an art magazine, is possibly the most historic way of delivering thoughts about art to the public, but it encounters huge pressures both internally and externally. For example, topics that are oriented to select groups could cause self-marginalization, or the magazine could loose its advantages in the face of the efficiencies and the low costs of other mediums, or there could be awkward and destabilizing situations caused by shifts in the interests of investors. We have seen the many ups and downs, births and deaths of art magazines.

It is clear that *Art and Investment* is a real-life version of a 8os' dream about magazines. Which is to say that it carries a strong confrere-kind of approach (we are too ashamed to call it an "idealist approach"). Having said that, we haven't given up on tFhe idea of building a "contemporary ecological art system" on paper. In our origin set-up for the columns, "Focus", as the most important column, paid close attention to the current trends in the art world (and rarely the "elite art world") and we allowed ourselves to follow our interests. "Case Study" [1] was dedicated to presenting different periods in the career's of important selected artists, with an attempt at placing their productions within related historical contexts. "Project" emphasized the introduction of young artists and their thoughts. "Concept" was devoted to displaying artists' drafts, notes, and plans for works that existed as concepts; it previewed what was anticipated. "Curating" was a column for curators, with the intent of providing an in-depth introduction of a selected curator and his/her philosophies every month. It sometimes includes journals, notes, or dialogues with artists, even the challenges that one could face during the process of putting up an exhibition. Other times, it could be just a virtual exhibition on paper. "The Space" column identified independent spaces and described what they were doing, their aesthetic approaches, and operational models. "The Group" was a section devoted to reviewing independent art organizations, including their key figures and activities. "Videos" was a place for special attention on Chinese independent filmmaking.

The Magazine has a committee structure. For the past three years, most of committees made solid contribution to the growth of the magazine. Most of the members come from outside of the art world (rarely from the elite art world), and worked in areas including design, architecture, film, music, dance, philosophy, literature, and others. These wide-ranging backgrounds reflect our belief in "the production of discourse". We feel that development should stem from an interdisciplinary, "intellectual community" spirit. Of course, time keeps moving, we are not so naïve as to run a magazine with a mindset from the 80s'. I've always believed that the ever-changing "ecological chain" that grows around the magazine will surely introduce many new possibilities. The persistent accumulation of energy can lead to new initiatives being triggered.

In March 2007, through Carol's introduction, Yao Jiashan (the curator of the exhibition "Fake!") became interested in our magazine. To substitute a magazine for a catalog that is normally produced in conjunction with an exhibition is not a new idea. But what makes this project intriguing is that the theme of the exhibition is about "copying, counterfeiting, and falsification in contemporary art". The question arose: how can we turn a magazine into a "fictional" publication? Yao and her artists discussed these concepts and moved into action. They used essays to introduce debates about artistic and philosophical questions concerning the real and the fictional. To be more specific, they edited texts that mixed truthful and false content, directing the content in a self-referential manner in order to reveal a so-called "truth". In the fourth edition of 2007 many "fake" items appeared in our magazine. This included a "fake" article that dealt with totally fictional questions, fake advertisements (not unlike Hong Hao and Xu Zhen's often-used style), fake exhibitions that were to have "happened" in a hotel but never really occurred, fake news (that Li Qing was commissioned to make a statue for the Queen of England), along with other items. So, the magazine became a space for artists and art critics to create experimental text. This was the most fascinating and unique edition of *Contemporary Art and Investment*.

In April 2008, Iberia Contemporary Art Center was opened, and we were asked to curate the first exhibition. It originated from our "Case Study" column and was entitled "Community of Tastes – Iberia Contemporary Art Center's Inaugural Exhibition". In an article that followed the exhibition, I mentioned the relationship between the exhibition and the magazine as such:

In our philosophy for running this magazine, we want to make it clear that the contemporary art this magazine presents is understood through an experimental, interdisciplinary, and spontaneous spirit. It is our aspiration to create a magazine free from conventional definitions, so that the essence of the magazine can develop to become an active and open independent voice. It is not only a cold, passive medium on paper, but also a framework based on which exhibitions, activities, publishing, and many other options could be opened up. I could call this exhibition a "Magazine – Curating practice.[2]

This exhibition (abbreviated as the "Work in Progress" exhibition) is the second example of this "Magazine – Curating practice" model. ("Gallery on Paper" in 2010 will be the third one developed from this model). Unlike "Community of Tastes", the "Work in Progress" exhibition created "the third option for exhibition" (as academic type of exhibition and commercial type are the first two options). As someone stated later, "'Community of Tastes', 'Independent Film Unit', and 'Spanish Artist Unit' don't comfortably go together, but they reflect Iberia's professional influence, academic pursuit, and institutional sponsorship." I sincerely hope to make "Work in Progress" exhibition into an academic one. As an important element in the "contemporary ecological art system", the artists we choose for the "Project" column are younger and more adventurous compared to the senior artists selected for the "Case Study" column. They represent different ideas about 'the now', and present the endless possibilities of what is unfolding before them. They represent China's future. Having said that, to curate all the artists from the "Project" column into a group show could easily create a convoluted, but dull medley. So in the past few days, consistent with what casual curators do, I spent a few hours browsing over all the artists from the column; their works and texts, and I wrote down my fragmented and instinctive notes. Here is what I got: "Qiu Anxiong – east and west cultural challenges, ancient mythology; Zhou Xiaohu – temporary sculpture, interventions with the public and society, photography as auto-writing; Zhang Qing – personal adventure and social intervention, neutral perspective; Liu Bo, Li yu – moving performance, social concerns with strong personal preference; Jiang Zhi – violence and control, the metaphor of light, intentional remembering happenings; He Yunchang, self-adventure, time and endurance; Shi Qing – historical imagination and thoughts on grand narration drawn from ancient texts; Wu Junyong – circus, humor, sexuality, and politics; Li Yongbing – time; Ma Qiusha – body; Li Ming – daily experience; Yang Jun – research on imagination; Dong Wensheng – Jiang Nan (regions south of the Yangtze River) aesthetic; Su Wenxiang – compulsion effects from machine to human; Sun Jianchun – personal preference vs social survey; Tang Yi – verbal masochistic and scientific addition; Wang Guangle – metaphysics painting; Li Jinghu – from the mundane (meaningless) to power (meaningful); Wu Jian'an – structure and material, folkart; Liang Shuo – art itself, the debate between the meaningful and the meaningless; Chang Kenhau & Chang Genhwa – interactive; Li Chao – perspectivism and its visual practice; Jin Shi – art discourse and grassroots politics; Wu Xiaojun – incident, and happenings…"

Should we, as we used to, step by step, categorize, sum up, and narrow it down to a theme, then separate them into different units? Obviously, this is not what we want. Should we start from the artists' intentions, methodology, and process? How about putting the final presentation into a relatively minor position, focusing more on the realization of the artwork. The presentation could be spiritual (expressed through material), materialistic, or a view to the evolution of contexts during the course of the artist's production. It is like using a series of artworks to present how artist's work; the evolution of their concepts, which could be fragmented or consistent. Another possible approach is to adopt what Prof. Wu Hung did in his case study in "Zhang Huan's Studio". Wu departs from the structural and functional meaning of an artist' studio, revealing different models and systems within the artist's creative process. By doing this, Wu opens up a discussion surrounding the relationship between artists and their art. That is how we found the subtitle for this exhibition "How do Artists Work", and as a result our vision became richer and clearer. But immediately we encountered a new challenge, namely how to visually present the theme of "how do artists work"? I realize that I set myself up for a mission impossible, just like when Sergei

Eisenstein said he would make Karl Marx's *Capital* into a film.

Artists' notes? Processes? Failed art? Abandoned draft? Sketches? Plans? Photos? Interviews? What is the holistic, identifiable thread that links all of them? Or should one forgo building interrelationships and simply display selected works, with an indication of their individual inner logic? Is our goal simply to accomplish the task of assembling, or is it to display the results of our research (or is that possible in this context)? Could the presentation dominate over the content? Or could the work lose its visual independence, and become just another show that "documentations of process"? How should one approach the catalogue? How should one install and design the show? What perspective on "the future of contemporary art" are we trying to present? To what degree would an exhibition as innovative as this turn into a failed attempt because of a shortage of preparation time. Or will we, in the end, have to lower expectations, and start a new discussion by learning better rhetoric? All these questions will likely emerge. The issue of privacy, the unaccountable to artistic processes, and other unexpected factors will make this exhibition a risk-taking challenge. We will be on a journey without knowing the destination. All these questions, academic and political, won't find their answers until the show is set up. And we hope there will be people to "clean this battlefield", offering what our community is expecting in order to deepen the knowledge of art.

Last but not the least, I want to say that the reason for using the first half of the essay to look back at the brief history of the magazine is that I wanted to outline that, in addition to accomplishing its own mission, there are other possibilities for this magazine. As well, I wanted to take the opportunity on the fourth anniversary of *Art and Investment*, and third anniversary for *Contemporary Art and Investment*, to write a "self-confession". It could be about the magazine, or about the exhibition.

2009-11-15

Notes:

(1) After the first edition in 2009, the column was renamed "Gallery on Paper" by the new Executive Editor, Dong Bingfeng. The content was changed. Each time, one artist is introduced by a different curator. The column focuses on artist's most updated projects and thinking, as well as the visual links between the text and the images.

(2) In that same article, I also mentioned the "magazine – publishing practice". At the 3rd anniversary of *Contemporary Art and Investment*, the publishing of nearly ten books based on the content in different columns of the magazine was planned. This series of books, entitled "Iberia Series" will be published by New Star Publishing House before the next Spring Festival.

Art Making Is My Profession

Carol Yinghua Lu

During my chat with Chu Chen, Han Dong's publisher, he described how Han Dong works. Han starts off by writing his first draft on a computer, prints it out, and deletes the file from the computer, then he re-types the text into the computer based on that original printout. He keeps repeating this process many times until he feels the writing is strong enough, and he does this even for a novel of three hundred thousand words. He forces himself into a self-created cul-de-sac, leaving no other paths to achieve a refined and distilled language. To know this particular detail about his process is essential in appreciating his writings. Widely known and praised by many for the content of his novels, the creativity and enchantment of his writing lies in the structure of his novels and the design of the plot. Even more so, is the texture, the refinement and accuracy of his language, which is possible only by this fastidious reworking. Another practitioner, a master in conceptual art, John Baldessari, destroyed all his "accomplished works", restarting from scratch. Using classical methods in sociology, American artist Alison Gerber, based in Sweden, did a three-year survey that was used to develop an evaluating system to define the "labor" of artists. As well, he published a manual to help the general public to understand the various degrees and combinations of "the creative", "the routine", and "labor" within the artistic process.

Here we are facing a question of how to understand art making as a profession. Art making always involves creativity, it is not an attitude, nor is it a representation of status. It demands "high goal" and other "basic requirements".[1] Here requirements refers to various qualities, including knowledge, technique, intelligence, methodology, attitude, sensitivities, persistence, dedication, and honesty. The pursuit of art making as a high goal relies on detailed duties in the different roles within the whole art system. It ranges from the responsibilities of gallery assistants to the security guards, to the museum organizers. All are basic, but instrumental. In all cases, artwork is the key element, but its presentation and distribution is not separated from these different kinds of support. It is important to realize the making of a professional artist calls for huge social resources.

A process of "demystifying" is required to understand how artists work. It could be the opposite of the artists' public image and their motivation. A well-known artist has describes art making as such: one picks an ordinary pebble, wraps with layers of gold leaf until everyone thinks it is gold, and no one can indentify it as a pebble. This kind of philosophy has become the goal and the core of his artistic practice. It is a tireless career effort towards establishing and consolidating an image as the "master", to spread the "myth" at all costs. He is one example of this type who actively creates a context for their artistic identities and practices. To analyze an artist's practice requires an awareness of the diversity of different creation types. What is the drive behind the practice: Is it his refinement in technique and medium, or his concept and theories? Is it his knowledge and analysis of the art system or his pursuits for questioning artist' identity? Is it the intellectual concerns and reflection towards to social issues, or an examination and a game between the existential self and the everydayness? Is it the result of his persistent efforts, or a sign of being objectified? Is it to satisfy art production rules, or simply to provoke controversies? How does the artist describe his practice? How many details and secretes does he want to have exposed? The deliberation and mastery of those boundaries also reveals how an artist works and how he thinks of his work.

In addition to observing the final "finished" artwork, joining the discussion and analysis of artists' processes and direction is helpful in developing greater understanding. It does not at all diminish or downplay the importance of the artists' works; on the contrary, it can provide a diverse framework that bridges to artistic creation. It reduces the obsession with myth building in artistic practices, and removes the overemphasis on artistic outcome. It promotes the idea of "process", develops an appreciation of the diverse approaches available in art making, and expands the possibilities in understanding and describing creative production. Some art works gain meaning from an understanding of the process of creation, others require an extensive timeframe of fermentation and accumulating before they shine. To discuss and present artists' creation as a profession opens up new possibilities for understanding artists' practice beyond just analyzing meaning and responding to visuals instinctively. Many of these factors can be taken into account, such as ideas, craftsmanship, technical capacity, theories, norms, and sense of professionalism.

For all roles in the field of the arts, including artists, curators, and art critics, a down-to-earth mindset is necessary to treat art practice as a profession. This approach is a required, and will also help us to develop a holistic understanding of artwork through pluralistic means, as opposite to applying only one standard. Diverse research approaches will help inform us about individual artists. What is his daily working style, processes, location, his educational background, his family influence and childhood, the range and the depth of his reading experience, where he has travelled to, his personality and interests, his social life, his shopping habits, his awareness towards his own identity and how he plays with it, his source material, his taste and aesthetic experience, his procedure, his facilities, the issues that concern him, his pattern of thinking, his production, sales, the distribution of his art, where did he exhibition, his ranking, his galleries, his records in collections, his public image, etc? All these form a rich context for an artist's practice, as well as providing a doorway for others to join artist's thinking, and subsequently a possible dialogue.

As a profession, art demands professional standards and established peer norms. Unfortunately, a rather uncomfortable situation has developed in the art world in china. The art world now is congesting with collusion and hyperbole, and the disrespect for professional criteria is still encouraged, while independent thinking and professionalism are rare virtues. These professional sycophants are not reliable, nor are the standards they create. Market value is another standard that has been given inappropriate importance, and hence it is harmful. The value of artistic creation should not be judged by the scale of the market. However, most of the time in China, the depth of an artist's thinking and his/her importance is determined by his/her popularity in the market. The art practice that solely relies on this market standard is singular and counterproductive. To have a healthy, diverse, and democratic art ecology, to allow independent voice, to respect academic practices instead of sales and power brokering; these are premises needed to allow artists to work independently and deepen their ideas. To establish professionalism for art practice is an important challenge for artists, and also a duty that needs to be taken up by art critics and the whole art system.

Note:

① *This Kind of Literature*, Han Dong, 2009-05-18, "Han Dong's Blog" http://blog.sina.com.cn/s/blog_4fe548220100cxos.html~type=v5_one&label=rela_prevarticle

Artist at Work

Dong Bingfeng

These days, are artists still "working"?

This question sounds very ambiguous and paradoxical. Of course, our discussion is confined to the topic of contemporary art. We haven't found a better word to replace this concept though it now looks very banal, bureaucratic and conservative.

The younger generation of artists who are rapidly rising in China either firmly embrace everyday life and pop culture and keep thinking about this dynamic background; or they just stop "working", thus eliminating the connection between art and reality. In this way, they keep their mind sharp. All this sounds to bear the utopian characters, but compared with their predecessors who carried on grand social responsibilities in avant-garde experimental art or turned underground with ideologically rebellious spirit; it seems so easy, simple and true. Actually, what the younger generation believes in is freedom, a new identity and communication without obstacle.

Similar to the reality of China, new art conceptions and forms are surging out everyday in this country. They are not merely taken from the West, nor are they simply an extension of Chinese philosophy in modern times. Rather they are a new art which attempts to transcend all the rules set by museums, the market and art criticisms. They are a spectacular hybrid. Brandon Taylor, author of Art Today, points out in his book, that this trend took place in global art development between 1999 and 2004; it happened later in China. One reason is that the revolts carried out by individual artists were quickly eliminated and replaced by consumerism. Even more ironically, the artists, under the influence of flourishing art market, set up numerous "studios" for massive art production. In Beijing, for example, the most conservative estimate for the number of artist studios is over 10,000. The world's increasing interest in Chinese contemporary art reached its peak in the past few years when the global economic recession had not yet taken place.

To some degree, this has prevented serious thinking from moving on. It has developed to such an extent that any serious exhibition or work needs to prove the artists' readiness to embrace the mainstream culture or consumerists' tastes, otherwise they'll be labeled as a "house built on sand".

Never has the concept of contemporary art been so rich, intertwined and baffling as it is right now in China. As it shakes off its potential cultural or spiritual responsibilities, it has become entertainment, indulging in the making of "scenes". In this way, it takes on its part in the social symbols of the rapid economic development of China. All the parties—government associations, art academies, commercial galleries, and even the marginal groups in a real sense, are claiming that they possess the right view and judgment about contemporary art. At the same time, the government, with the hope to turn "contemporary art" into an important component in the production of cultural industry and its message of open-mindedness to the world (forbidden topics not included), has become a major propellant. For the ordinary people who are confused by the soaring prices of Chinese contemporary art in action markets, will the truth be their concern? Everything looks unavoidable.

Today, how should artists begin their work?
This seems to be a good question.

2009-11-15

In What Way Does the Artist Work?

Su Wenxiang

In what way does the artist work? This is a topic discussed by art researchers and even by the most basic art lovers. It has been approached by art historians in essays and books, by artists themselves in their autobiographies, and by art institutions like museums and galleries in their education and promotion programs. Whatever the purpose is, they are trying to do the same thing: reveal the creative way in which the artist works and survives. Such a mysterious subject like art, altogether with artists, continues to provoke people's curiosity. In fact, people are more interested in how things become "art" in the hand of this special group (artists), than they are in the way in which artists work.

To see the world from one single perspective results in insufficient understanding. It would be the same if we look at art in this way. However, in our experience of approaching art, especially when we go to see an exhibition, what we can rely on in the exploration into the production of the artworks is only the exhibition catalogue, which is more like a report about the result of the artists' practice than anything else. You hardly gain any knowledge simply from looking at the catalogue.

What is the way the artist work? I have to admit, the current institution of the art exhibition can hardly reveal the answer. It has possibly even become an obstacle preventing people from understanding how the artist works. Most exhibitions show only the result of an artist's work; giving no hint as to how the result is achieved. There has even been a common recognition art circles that the best the way to understand an artist is to see his or her solo exhibition. Group exhibitions then are highly underestimated as what viewers are supposed to see. There are only intersections, or fragments of the each artist's work. This is, of course, partly due to the curating method of contemporary art that has lagged behind. Most group exhibitions look like expositions which are nothing but a hybrid of unrelated works, though better ones try to focus on one theme. There could be more discussions about the peculiarity of culture, absence of initiative from the organizers, and influence from commercial concerns, etc., which are all reasons of this consequence.

When we examine this question from the viewpoint of an artist, we find the way of their work is the process in which they conceive an idea, develop it, and finally present it as artwork. As far as I'm concerned, to find the consistency or the changes in the topics of the artist's work, is the biggest concern of this exhibition. This is like a chronological research method: the imperative is not to arrive at a presumed result, but to collect proofs for them. When the proofs are put together, they show an apparent result in themselves, which may diverge from or transcend our presumptions. A decision is seldom made all at a sudden and in the decision-making process, even trivial things can lead to totally different result. The final decision is nothing but a choice made at certain moment, maybe it is just accidental. That is also why we say that history is the result of both necessity and contingency. Such analysis can be seen in the biographies of the artists or monographs of art history. Our knowledge about an artist from his or her solo exhibition, therefore, is also based on his past works or our impressions about his or her personality. All this will finally lead to our overall understanding of the work presented in front of us.

I need to point out that this exhibition is not the same as the progress of those popular conceptual art practices, which tries to fix a concept first and then searches for the evidence to prove the concept and display them to the audience as a work. The most important thing is to show to the audience through the exhibition and the catalogue how the works of an artist achieve consistency, which, in turn influences the ideas of the artist and finally help him or her to arrive at what his or her art is now.

It is known to all that we are experiencing a "crisis". I think this crisis has properly let people realize that rather than focusing simply on the commercial part of art, they should also try to know more about the other side of art: the artist, and the way they work and carry on their work. Perhaps all are trying to change this boring situation. I, myself, also an artist, am particularly looking forward to this change.

2009-11-14

图版（艺术家、作品、问卷）

PLATES (ARTISTS, WORKS AND QUESTIONAIRES)

董文胜

DONG WENSHENG

作为艺术家，你在创作中所关心的是什么？以一件作品为例，分享你的创作过程。

我关心我的作品是否在实验的和社会学以及诗的层面。

以《精神现象学》为例，整个创作过程其实也就是一个在尸骨上种花养草的过程，我有一个可以搞到出土尸骨的渠道，我先在骷髅上培土，然后在少许种一些盆景植物，接下来就是要天天洒水养护了，只要保持潮湿，一些小草和青苔会长得越来越好。

如果你是一个批评家，你会从什么角度来阐释和讨论你自己的创作？

都可以，最好是我没有想到的角度。但有一点是肯定的，我并不希望从单纯摄影语言的角度。

在你的创作和思考中，什么书籍和艺术家曾经或正在影响着你？

挺多的，总有我喜爱的书籍和艺术家伴随我的各个时期。我是因为崇敬他们才走上创作之路的。

你是怎样判断和决定在什么语境下呈现你的哪些作品的？你是怎样看待作品呈现的语境和作品的关系的？

这是我近期才开使意识到的问题，我以往只凭感性的判断。

如何在创作上形成了现在的面貌，描述一下最近年来作品的发展和变化？

磨出来的，我是个慢热型的人，先是由着性子信马由缰，然后再逐渐梳理并明确，我用了十年才形成现在的面貌。而且我每个时期的作品都是环环相扣的。近年来我从对江南传统文化的当下思索渐渐衍生至存在与时间的哲学命题以及对当下的城市化进程的思考上。

你会在什么情况下摧毁你自己的作品？

任何情况皆有可能！

你怎么看待艺术史和艺术家创作的关系？

有才情的艺术家太多了，只有明晰艺术史的人才不会被感性的冲动所左右，才能驾驭自己的激情！

在你的工作中，理性和情感冲动各自扮演着什么样的角色？

相互制约，冲动有时会产生一些令人兴奋的念头，理性会让我遵循自己的体系，放弃一些面目模糊的创作方案。

As an artist, what do you care most during working? Could you please give an example to introduce the process of your work for us?

I care about whether my work stays on the experimental, sociological and poetic layer.

Take *The Study of the Phenomenology of Spirit* as an example, the whole creating process is just a process of planting flowers and grass on a skeleton. I have access to getting unearthed skeletons. First I earth up the skeleton, plant some bonsai plants and then water them everyday. So long as you can maintain the humidity, the grass and moss will grow better and better.

Suppose you are a critic, what perspective would you talk about and explain you work from?

Any angle is ok. Better be some angle that I've never thought of. But there's one thing I can be sure: I don't want it to be the single angle of photography.

What books and which artists have had, or are having an influence on your way of thinking and working?

There are quite a lot. There are always favorite books and artists that accompany the days of my life. Because of them, I chose to be an artist.

How do you decide the context in which your work is to be presented? How do you consider the relation ship between context and your work?

This is an issue that I've just realized recently. Before this, I only

董文胜在拍摄作品《无关紧要的一天》

地点：常州竺山湖

时间：2008年

The artist filming *A Day of No Significance*,
Zhushan Lake, Changzhou
2008

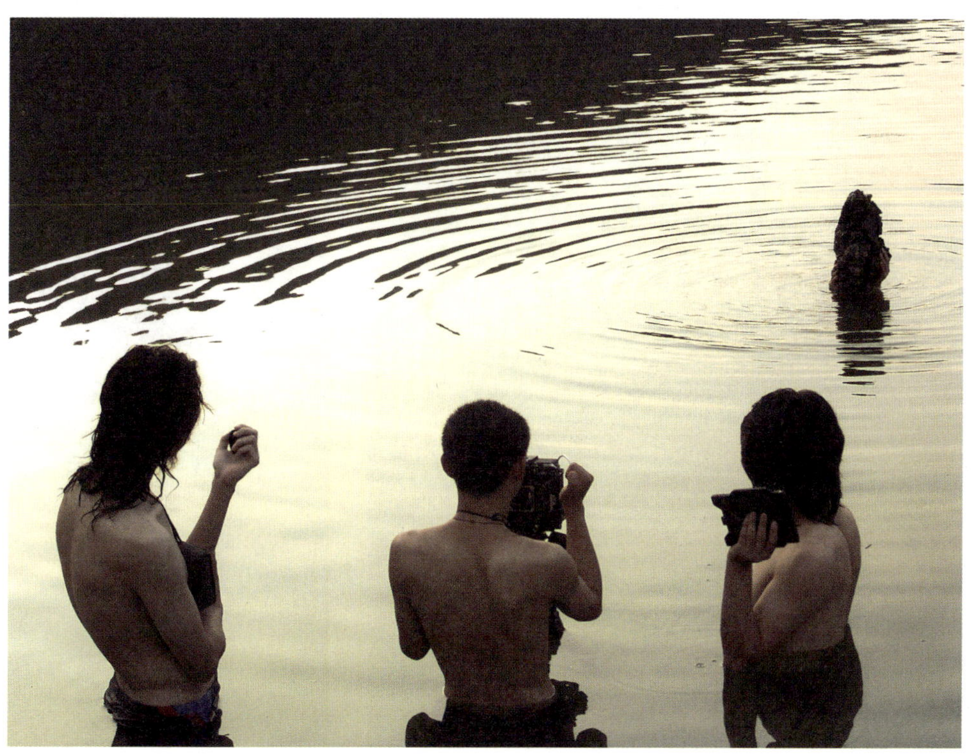

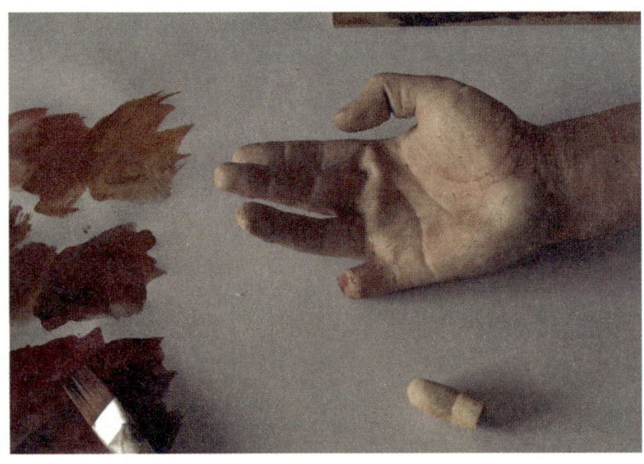

《皈依者》作品道具的搜寻与制作1

Making props and making preparations before filming *The convert*, photo 1

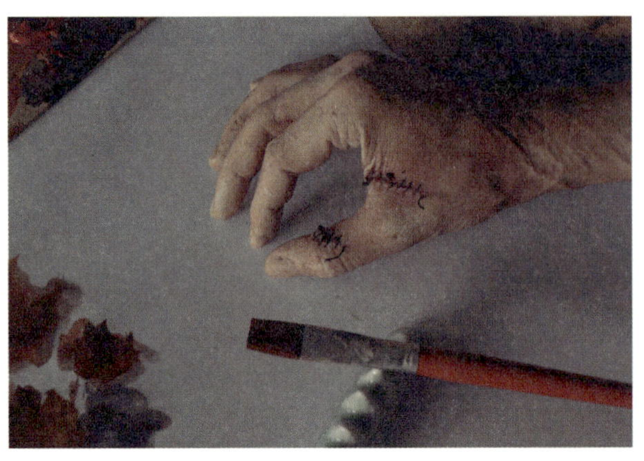

《皈依者》作品道具的搜寻与制作2

Making props and making preparations before filming *The convert*, photo 2

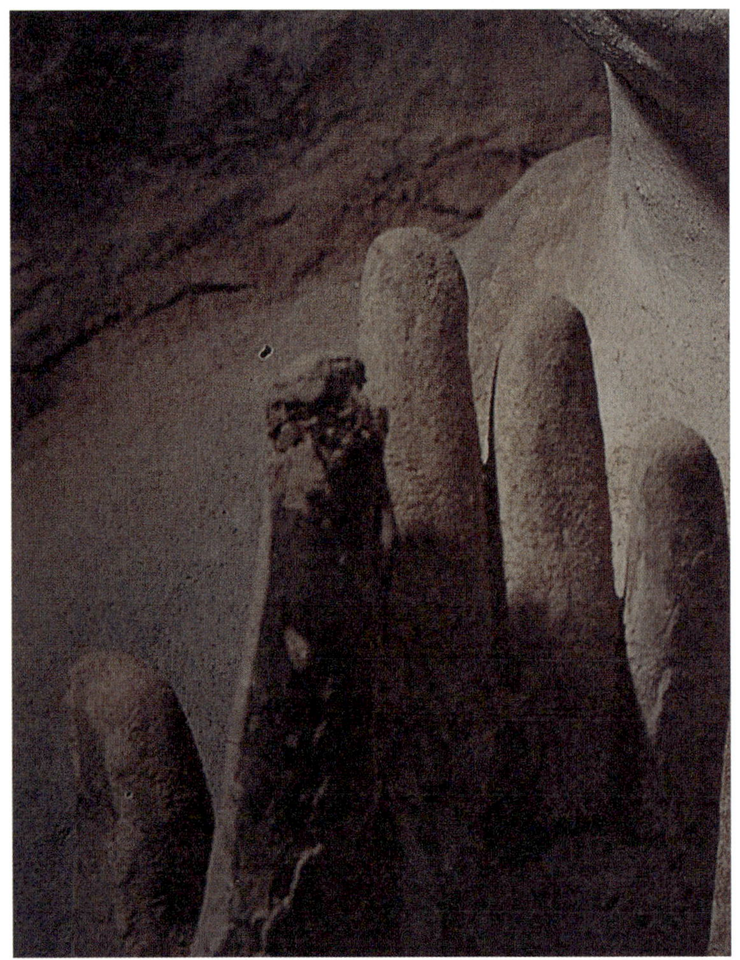

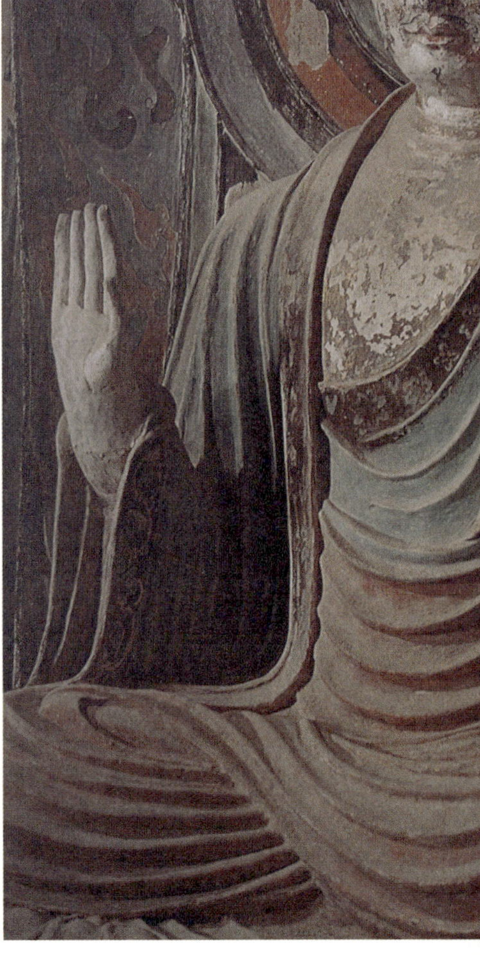

judge things emotionally.

How does your work take the present shape? And please give a few words about the latest development and changes in your work.

I've gone through the mill. I am a slow person. I follow my instinct at first, and then gradually make clear what I should do. I spent ten years to form how my work look now. Besides, the works of each period are closely bound to each other. Lately my thinking about traditional Jiangnan culture has gradually transferred to the philosophical topics of time and existence, as well as the current process of urbanization.

In what circumstances would you want to destroy your own creation?

Any situation is possible.

What do you think about the relation between the art history and artist's work?

There are so many talented artists, but only those who have a clear understanding of art history will not be driven by emotional impulses and therefore can take control of their own talent.

What kind of roles would rational thinking and emotional impulse respectively play during your work time?

They restrict each other. Impulse sometimes will generate some exciting ideas, but rationality will make me follow my own system and abandon some ambiguous plans.

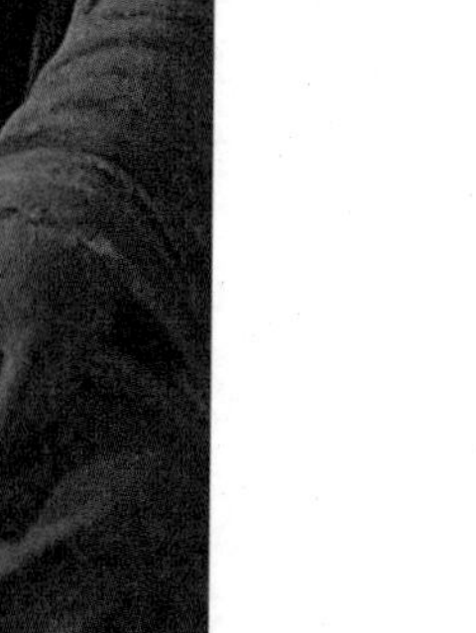

《皈依者》作品素材

Materials for producing *The convert*

《皈依者》作品素材
佛像手印

Buddha's hand print

Materials for producing *The convert*

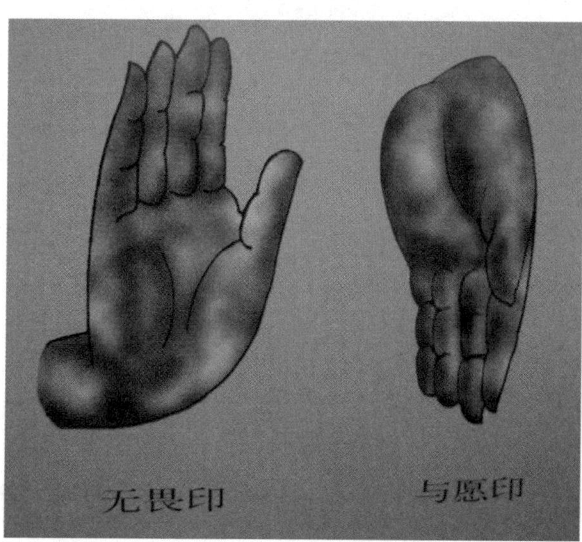

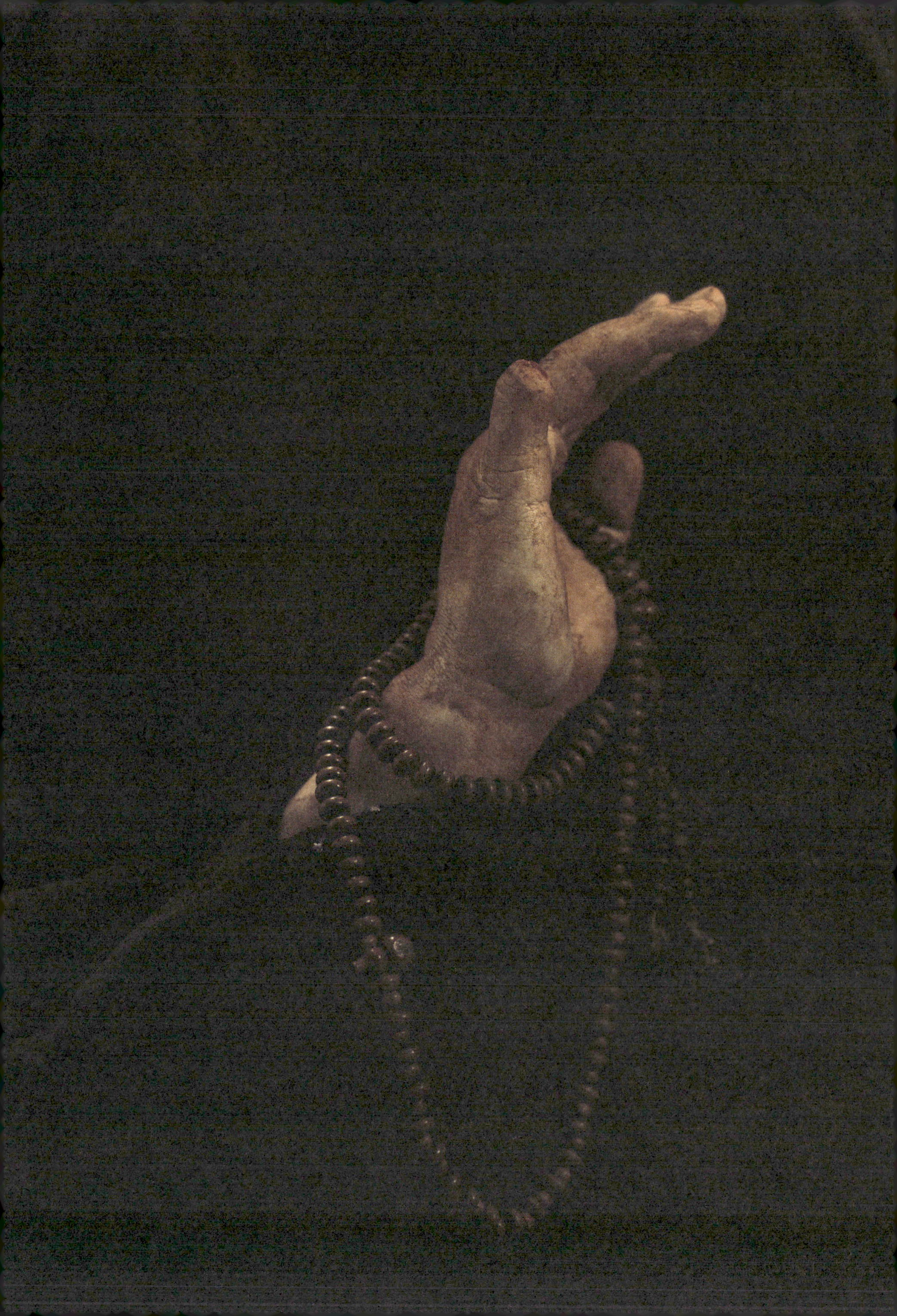

皈依者1， 2009
摄影

The Convert No.1, 2009
Photography

皈依者2，2009
摄影

The Convert No.2, 2009
Photography

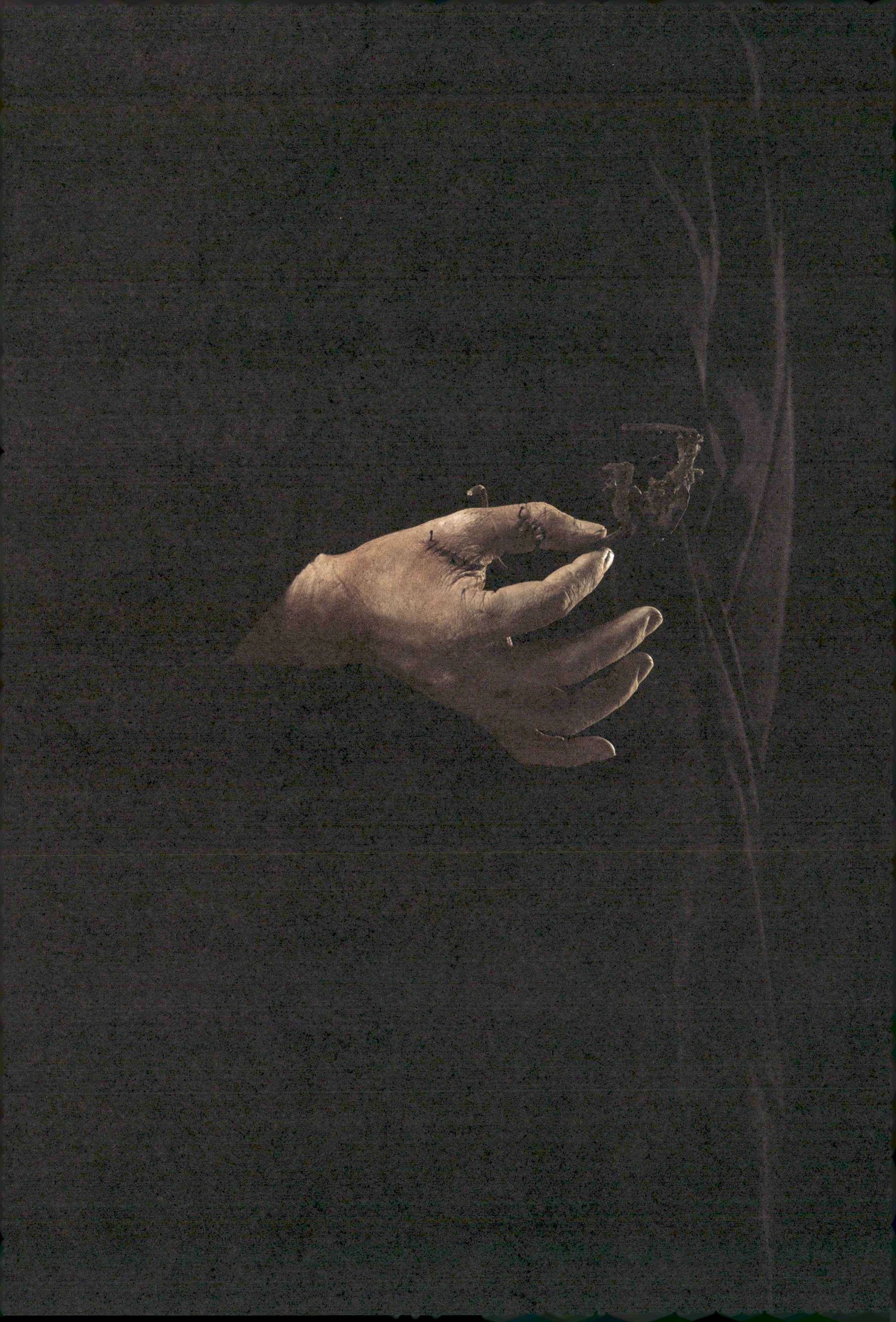

何云昌

HE YUNCHANG

作为艺术家，你在创作中所关心的是什么？以一件作品为例，分享你的创作过程。
新作品能呈现我当时最好状态就很开心。
《石头英国漫游记》近乎颠狂、浪漫。

如果你是一个批评家，你会从什么角度来阐释和讨论你自己的创作？
不是人人都可以当批评家，当村长也很好。我花心思在作品实施之前。

在你的创作和思考中，什么书籍和艺术家曾经或正在影响着你？
以前不重要，现在没有。

你是怎样判断和决定在什么语境下呈现你的哪些作品的？你是怎样看待作品呈现的语境和作品的关系的？
有条件实施作品就好，顺其自然。

如何在创作上形成了现在的面貌，描述一下最近年来作品的发展和变化？
一半用心，一大半瞎蒙。每件作品都想有一些变化，虚实相间。

你会在什么情况下摧毁你自己的作品？
清醒的时候。

你怎么看待艺术史和艺术家创作的关系？
就像烂苹果和土地一样。

在你的工作中，理性和情感冲动各自扮演着什么样的角色？
都重要，有时均衡，有时反之。

As an artist, what do you care most during working?
Could you please give an example to introduce the process of your work for us?
I'd be happy to find a new piece has me at my best.
The Rock Touring around Great Britain is close to madness, yet romantic.

Suppose you are a critic, what perspective would you talk about and explain you work from?
Not everyone can do a critic's job. It would be nice still to be just a village head. I usually spend lots of time on every project before I start to make it.

What books and which artists have had, or is having an influence on your way of thinking and working?
Those from the past became unimportant, and for now, I have nothing to tell.

How do you decide the context in which your work is to be presented? How do you consider the relation of the context with your work?
It will be nice as long as there is a chance to realize my project. Just let nature take its course.

How does your work take the present shape? And please give a few words about the latest development and changes in your work..
I'd say half is through following my heart and half is wild guess. For each piece, I'd like to see some changes, something between fiction and reality.

In what circumstances would you want to destroy your own creation?
When I get sober, I probably would do that.

What do you think about the relation between the art history and artist's work?
The relationship is like that between rotten apples and soil.

What kind of roles would rational thinking and emotional impulse respectively play during your work time?
Both are important and balanced, but, sometimes, it just goes to the opposite.

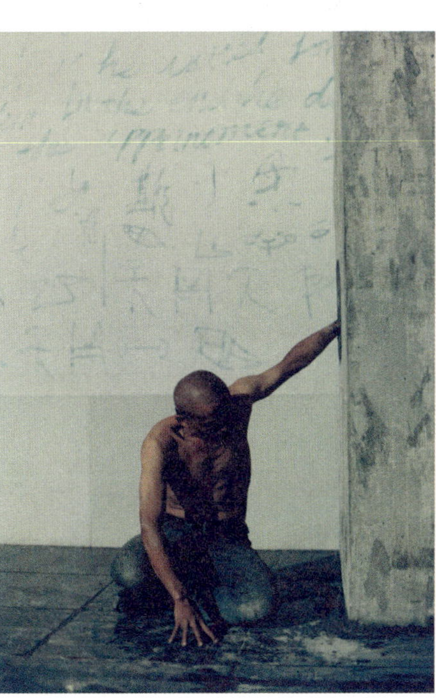

左图
抱柱之信，2003
行为：2003年10月24至25日
地点：中国云南丽江
何云昌把自己的一只手浇铸在水泥里，保持24小时。

Keeping Promise, 2003
Performance: October 24 – 25, 2003
Venue: Lijiang, Yunnan, China
He Yunchang had one of his hands cemented inside a concrete block for 24 hours.

右图
预约明天，1998
行为
地点：中国云南丽江
何云昌全身涂满泥巴，不停拨打电话30分钟，电话号码是随意编的。

Appointment with Tomorrow, 1998
Performance
Venue: Lijiang, Yunnan, China
He Yunchang covered himself with mud and kept dialing a telephone for 30 minutes. All the called numbers were randomly made up.

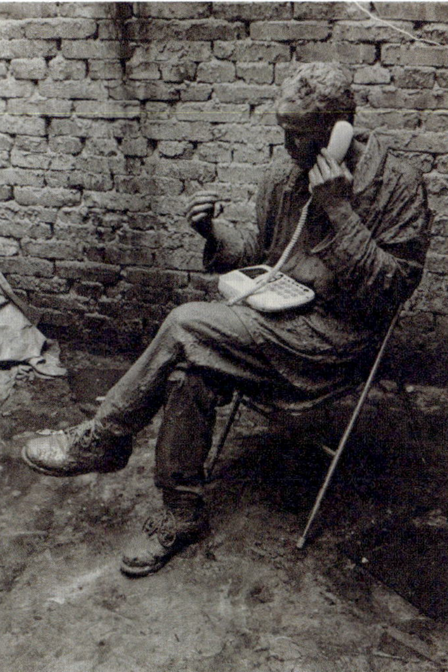

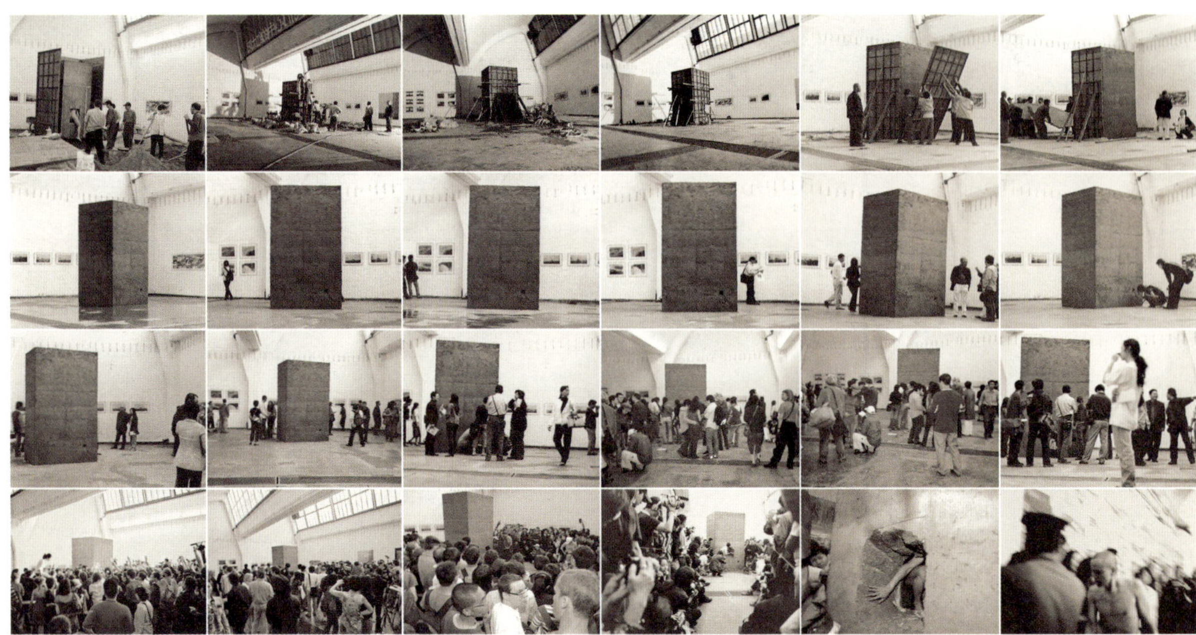

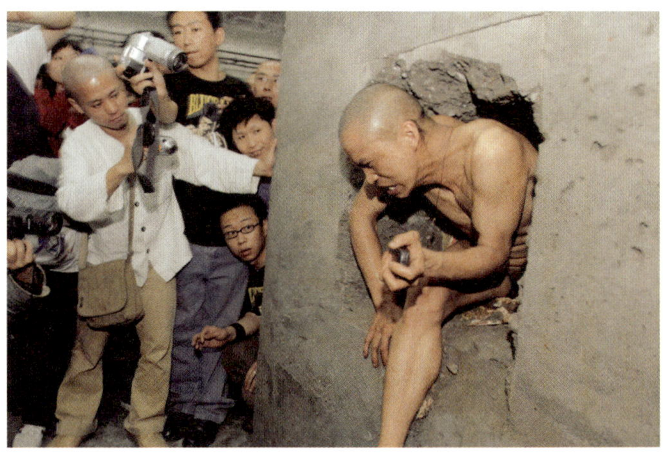

铸（No.2），2004
行为：2004年4月23至24日
地点：中国北京东京画廊
何云昌把自己整体浇铸在水泥墩
里，在水泥墩里停留24小时。

Cast (No.2), 2004
Performance: April 23 – 24, 2004
Venue: Beijing Tokyo Art Projects,
Beijing, China
He Yunchang sealed himself inside a cement
block and stayed inside for 24 hours.

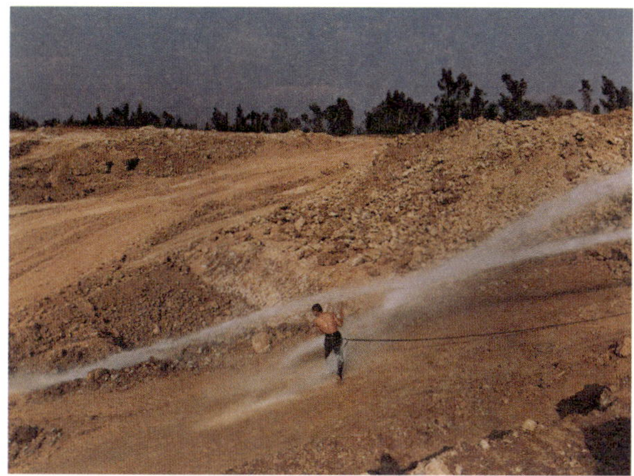
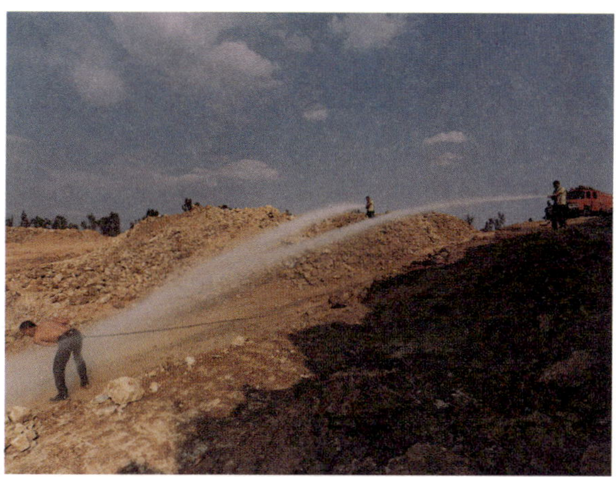
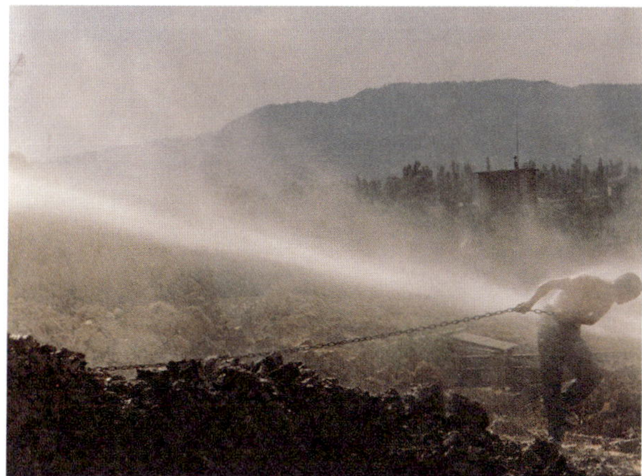
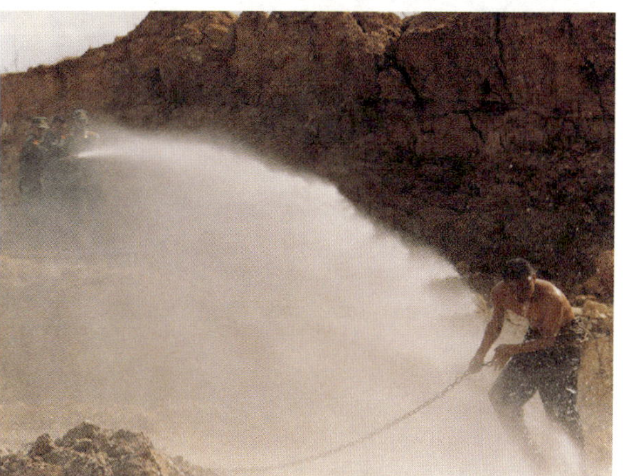

枪手，2001
行为：2001年3月31日
地点：中国昆明
何云昌与消防车和高压水枪
对峙30分钟。

Gunman, 2001
Performance: March 31, 2001
Venue: Kunming, China
He Yunchang was sprayed with a fire engine's
high-pressure water hoses
for 30 minutes

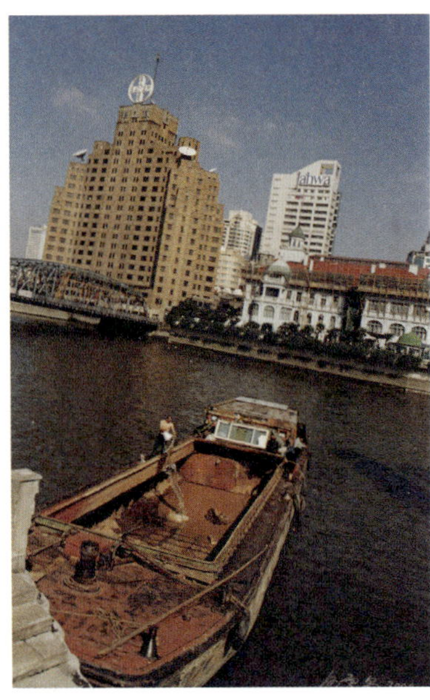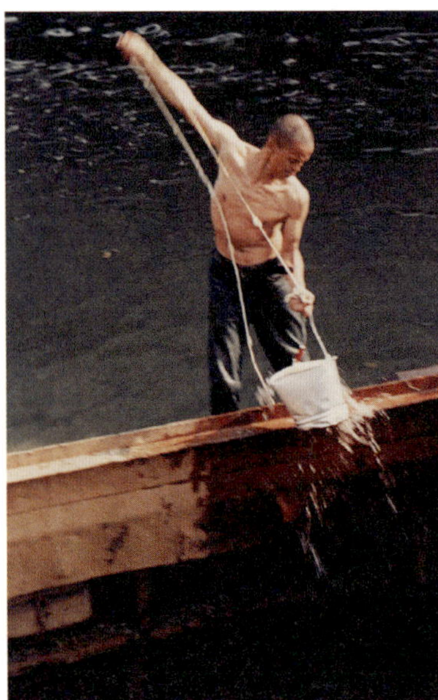

上海水记，2000
行为：2000年11月3日
地点：中国上海苏州河
何云昌从上海苏州河下游用水桶取10
吨水，倒入船舱中，
运往上游4公里处，
再倒10吨水入苏州河中，
使其重新流淌5公里，
全过程历时8小时。

River Document, Shanghai, 2000
Performance: November 3, 2000
Venue: Suzhou River, Shanghai, China
He Yunchang brought ten tons of water with a
bucket out of the Suzhou river into the cabin in
the lower reaches of Suzhou River, transported
it for 4 kilometers to the upper reaches, where
he poured all the water back into the river,
making them re-flow for 5 kilometers. The
whole process lasted for 8 hours.

与水对话，1999
行为：1999年2月14日
地点：中国云南梁河
何云昌企图将河水分为两半，左右臂开一厘米深刀口，
血顺手臂流入水，历时90分钟。

Dialogue with Water, 1999
Performance: February 14, 1999
Venue: Lianghe, Yunnan, China
He Yunchang attempted to divide the river into two halves,
 with his left and right arms cut 1cm deep and his blood dripping down his arms and into the
river. The performance lasted for 90 minutes.

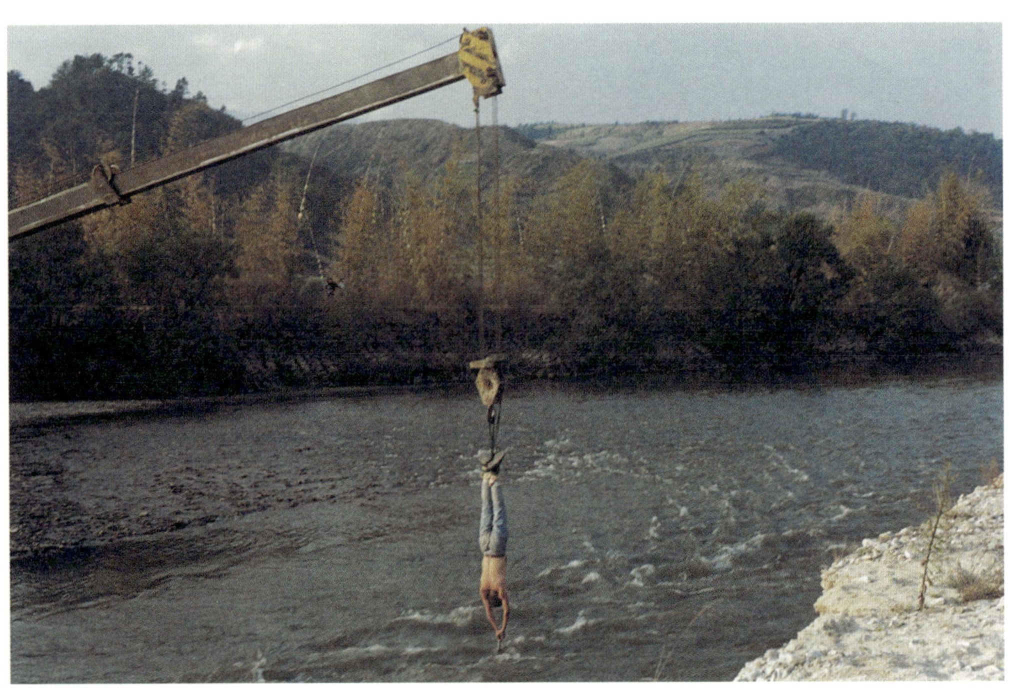

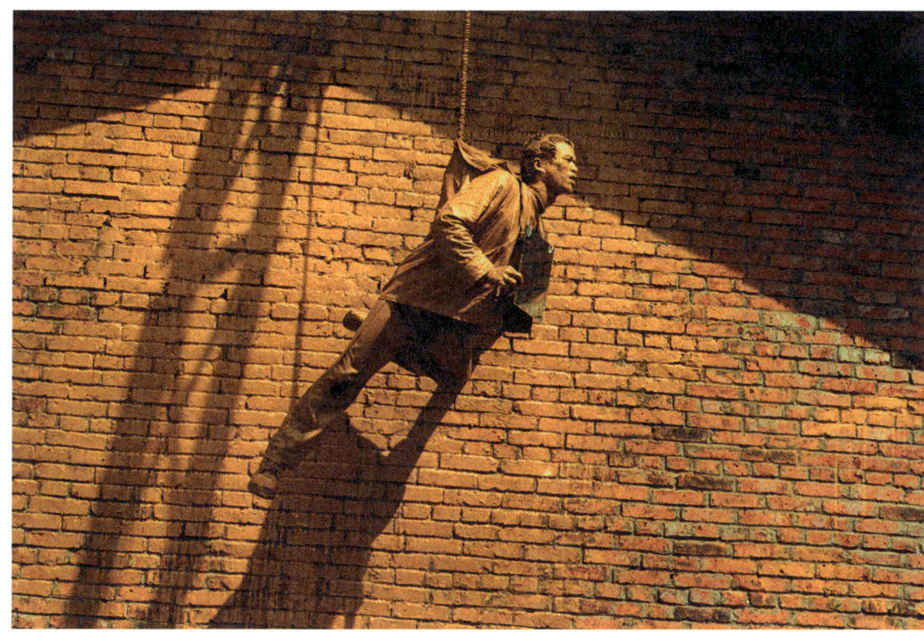

金色阳光（No.2），1999
行为：1999年10月3日
地点：中国云南安宁监狱
何云昌试图移动阳光，
历时127分钟。

Golden Sunshine (No.2), 1999
Performance: October 3, 1999
Venue: Anning Prison, Yunnan, China
He Yunchang attempted to move the sunlight
for 127 minutes.

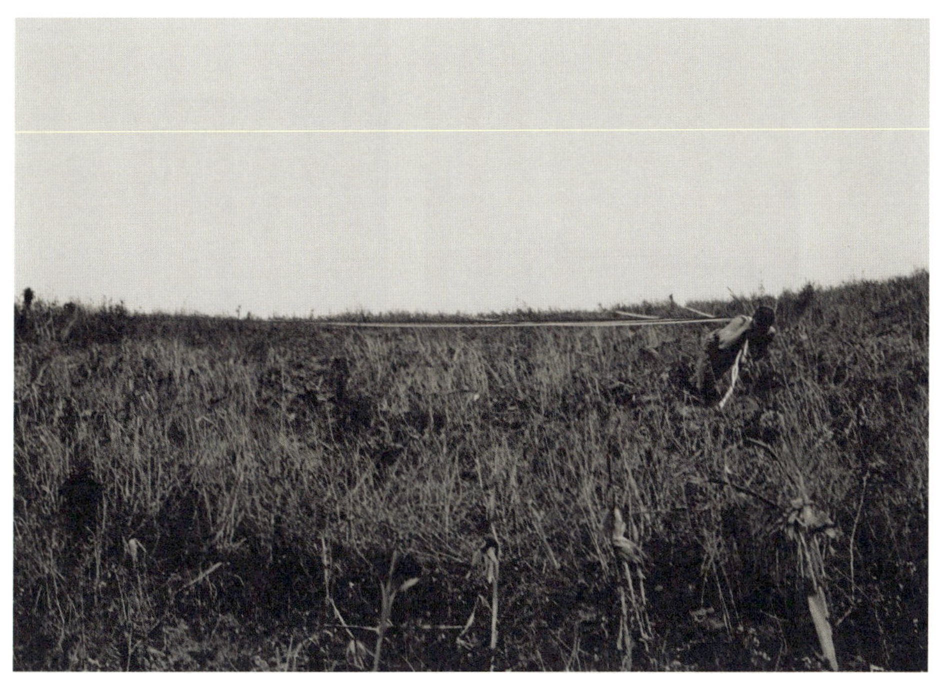

移山，1999
行为：1999年2月26日
地点：中国云南梁河
何云昌用木桩和绳子将一座山捆
住，用力拉扯30分钟。地球自转为
1670公里／小时，30分钟后此山自
西向东移动了835公里。

Moving a Mountain, 1999
Performance: February 26, 1999
Venue: Lianghe, Yunnan, China
He Yunchang fastened a mountain with a
wooden stick and a string and pulled it for
30 minutes. As the earth rotates 1670
kilometers per hour, the mountain moved
eastbound for 835 kilometers after 30
minutes.

石头英国漫游记， 2006-2007
行为：2006年9月24日至2007年1月14日
地点：大不列颠岛
何云昌在英国东海岸一个叫布姆的地方随意拣了一块
石头，拿着这块石头围绕着英国外沿大致绕行一圈，
回到布姆把那块石头放回原处，历时112天，行程约
3500公里。

The Rock Tours Round Great Britain, 2006 – 2007
Performance: September 24, 2006 to January 14, 2007
Venue: Great Britain
He Yunchang picked up a random rock from Boulmer, located on the
east coast of England, and carried it on foot around the perimeter of
the island of Great Britain. Eventually,
he returned the rock to its original location.
The pilgrimage took 112 days and covered
approximately 3,500 kilometers.

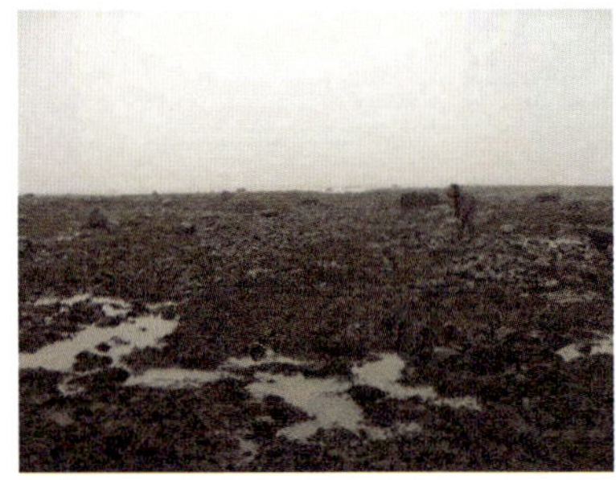
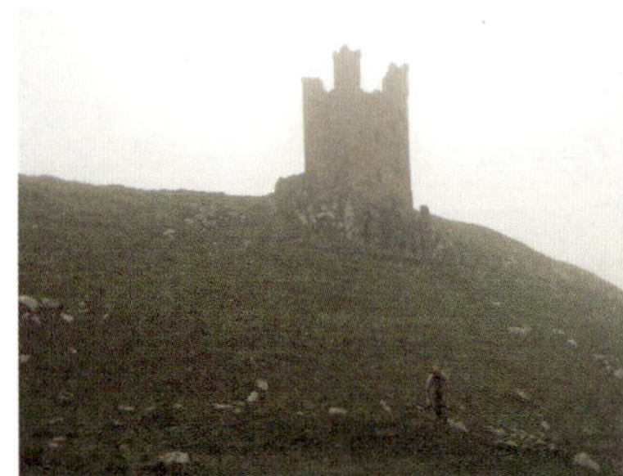

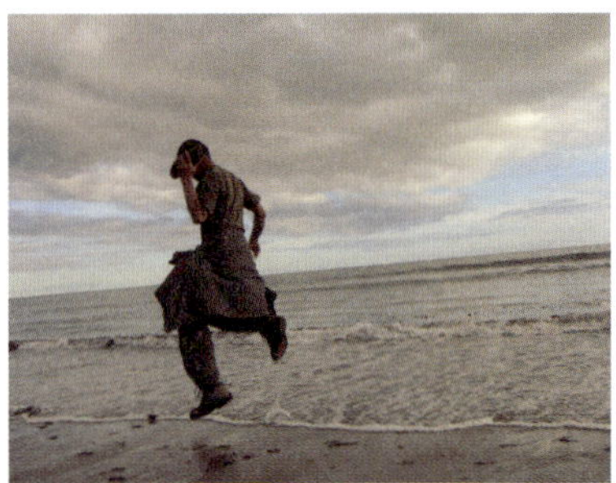
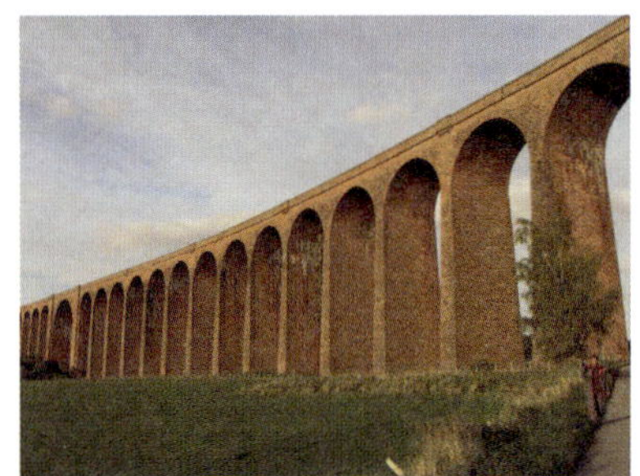
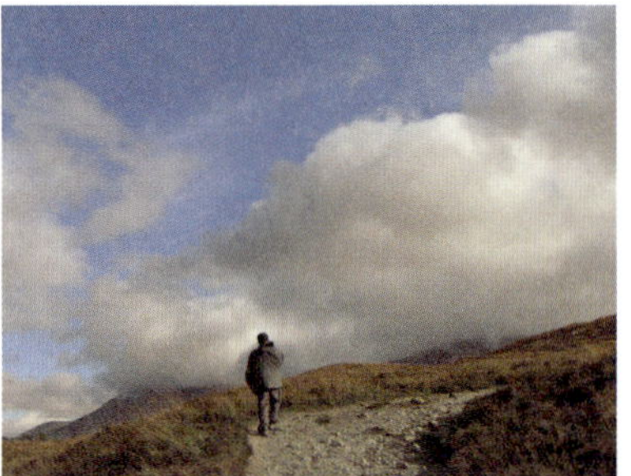

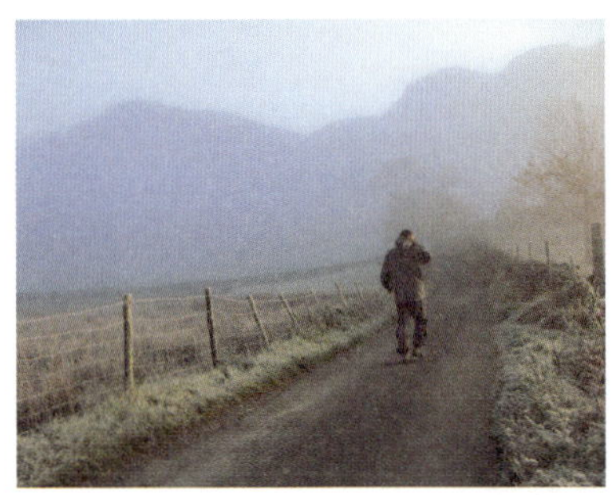
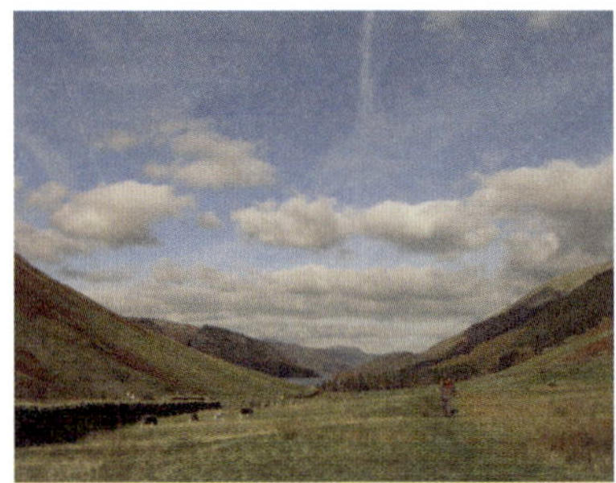
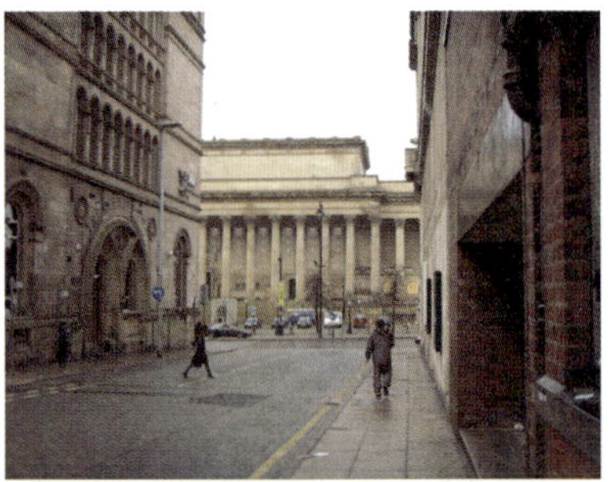

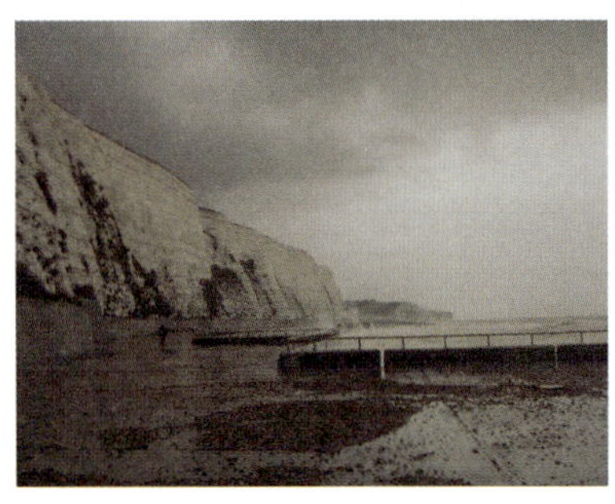
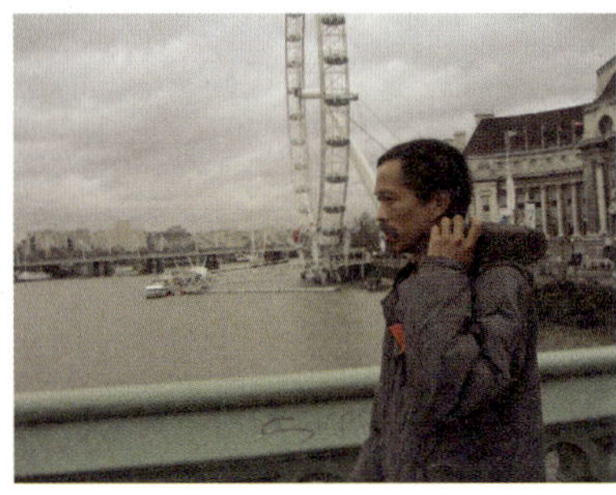
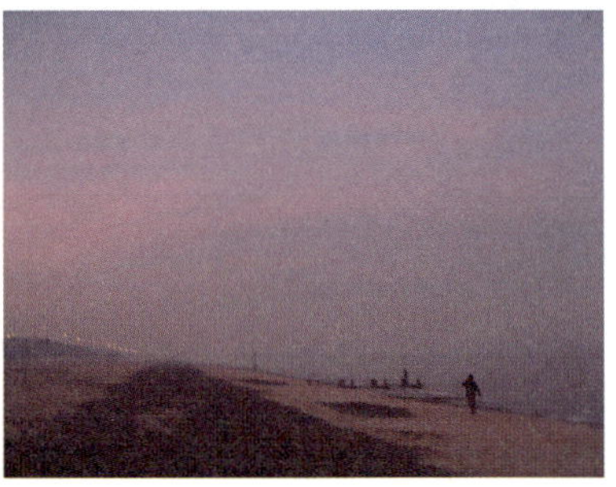

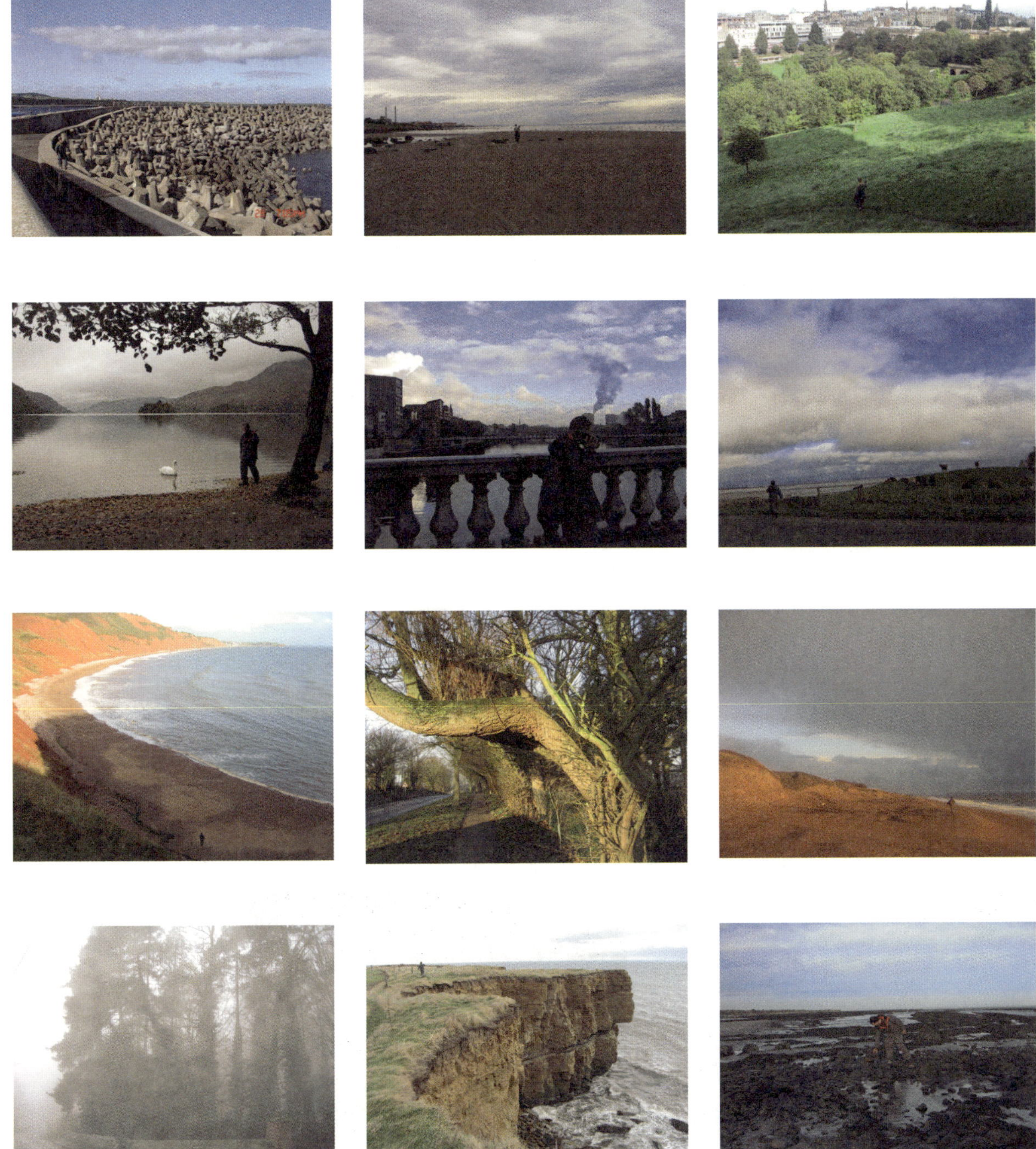

《一根肋骨》资料文件照片， 2008-2009
照片
何云昌用手术取一根肋骨制成项圈。
图片提供：麦勒画廊 北京-卢森

One Rib Photo Documentations, 2008-2009
C-print
He Yunchang had a surgeion rmove one rib from his
body. He used the rib to make a necklace.
Courtesy of Galerie Urs Meile, Beijing-Lucerne

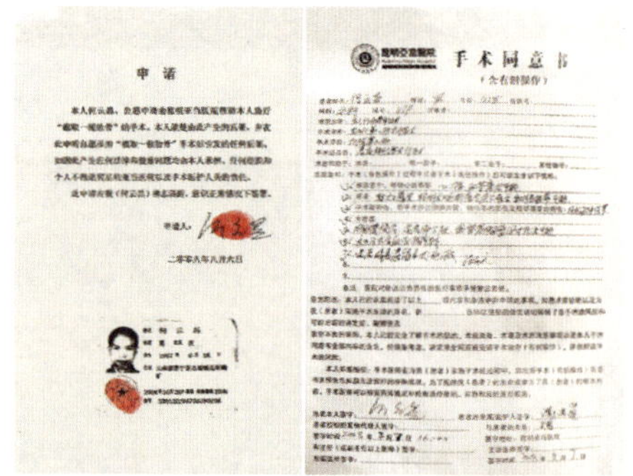

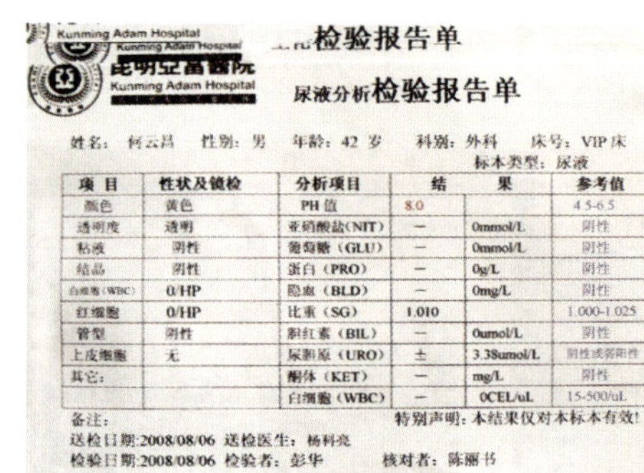

Kunming Adam Hospital
Kunming Adam Hospital
昆明亚富医院
Kunming Adam Hospital

检验报告单

尿液分析检验报告单

姓名：何云昌　性别：男　年龄：42 岁　科别：外科　床号：VIP床
标本类型：尿液

项　目	性状及镜检	分析项目	结　　果		参考值
颜色	黄色	PH 值	8.0		4.5-6.5
透明度	透明	亚硝酸盐（NIT）	—	0mmol/L	阴性
粘液	阴性	葡萄糖（GLU）	—	0mmol/L	阴性
结晶	阴性	蛋白（PRO）	—	0g/L	阴性
白细胞（WBC）	0/HP	隐血（BLD）	—	0mg/L	阴性
红细胞	0/HP	比重（SG）	1.010		1.000-1.025
管型	阴性	胆红素（BIL）	—	0umol/L	阴性
上皮细胞	无	尿胆原（URO）	±	3.38umol/L	阴性或弱阳性
其它:		酮体（KET）	—	mg/L	阴性
		白细胞（WBC）	—	0CEL/uL	15-500/uL

备注：　　　　　　　　　　　　特别声明：本结果仅对本标本有效！
送检日期:2008/08/06 送检医生：杨科亮
检验日期:2008/08/06 检验者：彭华　　　核对者：陈丽书

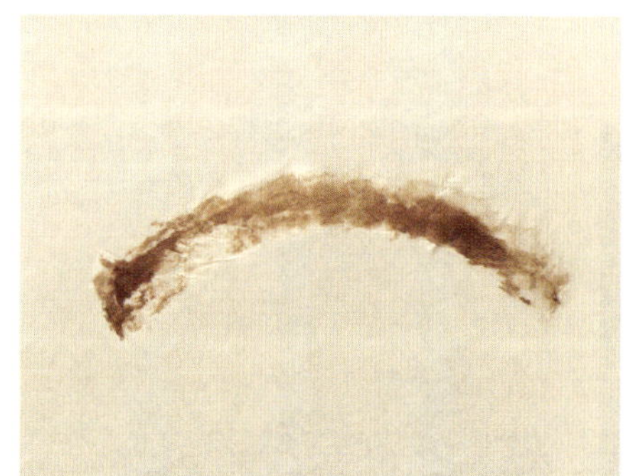

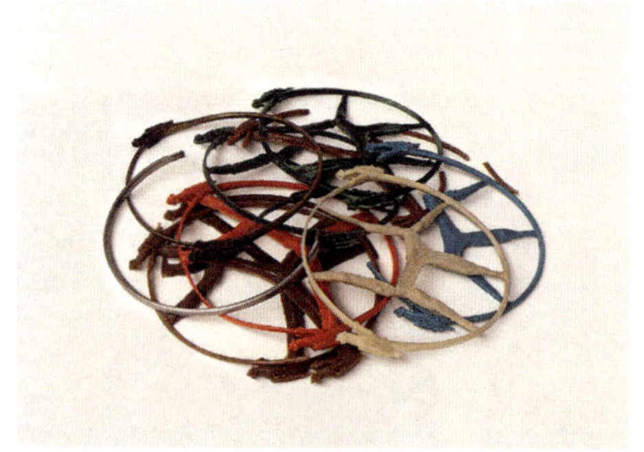

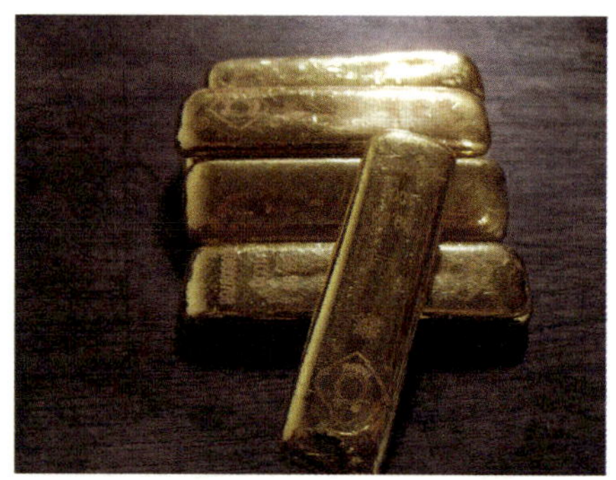

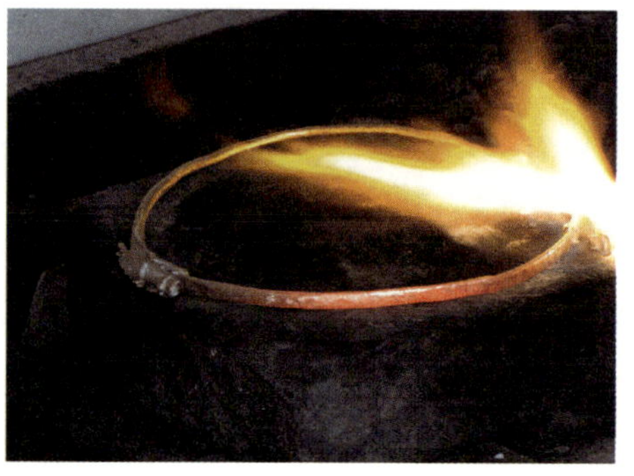

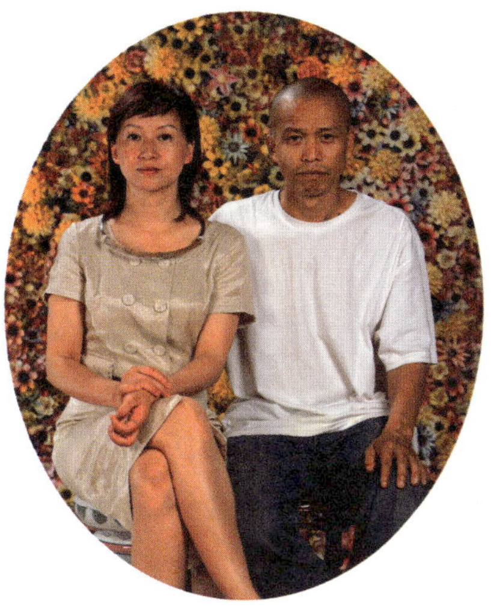
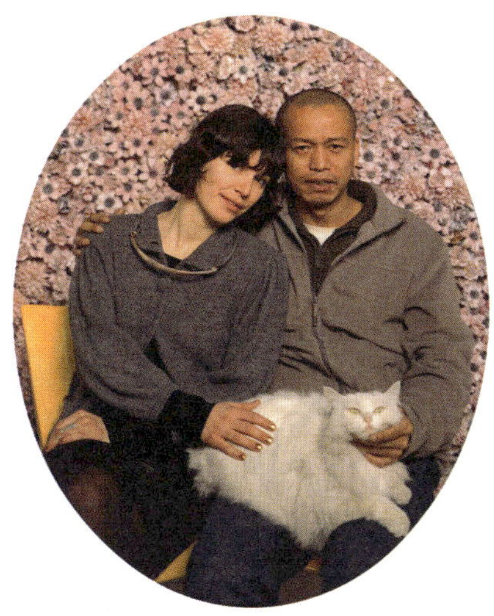
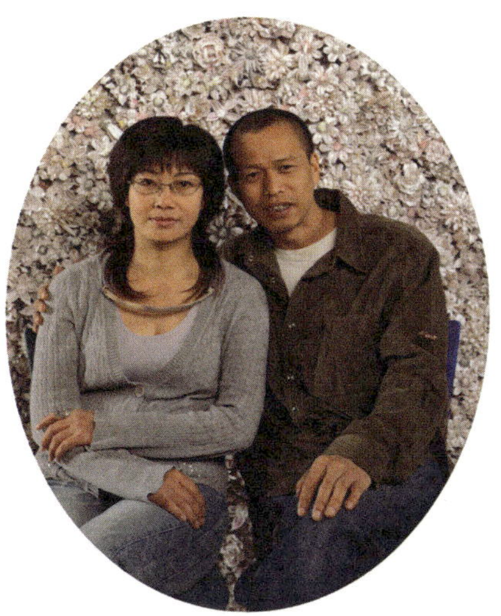
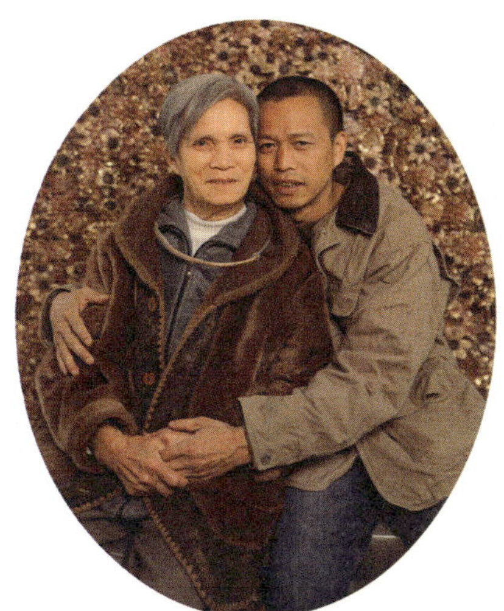

一根肋骨（No 1-5），2009
照片
图片提供：艺术家和麦勒画廊
北京-卢森

One Rib (No 1-5), 2009
C-print
Courtesy of the artist and Galerie Urs Meile,
Beijing-Lucerne

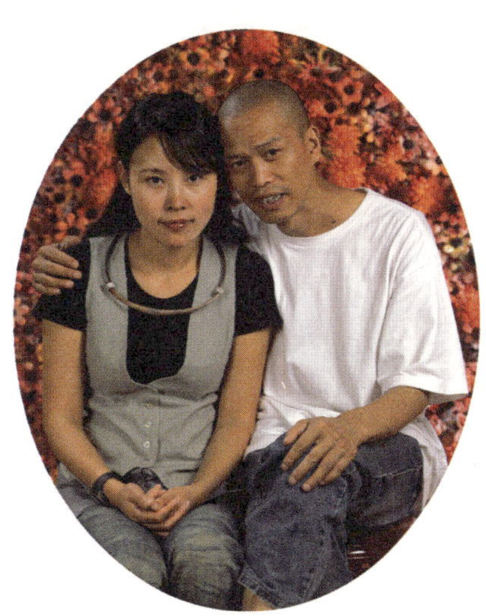

蒋 志

JIANG ZHI

作为艺术家，你在创作中所关心的是什么？以一件作品为例，分享你的创作过程。

人所关心的事物和问题，我都关心。就创作本身而言，我关心的是自己是不是以很私人的角度观察到了什么，是否是一个值得为之工作一段时间的新方向。我希望做出来的作品，不是要传达个人的某种意见和道理，而是我仍可以从中能不断看到什么，能从中学习的，能获得新感受的……那种东西……它的出现，能带来那种就像我曾体验过的冲破阻碍的震惊。

我有一件作品叫《一件作品》，应该是把它当小说看更好。2007年的时候我为一个主题展想作品方案，当时的情况很有意思，像是接了一单生意在为提案冥思苦想。我对着一张白纸，几天都写不出一个字，有天我上完洗手间重新坐到这张白纸面前，我想，去他的，我就展出一张白纸好了。于是我开始写方案、写作品阐述、写创作经过、写展示方式……为了让这张白纸有"现成品"的元素，"我"说它的前身是一件老棉衣；为了有"社会性"和"底层关怀"，"我"说这件棉衣是一个孤苦老头穿了十几年一年四季都没有脱下的来；为了有"和艺术家的紧密的生活联系"，"我"把这个老头说成我很小的时候就认识的；为了具有当时流行的"极简主义"，"我"让它就是一张方方正正的白纸出现……越写越觉得有问题，关于艺术家把"底层人物"当作作品材料的"道德"和"伦理"问题、当代艺术的作品范式问题、艺术家面对社会改造的能力问题、艺术家试图影响社会现实的心态问题……只不过，"我"觉得这张白纸仍是一件与当代艺术作品的成功条件丝丝入扣的"杰作"……因为如此，所以当我开始写第一个字的时候就没有打算要把"这张纸"制作出来。

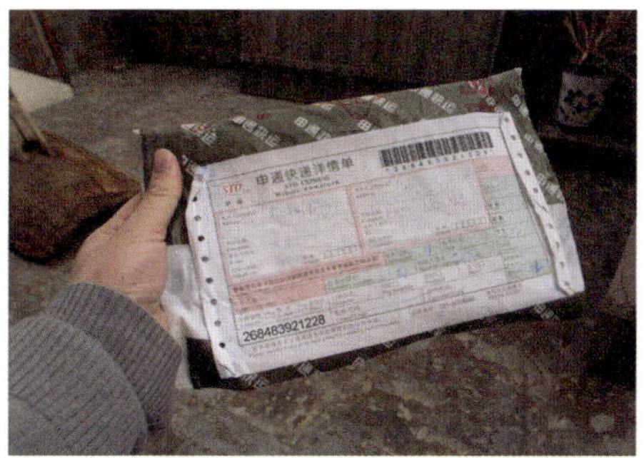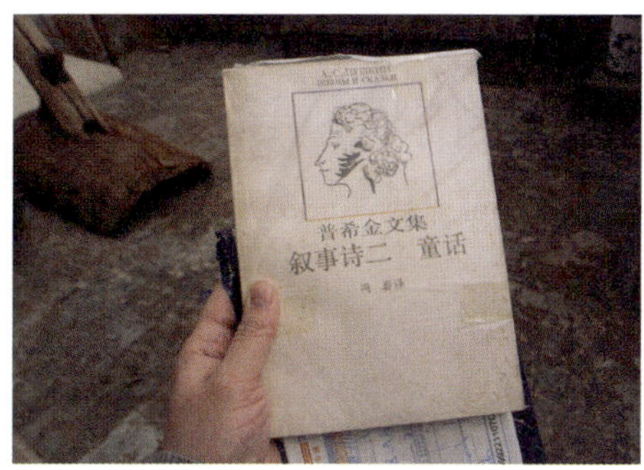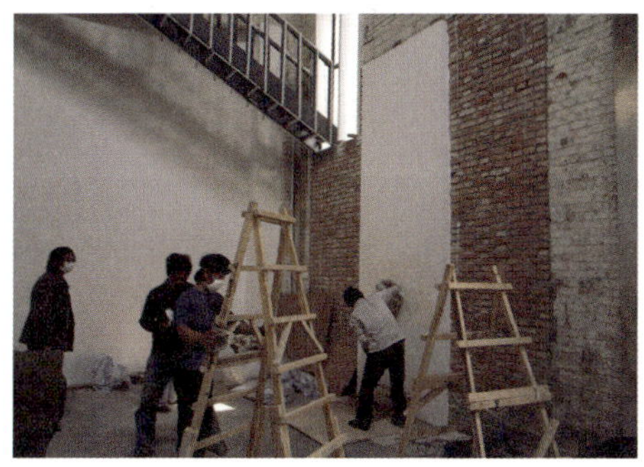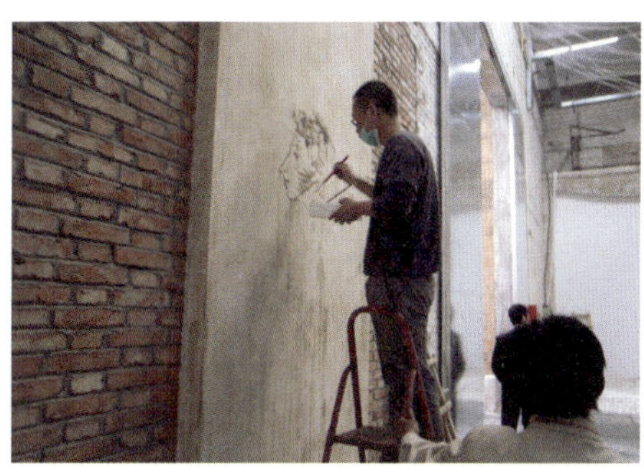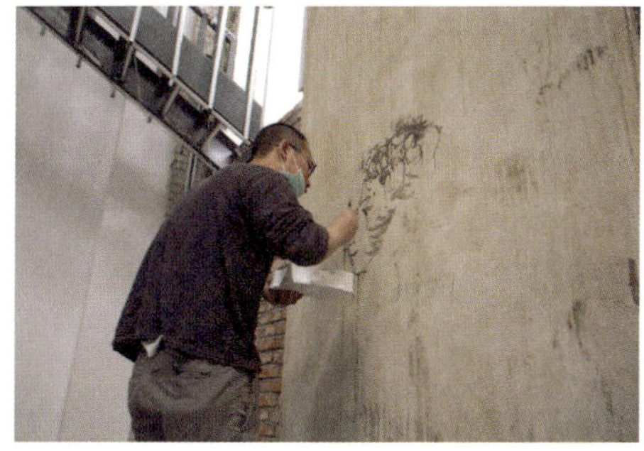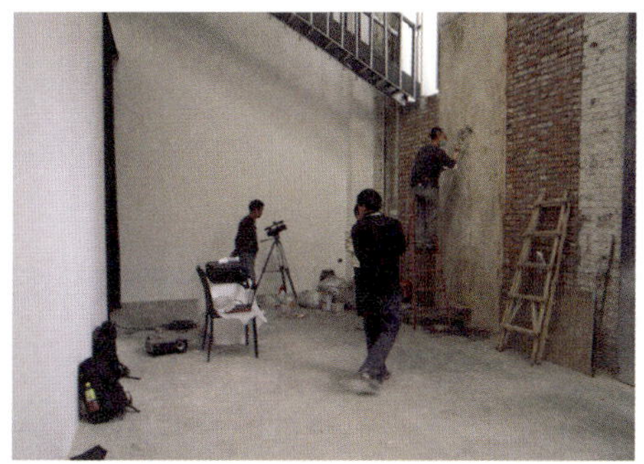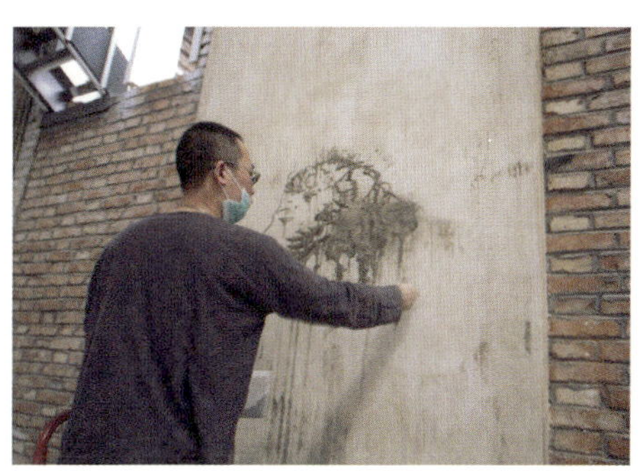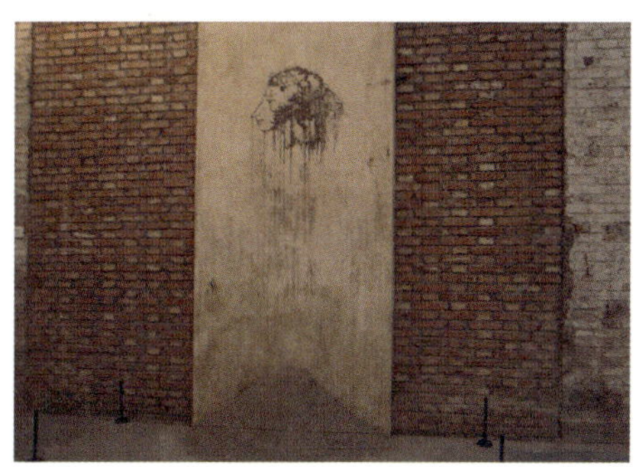

《假如生活欺骗了你》作品的制作过程　2009
地点：伊比利亚当代艺术中心
时间：2008年4月

If by Life You Were Deceived in installation process, 2009
Iberia Center for Contemporary Art
April 2008

一件作品

1

几个月前，策展人告诉我，邀请我参加的展览的主题是"四季"，等他走后，我打开电脑，想在博客上写点什么，想恢复一下对季节的感受，真不好意思说出来，自从世界有了空调和暖气设备，冰箱充满不同季节（以前的那种季节）的蔬果之后，对季节的感受开始淡漠了。而且，全球都在变暖，甚至南北的季节开始有错位的迹象了。

我藏下了一句："毕竟是春天了，我们园子里干燥的土地上开始有些绿色。"我立即发现这样的说法有些矫情。问题不是出在我对"春天"文艺青年般的"情怀"，而是"我们的园子"上。它带有一种危险感。它有炫耀的嫌疑。说在这个城市拥有自己的园子，会被眼明手快的网民骂得狗血喷头的。在20年前，你说"自己的园子"，这没什么不妥，尤其像我这样在农村长大，摘辣椒当玩具的人来说，这是对土地的热爱的表现。我现在这块土地———巴掌大小的——是开发商对我们一楼的住户在阳光上损失的歉意。

不管怎样，我还是换了一个说法："毕竟是春天来了，公园里干燥的土地开始有些绿色了。"但是公园和我有什么关系呢？有好几年都没去过公园了。我和公园的关系虽然比不上公园的清洁工。虽然他们和公园的关系不是一般的紧密关系，而更多的是紧密的紧张关系，或紧张的紧密关系。怎么说都可以，反正就那个意思。

还是要回到一个恰当的关系位置来写一句关于"春天"，……时间过得真快，阳光快要落到前面那幢楼的背后去了。我一般是以这个光线的消失来确认是不是到了下午两点。所以我要抓紧一点时间，来完成"一个表达"。我想了一会，写到"毕竟是春天了，祖国大地开始有些绿色了"。太傻了，我划掉了这句。改写成："毕竟是春天了，在亚洲———亚洲的中国———亚洲的中国的北方———亚洲的中国的北方的北京———亚洲的中国的北方的北京的朝阳区———望京地区———一个住宅小区———一个角落的干燥的土地上，开始有些绿色了"。不错，虽然不是很完美，但也勉强达到了我一直对艺术创作的独特角度的追求。卫星地图的视角。

完成了对季节的思考程序，我开始设想一些方案……

2

一个月过去了，我仍然想不出半个"四季"的方案，我只好打电话给策展人诉苦，他回答说"根本"不需要作品和四季有什么关系。他怕我仍然不明白，举了一个例子说，我这个火锅是麻辣火锅，不管你端来的是肥羊、鸭舌、土豆片，还是耗子鱼、金针菇，它仍然还是麻辣火锅。我觉得豁然开朗了。

那一刻，我觉得我的脑海里马上要产生四十个方案。

过了一天，我突然又为方案和主题太没关系而忧心戚戚。

3

在"四季"的展厅里，有一件这样的作品，就是一张一人高的白纸，纸的边缘不整齐，看得出不是现代工艺的流水线上出来的，而是纯手工的纸。它夹在两块玻璃之间的真空层里。作品的 Title 在旁边的小标签上：《棉衣》。没错，这就是我的作品。那张小标签上，还有作品的材料说明以及对作品简单的阐释。大致内容是，这张白纸来源于一个一穷二白的老头身上一件一年四季都穿着的棉衣，它经过了浸泡、捣烂、磨浆、漂白、滤网……等一系列工艺之后，做成的一张白纸。

其它的阐述文字难以在这复述了，因为那是特殊的文本——我用一个秘密软件在电脑上自动生成的。这个软件的资料库有三千多篇/本艺术评论的著作，我只要输入一些关键词和所需要的字数，就能得到一篇学术性不错的文章。而且，这个软件还能自动上网搜索资料并分析批评家在艺术界影响力的排名，更新候选文章的次序。这是一个"智能"软件。它还有"理解难度"强、中、弱三个可调等级。我一般会让它令人费解点。太白白会影响效果，这无疑会损害对此有智力要求的观众的利益。

我输入的关键词有：问题、社会、城市、全、球、时间、艺术家、代、化、后、感、严肃、换句话说、60、70、80、90、果冻、不朽、存在、新、性、型、迷你裙、殖民、技术、工业、农业、信息、进一步说、消费、很显然、非常、探讨、历史、在这个意义上、转换、本土、世界、政治、剥离、真实、反过来、展开、时代。就这些。字数要求是200字内。这些关键词效果不错，用了两年了（除了"60"因使用率不高很快被淘汰了）。

4

若有所思。我望着这张在两块大水晶玻璃和做工考究的白色木框之中的这张白纸。

它起码获得了物理上尊重。在豪华镶金的马桶上和在劣质陶瓷的马桶上获得的自尊感是不一样的。

看到它那么有尊严，那么平整，那么没有一点折印。我就明显感觉到了来自虚荣心的辐射波一阵阵荡漾过来。

把作品用图钉摁在墙上的时代一去不复返了。我甚至有了1949年的豪迈之情。这件作品不久后还将去纽约一个美术馆展出，我的画廊还给对方慎重地提出了展厅的光线、温度和湿度的要求。我得承认，它获得的待遇有点太过分了。

5

我需要给观众们记者们介绍这件作品的来龙去脉，首先，这张白纸的前身是一件穿了十几年的棉袄。棉袄的主人我从小就认识，现在七十多岁了。我小的时候他还抱过我，经常喜欢把我高高地抛起来然后双手接住。后来他觉得这个技术太娴熟了，就尝试用一只手来接。幸好他还是抓住了一条腿，要不然我就完蛋了。他以后再也没有

得到抱我的机会。他一直没有离开过那个村子，没有娶老婆，没有孩子，十几年只穿同一件棉袄，过着现在很时髦很环保的"简单生活"。

在这个作品方案想出来之前，开始我找这么一件棉衣之前，我从来没有想到过这个差点把我摔死的老头会进入我的艺术创作中来。我从来没有记起过他，他对我是没有意义的存在，我知道这种残酷性也正发生在我和其他人之间。

他，刘青山，也对我千里迢迢来找他感到非常的意外。我四岁离开了那个村子，他仍然完整地保留了对我那时候的所有记忆，我请他喝酒，请他讲述这件棉袄的故事。他竟然说这件棉袄是菩萨赐的，十年前因为村子里有个农民觉得他老要有"老不正经"的行为，一把火烧了他的住了几十年的房子，而这件棉衣奇迹般的完好无损（我想是因为那时他刚好正穿在身上）。现在他住在一座能靠自己一人之力搭起的楼房里，花了十年时间，每天他都在村子里捡来一些木头、灯砖块、竹子、矿泉水瓶、可乐罐、草等等，依傍一棵大树慢慢堆砌，现在已是2层的复式楼。工程还在继续。

我给他带来了四套服装，春夏秋冬他都有合适季的衣服了，他答应把他那件穿了十多年的棉衣送给我，他喝了酒之后开始兴奋起来，讲他的孤独，别人都不愿意和他来往；他的委屈，村子的人丢了东西都会首先怀疑他；他的担心，村委会要把他的房子那块地卖给一个老板作化工厂；他的愿望，他能去天安门看看毛主席……我对他的故事的需求其实没有这么多，只要能满足我的作品阐释和应付一些记者就可以了。所以，当他的话溢出这个容器的时候，我开始心不在焉。我相信大多数艺术家的感受和我一样，他们，民工、残疾者、失业者、乞丐等等那些所有家什财物可以堆满展厅几个平方的人，其实都属于一个种类：艺术作品的材料。

如果他的痛苦不是你的痛苦，他的快乐不是你的快乐，有效的交流将会是短暂的。这意味着，有需求关系的交流，才不会是虚假的。平心而论，我觉得这一点也十分正常。我想起几个月前和一个叫米娜娜同学的交流，我们在酒吧里热切地交流了几个小时，都觉得和对方勾起还有几个不是夜的话题倾诉，但是第二天上午，我们在酒店房间各自穿好球衣之后，再也无话可说，那天晚上我还讲了自己的一个作品的方案，我要和一个妓女一起搞艺术，让它带我的助手，让它完成一些画。米娜娜同学幽幽地问，"这样做多少年呢？"我说，"几个月，最多一年吧。"我说，"然后呢？"我说就还会骑嫂的人啊。她水汪汪的大眼睛望着我，"你不觉得太残酷了吗？""为什么呢？"我问。她说，"它对你产生了感情怎么办？"然后我开始真正反思了。面对这么一个漂亮的女孩我不能表现出没有情感。美貌是有说服力的，越美貌越有说服力。这点对一个"健康的男人"来说尤其如此。我们几乎就只有肉体。肉体的状况构成了我们精神和道德观念。在这个荷尔蒙的晚上，我追随她信奉了动物保护主义。

6

一张白纸很快就制作出来了。一开始我想在那上面做点什么，我本来没有想做得那么极简的。涂点什么呢？我想起刘青山曾提起过这一辈子的梦想就是去天安门，但是这个也太"中国"了，太"符号化"了，太有"后殖民主义"嫌疑了。这会把事情搞砸。

也许他心目中还有个女人？一个念念不忘的女人。我马上飞过去和他见面。这样，作品的成本又增加了。他看见我又出现在他面前很吃惊，非常高兴地说，以后他要把他的楼房留给我。他接过我带给他一张天安门的明信片看了半天，但没有说什么。我请他去镇上喝酒，他说自从穿了我给他的新衣服之后村里人对他不一样了，见面也会点点头，甚至还有一个五十多的寡妇对他抛了几个有意思的眼神。他说并不是几件新衣服的原因，而是村里人觉得他在北京有人。我接着他的话头把"交流"引向女人方面。出我意料的是，他好像很喜欢谈这方面的话题。他说他的初恋情人是人民币上的一个女拖拉机手，对这那张一元钞票一天可以手淫七、八次，他说他一直很穷，没有姑娘愿意嫁给他，只有自己的手愿意和他过性生活。他当时愿意那辆拖拉机从他身上压过去。我告诉他其实那个女拖拉机手和你差不多大哩，现在哈尔滨，都儿孙满堂了。他略微表现出一点不好意思。解释说那个时候的人都很不开放，想得不多，想得最多的是那张圆圆的脸，然后有时能想到乳房部分，阴毛部分根本没想过……我开始想象我的那张白纸，上面出现了用阴毛勾勒的一副女拖拉机手的形象。

我开玩笑说："你对人民币做那些事情，难怪人民币不喜欢你。你就没有喜欢过一个活生生在你面前的女人吗？"他说有的，年轻的时候他在村办学校的食堂做过炊事员，有个女教师长的很漂亮，每次她来打饭他都会特意给她双份的菜。那个姑娘也明白他的心意，每次见到他都会不好意思地对他笑笑。后来那个女孩被调到镇上的学校去了，临走前还送给他一张照片作留念。我很期待地问："那张照片现在还在吗？"

他带我去他树上的楼房里。这个"树楼"很小，只有不到4平米，大概有5米高。里面像个博物馆一样有很多奇怪的东西，他从房子中的半截树枝上挂着一个竹篓里拿出一个有小脸盆大小的贝壳，小心地打开它，我看见一张一寸黑白照片像珍珠一样躺在里面。但是因为磨损和褪色，已经看不清五官了，只看得出有条长辫子，照片上的脸部分的显影膜完全没有了。他说这是十年前那场火，他唯一救出来的东西。我问："她到底长得是什么样子呢？"他用奇怪眼神看着我，指着照片说："这不是很清楚吗？你看她的眼睛大大的，多么长的眼睫毛啊，还有鼻子，你看，多挺，这儿，她的嘴，嘴角是上翘的，平时她都这样……"

我半天都没说出话来，真的觉得被感动了。

最后，我还是狠下心向他借出这张照片，答应他一个星期就给他送回来。

7

我一回到北京，马上把这张照片拿去电分。另外我还请了一个法医根据这张模糊的脸形来做电脑复原绘图。我就接到老家的人的电话说我走后的第2天，刘青山就去世了。

一瞬间我的感觉成了一种空无的状态，世间的一切对这个人来说都逝去了。人生就是一本有限的日历。在上面曾经留下过也许有意思的线条，但没有记忆的参考，它们最终也是无谓的。他的那些大大小小的灾难和幸运、食堂里的心跳、那些几千次孤独的勃起、他的树上的宫殿……其实都是虚构。从空白的第一页到空白的最后一页，不同的人或厚或薄的日历内容，都是个体的虚构。

所以，这件作品，就是这张白纸了。我仿佛觉得他的一生都在里面，这是我彻底感到的虚空。

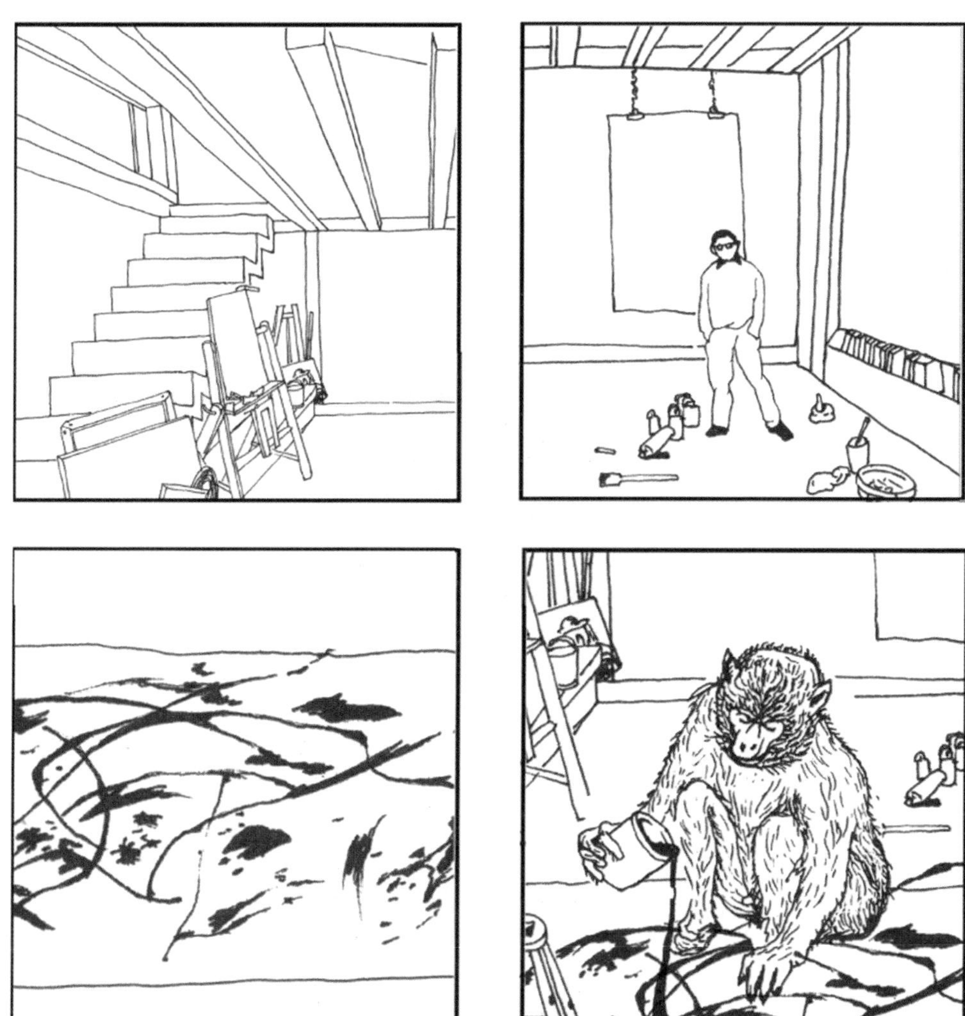

4，我有個計畫，找一隻猴子當我的助手，讓它幫我畫一些畫。

《一件作品》打印稿
一篇以小说形式记录的《四季》创作过程的文本

A Work, printout record
A fictional text recording the production of Four Seasons

《一件作品》（出版物）插图
绘图 / 江奕

A Work, (Publication) illustration
Drawing by Jiang Yi

《0.7％的盐》的拍摄现场
地点：香港观唐奥沙画廊
时间：2009年5月12日

0.7% Salt at filming site
Osage Kwun Tong, Hong Kong
12 May, 2009

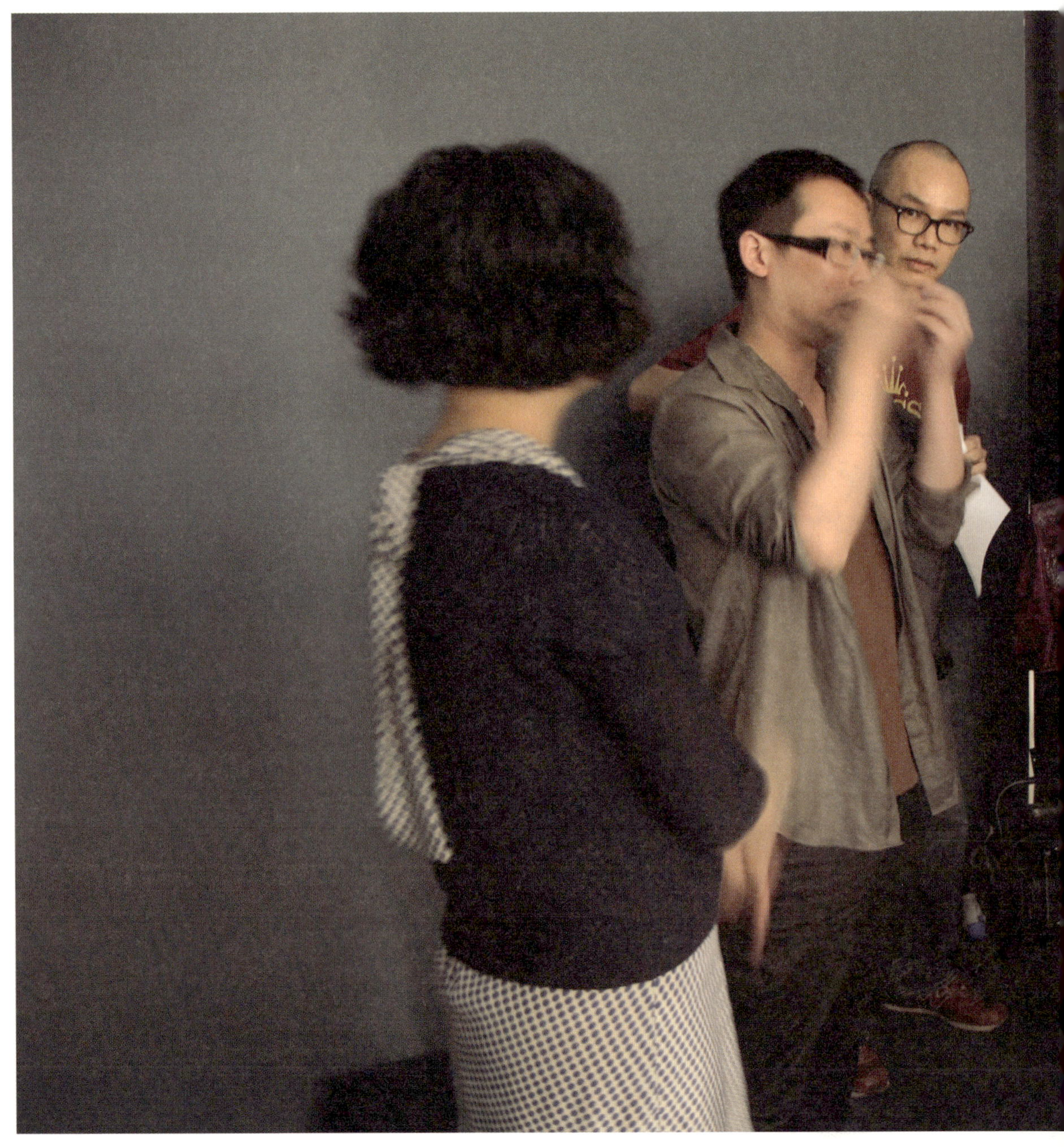

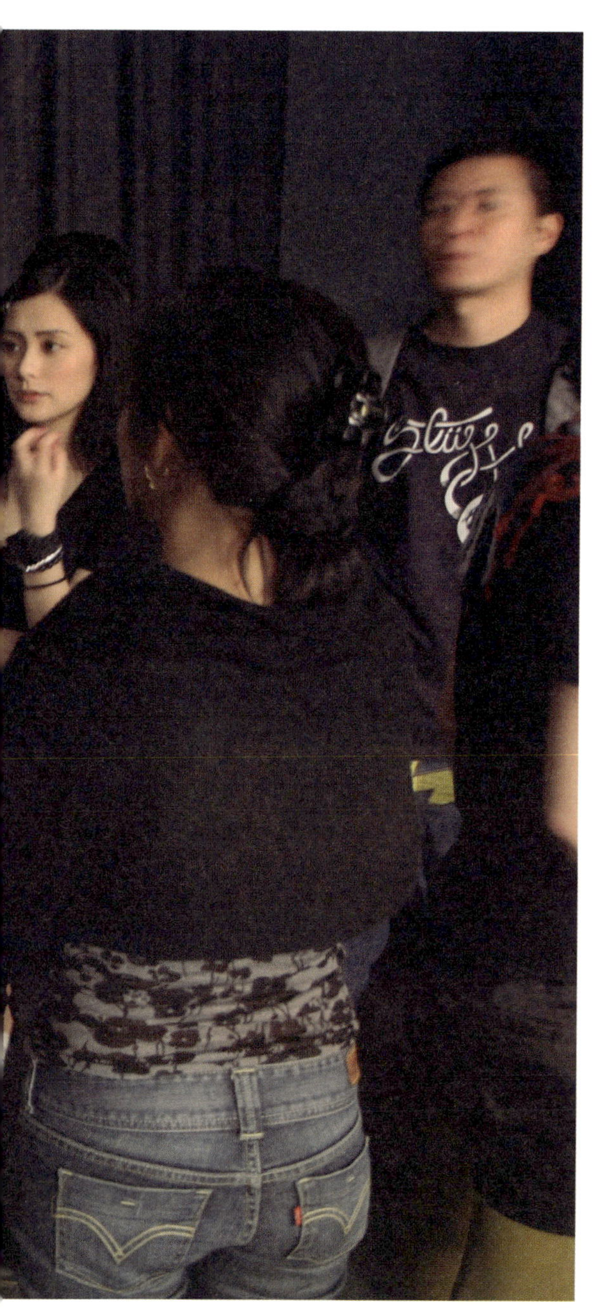

如果你是一个批评家，你会从什么角度来阐释和讨论你自己的创作？

我经常会假想很多种批评，从很多种角度来阐释和讨论，政治的、社会的、心理的、生理的、哲学的、历史的、修辞的、诗学的……但是我发现这毫无意义。最好的方式，是你找几个真正有想法的朋友聊聊。

在你的创作和思考中，什么书籍和艺术家曾经或正在影响着你？

太多了！看过的所有书（其实看得很少）都或多或少对我产生了影响，对我有影响的艺术家起码有上百个。就只算中国的话，起码有十个以上，而且这些都是我的朋友。

你是怎样判断和决定在什么语境下呈现你的哪些作品的？你是怎样看待作品呈现的语境和作品的关系的？

"时过境迁"，永远都是这个规律，作品得到怎样的呈现，依赖的是时间和空间。比方说，以讽刺的方式做老毛，现在已经没有太大意思了。

如何在创作上形成了现在的面貌，描述一下最近年来作品的发展和变化？

我不想说傻话。因为它很容易被搞成进化论式的回顾。我以前在一个采访中说过自己的所谓"发展和变化"，哦，从以前的很个人趣味和诗意到关注社会现实和政治……这类让人脸红的蠢话。我也不好说现在的面貌如何，因为我觉得一切都在形成之中。

你会在什么情况下摧毁你自己的作品？

摧毁作品？这样太矫情了。自生自灭是它们最合理也是最完美的命运。

你怎么看待艺术史和艺术家创作的关系？

尽量去了解以前和现在艺术家们的作品，我个人觉得这是该做的功课。历史一般是这样记载的：那个人在那个年代做的事情很突出。

在你的工作中，理性和情感冲动各自扮演着什么样的角色？

不知道，我只能听这俩无赖安排。

As an artist, what do you care most during working? Could you please give an example to introduce the process of your work for us?

I pay attention to all things and problems that man is concerned with. In respect of my work, the primary concern is whether my observation is made from some sort of personal perspective and whether the direction of work is truly something deserving of future attention. I hope my art is not trying to express personal opinion or reasoning, but rather something ... new that gives me inspiration and knowledge and evokes novel sentiments in me. It should be something that can help me land on a shocking experience that I once had after a break-through in my art career.

I once made a piece titled *A Work*. We'd better call it a fiction, actually. Back in 2007, I was conceiving a plan for an exhibition. The situation was very interesting, just like preparing a presentation for a client. Sitting before a white sheet of paper for days, I barely wrote a word. One day, I came back to my desk after going to toilet, thinking, "Damn it, I'll just exhibit this blank sheet." Then I started to draw out a plan, write explanation, working process and installation method... To make it resemble a "ready-made", "I" introduced the white sheet was made from an old winter coat made by cotton. To add elements of "social concerns and care for lower rungs of society" to the work, "I" made up a story that this coat was worn by an uncared poor old man four seasons out of the year. To make it have "direct relation to artist's life", "I" wrote that this old man knew me since I was a baby. To give it a touch of "minimalism", the prevailing movement at that time, "I" planned to show the white sheet in its original clean square form... The more I wrote, the more questions I got on my mind, such as the "moral and ethic" controversies involved in using "subordinate groups" as material for artwork, the customary paradigm of contemporary art-making, artists' capacity for social innovation, and the mentality of artists attempting to engage with reality... Even so, "I" believed this white sheet of paper still can be rated as a "masterpiece" as it perfectly incorporates all secret ingredients of a successful contemporary artwork... For that reason, it never occurred to me that I should actually produce "that blank sheet". I never gave it a thought even from the very beginning.

Suppose you are a critic, from what perspective would you talk about and explain you work?

I had speculated about many critical methods and tried to interpret my work in light of different disciplines, like politics, sociology, psychology, physiology, philosophy, history, rhetoric, poetics, etc. But they led me nowhere. The best way is to go and find some friends who have got their own way of thinking, and have a talk together.

What books and which artists have had, or are having an influence on your way of thinking and working?

There are too many! I can say all books I read (actually very few) more or less gave me influence, and I've learned from at least over a hundred artists. More than ten of them are Chinese artists, who are my friends also.

How do you decide the context in which your work is to be presented? How do you consider the relation of the context with your work?

"Circumstances alter cases." This is the rule for everything. The presentation of work is dependent on the factors of time and space. For example, using irony to produce a work on the subject of Mao will not be considered interesting now.

How does your work take the present shape? And please give a few words about the latest development and changes in your work.

I'm not going to say something silly, because the answer to this question will be easily turned into a Darwinistic retrospective. I talked about the so-called "changes and development" in an interview some time ago. I still remember what I said was the shift from a very personal taste to concerns about social reality and politics... silly enough to make me blush. It's hard to describe my present state because it's still in progress.

In what circumstances would you want to destroy your own creation?

Destroy them? This sounds too hokey. Let the nature take charge will be the most reasonable and ideal fate for them.

What do you think about the relation between the art history and artist's work?

Personally, I think as an artist I must try to find out what other artists have done in the history and at the present. Usually in a book history would be told in this way: that guy has made impressive contribution to his age.

What kind of roles would rational thinking and emotional impulse respectively play during your work time?

I don't know. All that I can do is only to do what the two rascals tell me to do.

《0.7％的盐》的拍摄现场
地点：香港观唐奥沙画廊
时间：2009年5月12日

0.7% Salt at filming site
Osage Kwun Tong, Hong Kong
12 May, 2009

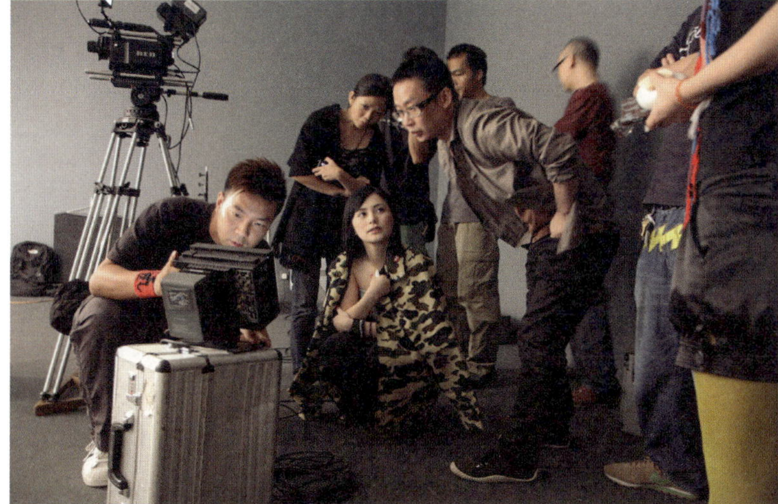

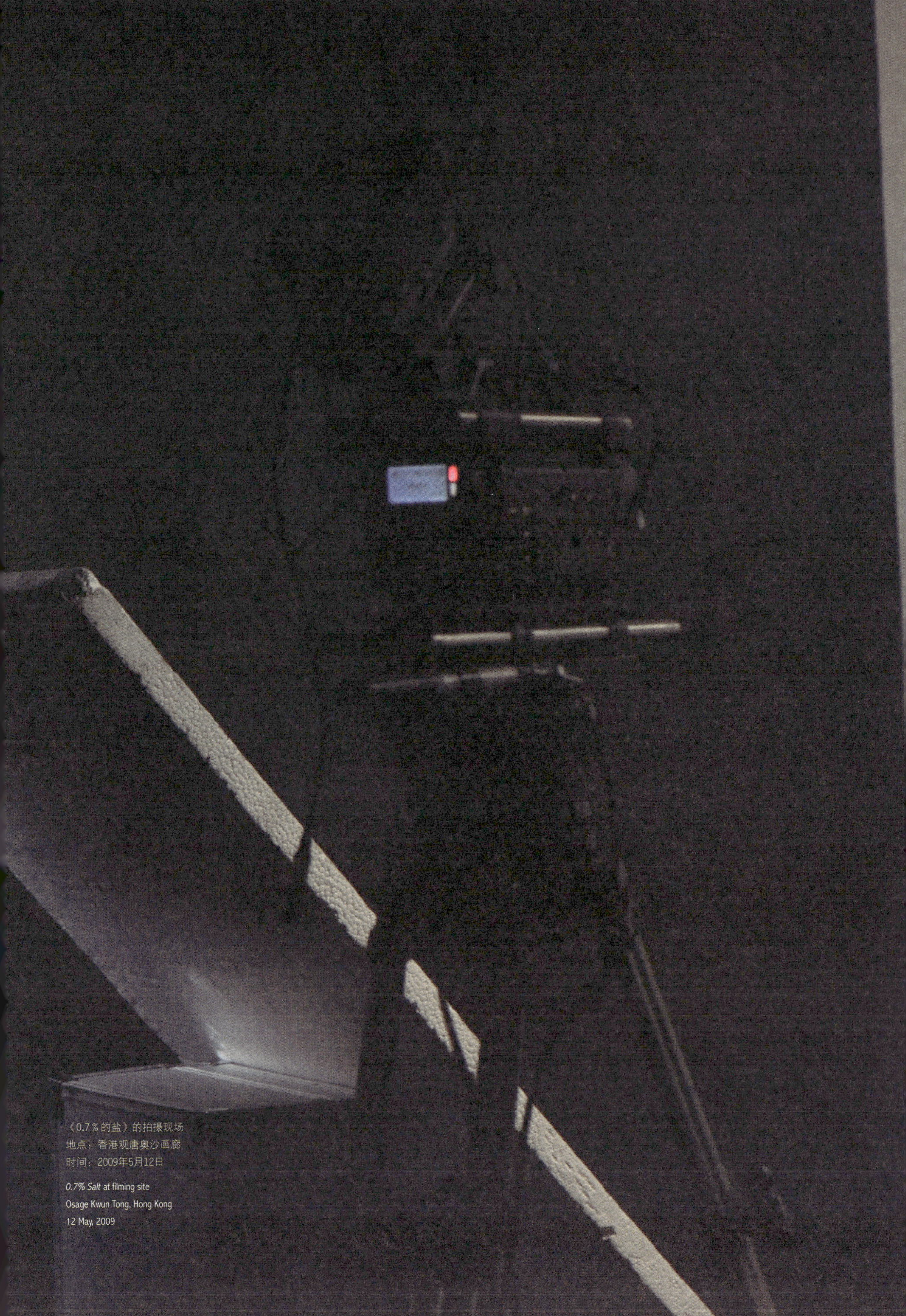

〈0.7％的盐〉的拍摄现场
地点：香港观唐奥沙画廊
时间：2009年5月12日

0.7% *Salt* at filming site
Osage Kwun Tong, Hong Kong
12 May, 2009

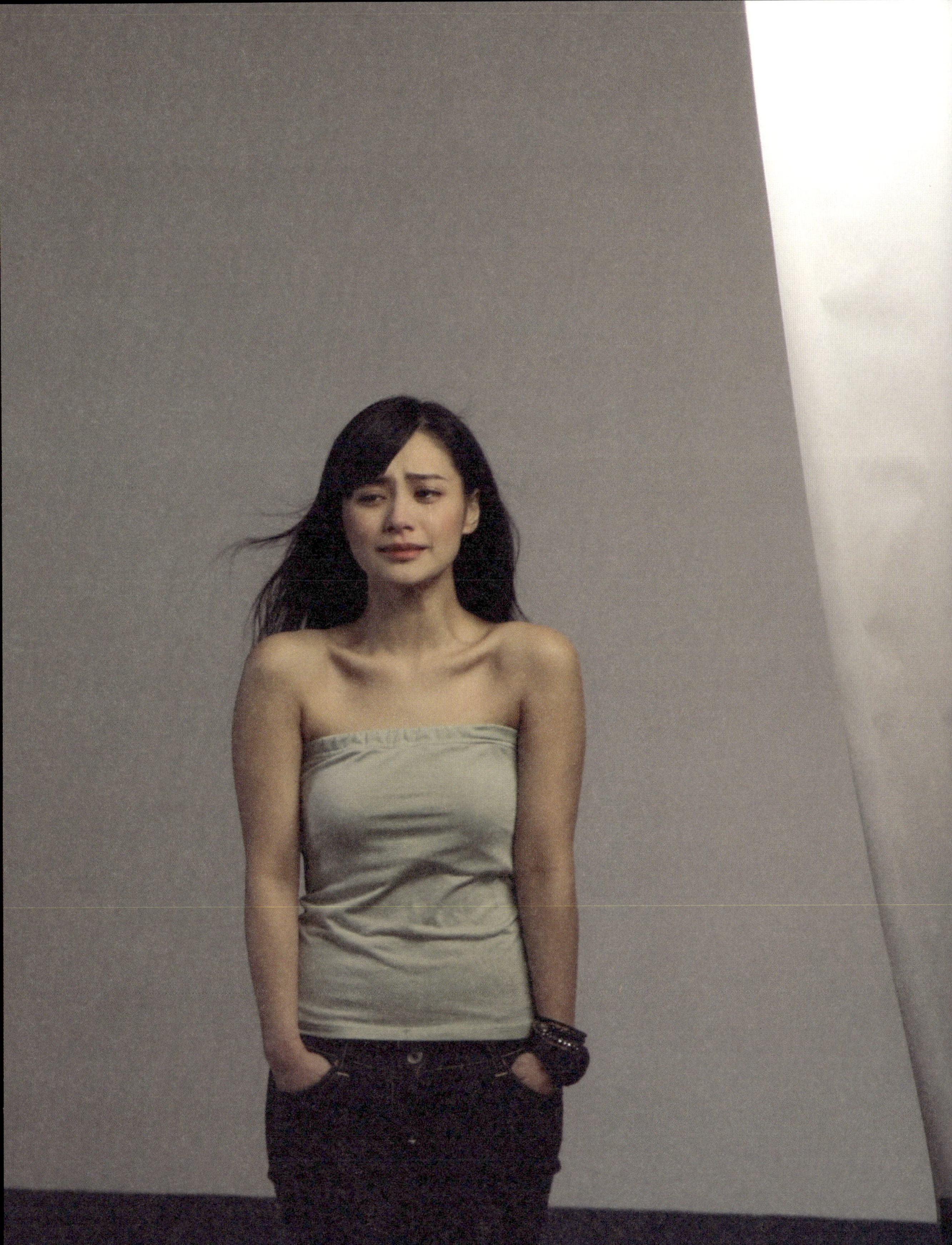

J
J
金 石

S
S
JIN SHI

作为艺术家，你在创作中所关心的是什么？以一件作品为例，分享你的创作过程。

在创作中，作品里所能体现出的现实的能量有多少是我最为关心的一点。艺术不应该是脱离生活的一种自言自语，和现实联系越紧密，越让我感觉塌实。

我一直关注平平淡淡的生活中所显现出的荒诞的那一面。这在我的作品《小买卖》系列之前表现的并不明显，因为我给这些背后的荒诞以现实的表象，以至于很少人会留意这些。作品《小买卖》系列就是主要凸现现实中荒诞的一面。总体结构是荒诞的，细节是真实的。用三轮车做小买卖在我们城市各个角落都是比较常见的，但是主要做有关饮食和日用品的生意，这些所满足的都是底层人群生活的最基本物质需求。如果我们顺着这个思路想下去，那么这个人群也同样有精神生活的需求，比如娱乐，像城市里比较小资的卡拉OK、洗脚等，但是这些娱乐一般都在灯红酒绿的豪华包间里。当这些娱乐设施和三轮车这样一个日常的小买卖载体结合在一起的时候，一种荒诞的效果——廉价的"奢华"就强烈的凸现出来，而我要做的就是给这些离奇的结合添加现实的细节。由于在整体概念的构思上是荒诞的，细节的添加并没有削弱这一点。在《小买卖之卡拉OK NO.3》的制作过程里，我使用了各种彩色霓虹灯具，增加娱乐的气氛，另外，这些灯具的布置上借用了摄影布光的方法，保证整件作品的每个部位都相应的被照明。这样在相对较黯淡的展厅里作品会出现很灿烂的视觉效果。这个效果和卡拉OK的廉价样式形成强烈的反差。如果站在经营者的角度来看，把一个卡拉OK的娱乐设施完全放置在一辆小三轮车上是有难度的，我尝试把整个车体后部设计成一个可以开合的箱体，并且把桌子

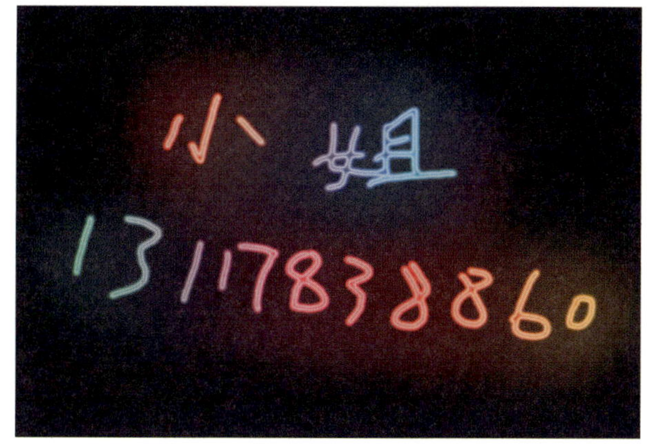
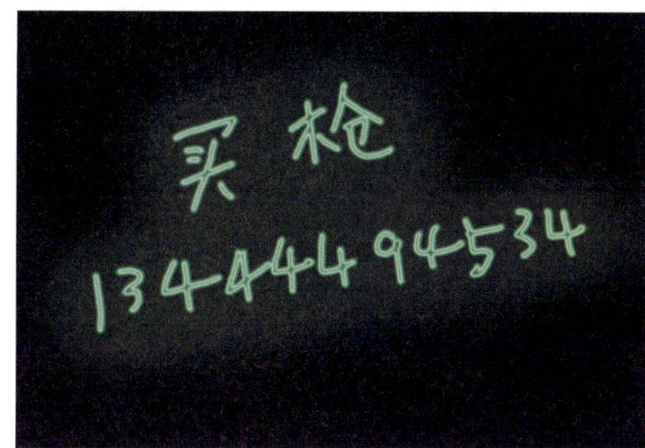

后巷，2009
霓虹灯管
效果图

Back Alley, 2009
Neon light tubes
Drawing

《小买卖之趣味钓鱼》作品的草图
Drawing of *Small Business: Fishing Game*

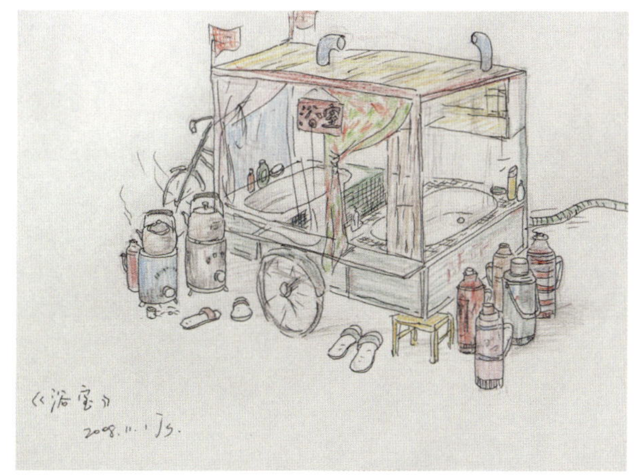

作为箱体的一个可以开合的面，桌腿可以折叠。如此以来几个部分自然结合在一起，节约了空间，这样的做法在现实中很常见，是生活中的智慧，我借来用了。

如果你是一个批评家，你会从什么角度来阐释和讨论你自己的创作？
因为我的作品很少表达而多叙述（对真实的呈现），所以对于自己创作的讨论就有很多可能的角度。以《1/2生活》为例。如果从社会学的角度，你完全可以把这件作品当成一个时期底层生活的记录，其中每件物品都多少的在传达这个时代的信息；你也可以把它当成一个模型来看：缩小的比例是主要的特征。我也尝试通过这些私密的房间来营造一种底层人的肖像的感觉，今天的人们越来越被物质量化了。在材料的使用上，我则毫无创新可言，一切材料都回归其最日常的状态。如果你喜欢故事，那么这其中丰富的物件以及各种痕迹可以让你像侦探一样编织联想出一个个小故事。

在你的创作和思考中，什么书籍和艺术家曾经或正在影响着你？
去年看了德国作家帕特里克·聚斯金德的小说《香水》，除了作为小说的故事所具有的吸引力之外，作者平静而细腻的描绘能力让我感觉到叙述的魅力——艺术不只是表现才可以有力量。
最近刚看了一本书，是导演贾樟柯的《贾想》，里面写有很多他的创作心路历程，更多的是他自己对生活细节敏锐的洞察力，其中所流露出的一种艺术家特有的敏感让我学习不少。
英国的RON MUECK和意大利的MAURIZIO CATTELAN都是我曾经狠喜欢的艺术家，其实很多艺术家都有非常不错的作品。然而

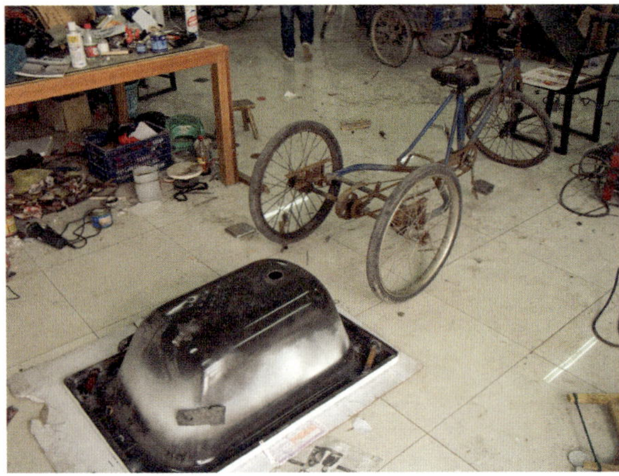
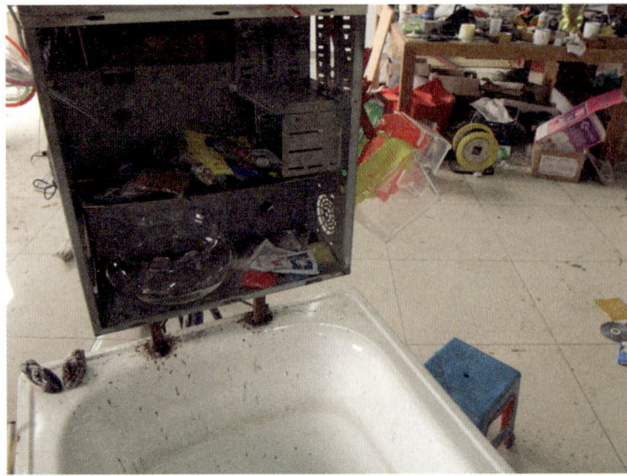
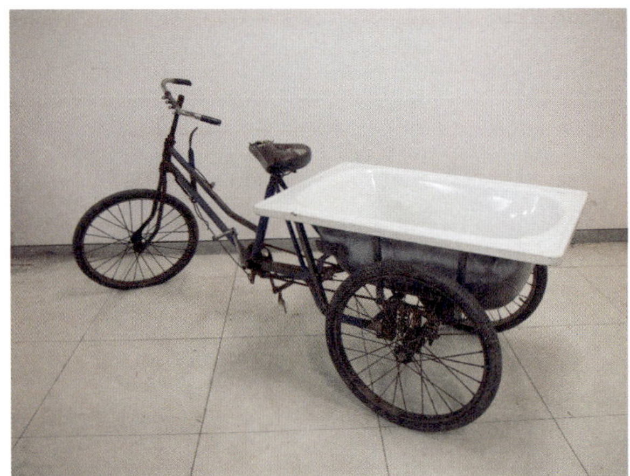
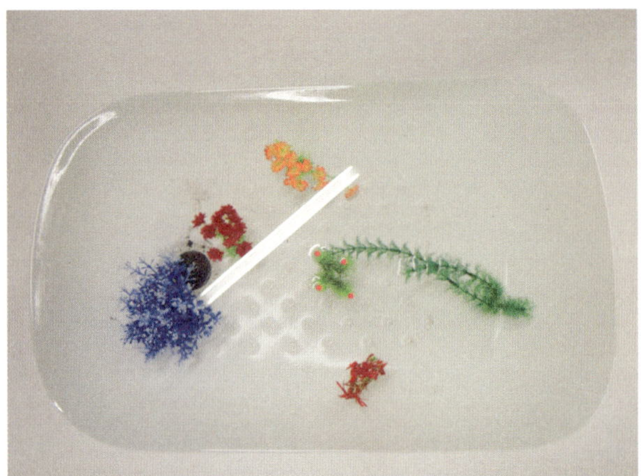
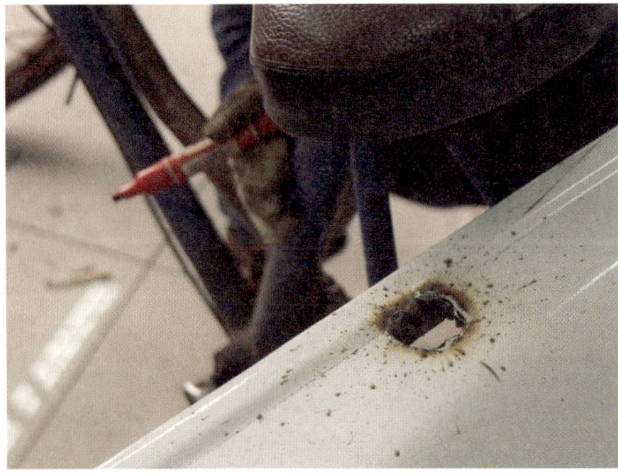
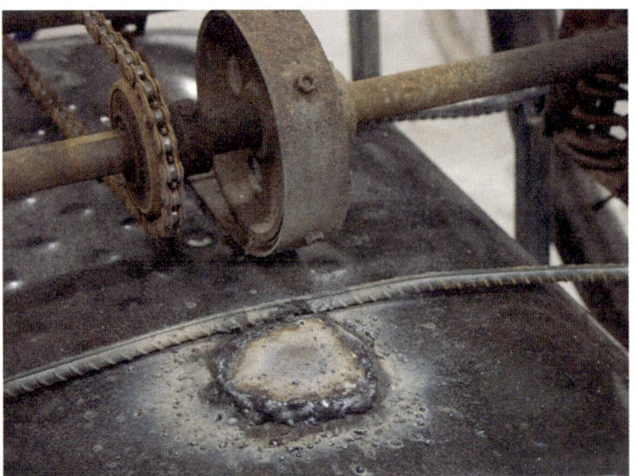

《小买卖之趣味钓鱼》作品的制作过程
Production process of *Small Business: Fishing Game*

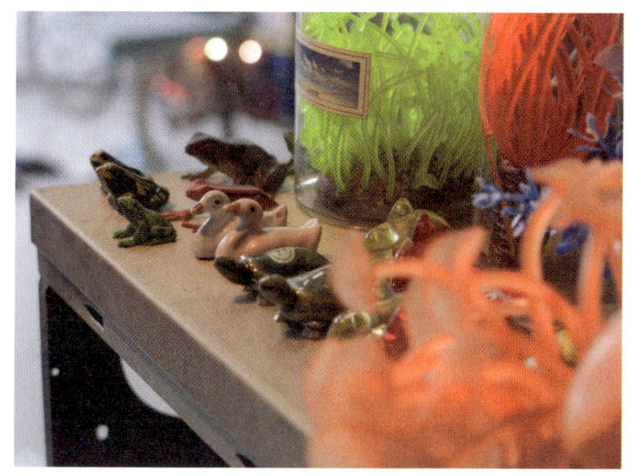
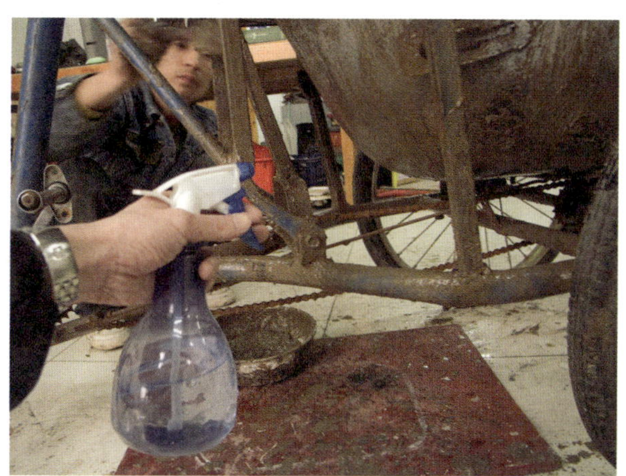
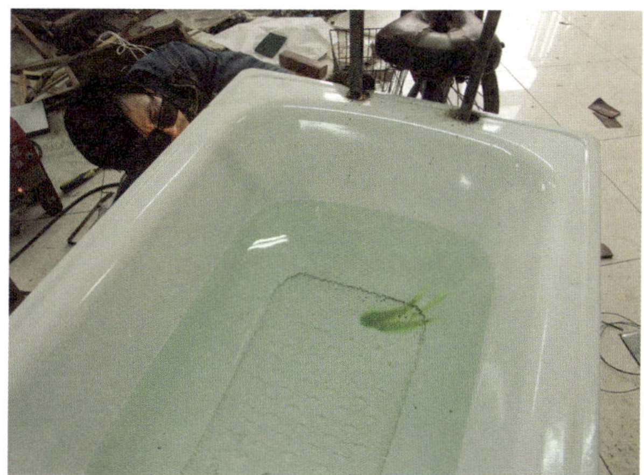
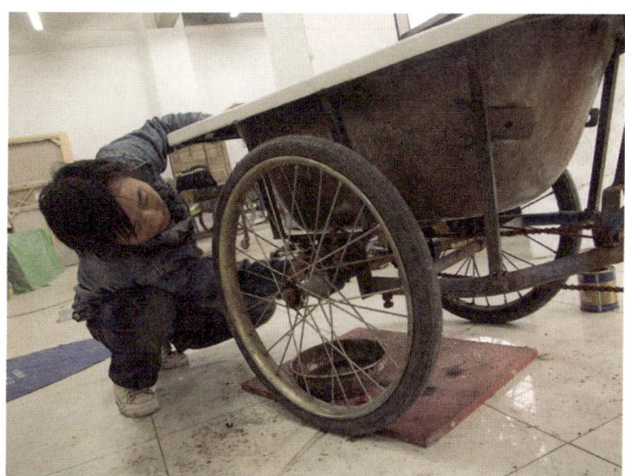
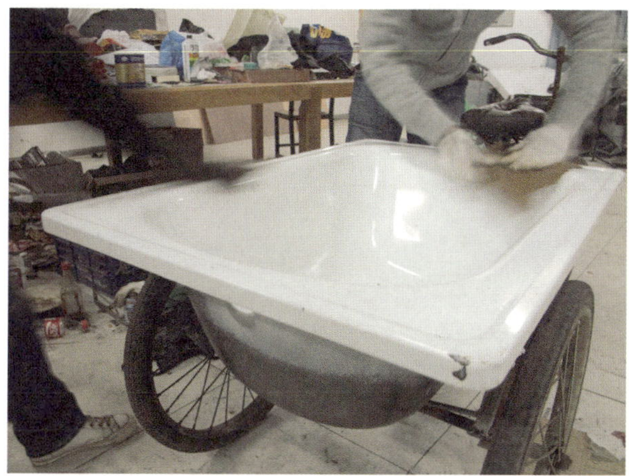
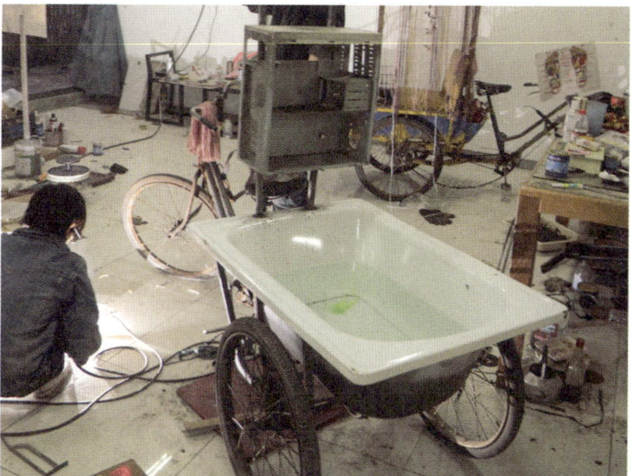

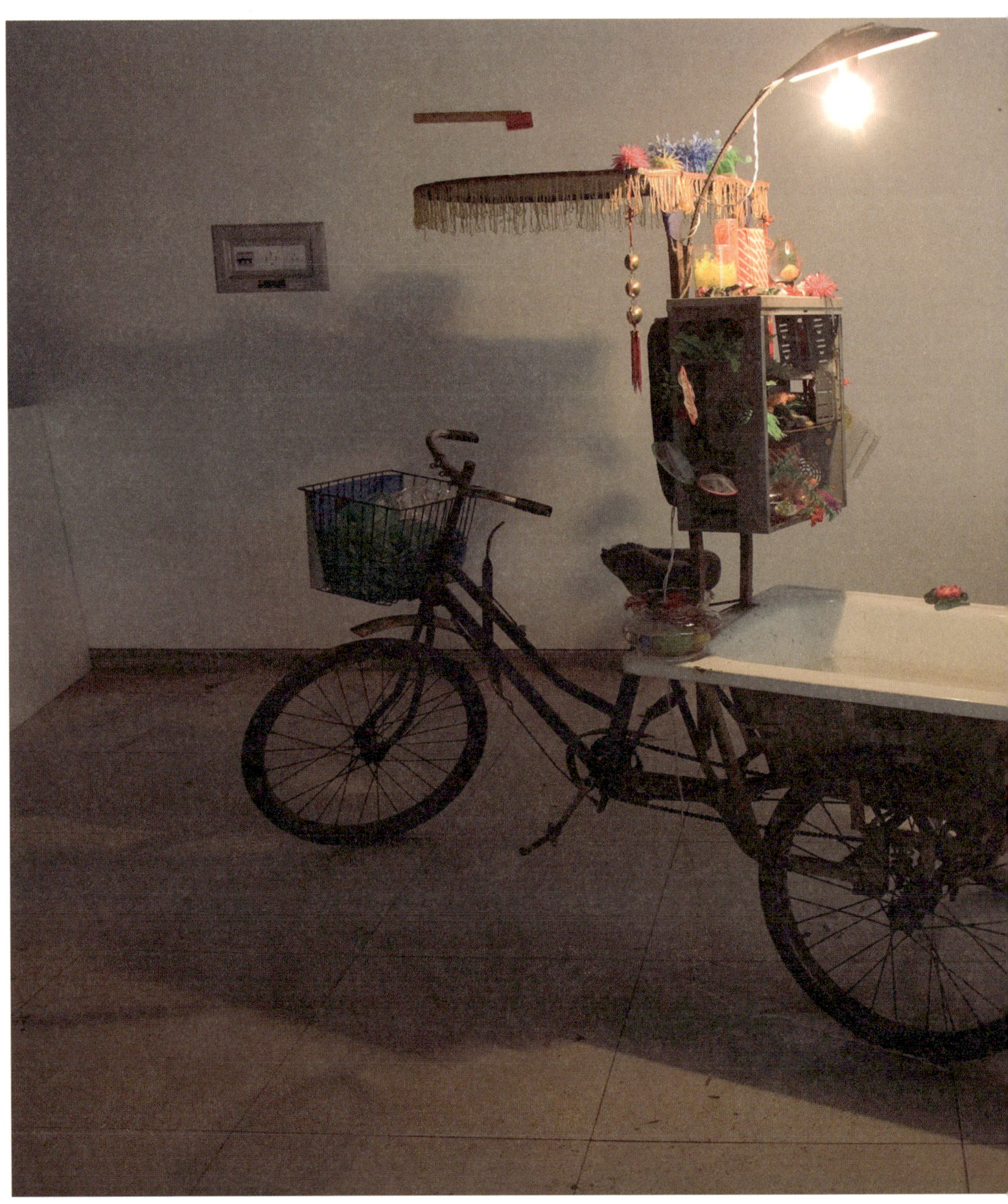

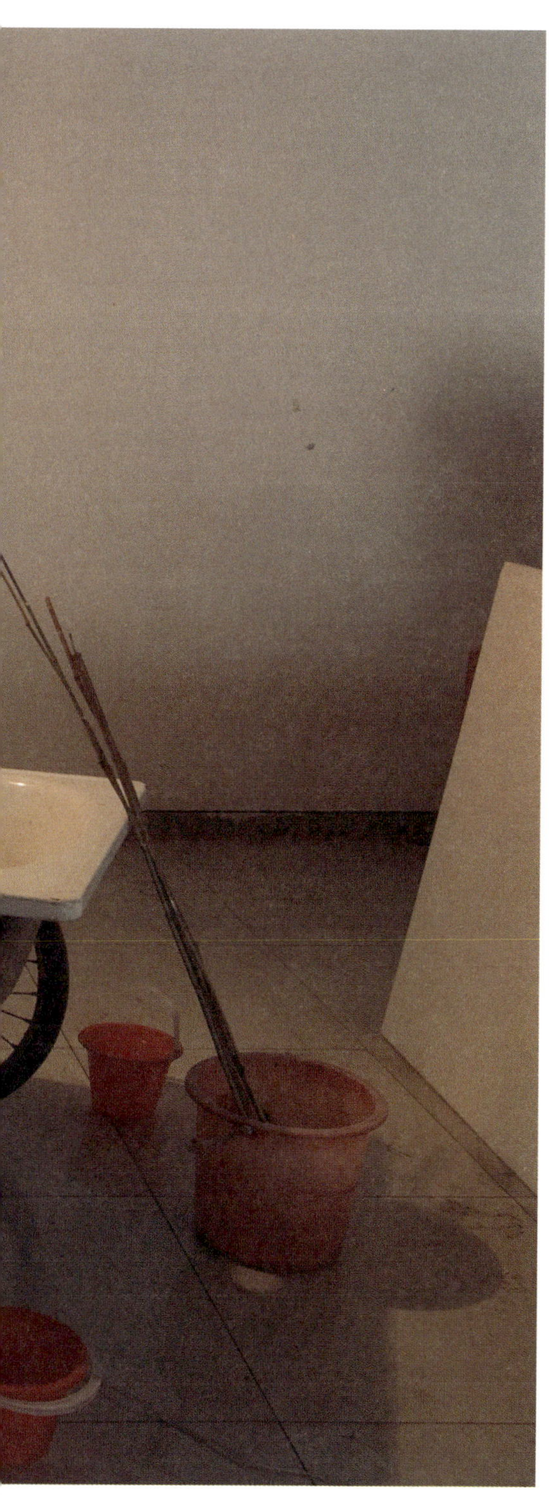

能给人启发的不一定都是那些伟大的作品，有时候可能只是一个小图片而已。

你是怎样判断和决定在什么语境下呈现你的哪些作品的？你是怎样看待作品呈现的语境和作品的关系的？

每一件作品都应该有它适合被接受的人群和地域范围。这就如同方言，换一个地方，你讲出来可能就很少有人听得懂。因为我的作品更多是和现实紧密相关，很像普通话，所以在呈现作品的时候不是很担心语境的问题。

如何在创作上形成了现在的面貌，描述一下近年来作品的发展和变化？

目前我的作品不多，所以基本谈不上什么面貌，主要是底层生活为主的一些创作；但是所反映的内容上，从开始的以复原室内生活场景为主到后来逐渐把目光转移到底层生存手段的层面上来。在作品的形式上也试图突破模型化的面貌，逐渐和现实拉开距离。

你会在什么情况下摧毁你自己的作品？

我没想过要摧毁自己的作品，倒是不愿意总看见自己那些关于底层生活房间的作品，在视觉上，他们非常不招人喜欢，但是这也正是我想要的效果。

你怎么看待艺术史和艺术家创作的关系？

艺术史上很多作品都是今天艺术创作的资源，但不应该成为创作上的障碍。艺术创作的前提应该是艺术家的表达需要而非艺术史的需要。

在你的工作中，理性和情感冲动各自扮演着什么样的角色？

情感的冲动总是在先的，有时候一个小小的灵感会让自己莫名的兴奋，紧接着就会天马行空的一顿乱想，甚至会有马上动手的念头在作品制作过程也会遇到这样的情况，脑筋总是会漫无边际的乱跑，有时候还很自鸣得意，理性这时候是很关键的，否则别人最终面对你的作品可能会觉得莫名其妙。

小买卖之趣味钓鱼，2009
综合材料
190×79×185 cm

Small Business: Fishing Game, 2009
Mixed Media
190×79×185 cm

As an artist, what do you care most during working? Could you please give an example to introduce the process of your work for us?

During the creation, what I care the most is how much of the reality energy can be shown in my work. Art is not supposed to be a kind of monologue that deviates from life. The more it is connected to reality, the safer I feel.

I always pay attention to the absurd side that plain life shows. This is not obvious before the *Small Business* Series. Because I give the absurdity hidden behind a realistic and superficial look, few people will pay attention to these. *Small Business* Series is mainly aimed to show this absurd side of reality. The general structure is absurd, while the details are true. Using a tricycle to do small business is common in each corner of the city; but most of the people sell food, drinks and other daily items, which satisfy the most basic needs of the people living at the bottom. If we follow this thought, then this group of people should also have needs for their spiritual life, for example, entertainments like karaoke and foot massage. However, entertainments like this usually happen in luxurious rooms full of lights and wine. When these entertainment services combine with a carrier of small daily business, a kind of absurd effect-a cheap "luxury"-is shown to the audience. What I do is just to add realistic details to these strange combinations. The plan for the general conception is absurd and the added details will not reduce the absurdity. During the process of making *Small Business: Karaoke No.3*, I used all sorts of colorful neon lights to add the entertaining atmosphere. Besides, I arranged the lights in the same way as photographers do so that every part of the work can be lightened. In this way, the work will have a splendid visual effect in a comparatively dim exhibition hall. This effect forms a sharp comparison to the cheap form of Karaoke. It was difficult to put the whole karaoke devices on a small tricycle. I tried to design the whole behind part of the tricycle into a case that can be opened or closed. The table is also part of the case that can be opened or closed. The legs of the table and the chair can be folded. In this way, several parts are combined naturally and save some space. This is very common in realistic life; it's the wisdom in life and I borrowed it.

Suppose you are a critic, from what perspective would you explain and comment on your works?

Because my work always narrates while seldom expresses, the discussion about my creation could have many possible angles. Take *1/2 Life* as an example: from the sociological angle, you can totally regard this work as a record for the life at the bottom during one period of time; every item in it more or less delivers some message of this era. You can also treat it as a model: the principle character is the reduction proportion. I also try to create a portrait of these people living at the bottom through these private rooms. People today have been materialized more and more. As for the application of materials, I don't have any new creation. All the materials go back to their daily status. If you like stories, the abundant objects and all sorts of traces can make you associate them with several stories, like an inspector does.

What books and which artists have had, or are having an influence on your way of thinking and working?

I read German writer Patrick Süskind's novel *Perfume*. Besides those attractions as a wonderful story, the author's calm and delicate ability of narration makes me realize the charm of narration-not only expression can show the strength of art.

I've just finished reading a book *Jia Xiang* by director Jia Zhangke, in which Jia tells many of his feelings and experiences during the process of creation. His acute insight shows a unique sensitivity of an artist, from which I have learned so much.

British artist Ron Mueck and Italian artist Maurizio Cattelan are both my favorite artists. In fact many artists have nice works, however, those that can inspire people are not necessarily the great ones. Sometimes it might be only a little picture.

How do you make judgment and decision as to in what context you'd like to present your works? According to you, in what way is the context created by the work related to the work itself?

Each work is supposed to have its suitable audience and place. This is just like dialect. If you go to another place, what you speak might not be understood by most of the people. My work is closely bound to reality and assembles mandarin. Therefore I don't worry about context much when presenting my work.

How does your work take the present shape? And please give a few words about the latest development and changes in your work.

At present I don't have many works, so it's hard to say. Most of them are based on the life at the bottom. As for the content, from copying the indoor daily life scenes to paying attention to the living methods of the people living at the bottom of the society, the forms of my work attempt to break the model-liked look and gradually keep a distance with reality.

In what circumstances would you want to destroy your own creation?

I never thought of destroying my work, but I am unwilling to all the time face to my works about the life at the bottom layer. People don't like their appearance, which is just the effect I want.

What do you think about the relation between the art history and artist's work?

Many works in art history are the resources for creation today, but they are not supposed to become obstacles for creation. The precondition of art creation should be the artist's need to express rather than that of art history.

What kind of roles would rational thinking and emotional impulse respectively play in your work?

The emotional impulse always comes the first. Sometimes a trivial thought might make me feel much exited and then my imagination will go wild. I have the impulse to implement it right then. During the process of making a work, I will also encounter the same situation. My thoughts are not restricted by anything and sometimes I am even contented and proud. Rationality becomes critical at this point, otherwise people will feel strange when they face your work.

三轮车因为其相对低廉的成本和机动性（流动性），成为城镇最为普遍的运输工具，同时也成为小夜市做买卖的最佳载体。这种载体既具有因市场需求而流转城市各个角落的便利性，也具有因买卖的某些不合法性而迅速逃离现场的可能性。卡拉OK，洗脚，台球，趣味钓鱼等便是其中应该有的小生意。每个人都有自己娱乐的权利和方式，无论是在街头还是豪华包厢。

Three-wheeled bikes due to the cheap cost and high mobility have become not only the most favorable transportation vehicles in many small cities, also the best gear to carry on small business in night-market. This kind of bikes provides convenience for the businessmen to travel to different markets and sell their business to people in all corners of the city; in addition, the bikes ensure them to escape from the markets easily before the patrolmen arrive. Karaoke, Foot-massage, billiards, fishing game, etc. are some of the small business they are running. Everyone has the rights to have fun and choose his/her own way of entertainment. This is a rule that is universally applicable either in the street or deluxe box.

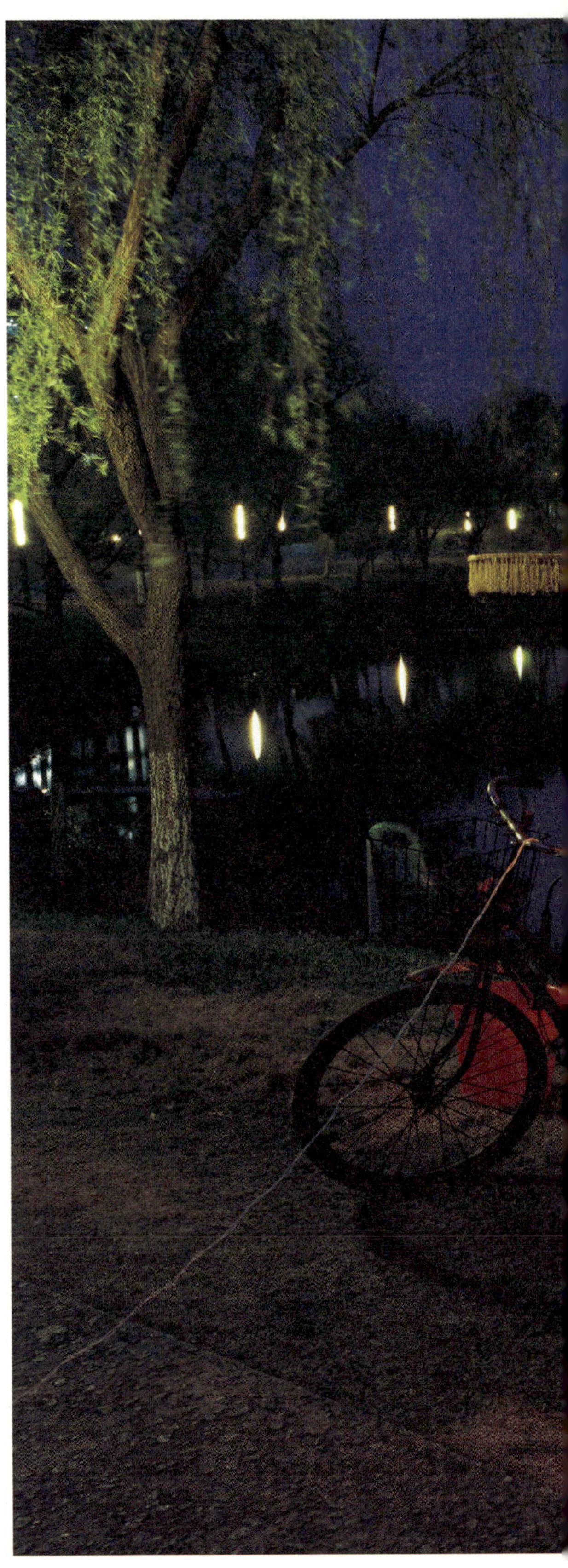

小买卖之趣味钓鱼，2009
摄影

Small Business: Fishing Game, 2009
Photography

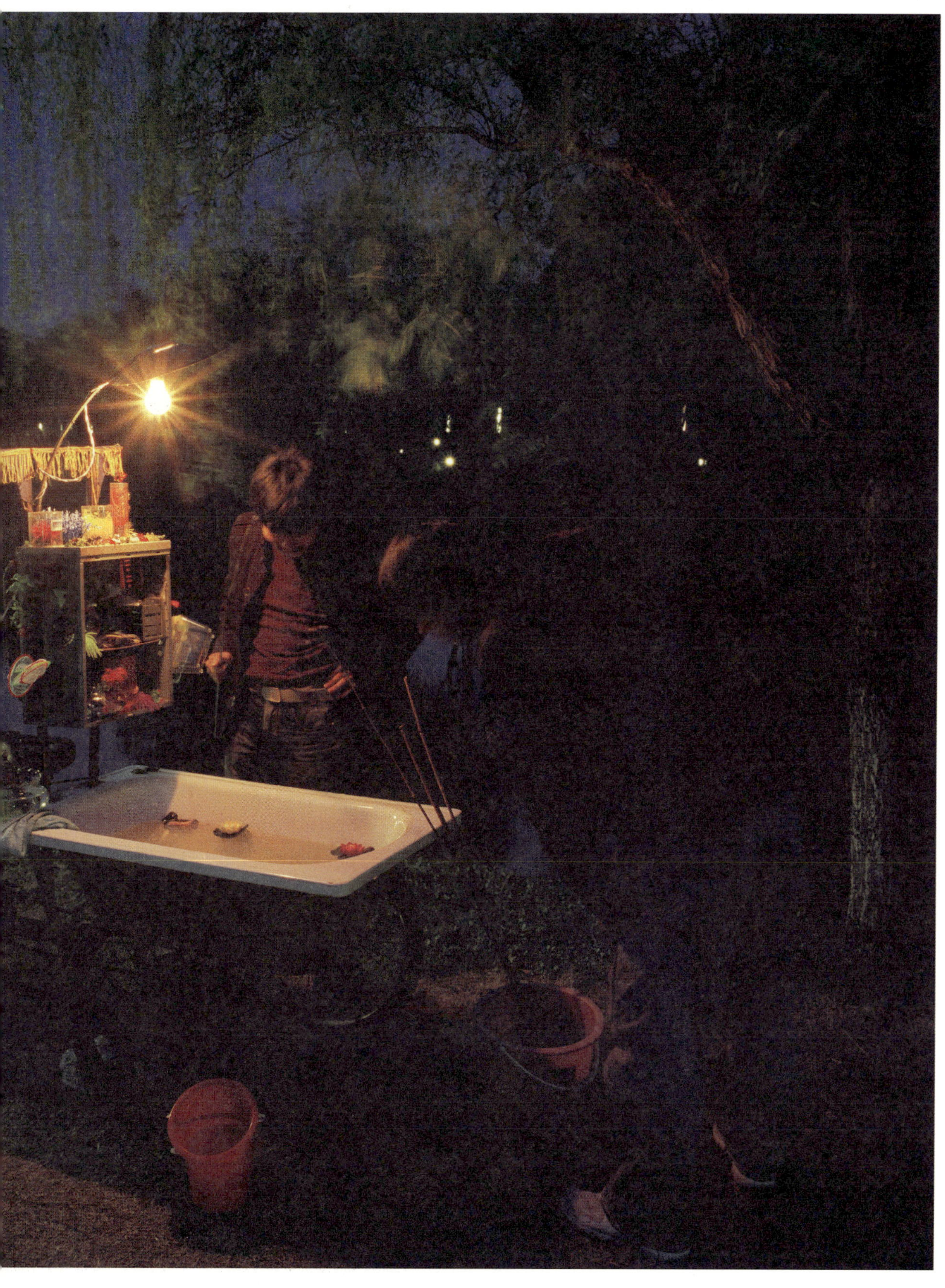

李 超

LI CHAO

作为艺术家，你在创作中所关心的是什么？以一件作品为例，分享你的创作过程。
关心的是视觉的变化，和个人经验的表达。比如《狗咬狗》在三张不同视觉感受的不同质感的画面上做到不同的效果。狗咬狗的想法是很暴力的，这完全是自我经验的一种感悟。

如果你是一个批评家，你会从什么角度来阐释和讨论你自己的创作？
观念和技术这两个角度。更多的希望来阐释自己内心细腻的感觉。

在你的创作和思考中，什么书籍和艺术家曾经或正在影响着你？
透纳、委拉斯贵兹、德加、杰夫·沃尔。

你是怎样判断和决定在什么语境下呈现你的哪些作品的？你是怎样看待作品呈现的语境和作品的关系的？
作品一旦呈现就已经没有语境可谈，美术馆、画廊其实就是那么回事，都一样。白墙、老板、利益关系，红酒、美女，扯淡。

如何在创作上形成了现在的面貌，描述一下近年来作品的发展和变化？
这个说不清楚，各种关系的相互影响，就慢慢如此这般啦。
最近一年，更加强调绘画本身的笔触质感以及视觉角度的多样性。

你会在什么情况下摧毁你自己的作品？
几年后回头看自己的作品，突然发现很烂，就必须毁掉。

你怎么看待艺术史和艺术家创作的关系？
艺术史是前人的东西，可以了解，更多的是自己的创作要创造艺术史的思考。

在你的工作中，理性和情感冲动各自扮演着什么样的角色？
理性更多支持着我对绘画本身的研究，情感冲动会带来观念上的思考。

As an artist, what do you care most during working? Could you please give an example to introduce the process of your work for us?

I care about the visual changes and the expression of personal experiences. For example, Dog Bites Dog has three different visual effects on three different pictures with different textures. The idea of *Dog Bites Dog* is violent. It's completely a kind of understanding of personal experience.

Suppose you are a critic, what perspective would you talk about and explain you work from?

From the two angles of concept and technique. I hope to interpret the delicate feelings in my heart more.

What books and which artists have had, or is having an influence on your way of thinking and working?

Turner, Velázquez, Degas and Jeff Wall.

How do you decide the context in which your work is to be presented? How do you consider the relation of the context with your work?

Once the work is presented, there will be no context. Museums and galleries are not that mysterious. They are all the same-white walls, owners, beneficial relations, red wine, beautiful women and bullshit.

How does your work take the present shape? And please give a few words about the latest development and changes in your work.

It's hard to explain clearly. Different things influence each other and then here I am.

This year, I concentrate more on the brushwork of the painting and the diversity of visual angles.

In what circumstances would you want to destroy your own creation?

After several years, when I look back on my works and find them very lousy, then they should be destroyed.

What do you think about the relation between the art history and artist's work?

Art history is history. You can learn something about it, but what's more important is that your own creation must develop the thinking of art history.

What kind of roles would rational thinking and emotional impulse respectively play during your work time?

Rationality supports my painting research work, while emotional impulse will bring conceptual thinking for the audience.

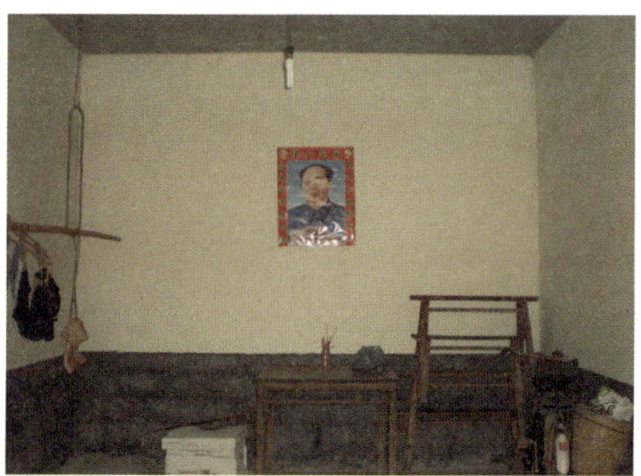

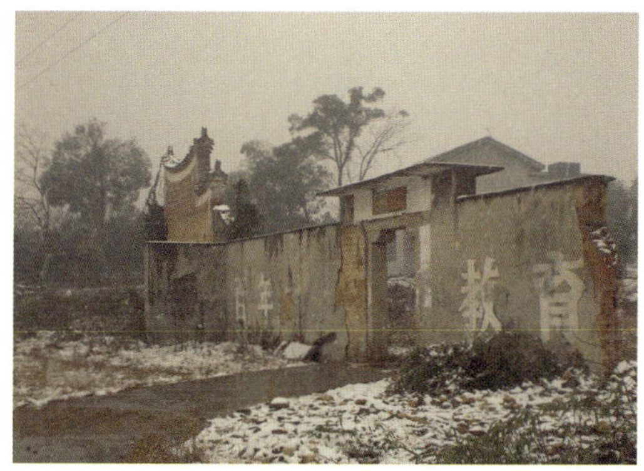

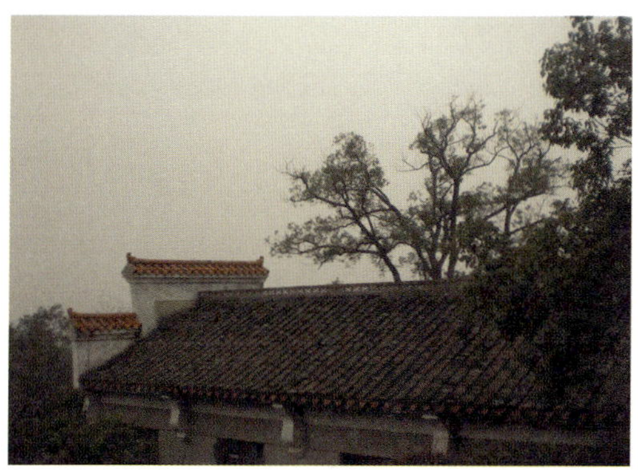

作品素材之湖南农村。

Photo of Hunan countryside by the artist

布褶，2009
油画
直径80cm

Fold of Clothes, 2009
Oil on Canvas
Diameter 80cm

《室内布置背景》 铅笔稿，2009
布上 铅笔
60×80cm

Pencil Sketch of *A Sitting-room Setting*, 2009
Pencil on Canvas
60×80cm

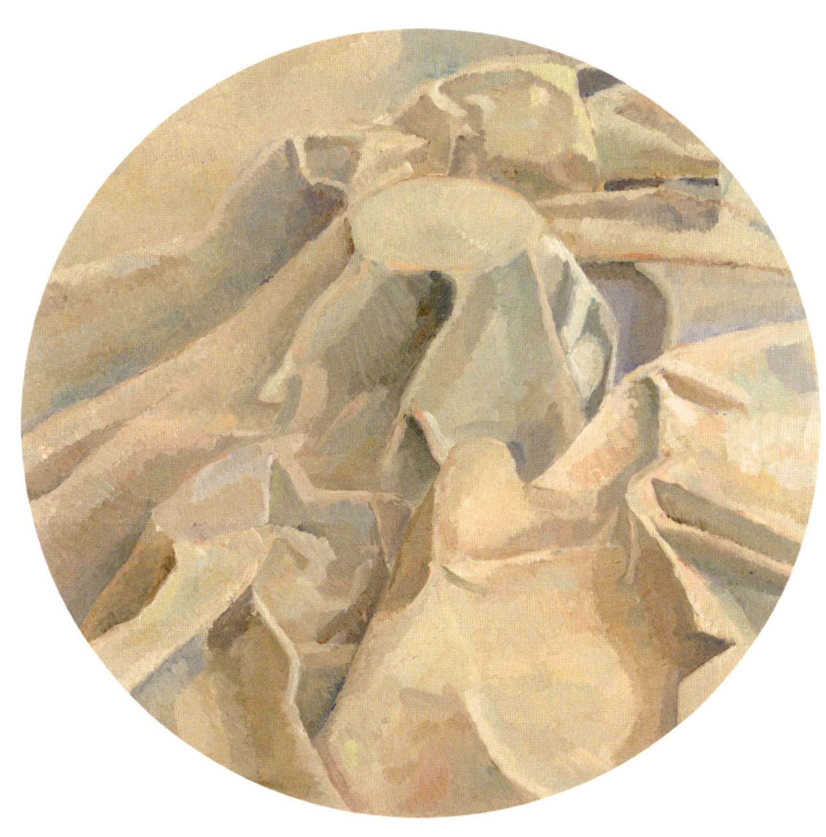

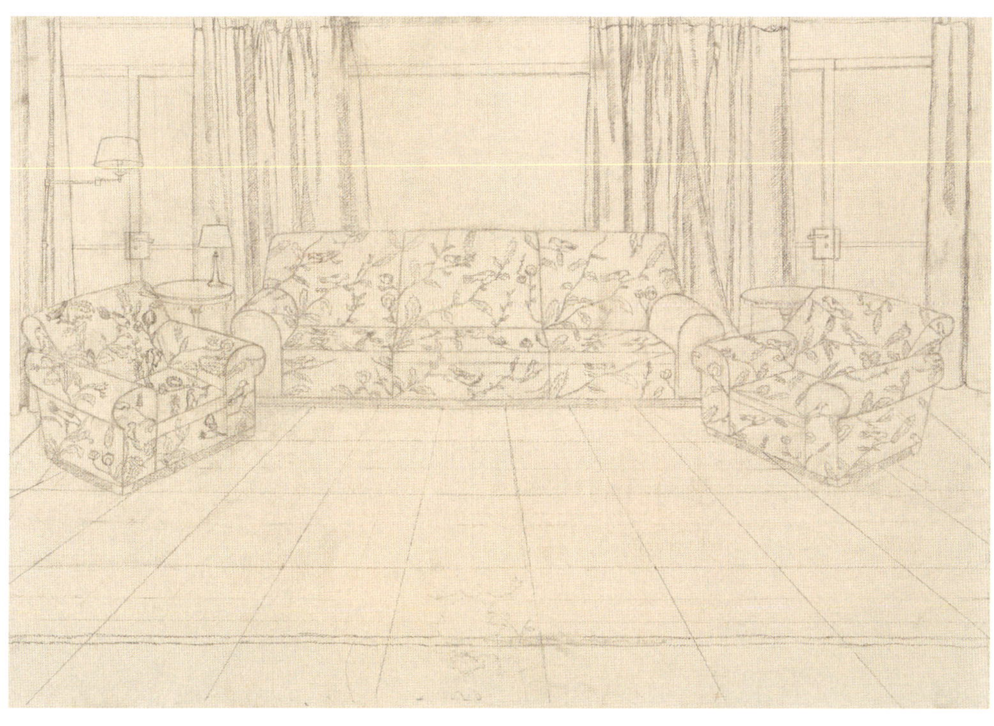

《拨云见日》之草图，2009
布上油彩
60×80cm

A Sketch of *Dispell the Clouds and See the Sun*, 2009
Oil on Canvas
60×80cm

斜靠的僧人（未完成），2009
布上油彩
30×30cm

A Recumbent Monk (unfinished), 2009
Oil on Canvas
30×30cm

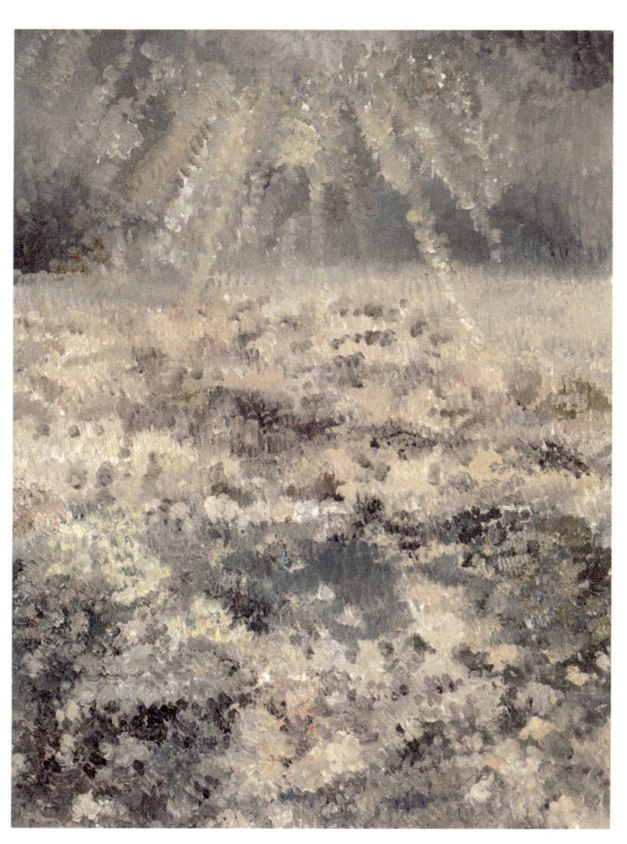

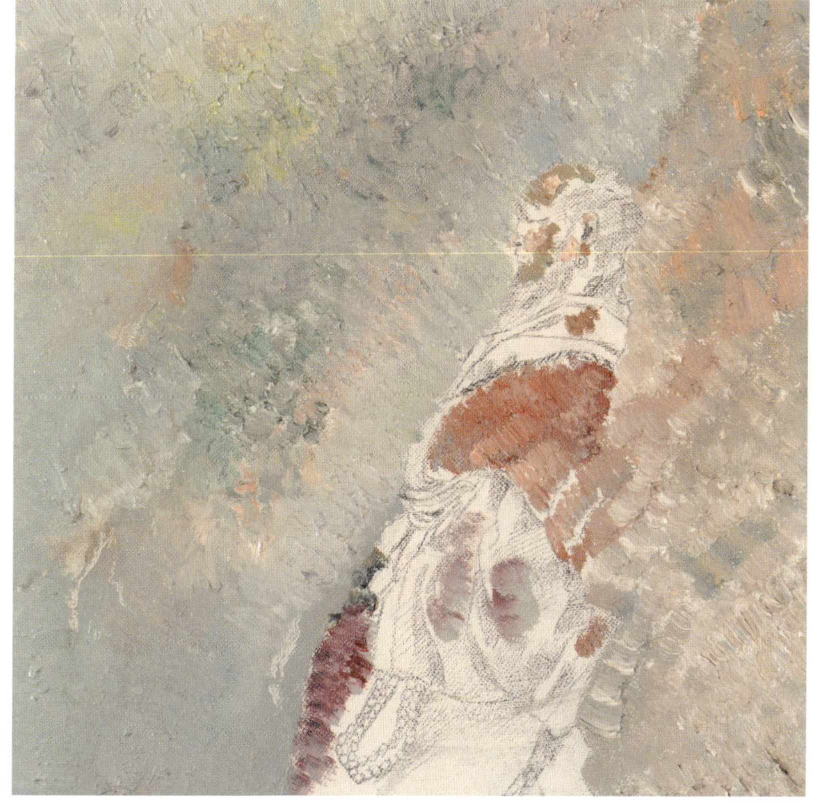

一年的废颜料，2009年
综合媒介
80×50×40cm

Waste Paint per Year, 2009
Mixed Media
80×50×40 cm

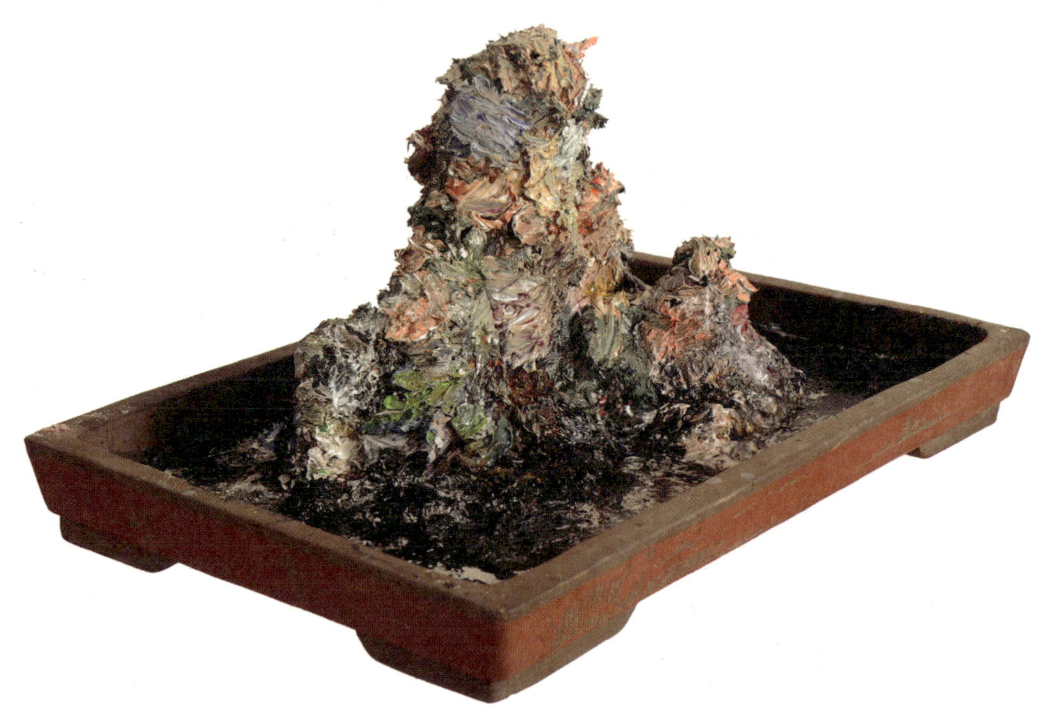

艺术家在工作中。
The artist at work.

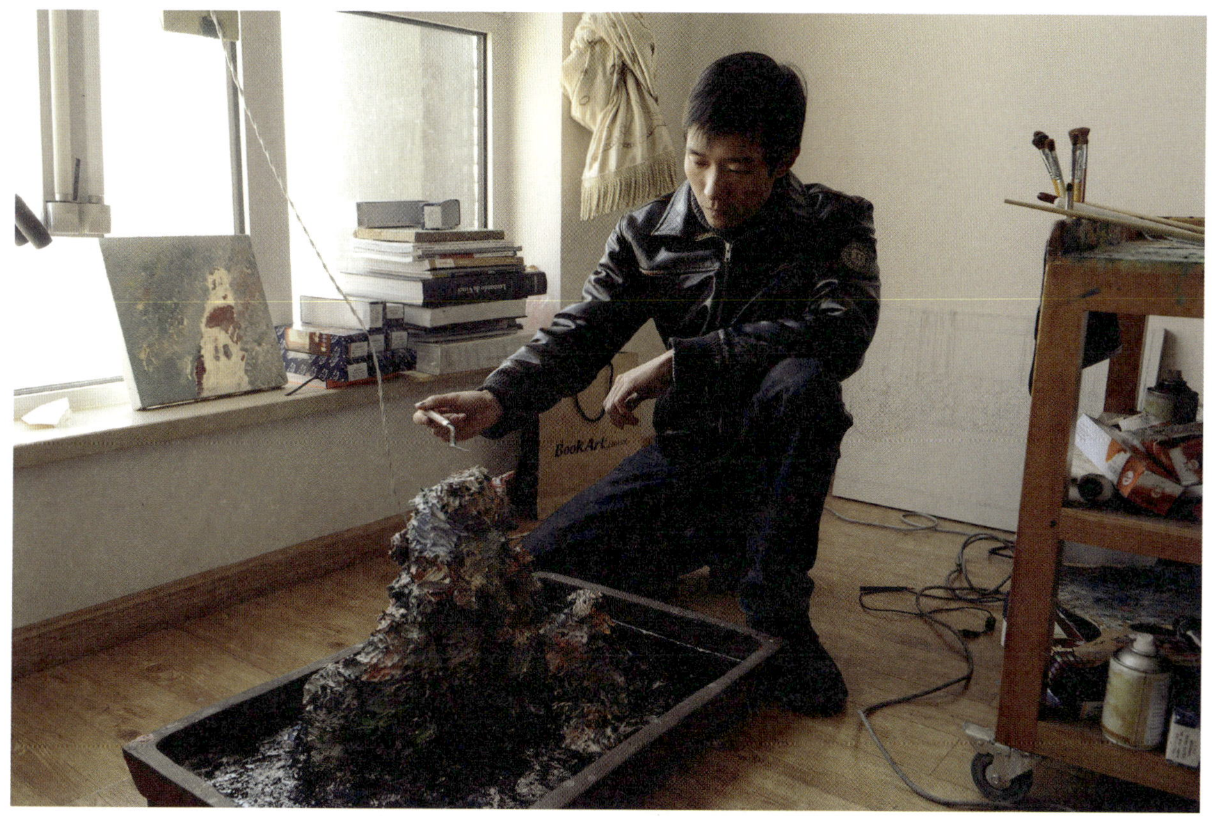

李景湖

LI JINGHU

作为艺术家，你在创作中所关心的是什么？以一件作品为例，分享你的创作过程。

作品能否反映我对现实的真实感受。或者说能否清晰的传达出我想表达的东西。

我的创作过程大概是这样的，每天基本无所事事，按日常做要做的事，看想看的东西，想感兴趣的问题，第二天早上醒来意识还不是十分清晰的时候，出现在脑海里的想法或图像到中午还能保留在脑海里的，我会记录下来，很多天以后还会想起的可能会转化成一个方案，再经过一些时间认为还有意思的话可能就是下一个作品，我大多数作品都是这样做的。

如果你是一个批评家，你会从什么角度来阐释和讨论你自己的创作？

批评家是一个要求非常高非常专业的行业，所以我从来不想这个问题。无论从什么角度来阐释和讨论都是批评家的权力。

在你的创作和思考中，什么书籍和艺术家曾经或正在影响着你？

《资本论》和杜尚。

你是怎样判断和决定在什么语境下呈现你的哪些作品的？你是

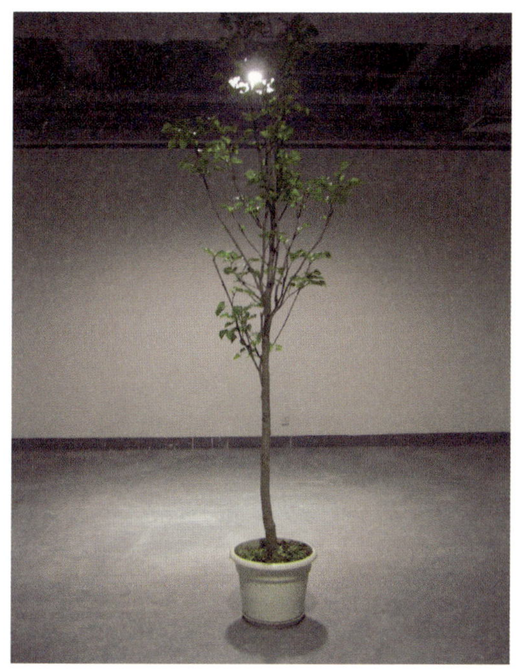

不要说出来，2006
装置
材料：树

Do Not Speak Out, 2006
Installation
Materials: Tree

怎样看待作品呈现的语境和作品的关系的？
作品呈现的语境和作品的关系我觉得像子宫和受精卵的关系，
没有了子宫，受精卵只是一堆蛋白质。

**如何在创作上形成了现在的面貌，描述一下近年来作品的发展
和变化？**
我想我创作上的面貌是自然而然形成的，可能跟个人感兴趣的
东西有关，前期感兴趣的是个人对私自生活的感受现在更感兴
趣的个人跟所生活的大环境的关系。

你会在什么情况下摧毁你自己的作品？
在绝望的情况下。

你怎么看待艺术史和艺术家创作的关系？
艺术史是工具，艺术家是使用并发明工具的人。

在你的工作中，理性和情感冲动各自扮演着什么样的角色？
我不太明确自己哪些时候是理性哪些时候是冲动，因为基本上
总是同时出现的。如同人的双脚。

不知道关于参展的作品你有什么样的想法？
如果参加展览，我想做一个很东莞的作品。

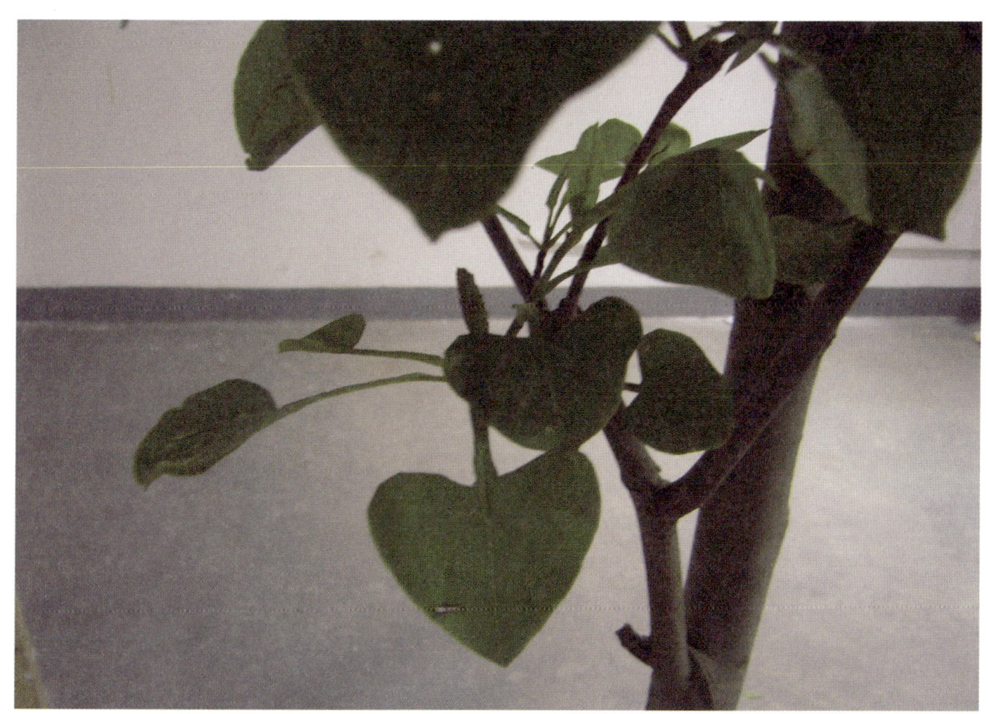

不要说出来（局部），2006
装置
材料：树

Do Not Speak Out (Detail), 2006
Installation
Materials: Tree

石屎（局部），2008
装置
材料：混凝土、涂料

Concrete Shit (Detail), 2008
Installation
Materials: Concrete, paint

石屎，2008
装置
材料：混凝土、涂料

Concrete Shit, 2008
Installation
Materials: Concrete, paint

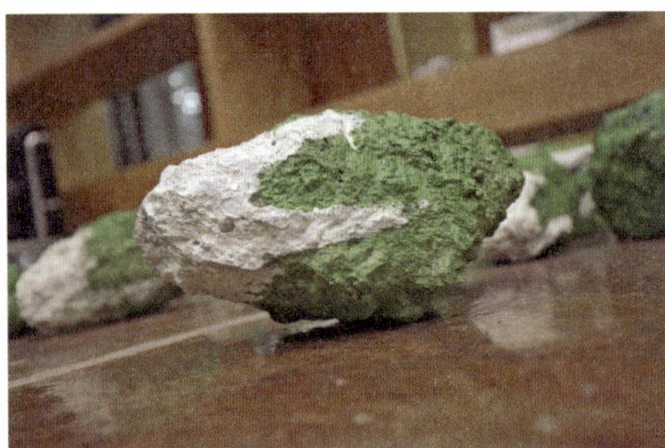

What is your major concern as an artist? Would you please take a work of yours as an example, so that we can share your artistic practice?
My works truthfully reflect my feelings about life, or put it another way, clearly convey what I want to express.
Generally, I don't engage in anything particular, following the routine by reading what I like and thinking about what interests me. I will note down the ideas or images that are not clear the moment I wake up but still remain until noon. They will become part of my project if I still remember them after some days and will probably appear in my next work if they still interest me. This is how I get most of my works done.

If you were a critic, from what perspective would you explain and comment on your works?
Only those who are highly specialized are worthy of the name, so I never think about being a critic myself. Critics are free to decide from what perspective to make criticism.

Are there any books or artists that greatly influenced or are influencing you in your artistic practice and thinking?
Capital and Duchamp.

How do you make judgment and decision as to in what context you'd like to present your works? According to you, in what way is the context created by the work related to the work itself?
Context to a work is like the womb is to a fertilized egg. Without a womb, the fertilized egg is only protein.

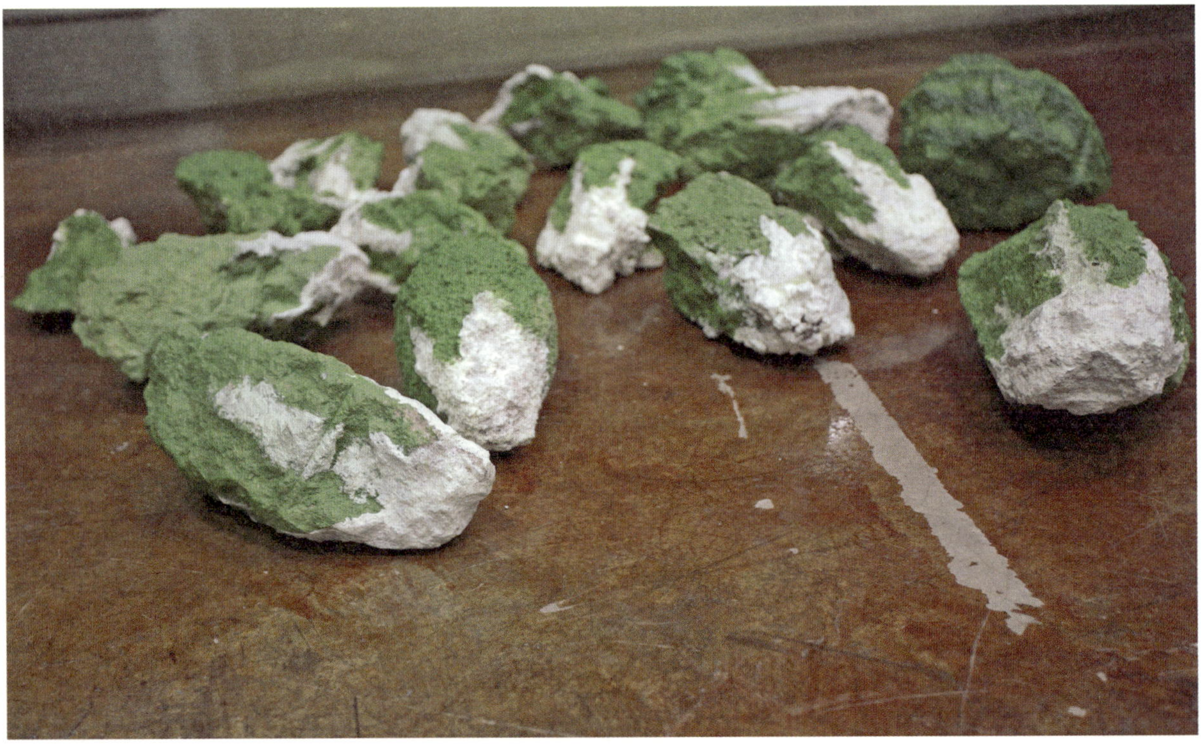

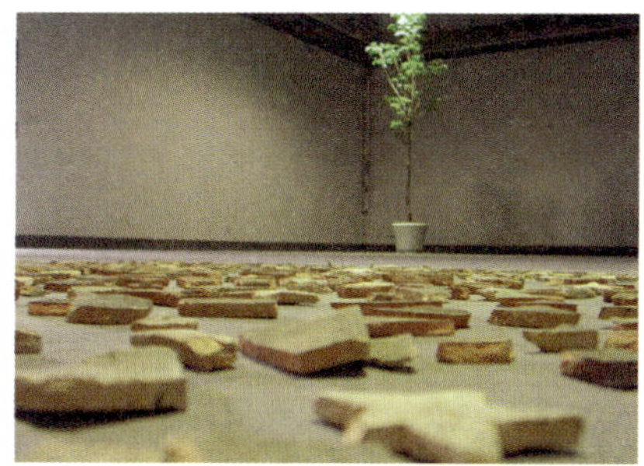

数星星（局部），2005
装置
材料：瓦片

Counting Stars (Detail), 2005
Installation
Materials: Tiles

数星星，2005
装置
材料：瓦片

Counting Stars, 2005
Installation
Materials: Tiles

How is your artistic style formed? Can you describe the changes in your works in recent years?
It follows a natural course, I think. Probably it is related to my interest. I used to take an interest in how an individual feel about his/her private life, but now it interests me more to explore how an individual is related to a broader life context.

Under what circumstances will you destroy your own works?
I will when I'm in despair.

What do you think of the relationship between history of art and artists?
History of art is a tool invented by artists for their use.

What roles do reason and emotion play respectively in your creation?
It's hard to tell when I am rational and when I am impulsive, for they are always simultaneous, just like our feet.

Would you like to share with us something about your contribution to the exhibition?
I prefer something that can stand for Dongguan if I participate in this exhibition.

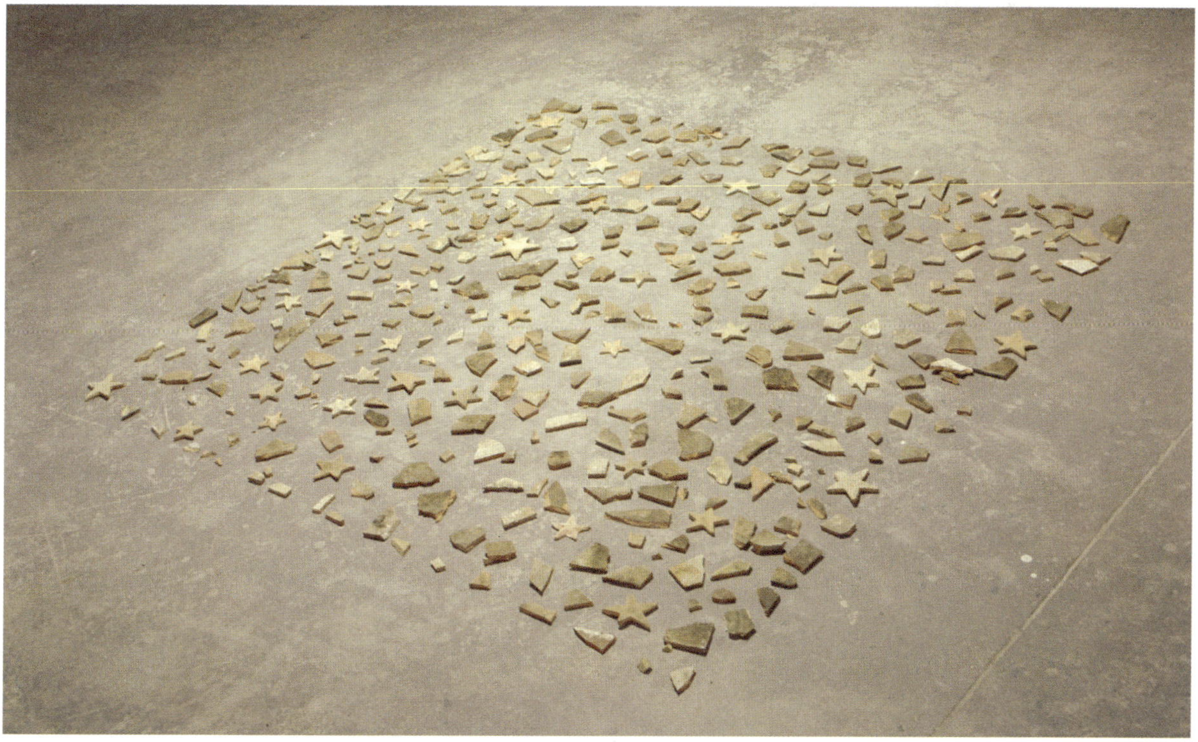

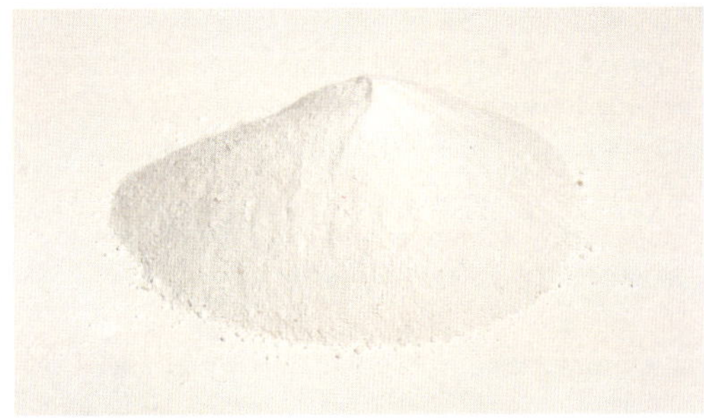

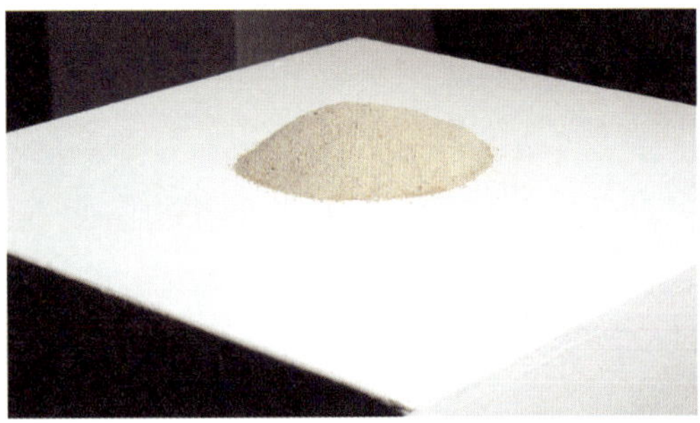

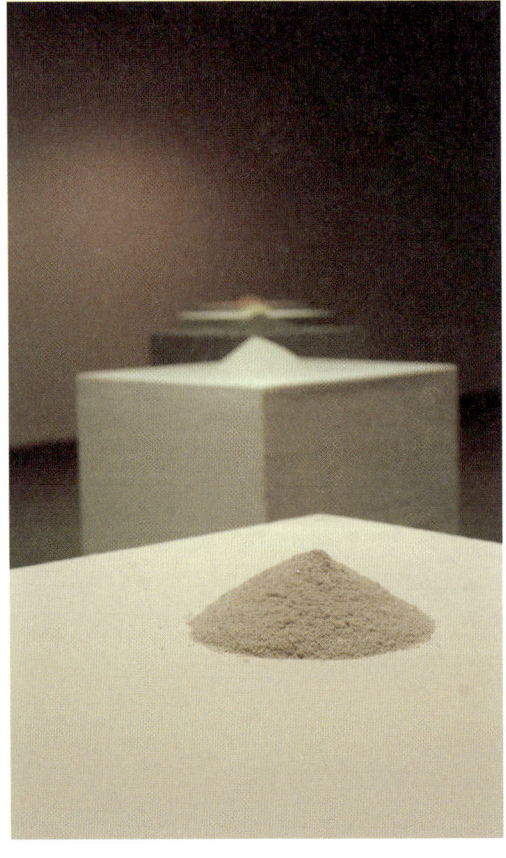

粉末，2003
装置
材料：大米，瓷碗、日光灯管、金
鱼缸、石子、石膏天花板、啤酒瓶
艺术家分别将以上罗列的物品研磨
成粉状。

Powder, 2003
Installation
Materials: Rice, porcelain bowl, fluorescent
light, goldfish bowl, stone, plaster ceiling,
beer bottle
The artist has grounded the above items
respectively into powder.

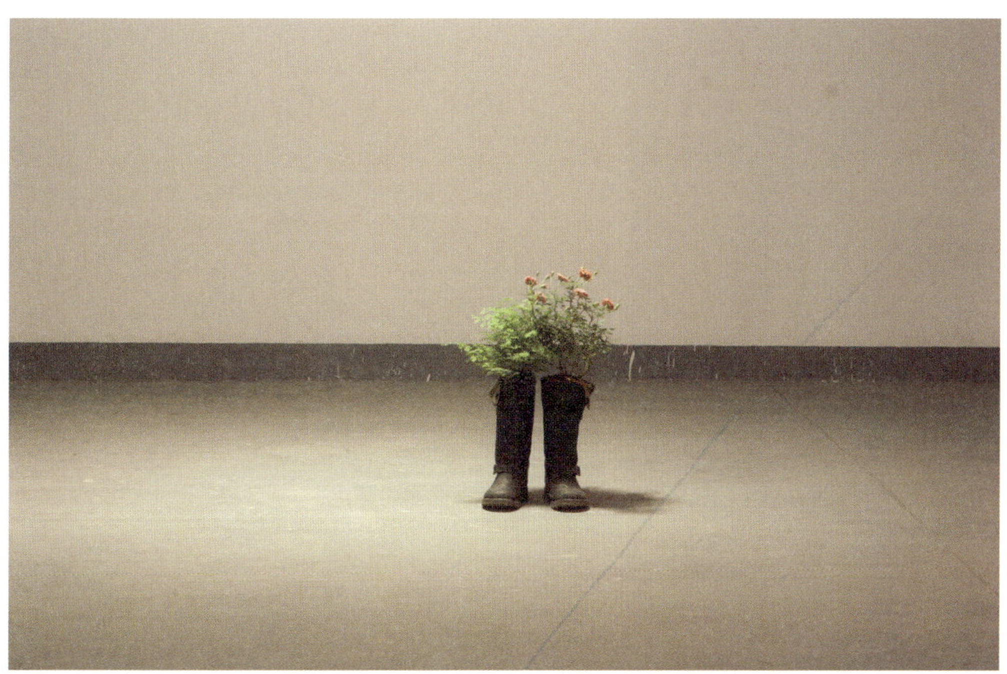

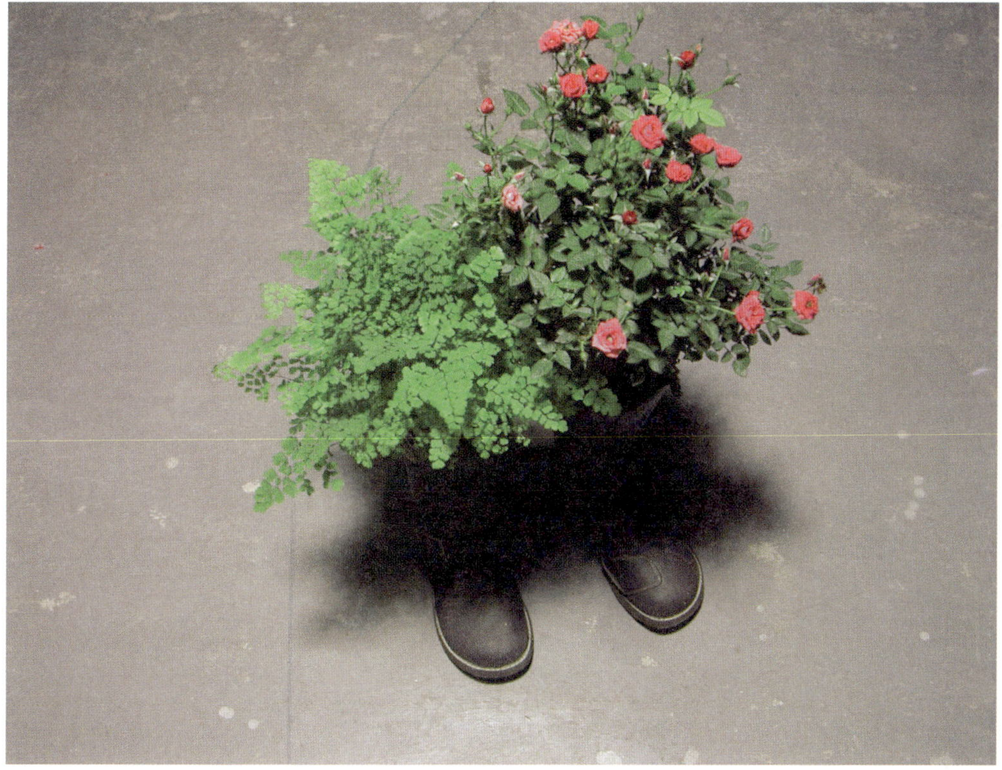

鲜花，2005
装置
材料：花卉、女式皮鞋

Fresh Flowers, 2005
Installation
Materials: Flower, female leather boots

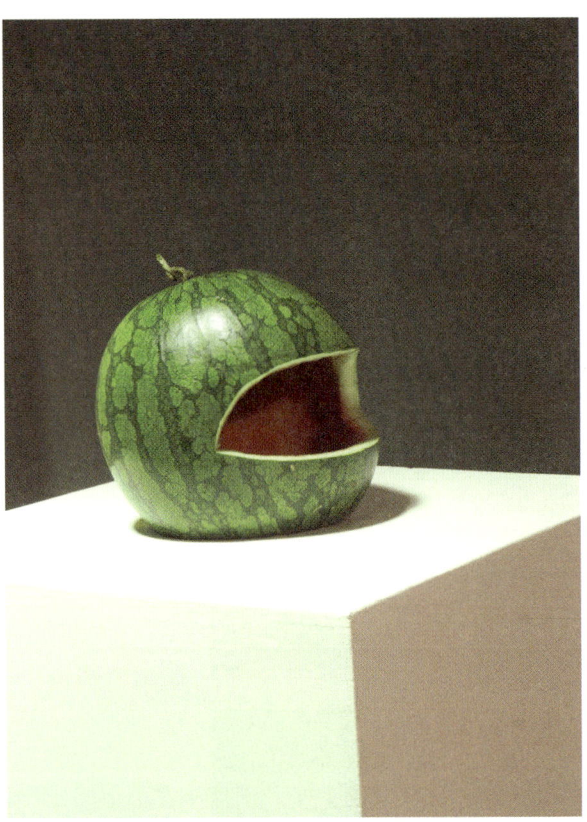

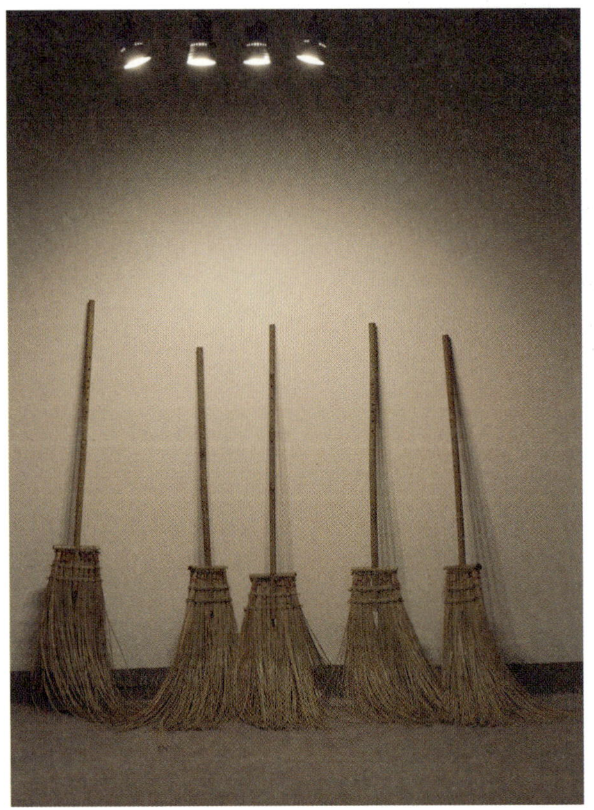

头盔，2006
装置
材料：西瓜

扫帚，2005
装置
材料：扫帚

Helmet, 2006
Installation
Materials: Watermelon

The Broom, 2005
Installation
Materials: Broom

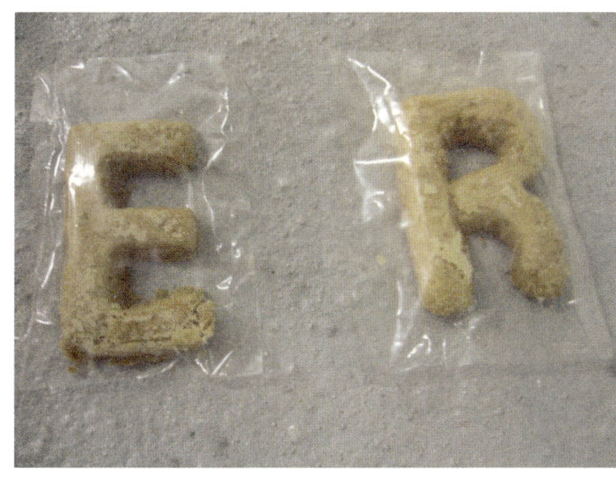

Tobias的来信（局部），2006
装置
材料：面粉、糖、食用油

Tobias' Letter (Detail), 2006
Installation
Materials: Flour, sugar, cooking oil

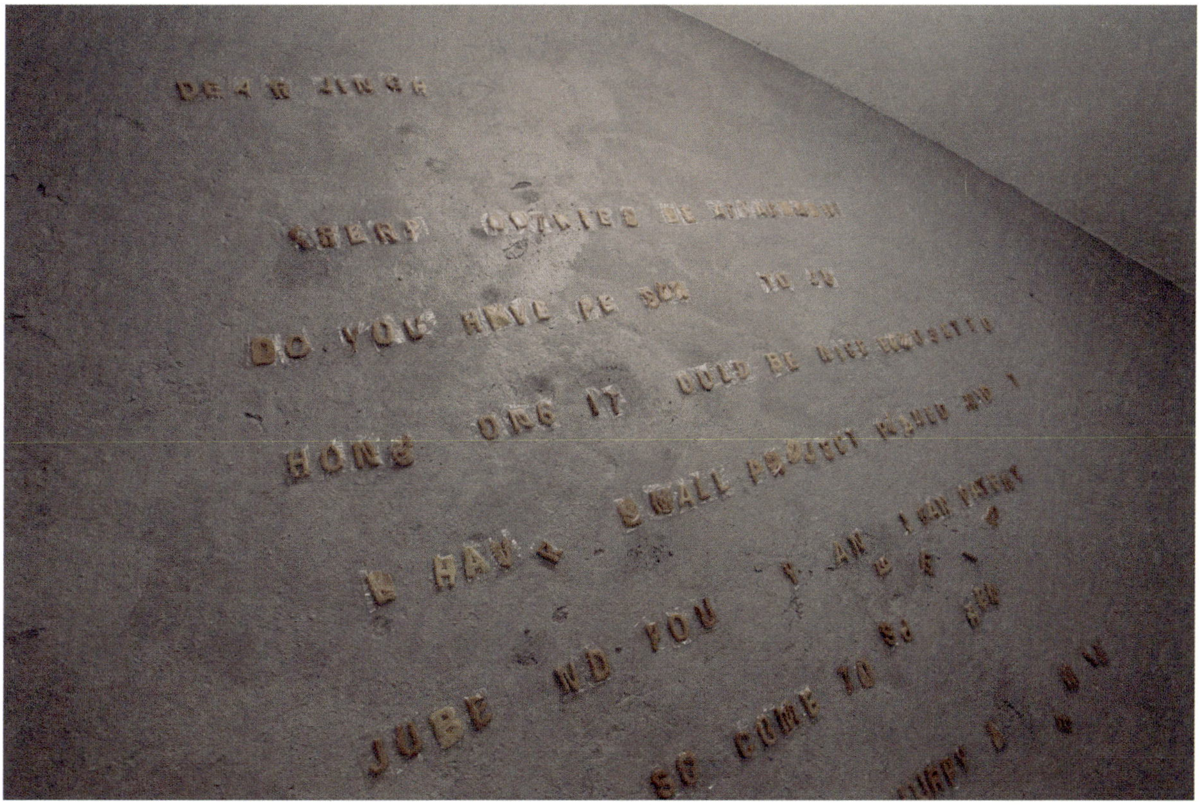

Tobias的来信，2006
装置
材料：面粉、糖、食用油

Tobias' Letter, 2006
Installation
Materials: Flour, sugar, cooking oil

李 明

LI MING

作为艺术家，你在创作中所关心的是什么？以一件作品为例，分享你的创作过程。

从创作开始启动到后期收尾的整个变化过程是我感兴趣的地方，因为我总是摇摆不定的临时改东西，各种客观阻力需要克服，不然就得妥协，创作过程变成一个斗争的过程，最初的想法也在同客观斗争的时候变了模样。《挡潮》刚开始的时候只是有这样一个想法，我以挡潮的出发点，在一段时间到岛上用不同的材料建筑一些围墙性质的雕塑，伫立在岛边缘，挡住潮水，每次挡潮的成果都保留在岛上，时间久了后就会有不同的雕塑在岛上，像一个露天陈列馆。而现实是，当我做完第一次的时候，第二次再去做时发现东西消失了，被滨江区政府环保局的负责人拆走，有次在岛上做时正好江水管辖员赶来，把我驱逐下岛，东西也要销毁，因为影响到了江面的环境。那次后，我只能在管辖员的工作时间外偷着去做这个行为了，早晨7点前，中午12点到14点间或者晚上19点后。因为工作时间，水路运输，人工体力等这些因素的不方便，我考虑的材料也只能是简便易带的或者是就地取材，后来就发展成录像装置这样的一个形式 — 把不同时间和不同地点的工作同时摆放到小岛的投影上，在形式上建立起同一个时间和地点感。一旦有新想法，我将继续补充这个体验过程。

如果你是一个批评家，你会从什么角度来阐释和讨论你自己的创作？

不知道，看针对哪些作品，我现在的能被阐释和讨论的创作太少，难以建立起一个比较宏观的线索。

在你的创作和思考中，什么书籍和艺术家曾经或正在影响着你？
关于读书，我非常欣赏杨福东常常提到的"断章取义"的学习
方式，这跟把线性时间处理成非线性似地。对我影响比较大的
艺术家，我想是阚萱和徐震吧。

**你是怎样判断和决定在什么语境下呈现你的哪些作品的？你是
怎样看待作品呈现的语境和作品的关系的？**
老金锋有一次说我"弹药备齐，枪膛也上好，只是子弹射偏，
大家都在桌子上面讨论这个东西，而你在桌子底下发出声
音"，语境是格局内的东西，是你在游戏里多少行为遵守了游
戏规则，我们总是要严格遵守游戏规则，只有发明游戏的人才
可以制定规则，或者是他们一边玩游戏一边改规则，参与者很
少有话事权。

**如何在创作上形成了现在的面貌，描述一下近年来作品的发展
和变化？**
"面貌"实指体系，休系需要规则，规则来自经验和习惯性，
我很多的想法和出来的东西都是直觉的，自然而然的，都是细
节的累积，这些细节是一些"偶遇"，碰撞之后延伸很多可能
性，这些"偶遇"来自生活中的不经意的瞬间；来自不断变换
情绪中的不经意间；以及剪辑时候对线性素材的某几秒局部的
重新定义从而改变整个时间轴等等。总之，这些直觉的自然的
带点的惯性的重复，使得这种"模式"不断扩大，新的经验也
不断累加。
至于"描述一下最近年来作品的发展和变化"，我做得太少，
还不能谈发展和变化。

你会在什么情况下摧毁你自己的作品？
我理解这个问题的"摧毁"非指对作品的主观蓄意破坏或毁
灭，当我遇到的客观阻碍自己不愿意绕弯回避的时候会失去兴
趣和想继续这个作品的欲望。

你怎么看待艺术史和艺术家创作的关系？
很少去想这两者的关系。

在你的工作中，理性和情感冲动各自扮演着什么样的角色？
拿录像的创作过程来说吧，当一切就绪所有的客观都能为你服
务并能达到自己舒服的状态，当时的情绪已经偏离了拍摄前的
详细计划，想要的东西也开始摇摆不定。而到后期的剪辑则是
非常理性的收拾，对素材的观察，打乱，重组，甚至是后期的
剪辑否定前期的拍摄。最后总是理性吞噬掉情感。

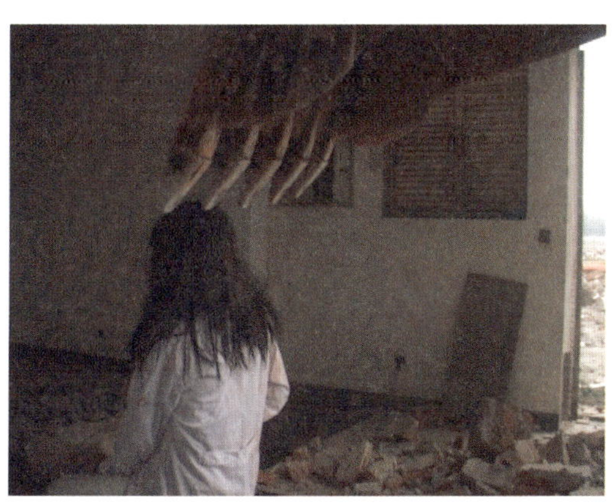

梳，2008
录像
7分15秒

Comb, 2008
Video
7'15"

屋顶上的风景，2009
装置
800×75×100cm

View on the Roof, 2009
Installation
800×75×100cm

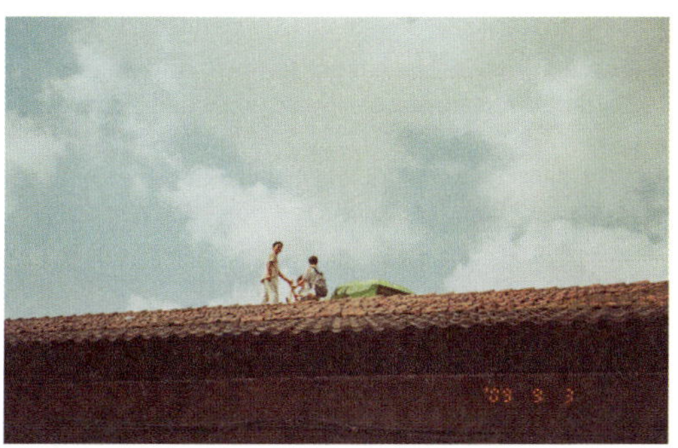

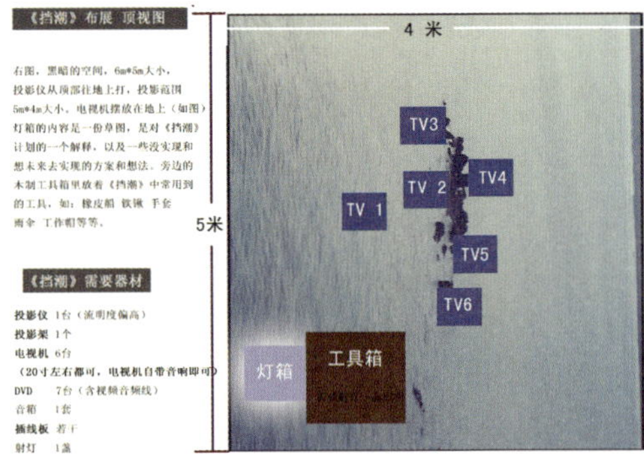

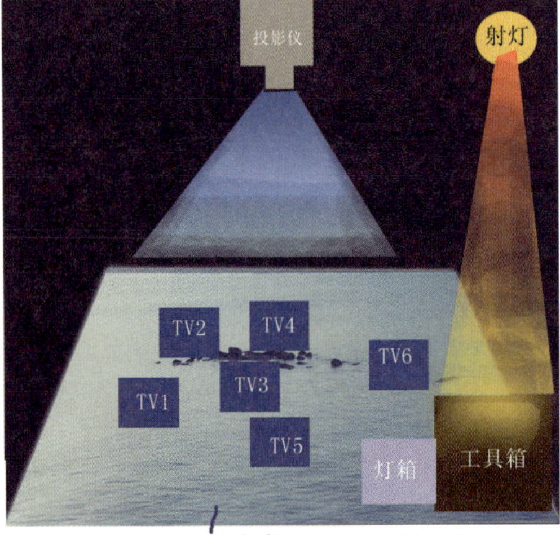

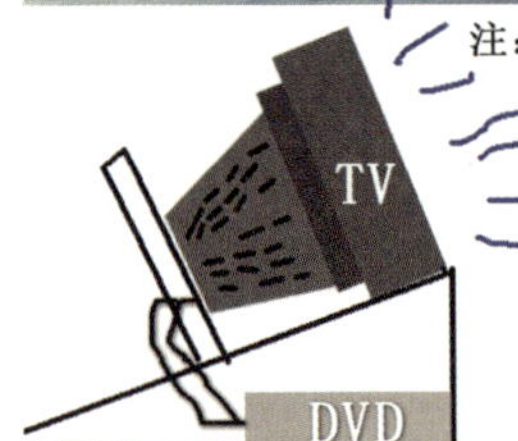

挡潮，2009
方案

Breakwater, 2009
Plan

As an artist, what do you care most during working? Could you please give an example to introduce the process of your work for us?

From the initiation of the creation to the end of it, the whole process is what I'm interested in, because I always want to change something. There are all sorts of objective resistance forces that need to be overcome; otherwise I'll have to compromise. The process of creation thus becomes a process of fighting. The initial idea changes when fighting with those objective things. The initial idea of *Breakwater* is like this: during a period of time, I use different materials to construct some sculptures on an island that will function like a fence and block the tide; each fruit of this "tide-obstructing" will be preserved on the island and after a period of time, there will be different sculptures there, like an open-air museum. But the reality is: after I finished my first work and went there for the second time, I found my things disappear-torn down by the Environmental Protection Bureau of the Government of Binjiang District. There was also one time that I was driven off the island by the water supervisor; my work would be destroyed, too because it influenced the environment there. Later on, I could only carry out this plan when the supervisor was not working-before 7 am, between noon and 2 pm or after 9 pm. Due to the inconvenience of the work time, transportation by water and manual work, the materials I had in mind were just simple things that were easy to carry or things that I could find on the island. Later the form became video installation-putting works at different places and dates on the projection of the island and establishing a feeling of the same time and place. Once I have new ideas, I will continue to supplement this experiencing process.

Suppose you are a critic, what perspective would you talk about and explain you work from?

I don't know. My creations that can be interpreted and discussed are too few and hard to establish a relatively macroscopic clue.

What books and which artists have had, or is having an influence on your way of thinking and working?

As for reading, I appreciate the learning style of "interpreting out of context" mentioned by Yang Fudong. This is like treating linear time as non-linear. The artists that have influenced me much are Kan Xuan and Xu Zhen.

How do you decide the context in which your work is to be presented? How do you consider the relation of the context with your work?

Lao Jinfeng once said, "You have everything ready for a gunshot, but your shoot deviated from your target; everybody is discussing this openly, but you speak under the table." Context is something that lies within the frame. We are supposed to strictly obey the game rules, but only the people who invent the game can set the rules; maybe they change the rules while playing the game. The participator seldom has the right to speak.

How does your work take the present shape? And please give a few words about the latest development and changes in your work.

"Look" is actually referring to system. System needs rules and the rules come from experience and inertia. Most of my ideas and creations are instinctive and natural; they are the accumulation of details. These details are some "coincidences" that extend many possibilities after colliding with each other". These "coincidences" come from the thoughtless instants of life and of the constantly changing emotions; they also come from the redefinition of some seconds of the linear materials when editing so as to change the whole time axis. In a word, these instinctive and natural repetitions continuously enlarge this "mode" and new experiences are also constantly accumulated.

As for the question about the development and change of my recent works, what I have done is not enough, so it's hard to talk about development and change.

In what circumstances would you want to destroy your own creation?
I understand the "destroy" in this question does not refer to a subjective and intentional damage to the work. When I don't want to avoid the objective obstacles that I face, I will lose the interest and desire to finish that work.

What do you think about the relation between the art history and artist's work?
I seldom think about their relationship.

What kind of roles would rational thinking and emotional impulse respectively play during your work time?
Take the process of making video as an example, when all the objectivity can serve you and reach a comfortable status, the emotion at that time has already deviated from the detailed plan before filming and the things you want also become unstable. The editing part is a very rational process-observing the materials, throwing them into confusion and re-organizing them; some later editing work even denies the previous editing. In the end, rationality always swallow emotion.

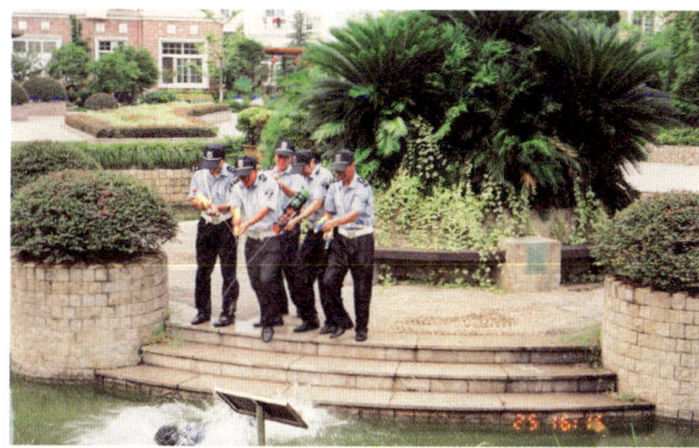

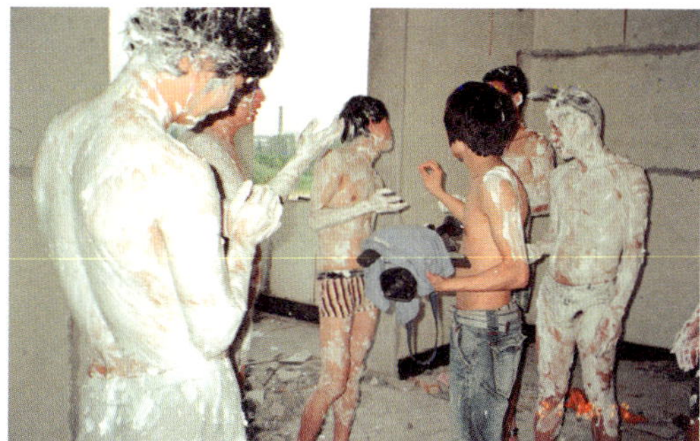

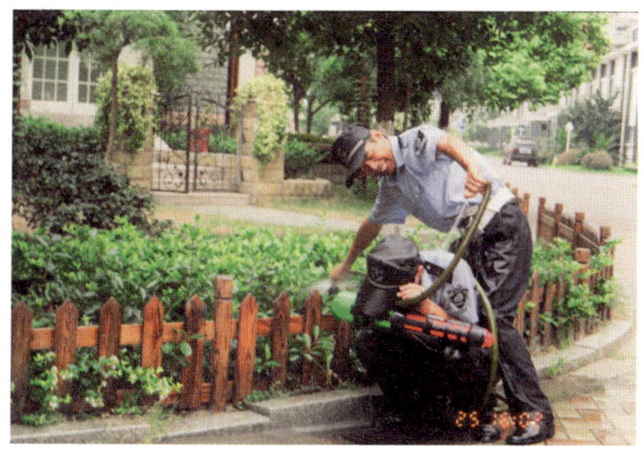

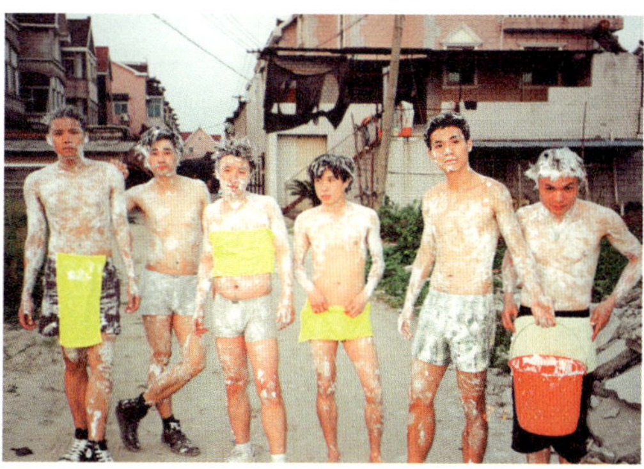

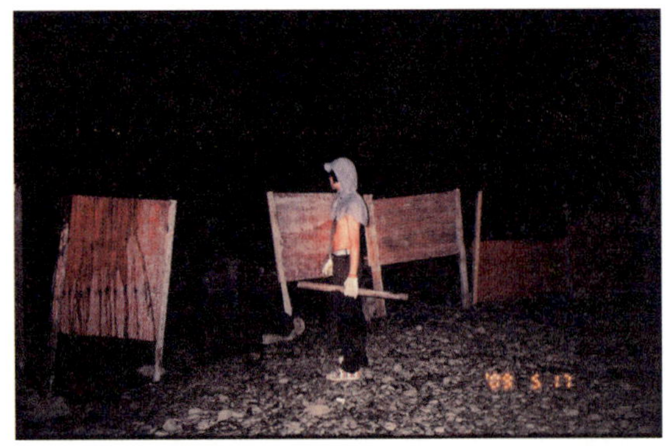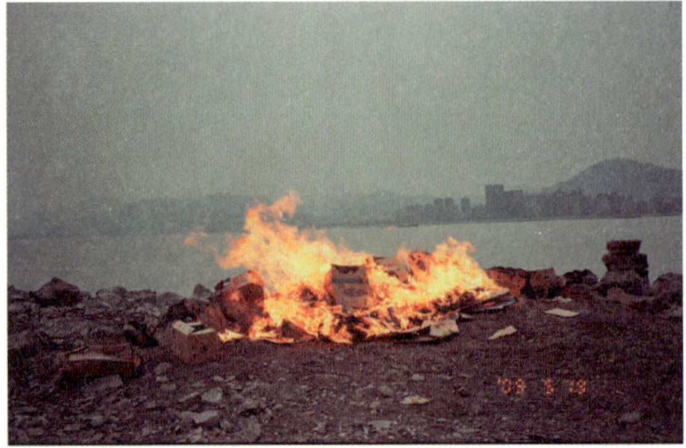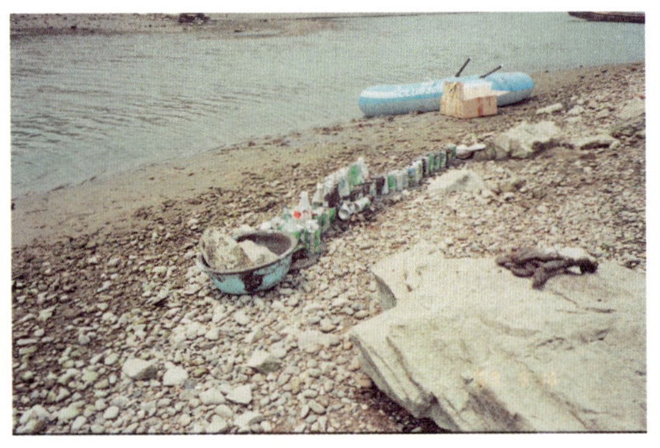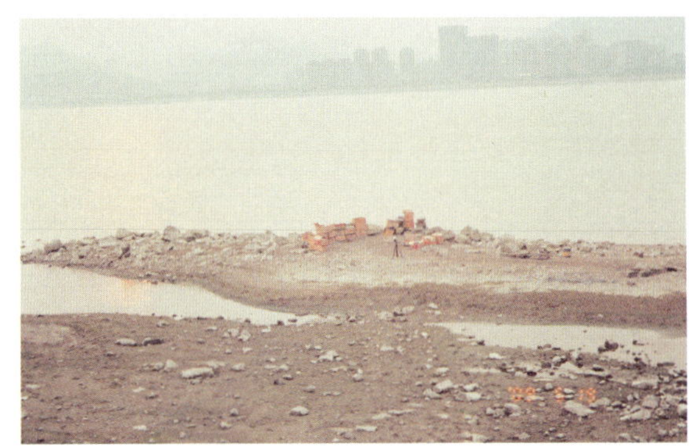

《挡潮》实施过程，2009
Documentation of performing *Breakwater*, 2009

萨特说："艺术是价值，因为它是召唤，它是作为一项有待完成的任务提出来的，它一上来就处于绝对命令级别"。我关心的是创作本身，把"要做一件东西"看成出发点，一旦迈出第一步，就会顺着往下走，要么完成任务，要么放弃任务。

本次展览的作品我想提出的是我对重复的看法，对劳动性的热爱。重复是一种力量而不是无意义，过程中的单调，枯燥无聊到最后都将升华成经验和个人习惯，这如同是面对一个电脑游戏，兴趣只是停留在刚上手的时间，长时间一如既往保持对它有激情的都是个人习惯和个人经验，无数次体验重复的乐趣。不可避免惯性和模式化会在这时候产生，体力的劳动难免不把人的身体惯性暴露出来，我将创作中的大量重复劳动看成是武侠片中武士们的修身练习，在"修身"过程中体验当下，单纯直接的与客观做斗争，把剩余体力输出给这些困难。当创作结束时，便能享受到困难过后的舒畅。

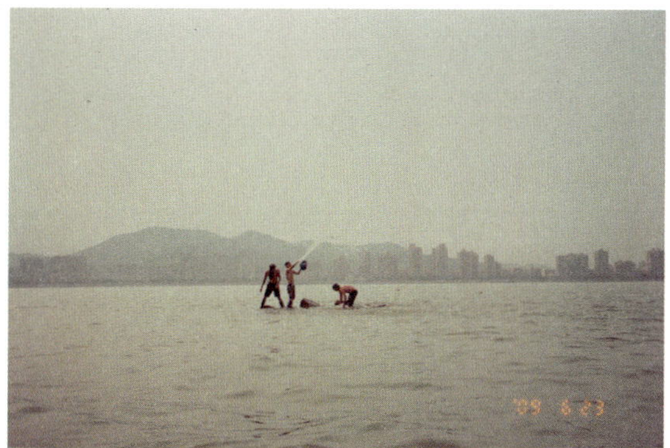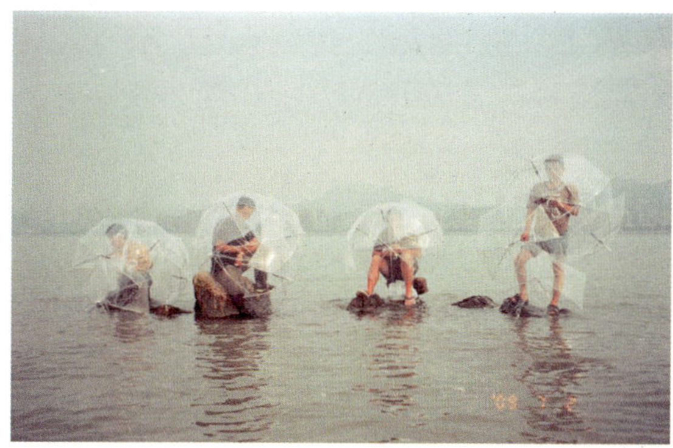

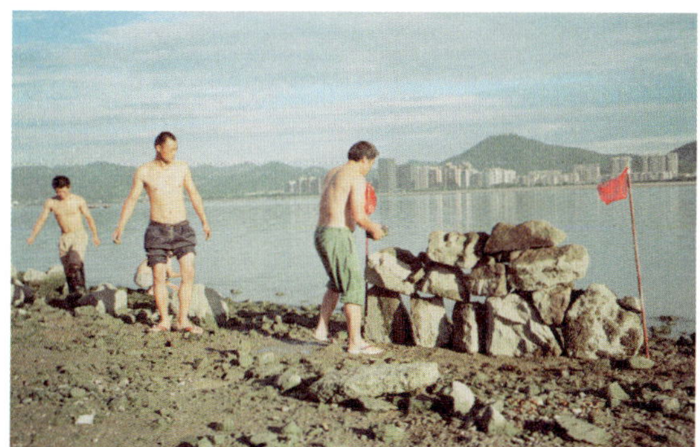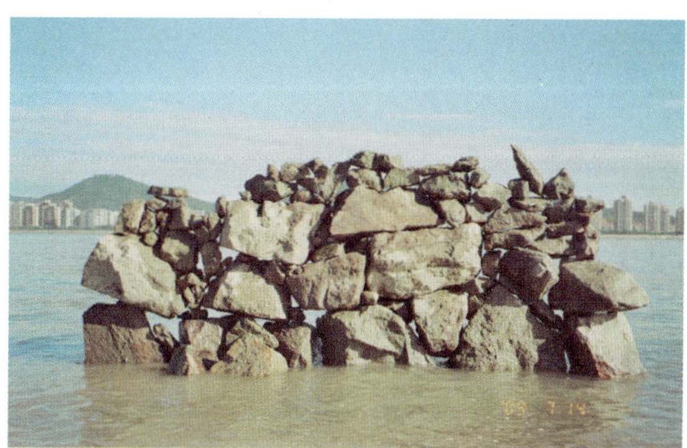

Sartre once said, "Art is value, because it is summoning and is raised as a task to be finished. It is already at the 'absolute command position'." What I care about is the creation itself. "To make something" is my starting point. Once I make the first step, I will continue walking along this path, and then either finish the task or give it up.

The work I want to present in this exhibition is my understanding of repetition and passion for labor. Repetition is a kind of power and is not meaningless. The monotony and dullness will eventually sublimate into experience and personal habit. This is like facing a computer game-your interest only exists when you just begin to play it. Long-term passion for it is just personal habit and experiencing the same fun again and again. At this time, unavoidability and stereotypes will be generated. Physical labor tends to expose one's physical inertia unavoidably. I regard the great deal of repetitious labor in the creating process as a kind of exercise and cultivation, like warriors do in a martial art film: experiencing current life during the course of that exercise, fighting the objective world directly and outputting one's physical strength in dealing with those difficulties...When the creation is over, one can enjoy the comfort after those difficulties.

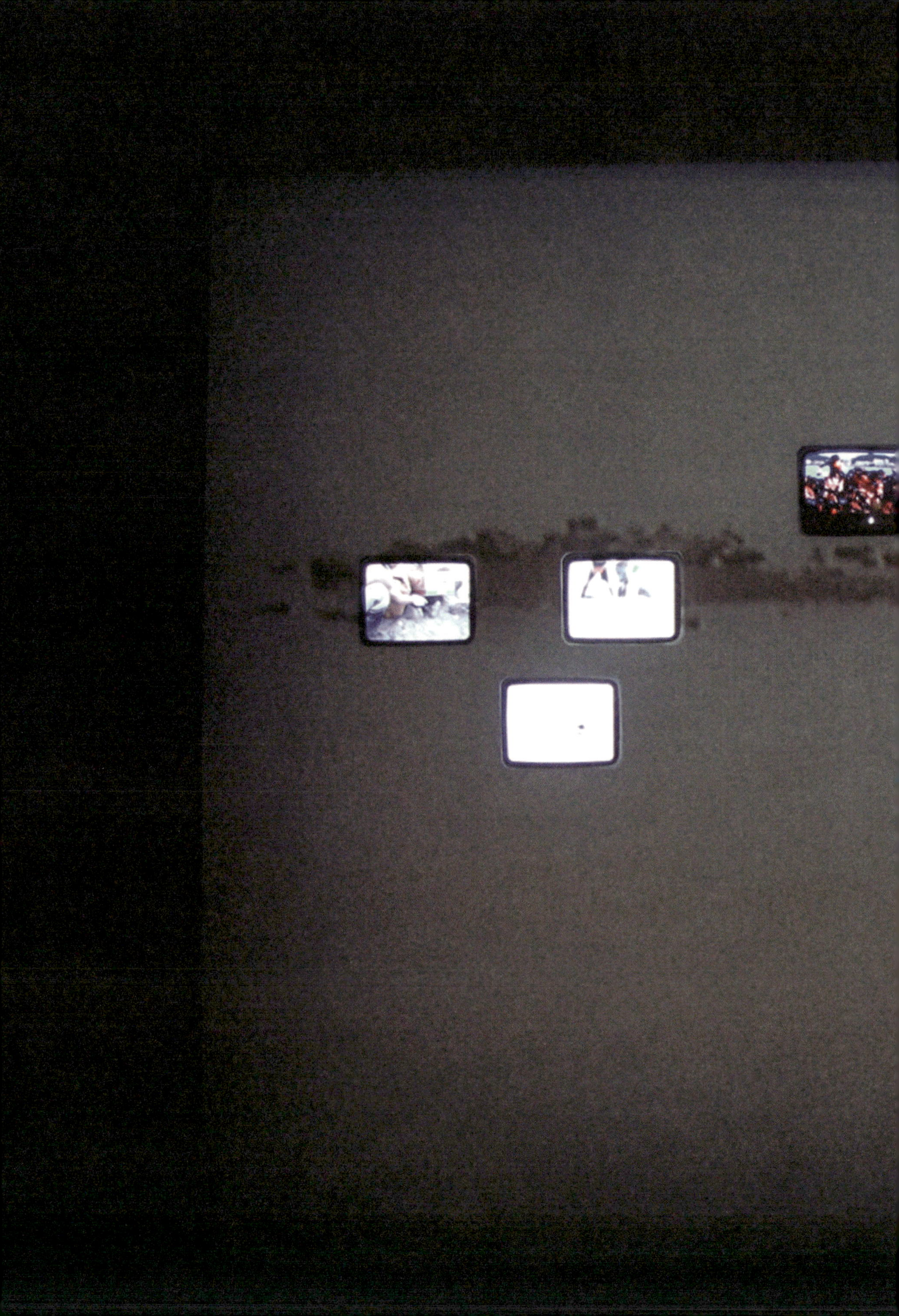

梁 硕

LIANG SHUO

作为艺术家，你在创作中所关心的是什么？以一件作品为例，分享你的创作过程。

我想我只能回答"在制作中关心什么"，因为创作的状态不大好界定，也许胡思乱想的时候也在创作，但之后肯定想不起来之前关心什么。在制作过程中，有时候关心手里的活儿会对下一步造成怎样的影响；有时候会想手里的活儿跟游戏规则是什么关系；有时候想什么之后就忘了，但大多数都跟技术有关。

就拿《什么东西》说吧，我主要关心手里的活儿会对下一步造成怎样的影响。首先，我做一个写实雕塑（步骤1），尽量的写实，尽量的细致入微，还要考虑尺寸，因为做小了细节出不来，做大了下一步和以后所有的步骤就很难继续。然后把雕塑往泥里杵（步骤3），为的是印出个雕塑的负形。在这之前要在塑料桶里塞满泥（步骤2），泥塞得不能太松也不能太结实，太松了得到的雕塑的印记太少；太结实雕塑杵不进去，而且泥的软硬度还要适中。在做这一步的时候还要兼顾两件事：一是事先在塑料桶底部挖个合适的洞；二是塞泥的时候要留出一个连接最底部和最上部的通道，这些都是为步骤6服务。雕塑完全被杵进泥里之后就往外拔（步骤4），要晃悠着往外拔，不然人力根本拔不出来，拔出来后就得到了雕塑的负空间，也就是一个泥质的容器。雕塑被拔出来之后就准备蜡（步骤5），原料蜡是块状固体，要煮，直到蜡化为液态，液化的程度要控制，这点至关重要，因为液化过了会使周围的泥变质，也会由于流动过快而难于成型；液化不够流动性就差，就得不到清晰的负空间的造型，这都决定了步骤6的成败。在蜡的温度合适的时候就可以往负空间里灌了（步骤6），灌蜡的时候速度要适中，让液态蜡均匀的附着在泥的表面，然后让多余的蜡流出负空间，这样就形成一层厚度均匀的蜡壳，蜡壳的厚度是步骤8成败的关键，太薄了强度不够，太厚了无法完成金属铸造，薄厚不匀也会毁掉整个雕塑的完整性。等蜡凝固冷却就可以把塑料桶拿掉然后拔掉附在蜡壳外边的泥（步骤7），因为泥块之间的空隙会与雕塑的负形连结成一体的负空间，所以最终雕塑的正空间会呈现出如此出人意料的面貌。清理掉所有蜡壳表面的泥之后就可以把它交给金属铸造厂了，由工人们完成最终的铸造工作（步骤

8），金属铸造工艺还要经历若干复杂的工序，任何一步的闪失
都会使整个工作前功尽弃，但这就不由我控制了，只能听天由
命了。我在大概一年半的时间里反复试验了三、四十次这样的
工序，最终只得到了这样几个成品，即使如此还没出现完全令
我满意的结果。

**如果你是一个批评家，你会从什么角度来阐释和讨论你自己的
创作？**
我会完全忽略复杂的制作过程，直接从作品呈现的面貌入手，
分析我所得到的信息以及这些信息的意义。

**在你的创作和思考中，什么书籍和艺术家曾经或正在影响着
你？**
我看的书很少，影响我的艺术家也都不是在工作方法和技巧方
面的。避不开的两个艺术家是布鲁斯·瑙曼和怀特里德，因为
我知道他们都做过有关负空间的作品，但这对我来说没那么重
要，我不想拿负空间来说事儿，这些技法和方法都是在雕塑制
作实践中慢慢掌握的，你要对雕塑制作工艺不了解的话即使用
到一些其中的办法也只是偶然的，不会对其有进一步的挖掘和
展开，也不会了解其中的可能性。这些活儿只有做雕塑的才干
得出来。

给老婆的信和给恋人的信，
2005
录像展览现场
给老婆的信，长度78分48秒
给恋人的信，长度45分51秒

*Letter to My Wife and Letter to My
Lover,* 2005
Exhibition view of the video
Length of *Letter to My Wife*: 78 min
48 sec
Length of *Letter to My Lover*: 45
min 51 sec

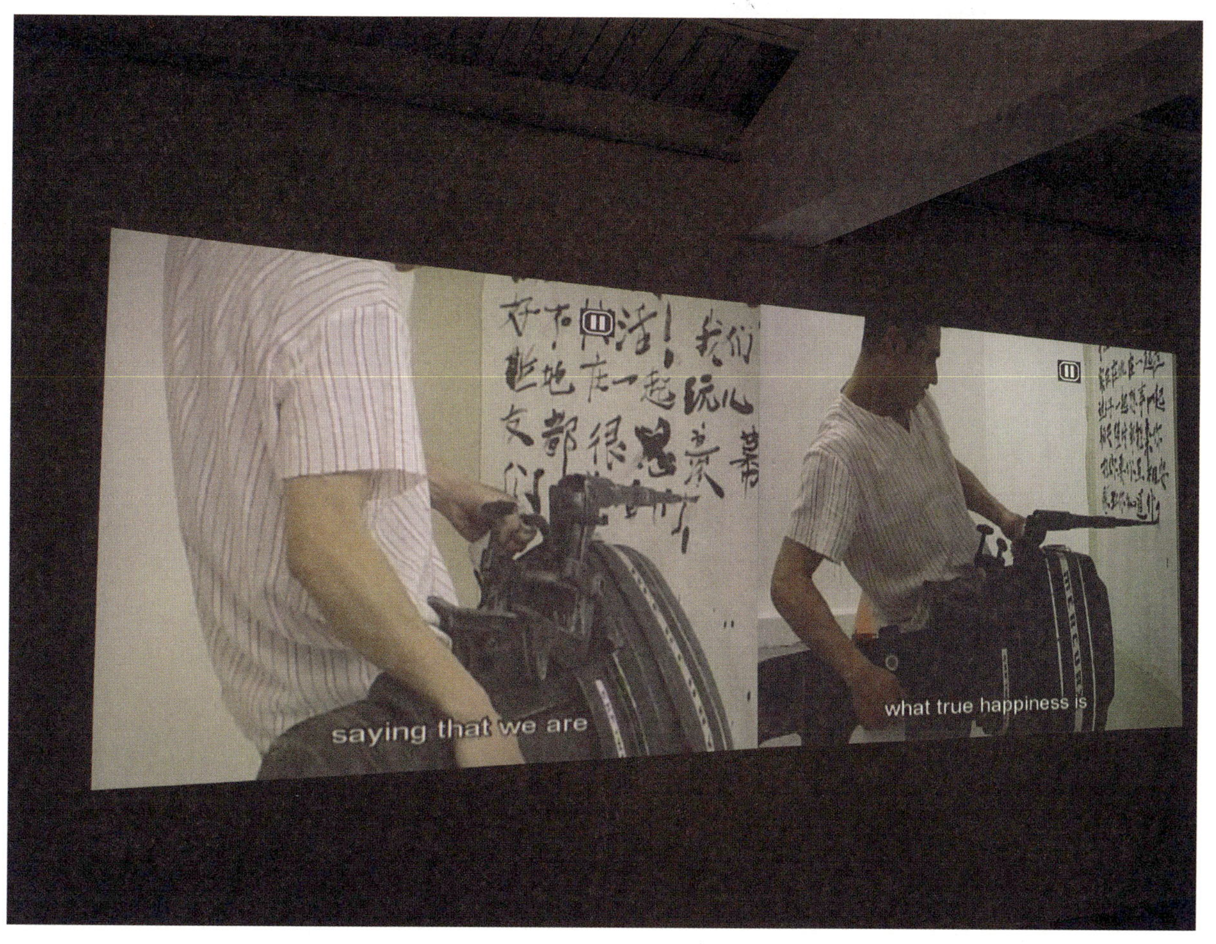

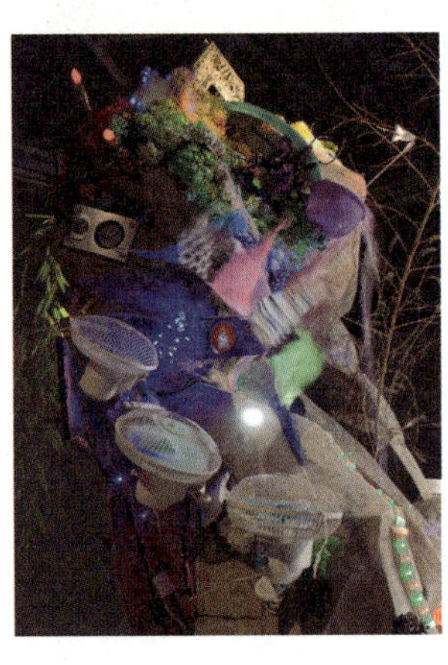

臭美三号，2008
混合媒体
360×350×350cm

I am Fucking Beautiful No.3, 2008
Mixed Media
360×350×350cm

你是怎样判断和决定在什么语境下呈现你的哪些作品的？你是怎样看待作品呈现的语境和作品的关系的？

我首先想到自己是个中国艺术家，但又没必要给自己贴个标签。我有自己的思路和问题，这是我自己的语境，但别人如何进入？这些我都把握不了。更要命的是我说着洋不洋土不土的话跟别人交流，实在是不好弄，我只能尽量避免操着土话让别人听不懂，也尽量避免非得用对方的方言跟人家交流。这个事儿解决了才涉及到具体语境问题。

我不想把作品的语境设置在具体的民族、国家、文化这些概念里，因为我自己都摘不清楚这些问题，我想让它们与人的普遍经验发生关系，所以我使作品尽量少携带它背后的文化背景（比如《什么东西》）。

虽然作品避免不了受到社会和文化语境的影响，但这不等于作品就一定要为它们服务，就像我们吃鱼香肉丝是文化的影响，但绝不是为了这个文化而吃。

如何在创作上形成了现在的面貌，描述一下近年来作品的发展和变化？

我不觉得自己的作品有什么面貌，我也不在这上面费心。我只关心自己面对的问题，追踪这些问题未必导致作品有一惯的面貌。

关于近年来的变化，就从05年说起吧。之前我主要关心"民工"的事儿，后来我越来越觉得做民工那样的一套思维方法不好用、不够用了，而且心里被越来越多的"怀疑"占据，越来越不知道什么事是值得去做的，但同时我对世界的好奇心也跟着滋长。我意识到这种纠缠要不面对它就只有等死。这段时间我主要做的事就是触及那些个聚集着疑惑的点，让问题一个个暴露出来。思路的转变可以从两个角度说：1，对作品的态度。总的来说《给老婆的信和给恋人的信》之前我习惯把想法、效果都想好了才实施作品，呈现脑子里已有的东西，从这个作品开始我就不再依靠"成熟"的想法和预设的结果。因为我把作品当作"一件事"来做，重要的是从这件事里暴露问题得到启发，而不是证明一个成型的概念。2，具体的问题具体的转变。我曾面临的双重问题是爱情和做艺术的理由，这两个问题把我逼到了一个死角，这时艺术和生活变成了同一个问题：怎么办？回答是：只能做一件事。而且当时只有唯一的一件事可以做：《给老婆的信和给恋人的信》。由此艺术第一次帮我呈现了最切身的生活问题，最切身的生活问题也给了艺术一个不容怀疑的理由。这个作品做完之后我有种被掏空的感觉，变得无所事事，接下来的问题便是：当内心无情感可表达的时候艺术的理由何在？这种空空的状态让我有机会对身边普通的物体发呆，我开始漫无目的地摆弄那些东西，《物质练习——墨汁石膏粉》是个开始。我慢慢意识到作品可以仅仅来自好奇，对自己的思维结构的好奇和对外部世界的好奇。只有不预设结果的行为才会让我好奇。我不再关心作品有什么"意思"，我关心行为与物质间的逻辑关系、物质与身体间的接触方式、控制与失控间的交叉作用，它无关乎人情，但它同样可以引导我对世界进行深层感知。由于这批东西很容易被人误解，就逐渐对观众与作品之间的关系有了兴趣，那几个《什么东西》就是使误读不再成为问题的尝试。

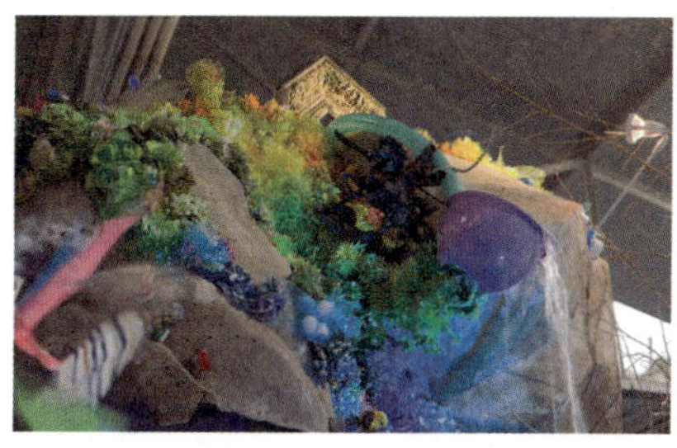

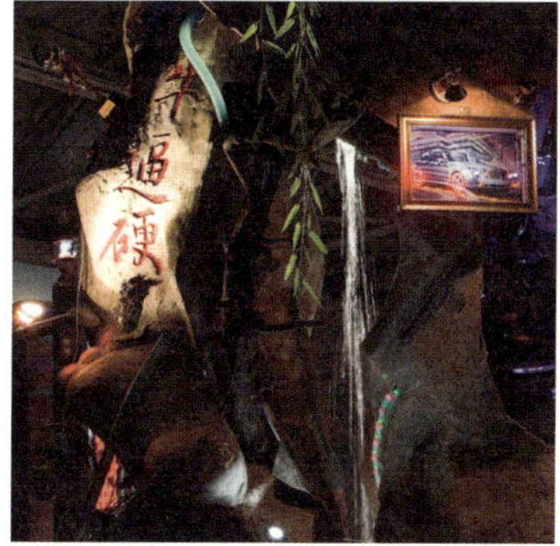

后来07年回国，空前地被国内火热杂乱的社会生活触动得不行，突然感到几年来苦苦向内追寻的那个"自我"突然变得极其弱小，在这种力量面前那个"纯艺术"也显得很牵强。我就寻思能不能到更开阔的社会空间里找点东西，就弄了个《庙会购物》。从这件事我重新发现关注别人的快感，其实只要你一关注，不管那个事物跟你有多大关系，你的那个"自我"就已经在它身上显现了，可以说"自我"根本不用找，简直到处都是，更不用担心把它丢了。

顺着这个意思我展开了对周围人的状态的关注，不知不觉就关注起"山寨"。"臭美"系列是这样产生的。在这些作品中，我曾用混杂的物体和媒介相互作用呈现一种气质，我想以这种气质体现周围人们的主流心态。我自认为作品的气质是有了，但问题也就出来了：我发现这些东西跟几年前的"民工"那些东西太像了，尽管媒介不同，但仍然是一种简单的"反映"社会的那套思路：反应准确了就ok，不然就失败。我就感觉特"土"，说白了就是"第三世界"的味儿特浓，这多少有点缺胳膊少腿的乞丐露胳膊露腿的嫌疑。我就想一个作品除了艺术语言和它所反映的社会背景之外是不是还有点"别的"什么东西，那好像更有意思。

但"山寨"的方法没问题，只是作品不能"山寨"。"山寨"的糟粕是抄袭，精华是创造力，它呈现的面貌是荒唐的但思路是有理的手段是直接的。我身边的这些东西明显很土，但它们未必只说土话，同时也不时说英语。这是有方法的。而且这时候我意识到可以把以前的思路综合起来用：用普通的信息、携带感情的信息、不预设行为结果等等。我尝试把身边的这些东西按照一定的规矩组合起来，让这个规矩决定作品的形态（规矩就是他们恰好能互相插在一起）。这个规矩好像有点像"别的"什么东西。《临时结构》是这种尝试的结果。这些东西呈现的是荒谬和陌生，但确实是按道理弄的，这道理一说谁都明白。

促成以上思路转变的因素其实远非说的那么简单，有时要向前追溯很多年，有些东西记不清楚也说不清楚，其实生活本身更强大，它会莫名其妙地改变一个人。

你会在什么情况下摧毁你自己的作品？

当我发现那东西是个陈词滥调。

你怎么看待艺术史和艺术家创作的关系？

不同的人写不同的艺术史。我们都了解一点艺术史，同时我们也了解一点自己拉的屎，只要跟自己的思维和意志扯上关系就行。想进谁的艺术史就吃谁的屎。

在你的工作中，理性和情感冲动各自扮演着什么样的角色？

人要真冲动了根本没理性这码事儿，倒是冲动不起来才找理性出来帮忙。通常情况下没谁老是让自己冲动着，除非疯子和装疯；也没谁事事保持理性，那也不是人。感情充沛的时候干事儿确实很爽，但坚持不了太久，所以平时大多用理性，它能整出不同的工作方法，以备下次冲动的时候用。有时候做一件事也很难区分理性感性哪个更用劲，两者是相互作用的，甚至很难搞清楚。肯定的是两者配合好了才能把事儿办好。

臭美三号，2008
混合媒体
360×350×350cm

I am Fucking Beautiful No.3, 2008
Mixed Media
360×350×350cm

家无处，2006
窗帘布上丙烯、钢管、钢丝
300×700×350cm

Home in Non-place, 2006
Materials: Acrylic on curtain, steel tube, steel wire
300×700×350cm

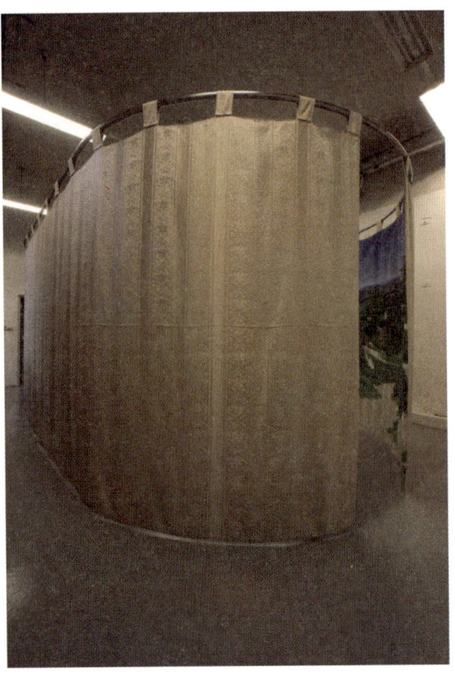

**As an artist, what do you care most during working?
Could you please give an example to introduce the
process of your work for us?**

I think I could only answer the question "what are you concerned in producing" because it's not easy to define "the status of creation". I might create something while I was thinking about nonsense. But I am sure I couldn't remember what I was thinking afterwards. During the producing process, I might think about what I was doing would have what impacts on the next stage. Sometimes, I was thinking about the relationship between what I am doing and the rules of the game I am playing. And sometimes I just forgot what I was thinking. However, most of time, they were all about the techniques.

Let's take the example of *What-thing*. I am concerned about the impact the current work has on the next stage of the process. Firstly, I create a sculpture model (Stage 1), this will be duplicated in as accurate a way as possible to the subject matter, I would even have to consider issues such as dimensions and measurements. This is because if I cannot even capture the smallest details in the right manner, I will encounter great difficulty in the next stage of the sculpturing process.

At Stage 3, I will take the sculpturing model and place it in the mud/clay imprint device/spinner. This is to create the actual model in shape and size. However, in order to do this, Stage 2 has to be in place. Stage 2 involves filling the mud imprint device/spinner with mud/clay. One must prepare the optimum amount of clay as if there is too much clay, it will be too relaxed, if there is too little clay, it will be too tight. When the clay is too relaxed, the imprint will be too small; on the other hand, when the clay is too tight, the imprint cannot be made. It must be noted that the flexibility of the clay is very important as well (whether the clay is soft or hard).

In order to achieve this, two conditions must be in place. Firstly, there must be an appropriately sized hole created at the base of the mud/clay device/spinner. Secondly, when clay is put into the device/spinner, there must be continuous link between the bottom and the top. This is done in preparation for Stage 6.

At Stage 4, once the model has been completely submerged in clay. Shaking must be done vigorously towards the exterior; this is to ensure that it can be extracted by human efforts.

After extracting the sculpture you will obtain an empty space in the middle of the model, next you prepare the wax (Stage 5). In its natural state, raw paraffin is a massive solid, to change it into its liquid stage which is wax, you must boil it.

One important note is that the degree of liquification must be closely controlled; this is because if there is too much liquification, this will cause deterioration which will also result in excessive flow, too rapidly and will cause great difficulties in the wax taking shape of the model. To decide the success of Stage 6, the important factor would be whether the liquified wax has sufficient or insufficient fluidity.

Once the correct wax temperature is achieved, it is also the appropriate time to fill the model with wax (Stage 6). The time taken and the speed used to fill the model with wax has to be moderate, the liquid wax must attach itself to the surface of the model, followed by allowing the unnecessary, unwanted wax flow out, this will allow the formation of an wax shell with even thickness throughout. Stage 8's crucial factor is determined by the thickness of this said-wax shell. There is undercapacity when the wax shell is too thin, and when it is too thick, this is an inability to complete the metal founding. Also when thickness is not uniform, it will ruin the entire sculpture's integrity.

Once the liquid wax cools and coagulates, the sculpture device can be removed. This is done to prevent any unwanted sections being part of the sculpture, and present an unwanted surprise beyond what is expected.

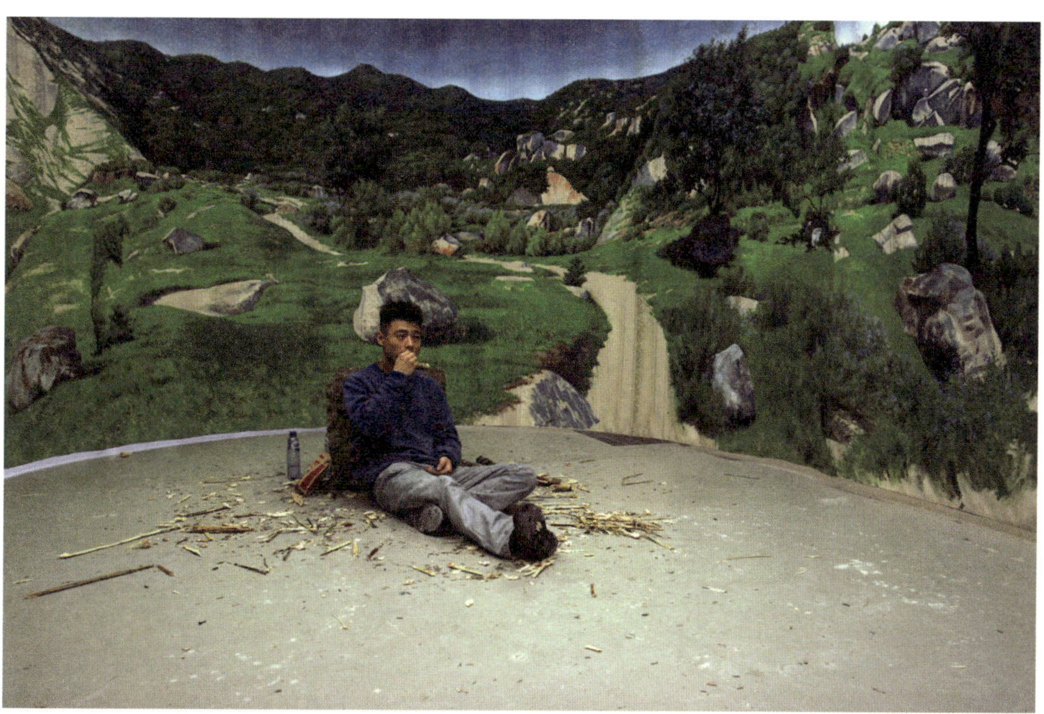

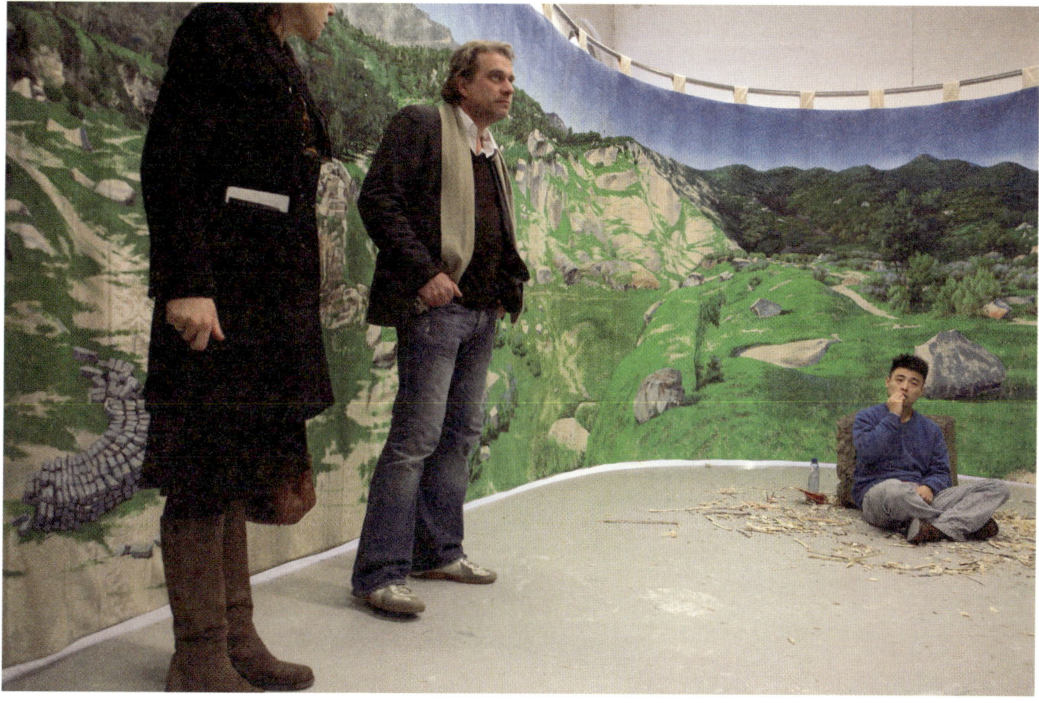

家无处，2006
表演现场
磕瓜子、喝水、休息、不与观众对话

Home in Non-place, 2006
Performance
Crack sunflower seeds, drink water, and rest, with no
communication with the audience

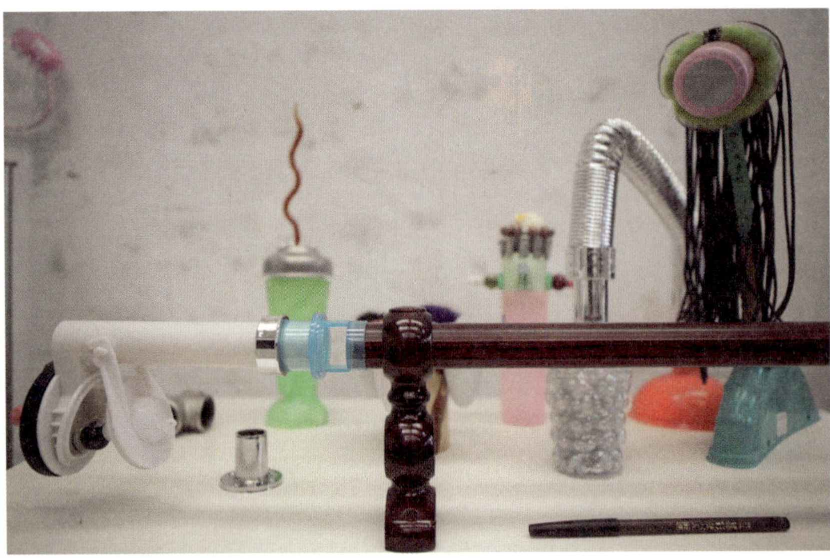

临时结构（局部），2009
装置
现成品

Temporary Structure (Detail), 2009
Installation
Ready-mades

After cleaning up the final metal works can be performed by the workers (Step 8), this involves complex work procedures. At this stage, any negligence will cause failure in the whole project. This however is beyond my control. Over a period of a year and a half, I have experimented close to 30 or 40 times and finally, I have only gotten just a few completed products. In fact, out of these few completed products, there isn't one which is satisfactory.

Suppose you are a critic, what perspective would you talk about and explain you work from?
I would absolutely ignore all the complicated producing processes. I would start from the very outside of the work and then analyze the information I have got and the meaning of it.

What books and which artists have had, or is having an influence on your way of thinking and working?
I read few books. The artists who influenced me however, didn't have influences on my skills and techniques. Bruce Nauman and Rachel Whiteread are the two artists who I have to mention here because they both did their works on the negative space. But it's not very important to me. I don't want to use negative space as an example as the skills and techniques are learnt gradually from the practice of sculpting. If you are not familiar with sculpting, even if you used some of the techniques by chance, you wouldn't explore and develop them further. Those can only be developed by the people who are actually doing sculptures.

How do you decide the context in which your work is to be presented? How do you consider the relation of the context with your work?
Firstly, I know I am a Chinese artist but I don't want to have a tag on me. I have my own problems and my own way of thinking. That is my context.
But how can other people come into my context? I am not too sure. Even worse, I am communicating with others using my crappy mandarin. It's very difficult. I try to avoid making confuse to people with my own dialect or using their dialects when I talk to someone. Once these are solved and then we can talk about the context. I don't want to put my work's context into the concept of any specific nation, country or culture because even myself don't

understand those problems. I want my works to have relationship with the ordinary man's experiences. Therefore, I made my works with less culture background as possible.

Although works are not avoidably influenced by the society and the cultural context, it doesn't necessarily mean that works have to serve them. It's just like you eat "Sauteed Shredded Pork in Spicy & Chilli Sauce" which is affected by the culture but it is absolutely not to eat it for the culture.

How does your work take the present shape? And please give a few words about the latest development and changes in your work.

I don't think my works have unique characters and I don't pay any attention to it as well. I only care about the problems I am facing. Pursuing these questions won't necessarily make my works have consistent shape characters.

About the changes of recent years, let's start from 2005. I was mainly focused on the Migrant Laborer issues. But I found out later that it wasn't good enough or adequate if I keep going on the same way of thinking which I used for migrant laborer issues. My heart was full of doubts and I wasn't sure what was worth doing. But in the same time, my curiosity of the world was growing as well. I realized that I would be died if I don't face the problem.

During this period, I was mainly focused on the points which puzzled me and exposed them one by one. The change of thinking can be described into two different perspectives: 1. the attitude to the work. Before the Letter to the *Wife and the Letter to the Lover*, I used to created my works after I had all the thoughts in my mind. But starting from this one, I don't rely on those mature thoughts and pre-planned results any more. Because I treat my works like something which are still happening. It is more important to be inspired by exposing issues during this process other than to prove a mature conception.

Specific Problems need specific solutions. Love and doing art once were the double questions I faced. Those two questions forced me into a corner. At that point, art and life become into a same question: How? The answer was: pick only one. Therefore *the Letter to the Wife and the Letter to the Lover* was the only thing I could do at that time. It was actually the first time that the art helps me to express the deep inside of my life. But it also provided me an undoubtable reason towards art. I felt I had been emptied inside my body after I finished the work. I felt I lost my directions and became aimless. Then the next question was: How does art exist when there is no emotion to express? My emptiness gave me the opportunities to observe ordinary things around me without any purposes. *Study of Substance - Ink Plaster* is a beginning. I gradually realised that the art can even come from curiosities, the curiosities of thinking and the curiosities of the outside world. Only things which weren't planned could arouse my curiosity. I don't care about the meanings of an art work but the logical relationship between behaviors and material, the contact between material and the human bodies, the cross relationship between under control and out of control. It sounds have nothing to do with human nature but it does guide me into another deep perception level of the world. Because these are very easy to be misinterpreted, I gradually have interests in the relationship between the audience and the art works. The *What-thing* works were the trials which designed for audience to avoid misinterpretation.

When I was back in China in 2007, I was unbelievably moved by the high spirits and the chaotic social life. Suddenly I felt the inner me I pursued badly in the last couple years became extremely small and weak. In front of this, the pure art appeared to be far-fetched. I was wondering whether I could find something in a wider open society space and then Shopping in the Temple fair was born. From then

临时结构（局部），2009
装置
现成品

Temporary Structure (Detail), 2009
Installation
Ready-mades

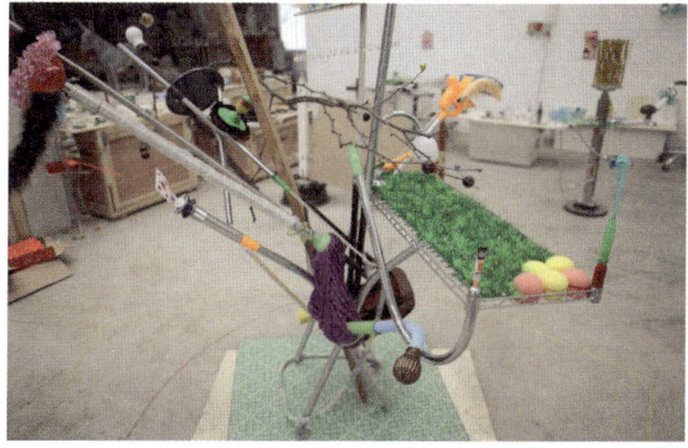

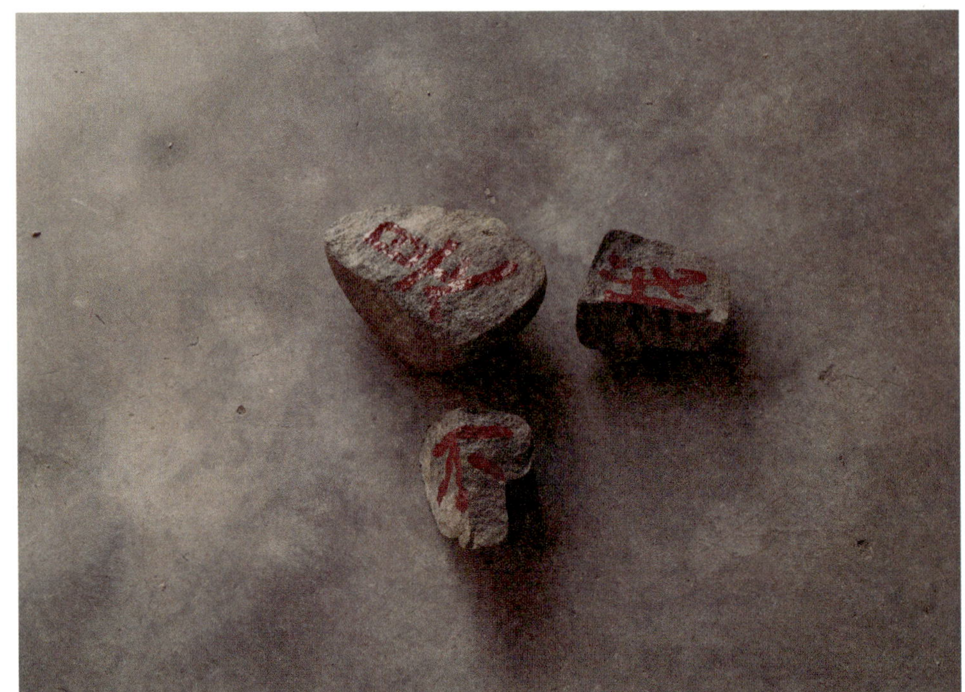

物质练习—鹅卵石（打开），
2007
鹅卵石，油漆
直径13cm

Study of Substance - Pebble (open),
2007
Materials: Pebble, oil paint
Ø13cm

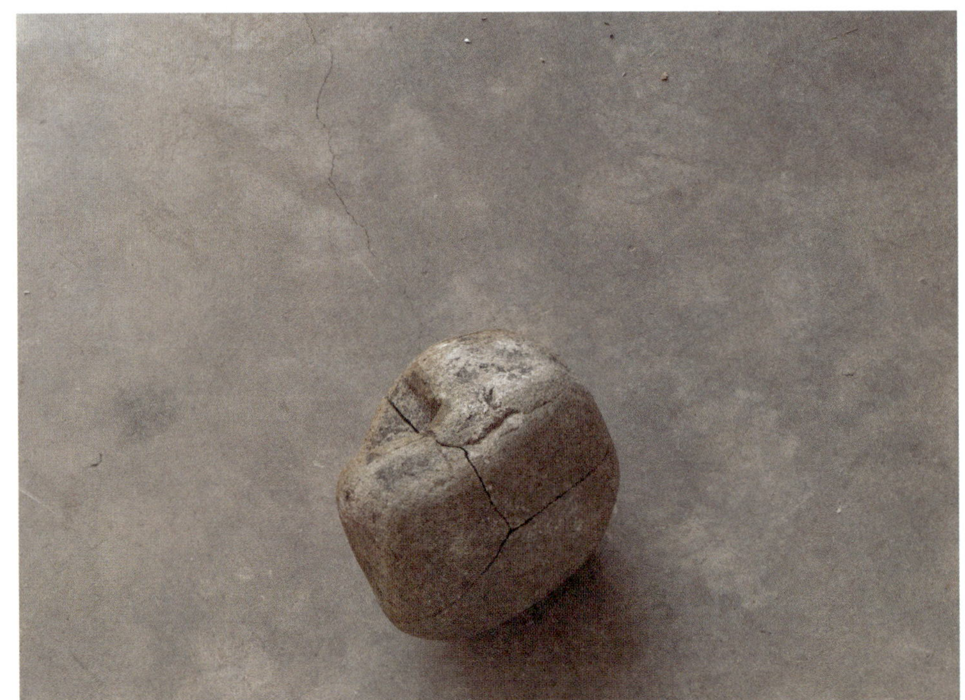

物质练习—鹅卵石（拼合），
2007
鹅卵石，油漆
直径13cm

Study of Substance - Pebble (close),
2007
Materials: Pebble, oil paint
Ø13cm

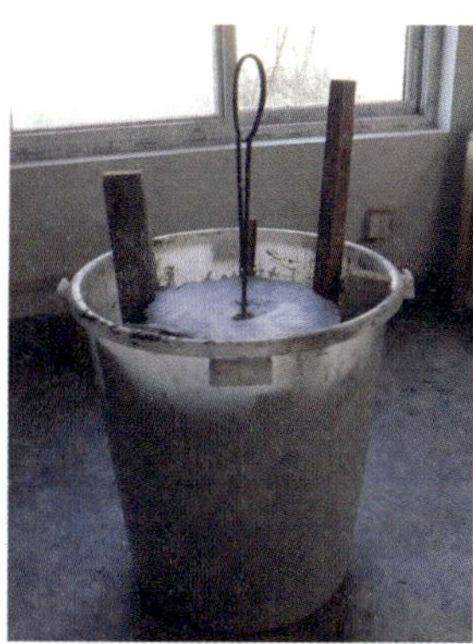

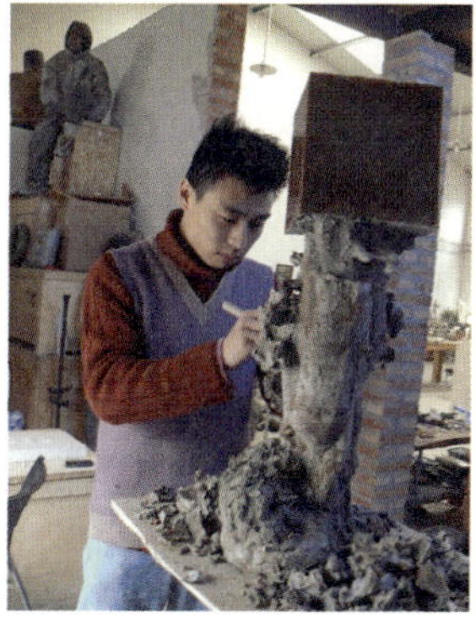

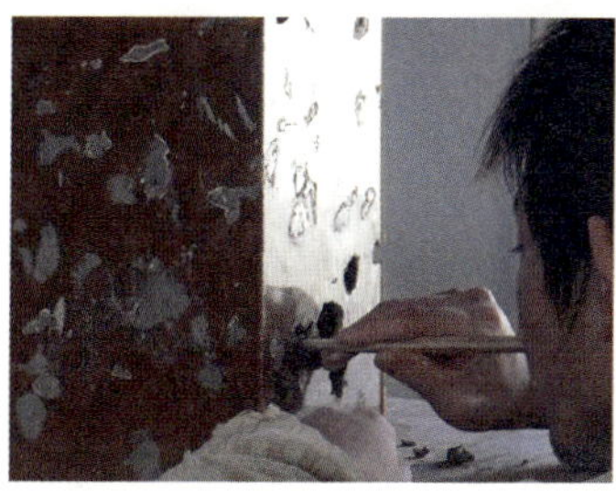

《什么东西》工作图
The Making of *What-thing*

on, I rediscover the pleasure of observing others. In fact, once you observe, no matter how close to you, you will find yourself on it. In other words, you don't' need to look for it, it's everywhere. No need to worry about losing it at all.

Following the thoughts, I started to observe the people around me and had more and more interests in Copycatting phenomenon. My I am Fucking Beautiful series were done under that circumstance. I tried to express sort of Characters by mixing objects and intermedium in these works. I thought those Characters could represent the mainstream mentality. I thought I got all the Characters but problems came out: These were too similar to the work Peasant Laborers I did a few years ago. Although the media are different, it is still in the same way to simply reflect the society: it's a ok if it is reflected precisely otherwise it is a failure. I think this is vulgar or in the directly way, it's too Third World. It's like a disabled beggar showing off his disabled body to get sympathy. I assume the work would be more interesting if it reflects something else except art language and the social background.

The method of Copycatting is no problem but art works couldn't be copycats. The dross of the Copycatting is copy but the essence is creativity. The presentation is ridiculous but the thinking is reasonable and the method is straight. Those things around me look vulgar but at least they don't only speak either dialect or stiff English. There are ways to do it. And at that time, I realized that I could mix up my thoughts: the use of common information, messages with feelings and unplanned behaviours etc. I tried to assemble those around me under certain rules and let the rules decide the shape (the rule is, as long as they could be assembled). These rules seem like something else. *Temporary Structure* is the outcome of this trial. These works appear to be ridiculous and strange but they were made under the rules. It's easy to understand by anybody.

What made the changes of said-thoughts is not as easy as I explain. Sometimes I need look backward many years. I couldn't remember and explain all. In fact, life itself is full of power and influences people unaccountable.

In what circumstances would you want to destroy your own creation?

When I realize it's a cliché (rubbish).

What do you think about the relation between the art history and artist's work?

Different art history is written by different people. We all understand a little bit about the art history as we understand a little bit of our own shit as long as it is related to our thinking and will. Involving into someone's art history means eating his shit.

What kind of roles would rational thinking and emotional impulse respectively play during your work time?

There is no rational at all if people are really impulsive. Actually if we could not be impulsive, we will rationally ask why. Unless you are mad or pretend to be mad, generally speaking no one want themselves to be impulsive at all the time. And no one wants to be rational at all the time either. Otherwise, they are not human beings. It is fun if you are full of feelings but it won't last long. Therefore, please be rational at usual times and it would lead to the different way of working. But prepare for the next impulse. Sometimes it's difficult to say which one is better between rational and emotional. They interact each other. But I am sure that things will be done well if they both could cooperate.

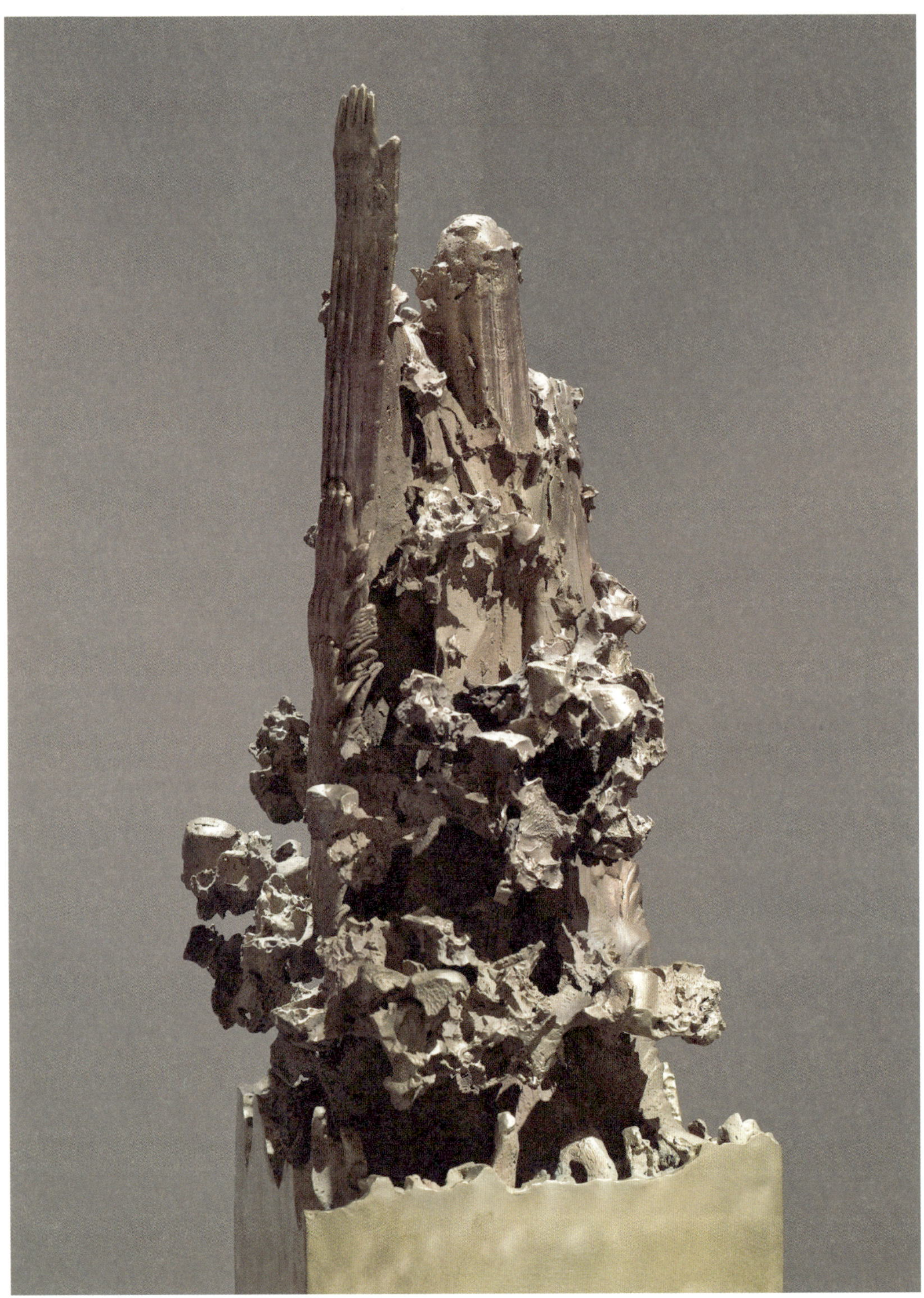

什么东西#3（局部），2008
铝
79×40×34cm

What-thing #3 (Detail), 2008
Materials: Aluminum
79×40×34cm

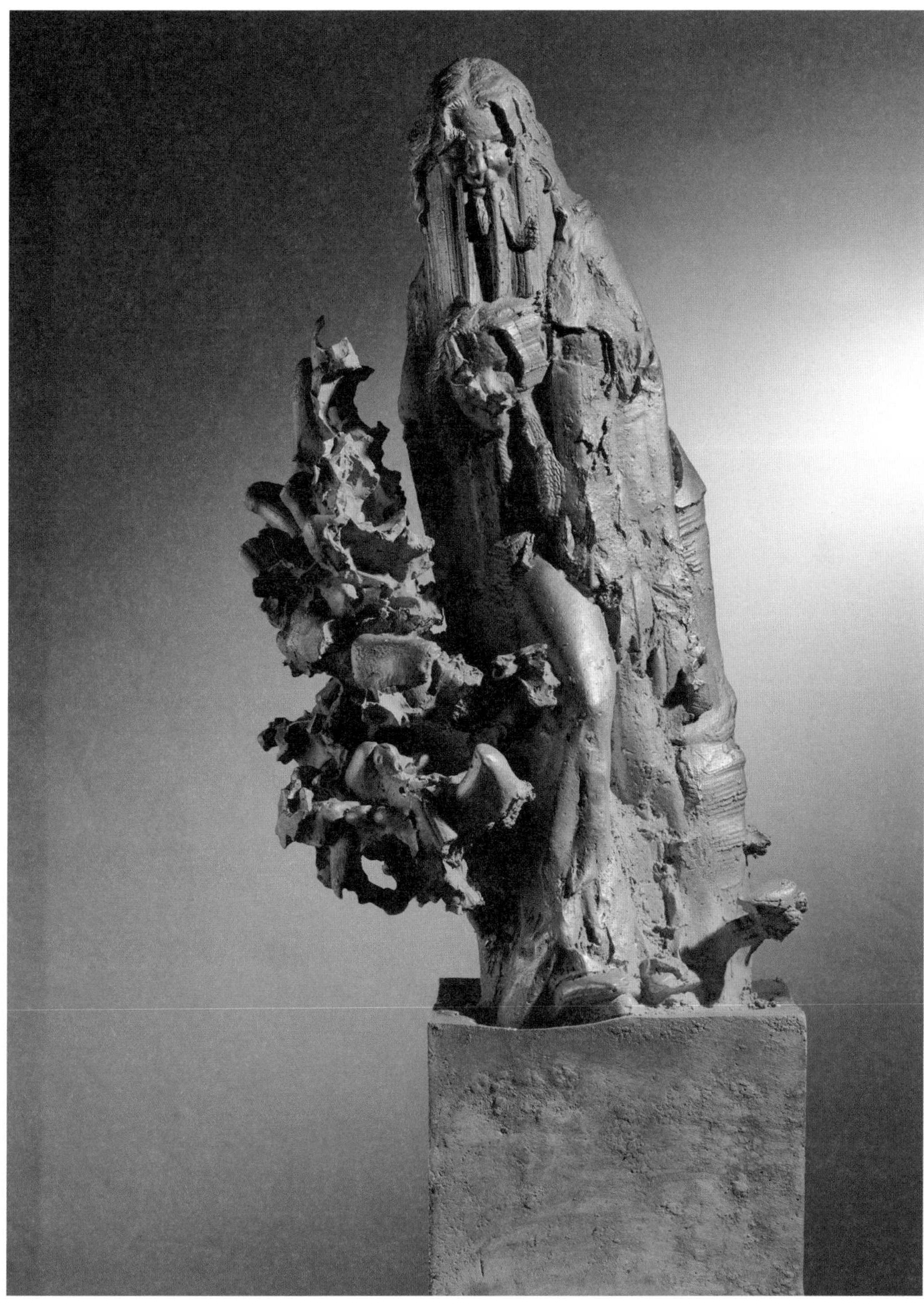

什么东西#4，2008
铝
68×28×21cm

What-thing #4, 2008
Materials: Aluminum
68×28×21cm

李 郁 / 刘 波

LI YU & LIU BO

作为艺术家，你在创作中所关心的是什么？

李郁：关心创作中的偶然性因素，特别留意在做的过程里产生的新的想法，以及技术层面的问题。因为我们的作品由一系列的图片组成，需要在较长时间内完成，这个过程中必须考虑很多技术问题。虽然我们采取舞台化的摆布拍摄手段，但实际上也具有很多的即兴和偶然的东西，这些东西有时候是头脑里闪现出来的，有时候是在制作现场中突然的出现，要抓住这些瞬间，从某种角度来讲，也是布勒松所说的"决定性瞬间"。

刘波：关心创作时作品整体性和延续性的问题，这几年和李郁合作作品中我们都是以一年或几年为一个创作单位来实施完成整套作品，特别在08-09年《受害者 II 》中，新闻主题选择、画面场景对应式的布置，作品选择的角度，在前面两年是未曾遇到的。我们需要共同去解决这些问题，并展现出来。

以一件作品为例，分享你的创作过程。

李郁：讲个失败的例子。我们看到一则新闻：

楚天金报2006-03-30

昨晨青山发生离奇凶案 四男子当街追打枪击的哥

我们设想这四人行凶后，穿过斑马线离开的那一刻。可以拍成披头士乐队的那张著名唱片Abbey Road封套的样子，四个凶手依次迈开大步，手里拿着裹着报纸的刀或枪。远处路边躺着受害者。我们找了湖北美院国油版雕四个专业的朋友来演这四个歹徒，找到了很好的场景，准备好了道具。但是最后拍摄失败。

刘波：举一个拍摄制作上的例子

楚天金报2007-08-13

被人追赶纵身跳下 洞穿楼顶吓坏众人

07—08年的《受害者》作品中，这样的暴力新闻在武汉小报上几乎每天都有，我们选择这样一个具有代表性的新闻来拍摄，我们确定好表现主题后，分头去找拍摄场地，李郁找到一个朋友，他那边有个四面墙全是落地玻璃的房子，视线通透，但这个简单的房子离我们所想表现的场景还有比较大的区别，需要找工人来进行详细的布置和装修，以确保能和我们想象中的场景更加接近，之后我们俩和装修工人一起完全依照我们想象中的要求来重新布置了房间，在整个作品的前期准备、制作、拍摄中我们共同讨论去解决一些实际遇到的困难，这整个过程是很有意思的。

如果你是一个批评家，你会从什么角度来阐释和讨论你自己的创作？

李郁：我会通过我们的创作来讨论摄影和媒体的关系、摄影和电影的关系、摄影和叙事的关系。

刘波：通过我们的创作来讨论事件本身与社会的关系、摄影记录与社会的关系、摄影主题与政治的关系，摄影作品表现中隐喻的事件等关系来阐释。

在你的创作和思考中，什么书籍和艺术家曾经或正在影响着你？

书籍包括《景观社会》、《希区柯克论电影》、《反对方法》。

艺术家包括布勒松、迪克西亚、杰夫·沃尔，艺术家的影响一方面来自他们的作品，一方面也包括批评家对他们作品的解读。

刘波：我们俩平时关注的艺术家都比较接近，艺术家包括卡梅隆、希区·柯克、昆汀·塔伦蒂诺和科恩兄弟等很多优秀的摄影师和电影导演。

你是怎样判断和决定在什么语境下呈现你的哪些作品的？你是怎样看待作品呈现的语境和作品的关系的？

李郁：当代艺术重视上下文关系，在特殊语境下，平常物品也能成为艺术作品。艺术作品经常借助语境生成意义，但语境也可能会遮蔽作品，而作品也可以脱离语境，变得更加高深莫测。但我很少做这样的判断和决定，我更相信独立的作品，或者说是在一个大的语境下的艺术作品成立的可能。这个大的语境不是靠一个展览或一次会议建立的，它也许本来就存在，也许需要在整个人类的文化体系中发育形成。

刘波：这个我很赞成李郁的观点。

如何在创作上形成了现在的面貌，描述一下近年来作品的发展和变化？

李郁：前几年我先是零星的创作了一些图片和录像作品，其中的一条线索表现了两个稍微有那么点与众不同的中老年男女的生活，借由他们的白日梦般的呓语和行为，探讨虚幻和纪实之间的关系，主要手法也是游离在记录和扮演之间。近几年我和刘波合作，创作了一系列完整的作品，逐渐形成了现在的面貌。我们合作的三件作品，都是以一到两年为周期。这期间我除了拍摄半部DV作品之外，没有再做其它作品。

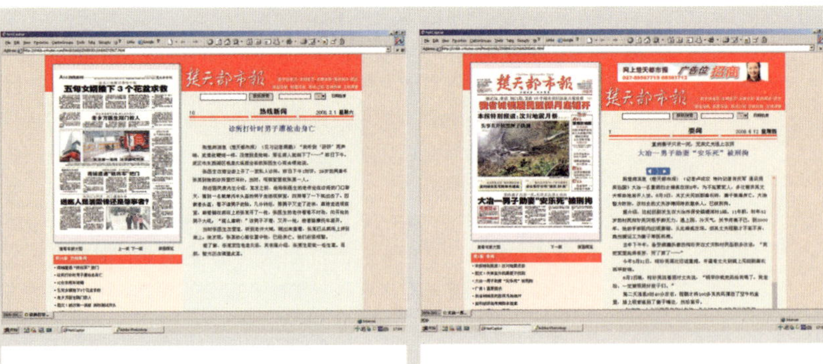
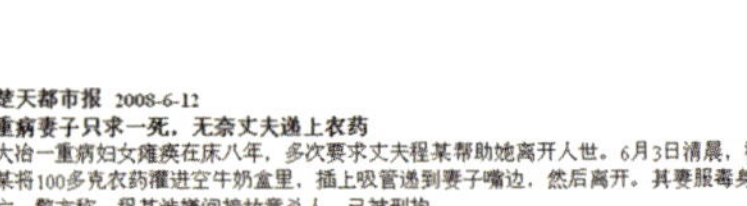
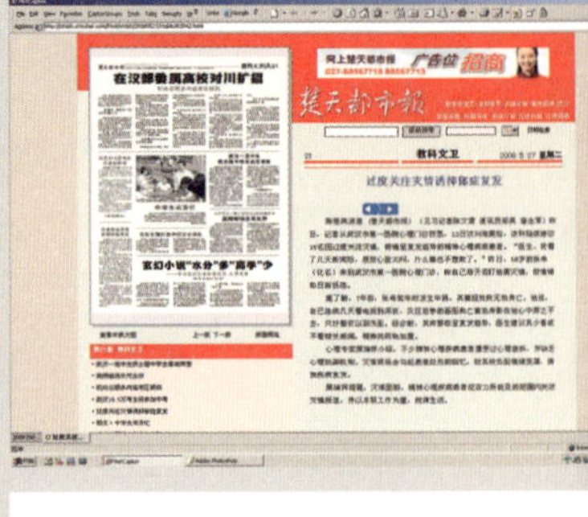

楚天都市报 2008-3-1
诊所打针时男子遭枪击身亡
昨日下午1时许，28岁男青年张某，在东西湖区柏泉农场一私人诊所内打吊针。突然，一名男子走进观察室，朝躺在病床上的张某开了两枪，然后骑摩托车离开。里屋的张医生跑出来查看，发现张某的心脏位置中枪，已经身亡。

楚天都市报 2008-6-12
重病妻子只求一死，无奈丈夫递上农药
大冶一重病妇女瘫痪在床八年，多次要求丈夫程某帮助她离开人世。6月3日清晨，程某将100多克农药灌进空牛奶盒里，插上吸管递到妻子嘴边，然后离开。其妻服毒身亡。警方称，程某涉嫌间接故意杀人，已被刑拘。

楚天都市报2008-5-27
过度关注灾情诱抑郁症复发
昨日，56岁的张某来到武汉市第一医院心理门诊，称自己每天从电视里观看四川地震灾情，情绪日渐低落。经诊断，其抑郁症呈复发趋势，医生建议其少看或不看相关新闻，精神类药物加量。

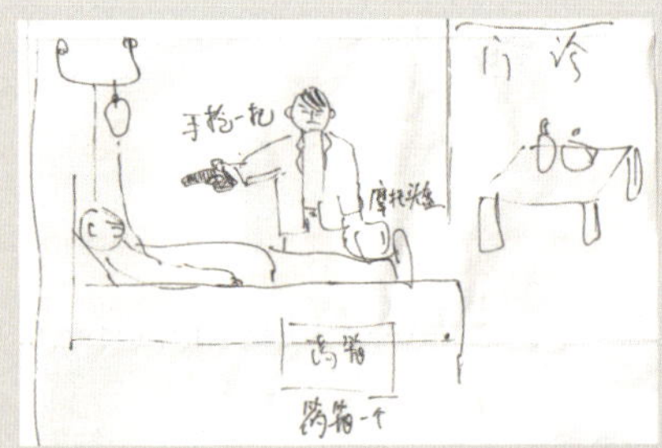

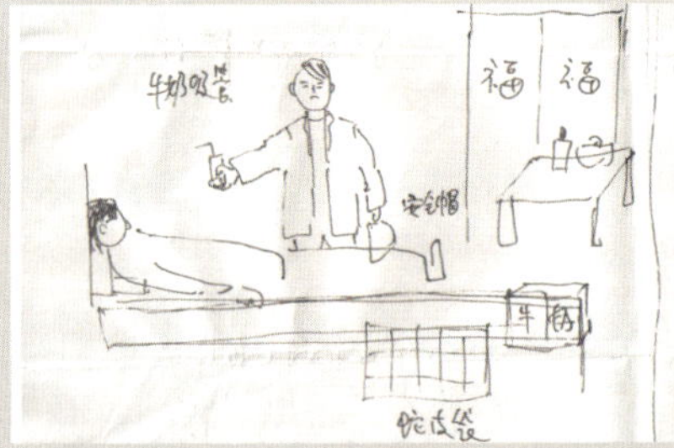

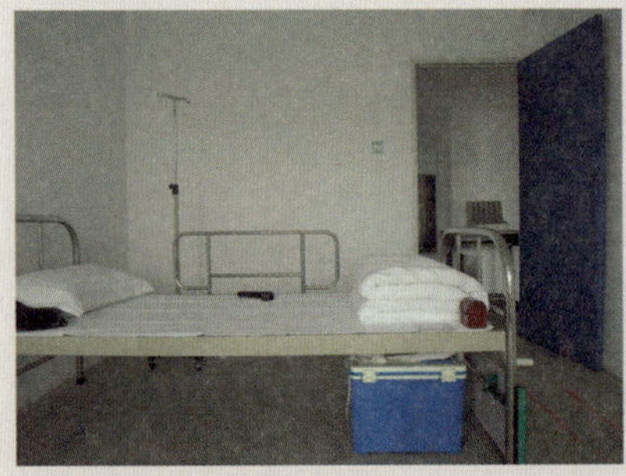
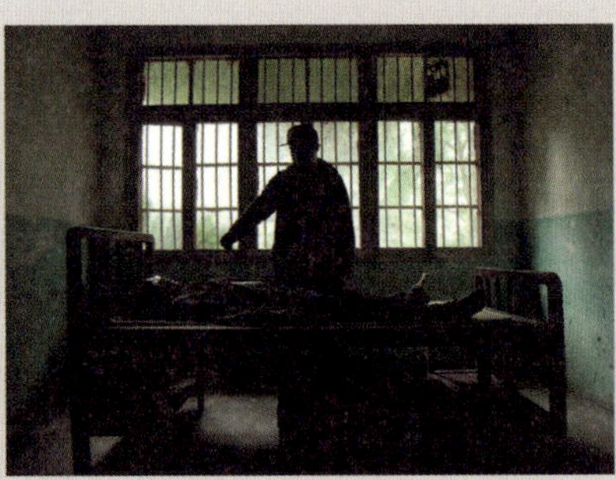

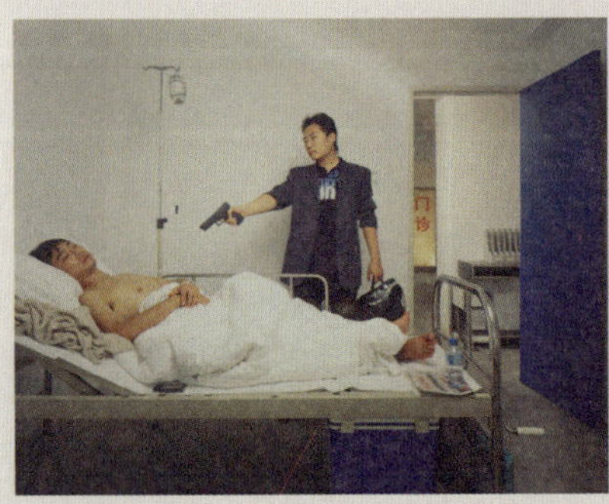
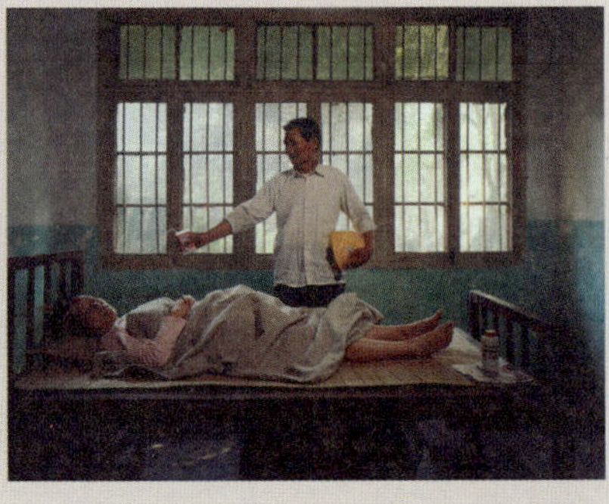
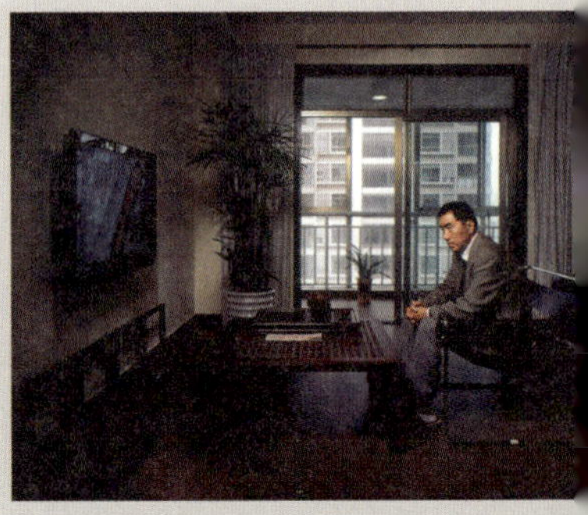

《受害者II》工作流程

Working Procedure for Victims II

刘波：虽然在美院读书期间学习的是油画专业，但在校大多时间是利用摄影这个方式在进行我的个人作品记录和创作，早期我个人比较关注的是伤害、暴力等主题。在和李郁合作作品之前我们都在进行各自摄影作品的创作，同时也经常一起组织和参加活动。在2005年底开始商量我们合作拍摄作品的计划，并在06年开始了我们《狗年十三个月》作品的拍摄和制作。在我们合作作品中全力汇集两个人的力量来制作和拍摄合作的作品，花费了大量的时间和精力。在作品的延续中我们尽量保持作品系列的完整性，在《受害者II》中我们突出寻找新闻内容、情景的对应关系，并在我们拍摄中呈现出来。

你会在什么情况下摧毁你自己的作品？

李郁：不知道是否有艺术家是因为觉得自己的作品太好了而摧毁它，除非摧毁也是作品的一步，但那实际上又是在创建而不是摧毁。对于好或不好的作品，遗忘和摧毁的结果也许是一样的。

刘波：我们在制作中有多次失败的拍摄，只会把自己觉得失败的作品不呈现出来而已。

你怎么看待艺术史和艺术家创作的关系？

李郁：今天的生活是明天的历史，对于艺术家来讲，应该更多的关注当下，当然艺术家也善于从艺术史中寻找创作的资源。艺术史的当代部分都是当代人写的，而对于这个部分上存在或缺席的名字，总让人想起那句"有的人把名字刻在石头上想不朽，有的人情愿作野草，等着地下的火烧"。

刘波：这个我很赞成李郁的观点。

在你的工作中，理性和情感冲动各自扮演着什么样的角色？

李郁：美国科学哲学家保罗·费耶阿本德在《反对方法》中，论证了最成功的科学研究从来不是按照理性方法进行的。对于科学如此，对于艺术来说也是这样。理性就像一个独裁者，总会有人甘愿接受他的统治，而情感冲动就像天使，越来越少降临，但总是带来希望。

刘波：这个我很赞成李郁的观点。

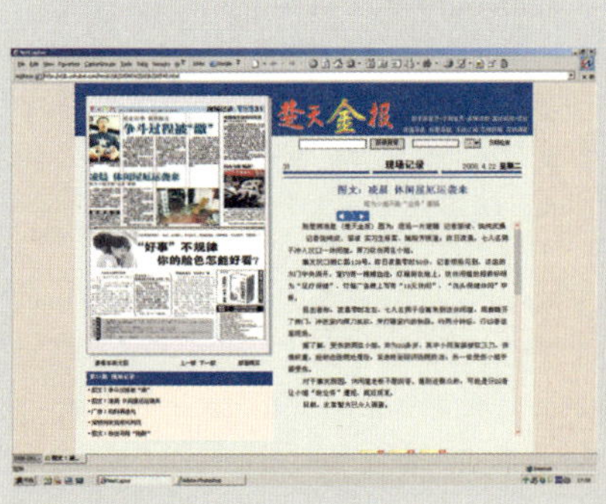

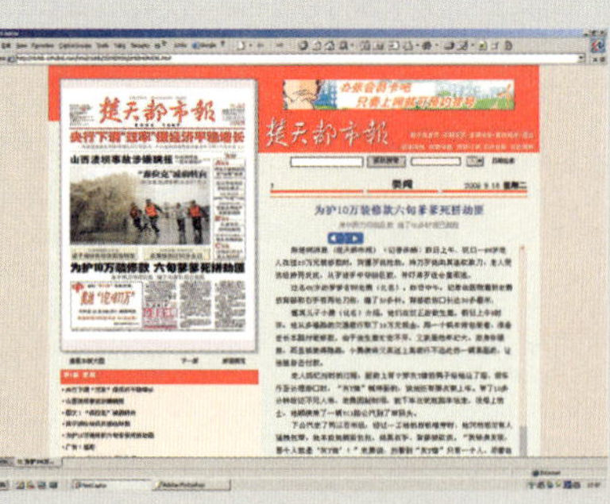

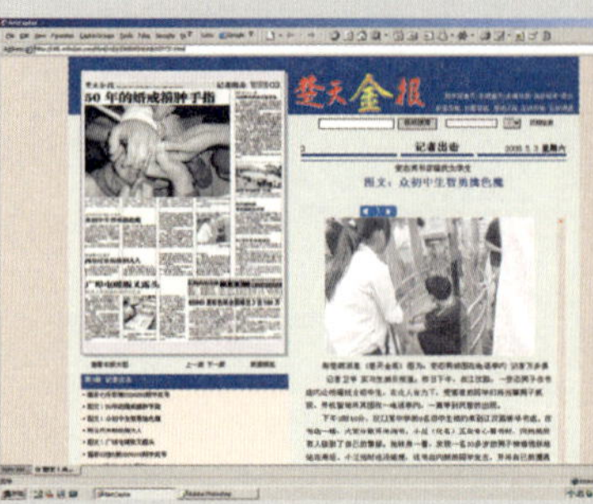

楚天金报2008-4-22
休闲屋厄运袭来 疑为小姐不做"业务"惹祸
昨日凌晨，七八名男子冲入汉口崇仁路128号一休闲屋，挥刀砍伤两名小姐，其中小凤背部被砍三刀，伤情较重，另一位小姐手部受伤。据附近群众称，可能是行凶者让小姐"做业务"遭拒，疯狂报复。

楚天都市报 2008-9-16
为护10万装修款 六旬爹爹死拼劫匪
前日上午在汉口常码头，一位66岁老人在送10万元装修款时，突遭歹徒抢劫。老人拼死反抗，最终夺回巨款。但其右手和背部被砍伤，缝了50多针，背部的伤口长达30多厘米。

楚天金报2008-05-03
男子书店骚扰女学生 众初中生智勇擒色魔
昨日下午，在江汉路，一男子在书店内公然骚扰女初中生，在众人合力下，受害同学们将当事男子抓获，并机智地将其围在一电话亭内，一直等到民警的出现。

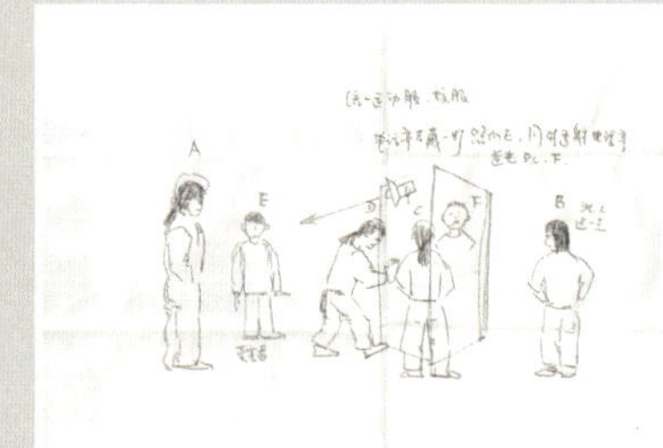

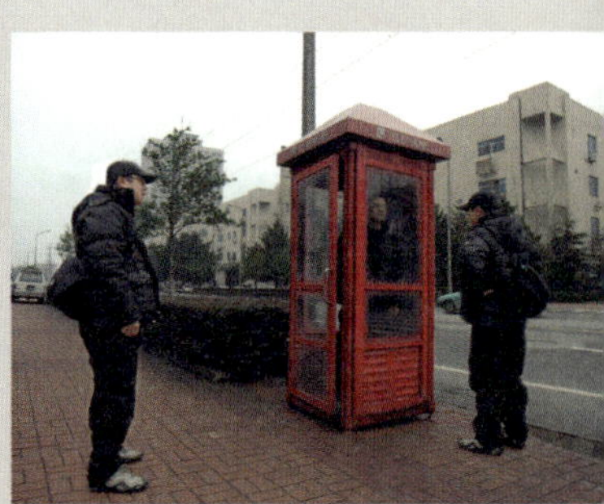

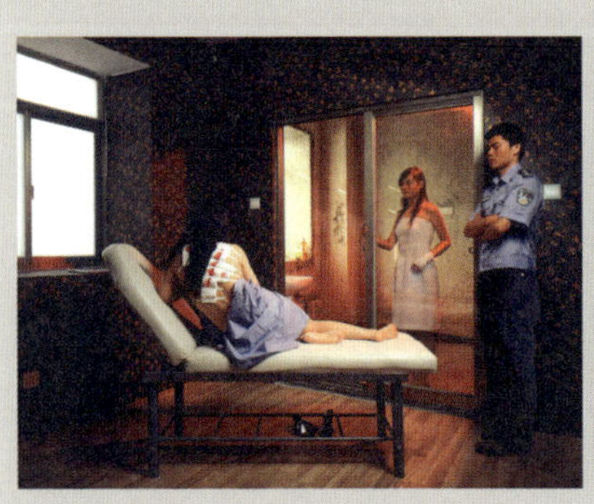

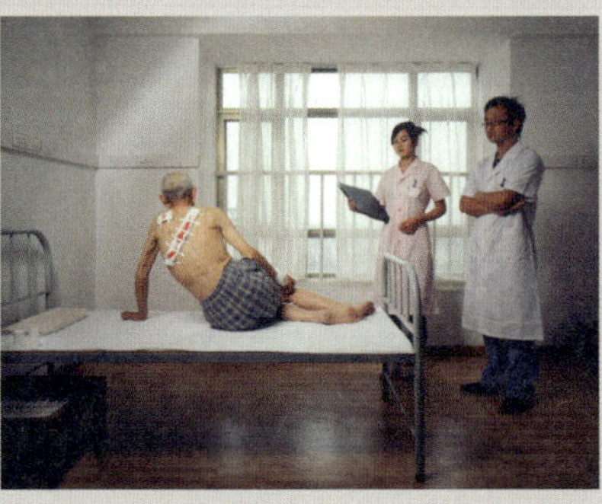

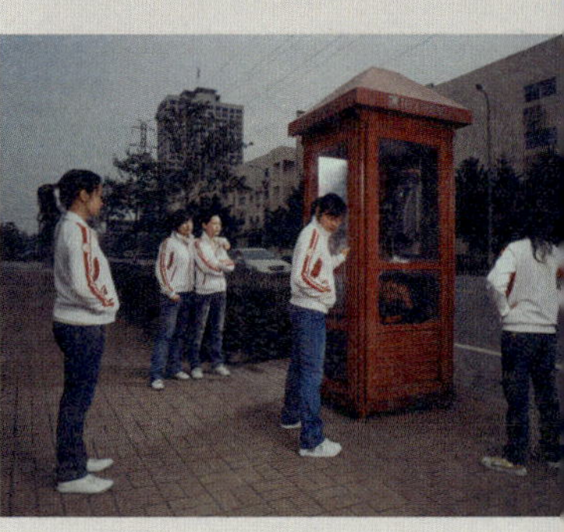

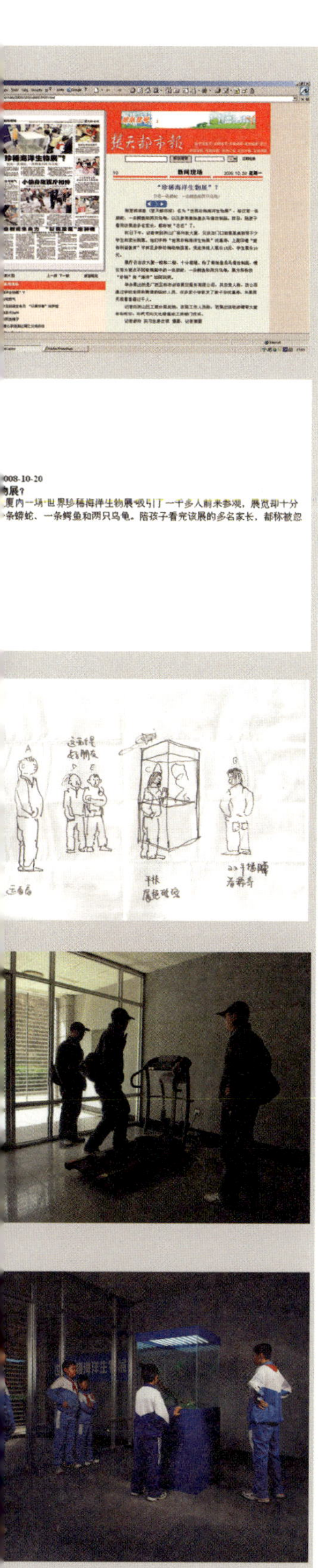

《受害者II》工作流程

Working Procedure for *Victims II*

As an artist, what do you care most during working?

Li Yu: I'm particularly interested in those acccidental matters and care more about fresh ideas emerging in the working process, and technical problems. There are lots of technical problems to deal with during the process because our work consists of photo series that require lots of time to complete the work. Although we employ staged photographic shooting devices, improvised and spontaneous factors still occupy a big part of the creating process. Many of them just popped into our minds like a flash. Sometimes they came to us while working. Speaking from a certain point of view, to capture these inspirational moments is equal to a passage to Henri Cartier-Bresson's "decisive moment".

Liu Bo: My concern is mainly about the integrity and continuity of a work. In recent years Li Yu and I have been collaborating on a basis of one year or several years, to complete a series. Especially in the work *"The Victim II"* (2008-2009), we met with some new problems, such as how to select the subject matters from newspaper, how to create a setting with corresponding relation, and how to choose the angle for each work. We have to face these issues together and represent them.

Could you please give an example to introduce the process of your work for us?

Li Yu: I'll give a failed example. At that time, we saw a news report:
Chutian Golden Paper 2006-03-30
An Odd Homicide Case Happened in Qingshan Yesterday Morning, Four Men Killing a Taxi Driver with Guns on the Street.
We conceived a scene depicting the moment when the four men walked across the zebra stripes after having committed the murder. We planned to imitate the picture on the sleeve of the famous disc "Abbey Road" by the Beatles, with the four murderers striding forward in turns, holding knives and guns wrapped up in newspaper, while the victim lying on the shoulder of the road. We've found four art student volunteers from four departments of Chinese Painting, Oil Painting, Printmaking and Sculpture at Hubei Institute of Fine Arts to act the roles of the four gansters, and prepared a good shooting view and props. But in the end things didn't work out.
Liu Bo: I'll introduce one of our shooting experiences.
Chutian Golden Paper 2007-08-13
An Escapee Being Chased Dropped through the Top Floor of a Building and Scared Everybody Inside
The work *"Victim"* made in 2007 – 2008 was based on this kind of horrifying news story that can be found on local newspapers in Wuhan almost every day. We decided to shoot a representative story like this. After we agreed on the motif to be represented, we looked for shooting sites separately. With help from a friend, Li Yu found a room with glass walls with light coming through from all sides. But this scene was still greatly different from the view we wanted to recreate. We needed to have workers decorate this house tailored to our specific plan, making the scene look like the one we expected. Then we redecorated the room in the way as strictly as required by the plan together with workers. During the process of preparation, production and shooting we settled each difficult matter through discussions, which was fun by itself.

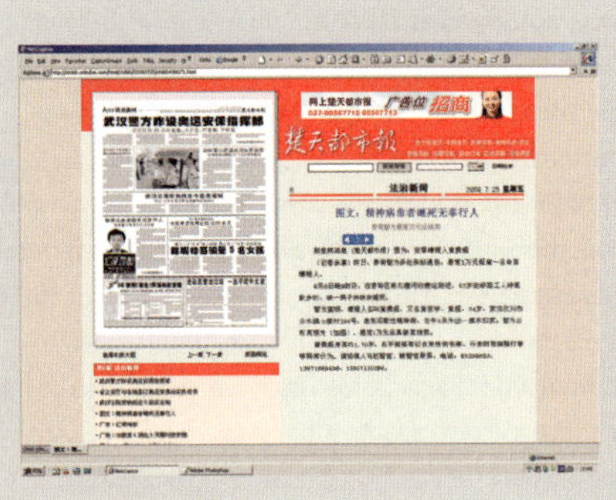
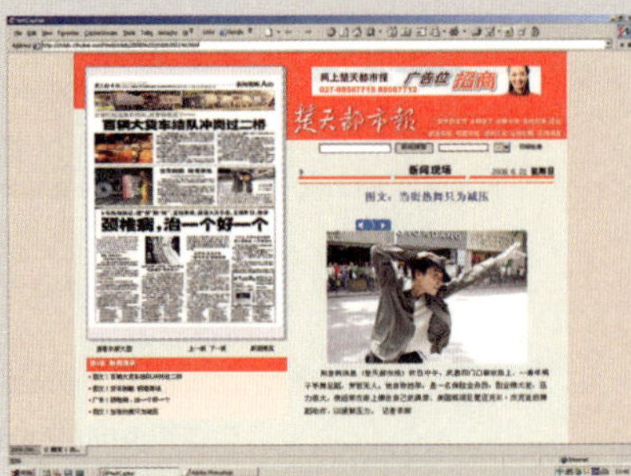
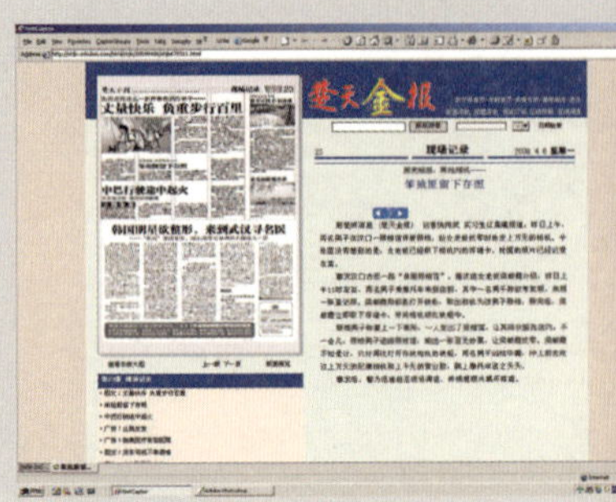

楚天都市报2008-7-25
精神病患者砸死无辜行人
6月6日晚8时许，蔡甸区唐河收费站附近，52岁修路工人钟某被一男子持砖块砸死。警方查明，嫌疑人黄某患间歇性精神病，自去年3月离家未归，其行走时有踢腿打拳等异常行为。请知情人与赵警官、熊警官联系。

Chutian Metropolis Daily 2008-7-25
A mental patient struck down an innocent passerby
Around 20:00 p.m. on the 6th of June, a 52-year-old roadman, Mr. Zhong was struck dead by a man with bricks near to Tanghe toll station, Caidian district. The police found out that the suspicion, Mr. Huang has been suffering from intermittent psychosis. Since leaving home last March, he has been wandering everywhere with some deviant kicking and striking action. Please contact the policeman Mr. Zhao or Mr. Xiong if someone knows this mental patient.

楚天都市报2008-6-22
当街热舞只为减压
昨日中午，武昌司门口解放路上，一青年男子手舞足蹈，旁若无人。他自称姓李，是一名保险业务员，因业绩太差，压力很大，便经常在街上模仿自己的偶像、美国摇滚巨星迈克尔·杰克逊的舞蹈动作，以缓解压力。

Chutian Metropolis Daily 2008-6-22
Dancing in the street for decompression
Yesterday noon, a young man was waving body fanatically in Jiefang Road, Simenkou ,Wuchang, disregarding other people present. He proclaimed himself Mr. Li, an insurance salesman. To relieve the tremendous pressure from his poor work performance, he often imitated his idol, Michael Jackson, the American pop music superstar, dancing in the street.

楚天金报2009-04-06
照完相后抢相机 笨抢匪留下存照
昨日上午，两名男子在汉口古田一路佳丽照相馆伴裘照相，趁女老板找零时抢走元的相机。令抢匪没有想到的是，女老板已经取下相机内的存储卡，抢匪的照片记录在案。

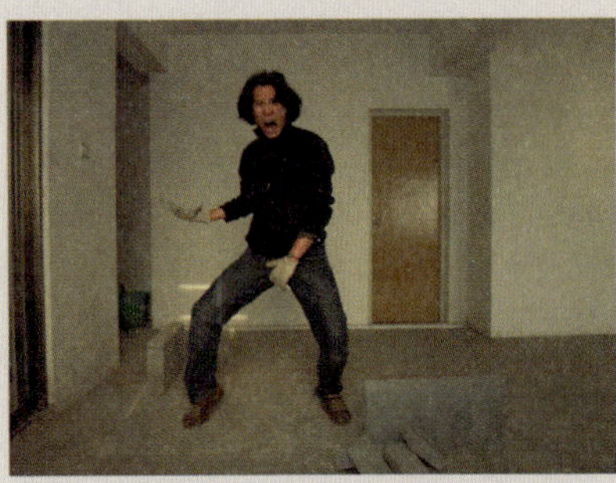
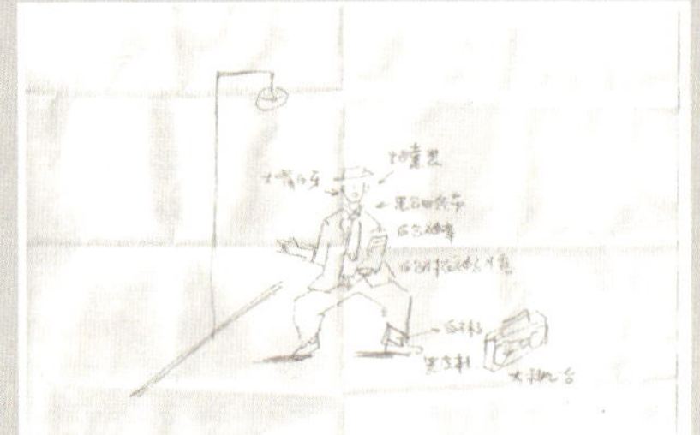
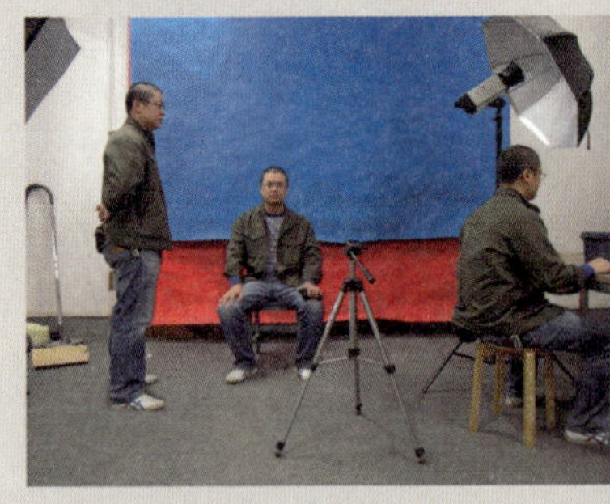

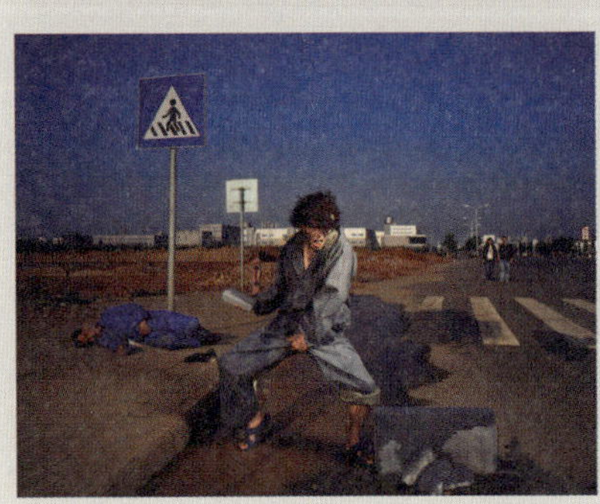
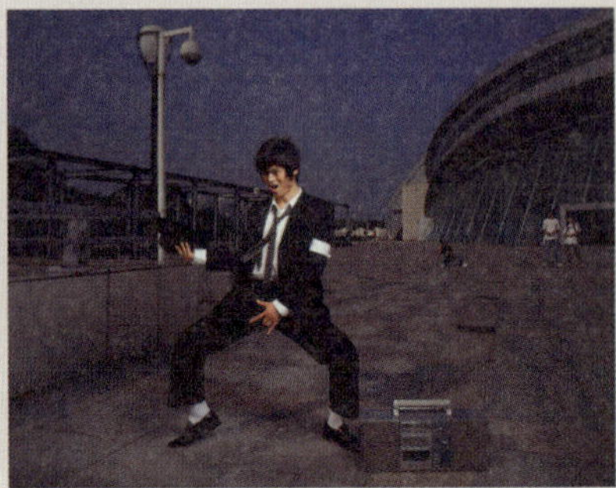
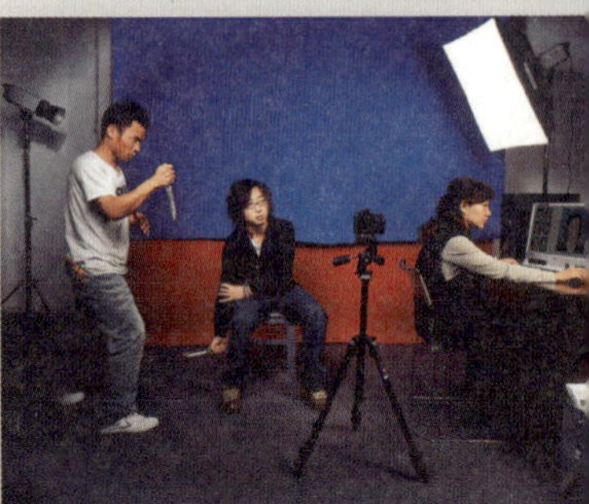

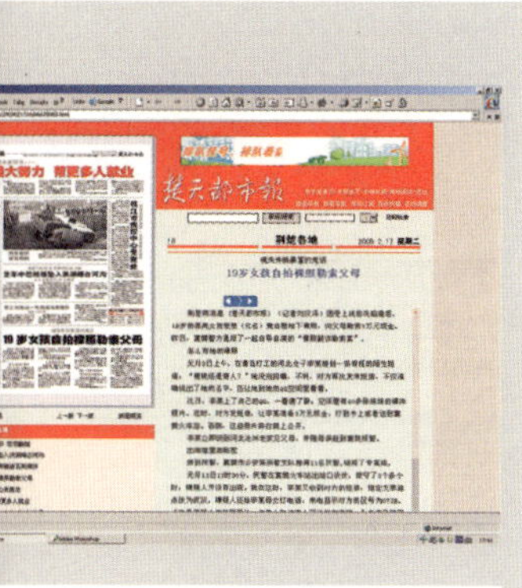

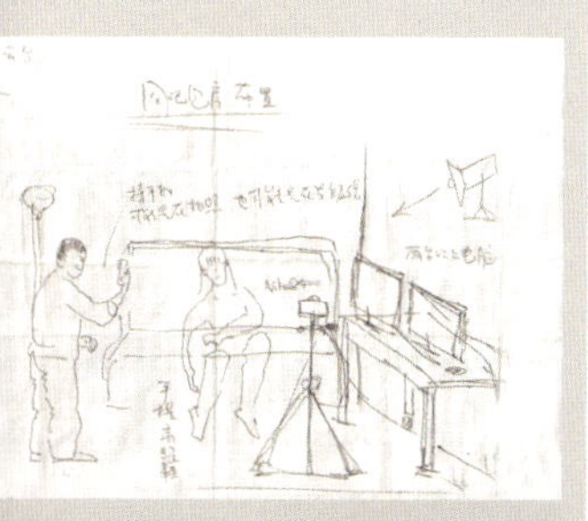

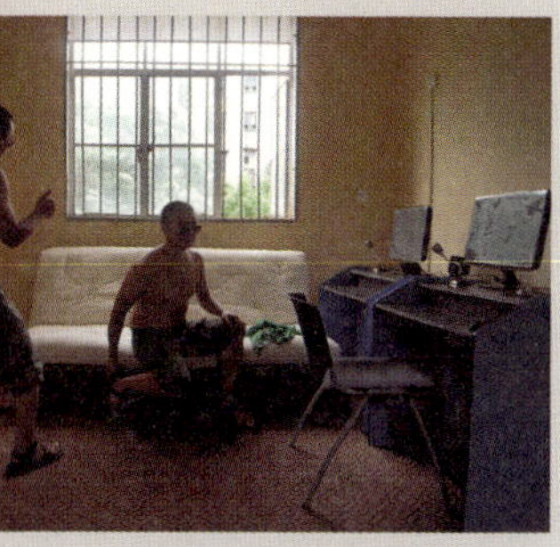

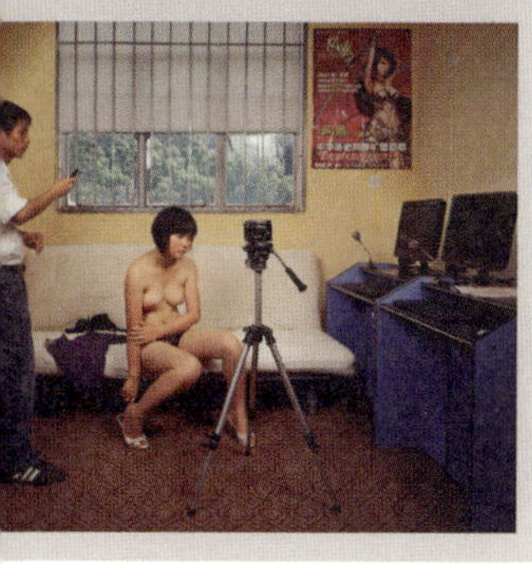

《受害者II》工作流程

Working Procedure for *Victims II*

Suppose you are a critic, what perspective would you talk about and explain you work from?

Li Yu: I would use our work as a case to analyze the relation of photography with media, with cinema, and with narrative.

Liu Bo: I would examine through our work the relation between events and society, between photo recording and the reality, and that between photographic subjects and politics, and metaphors of events in the photographic representation.

What books and which artists have had, or is having an influence on your way of thinking and working?

Li Yu: Books include *The Society of the Spectacle*, *The Cinema According to Hitchcock*, and *Against Method*.

Artits like Henri Cartier-Bresson, Philip-Lorca diCorcia, and Jeff Wall all had an influence on me, either through their work or through the criticism over them.

Liu Bo: Most of the artists we like are the same. They are photographer and film directors, such as Cameron, Hitchcock, Quentin Tarantino, and Coen Brothers.

How do you decide the context in which your work is to be presented? How do you consider the relation of the context with your work?

Li Yu: For contemporary art, context is an important dimension. Given a particular circumstance, an everyday object can be an art piece. Though the significance of a work often is subject to the context, sometimes the situation may well be the opposite. And a work could be independent of the context, thus getting unfathomable. But I don't think about the difference often. I place greater faith in the autonomy of a work; in other words, the potential of the validity of a work in a larger art environment, which is not built by one exhibition, or a conference. Maybe it's been always there. Maybe it has to grow and take shape within the cultural networks of the entire human race over time.

Liu Bo: I agree with Li Yu on this point.

How does your work take the present shape? And please give a few words about the latest development and changes in your work.

Li Yu: In the past few years, I have made some pictures and videowork with a loose structure. Some of them seek to depict lives of a middle-aged man and woman, who are somewhat distinctive from the rest of people. The work explore the boundary between fiction and reality with their daydreamy murmuring and behaviors, mainly using a technique blending documentary and staged photography. In recent years, Liu Bo and I formed a working team and several complete series were developed and take the present shape. The three works we produced together were made over a time period of about one or two years. During this time, I didn't make any other work on my own apart from a half-done DV-film.

Liu Bo: Although I majored in oil painting at college, I've been spending most of my time on using photography to make individual recording and produce works. My early interest foamed motifs of violence and injury. Before collaborating with Li Yu, we've

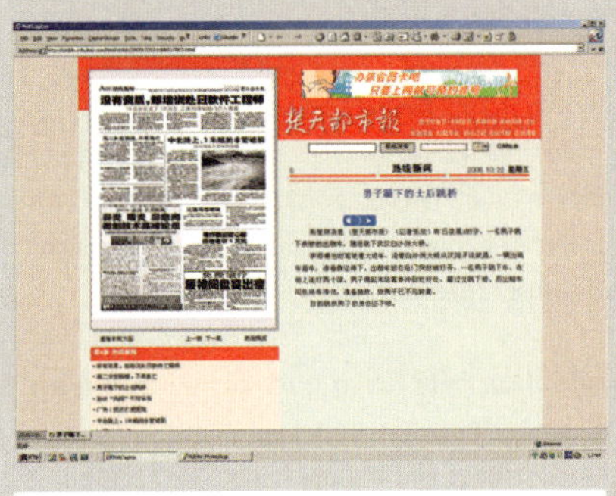

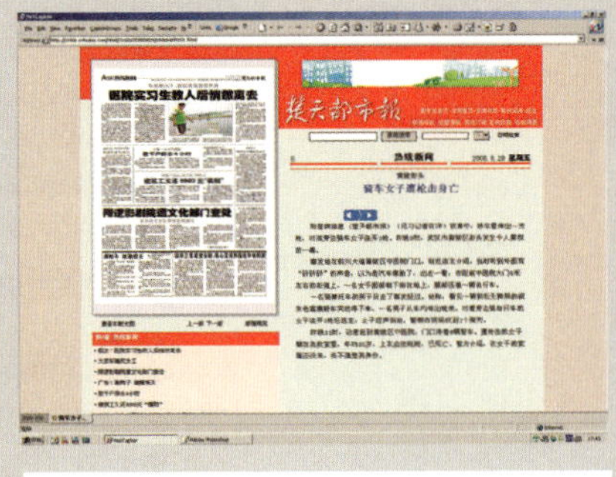

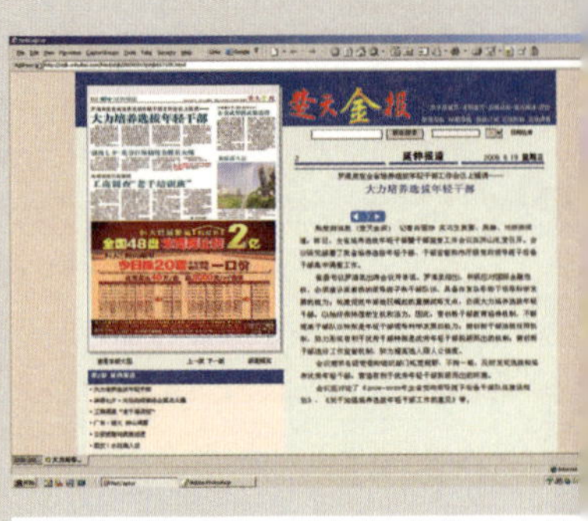

楚天都市报2008-10-22
男子蹦下的士后跳桥
目击者李师傅称，昨日凌晨2时许，他驾车沿白沙洲大桥从汉阳开往武昌，看到前方一辆的士靠边准备停车，其后门突然被打开，一男子从车内跳下，翻过栏杆就跳下大桥。出租车司机准备施救，但该男子已不见踪影。目前跳桥男子的身份还不明。

楚天都市报2008-08-29
骑车女子遭枪击身亡
昨晚9时，武汉市黄陂区街头发生令人震惊的一幕。一辆前后无牌照的银灰色富康轿车突然停下来，一名男子从车内伸出枪来，对着旁边骑自行车的年轻女子连开三枪后逃走，女子倒地身亡。警方介绍，现场发现三枚弹壳。

楚天金报 2009-8-19
大力培养选拔年轻干部
昨日，全省培养选拔年轻干部暨干部监督工作会议在洪山礼堂召开。会议要求各委和组织部门拓宽视野，不拘一格，及时发现选拔和培养优秀年轻干部，营造有优秀年轻干部脱颖而出的环境。会议还讨论了《2009-2020年全省党政领导班子后备干部队伍建设规划》、《关于加强培养选拔年轻干部工作的意见》等。

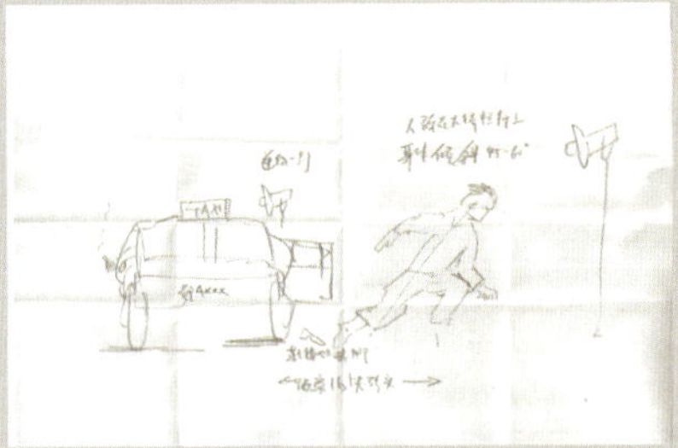

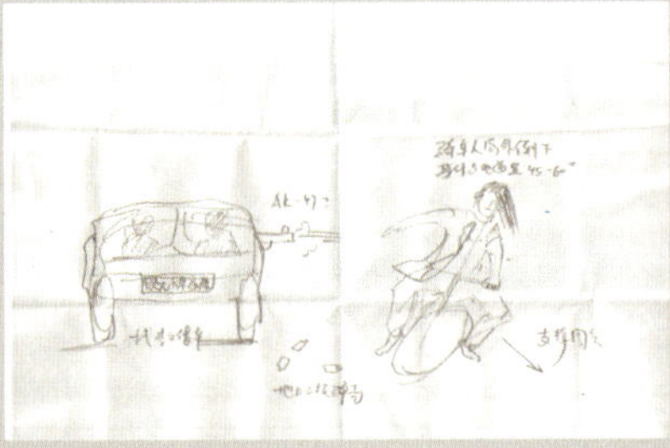

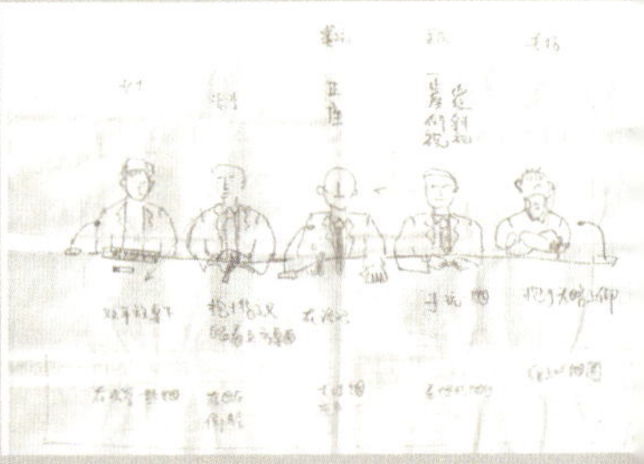

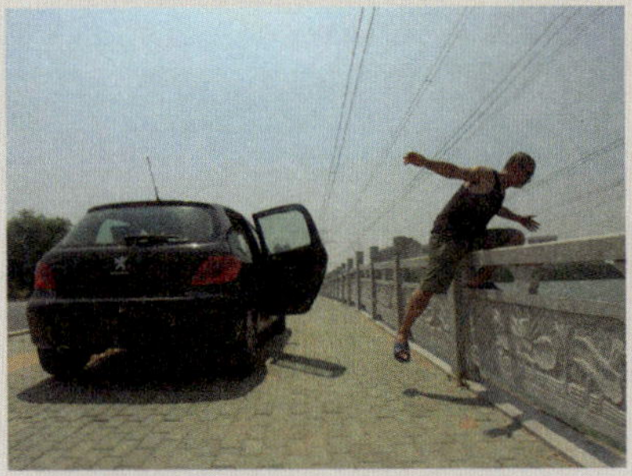

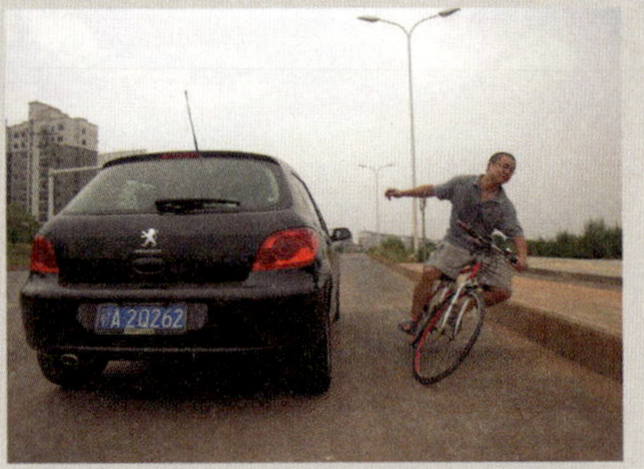

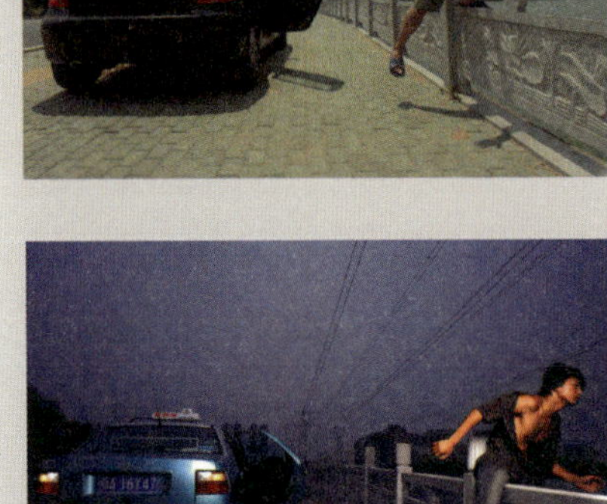

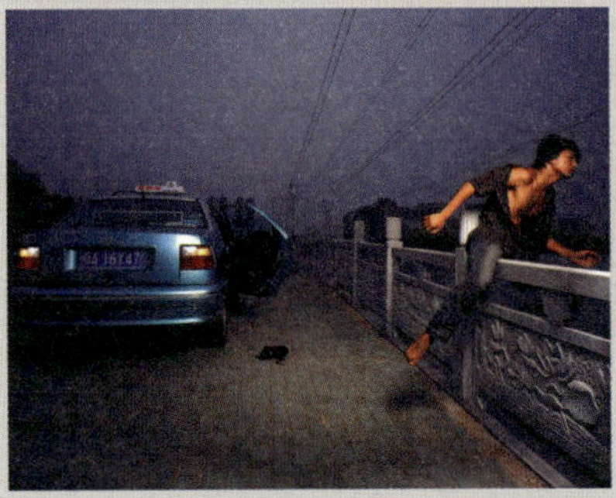

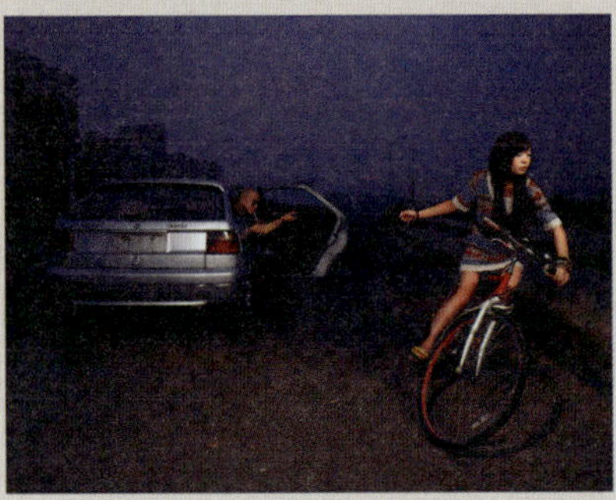

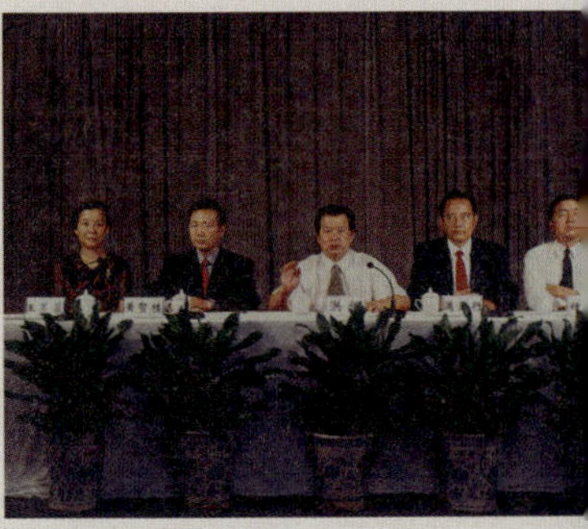

already been working seprately in photography and also we often participate in and organize events together. By the end of 2005, we started to consider the possibilties of collaboration. Next year, we began to make *13 Months in the Year of the Dog* as a team. It cost us lots of time and energy to gather the strength of two persons in the working process. In the on-going project, we try to preserve the integrity of a series work. *Victim II* seeks to foreground and represent the correspondence between the news' content and the context.

In what circumstances would you want to destroy your own creation?

Li Yu: I don't know whether there would be any artist who'd like to detroy his work just because it's too perfect, unless the action of destruction is also part of the work. In that case, doing so actually is constructive, rather than destructive. To a work, no matter it's good or bad, either being forgotten or being demolished are just the same.

Liu Bo: We had several unsuccessful shooting experiences before. If the work is not good enough, we would put it away.

What do you think about the relation between the art history and artist's work?

Li Yu: Today will become the history of the future. An artist should focus on the present, though art history may well become an artist's creative sources. Contemporary history is written by contemporaries. The names included in the history and those excluded from it always remind us of the famous lines by the Chinese modern poet Zang Kejia:"...Some people / Want to be immortal by carving their names in stones; / Some people / Are willing to be grass for the fire to burn./..."

Liu Bo: I totally agree with Li Yu's opinion.

What kind of roles would rational thinking and emotional impulse respectively play during your work time?

Li Yu: The American science philosopher Paul Feyerabend in his book *Against Method* observes that the most valuable science research never followed the rule of reason. The same for the art. Reason is like a dictator. There always will be some people who are willing to accept his despotic rule. Sentimental drive is an angel, who seldom descends on the earth, but he never fails to shine the light of hope upon us every time.

Liu Bo: Yes, Li Yu is quite right on this.

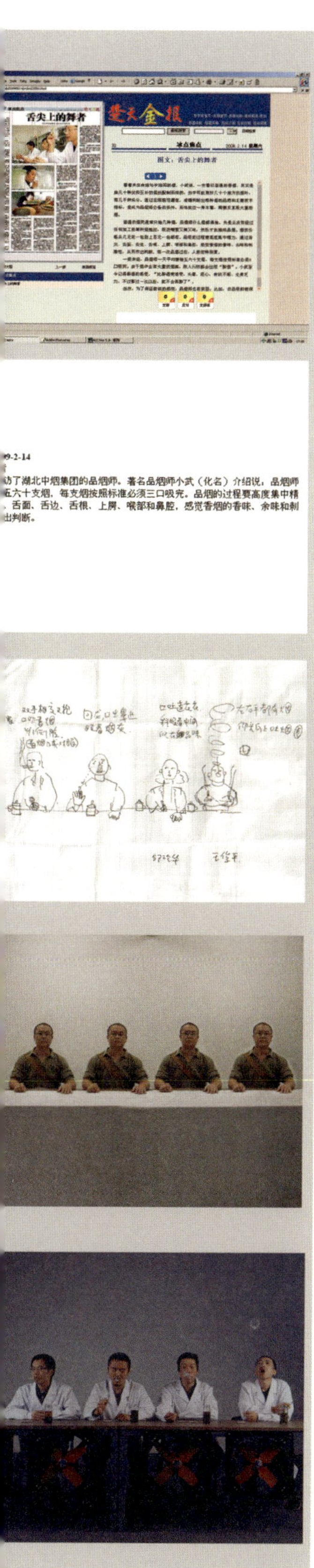

《受害者II》工作流程

Working Procedure for *Victims II*

卢征远

LU ZHENGYUAN

作为艺术家，你在创作中所关心的是什么？以一件作品为例，分享你的创作过程。

触碰到艺术和各种事物的边界并挑战它们，讨论既有观念新的可能性。

在思考漂浮在顶端的艺术系统它们是由什么支撑的以及它们的关系，我做了《XXX》。找来一个没有接触过艺术的工人，给他国内外著名艺术家的作品的图片，让他独立的绘制他所能理解的这些作品的绘画，并把对这些作品进行报道和描述的文字一起展出。但把文字里艺术家的名字替换成XXX。

如果你是一个批评家，你会从什么角度来阐释和讨论你自己的创作？

是一个各种风格混杂，不易辨别，需要有长期工作和深入了解才能把握的艺术家。工作是基于思考和切身经验，而不是某种风格或媒介（因为我对风格也是抱有怀疑）。在不断建立一个面貌多变，充满想象和矛盾，同时拥有相同气质的艺术系统。并用这个系统与固有的认识体验不断碰撞。

在你的创作和思考中，什么书籍和艺术家曾经或正在影响着你？

《西游记》，有着东方哲学精神，探索意识，丰富想象力。隋建国，引导我进入当代艺术语境。

你是怎样判断和决定在什么语境下呈现你的哪些作品的？你是怎样看待作品呈现的语境和作品的关系的？

作品与语境的关系，一种是和谐的，一种是矛盾的。我会在这两种条件下的关系发生有效关系的时候呈现。语境与作品并没有固定的条件关系，或有衬托加强，或有破坏，都可，但要达到一种力，只要作品和语境能形成这种力，并达到一定强度就可以。

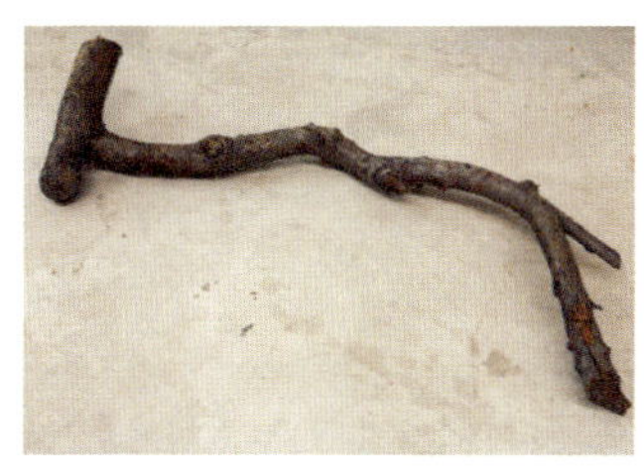

树枝，2008
装置
材料：树枝，油画
120×50cm
在一根树枝上用油画的方式画画，希望
把它画得像一根真的树枝。

Twig, 2008
Installation
Materials: A twig, oil paint
120×50cm
Paint on a twig to make it look like a twig

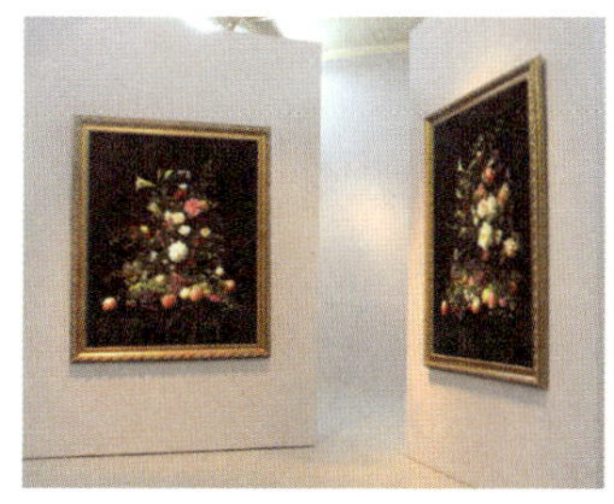

谎言，2007
摄影装置
150×170cm，两张
两张外表一致的摄影，一张拍摄的
是真实的水果和鲜花，另一张拍摄
的是人造的水果和鲜花。

Lie, 2007
Photography installation
150×170cm, two pieces
Two identical photographs, with one featuring
real fruits and flowers, the other artificial fruits
and flowers.

蛋，2008
布面油画
每幅20×20cm
数量无限，尽力绘制相同的画，对绘
画手工性的挑战。

Egg, 2008
Oil on canvas
20×20cm per piece
Painting after the first painting of egg, trying to
look as close to the first one as possible.

如何在创作上形成了现在的面貌，描述一下近年来作品的发展和变化？

形成现在面貌的原因，可能是有"100天"的训练，自己的性格，教育背景，可把握的资源，思考的方向构成。

在多面的创作中，还是存在一个摆脱不掉的自身系统，我也在和这个系统对话，建立系统的立体性和多面性也是在争取更大的自由，这也是我认为的艺术魅力之一，我承受不了单调的"个人风格"。

近年的作品仍然是在持续的探索，自身系统仍处在"青春期"，我希望能更久的保持这种"未成熟"，这样才会让我始终亢奋的寻找。

你会在什么情况下摧毁你自己的作品？

做"摧毁你自己的作品"的作品的时候。这里指的作品应该是指物化的作品，相当于摧毁"精神化的作品"的影子，影子是可以消失，但也随时可以出现。

你怎么看待艺术史和艺术家创作的关系？

宏观的看，任何艺术家都无法回避艺术史，无论你是愿意还是反抗。具体地看，艺术史可以成为我创作的资源，有时会为我做一个支点。

在你的工作中，理性和情感冲动各自扮演着什么样的角色？

在工作中，理性和情感冲动就像做红烧肉时火候和酱油的关系，用火一直烧着，快熟时加上酱油翻煮上色，一下子味道就都出来了，就成了。很多时候是对一个问题有了很久理性的思考，突然某刻有了情感冲动，可能也称之为灵感，最后形成作品。

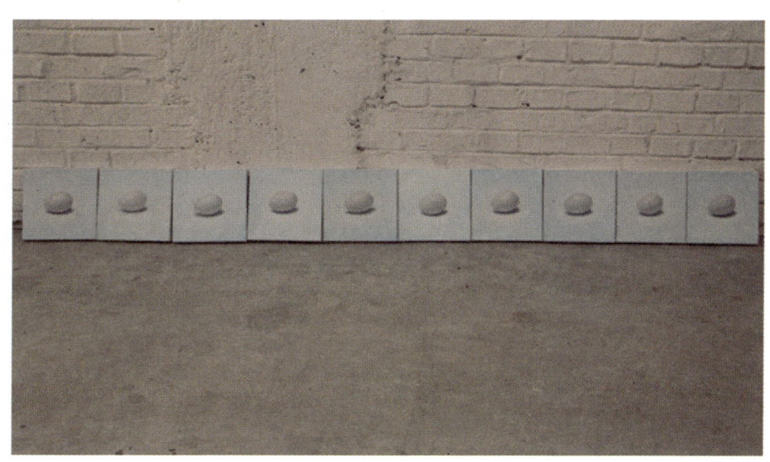

心，2009
布面油画
200×200cm
将被符号化了的心还原。

Heart, 2009
Oil on canvas
200×200cm
To depict a real heart as it is instead of
one being symbolized.

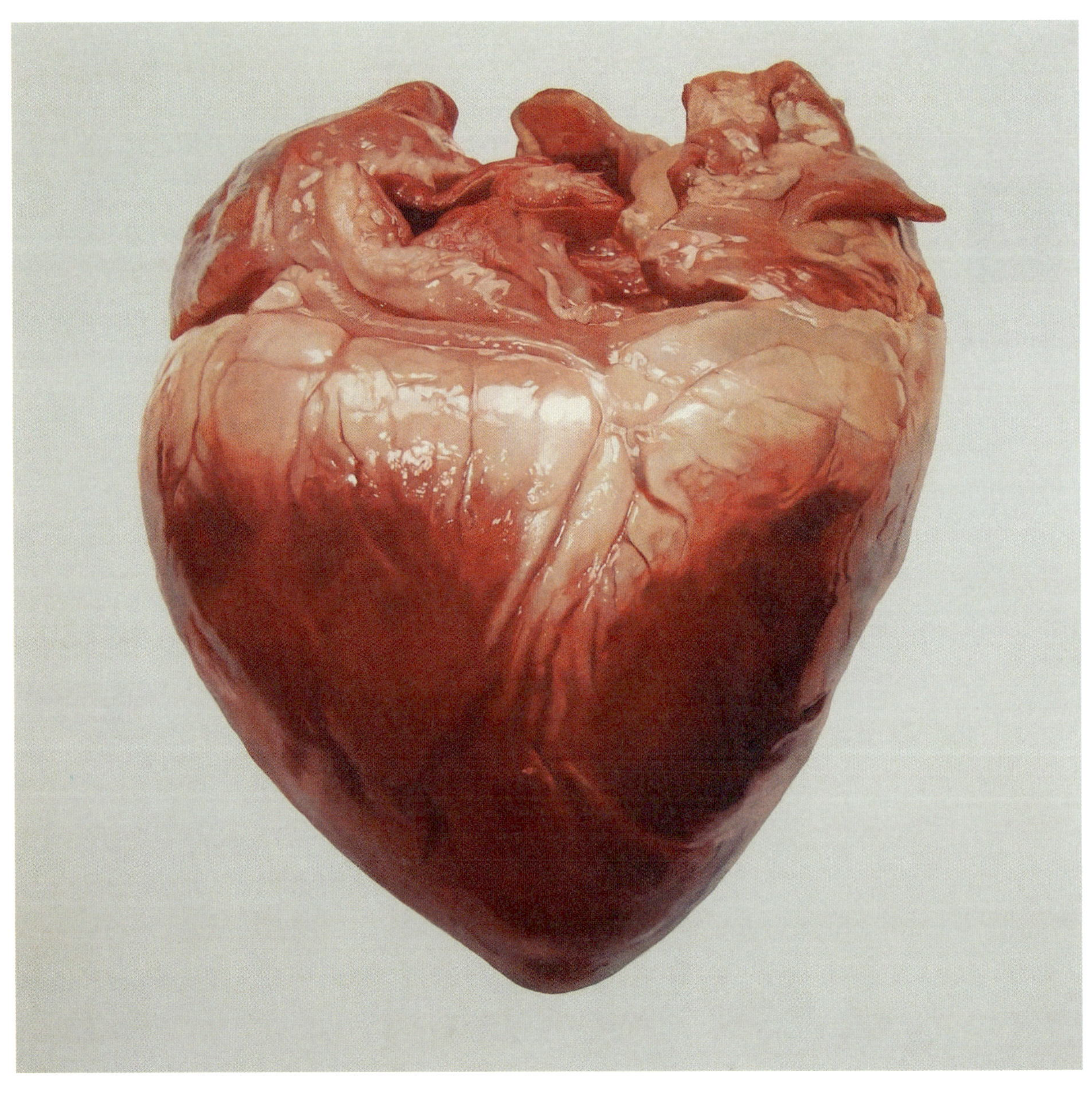

心，2009
布面油画
将被符号化了的心还原。

As an artist, what do you care most during working? Could you please give an example to introduce the process of your work for us?

I'm interested in reaching out the boundaries of the art and various things and challenging them. Also my concern is to explore new possibilities in existing concepts.

Based on inquiries about what is giving support to the art system and allows it to be visible to the public I made the work *XXX*. I employed a worker, who has never been in contact with art, and gave him images of artworks created by famous artists from all round the world, asking him to draw paintings about these artworks according to his own understanding to them. The paintings produced by the worker were to be exhibited along with texts and descriptions of the original works, but all the artists' names were removed and replaced with "XXX".

Suppose you are a critic, from what perspective would you explain and comment on your works?

I would comment in this way: I'm an artist with a difficult understood and hybrid style, who can only be understood through a long time observation and in-depth study. My work is based on thinking and keen personal experience, rather than a fixed style or medium (as I also have doubts on 'style'). I'm making a continuous attempt to build up an artistic mechanism of an average artistic temperament alive with imagination, contradictories and changes, and then allow it to confront with established understanding and experiences.

What books and which artists have had or are having an influence on your way of thinking and working?

Journey to the West is a book imbued with oriental philosophical spirit, exploration awareness and rich imagination. The artist Sui Jianguo has guided my way to contemporary art context.

How do you make judgment and decision as to in what context you'd like to present your works? According to you, in what way is the context created by the work related to the work itself?

A work and the context share a harmonious relationship with each other, but sometimes they are in conflict. I would try to find the moment when their relation helps to construct validity for the exhibition of the work. Between them there isn't a permanently conditional relation. Sometimes the relation is supplementary, and sometimes can be destructive. Both will do, as long as a force that is intense enough can be found between the work and context.

How does your work take the present shape? And please give a few words about the latest development and changes in your work.

One of the reasons contributing to the formation of my present artistic practice could be the "A Hundred Days" training at college, and my character, educational background, available resources and the structure of my thinking methods.

While practicing art in different directions, I found it's hard to disengage from an inner system. I'm trying to dialogue with the

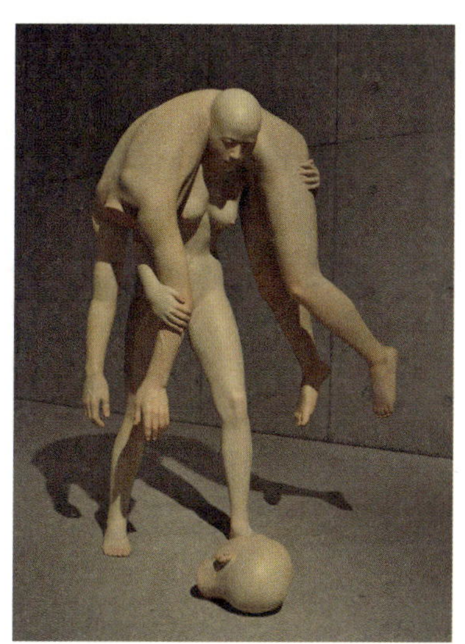

鸵鸟，2009
雕塑
树脂上色
等身大

Ostrich, 2009
Sculpture
Resin with paint
Life-size

对话，2009
雕塑
树脂上色
等身大

Dialogue, 2009
Sculpture
Resin with paint
Life-size

system. The effort of creating more dimensions and facets in the system also helps to win back greater freedom for my work. Here lies in the true glamour of art. A bald "personal style" is the least thing I can bear.

My recent work still continues my on-going exploration. The artistic structure of my work is still at the "age of adolescence". I wish I could keep staying in this "immature" state longer, so that I can continue this exciting journey of pursuit.

In what circumstances would you want to destroy your own creation?

I may do that when I'm making a work entitled "Destroy Your Own Work". Here the work refers to a physical object. This is equal to destroying the shadow of "spiritualized work". The shadow can vanish and reappear at will.

What do you think about the relation between the art history and artist's work?

Generally speaking, all artists have to face the issue of art history, no matter your attitude is against it or for it. Particularly speaking, the history of art can be utilized as resources for my creation, and sometimes it can serve as a fulcrum in my work.

What kind of roles would rational thinking and emotional impulse respectively play in your work?

In my artistic practice, the relation between rationality and impulse are like that between the duration of heating and soy sauce in making the braised pork with soy sauce. First cook it on the fire, add soy sauce before it's almost done and then stir-fry it. It's done when it smells lovely. Many times, the case is creative urge, or inspiration, come to me uninvited after I've been rationally reflecting on a question for a long time. That leads to the formation of the final work.

彩轮，2008
颜料
60×60cm
把颜料挤到板子上，刮。刮出一块颜料，也可以说它是一张画。

Color Wheel, 2008
Paint
60 × 60cm per piece
Squeeze paint onto a board and rub it even over the surface of the board to form a painting.

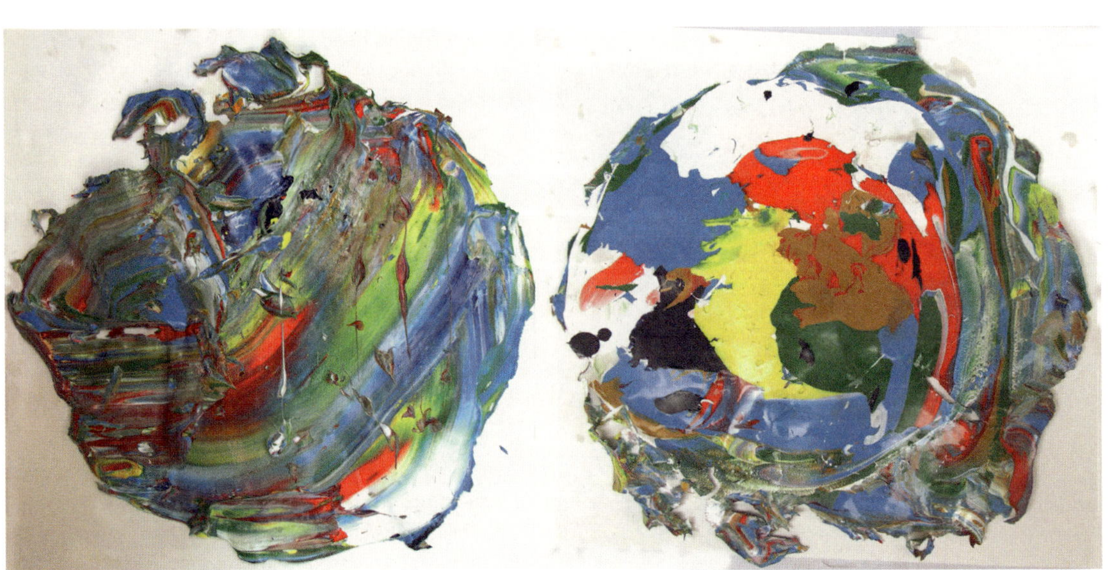

无题，2008
绘画装置
材料：沥青、霓虹灯、油画布、画框
250×300cm
把沥青涂抹在画布上，自然流淌，在背面安装上耀眼的霓
虹灯。

Untitled, 2008
Painting installation
Materials: Asphalt, neon light, canvas, frame
250 × 300 cm
Smeared asphalt onto a canvas and let it flow freely and installed neon
light in the back of the canvas.

XXX，2008
布面油画、文献
尺寸不定

XXX，2008
Oil on canvas, documentations
Size variable

我找来一位从未接触过当代艺术，甚至从未碰过画笔的工人作为这件作品的执行者。把一些著名当代艺术作品作为绘制图像，在绘画过程中不加入我的意图，让他独立完成，包括画面尺幅的选择，。画面产生了一种"野生"的气质。在一幅作品中，有人没有胳膊，他的解释是，那个地方再画出两只胳膊就不好看了。我整理出关于这些作品的阐释，并把其中作者的名字剔除，代以"xxx"，作为作品的文字部分。

I showed an untrained assistant printed images of the works of iconic artist figures such as Cai Guoqiang, Fang Lijun, Wang Guangyi, Damien Hirst and Andy Warhol and asked him to "copy" their styles to make paintings in their styles based on his own understanding and projection. The unnamed assistant's imitations are then exhibited next to a printout description of the artist's practice taken from magazines.

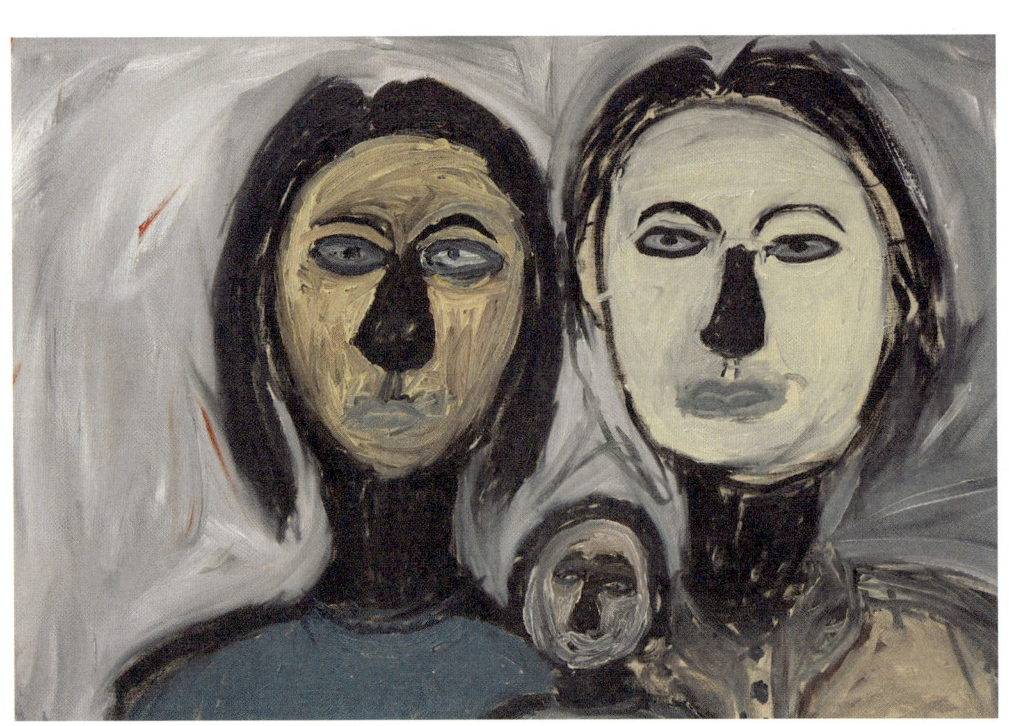

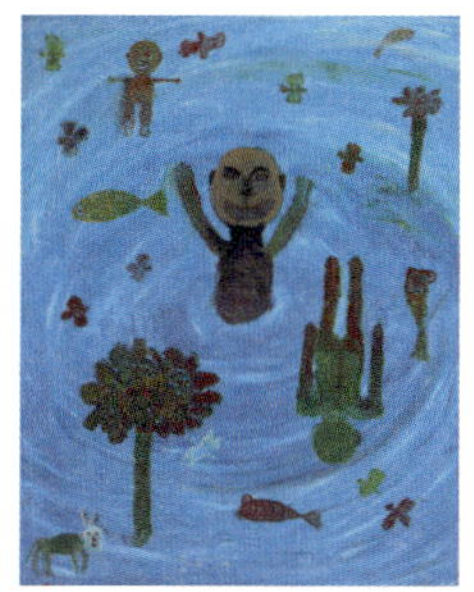
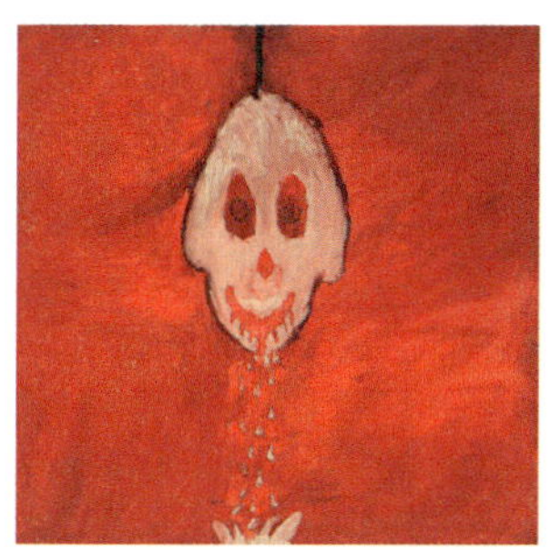
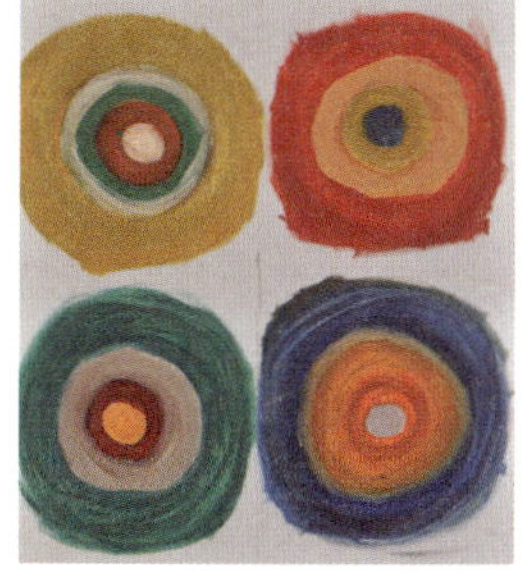
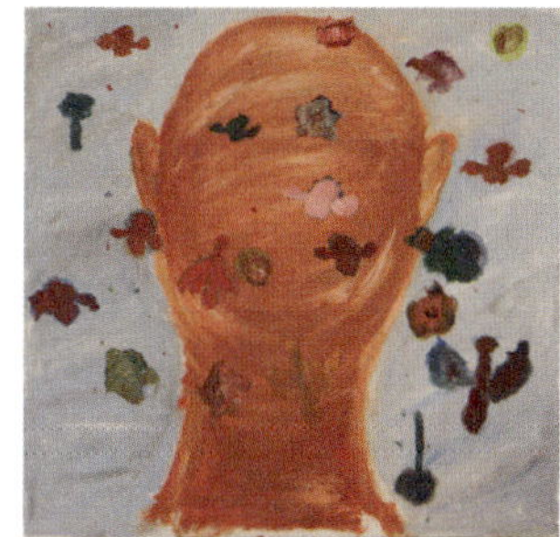
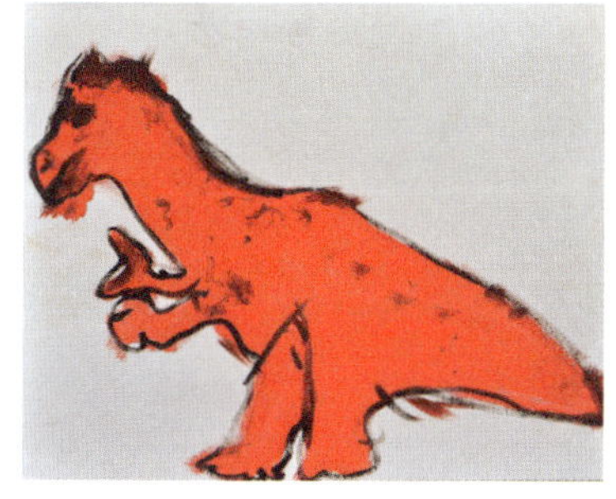
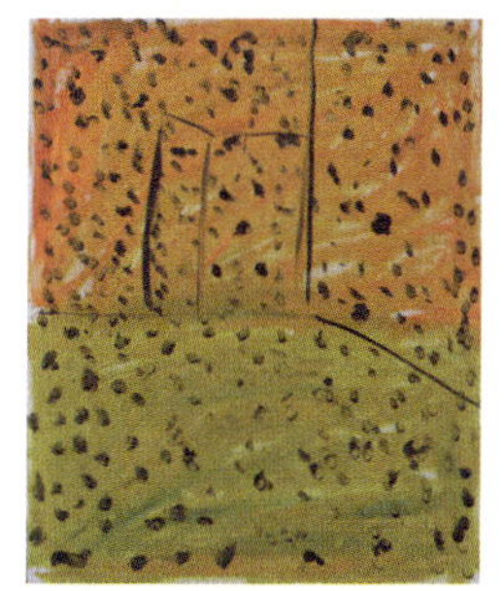
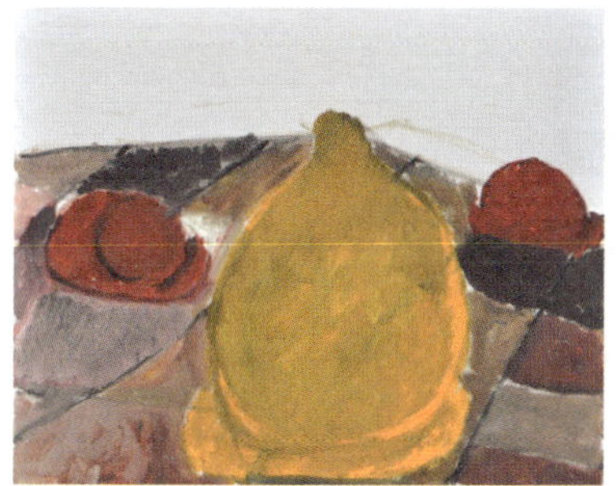
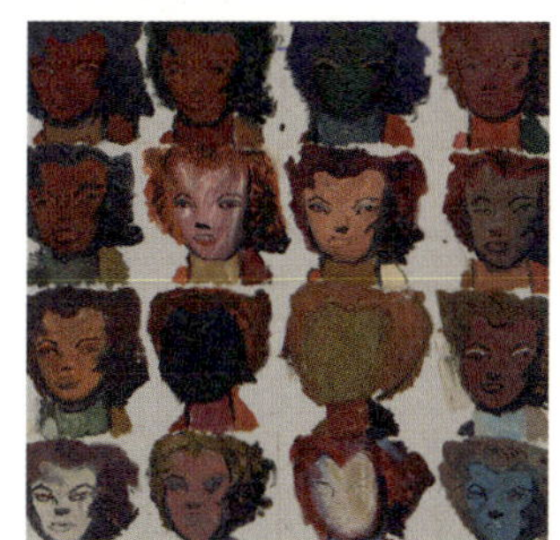
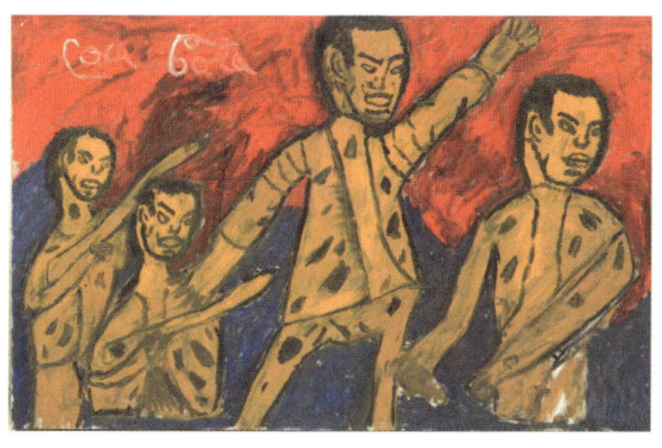

Coca Cola

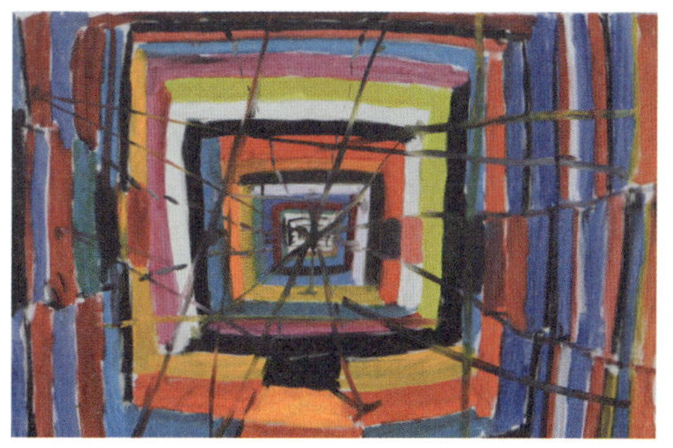

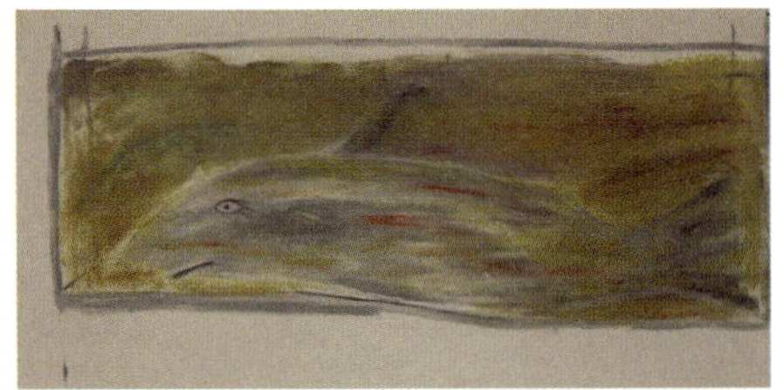

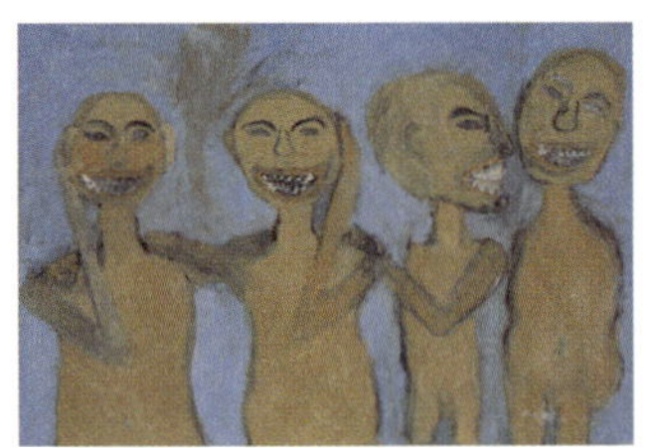

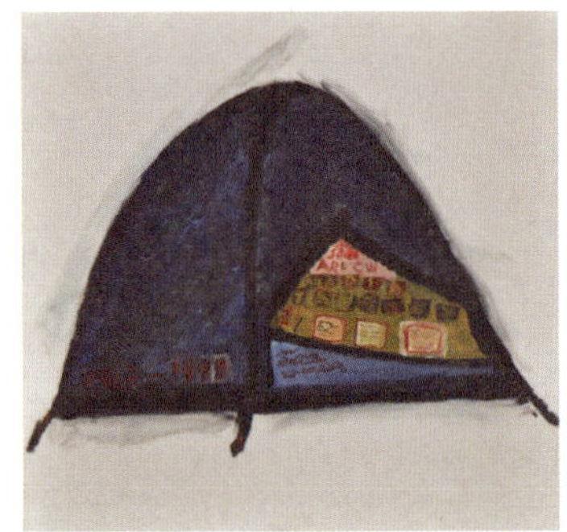

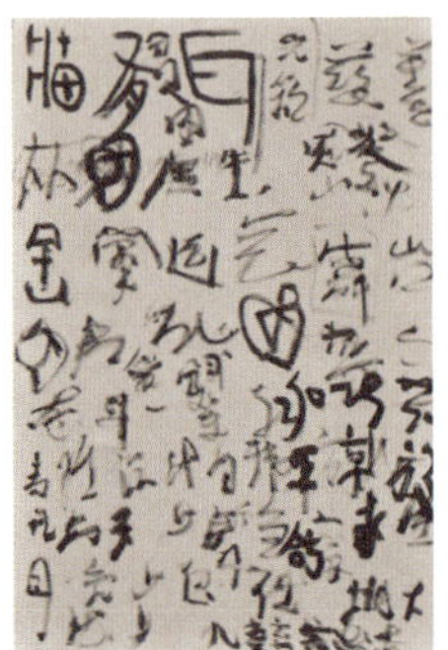

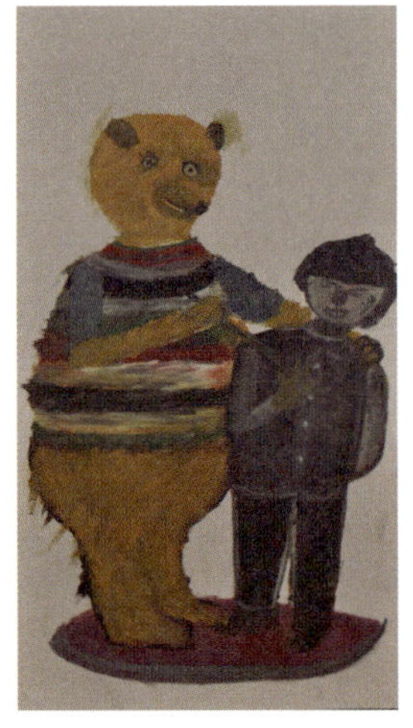

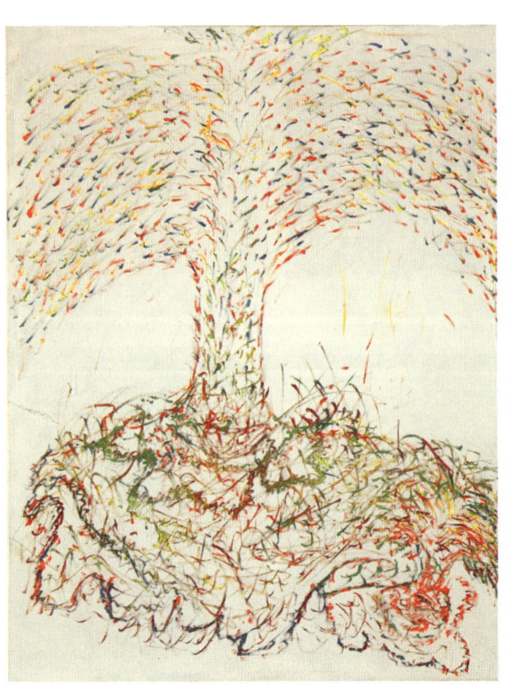

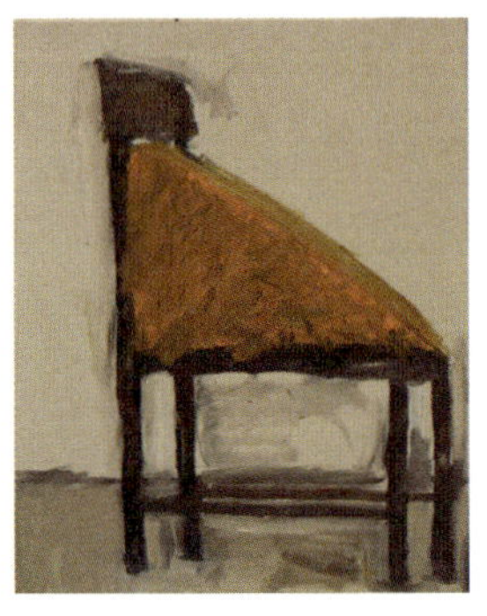

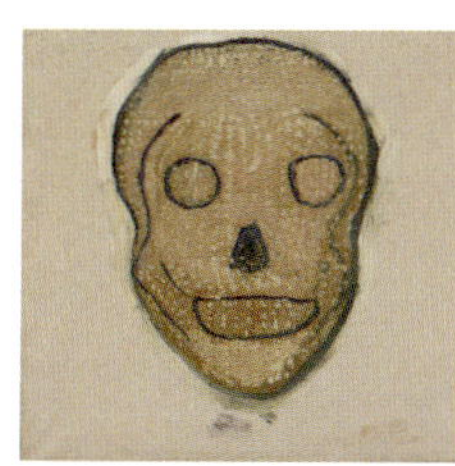
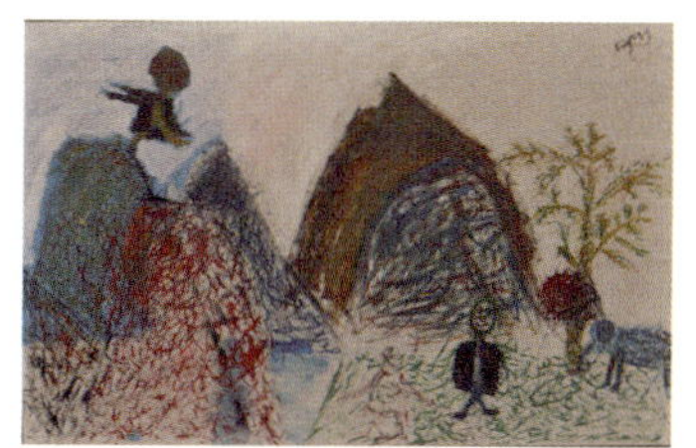
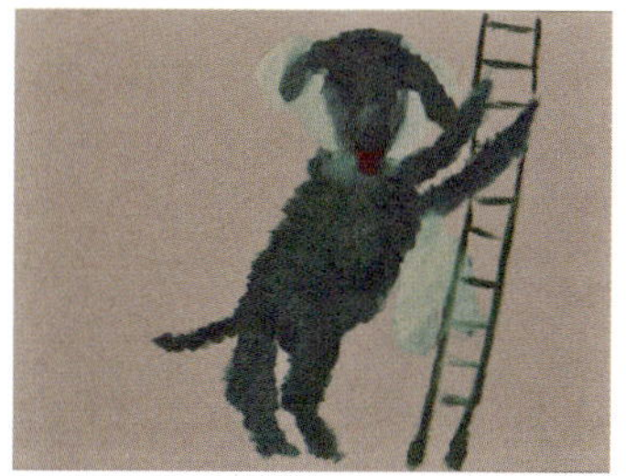
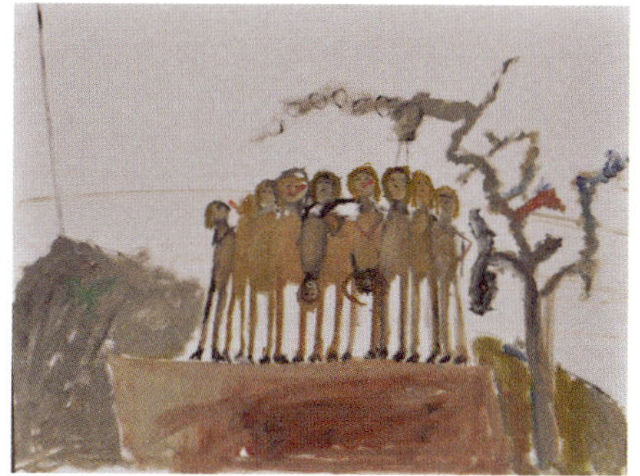
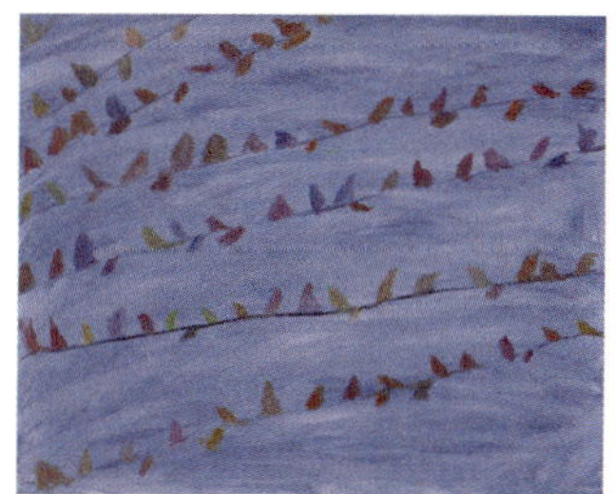
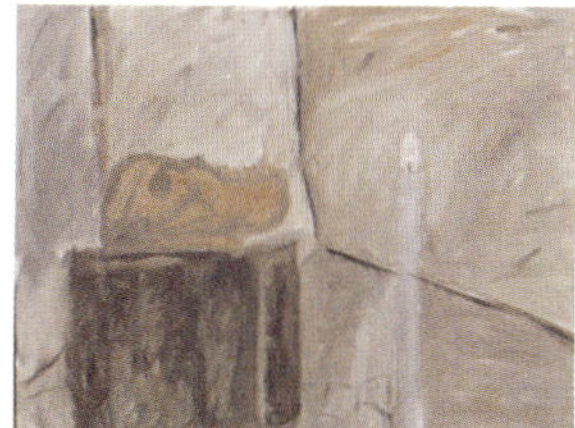
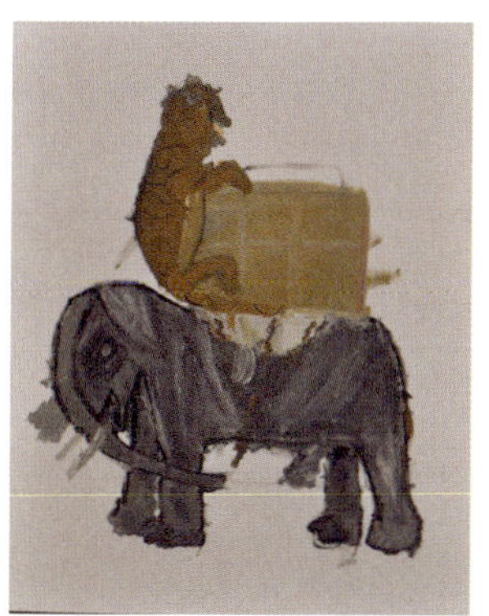
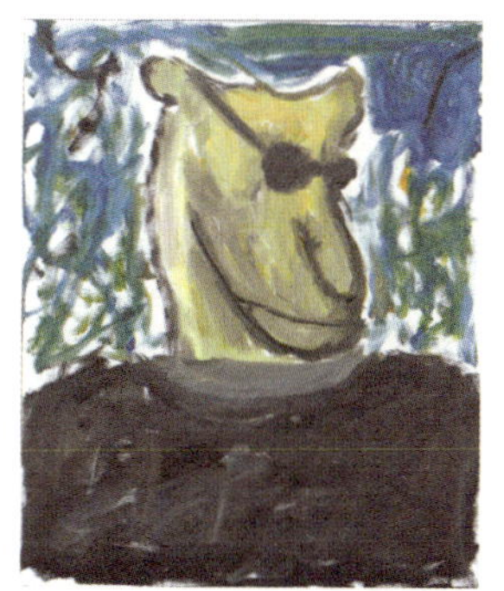
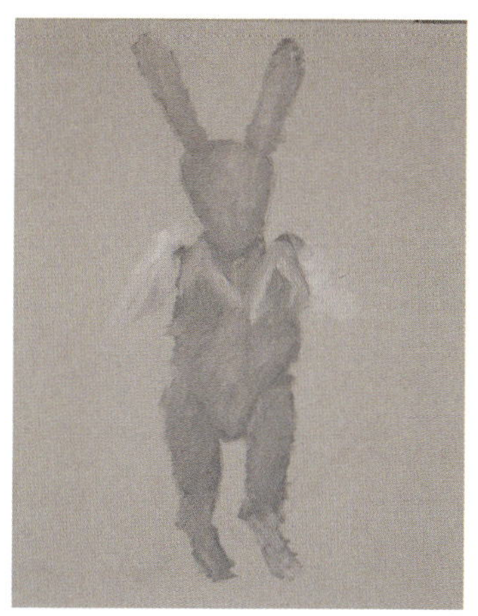
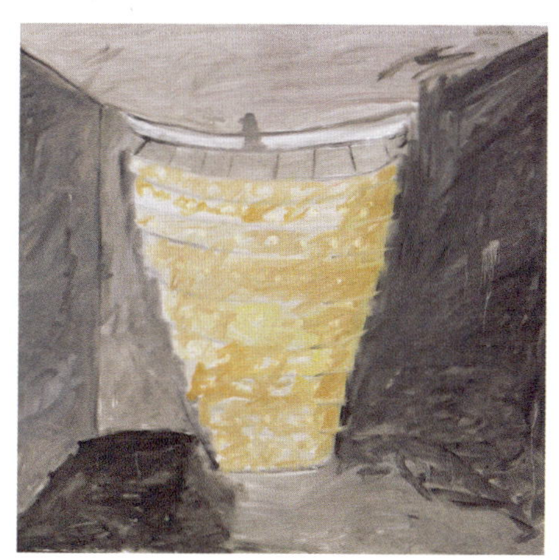

马秋莎

MA QIUSHA

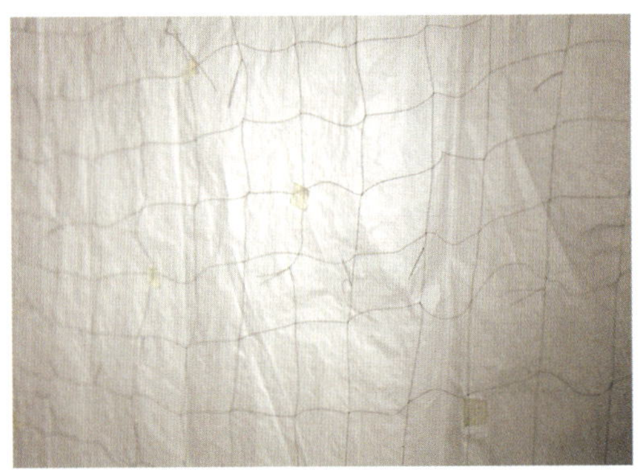

网（局部），2009
混合媒介
420 × 450 cm

Net (Detail), 2009
Mixed media
420 × 450 cm

作为艺术家，你在创作中所关心的是什么？以一件作品为例，分享你的创作过程。

如何将动机变得温和、平易近人，如何在过程中保持警惕，如何更有效的将私人的转化为可供公众交流的。

在《从平源里4号到天桥北里4号》中，我预设了一个简单直接的场景——个类似证件照片似的画面。语言与我的脸是两条路径。在这部片子中，故事性的叙述是一条明显可以追踪的路线，而藏在嘴里的痛是另一条时隐时现的线索。它们的终点都是伤痛，只不过一个是心理上的一个是生理上的。一个不懂中文的观众在第一次看的时候也可以到达终点，他可以完全感知我的生理上的痛（因为我诉说时表情的痛苦），他可以折返回片子的开始，认真的阅读字幕，这时字幕就成为对于疼痛的有效的补充；而对于中国观众，他可以通过阅读故事性来预见终点，（那更明显的是心理上的痛）而最后刀片从口中取出的那一刻就变成了另一条路的入口，它又返回到片子的最初。

如果你是一个批评家，你会从什么角度来阐释和讨论你自己的创作？

我不是批评家。

在你的创作和思考中，什么书籍和艺术家曾经或正在影响着你？

在创作中没有东西可以影响我。生活中的很多事情和人都会影响我。书是空闲时间的补充。

你是怎样判断和决定在什么语境下呈现你的哪些作品的？你是

怎样看待作品呈现的语境和作品的关系的？
这太理想主义了。

如何在创作上形成了现在的面貌，描述一下近年来作品的发展
和变化？
很多时候，性格中的缺陷导致在现实生活中的被动。而作为人
的敏感被激发。每天都有很多经验建立起来，同时又有很多经
验失去效力，焦虑感和疏离感充满整个生活。我更喜欢寻找那些
相对稳定的因素——那些模棱两可的、看似相互矛盾又互为补充
的东西，它自身的完整性和相对真空的状态很神秘，又长久。

你会在什么情况下摧毁你自己的作品？
不需要摧毁吧，不拿出来就好了。

你怎么看待艺术史和艺术家创作的关系？
艺术史是历史，艺术家的创作会成为历史。

在你的工作中，理性和情感冲动各自扮演着什么样的角色？
没有无缘无故的情感冲动，理性好像很难单独进入到我的世界。

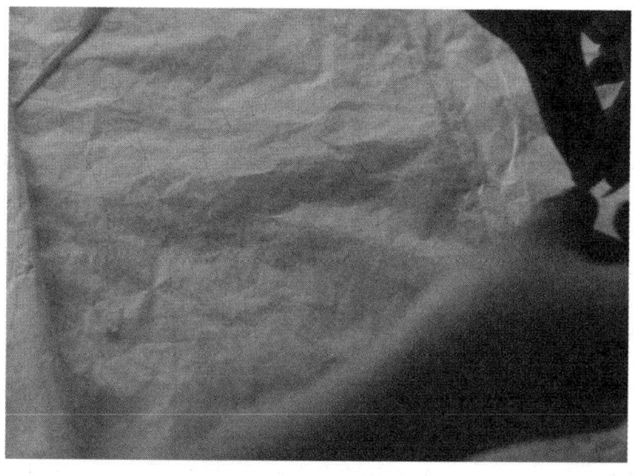

作品《网》在制作中，艺术家工作室，2009年。
The artist making the work *Net* at the studio in 2009

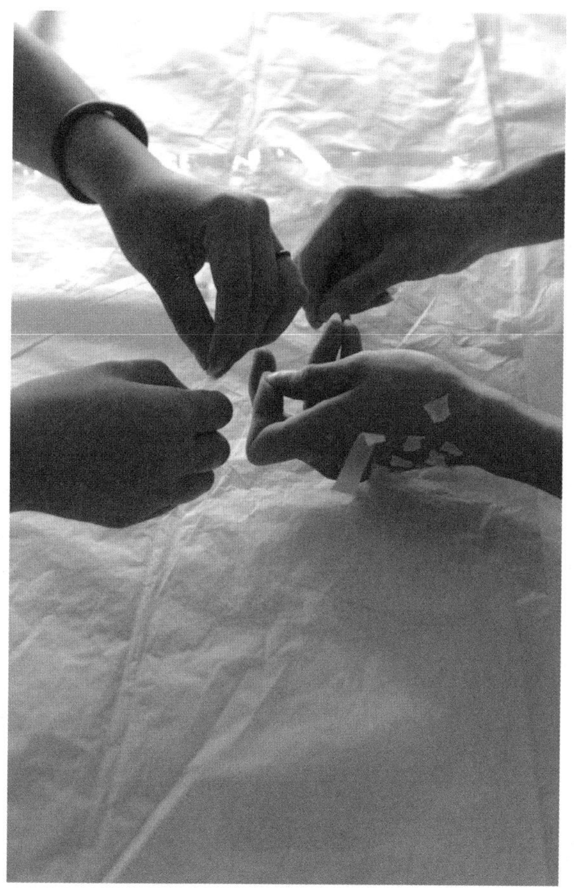

白雪公主, 2009
双频录像
3分30秒

Snow White, 2009
2-channel video
3'30''

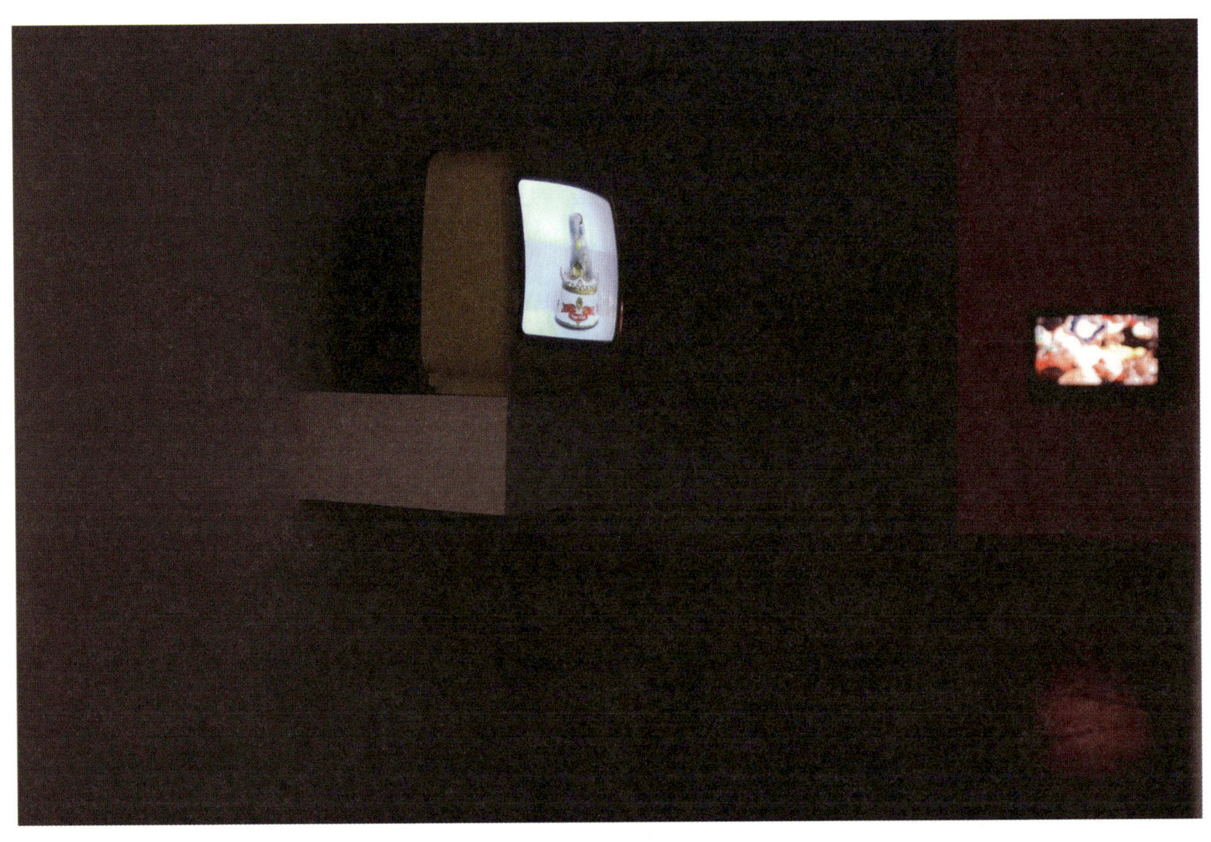

白雪公主, 2009
双频录像
3分30秒

Snow White, 2009
2-channel video
3'30''

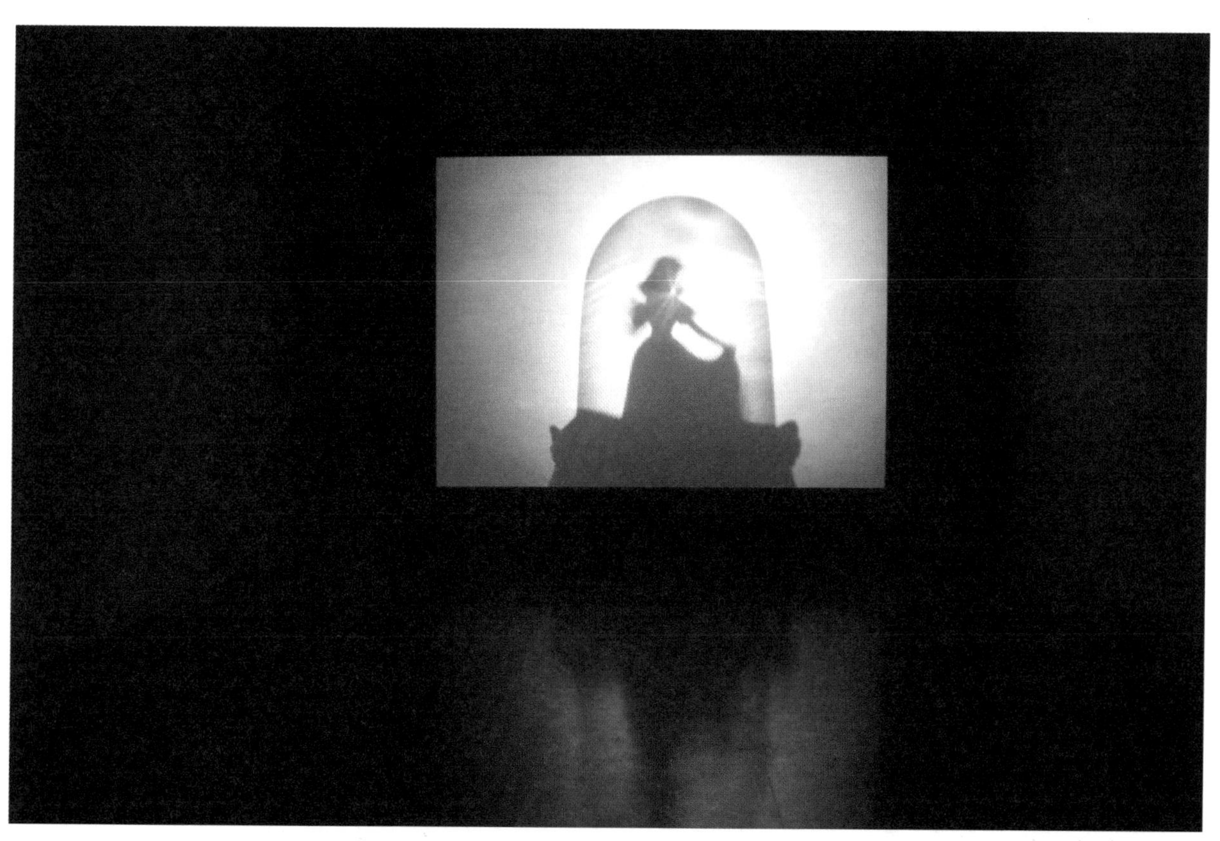

As an artist, what do you care most during working? Could you please give an example to introduce the process of your work for us?

My chief concern is how to make the motive of my work more friendly and easy to approach, how to keep my vigilance along the working process, and how to effectively allow the private to become public. In *From No.4 Pingyuanli to No.4 Tianqiaobeili*, I set up a simple scene — a view similar to certificate photos. Words and my face represent two different tracks. In this video, story narration creates a clearly visible thread for the viewer to follow, while the hidden pain inside my mouth serves as a flickering clue. Both of them lead to pain and hurt, except that one is on mental level. The other is physical. A non-Chinese speaking viewer might get to the end point immediately after viewing it and experience exactly the same amount of the physical pain as I did (because of the painful expression on my face accompanying the narration). Also he may return to the video's beginning and read the subtitles carefully, which at this time will be a useful supplement to the understanding of the pain. As for a Chinese viewer, he can come to the destination through the told story (which is more a pain in the heart). And at the end of the story narration, the moment when the razor is taken out from my mouth, a new pathway opens up and it takes the viewer back to the very beginning.

Suppose you are a critic, what perspective would you talk about and explain you work from?

I'm not a critic.

What books and which artists have had, or is having an influence on your way of thinking and working?

Nothing could give me influence while I'm working. Lots of people and things in my life could have influence on me. Reading books is an

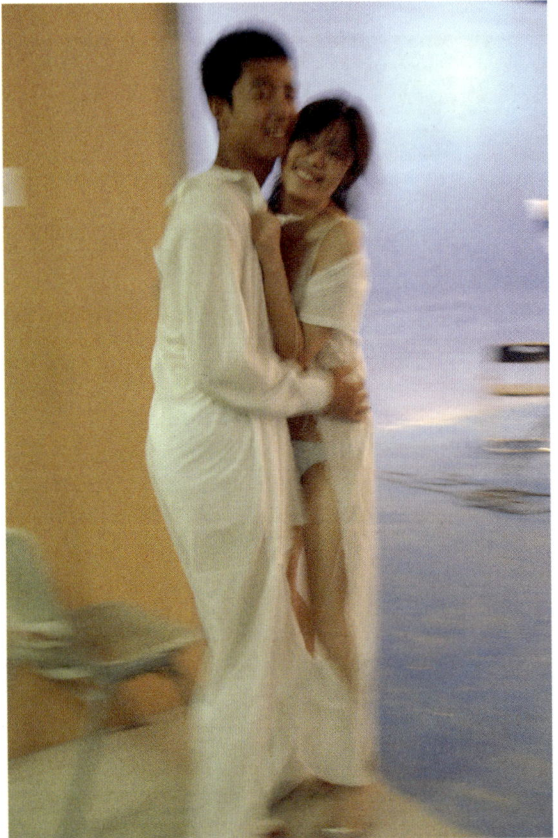

作品《我们》的拍摄现场，中央美术学院影棚，2009年6月26日。
Filming *We* at the studio of Central Academy of Fine Arts on 26th June 2009.

additional activity for leisure hours.

How do you decide the context in which your work is to be presented? How do you consider the relation of the context with your work?

This sounds too idealistic.

How does your work take the present shape? And please give a few words about the latest development and changes in your work.

Often man's defects in character make him a passive role in real life. Man's sensitivity thus is stimulated and intensified. Every day lots of experiences are being captured while many others are ceasing to be valid, leaving our life to be filled with this sense of anxiety and alienation. What I prefer to do is looking for elements with relatively more certain quality — those seemingly contradictory yet mutually complimentary things of ambiguity. The completeness in itself and the relatively vacuous state looks very enchanting and lasting.

In what circumstances would you want to destroy your own creation?

Maybe you don't have to do that. Just put it away then.

What do you think about the relation between the art history and artist's work?

Art history is the History as it is. Artists' work will become part of it.

What kind of roles would rational thinking and emotional impulse respectively play during your work time?

There always is a reason behind each emotional movement. It seems hard for rationality to go into my world separately.

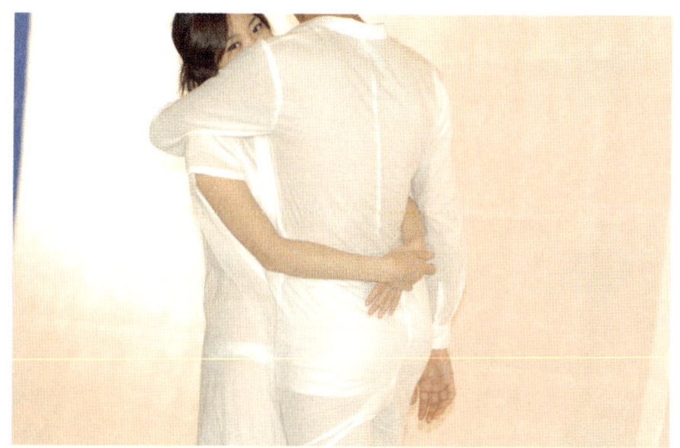

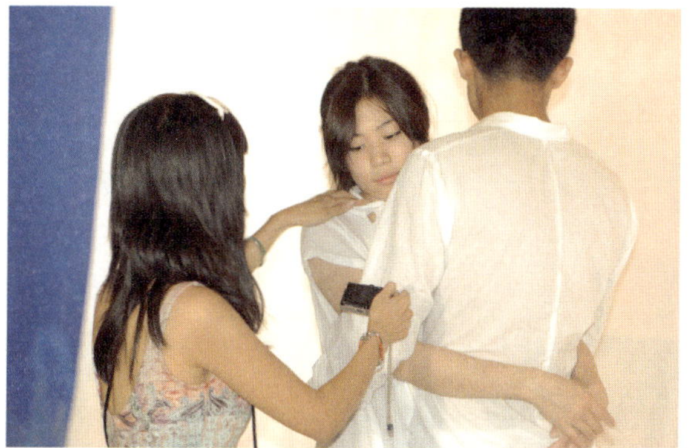

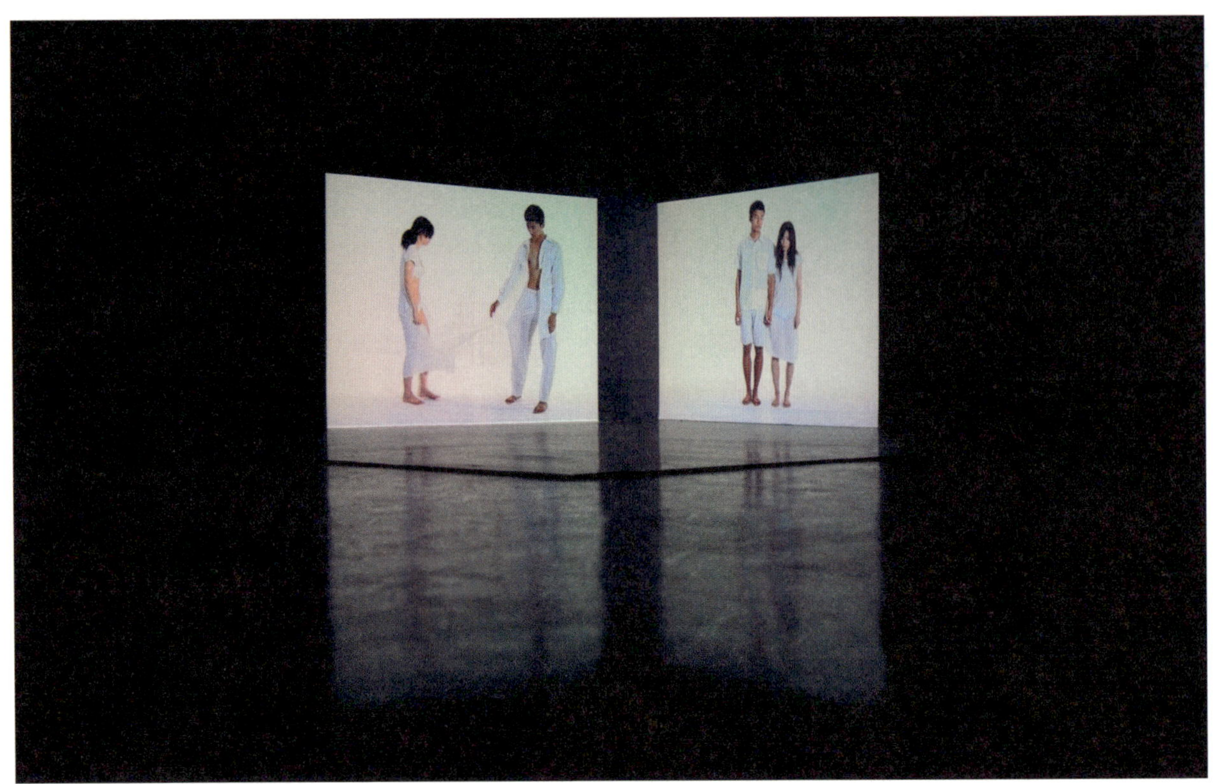

我们 NO. 1 & 2, 2009
3频录像
2分钟

We NO. 1 & 2, 2009
3-channel video
2'00''

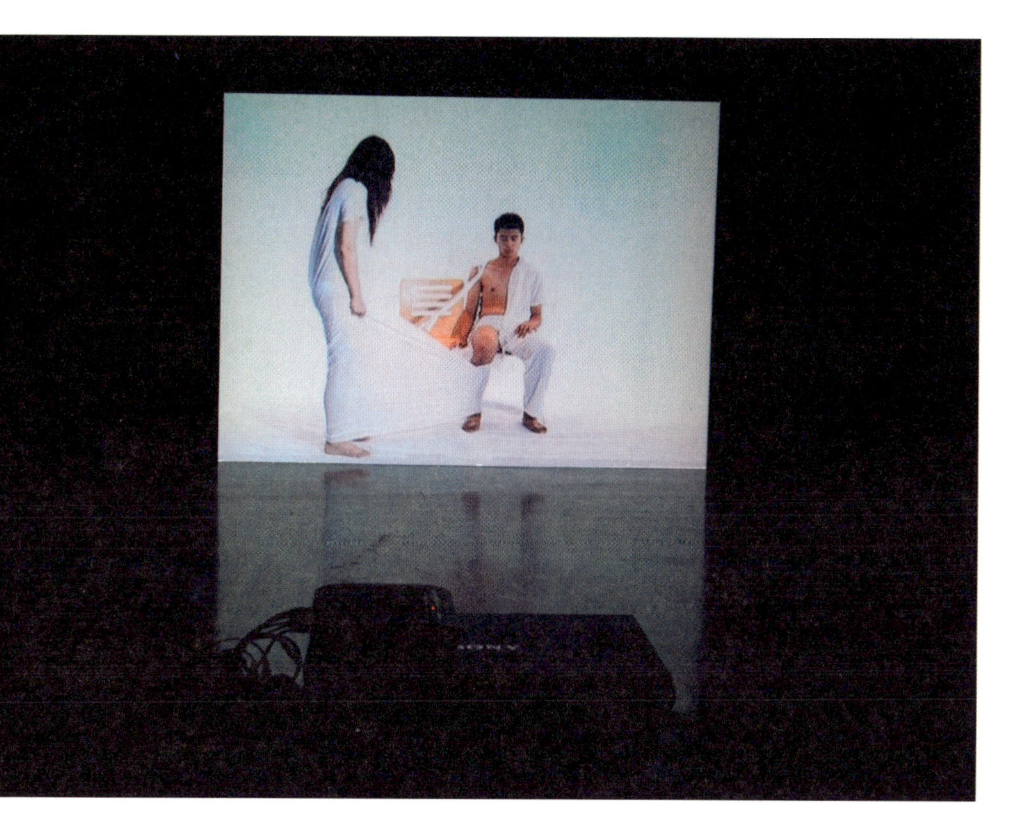

我们 NO. 3, 2009
3频录像
2分钟

We NO. 3, 2009
3-channel video
2'00''

邱黯雄

QIU ANXIONG

作为艺术家，你在创作中所关心的是什么？
当有一个想法时，是否有意义，然后怎样把自己的想法以恰当的方式呈现出来。

以一件作品为例，分享你的创作过程。
《新山海经》，最早画了一批纸上的鸟兽，配上文字，后开始动画构思，画分镜剧本两三个月，剧本定稿后，开始制作，原画画了两个月，后期用AE和premiere制作和剪辑，请音乐家作曲和制作音乐，最后合成。

如果你是一个批评家，你会从什么角度来阐释和讨论你自己的创作？
不知道，我不知道批评家的态度。我自己看作品是凭感觉多些，阐释是一种联想，属于反射面，从不同的角度都可以，不同的作品偏重也不同，比如从文本，从社会学，从诗学，都可以。

在你的创作和思考中，什么书籍和艺术家曾经或正在影响着你？
早期影响我比较大的是沈晓彤，波依斯，基弗尔，后来是肯特里奇，黄公望，书籍《论语》、《金刚经》、《坛经》。

你是怎样判断和决定在什么语境下呈现你的哪些作品的？你是怎样看待作品呈现的语境和作品的关系的？

我更关心的是作品本身是怎样呈现的，语境是在作品的呈现中成型的。

如何在创作上形成了现在的面貌，描述一下近年来作品的发展和变化？

主要是在影像和装置方面尝试，面貌谈不上，就是做了几个作品吧。《新山海经》是以文明之外的角度审视文明的产物。《民国风景》则虚拟了个人的历史风景，以质疑历史叙述的真实性。影像装置《为了忘却的记忆》是用记忆载体建造了一个唤醒记忆和提示失忆的复合体。历史在影像的流逝中失重，个人日常生活的真实存在也只是如影子般在记忆的底片上失真。

你会在什么情况下摧毁你自己的作品？

通常不会，只有自己觉得太差的又不知道放在哪里的，可能会这样做，但我印象里没有这么做过。

你怎么看待艺术史和艺术家创作的关系？

艺术史就是记录和梳理艺术发生的工作，艺术家对艺术史只需要知道他感兴趣的内容就可以了。

在你的工作中，理性和情感冲动各自扮演着什么样的角色？

不会分得很清楚，一个想法也很难说哪些是理性哪些是感性的，都会有吧。理性思考更多是事后的反省，做作品是比较感性的状态。

邱黯雄工作室一角
A corner of Qiu Anxiong's studio

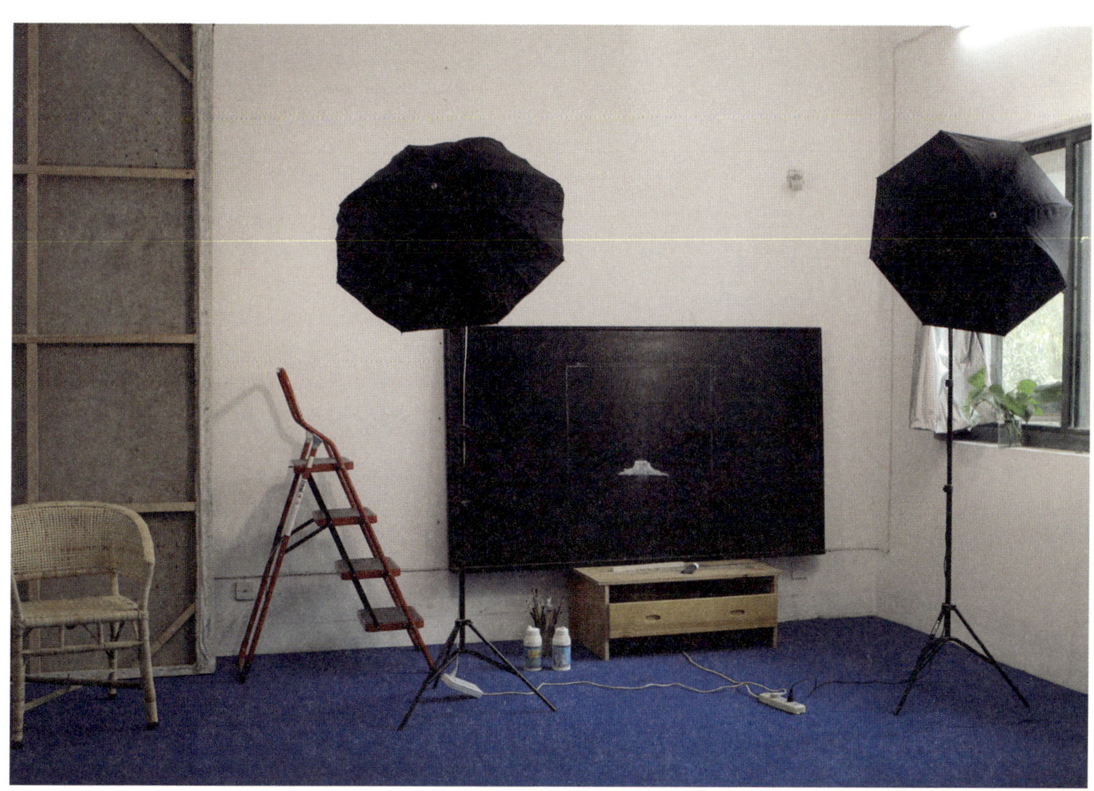

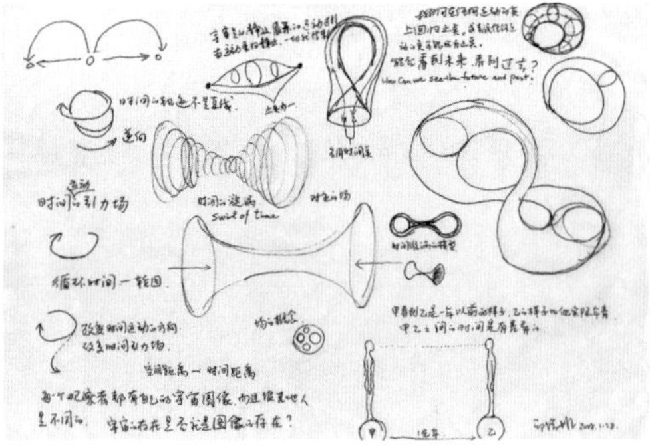

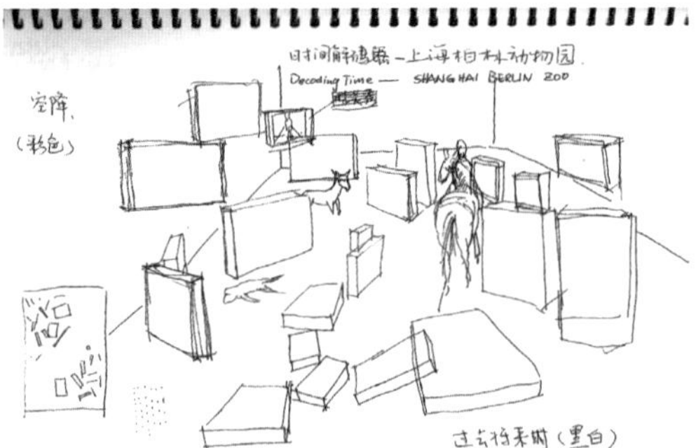

时间解码器—上海柏林动物园，2006
影像装置
草图及说明

Decoding Time — Shanghai Berlin Zoo, 2006
Video Installation
Draft and explanation

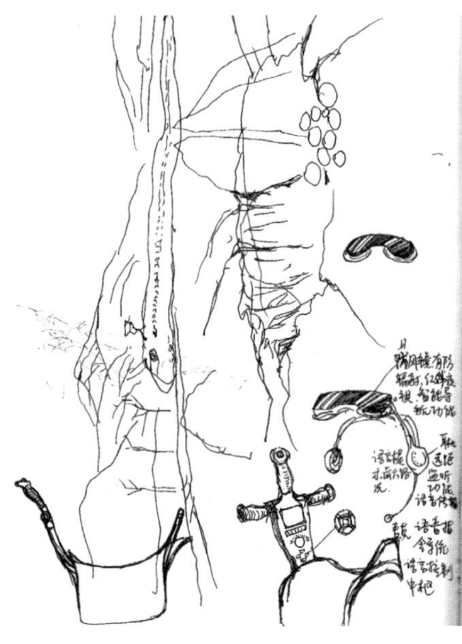

As an artist, what do you care most during working?Could you please give an example to introduce the process of your work for us?

When an idea occurred to me, (I'm concerned about) whether it makes any sense, and then how to express it in a proper way.

For the *New Classic of Mountains and Seas*, I drew a batch of birds and animals accompanied by text at the very beginning, and then started to design the animation. Before I started the production, it took me two or three months to draw the visual script and complete the final version. I drew the original paintings for two months, and then made into an animation and clip it with AE and Premiere. After that, I asked a musician to compose and produce the music for it, and finally combined them together.

Suppose you are a critic, what perspective would you talk about and explain you work from?

I don't know, because I do not know the critics' attitude. I appreciate works mainly by my feelings; while explanation is kind of association, which belongs to reflection level, thus can be made from different angles, with different emphasizes for different works: from text, sociology, poetics, and so on.

What books and which artists have had, or is having an influence on your way of thinking and working?

At early period, it's Shen Xiaotong, Joseph Beuys, Kiefer who impacted me a lot, and later Kentridge, Huang Gongwang, and books include the *Analects of Confucius*, the *Diamond Sutra* and the *Platform Sutra*.

How do you decide the context in which your work is to be presented? How do you consider the relation of the context with your work?

I am more concerned about how the work itself is presented, and the context is molded in the works' expressions.

How does your work take the present shape? And please give a few words about the latest development and

changes in your work.

Mainly in video and installation, I managed to do several creations, It's early to mention an outlook. The *New Classic of Mountains and Seas* is a production seeing civilization from beyond civilizations. *Minguo Landscape* makes up individual's historical views to question about the authenticity of historical narrations. And the video installation *Memory for Forgetting* builds up a complex with a memory carrier to wake up memories and remind of amnesia. The history loses its weight during the flow of videos, and individual's really existed daily lives also distort on the films of memories like shadows.

In what circumstances would you want to destroy your own creation?

Usually I won't. Only when I feel too bad for this work and do not know where to place it, I may destroy it. But I have never done this in my memories.

What do you think about the relation between the art history and artist's work?

Art history is to record and sort out events about art, while artists only need to know what they want to know about the art history.

What kind of roles would rational thinking and emotional impulse respectively play during your work time?

It can't be distinguished very clearly, since it is difficult to say about an idea-which part is rational and which is emotional-probably both. Rational thinking is more often made after creating, while doing a creation is in a more emotional state.

时间解码器—上海柏林动物园，2006
影像装置
草图及说明

Decoding Time — Shanghai Berlin Zoo, 2006
Video Installation
Draft and explanation

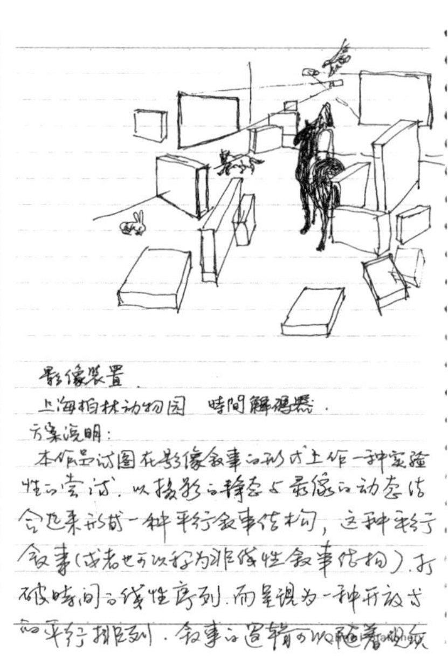

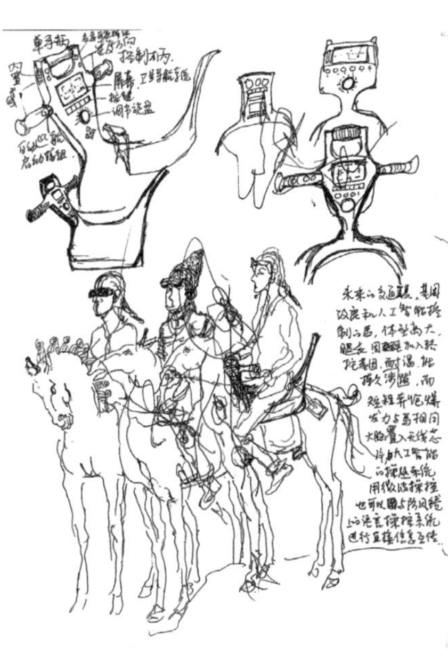

邱黯雄作品方案说明

题目：《时间解码器-上海柏林动物园》
影像装置
媒介：灯箱照片（彩色和黑白），录像（彩色），动画（黑白），雕塑，动物标本

释题
　　"上海柏林动物园"是一个人为设定的虚拟存在空间，是一个在记忆和幻想中的失乐园，是现实人类处境投向未来想象的隐喻镜像。
　　上海是西方对东方想象的一个充满梦幻嘉年华氛围的冒险乐园，一个随时可能出现奇迹的生命赌场，一个就算落魄流浪也能寻欢作乐的殖民地。对于中国，上海是先进，发达，速度，机会，财富的代名词，是中国的国际大都市，是通往外面世界的桥梁，是奔向明天的幸福世界的试验场。上海浓缩了这个时代人类乌托邦想象的各种可能，它是我们的空中之城，悬浮在明天的空气中。
　　柏林恰好是理想国破灭之后的废墟中重新认识人类精神的另一个起点，伫立在柏林动物园的教堂残骸还拖出不远的历史投过来的影子，柏林动物园也是离去和到来的车站，我们从何处来，向何方去，历史的坐标仍在迷雾中若隐若现。
　　动物园是现代人类社会对自然的最后乡愁之地，当人类渐渐逃进自己建构的城市笼葛，又把自然之物关进笼子里圈禁起来，以便记住与自然一丝仅存的关系，我们在动物园可以近距离的观察这些动物，而我们与他们的距离又是如此的远，我们对理想的企图带着我们走得太远，以至于要在城市中围出一块可以回望驻足的地方，而那些被圈禁的动物正好是我们内心自然之性的象征物，人类的每次理想的跃进都如虎兕出笼，凶猛而失控，我们既是灾难的缔造者又是受难者，是否我们的救赎者就是我们的圈禁之地？

作品构想：
　　时间的循环结构，开放的空间设置，叙事的非线性平行结构是整个作品的基本构架。作者试图在影像叙事的结构形式上作一种尝试，录像和动画的动态部分是整个作品的叙事框架和脉络，动态影像的内容是由一些相互关联的小情节组成的，可以前后互为因果，用静态的照片作为整个叙事的基础和背景，在空间上建构起一个叙事迷宫。而雕塑则为现场和这个虚拟空间提供了一个转换的角色，使现实和虚拟的界限更为模糊。这种平行叙事（或者也可以称为非线性叙事结构）区别于单屏影像作品的线性叙事特点，呈现为一种开放的叙事方式，叙事的逻辑可以随着观众观看线路的改变而改变，而叙事时间也就成为一个不确定的因素了，叙事的完成是在观看结束后得以实现的。

　　整个作品计划布置在一个约 150 至 200 平米的封闭无光源的空间里，可以有几个不同的出入口，作品分为两个部分，第一部分"空降"为彩色灯箱照片和彩色录像，灯箱尺寸大小不等（宽度 180cm—30cm），约 20 个，录像用 2 个投影仪和 4 个电视机（液晶为佳）放映，整个灯箱群占屋内 1/3 面积，倚角而生，高度较高，多用吊挂，部分摆放在地上，渐次向屋中空间低斜过渡，灯箱之间也留出空间，观众可以穿行。第二部分"过去将来时"为黑白灯箱照片和黑白动画片组成，灯箱尺寸与第一部分相仿，动画由 2 个投影仪和 6 个电视机（普通电子管即可）播放，大部分灯箱高度较低，有些灯箱倒放，斜幕。整个灯箱群比第一部分低，占整个空间 1/2 面积，动画投影一个在地上另一个在幕布上。雕塑和动物标本则散放在两个灯箱群里以及两者之间。

前期准备工作：

1，照片的拍摄，后期处理，以及灯箱制作
2，录像拍摄，后期制作
3，动画制作，动画后期
4，雕塑制作
5，标本购买

展示所需材料与设备：

名称	数量（估算值）	备注
灯箱片.	40	
灯箱	40	
投影机.	4	
幕布	4	
电视机	10	
雕塑	1	骑着未来的基因改良的马的年轻人
动物标本和皮毛	6	鹰，兔子 2，狐狸，狗

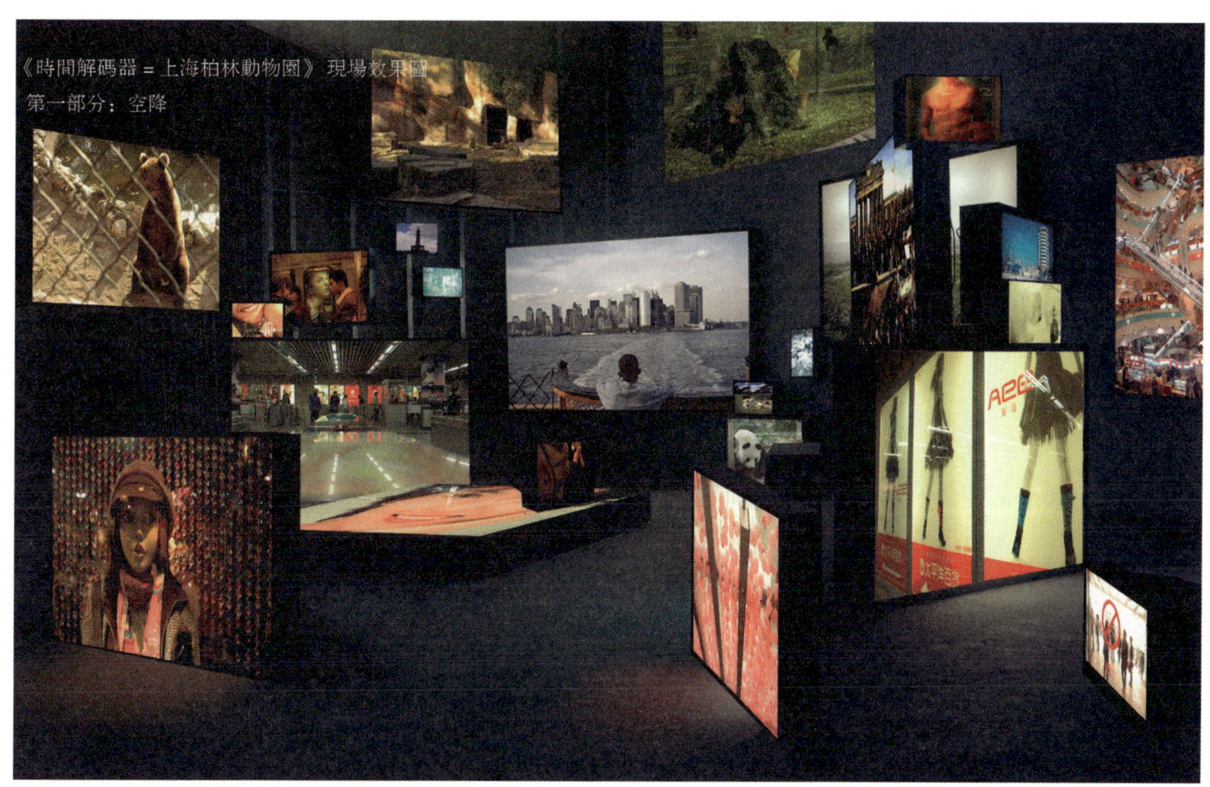

时间解码器—上海柏林动物园，2006
影像装置
现场效果图
第一部分　空降

Decoding Time - Shanghai Berlin Zoo, 2006
Video Installation
Drawing of installation view
Part I: The Airborne

《時間解碼器－上海柏林動物園》效果圖 2
第二部分：過去將來時

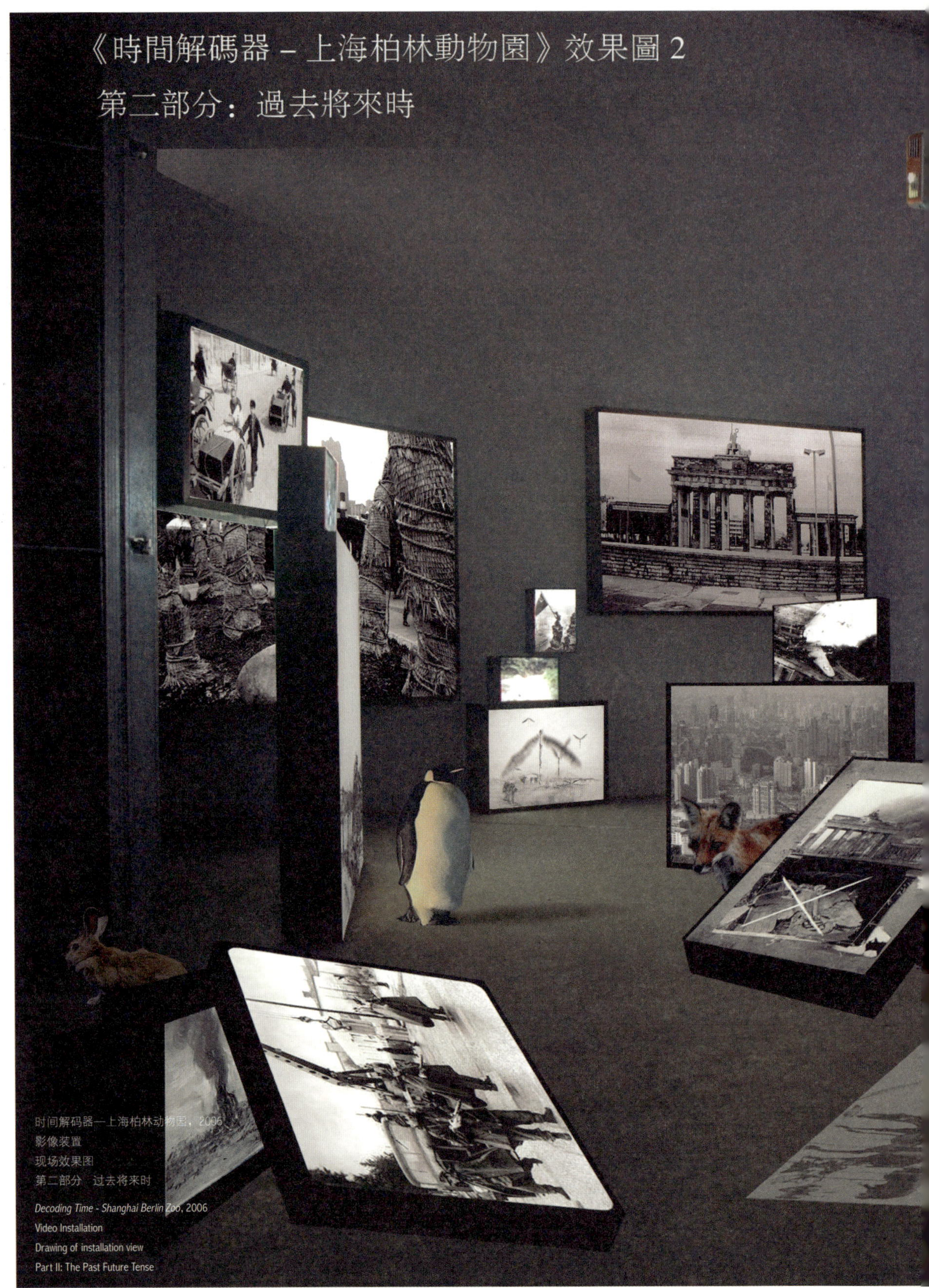

时间解码器—上海柏林动物园，2006
影像装置
现场效果图
第二部分　过去将来时

Decoding Time - Shanghai Berlin Zoo, 2006
Video Installation
Drawing of installation view
Part II: The Past Future Tense

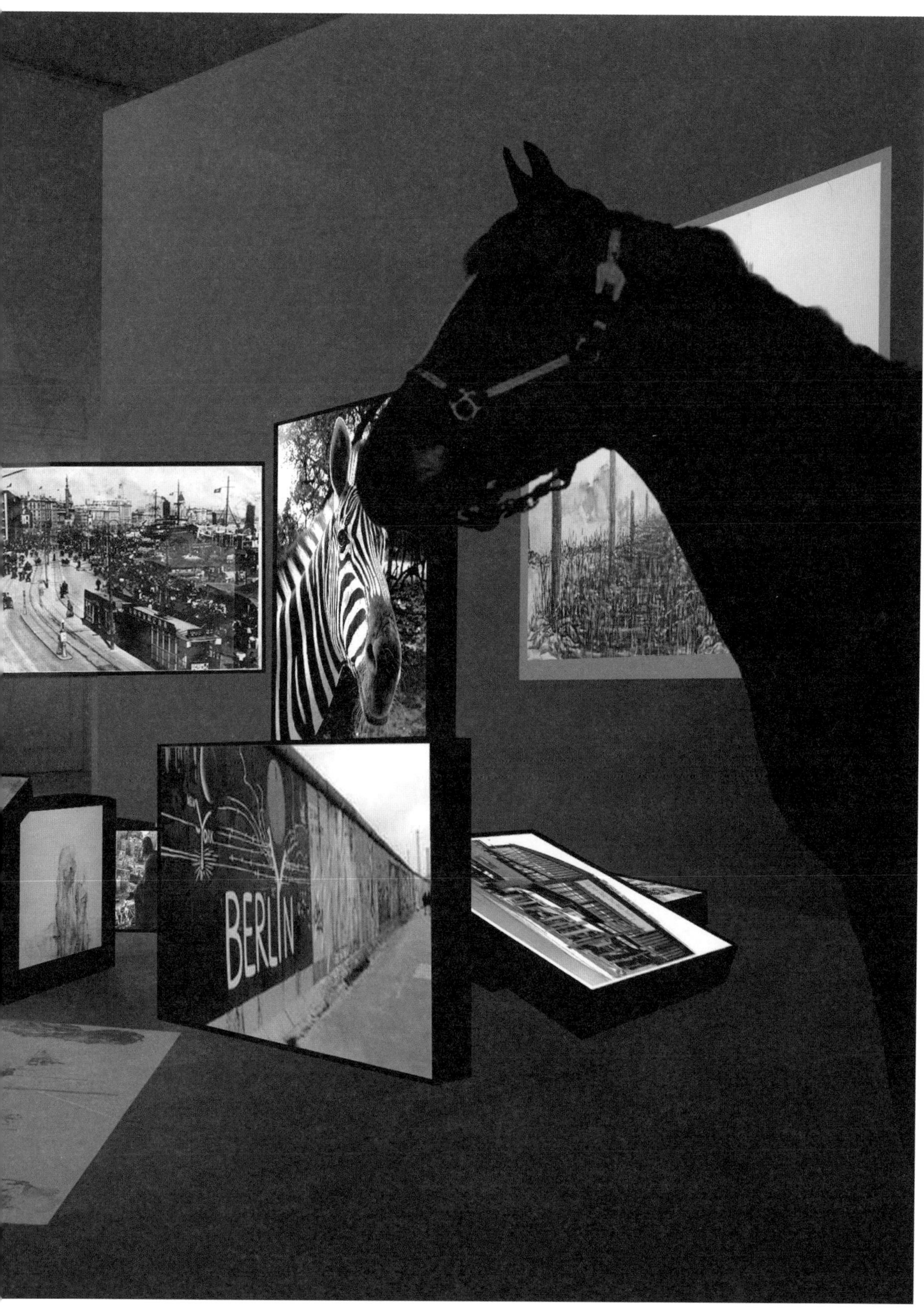
BERLIN

石 青

SHI QING

作为艺术家，你在创作中所关心的是什么？以一件作品为例，分享你的创作过程。

把事情想明白了比做作品要难得多，但全想明白了也就不用做作品了。

迄今作品还都达不到自己的要求。

如果你是一个批评家，你会从什么角度来阐释和讨论你自己的创作？

和作品保持距离，距离就是阐释，合理的阐释就是合理的距离。

阐释是魔术师的助手，应该帮着一起把游戏玩下去，而不是去揭老底。

在你的创作和思考中，什么书籍和艺术家曾经或正在影响着你？

每一次创作都是进入新领域的一种方法，一些书籍和艺术家，多多少少会临时扮演帮助者或阻碍者的角色；区别在于，当转向另一个领域时，有些书籍和艺术家也会一起转移阵地，或者说，人家早在那里等着你呢，这才叫影响。

你是怎样判断和决定在什么语境下呈现你的哪些作品的？你是怎样看待作品呈现的语境和作品的关系的？

现实中的语境不是固定靶子，是会跑的猎物，不断游动，视点模糊。这种情况下的判断和决定注定是无中生有的，不过没关系，这个判断会波及这个语境，甚至会主动迂回到你面前。

当你盯着这头游动的猎物时，猎物也在盯着你。双方在空间时间上对应着，离得太近和太远都有危险。

如何在创作上形成了现在的面貌，描述一下近年来作品的发展和变化？

面貌这个词模糊且可憎。前两年的试着把艺术变成一种社会实践并干预现实；现在继续与现实胶着，但拉开保持距离；以前是肉搏，现在是围场打援。

你会在什么情况下摧毁你自己的作品？

作品成尸体的时候，当肥料。很环保很营养。

你怎么看待艺术史和艺术家创作的关系？

一个艺术家就是一部艺术史。自家肥料养活自家田，质量好点的对邻居有用，但终归有限。

在你的工作中，理性和情感冲动各自扮演着什么样的角色？

感性和理性是一对陪练，随时倒地随时复活。

感性要灵活些，理性有滞后性，但随时反扑；但要警惕理性硬化和跟得太紧。

一直就在那里，2008
图片、改装自行车

Always there, 2008
Photography-modified bicycle

在上海的恒丰北路买一辆二手车，在这里的二手车大多是被偷的赃物。
买来的车进行一些加工，将部分零件（挡泥板、飞轮等）开刃或打磨成
尖（螺栓，车把等），这些零件的改造把自行车变成一组凶器的组合，
虽然从外表乍看与其他自行车无异。
2008年12月14日，将改装的自行车刚在恒丰北路的一个巷子口，即购车
的地点。等待车子被偷走，到17：30车子仍在；次日15日上午10：30，自
行车已不见踪迹。作品关注的是今天社会语境下潜在的大众暴力可能以
及这种情绪的传染性。

Bought a second hand bicycle on Hengfeng Bei Road where most second hand bicycles there were stolen goods.
Had some modification on the bought bike, edged some accessories such as mudguard, flywheel, etc. and sharpened bolt, handlebar, etc. The modification of these accessories transformed this bicycle into a combination of criminal weapons, although the appearance looks the same as other bicycles.
On 14th of December, 2008, left the modified bicycle at an alley on Hengfeng Bei Road, where the bike was bought.
Waiting for the bike to be stolen, but it was still there at 17:30.
Until 10:30am on the next day, 15th of December, the bike was gone.
The work is concerned about the possibility of potential public violence in today's society and the infectivity of criminal emotion.

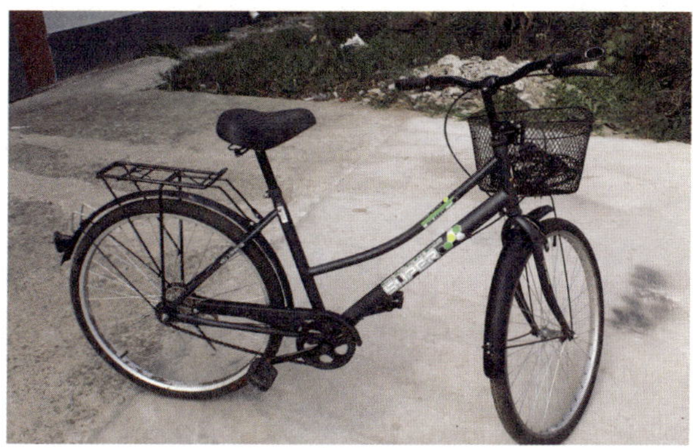

改装的自行车
Modified bicycle

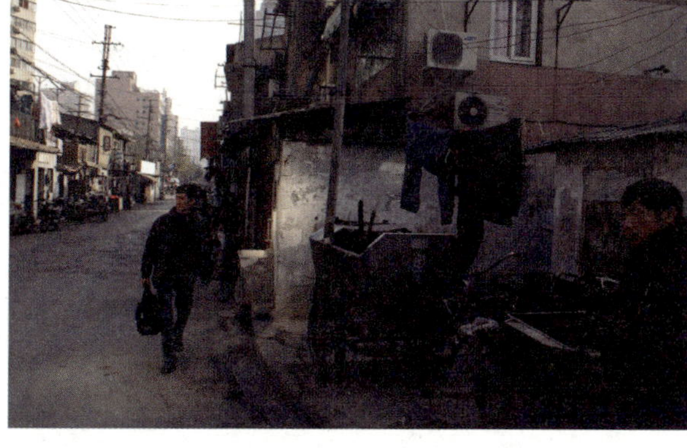

2008年12月15日上午，上海恒丰北路，自行车丢失的现场。
On the afternoon of December 15th, 2008, Hengfeng Bei Road in Shanghai, the spot where the bicycle was Lost.

自行车细部：被削尖、开刃的局部
Details on the bicycle: Sharpened and edged part

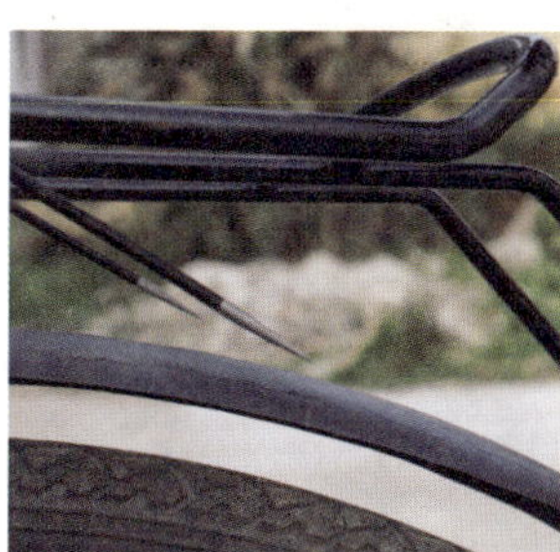
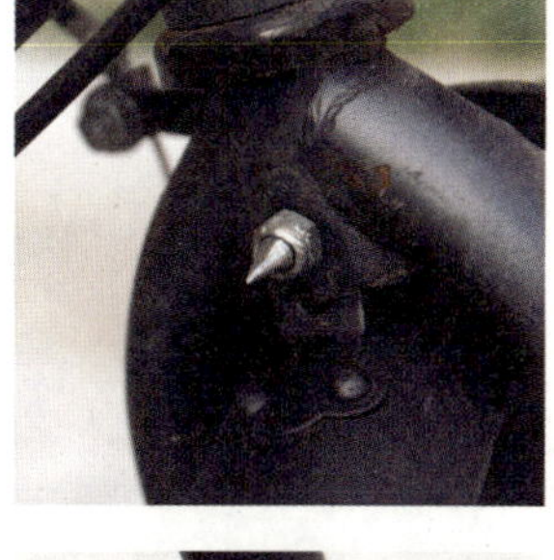
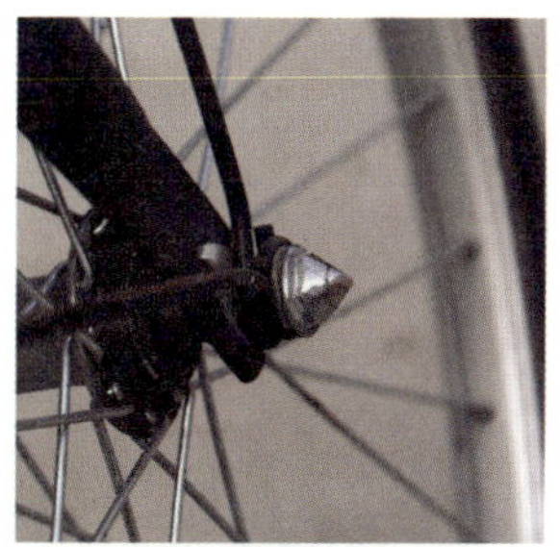
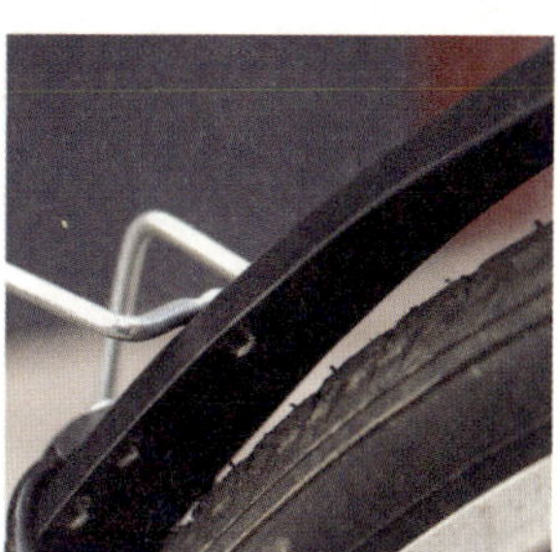
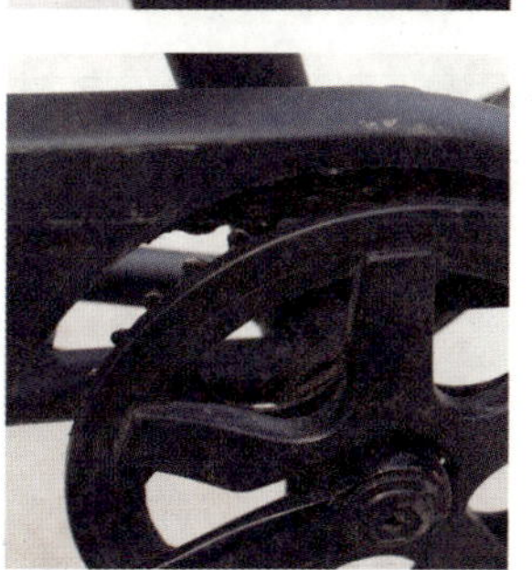
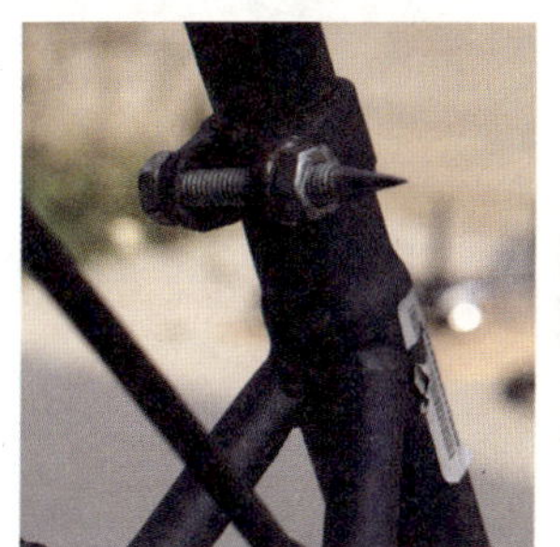
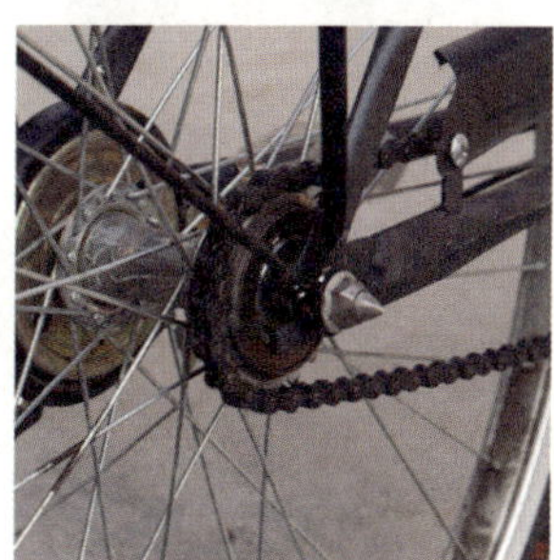

怪物总是硬邦邦的，2008
录像、竹子、日光灯管、电线、竹箩筐

重庆是有时空感的城市：传统农耕劳作的质朴与工业化的喧嚣；坡江林岸的地理与交错纵横的交通，如同各个历史形态的切片一样并置在这个城市。作品中一群当地的底层劳工（当地叫作棒棒），田园气息的城市服务者，把成筐的日光灯管挑下山岗，码头上船。在象征着工业化动力的电厂沙滩登陆，竖起一个竹子搭建的电塔，看上去又像一个待射的飞行器。沿着它的轮廓线装满日光灯管与远处的大桥争辉。

Monster is always blunt, 2008
Video, bamboo, light tube, electrical wire, bamboo basket

Chongqing is a city with senses of space and time, as all historical statuses co-exist in this city, such as modest traditional farming and uproarious manufacturing industry, geography with rivers and forests, and vertically and horizontally staggered transport. In the work, a group of lower working class (called as bangbang in the local area), who are pastoral city service workers, carrying baskets of light tubes to the dock at the root of hill, and loaded to the boats. Landed at the beach of the electricity factory which symbolizes the engine of industrialization, set up an electricity tower with bamboos, which looks like an aerocraft ready to be fired, and installed light tubes according to its outlines to compete with the bridge faraway.

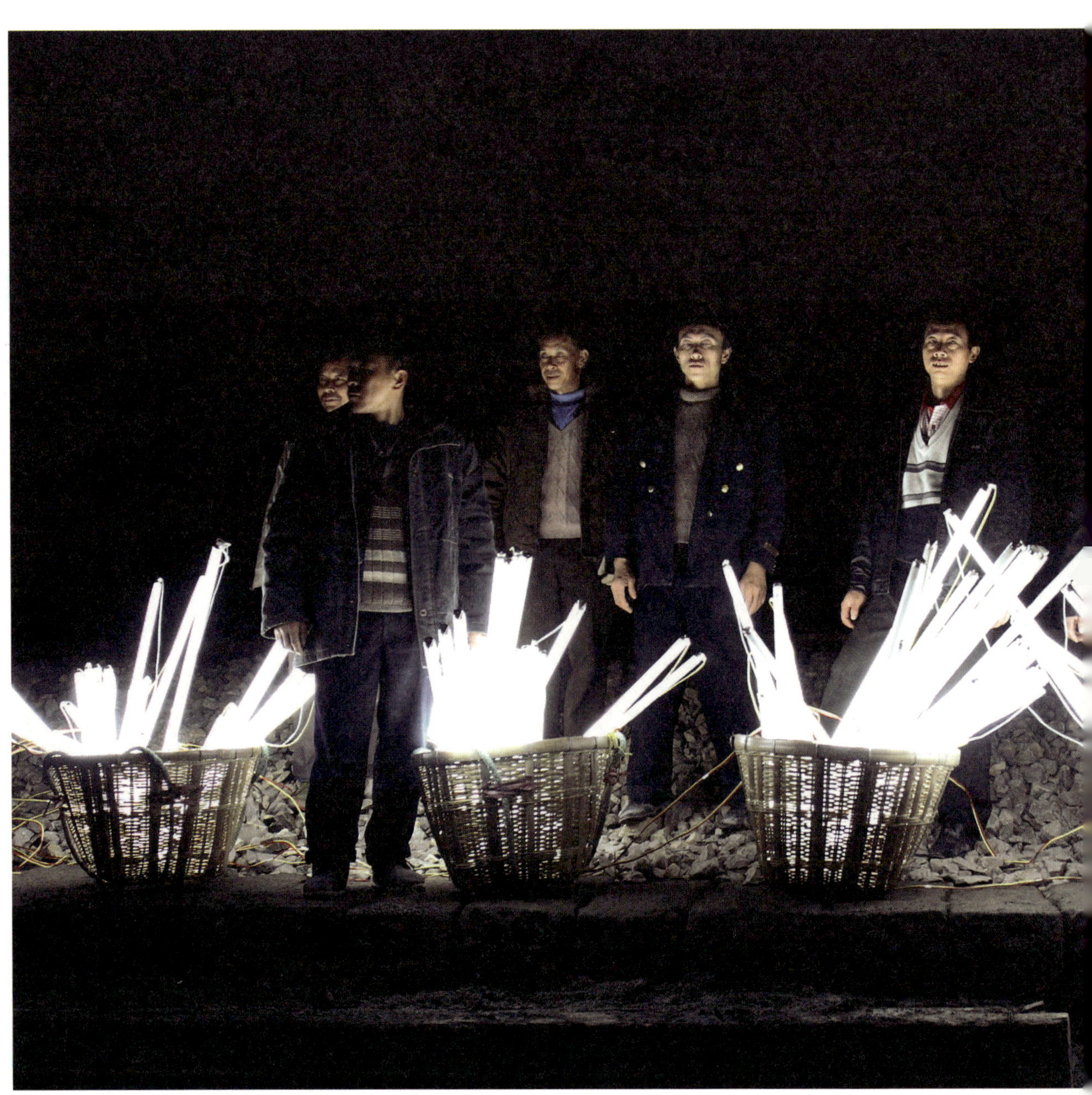

As an artist, what do you care most during working? Could you please give an example to introduce the process of your work for us?

To think things through is much harder than making art. However, there would be no need to make art if everything looks straight. So far I haven't made any work that is satisfying to me.

Suppose you are a critic, from what perspective would you explain and comment on your works?

Keep distance with the work. The distance is equal to an interpretation. A sound interpretation stands for a reasonable distance.

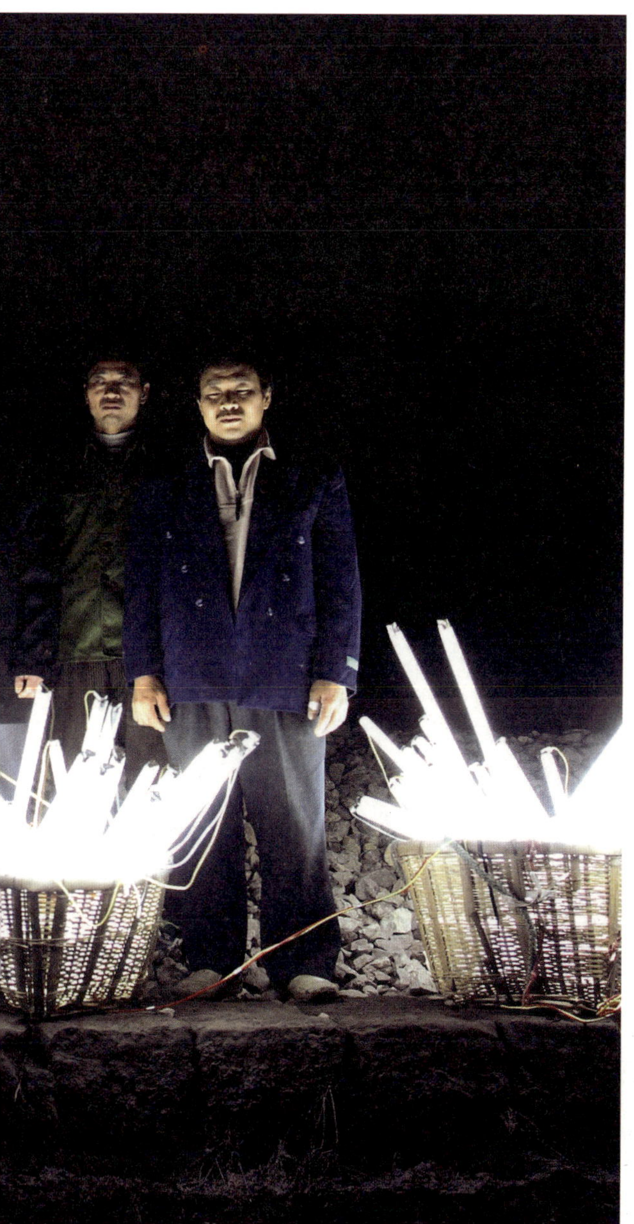

What books and which artists have had or are having an influence on your way of thinking and working?

Each time, making a new work offers an entry to a new field and some readings and artists will temporarily play the roles of either a helper or an obstructer. The difference lies in the fact that, when you turn to a new area, some books and artists will follow up immediately. In other words, they would be waiting for you there. This is how influence goes.

How do you make judgment and decision as to in what context you'd like to present your works? According to you, in what way is the context created by the work related to the work itself?

Context in real life is not a fixated target, but rather a running prey, whose location is under constant changes and whose view is out of focus. In this case, all judgments and decisions are doomed to be groundless. But it doesn't matter. The judgment will spread to the context and even bypass you voluntarily. As you are watching this moving prey, the prey is watching you as well. Both are correspondent in terms of time and space. A distance too far away from each other or too intimate will lead to danger.

How does your work take the present shape? And please give a few words about the latest development and changes in your work.

"Style" is a fuzzy and detestable word. In the past two years I was trying to transform art into a kind of social practice to engage the reality; now I continue to stick with reality, but try to keep a distance from it. Previously I was doing a close battle and now what I'm doing is besiege the stronghold and fight with reinforcements.

In what circumstances would you want to destroy your own creation?

I'll do it when my work turns into a corpse and becomes an environmental fertilizer with rich nourishment.

What do you think about the relation between the art history and artist's work?

An artist represents a book of art history. One's own manure feeds one's own field. If the quality is good, it might also be useful to neighbors (but it has a limit).

What kind of roles would rational thinking and emotional impulse respectively play in your work?

Sense and sensibility are two training mates, who can come back to life any time.

Sensibility seems to be more flexible while sense is hysteretic, but ready to fight back any time. We should try to avoid the stiffness of sense and also we should keep an appropriate distance.

蒙古信使：一次游牧式的饮食实践，2008
摄影、录像、印刷品、文字、食物与调味品

请一位蒙古籍（来自中国内蒙古）厨师去到圣达菲向当地印第安人、墨西哥人传授蒙古食品的作法，而且希望这些食品能在当地流传下来，所以使用的原料都是必须在当地买得到的，也只有这样这些被传授的食品才有可能在当地真正流传下来，同时也想请蒙古厨师找到他感兴趣的本地食品带回蒙古家乡去。

Mongolian Messenger: Experience Nomadic Style of Cuisine, 2008
Photography, video, print, literature, food, and seasoning

Invited a Mongolian chef (from inner-Mongolia in China) to Santa Fe to teach local Indians and Mexicans how to make Mongolian food. I hope Mongolian cuisine will get popular there, so all of the ingredients must be able to be purchased in the local area so that the cuisine can be really popularized in the local area. At the same time, the Mongolian chef will find his favoured local food and bring to his hometown in Mongolia.

蒙古厨师朝克图在圣达菲陶斯镇
Mongolian chef Chao Ke Tu visited Taos New Mexico

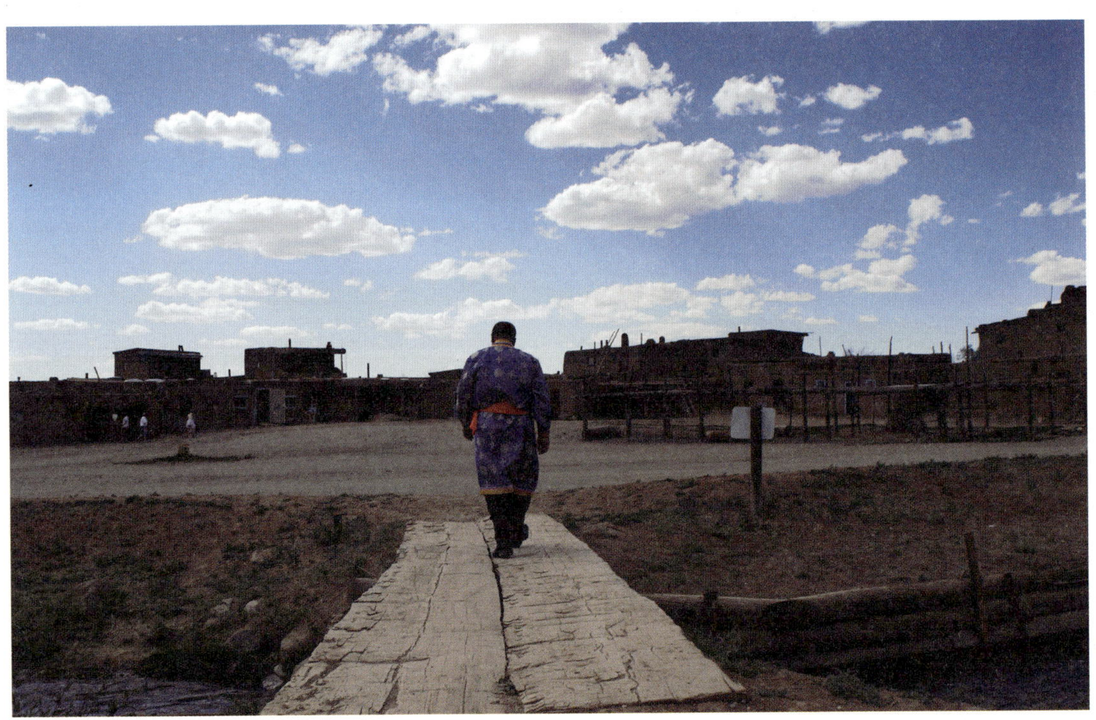

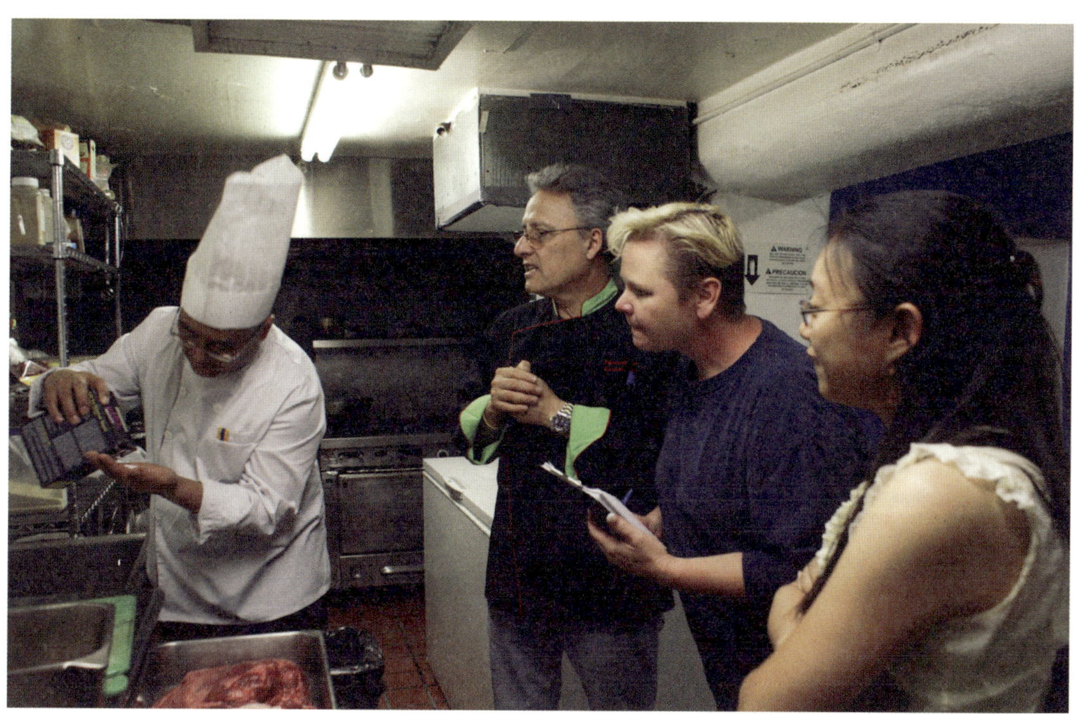

朝克图在圣达菲的LA TAQUERIA餐厅教授蒙古菜的做法
Chao Ke Tu teaches the Native American family how to cook Mongolian dishes

印第安家宴
Dining with Mongolian and Native American dishes at a Native American family

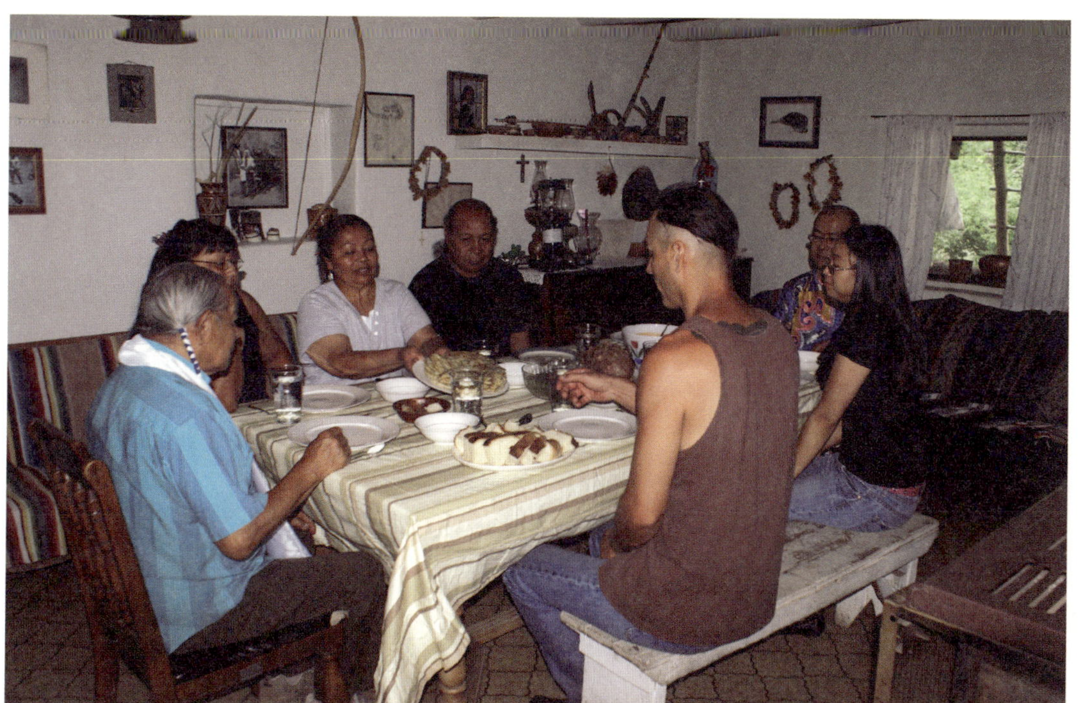

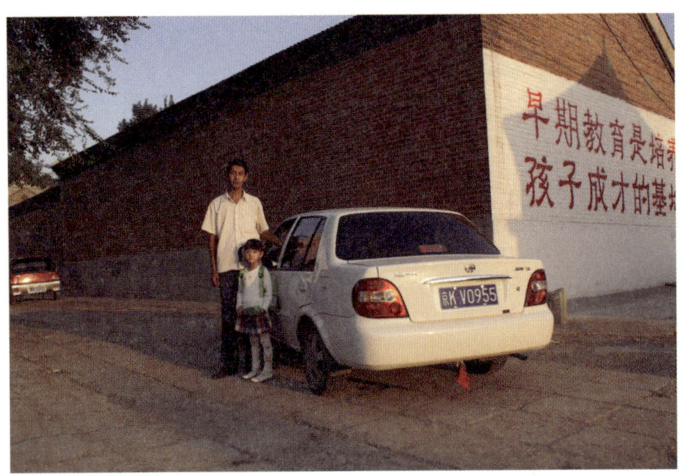

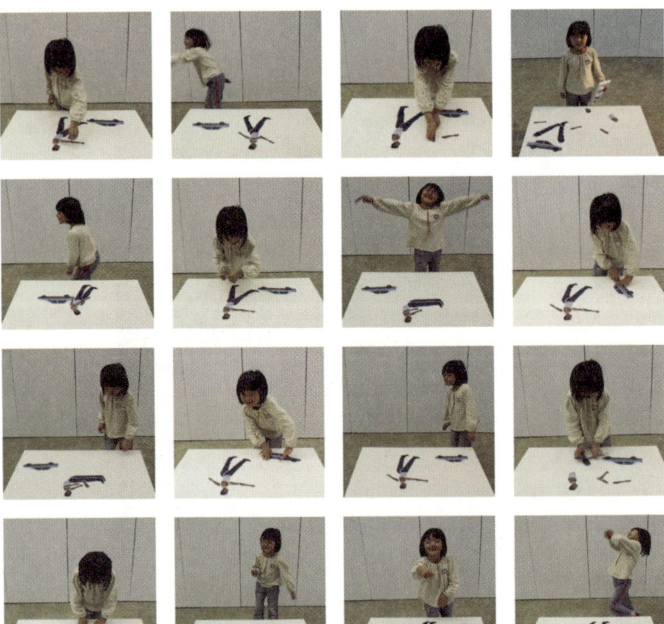

司机小王和女儿在幼儿园的合影
Photo of Xiaowang and his daughter in the kindergarten

小王的女儿在拼图
Xiaowang's daughter is playing jigsaw puzzle

司机小王和他的女儿，2007
摄影

司机小王来自河北，平时靠出租拉活维生，我经常雇用他的车。他有一
个4岁的女儿，在北京五环外的一个小幼儿园里，每天下班后小王都要去
接女儿。女儿知道她爸爸一天的生活吗？我问过她，看来她只熟悉爸爸
下班后和她在一起的情景，小王的部分生活其实是以想象方式进入女儿
的世界的。
我把小王的图片剪成头部四肢可以组合移动的，类似皮影动画的道具，
编上号码，让他的女儿来做拼图游戏，看看她脑海中爸爸的生活是什么
样的。

Driver Xiaowang and His Daughter, 2007
Photographs

Xiao Wang comes from Hebei and makes a living as a driver, I often use his
services. He has a four year s old little girl, going to a kindergarten out of the
fifth ring road in Beijing. Each day after work Xiao Wang goes to pick up his
daughter. Does his daughter know what he is doing? I asked her already. It
seems that what she is the most familiar with are the scenes with her father
after his work. In fact, part of Xiao Wang s life is constituted by what he
imagined to enter his daughter's world.
I cut Xiao Wang's pictures separating and reassembling head and members
like a shadow theatre's puppet, I numbered them and asked his daughter to
make a picture puzzle, to see her own vision of her father's life.

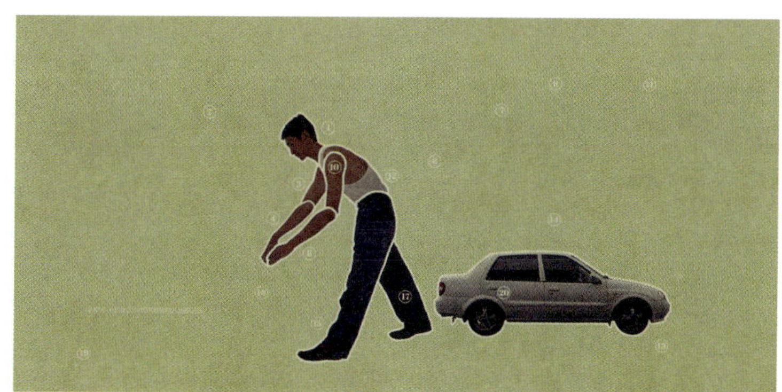

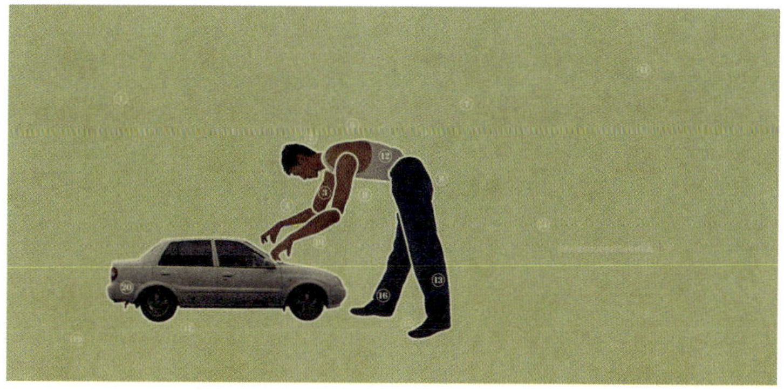

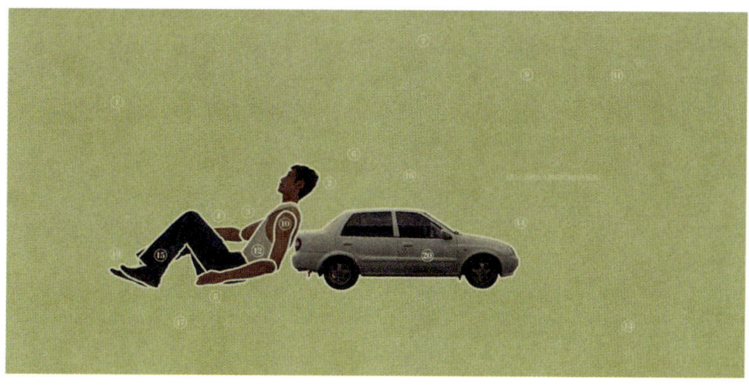

苏文祥

SUN WENXIANG

作为艺术家，你在创作中所关心的是什么？以一件作品为例，分享你的创作过程。
能否发现一些有意思的东西，一些秘密，然后可以跟别人分享这个东西还可以这样，或者那样。
比如对电视机长期监视和把玩，带着它从上海到了北京，最后做了一个东西叫《有限电视》。

如果你是一个批评家，你会从什么角度来阐释和讨论你自己的创作？
会从批评家的角度，会从非常特别的角度。

在你的创作和思考中，什么书籍和艺术家曾经或正在影响着你？
《射雕英雄传》、约翰·凯奇。

你是怎样判断和决定在什么语境下呈现你的哪些作品的？你是怎样看待作品呈现的语境和作品的关系的？
在哪里呈现哪些作品，大部分时候是由别人来挑选、来决定的。判断决定这个事就像是两股力量的博弈，尤其是艺术家年轻的时候。艺术家们一辈子都是在争取这个权利。

如何在创作上形成了现在的面貌，描述一下近年来作品的发展和变化？
还没有固定的面貌，隔一段时间就变化一下。从为一个展览创作或者为一个感觉创作变成为自己创作。

你会在什么情况下摧毁你自己的作品？

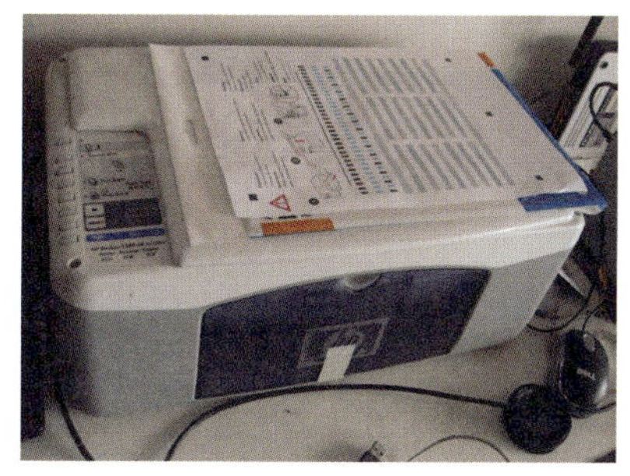

惠普Deskjet F388彩色打印机。
HP Deskjet F388 color printer

我不会毁自己的东西。一个东西要不要留下，其实是由他人来决定的，不仅仅是自己。如果是摧毁一个作品的想法那另当别论。

你怎么看待艺术史和艺术家创作的关系？
艺术家创作是正在吃东西，或者是正在做吃的。艺术史呢是一本的菜单，里面有一些关于菜的点评。

在你的工作中，理性和情感冲动各自扮演着什么样的角色？
一般不太会有莫名的情感冲动，只对人有这个。理性可以让你活着，偶尔有情感冲动会使你活的像个人。

逐渐消失的两元，2007
行为、装置

The Disappearing 2RMB, 2007
Performance and Installation

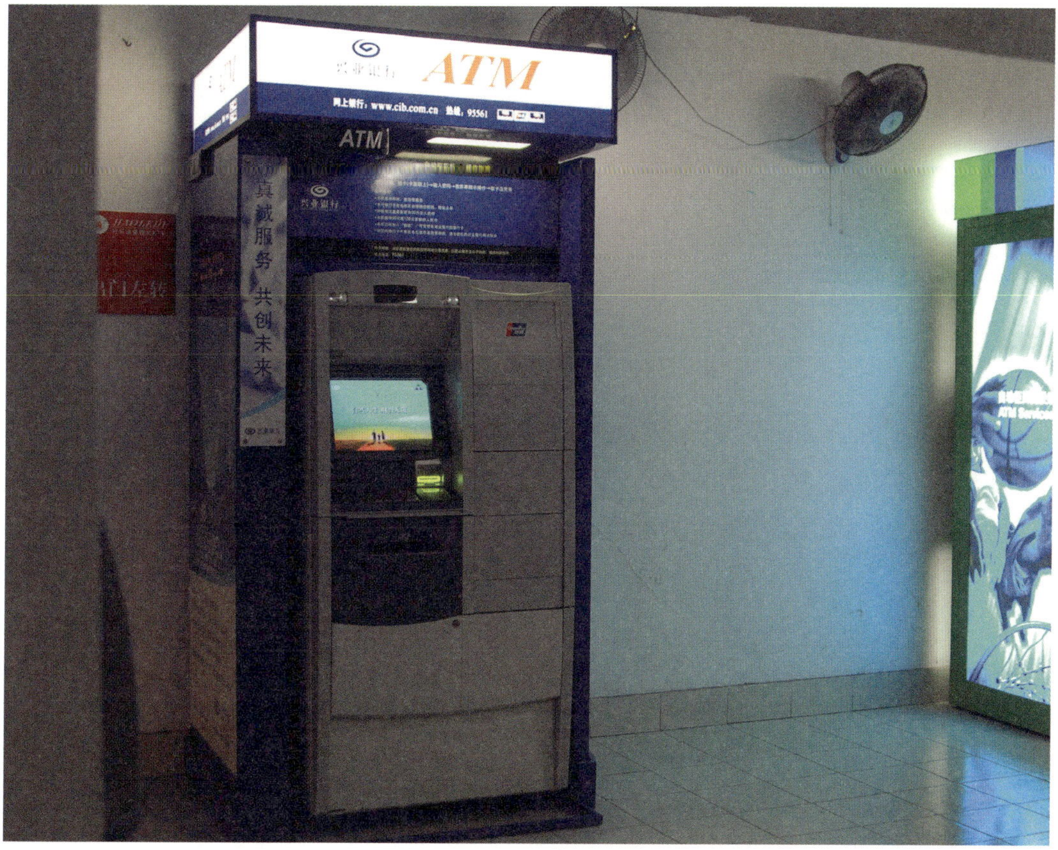

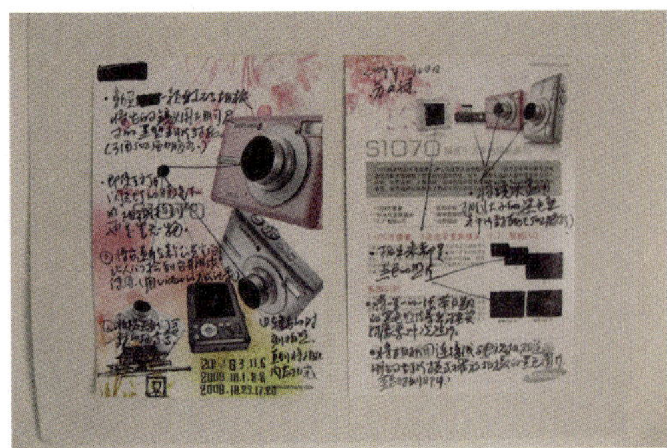

《北京时间》方案图，2009年
The graphic plan of *Beijing Time* (2009)

北京时间，2009
综合媒介，蒙住镜头的相机和它拍摄的照片
循环、有声、尺寸不定

Beijing Time, 2009
Mixed Meadia - Lens Covered Camera with Photoes Took By It
Loop, Sound, Undefined Size

As an artist, what do you care most during working? Could you please give an example to introduce the process of your work for us?

I care more about the possibility of discovering something really interesting, some secrets that I might share with others and that may create something out of my expectation.

For instance, I kept a long term observation on TV, playing with it like a toy and bringing it with me all the way from Shanghai to Beijing. This finally gave form to a work entitled *Limited TV Channel*.

Suppose you are a critic, from what perspective would you explain and comment on your works?

I would comment on my work from a critic's viewpoint and from a very unique angle.

What books and which artists have had, or are having an influence on your way of thinking and working?

The Legend of the Eagle Shooting Heroes and John Cage.

How do you make judgment and decision as to in what context you'd like to present your works? According to you, in what way is the context created by the work related to the work itself?

The decision of where to present which work is mostly subject to

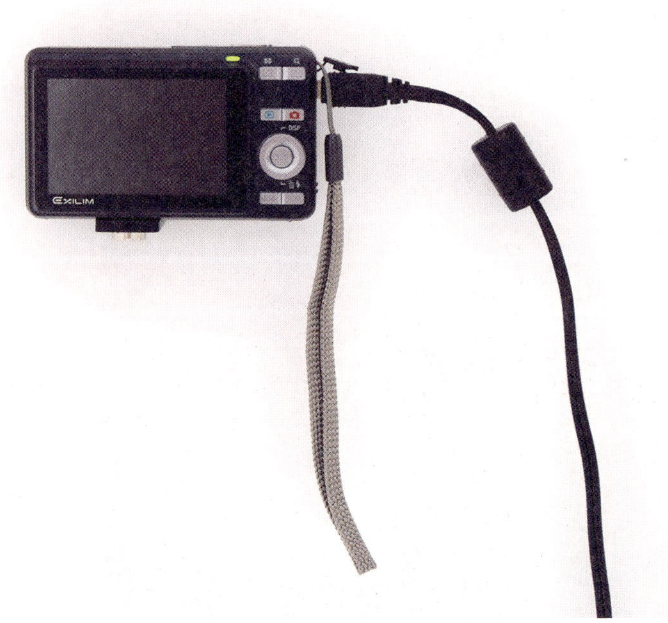

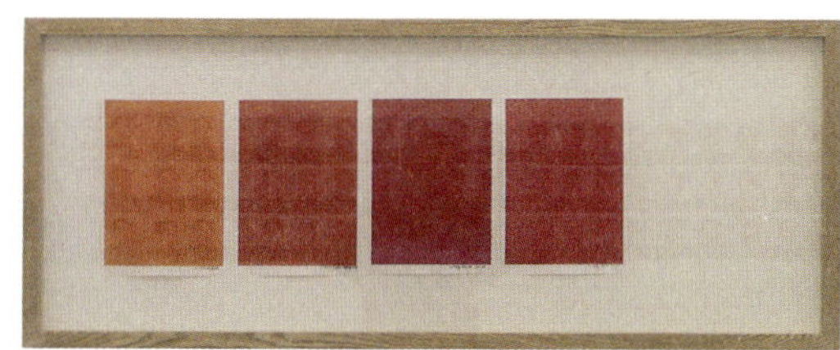

M100，Y100（未完成），2009
HP Deskjet F388彩色打印机打印的相纸
29.7 × 21cm × 12

M100, Y100 (Unfinished), 2009
Photo paper, color print by HP Deskjet F388
29.7 × 21cm × 12

五色令人目盲，2009
宝丽莱600相纸，8.8 × 10.8cm × 10张
将相机里装好的相纸取出，再装进去，得到自动曝光的照片。

The oneness of the five colors blinds the eyes，2009
Polaroid 600 photo papers, 8.8 × 10.8 cm × 10
Take out the photo paper which had already been equipped in the Polaroid
camera, then you get the white photos which are already automatically exposed.

choices by others. The judgment and decision of this matter is a bit like a game between two forces, especially for artists in the early stage of their career. Artists have been fighting for the right throughout their lives.

How does your work take the present shape? And please give a few words about the latest development and changes in your work.

I don't have any established style yet. I would change my focus after a period of time, now shifting from working for a show or a flash of sentiments to working for my own sake.

In what circumstances would you want to destroy your own creation?

I wouldn't do that. Actually the artist is not alone in deciding on the fate of a work; the right also belongs to the other people. But if that is a working concept, it will be another case.

What do you think about the relation between the art history and artist's work?

An artist's work is eating food or making some food to eat. The art history is a menu, which keeps a record of some comments on the food.

What kind of roles would rational thinking and emotional impulse respectively play in your work?

Usually I won't have impulse for no reason, except towards human beings.
Rationality keeps you alive; occasional impulse would make you live like a real man.

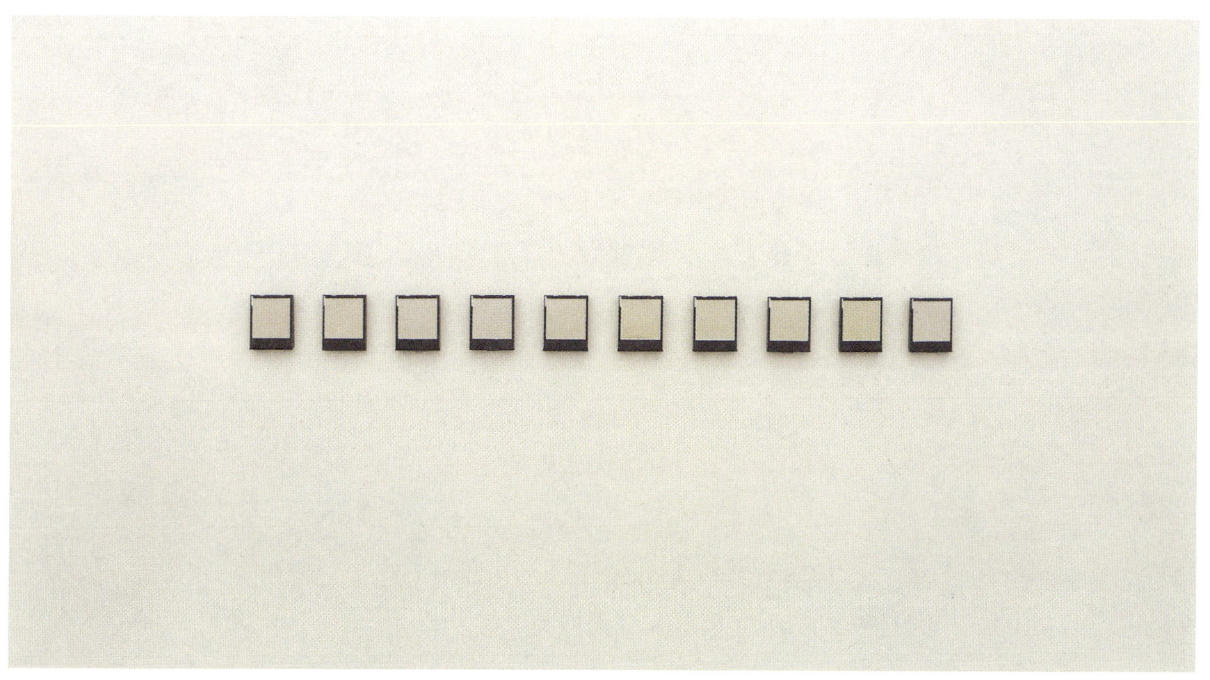

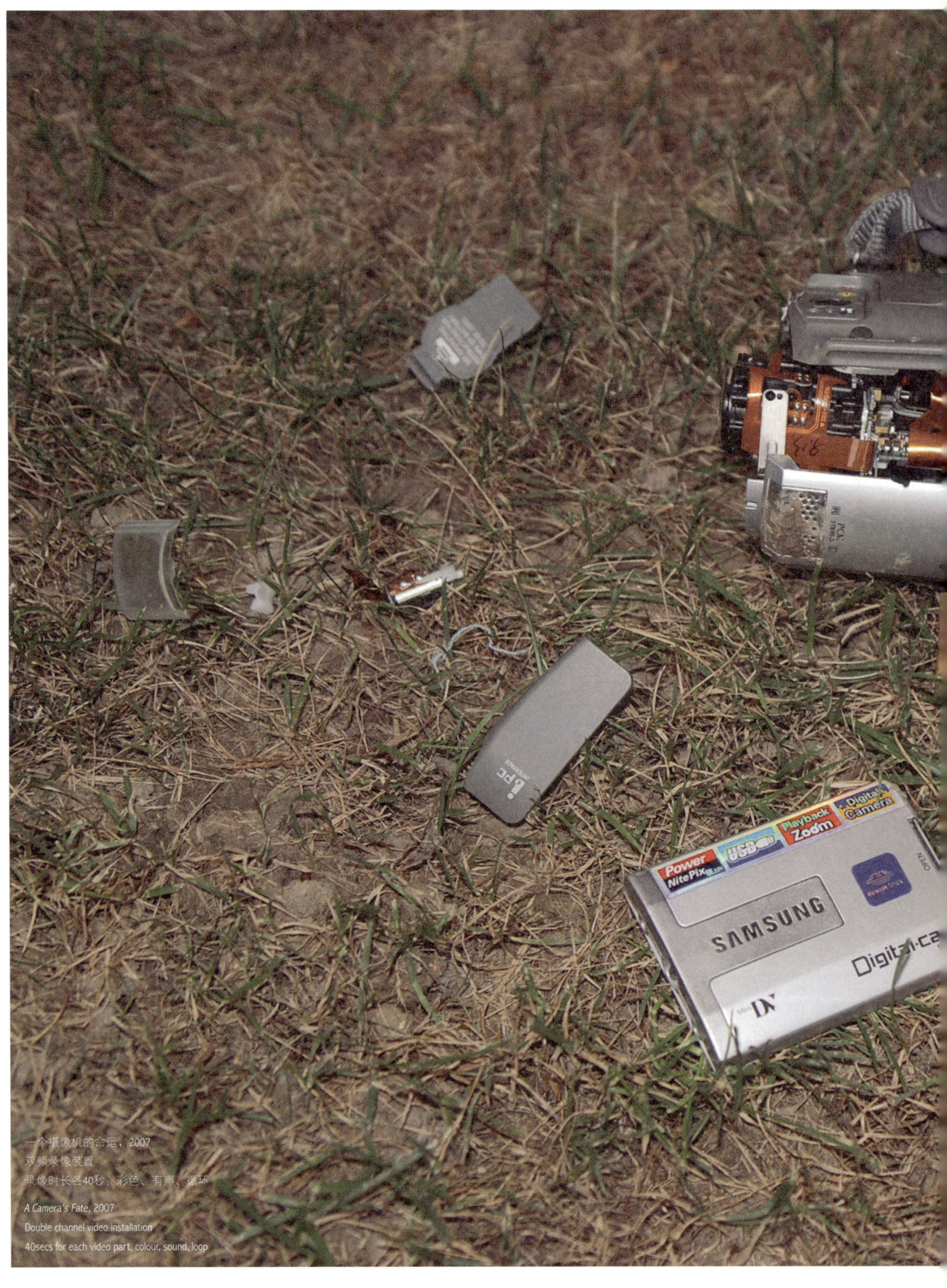

一个摄像机的命运，2007
双频录像装置
录像时长各40秒；彩色、有声、循环

A Camera's Fate, 2007
Double channel video installation
40secs for each video part, colour, sound, loop

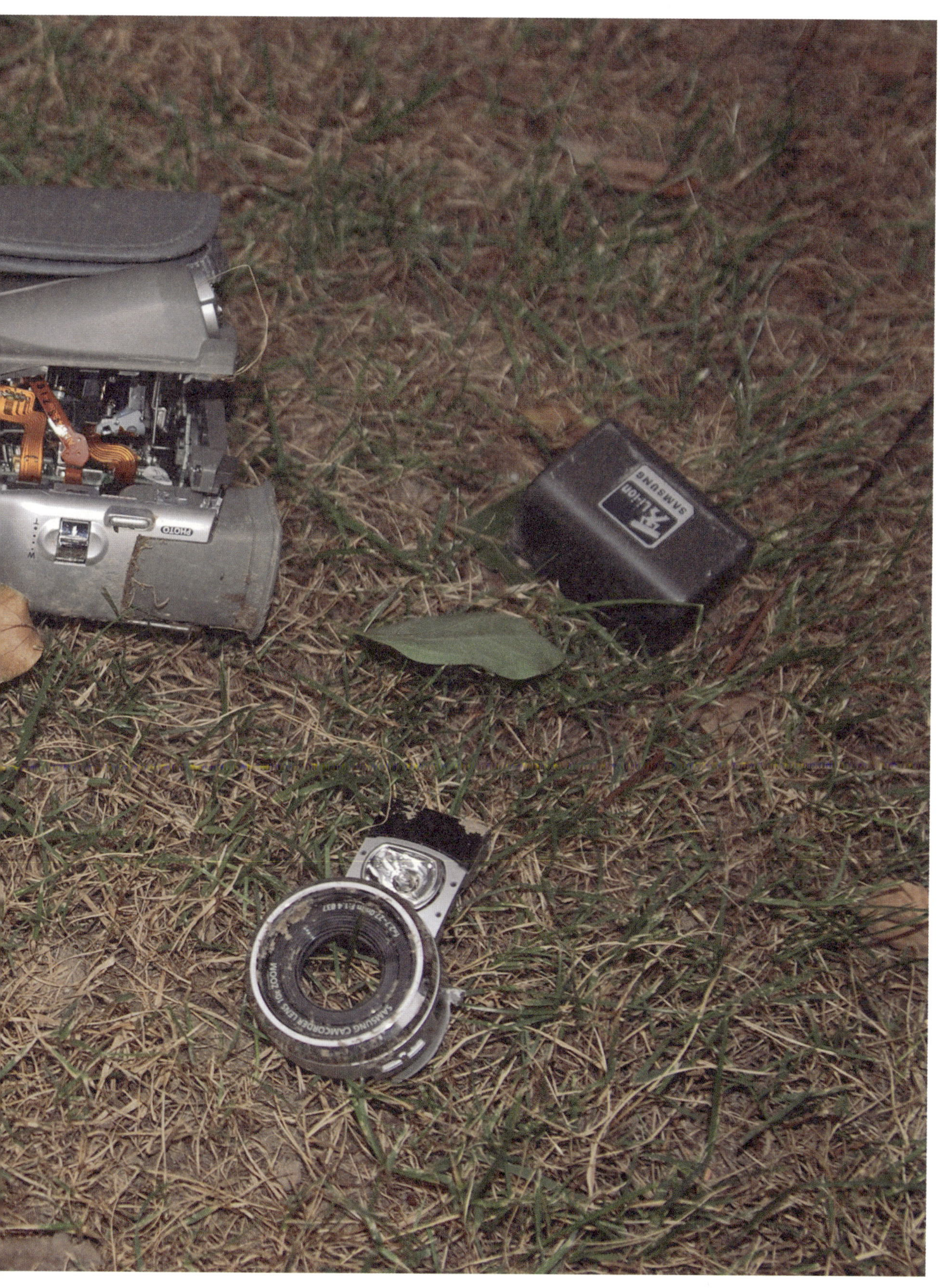
SAMSUNG
Li-ion
PHOTO
T W
SAMSUNG CAMCORDER LENS

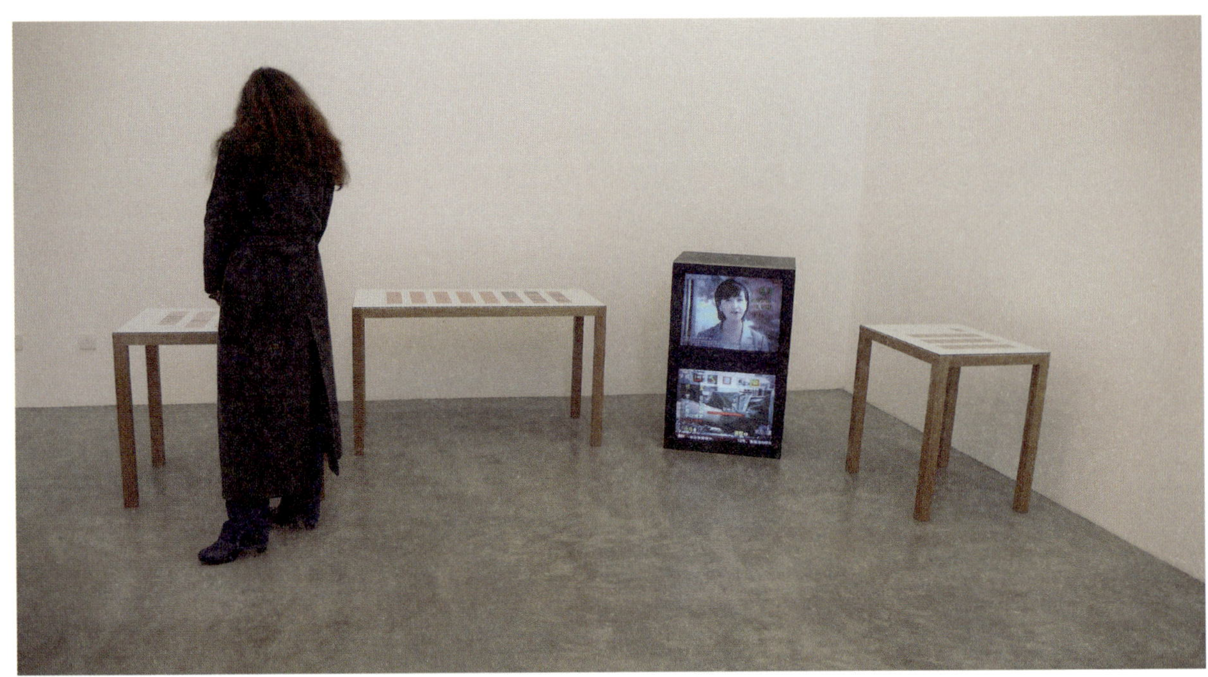

有限电视频道, 2008
录像装置
纸上数码输出3幅，122×55cm、80×55cm、65×55cm
两个电视机，录像Ⅰ，7分33秒；录像Ⅱ，3分07秒；均为彩色、有声、循环

Limited TV Channel, 2008
Video installation
3 prints on paper, 122 × 55 cm, 80 × 55 cm, 65 × 55 cm.
2 monitors; video Part I, 7min 33secs, colour, sound, loop; video Part Ⅱ, 3min 7secs, colour, sound, loop

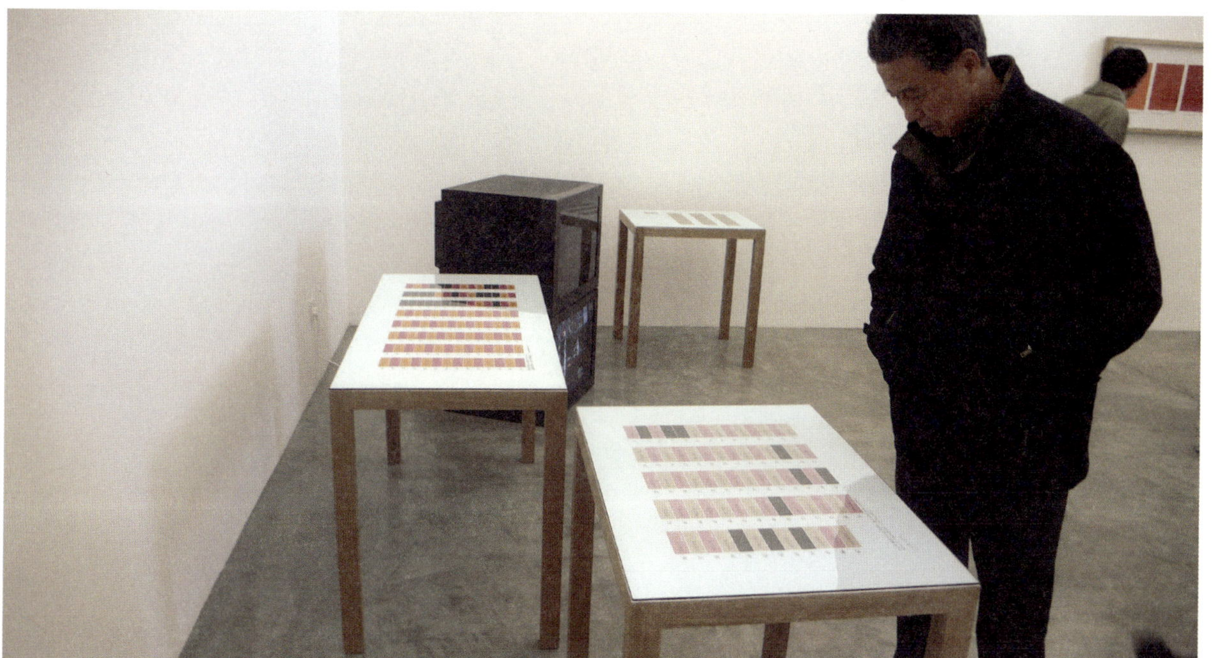

孙建春

SUN JIANCHUN

作为艺术家，你在创作中所关心的是什么？以一件作品为例，分享你的创作过程。

从现实层面看，我一直比较关心社会变迁形成的相对微观的社群政治和社群情感。

2006年，我创作了作品《中国，2006》，我每天都重复了一件同样的事，从互联网上选取了一张当日的新闻图片并把它以绘画的方式记录下来，当这年结束的时候，我有了一件由365个画面和相关的文字叙述构成的完整的作品《中国 2006》，有了一个我个人私辑的一个公元2006年的中国的"图像编年史"。这件作品完全是从微观社会学的角度来观察社会群体间在变迁中形成的观念变化，以此来考察中国独特的现代性。

如果你是一个批评家，你会从什么角度来阐释和讨论你自己的创作？

没有特别的角度，一贯性相对更重要。

在你的创作和思考中，什么书籍和艺术家曾经或正在影响着你？

中国宋代的绘画曾经并仍在影响我。

你是怎样判断和决定在什么语境下呈现你的哪些作品的？你是怎样看待作品呈现的语境和作品的关系的？

语境和作品的关系是相互依存的，具体的作品需要对应具体的语境，作品呈现的是一组复杂对应的关系，没有语境往往便没有作品。

如何在创作上形成了现在的面貌，描述一下近年来作品的发展

和变化？

创作面貌的变化是个相对复杂的问题，任何细节都可能导致认识上的变化，近几年，我更关注中国近三十年的社会变革中的个体的观念改变和呈现。我趋向于认为中国社会30年正在建立一种全新的美学体系，这一体系有待进一步认识和理解。

你会在什么情况下摧毁你自己的作品？

任何情况下我都舍不得，哪怕是碎片，我也收藏。

你怎么看待艺术史和艺术家创作的关系？

艺术家创作是个人的事，艺术史是公共的事。就创作本身而言，两者没关系；就认识而言，艺术史是艺术创作的上下文语境。

在你的工作中，理性和情感冲动各自扮演着什么样的角色？

理性放在面上，情感放在下面。

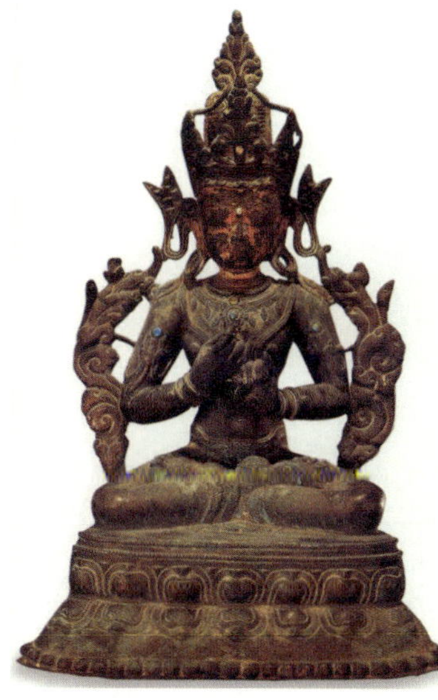

毗卢遮那佛像，元
铜
高36cm
北京故宫博物院

Vairochana Buddha, Yuan Dynasty
Copper
36 cm in height
The Palace Museum, Beijing

我很好
摄影

I'm fine
Photography

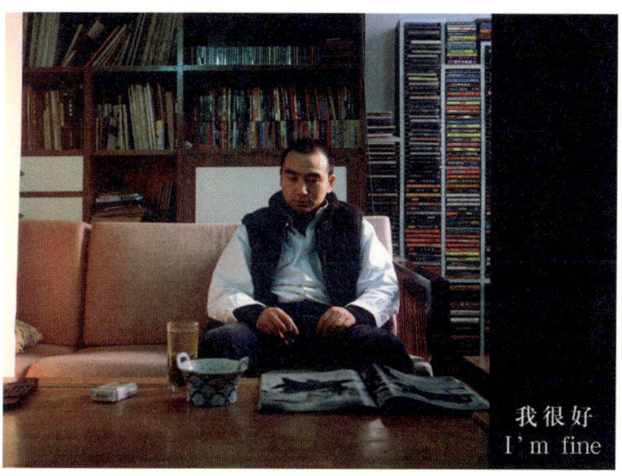

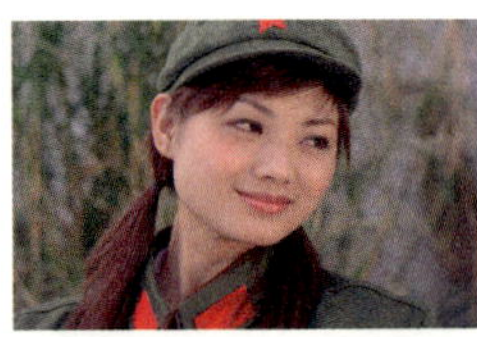

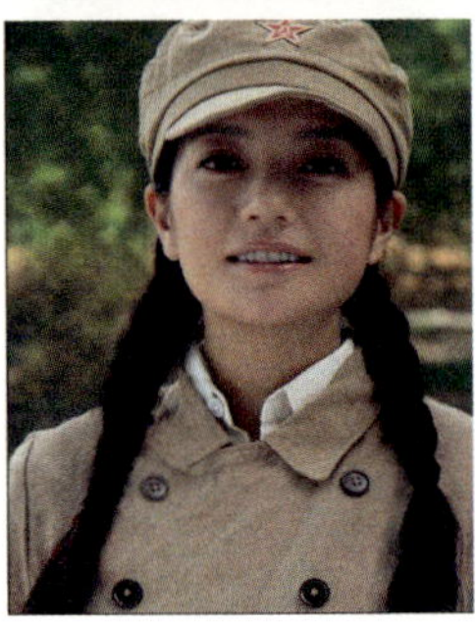

军装美女
（来自"东方军事"，URL: http.mil.eastday.com）

A pretty girl posing in military uniform
(Retrieved access: *The Oriental Military*, URL: http://mil.eastday.com)

作品草图
Work Plan

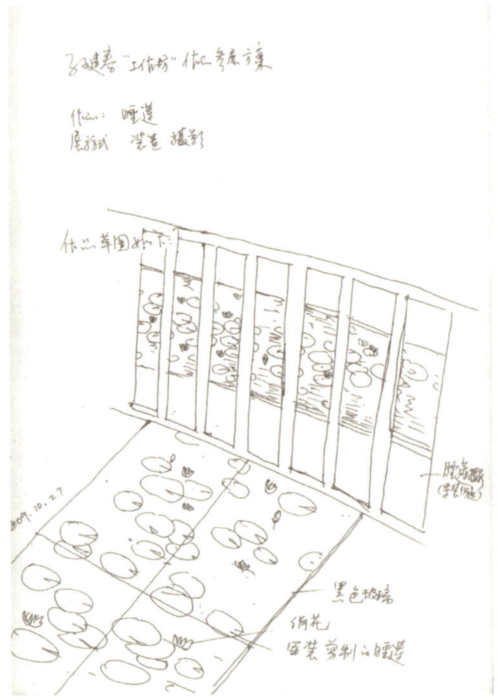

As an artist, what do you care most during working? Could you please give an example to introduce the process of your work for us?

Such relatively micro issues as group politics and group feelings as a result of social changes have always been my focus.

In 2006 I finished *China, 2006*. Every day I chose a news photo from the Internet and paint it. So, by the end of that year, I had a collection of 365 photos and captions. They make up a complete work *China, 2006*, an "image chronicle" about China in 2006, my private collection. From the perspective of micro-sociology, it reveals the unique Chinese modernity by taking notice of how social groups change their mentality as society transforms.

Suppose you are a critic, from what perspective would you explain and comment on your works?

To me, there is no specific perspective. Consistency is fairly important.

What books and which artists have had, or are having an influence on your way of thinking and working?

Chinese paintings in Song Dynasty.

How do you make judgment and decision as to in what context you'd like to present your works? According to you, in what way is the context created by the work related to the work itself? According to you, in what way is the context created by the work related to the work itself?

Context and works are interdependent. Different works require different contexts. What a work shows is a set of complicated correlations. Generally speaking, there would be no works without context.

How does your work take the present shape? And please give a few words about the latest development and changes in your work.

To talk about changes in my works is not something easy. Any detail may lead to changes in understanding. In recent years I have been focusing more on how the individuals changed and their mentality as society changed in the past thirty years. I tend to believe that a new system of aesthetics was being developed in these thirty years. There is a lot to learn about it.

In what circumstances would you want to destroy your own creation?

Under no circumstances will I part with my works, and I will keep everything, even the smallest bits.

What do you think about the relation between the art history and artist's work?

An artist's career belongs to an individual, but history of art belongs to all. As far as creation is concerned, there is no bond between them; in terms of knowledge, history of art provides a context for creation.

What kind of roles would rational thinking and emotional impulse respectively play in your work?

In my works, reason is made visible, while emotion is covered.

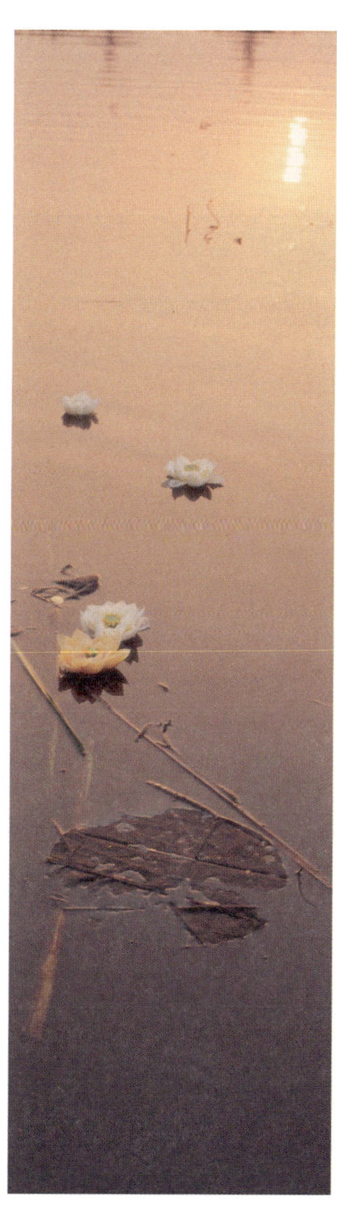

军装·睡莲
Military Uniform - Water Lilies

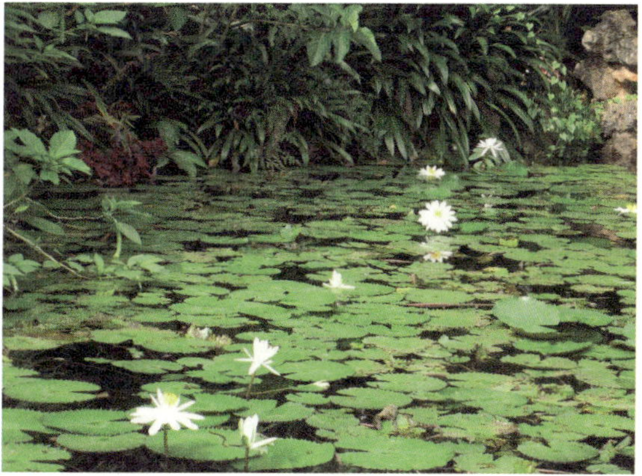

睡莲
Water lilies

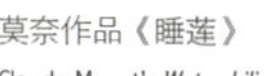

莫奈作品《睡莲》
Claude Monet's *Water Lilies*

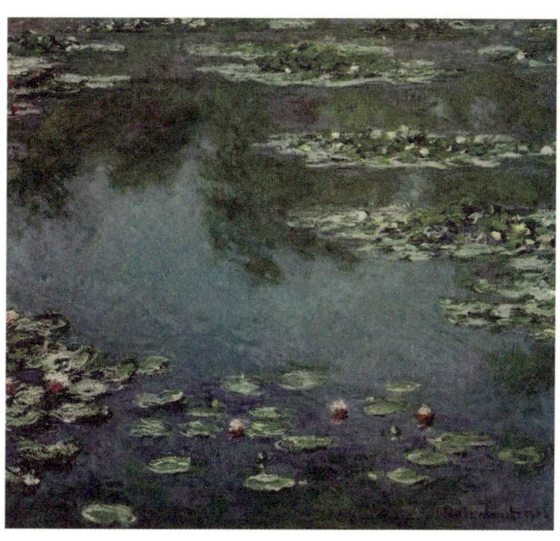

作品也许本身就是一个骗局。一个关于伪造和虚构的骗局。

在我的作品里,这首先是个关于距离的骗局，"睡莲"自身的文化符号和作品刻意的样式给人很直接的东方感。——一切都是伪造的。而伪造这美丽的图景的恰恰是现实的牢笼.

在东方的文化传统中,睡莲永远是美好的、浪漫的、静谧的、……在佛教中,它甚至是救赎的、极乐的。军装则是国家和毒品,无法摆脱的依赖,它在政治和国家的名义下炮制着罪恶又庇护着规则与秩序。它是政治的、权力的、暴力的、革命的、规训的、杀戮的……我的努力使它们获得了视觉上可能的和谐.

我一直试图寻找一种可能的方式来接续东方精神中的"静谧"和"超然"，那是被我们遗失的对世界的观看和判断方式，尤其在今天它对中国的现代性建设中对西方的"盲从"是有修正有着特殊的意义。这种观看和表达的一体性提供了一种可能的途径来弥补现代性带来的缺陷和危机.它所替代的不仅仅是视觉形式的东方化,更重要的是对本土的图像语言在今天语境下的探索。

军装·睡莲
Military Uniform - Water Lilies

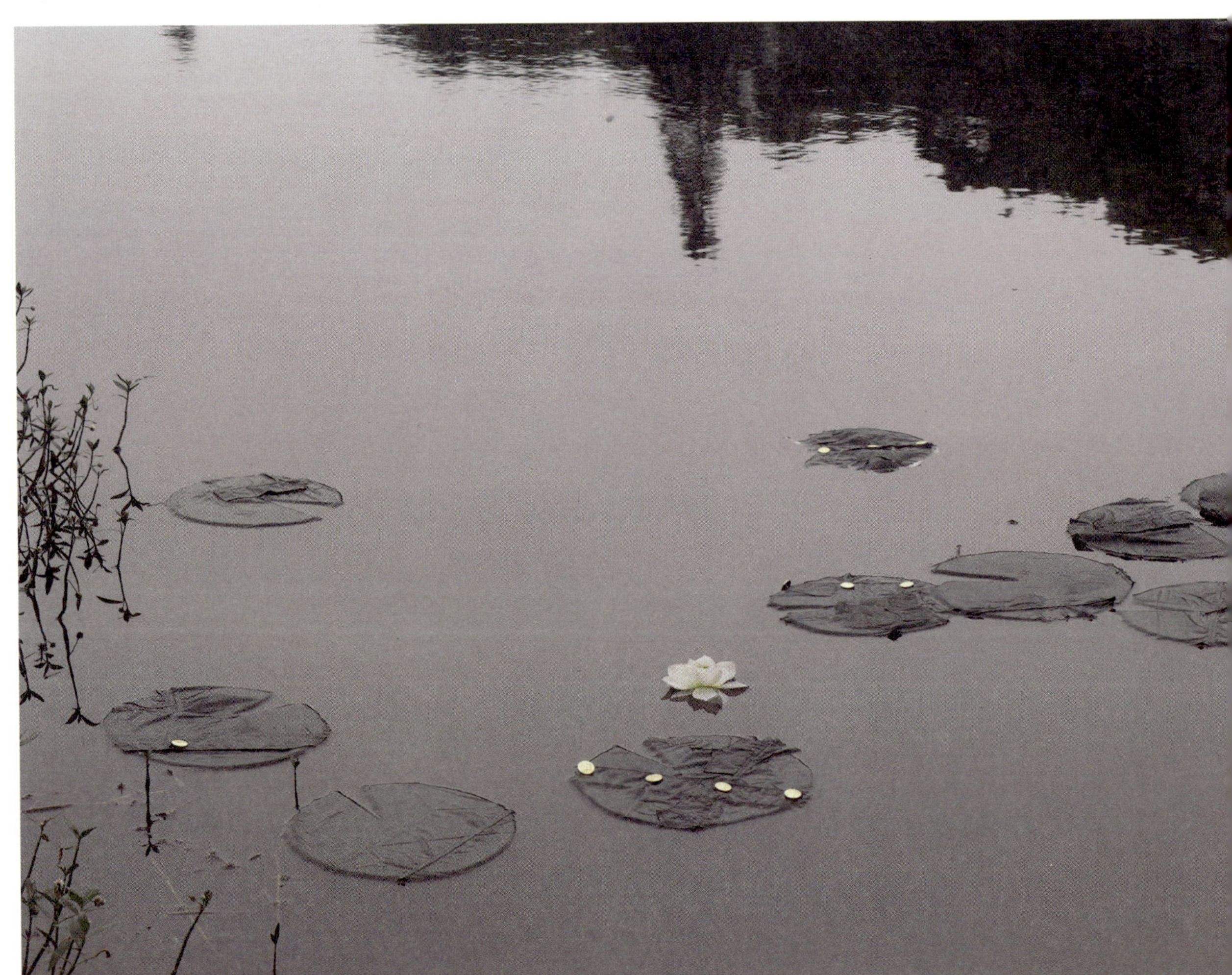

A work is a deception itself, a deception about fabrication.
In my works, it is, above all, a deception about distance. Both the "water lilies" as a cultural symbol and the particular organization as a work are easily associated with the Orient. However, it is all about fabrication. What fabricated the beautiful scene is nothing but the cage of reality.   In eastern cultural tradition, a water lily always symbolizes beauty, romance and tranquility; in Buddhism, it even stands for salvation and the seventh heaven. By contrast, a military uniform stands for the state and drug, as they are hard to do without. In the name of politics and the state, it brings about evil while keeping order. It involves politics, power, violence, revolution, discipline and killing... My efforts give them a kind of harmony that is visually possible.
I have been in the pursuit of a possible way to retain the "tranquility" and "transcendence" inherent in the eastern psyche. They used to constitute our way for observing and making judgment of the world but unfortunately got lost. In present China where modernization is on its way, it can surely offer great significance in redressing the "blind conformism" in relation to the West because the unity of observation and expression can help to make up for the negative effects and crisis as by-products of modernity. In addition to the visual feature of eastern style it replaces, it is more importantly an exploration of the native image language in a contemporary context.

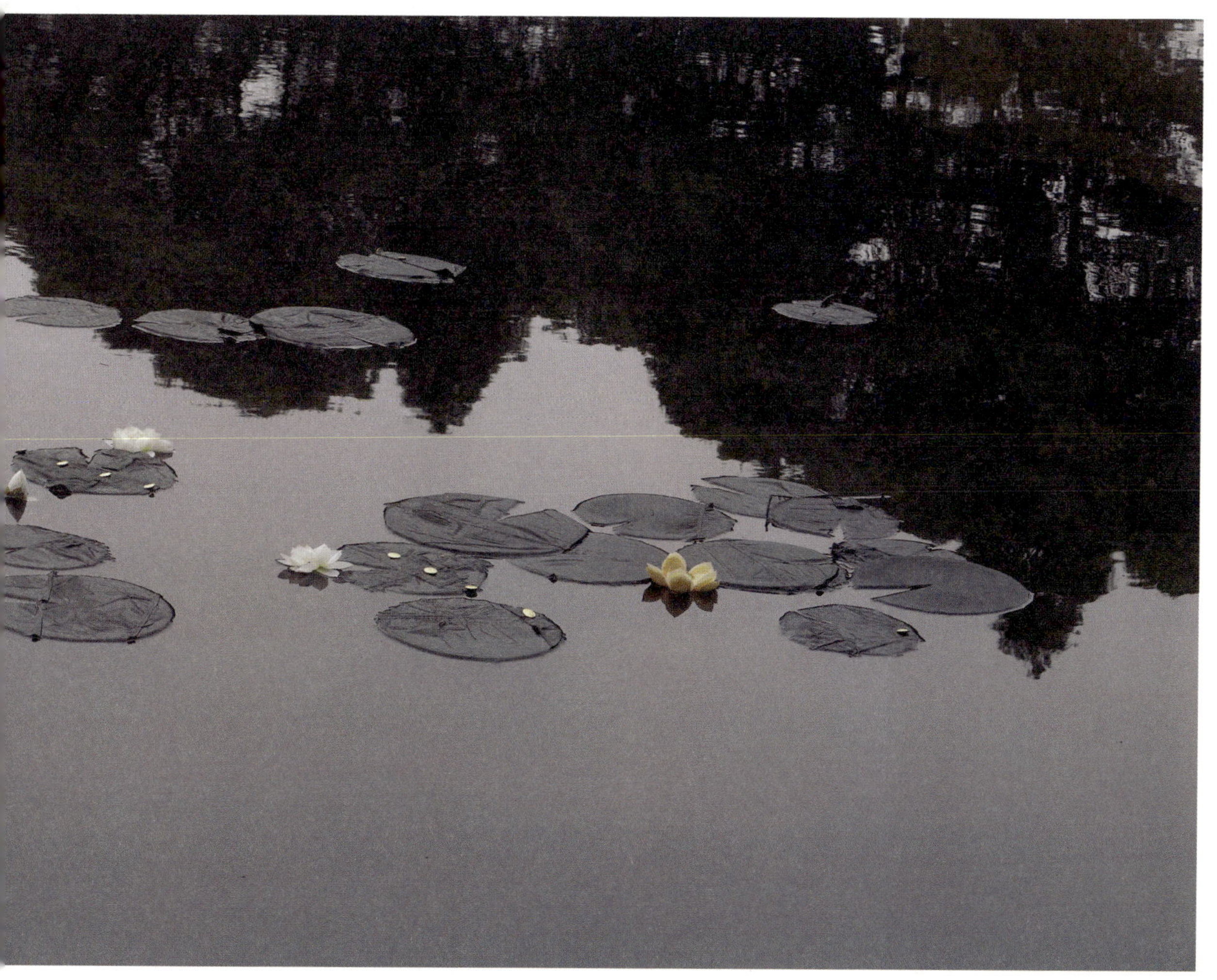

军装·睡莲
Military Uniform - Water Lilies

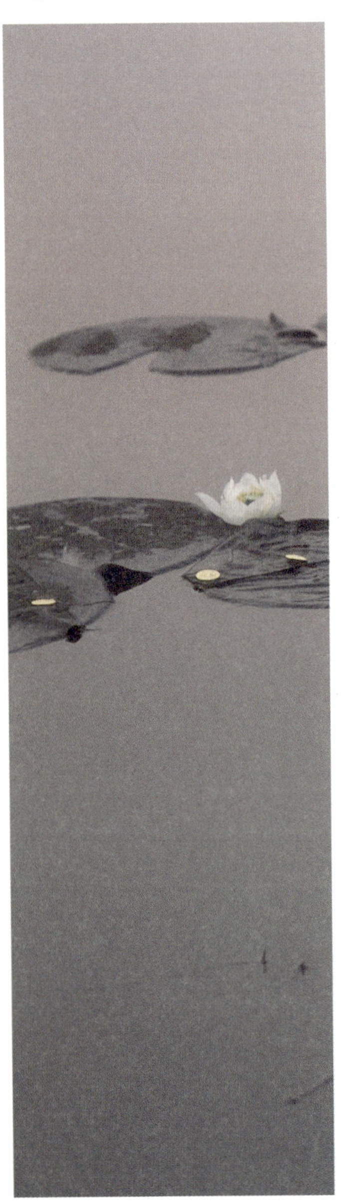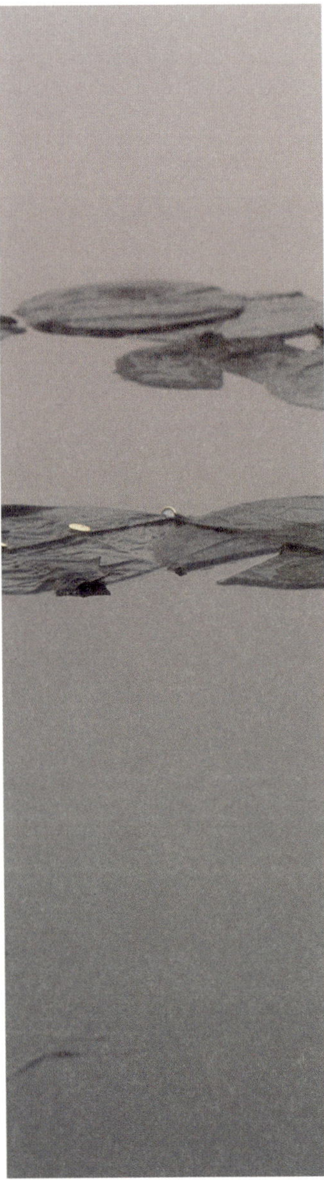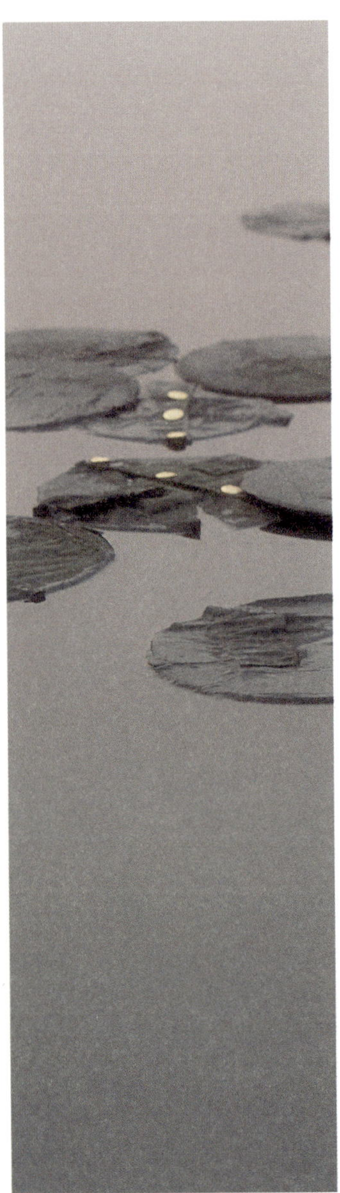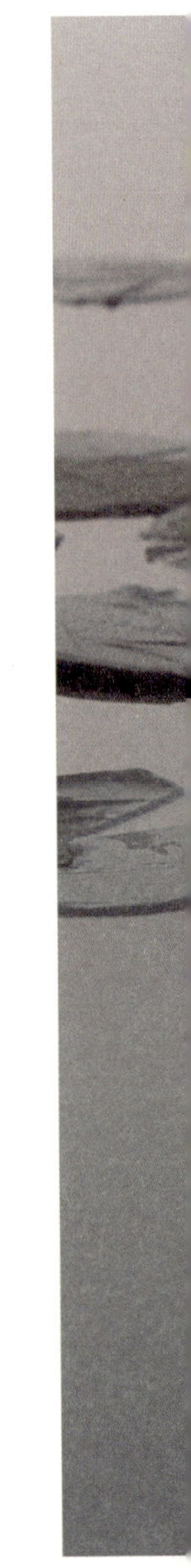

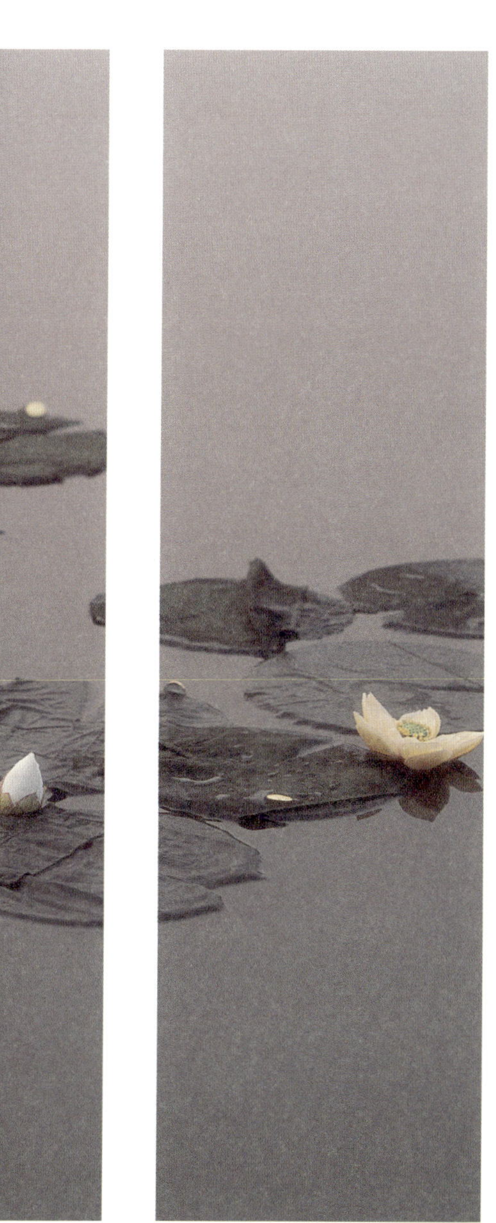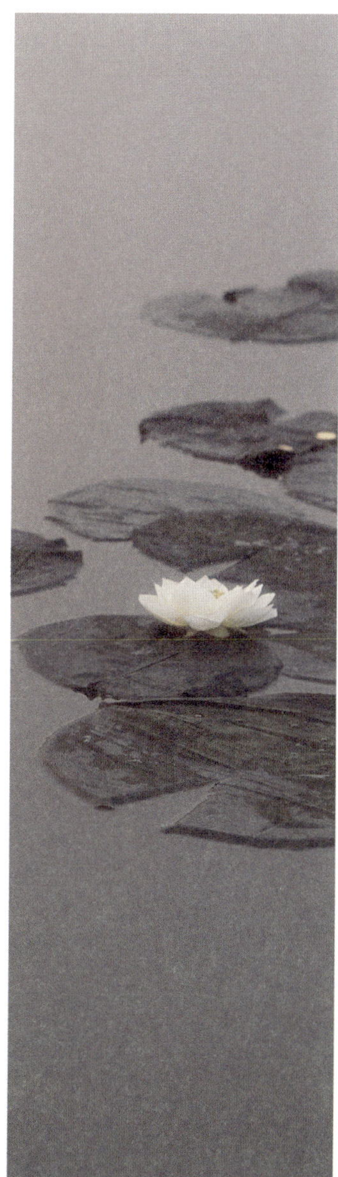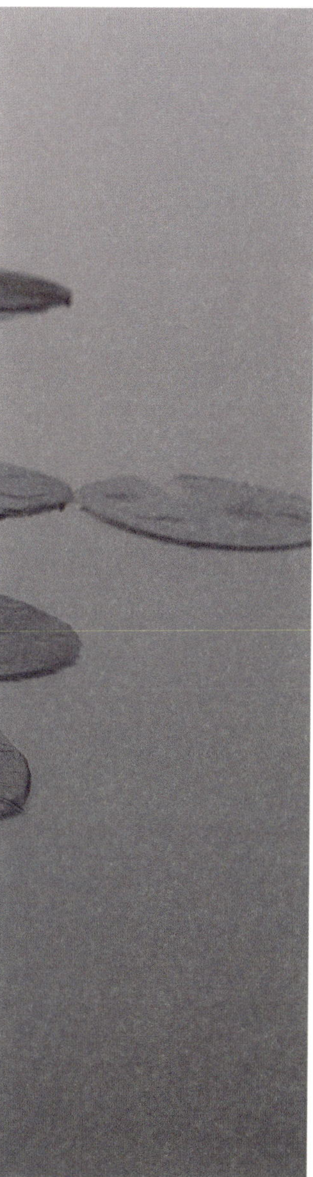

汤 艺

TANG YI

作为艺术家，你在创作中所关心的是什么？以一件作品为例，分享你的创作过程。

我关心的是在作品的构思、发问和答疑、成型和实施的过程中引发的思考和经验（结论）。当然更多的时候得不到经验（结论），只能得到体验，体验对他人来说难以表述而且毫无意义。所以偏执的思考和盲目的结论很重要。

创作过程可以陈述，但是很难分享。你的享受也许对他人是苦难。所以观者自酌吧。要说的话，我想提的是《一把药丸》，这是从《一颗糖》这件作品发展出来的。《一颗糖》是模拟一颗抽象的球状物体从同一个点出发弹跳出的四种（强——次强——次弱——弱）轨迹。而在《一把药丸》里，这些轨迹分为两组：一组轨迹来自于同一个点、朝向不同的方向，他们都规规矩矩、符合自然规律的正常的渐弱式微；在其对面的一组轨迹就是一把药丸假设在混乱的外力条件下发疯的乱弹，他们不符合任何自然规律，塑造他们的过程与其说是抽象创作，不如说是发疯发泄。

如果你是一个批评家，你会从什么角度来阐释和讨论你自己的创作？

这应该是在一个艺术家晚年的时候讨论的问题。如果必须要现在讨论的话，我希望能从尊重生物的多样性法则的角度和反进化论的角度来看待我的创作。我希望我的创作被看作类型的实验和状态的实验。

在你的创作和思考中，什么书籍和艺术家曾经或正在影响着你？

书籍很难说全，暂列两本：《爱因斯坦晚年文集》、《我为什么要写作》（奥威尔）

艺术家有：达芬奇、博西、博伊斯、霍普、Olarf Eliasson、Francis Aly。

你是怎样判断和决定在什么语境下呈现你的哪些作品的？你是怎样看待作品呈现的语境和作品的关系的？

当作品和当时的语境有所呼应或冲突的时候呈现作品才更有意思，这种呼应不是矫情的牵强附会的呼应，而是经得起客观和大多数观众推敲的。严格说来，作品呈的语境是作品的一部分，只有在特定的关联和呼应之下作品才成立。

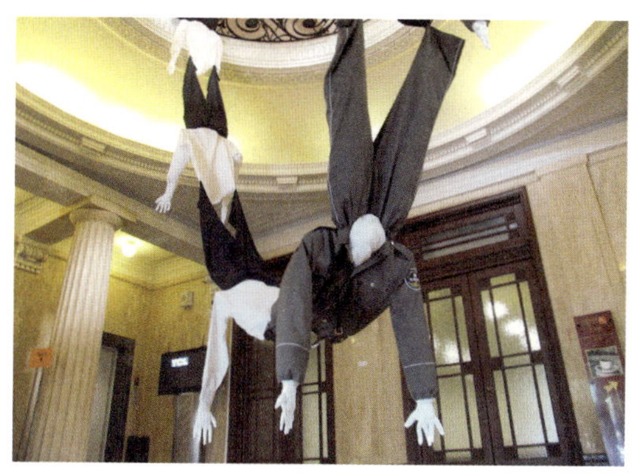

国王、奴隶和上帝，2007
装置
现成品衣物，木头，纤维棉

King, Slave and God, 2007
Installation View
Clothing, wood, fiber cotton

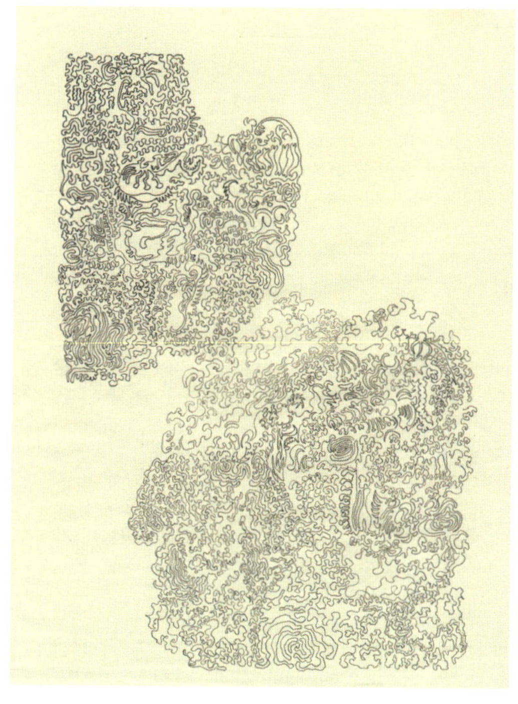

抽思，2003
纸本钢笔
28cm x 20cm x 16

Silky Mood, 2003
ink on flimsy by pen
28cm x 20cm x 16

如何在创作上形成了现在的面貌，描述一下近年来作品的发展和变化？

首先是对记录和描述宇宙规律的主题感兴趣。在科学的求知方向上反其道而行之，探索另一种假设条件下事物可能出现的形态和面貌。比如：重力失效、时间凝固、物质和能量转移暂停……呈现出来的比如：物体运动的轨迹、对自然现象的人工模仿、以及某种关于数据的景观营造……

其次是对人性的心灵化程度的追问。人究竟有多少种面目？人性是如何成长的？何为扭曲何为健康？价值观是如何被影响和误导的？为生产而生产、为消费而消费能否解释一切人类的阴霾？……很多人在宗教里找到了答案。体现在创作上就是关于自身精神状态的描述、摹画和表现。

这两个方向一直都同时存在、互相影响和渗透、有时密不可分。

你会在什么情况下摧毁你自己的作品？

不需要去摧毁作品，被自己否定的作品自然而然会被遗忘和忽略，就等于被摧毁了。

你怎么看待艺术史和艺术家创作的关系？

历史是个变量，艺术史亦然。关于历史，争论永远比结论更可靠、也更有意思。

艺术家的创作对于编撰史论者而言只是编写的材料，对材料的取舍有很多主观因素，很难真实客观的再现和评论艺术家的创作。

在全球化的当代社会，大致上是越接近社会上层建筑的金字塔顶端的艺术家，在艺术史上的名字越大。资本搭台文化唱戏是老生常谈的道理。但是在中国这样从物质生产到精神生产都十分混乱并急于转型的社会，最大的规律就是没规律。

在你的工作中，理性和情感冲动各自扮演着什么样的角色？

理性是骨架，情感冲动是肉，高兴了就多长肉，不高兴了皮包骨。一滩软肉或者一具骷髅也是有可能出现的。但我个人还是喜欢瘦骨嶙峋的作品，显得干练、仙风道骨。

**As an artist, what do you care most during working?
Could you please give an example to introduce the process
of your work for us?**

I care about thoughts and experience (conclusion) deriving from
the process of conceiving, questioning and question-answering,
forming, and completing of a work. Sure, more often what I get is
not experience (conclusion), only feelings, which are difficult to share
with others and thus is meaningless. So, eccentric thinking and blind
conclusion are very important.

It's possible to give a presentation for my working process, but to
share with others is hard, as one's enjoyment could become others'
suffering. So, just leave the question to viewers.

If I have to say a few words about it, I'll give *A Handful of Pills* as an
example, which develops from the work *Lemon Drop*. *Lemon Drop*
reproduces four trajectories (from strongest to less strong, from
weakest to less weak) of an abstract spherical object bouncing off
from the same spot, while in *A Handful of Pills*, there are two groups
of trajectories: one group start from a common point moving in
different directions, with changes based on the law of nature; the
opposite group simulate the courses of a handful of pills bouncing
wildly under a chaotic external force. The latter shows no sign of
natural laws. The process of creating them is not so much work of
making abstract art as a way of venting emotions.

**Suppose you are a critic, what perspective would you talk
about and explain you work from?**

This seems to be a question for an artist to ponder in his/her
remaining years. If we have to discuss this now, I wish my work can
be viewed from antievolution perspective and with respect for the
variety of life. I hope my artistic creation could be considered as
experimentation of type and state.

**What books and which artists have had, or is having an
influence on your way of thinking and working?**

It's hard to list out them all; I just give two books here: *Albert
Einstein: Out of My Later Years* , *Why I Write* by George Orwell.
The artists who have influenced me include Leonardo da Vinci,
Hieronymus Bosch, Joseph Beuys, Matt Hope, Olarf Eliasson, Francis
Alys.

**How do you decide the context in which your work is to be
presented? How do you consider the relation of the context
with your work?**

It will look more interesting when the piece responds to or even runs
in conflict with the actual context. The connection between them
must not be reluctant and forced, but must stand up to objective
critique from the majority. Strictly speaking, the viewing context
where the work is engaged is part of the work and the work is
dependent on the relation between them.

**How does your work take the present shape? And please
give a few words about the latest development and changes
in your work.**

My interest first of all lies in subjects of recording and depicting
patterns of the universe, following a path reverse to scientific way
of learning to explore the possible forms and appearances of things
under another hypothetic condition, such as the failure of gravity,
the freeze of time, the pause in material and energy transmission,
etc. Visual representations in my work include the trajectory of

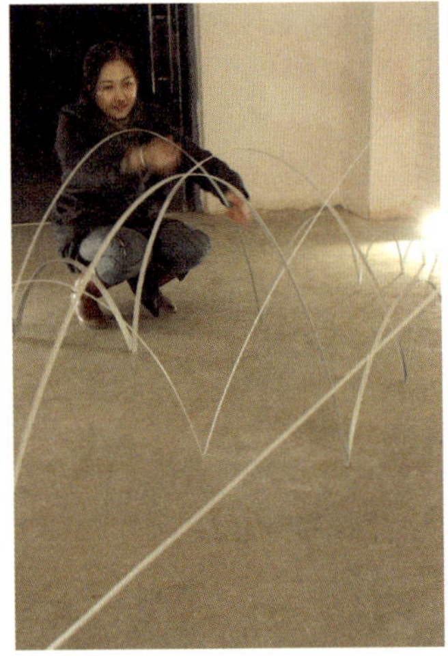

艺术家在工作现场。
The artist at work

moving object, artificial simulation of natural phenomenon, a sort of landscape-structure based on data...
My next interest is inquiries on the degree of spirituality of humanity. How many faces does man have? How does human nature evolve? How to define twisted soul and healthy mind? How does the view of value get influenced and misled? Will "production for the sake of production" and "consumption for the sake of consumption" provide omnipotent explanation for the haze lingering on the sky of human world? Many people have found the answer in religion. This kind of exploration can be found in the portrayal, depiction and representation of my own spiritual state through my work.
The two directions co-exist all the time, influencing and permeating into each other; sometimes, they are inseparable.

In what circumstances would you want to destroy your own creation?
There is no need to do that. The work I dislike will be gradually forgotten and thrown out of my mind, which is equal to destroying it.

What do you think about the relation between the art history and artist's work?
History is a variable; the same with art history. About history, controversy will always be more reliable and interesting than conclusion.
For history writer, artist's work is just material and the selection of the material involves lots of subjective elements, which make it very hard to represent and critique artist's work in an objective and faithful way. In this globalized modern society, approximately the artists whose positions are close to the social superstructure and the top of power pyramid will enjoy greater visibility in art history. It's the same old story: capital sets up the stage and culture puts in the show. However, in China where material and spiritual production are both in a mess and which is fast moving toward transition, the biggest rule is no rule at all.

What kind of roles would rational thinking and emotional impulse respectively play during your work time?
Our rationality and emotional impulse can be compared as skeletal structure and the flesh. Making a piece of 'fat' work contains more pleasure, while a 'skinny' one is less entertaining. Occasionally the result can be just flesh without bones, or only a skeleton. Personally, I prefer 'skinny' ones, because they look more settled and noble.

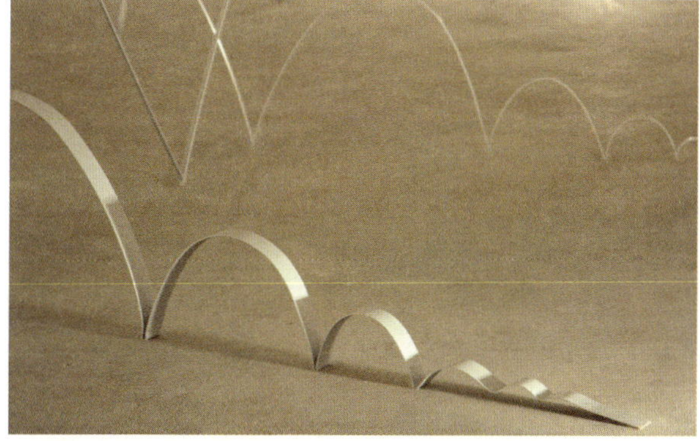

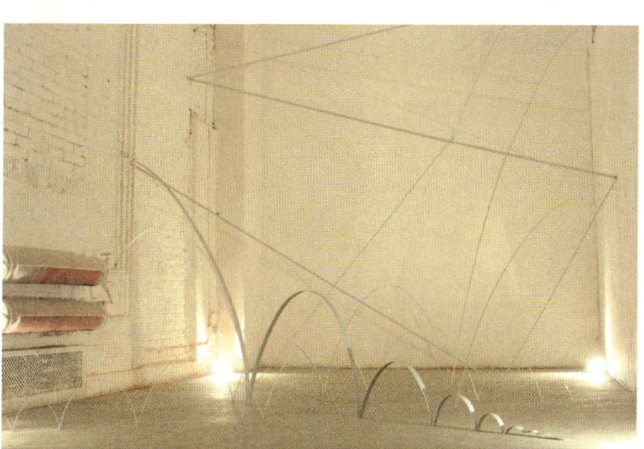

一颗糖，2005
装置
金属条
长征空间独立项目，北京

Lemon Drop, 2005
Installation view
Metal strip
Long March Space - Independent Project Space, Beijing

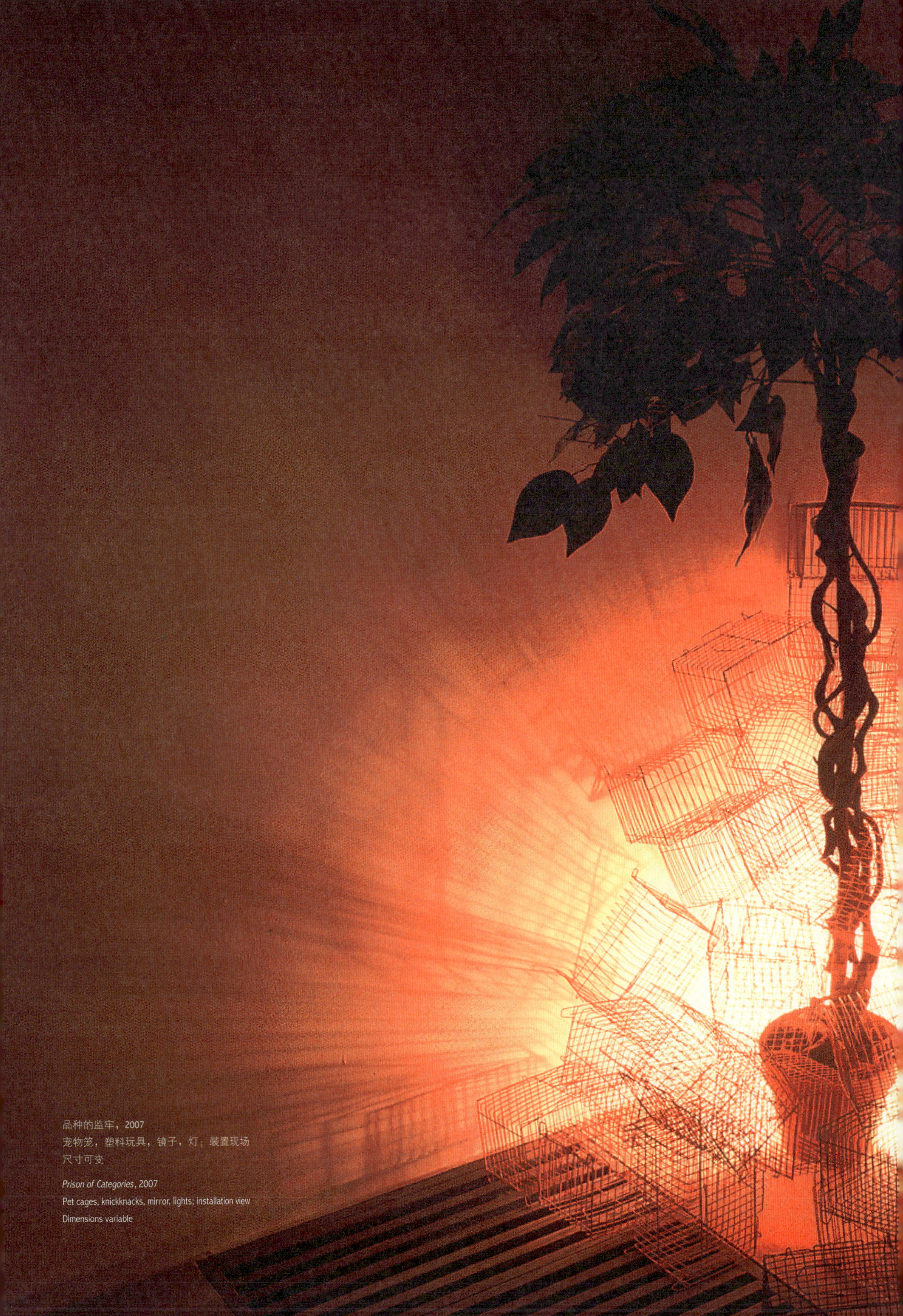

品种的监牢，2007
宠物笼，塑料玩具，镜子，灯；装置现场
尺寸可变

Prison of Categories, 2007
Pet cages, knickknacks, mirror, lights; installation view
Dimensions variable

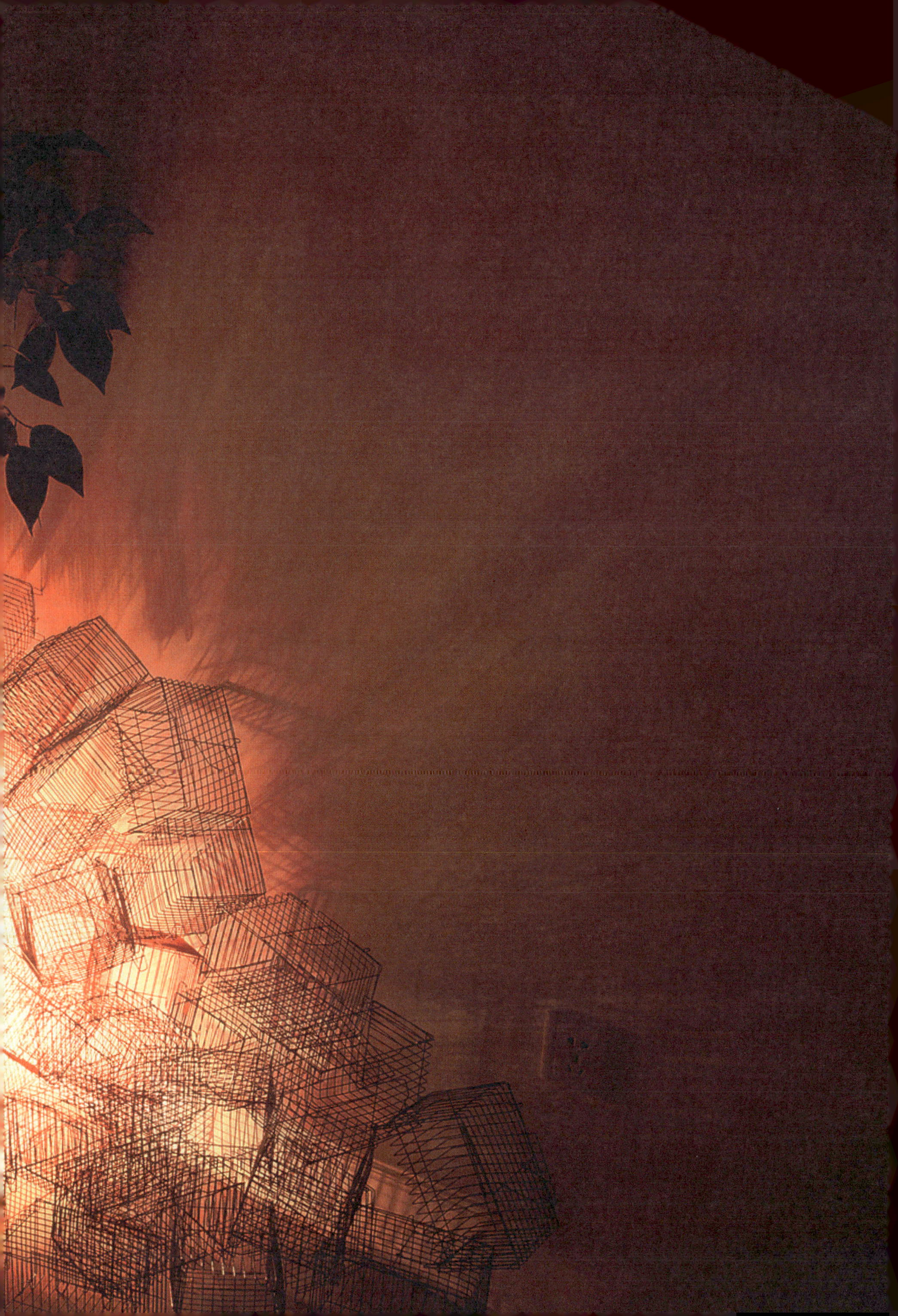

一把药丸，2006年
装置
金属条（铝）
第二届宋庄艺术节，宋庄，北京

A Handful of Pills, 2006
Installation view
Metal strip (aluminum)
Exhibited at "The 2nd Songzhuang Art Festival", Songzhuang, Beijing

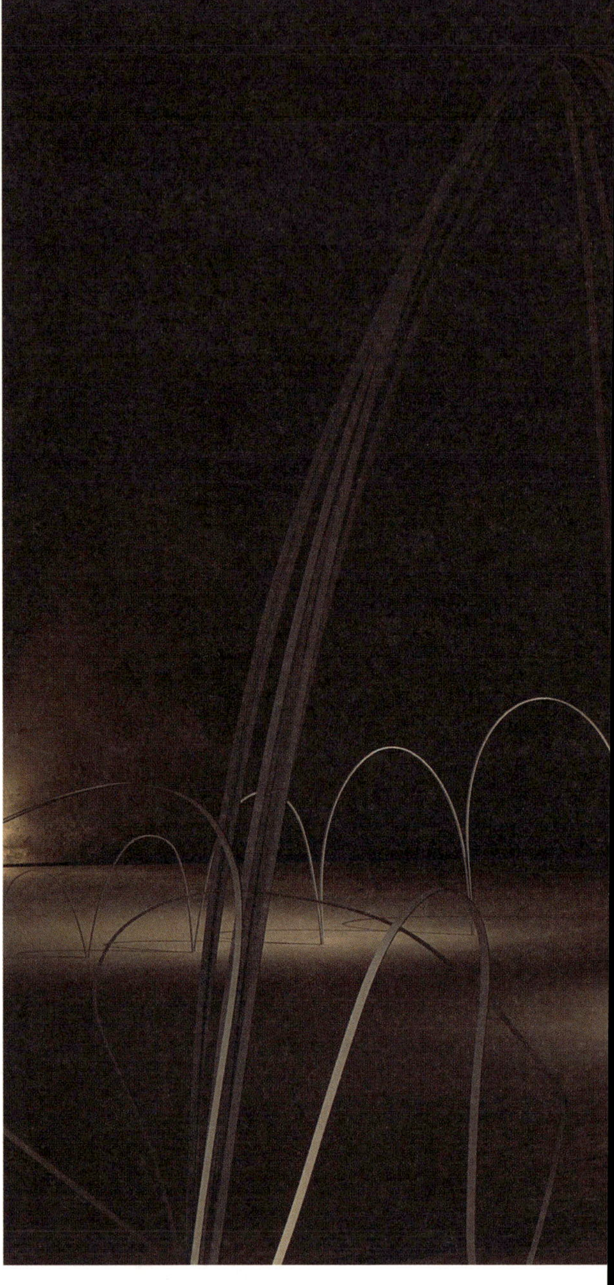

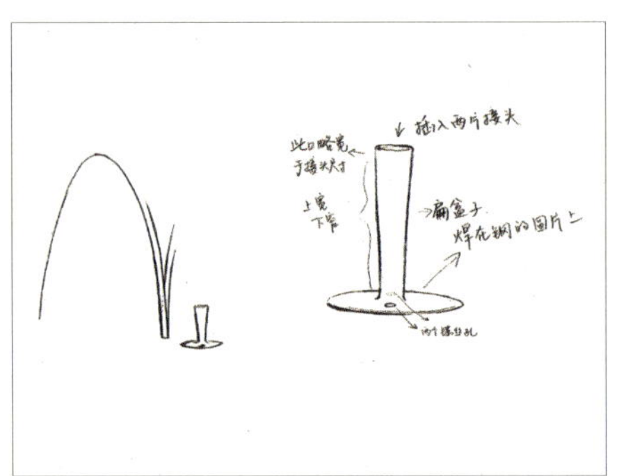

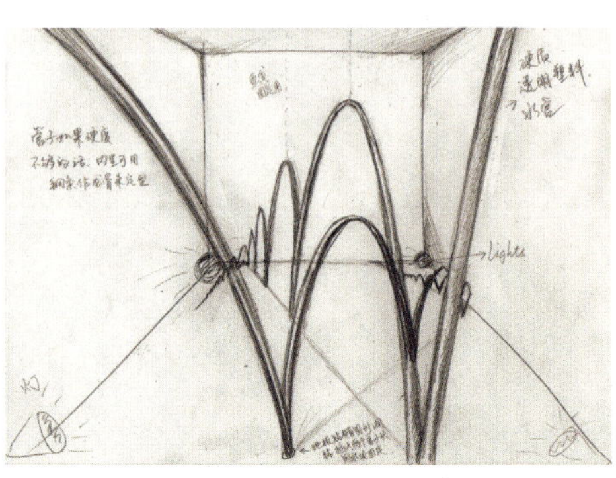

装置作品《一颗糖》手稿，2005年
Manuscript of Installation *Lemon Drop* (2005)

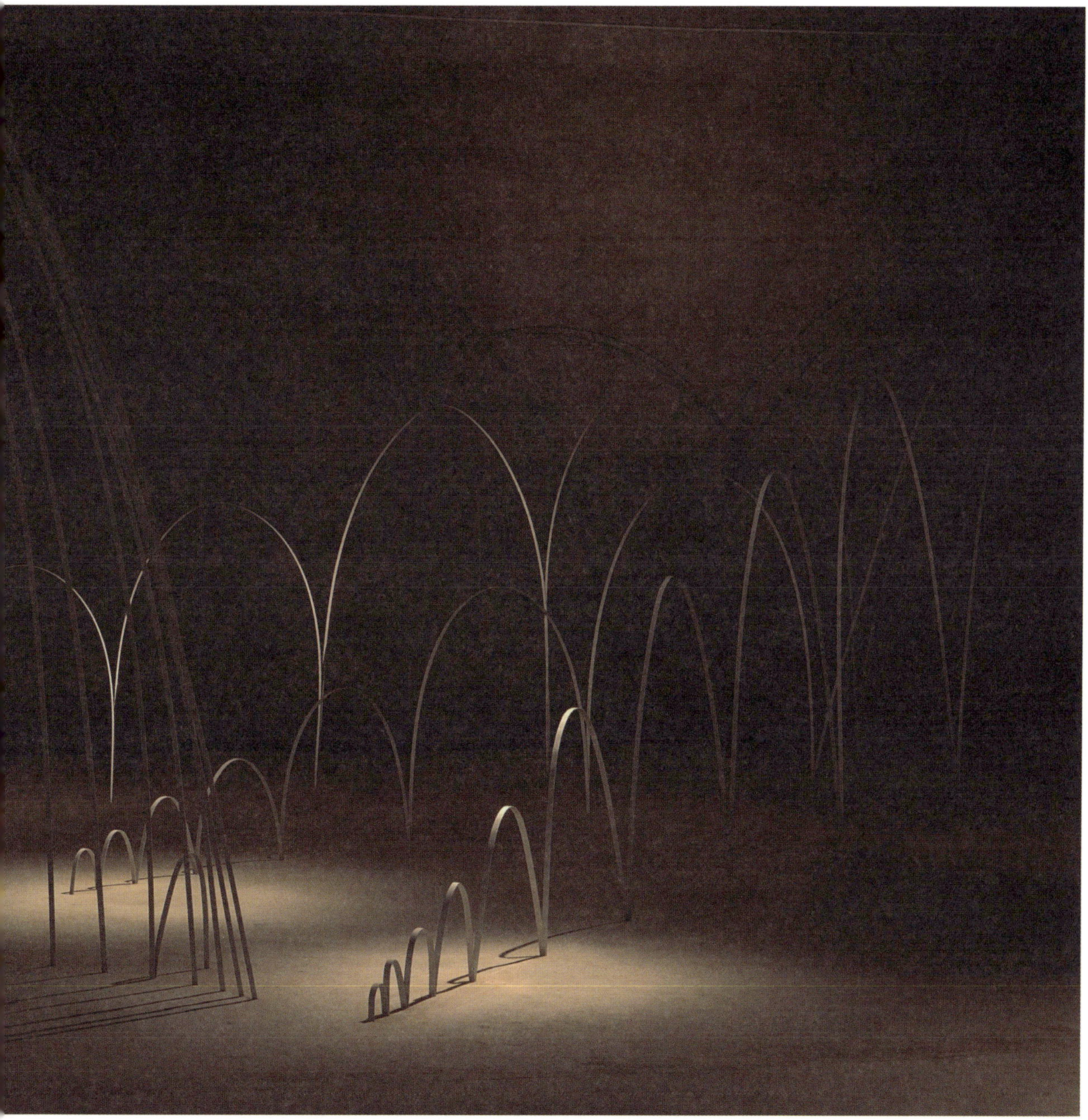

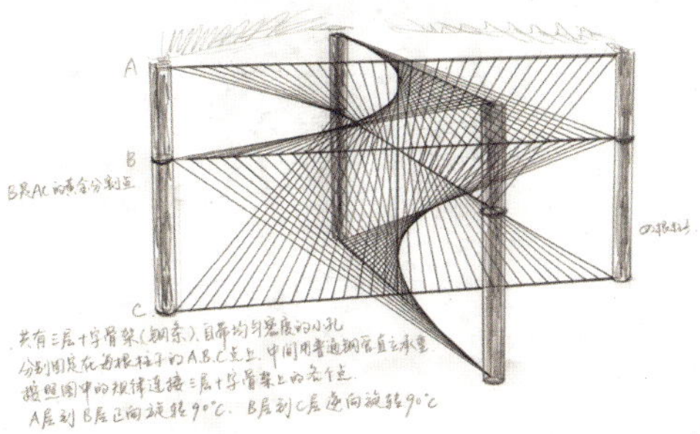

装置作品《Hoo-ha》手稿，2005
Manuscript of Installation *Hoo-ha* (2005)

屠宏涛

TU HONGTAO

**作为艺术家，你在创作中所关心的是什么？以一件作品为例，
分享你的创作过程。**

在创作的前期主要关心我自己是什么样的态度或是状态与对象
的交流。当调整好这样的感觉后，就开始具体工作。在进行时
里就不好说了，我觉得当对象可以刺激到表达的欲望时，肯定
就有冲动，这样的感觉会自己产生点什么吧。

我也想了很久，这个过程没有办法展示，因为过程本身就是语
言本身，呈现就是作品。画个步骤出来？好像就全变味了。但
展览的目的是展现过程。所以这次我尝试用一个烟灰缸来体会
一下。通过记录过程来表达过程。

**如果你是一个批评家，你会从什么角度来阐释和讨论你自己的
创作？**

我会写首诗来说明问题。我越来越觉得人是完全参与到了生活
当中，创造的才有其意义。而不是赋予的意义中可怜的等待。

**在你的创作和思考中，什么书籍和艺术家曾经或正在影响着
你？**

我看的书很乱，说不上来。艺术家我比较喜欢委拉斯贵兹和培
根。当然现在比较喜欢普林斯。他们都是神经病。做个高贵
的，有修养的神经病比正常的没修养的好。

**你是怎样判断和决定在什么语境下呈现你的哪些作品的？你是
怎样看待作品呈现的语境和作品的关系的？**

以前的问题正是在这里，我忙于表达，或被表达自己的冲动所
困。不太好。就是对语境的要求少了，呈现肯定是个整体的

事，可以调动所有感官的课题。我发现要近于变态的去追求那种感觉，可能会达到整体。

如何在创作上形成了现在的面貌，描述一下近年来作品的发展和变化？

人的知识越多就越自我，把自己就看得越重要。这样的创作是我反对的。但人又不能无知，那叫没教养。我觉得创作还是要自然点，我也在努力的追求教养和轻松之间的感觉，知识多点可以让自己看到事物之间更多的因缘关系，轻松的，自然的东西有时候比较真切。

你会在什么情况下摧毁你自己的作品？

这是个难题，不是不敢摧毁，过程中时常很焦虑，怎么会这么差，但往往隔段时间会觉得那样很好。有时候觉得很顺的东西，反而隔久了觉得不行，只好让时间自己来摧毁了。

你怎么看待艺术史和艺术家创作的关系？

我相信艺术家创作是听候神的摆布，而艺术史是人们相信这已经是神的意思了。

在你的工作中，理性和情感冲动各自扮演着什么样的角色？

理性的确可以解决很多具体的因果关系，比如在我了解的烟灰缸里，我们可以知道它是怎么被做出来的，在那里买的，怎么用，等等。但这一团泥巴怎么就没有变成其他的烟灰缸？或者就没有变成其他的用品？再或者它们就没有其他的用途？我能看到的只是这个时间里的东西。我不能相信它真的就是这样。

表达冲动包括了情感的东西，具体怎么安排，还真是说不上来。就好像明天约好了拜访朋友，难道我就一定知道了明天的过程。艺术作为一个职业真是奇怪，这个职业居然在追求经验之外的东西。

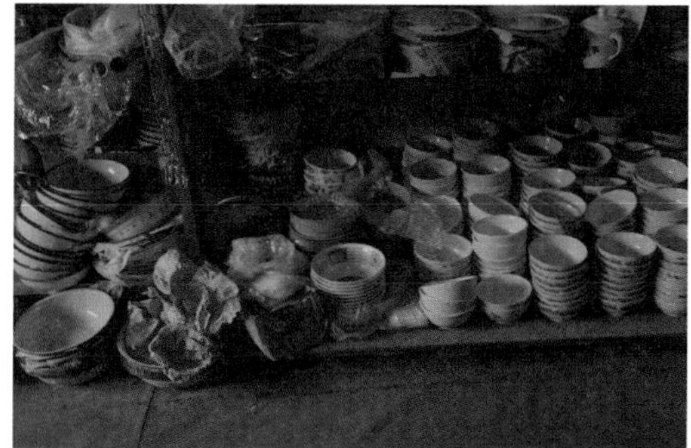

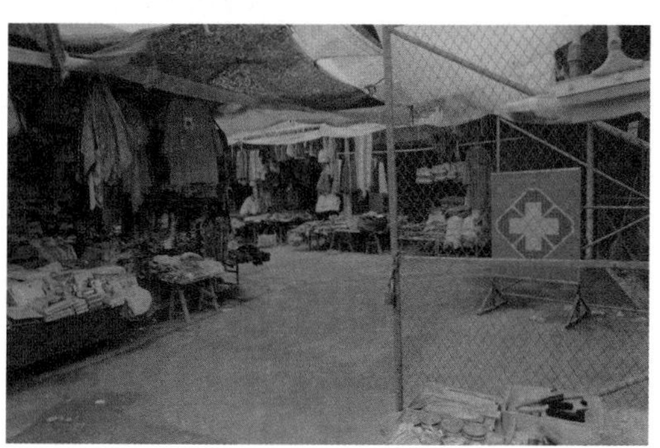

资料图片

Photo references

As an artist, what do you care most during working? Could you please give an example to introduce the process of your work for us?

During the beginning of my creation, I care about what attitude I have and what status I'm in when I communicate with the object. After adjusting this feeling, I begin to work. When I'm creating, it's hard to say. I think if the object can stimulate my desire to express, I will have the impulse to produce something.

I've been thinking about this for a long time. This process cannot be displayed, because the process itself is the language and the presenting part is a work. If I illustrate the steps here, then it is just not the same any more. The purpose of an exhibition is to show the process.

Therefore this time I attempt to use an ashtray to experience it; to express the process through recording it.

Suppose you are a critic, what perspective would you talk about and explain you work from?

I will write poems to state the point. I more and more think only when people totally join in life, what they create is meaningful. They shouldn't be waiting pathetically for some given meanings.

What books and which artists have had, or is having an influence on your way of thinking and working?

I read diversified books. As for artists, I like Velázquez and Bacon. Of course now I like Prince. They are all crazy. Being a noble and refined nut is better than being a normal but unrefined one.

How do you decide the context in which your work is to be presented? How do you consider the relation of the context with your work?

My previous problem is just this. I was busy expressing or being imprisoned by my own impulse. That's not good, having fewer requirements about context. Presenting is an issue about entirety, which activates all the sensual feelings. I find if I pursue that kind of feeling abnormally, it might reach to an entirety.

How does your work take the present shape? And please give a few words about the latest development and changes in your work.

The more knowledge a person has, the more important he consider himself is. Creation based on this is what I'm against, but people cannot be ignorant. I think the creation should be more natural and I'm trying to pursue a kind of feeling between refinement and relief. With more knowledge, I can see more causal relationships of things.

玻璃, 2009
综合媒介 / 摄影
130 × 40 cm

Glass, 2009
Mixed Media / Photo
130 × 40 cm

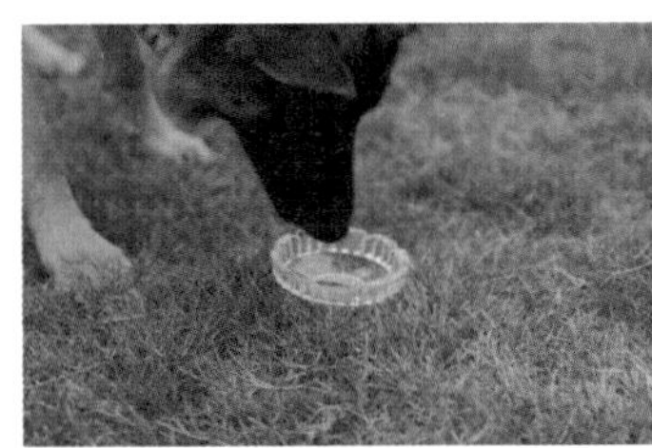
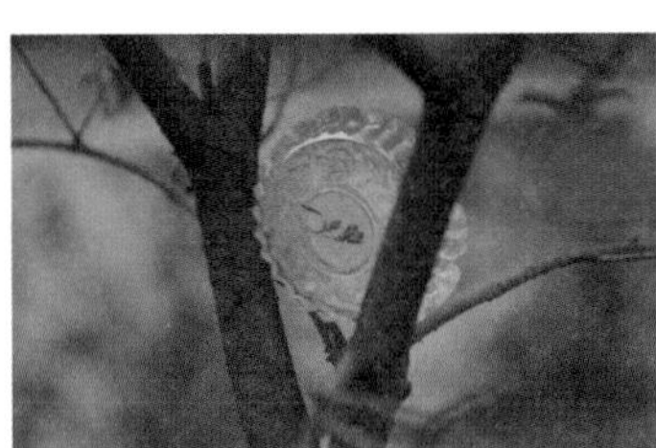
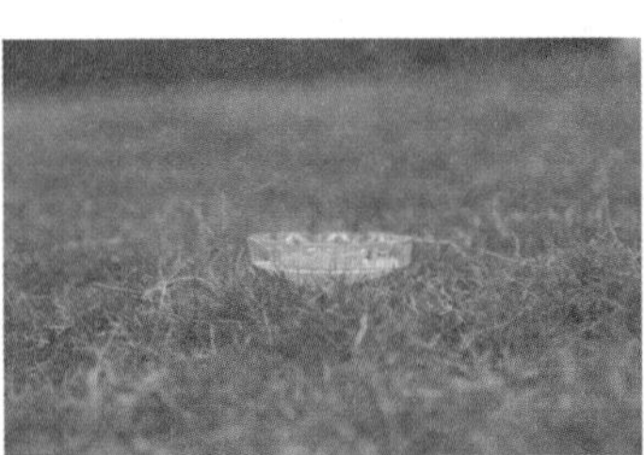
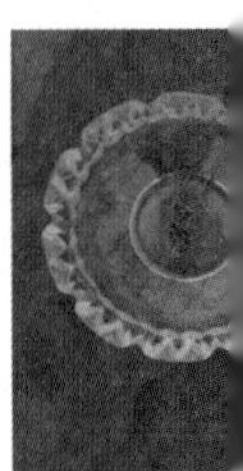

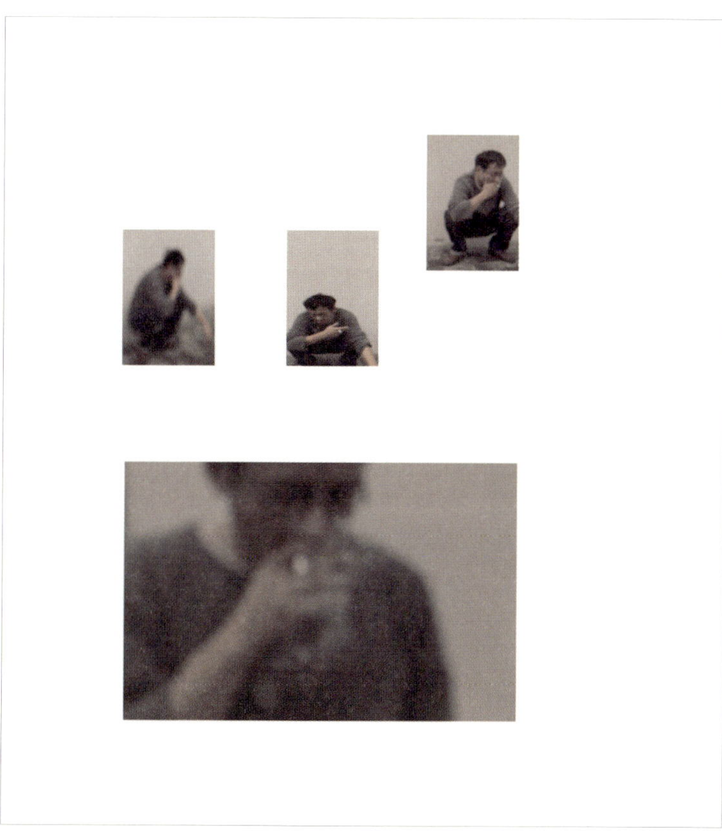

玻璃, 2009
综合媒介 / 摄影
70 × 50 cm

Glass, 2009
Mixed Media / Photo
70 × 50 cm

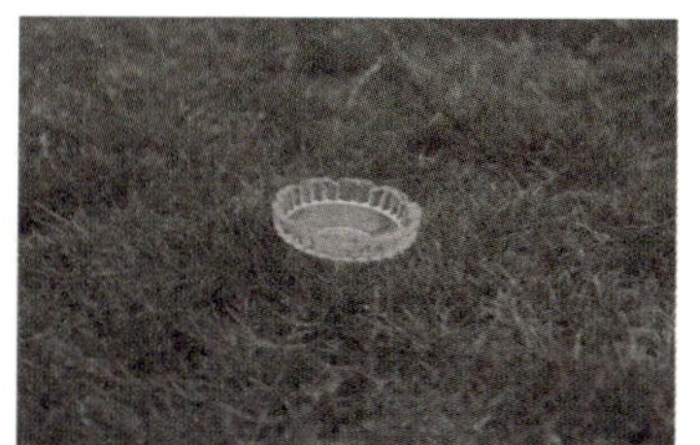

Relaxing and natural things sometimes are more distinct.

In what circumstances would you want to destroy your own creation?
This is a tough question. It's not that I don't dare to destroy my works. I am often worried during the process of creation: why is it so lousy? But after a period of time, I will think it is good. Sometimes I think those works that I created smoothly are not ok after a period of time. Then I can only let time destroy them.

What do you think about the relation between the art history and artist's work?
I believe artist's creation is in God's hands. Art history makes people believe it is God's will.

What kind of roles would rational thinking and emotional impulse respectively play during your work time?
Rationality can indeed solve many causal relationships. For example, we know how an astray is made; we also know where to buy it and how to use it, etc. But why this glob of mud hasn't become another ashtray or other items? Can't it have other usage? What I can see is only what I see in this time. I can't believe it really is this way.
Expressing an impulse includes emotional elements. How to arrange it is hard to explain. It's like going to pay a visit to a friend someday, it doesn't mean that I know exactly the process of that day. As a profession, art is really strange. This profession is actually pursuing something beyond experience.

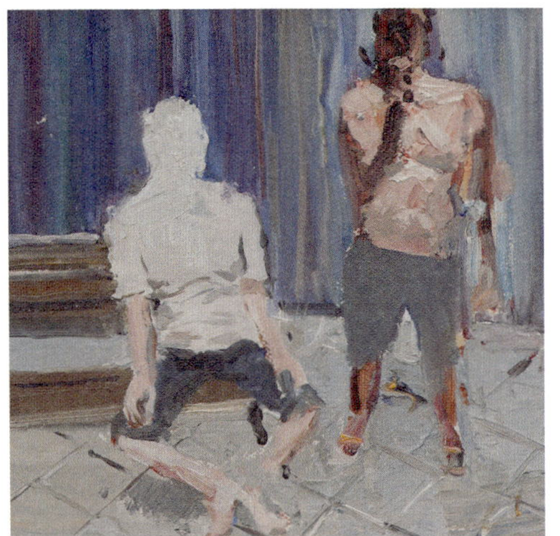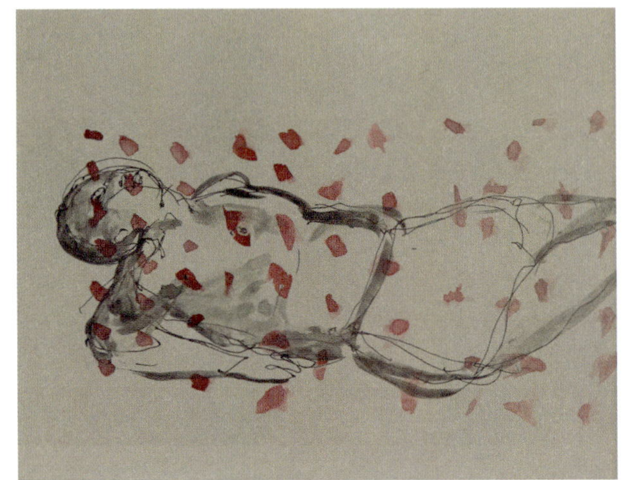

玻璃, 2009
综合媒介
绘画4幅：21 × 21 cm; 15 × 13 cm × 2; 75 × 56 cm

Glass, 2009
Mixed Media
4 Paintings: 21 × 21 cm; 15 × 13 cm × 2; 75 × 56 cm

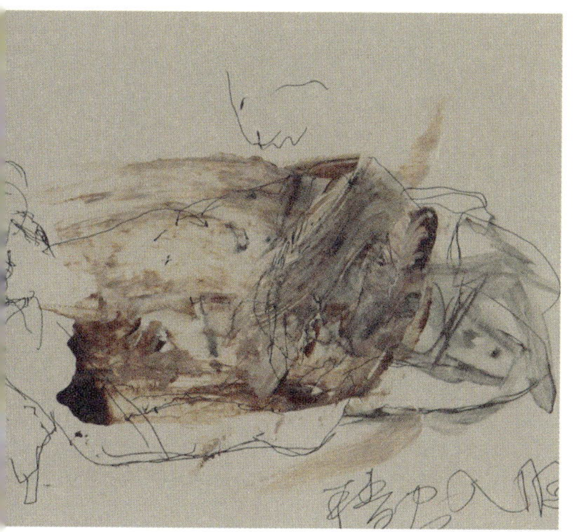

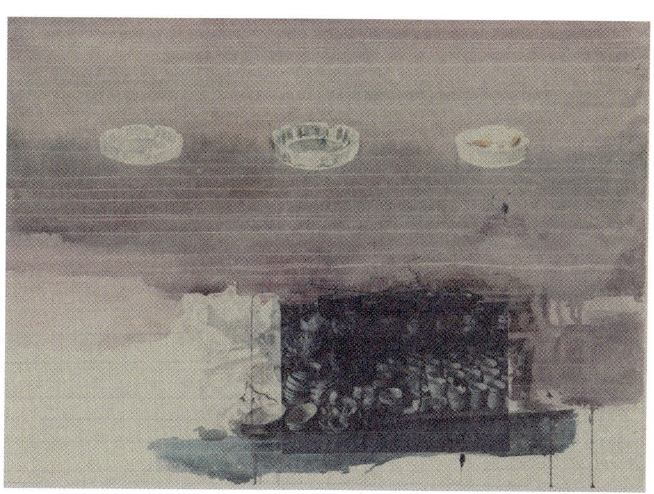

作品是通过对一个烟灰缸的观察，想象完成。在观察的过程中我更确定一些基本的物质与人的关系。比如图像意义，一支烟在几分钟的燃烧后转化成了青烟和灰尘。图像是物质的暂时的显现，物质是在世界里不断流转，变化。图像的意义是人赋予的，其实没有意义。而在变化中，人会产生体验和对世界的整体把握，催生出形式，那就是美。

The work was finished through the observation and then the imagination of an ashtray. During the course of observation, I became clearer about some basic relationships between materials and man, for example, the meaning of image. A cigarette turned into smoke and ash after several minutes of combustion. An image is the temporary display of a material. Materials keep changing in the world. The meaning of an image is given by man and is actually meaningless. During the process of changes, man will have his own understanding of the whole world and then form is generated. That is beauty.

作品是通过对一个烟灰缸的观察，想象完成。在观察的过程中我更确定一些基本的物质与人的关系。比如图像意义，一支烟在几分钟的燃烧后转化成了青烟和灰尘。图像是物质的暂时的显现，物质是在世界里不断流转，变化。图像的意义是人赋予的，其实没有意义。而在变化中，人会产生体验和对世界的整体把握，催生出形式，那就是美。

The work was finished through the observation and then the imagination of an ashtray. During the course of observation, I became clearer about some basic relationships between materials and man, for example, the meaning of image. A cigarette turned into smoke and ash after several minutes of combustion. An image is the temporary display of a material. Materials keep changing in the world. The meaning of an image is given by man and is actually meaningless. During the process of changes, man will have his own understanding of the whole world and then form is generated. That is beauty.

玻璃, 2009
综合媒介 / 摄影
40 × 40 cm

Glass, 2009
Mixed Media / Photo
40 × 40 cm

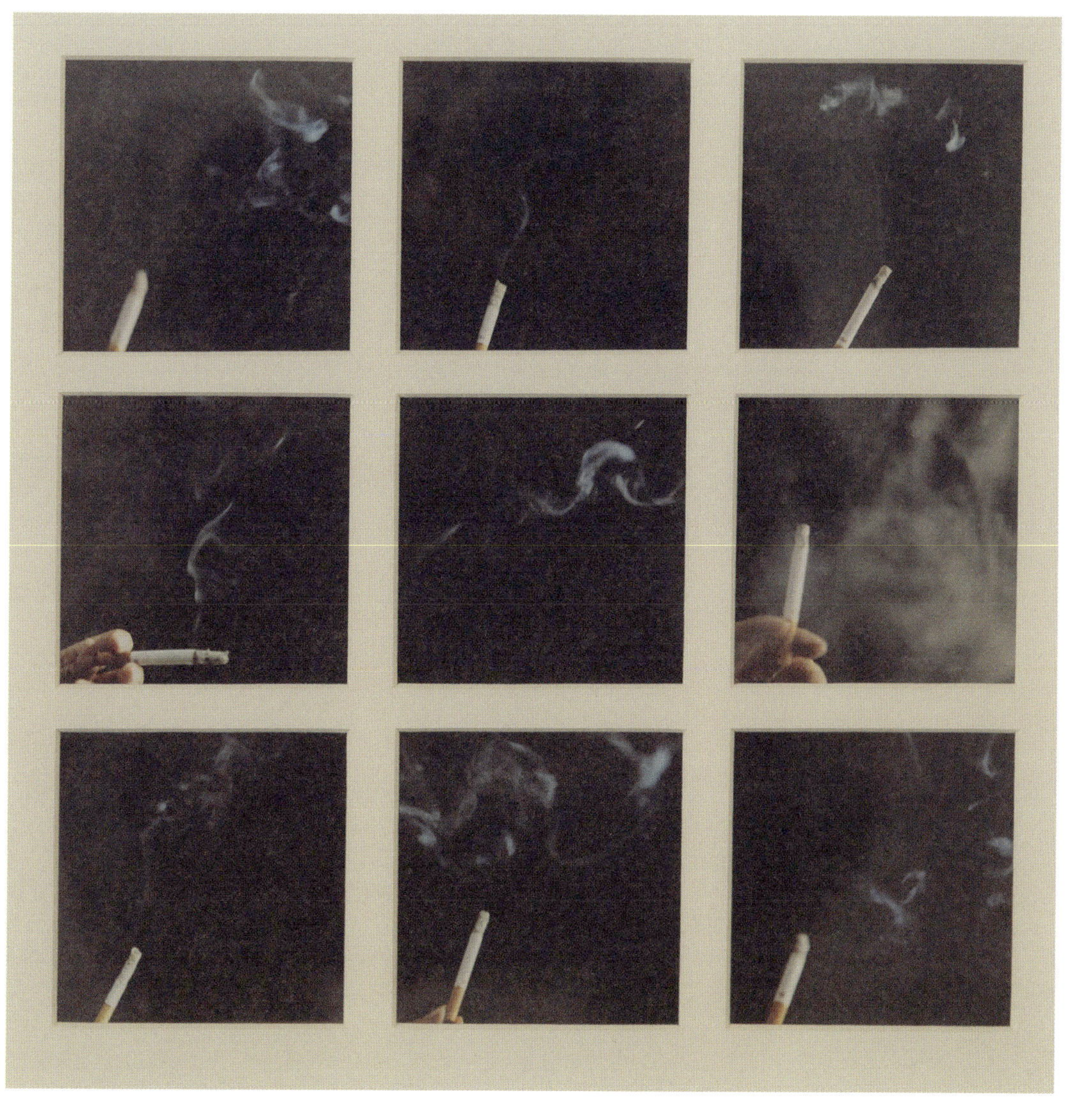

王光乐

WANG GUANGLE

作为艺术家，你在创作中所关心的是什么？以一件作品为例，分享你的创作过程。

形式。在《寿漆》这一系列作品中我要说的是"有限"这样一层意思，我在画布上重叠颜料，并且覆盖尽量多的层数，直到最后一层和刷子一样宽或颜料穷尽。为提示这个覆盖，每一层为上一层留出边缘，并且保留侧框的滴淌。

如果你是一个批评家，你会从什么角度来阐释和讨论你自己的创作？

系统学。

在你的创作和思考中，什么书籍和艺术家曾经或正在影响着你？

《老子》、《荒漠甘泉》、《辩证逻辑叙要》和一些小说，艺术家不胜枚举。

你是怎样判断和决定在什么语境下呈现你的哪些作品的？你是怎样看待作品呈现的语境和作品的关系的？

语境暗示作品，作品暗示语境。

如何在创作上形成了现在的面貌，描述一下近年来作品的发展和变化？

我主要围绕着"区别"与"无区别"这对范畴来工作。最初"水磨石"给我一个画面结构，我用无区别的态度来对待有区别的细微形状和颜色。工作的进展带出的却是后退的记忆——家乡老人的"寿漆"行为"重复涂刷"——我认为这是"无区

寿漆061213，2006
布面丙稀
116×114cm

Coffin Paint 061213, 2006
Acrylic on canvas
116×114 cm

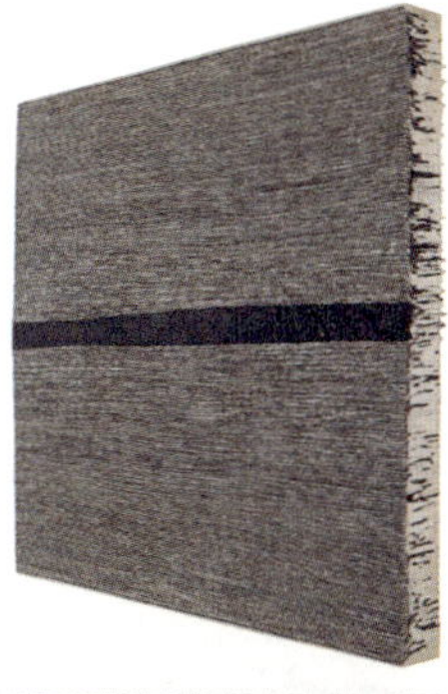

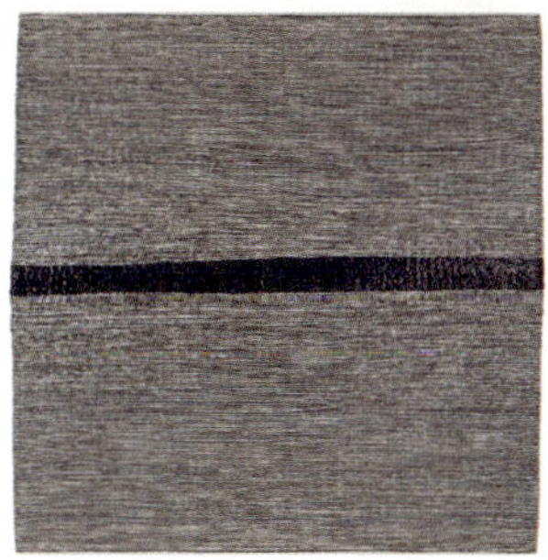

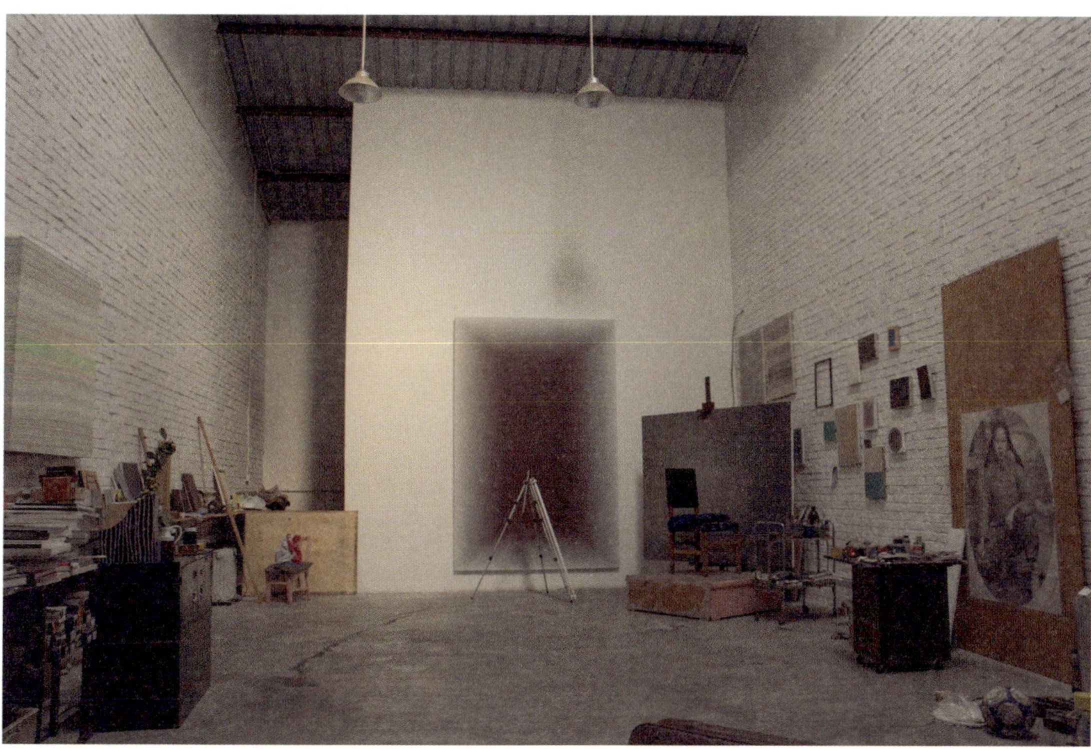

艺术家工作室。
The artist's studio

别"的更简单的形式。至今还在区分涂刷的微妙样态的不同。

你会在什么情况下摧毁你自己的作品？
不会。

你怎么看待艺术史和艺术家创作的关系？
艺术史是语境中的语言因素，艺术家从中学习基本语汇，但艺术史很难还原非语言因素。

在你的工作中，理性和情感冲动各自扮演着什么样的角色？
我的理性服务于我的情感冲动，赋予情感冲动一些形状。

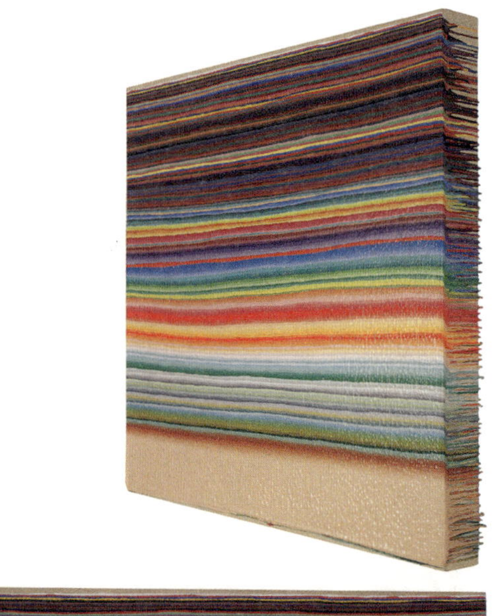

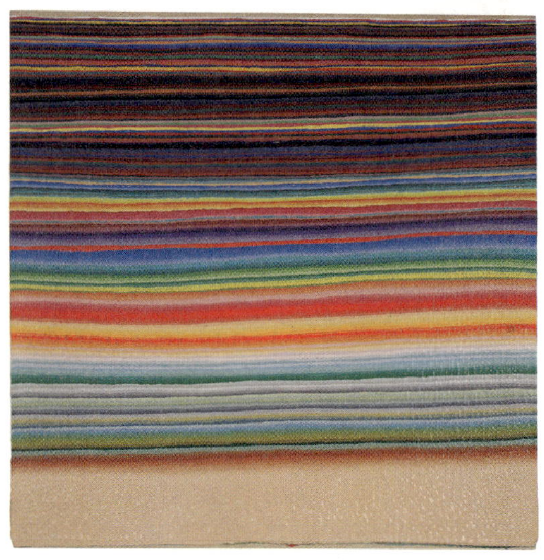

寿漆070613，2007
布面丙烯
116×114cm

Coffin Paint 070613, 2006
Acrylic on canvas
116×114 cm

水磨石2004.10-11，2004
布面油画
200×200cm

Terrazzo 2004.10-11, 2004
Oil on canvas
200×200 cm

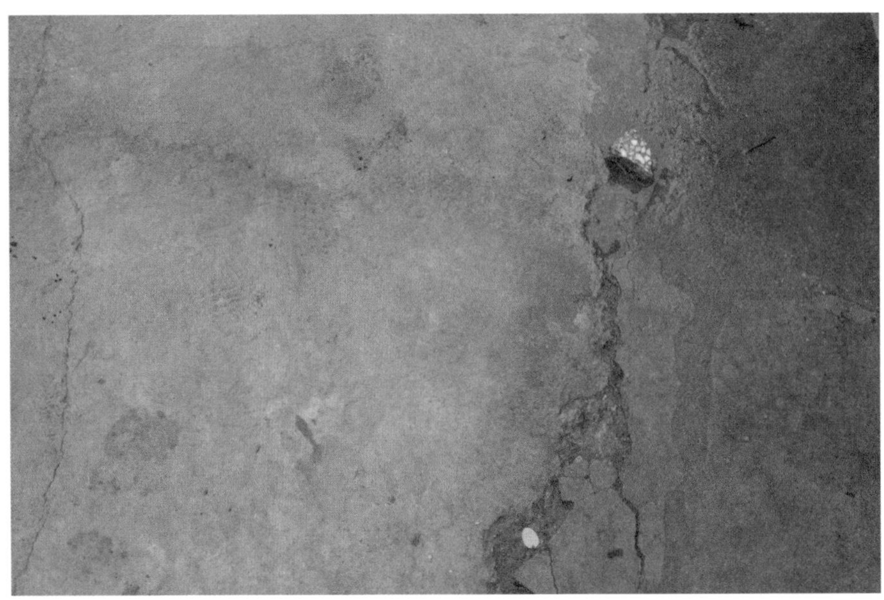

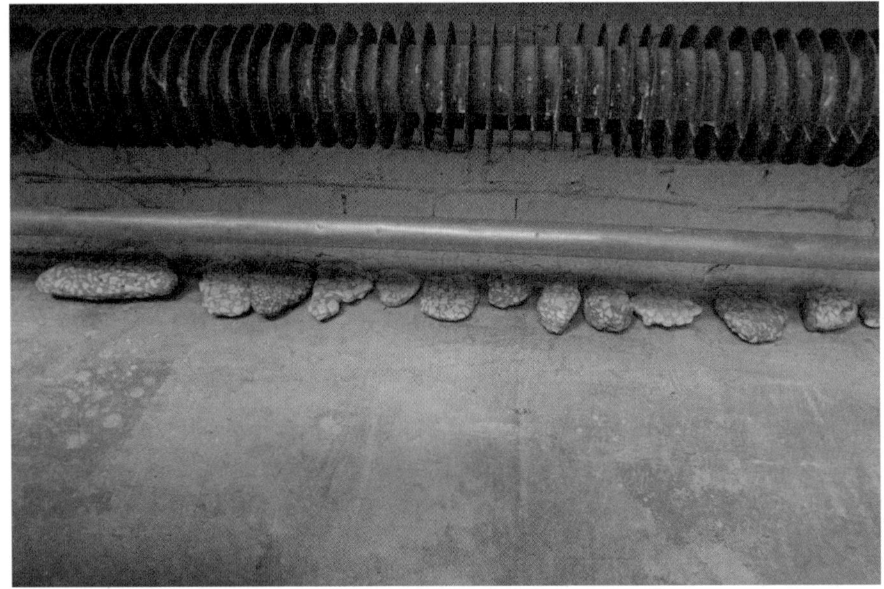

路上的水磨石碎块。
Broken terrazzo piece on the road

敲好的水磨石放在墙角暖气片下。
The finished terrazzo pieces placed under the heating radiator

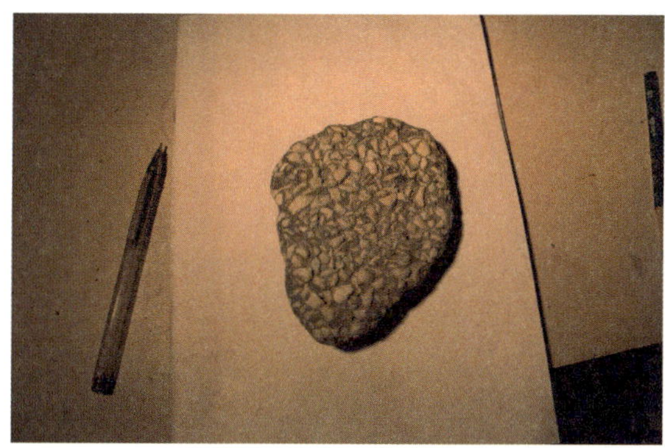

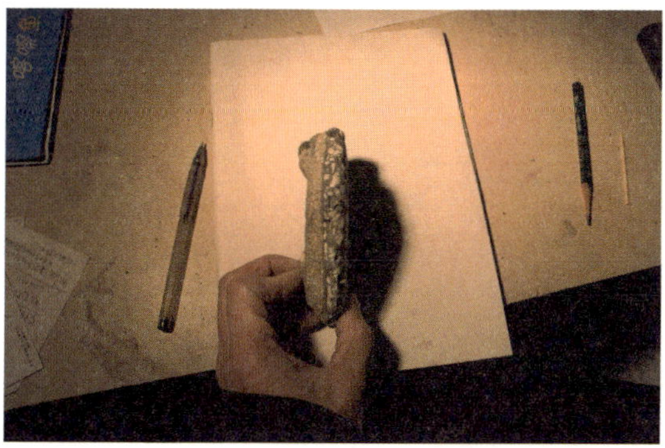

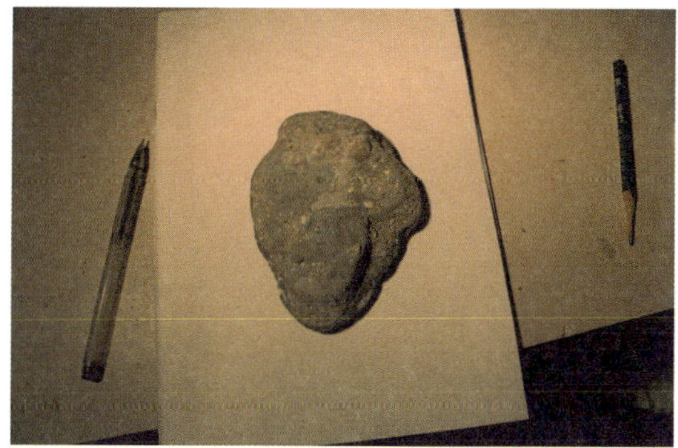

北戴河水磨石之正面、侧面、背面。

The front, sides and back of a terrazzo from Beidaihe, Qinhuang Island.

As an artist, what do you care most during working? Could you please give an example to introduce the process of your work for us?

Artistic form is the first concern in my work. In *Coffin Paint* series, what I want to articulate is a layer of meaning — "limitedness". I applied layers of paints as many as possible on canvas, until the breadth of the last layer became the same with that of my brush, or until the paint was used up. As a reminder, each layer was narrower than the previous one, leaving the margins of all layers visible in the final work. Besides, the traces of paint dripping on two sides of the painting's frame were kept on purpose.

Suppose you are a critic, from what perspective would you explain and comment on your works?

I would discuss my work from the perspective of systematics.

What books and which artists have had or are having an influence on your way of thinking and working?

The books include *Lao-tzu*, *Streams in the Desert*, *Dialectical Logic* and some novels. As for artists, they are too numerous to mention one by one.

How do you make judgment and decision as to in what context you'd like to present your works? According to you, in what way is the context created by the work related to the work itself?

Context and work simultaneously imply each other's existence.

How does your work take the present shape? And please give a few words about the latest development and changes in your work.

My work evolves around a pair of concepts "difference" and "non-difference". At the beginning, the series work *Terrazzo* set up a composition, in which I used undifferentiated attitude to treat different formal details and color. The progress of my work only took me back to the past memory — the "coffin paint" performance with "repeated labor of painting" by elderly people in my hometown, which could be considered as a simpler form of "non-difference". To date, I'm still differentiating the minor differences of form in the overlay of painting layers.

In what circumstances would you want to destroy your own creation?

I won't.

What do you think about the relation between the art history and artist's work?

The history of art is contextualized lingual factors, and artists try to learn the basic grammar from it. But art history seems to be hard to restore non-lingual factors.

What kind of roles would rational thinking and emotional impulse respectively play in your work?

My rationality serves my impulse through giving it forms.

你自己做过饭吗?

坐在餐桌前进餐,享受或评判这顿饭的色泽或味道,这个过程在我不是一个独立的事件,它前后联系着买菜,淘洗,烹炒,洗碗,倒垃圾这些环节。可以说垃圾没有及时清倒会影响到餐桌上的那道菜肴的成色。

艺术家来到工作室可能看到的是地面很脏。每天的调颜料,清理画笔,打扫工作室混淆了画画这个环节,画画与这个序列组成一个整体。既然是一个整体就不能有偏见:觉得画画比墩地重要,或墩地比画画更备普遍意义。

话是这样说,更多的时候,饿了,饭来张口是我喜欢的,这吃之前的做饭,做饭之前的买菜和吃之后的收拾餐具是我不喜欢的。

我在实践的是一心一意的去买菜,一心一意的做饭,一心一意的吃,一心一意的洗碗,把相关的各个环节中的每一环都相同对待,不产生情绪好恶。这个做法是基于这样一个整体观叫做吃饭的这个事情实际是一个系统,包含了很多的子环节,而独独喜欢吃会出现很明显的后遗症。而且在不可分割的整体里天天在做分裂,独独喜欢某一个局部而回避其它,这在逻辑上是也说不通的。

无题,2006至今
水磨石、雕塑
不规则尺寸

Untitled, dated from 2006
Terrazzo, sculpture
Variable dimensions

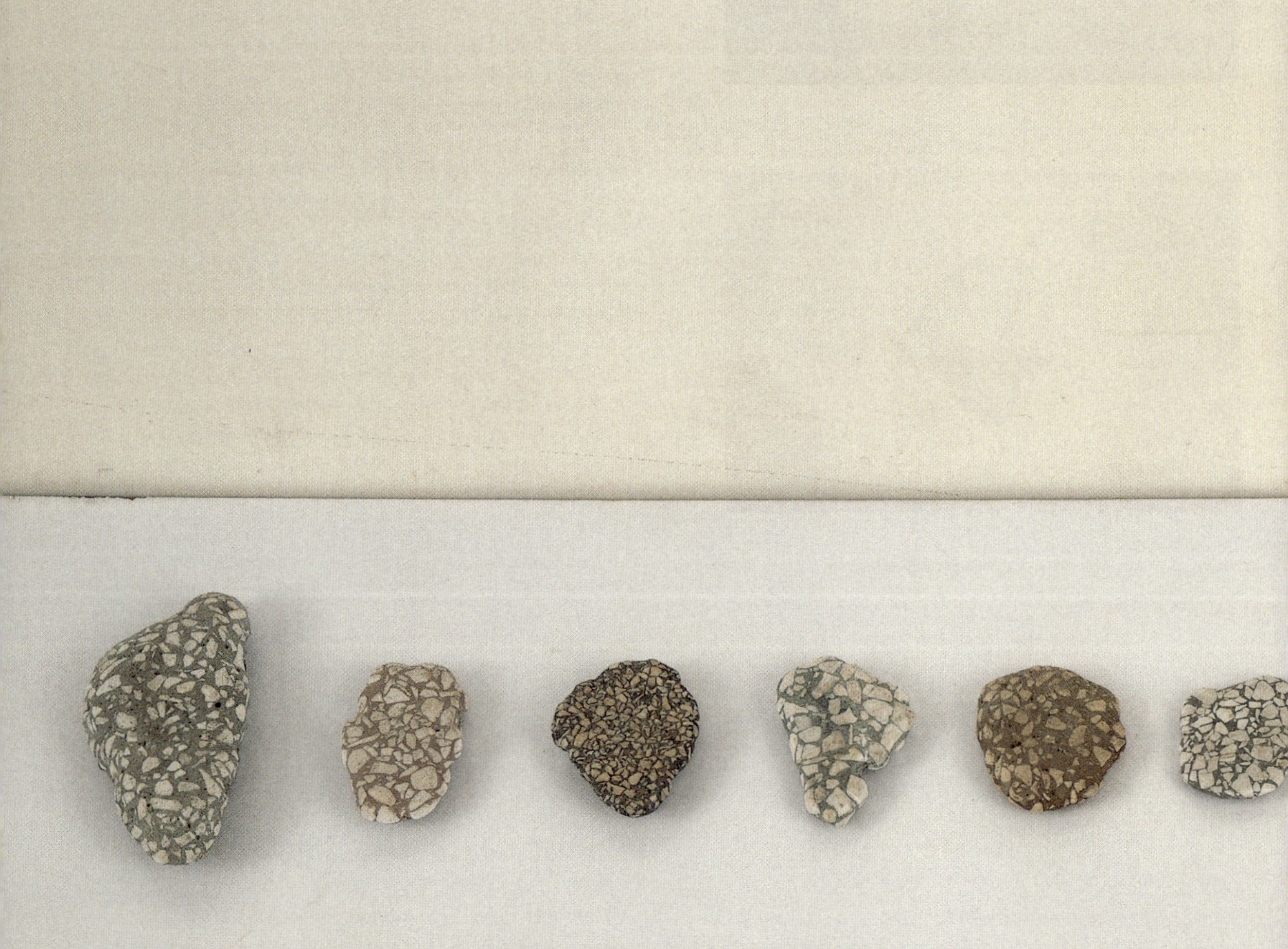

Did you cook meal?
Sitting at the table, enjoying and commenting on the color and taste of the meal, this is not a process with just a single thing to do. It involves many odd jobs like grocery shopping, washing, cooking and dumping the trash. I could say that the delay of emptying the trash bin may well affect the final quality of cuisine on the table.

The first thing the artist notices when he comes to his studio maybe is the dirty floor. Everyday chores like color-mixing, disposing brushes, and cleaning studio blend with the labor of painting and become integrated parts of the entire art-making process. Since they are parts of a whole unit, we shouldn't view them separately with prejudices, such as considering painting to be more significant than mopping floor, or vice verse.

By the way, more often I prefer to eat a ready-cooked meal when hungry and things such as cooking, shopping and clearing the table are not what I like to do.

What I do is wholeheartedly practicing grocery shopping, cooking, eating and washing dishes, and treat each part of the work equally without the slightest feeling of like or dislike. This practice is based on a concept of wholism, which believes the whole matter is actually a system containing many secondary chains while an exclusive interest in eating will cause an apparent symptom of hangover. What's more, the act of creating boundaries to divide an inseparable whole unit, showing an exclusive interest in one part and shunning from others, will make no sense either.

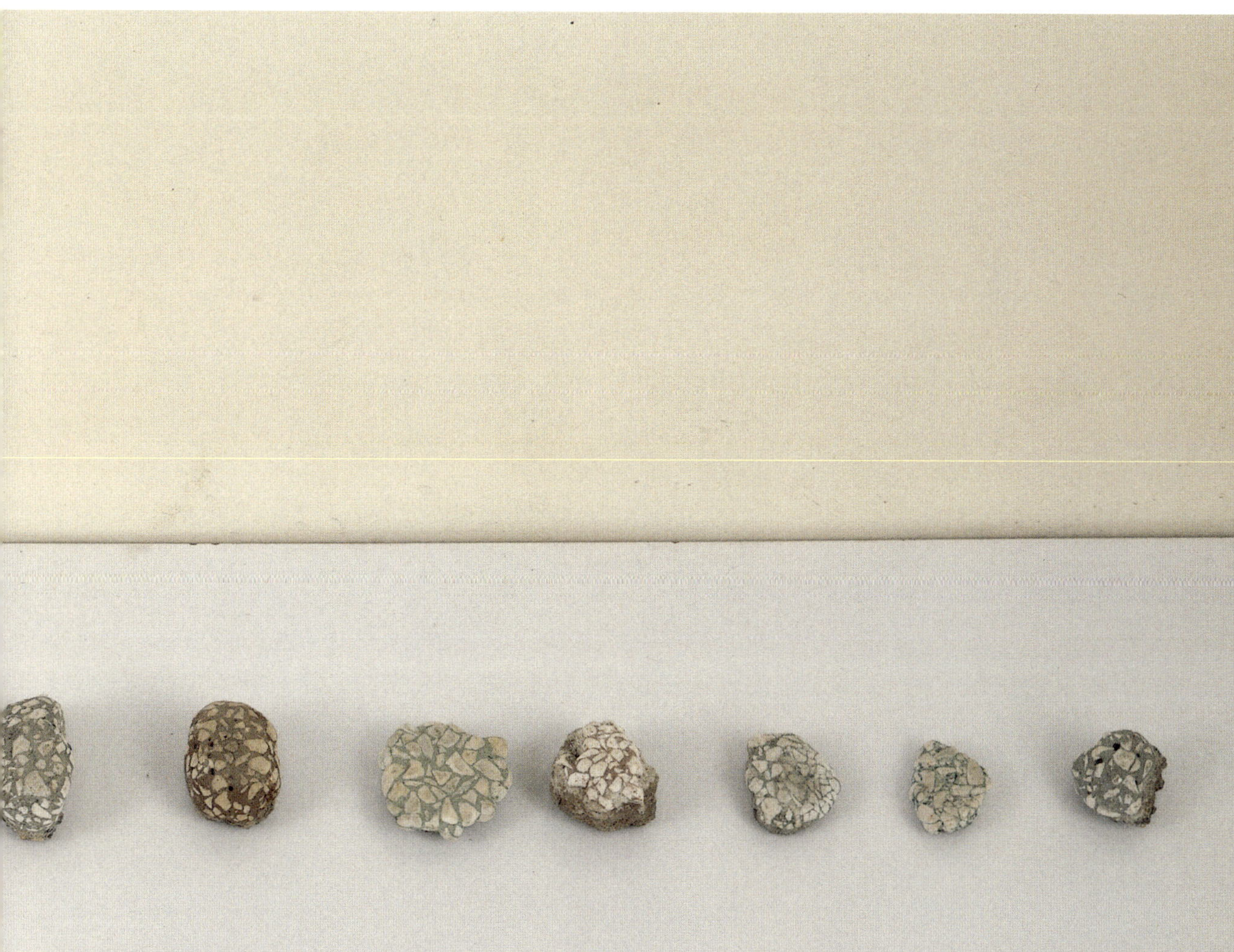

王宁德

WANG NINGDE

作为艺术家，你在创作中所关心的是什么？以一件作品为例，分享你的创作过程。

我经常无法判断自己是否在创作中，如果我意识到的话，会让自己的关心能够进入到一个巷道里，这个巷道暗无天日并且独自一人，这样就会避免重复的劳动。

在做这个参展作品《向上》时，我所关心的是巷道的曲度、深度和施工难度，这包括牛顿的运动三定律。

如果你是一个批评家，你会从什么角度来阐释和讨论你自己的创作？

既然是批评家，我自会用批评的角度来阐释和讨论。

在你的创作和思考中，什么书籍和艺术家曾经或正在影响着你？

法布尔的《昆虫记》。我容许杜尚偶尔影响我，因为在他真正影响我的时候，往往提醒我从影响中走出来。

你是怎样判断和决定在什么语境下呈现你的哪些作品的？你是怎样看待作品呈现的语境和作品的关系的？

我一般不去判断那是一个什么语境，在今天，呈现往往就是比创作稍晚的时候，而这些决定权往往不在我手上。

如何在创作上形成了现在的面貌，描述一下近年来作品的发展

和变化？

这个面貌大多是因为先天因素，也有一点后天的修正。最近因为"后天"的因素多了一点，所以开始不太想昨天、今天和明天。

你会在什么情况下摧毁你自己的作品？

我很早就明白，任何想毁灭证据的行为都是徒劳的，事情一旦败露势必遭到严惩。

你怎么看待艺术史和艺术家创作的关系？

艺术史是艺术家成为艺术家之前关心的问题，在艺术家成为艺术家以后，我认为，最好还是把那个问题放到艺术史本身比较好。

在你的工作中，理性和情感冲动各自扮演着什么样的角色？

每次我冲动之后都会回归理性，理性过久又会有抑制不住的冲动，周而复始，从无例外。

宁德年间-游乐场-1，2006
摄影
In the years of NingDe-Playground-1,2006
Photography

宁德年间-游乐场-4，2007
摄影
In the years of NingDe-Playground-4,2007
Photography

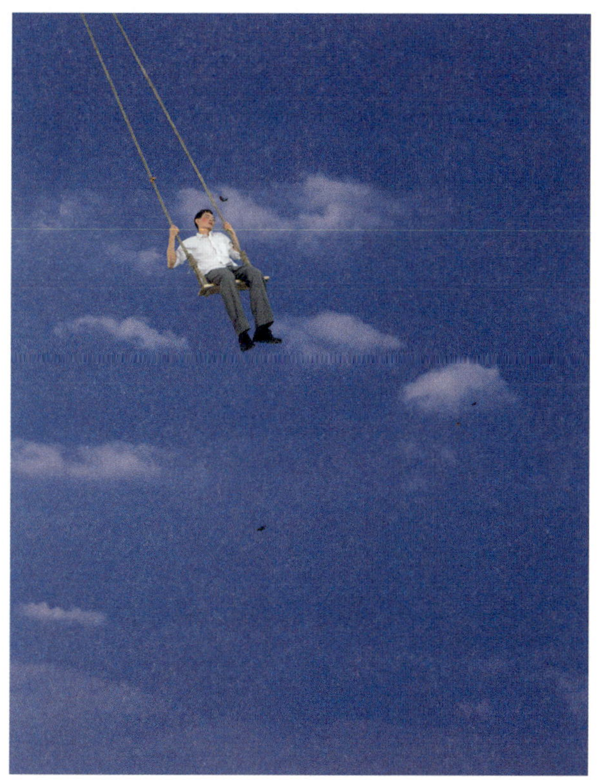

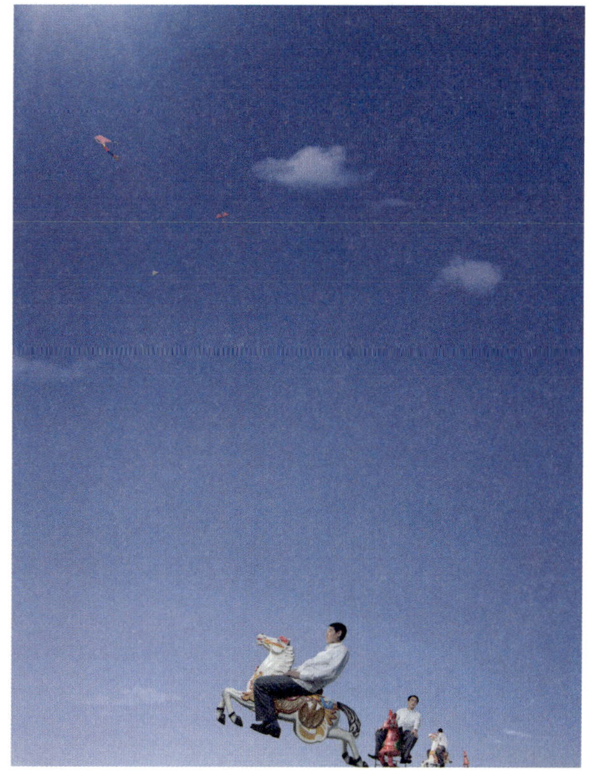

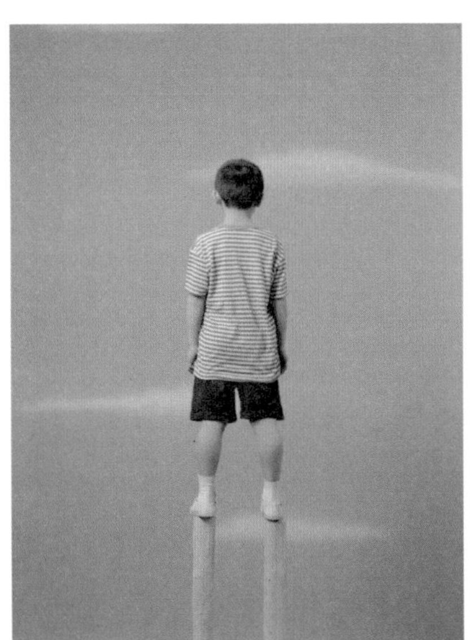

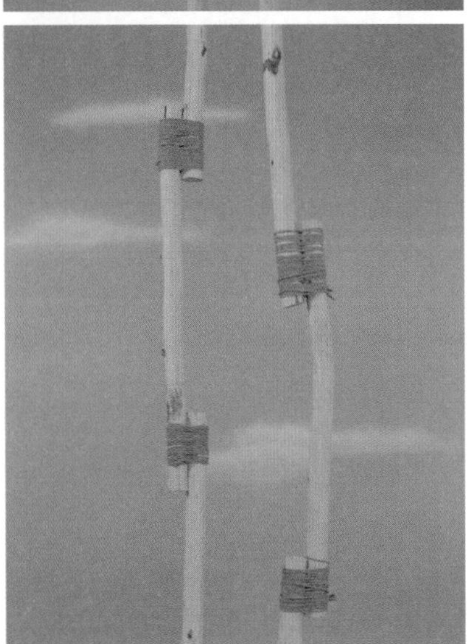

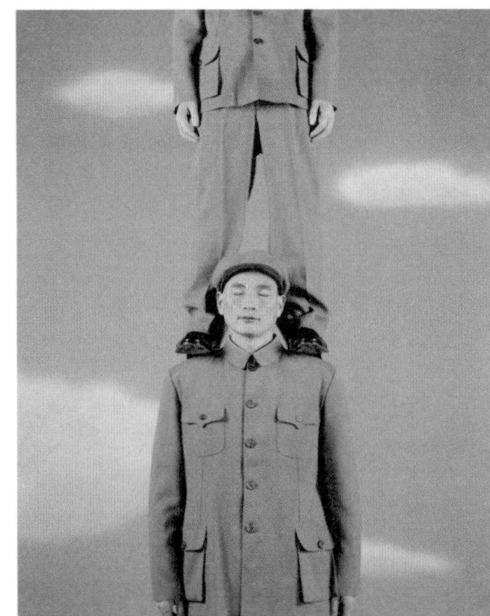

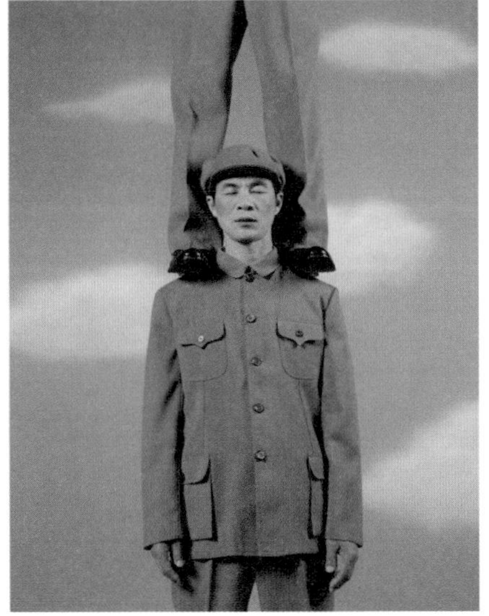

左图
某一天系列59，2009
摄影
left
Some days No.59，2009
Photography

右图
某一天系列60，2009
摄影
right
Some days No.60，2009
Photography

单片机控制中心电路板

Singlechip machine control center circuit board

主从式总线型单片机网络通信结构

Master-Slave bus type scm communications system

主机流程图

Master machine flowchart

从机中断通信流程图

Slave machine communications block-out flowchart

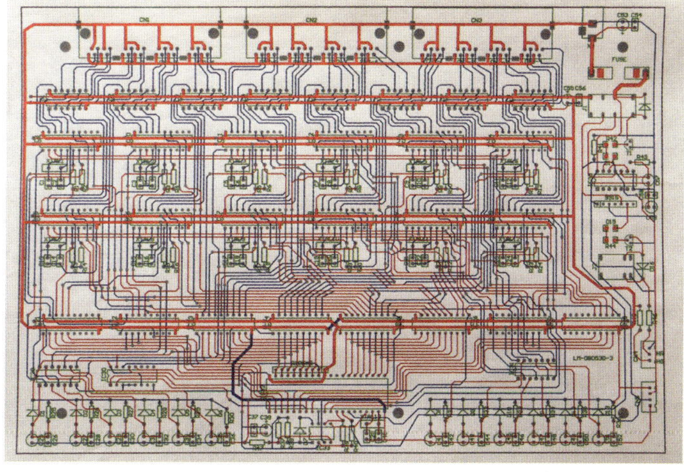

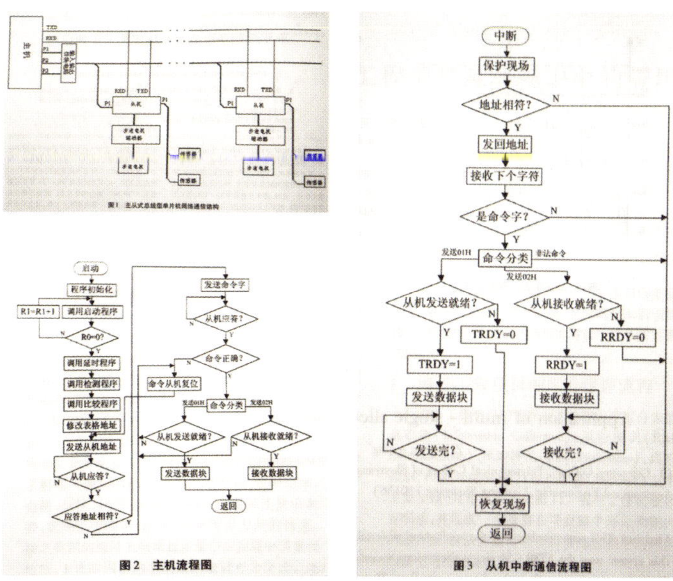

图2 主机流程图

图3 从机中断通信流程图

As an artist, what do you care most during working? Could you please give an example to introduce the process of your work for us?
I often cannot draw a clear line between life and work. If I'm aware of that, I may keep myself focused just like walking through an alley, where I'm all by myself in the darkness. In this way I can avoid duplication of effort.

Suppose you are a critic, from what perspective would you explain and comment on your works?
If I was a critic, I would undoubtedly comment on my work from a critical point of view.

What books and which artists have had or are having an influence on your way of thinking and working?
Jean Henri Fabre's *Souvenirs Entomologiques*, and sometimes I would allow some influence from Duchamp, as the true influence he has on me was reminding me of getting rid of the influence.

向上（局部），2009
装置

Up(detail),2009
Installation

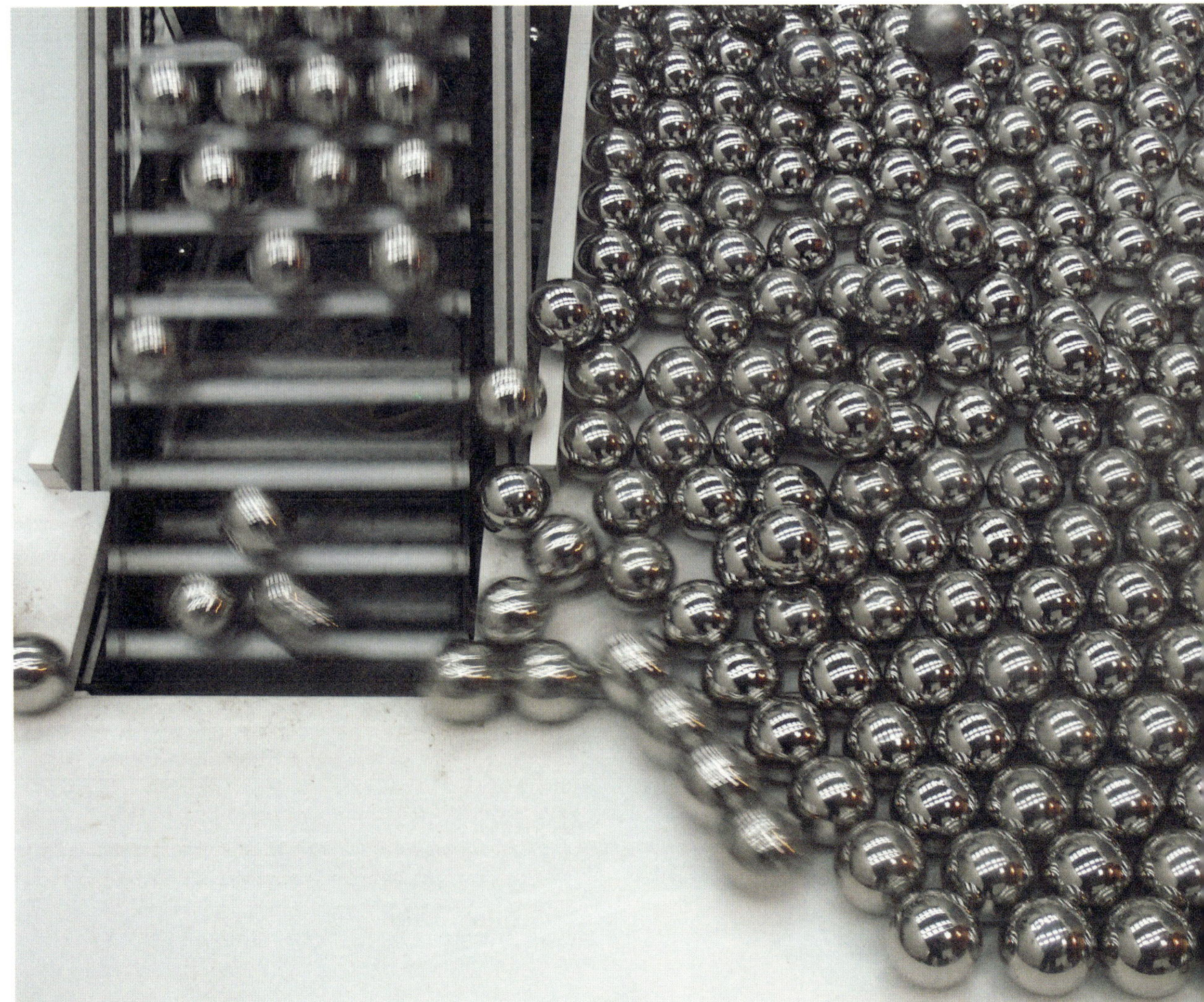

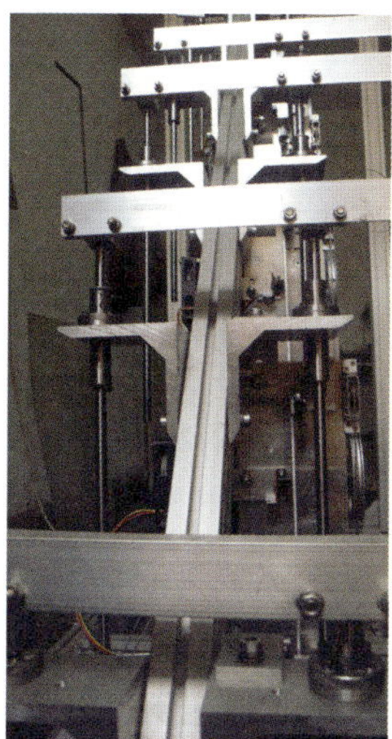 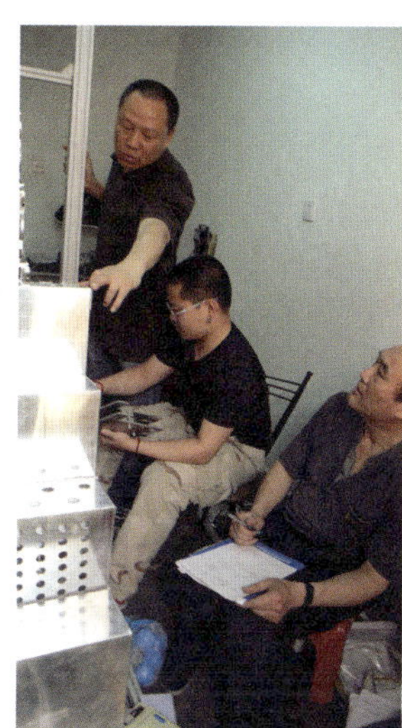

《向上》组装过程，2009

Up in working process,2009
Installation

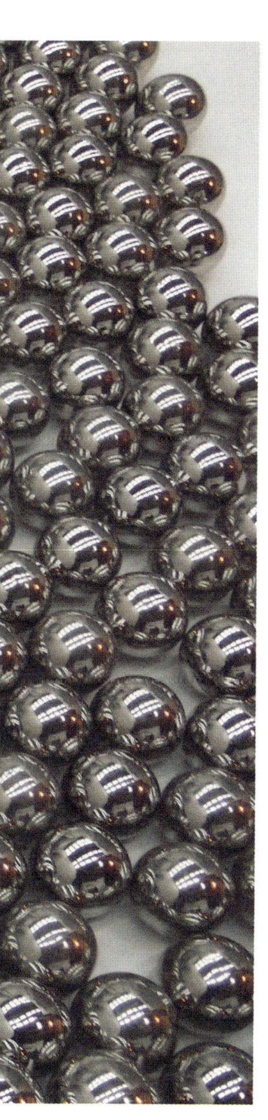

How do you make judgment and decision as to in what context you'd like to present your works? According to you, in what way is the context created by the work related to the work itself?

Normally I won't make such judgments. The present situation is the opportunity of exhibition often arrives after the completion of work and for most of time I don't hold the right to make the decision.

How does your work take the present shape? And please give a few words about the latest development and changes in your work.

The formation of the style mostly is due to innate factors with a bit acquired influence. Recently I found my work is getting greater influence from "acquired" factors. So I began to give up thoughts on the past, the present and the future.

In what circumstances would you want to destroy your own creation?

I knew since long time ago that any attempt of eliminating evidence will be in vain and you would be severely punished if it were brought to light.

What do you think about the relation between the art history and artist's work?

An artist might consider the questions about art history before he/she becomes an artist. As an artist, I think we'd better leave this question to the art history.

What kind of roles would rational thinking and emotional impulse respectively play in your work?

Each time I would restore my rationality after impulse, but soon I will have another wave of irresistible impulse. They occur in a circle, always like that.

以下的这些物理学概念保证了该作品的正常呈现和运行

加速度：速率 (有方向的速度) 的改变称为加速度。 一个物体加速，减速，或改变方向称之为加速度。 当下坡时物体可能提高速率或加速度。

能量(动能+势能)——能量使物体工作/ 动能- 正被使用的能量 能量产生运动/势能——被储存的能量 以后再使用。

能量的守恒定率： 能量可以从一种形式转化为另一种形式但是不会自动生成和消失。

球体能够运行是因为两个基本点:地球引力和能量守恒。

重力加速度:地球表面附近的物体，在仅受重力作用时具有的加速度叫做重力加速度，也叫自由落体加速度。

动量:物体的动量是质量乘以速率。如果质量或速率很大 物体的动量也很大。 物体的动量越大使物体停下来或改变物体的运动方向就越困难。

牛顿的运动三定律

第一定律（惯性定律）:物体在没有外力作用的情况下会保持原有的状态。

第二定律：F=ma ，物体的加速度，与施加在该物体上的外力成正比。

第三定律：作用力与反作用力大小相等，方向相反。

失重：物体对支持物的压力小于物体所受重力的现象叫失重。有两种失重的经历: (1)足够快的速度离开地球到足够高的距离使所受重力近于零（重力可以作用与无限距离人永远不可能脱离）。(2) 下落的速度和和重力加速度是一样的。 即在地球上的加速度是以 9.8 米/ 秒竖直向下行进。

要使人有重量人必须感觉到来自地面的重力反作用力。

作用力、摩擦力、重力、惯性、质量、速度、重量:（解释略)

The following concepts of physics provide theoretical feasibility for the successful installation and operation of this project.

Acceleration
Acceleration (a speed with direction) is the change in velocity over time. An increase and decrease in speed, or a change in the direction is acceleration. The object moving on a curved path may increase the rate of velocity, or acceleration.
Energy (Kinetic energy + Potential energy) — Energy enables an object to work. / Kinetic energy describes a working energy that sets an object in motion. / Potential energy is energy stored within a physical system to do work in a later time period.
The Conservation Law of Energy: Any form of energy can be transformed into another form, but can neither be produced nor destroyed by itself.
Two fundamental principles govern the movement of a sphere: Earth's gravity and the Conservation Law.
An Applied Force
The forces occur between two objects are called the Action and the Reaction, which are a pair of forces opposite in direction.

Friction
Friction is the force resisting the relative lateral motion of solid surfaces in contact.
Gravity
The force that pulls things towards the Earth's center is called gravity.
Acceleration of Gravity
The acceleration of gravity, also called the acceleration of free fall, refers to the acceleration that the Earth imparts to objects on or near its surface due to gravity.
Inertia
An object, such as a sphere, tends to maintain its state of rest unless acted upon by an external force. It is represented numerically by an object's mass.
Mass
Mass refers to the amount of matter an object contains.
Momentum
Momentum is the product of the mass and velocity of an object. The momentum of an object is proportional to its mass and velocity. The bigger the momentum is, the harder it gets to stop the object or change its moving direction.
Newton's Three Laws of Motion

《向上》设计草图，2009
装置
Design drawing *Up*，2009
Installation

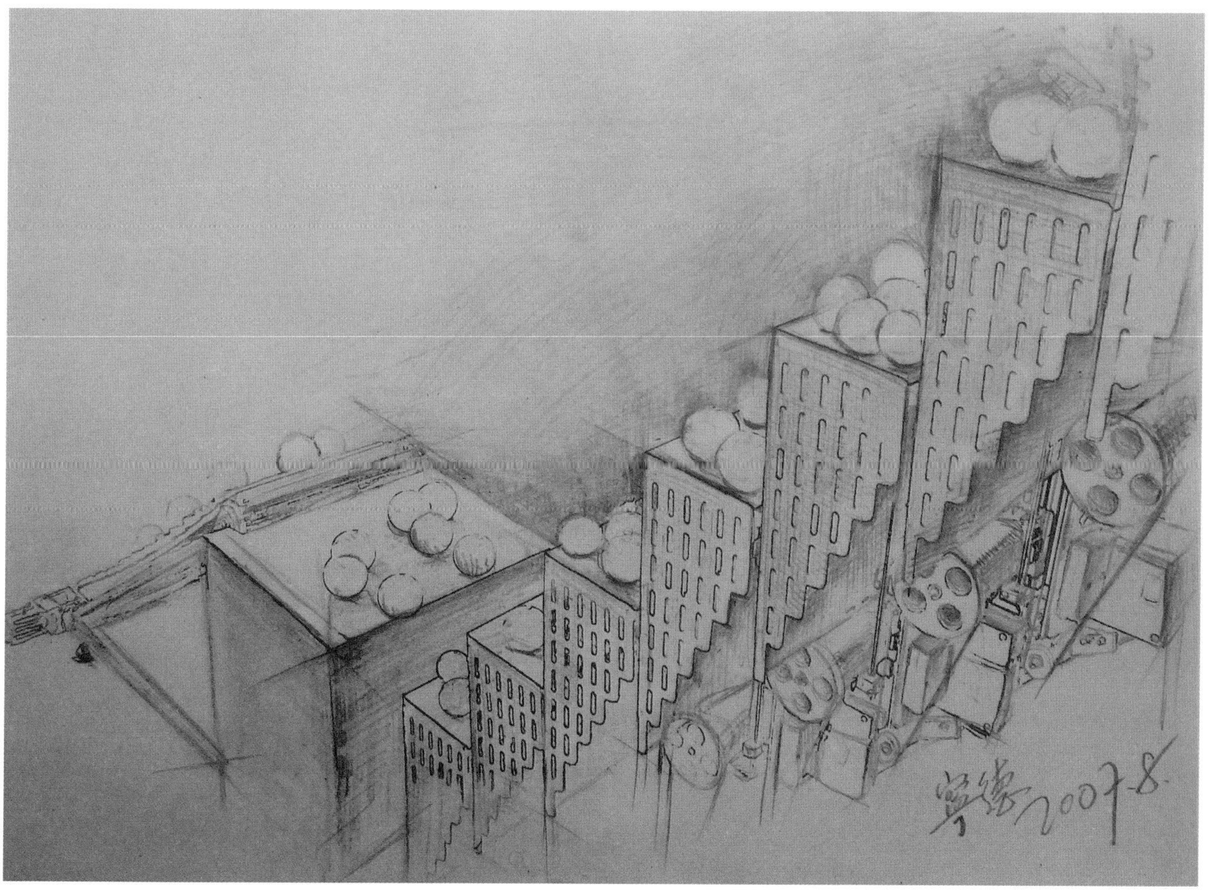

邬建安

WU JIAN'AN

作为艺术家，你在创作中所关心的是什么？以一件作品为例，
分享你的创作过程。
情绪的真实表达与思考的强度。

如果你是一个批评家，你会从什么角度来阐释和讨论你自己的
创作？
历史的，社会学的以及造型语言的。

在你的创作和思考中，什么书籍和艺术家曾经或正在影响着你？
啊，好多，《百年孤独》、《1984年》、《梦的解析》、保
罗·科埃略、博尔赫斯的小说等。
米开朗基罗、达利、毕加索、博伊斯、沃霍尔、阿尔默多瓦、
帕索里尼、库布里克、约翰·列农等。

你是怎样判断和决定在什么语境下呈现你的哪些作品的？你是
怎样看待作品呈现的语境和作品的关系的？
判断社会文化的具体情况，对个人感兴趣的问题需要进行客观
的评估，有些问题的提出会引发人们的思考而有些则不能，都
要看具体的语境。

如何在创作上形成了现在的面貌，描述一下近年来作品的发展
和变化？
其实还很难讲现在形成了什么面貌。近几年来的兴趣好像从特
别关注个人幻觉转向了对主客观结合的历史的关注。

你会在什么情况下摧毁你自己的作品？
不知道。

你怎么看待艺术史和艺术家创作的关系？
艺术家绝大多数情况下都会将自己创作的目标设定为对艺术史
的续写，在精神上获得与前辈英雄人物平等对话的机会。职业
的艺术家都会十分关注艺术史，并试图在其中寻找到证明自己
的创作有价值意义的证据。

在你的工作中，理性和情感冲动各自扮演着什么样的角色？
情感是动力，理性是工具。

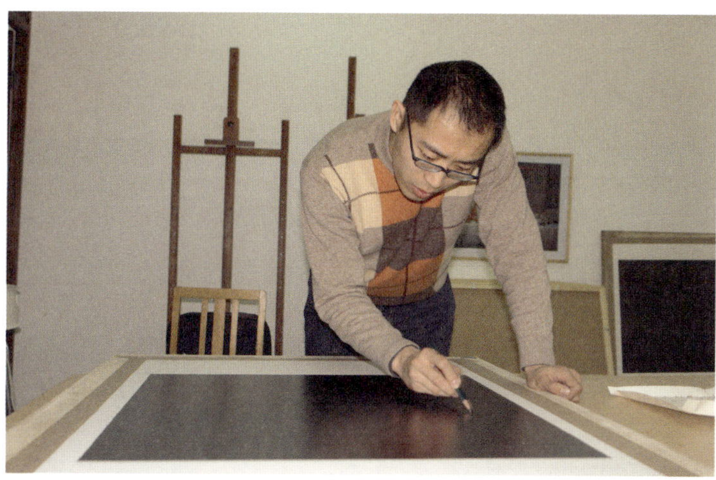

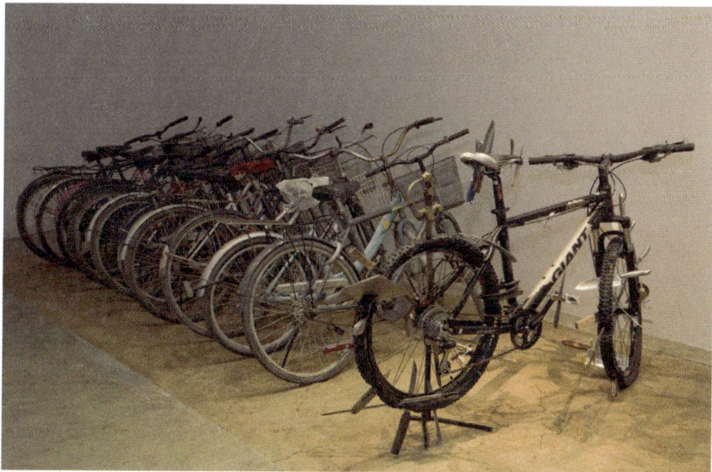

上图 艺术家正在创作《中华6B》
Top The artist working on the work *China 6B*

下图 作品《买辆好车得罪谁了》现场。
Bottom Installation view of *Who got offended when I bought a new bike?*

As an artist, what do you care most during working? Could you please give an example to introduce the process of your work for us?
The true expression of emotion and the intensity of thinking.

Suppose you are a critic, what perspective would you talk about and explain you work from?
Historical, social and linquistic.

What books and which artists have had, or is having an influence on your way of thinking and working?
There are many, such as *One Hundred Years of Solitude*, *1984*, *The Interpretation of Dream* and novels by Paul Coelho and Borges. Artists: Michelangelo, Dali, Picasso, Beuys, Almodovar, Pasolini, Kubrick, John Lenon, etc.

How do you decide the context in which your work is to be presented? How do you consider the relation of the context with your work?
To judge the specific situation of social culture and to evaluate objectively the issues that I have personal interest in, you need

左图
手脚（上），2008
黄铜板激光镂刻
96cm × 152.8cm × 0.15cm

Left
Hands and Feet (up), 2008
Laser cutting on brass plate
96cm × 152.8cm × 0.15cm

右图
驱魔的手法，2004
夹宣镂刻
120cm × 70cm

Right
The Way of Expelling Ghosts, 2004
Engraving on Jiajiang rice paper
120cm × 70cm

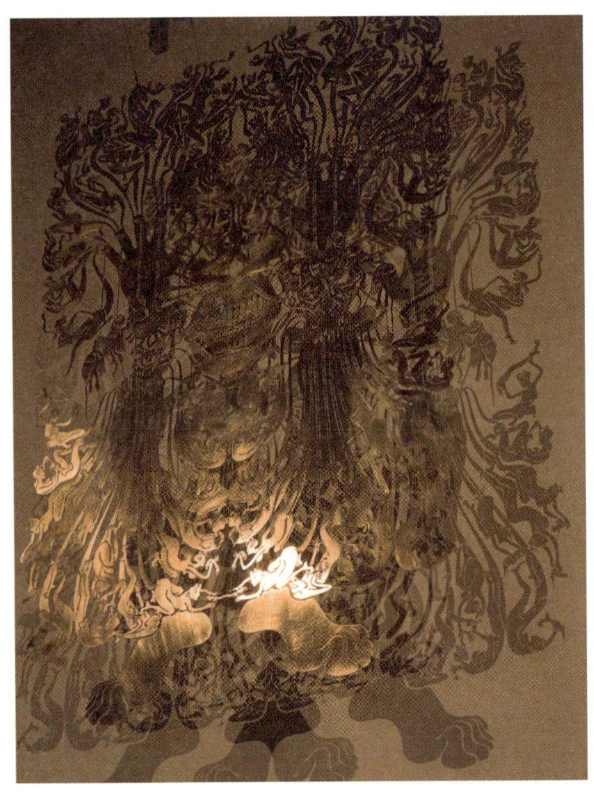

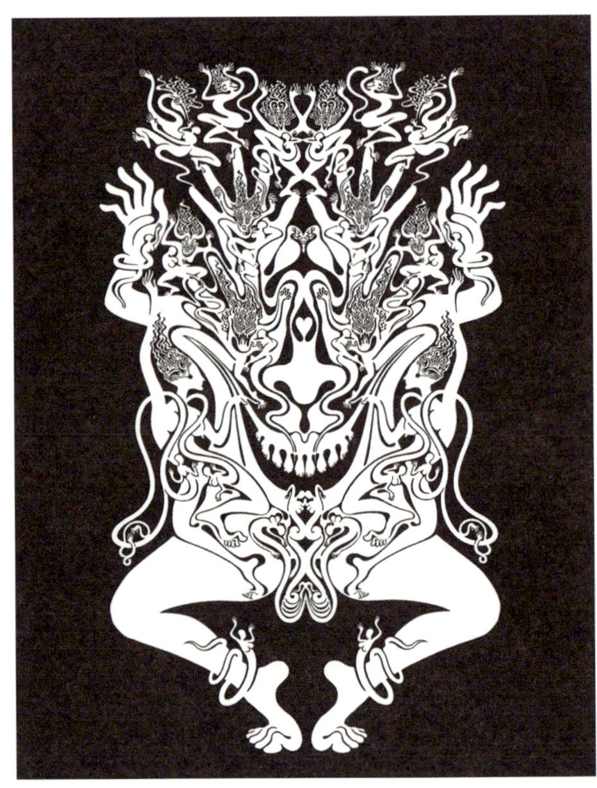

九重天，2007-2008
手工镂刻牛皮、LED灯箱
547.5cm × 390.9cm × 23.3cm

The Heaven of Nine Levels, 2007-2008
Hand engraving on ox hide, LED light box
547.5cm × 390.9cm × 23.3cm

to consider the specific context. Some questions raised will make people think while others won't.

How does your work take the present shape? And please give a few words about the latest development and changes in your work.

Actually it's hard to say what look it has formed now. For the past several years, my interest has changed from personal illusion to the history that combines objectivism and subjectivism.

In what circumstances would you want to destroy your own creation?

I don't know.

What do you think about the relation between the art history and artist's work?

Under most circumstances, artists will set their goal of creation as a postscript of art history so as to acquire an equal opportunity to converse with their heroic predecessors. Professional artists all care much about art history and attempt to find something there to prove their creation meaningful.

What kind of roles would rational thinking and emotional impulse respectively play during your work time?

Emotion is my motivation and rationality is my tool.

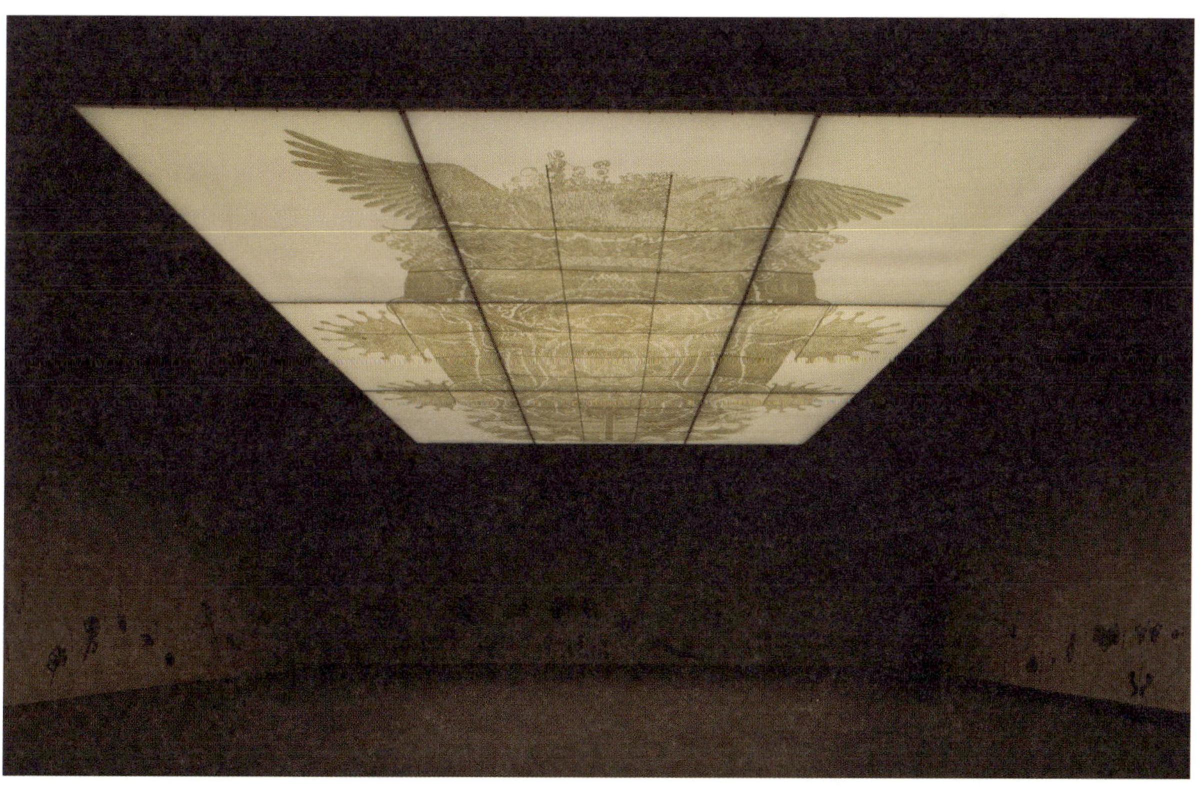

九重天，2007-2008
手工镂刻牛皮、LED灯箱
547.5cm × 390.9cm × 23.3cm

The Heaven of Nine Levels, 2007-2008
Hand engraving on ox hide, LED light box
547.5cm × 390.9cm × 23.3cm

刑天，2006-2007
手工镂刻牛皮、LED灯箱
275.2cm×165cm×14.3cm

Xingtian, 2006-2007
Hand engraving on ox hide, LED light box
275.2cm×165cm×14.3cm

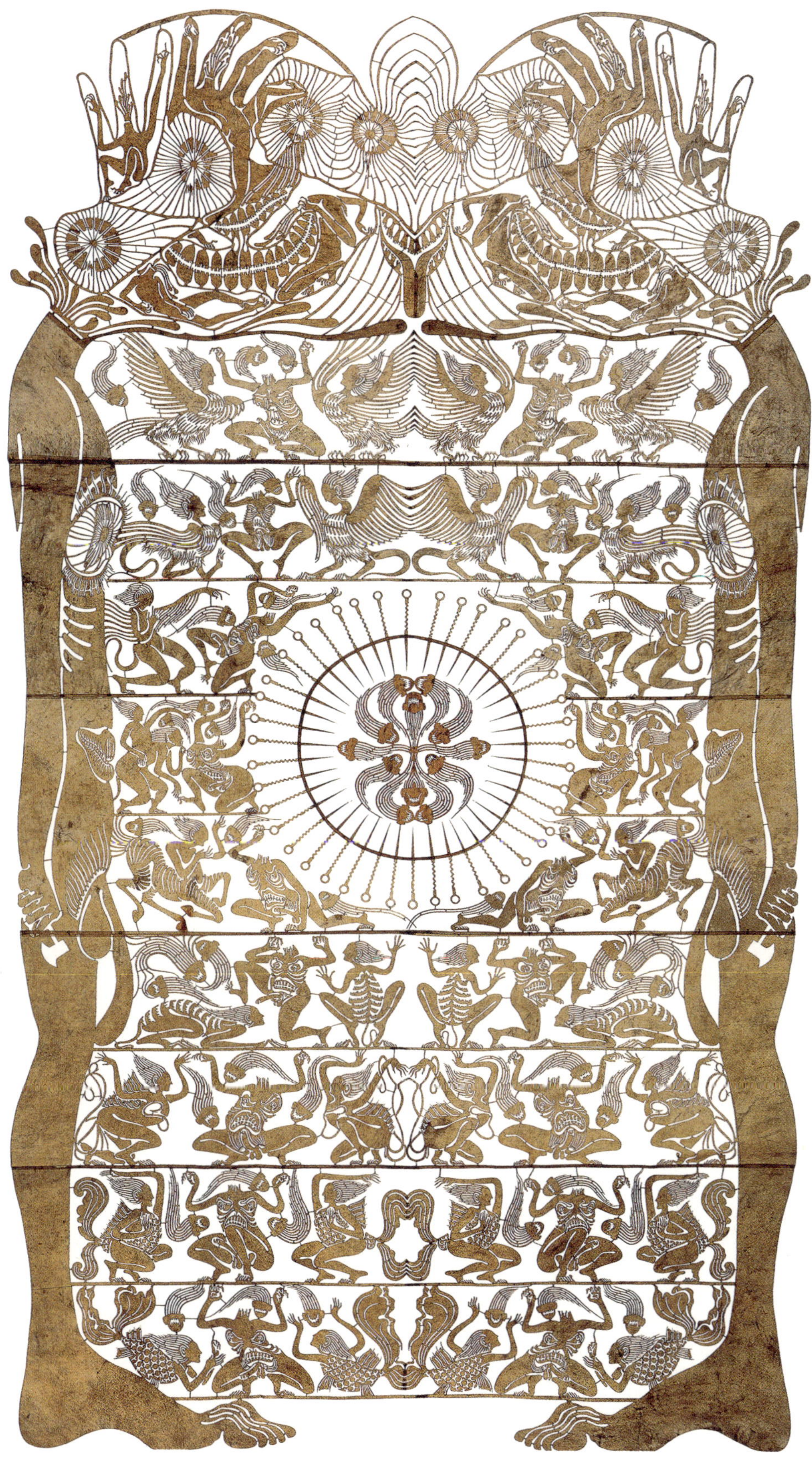

凌迟酷刑，对于我来说是最刺激凶猛的对于伤害的想象，这种酷刑在残忍之余还制造出了些许娱乐的因素。蚩尤在我们这一代人的所受的教育中是一个负面的神话人物形象，是华夏族最早也最大的敌人，是令人恐惧的对手。凌迟掉他，暗示一种彻头彻尾的征服，一方面洗干净了历史记忆里的恐惧，同时也让敌人变成了今天娱乐的材料。

To me, Ling Chi (put to death by dismembering the body) is the most stimulating and ferocious imagination about hurt. This penalty created some sort of entertaining element apart from its cruelty. Chi You is a negative fairy figure in the textbook of our generation. He is the earliest and strongest enemy of Huaxia nation, as well as a frightening opponent. Executing him by Ling Chi suggests a thorough conquer. On one hand, the fear in the memory of history is cleaned; on the other hand, the enemy becomes an object for amusement.

凌迟蚩尤，2009
纸本激光镂刻
200cm×110cm

Execute Chiyou by Lingchi, 2009
Paper Cut
200cm×110cm

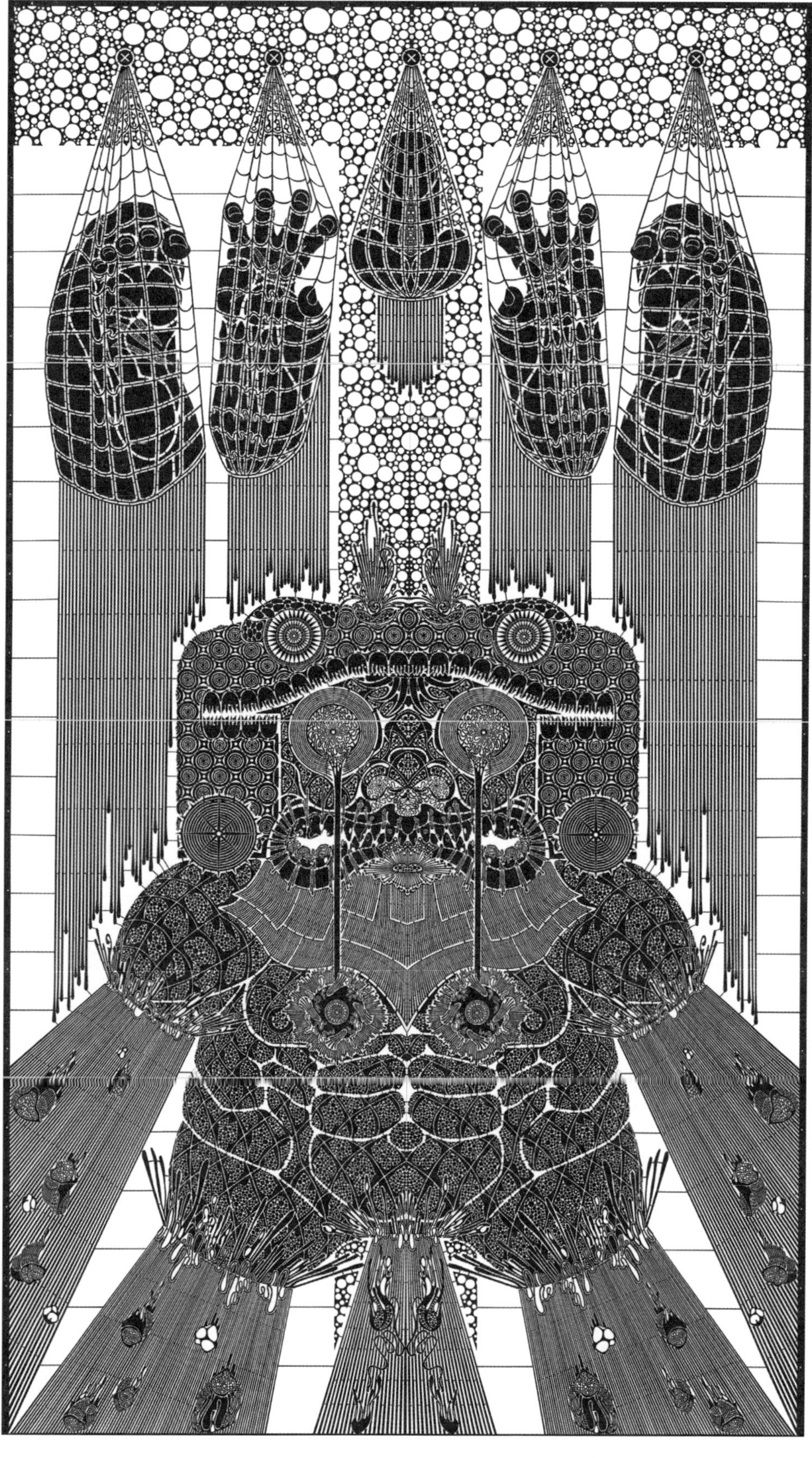

吴俊勇

WU JUNYONG

作为艺术家，你在创作中所关心的是什么？以一件作品为例，分享你的创作过程。

当一种谎言被冠以各种堂皇理由后出现的荒诞景致是我目前最感兴趣的方向之一。比如指鹿为马，我感兴趣的不是指使者的话语，而是受指者由此被衍生出来的新"物种"，一匹长角马成为公共景致。或者说这种理性之外的"怪异公共风景"，一种画蛇添足式刨根思维是我目前的创作当中最惯性的思路。又如："特色"如果是一种颜色，那它在色彩系谱中到底是什么颜色，这真让我百思不得其解，是个让人很着迷又懊恼的象。

如果你是一个批评家，你会从什么角度来阐释和讨论你自己创作？

如果可能的话，我愿意从批判现实主义角度来看。

在你的创作和思考中，什么书籍和艺术家曾经或正在影响你？

我的阅读属于杂食又碎片式的，不深也不成系统。很多的东西会影响到我，有些东西可能会马上进入我的创作，有些可能进入深层意识，在将来某个预期不到的机会浮现。影响我的东西又往往都是某些被忽略的细节，比如某个词、某张图片的局部，某个道具等等。个人的审美趣味也会筛选什么东西会吸引你，我更喜欢的是那种具有古典知识分子或手艺人气质的创作者，严谨而又优雅，严肃而又荒诞。艺术家当中我比较喜欢马格里特，布鲁盖尔之类型；书籍喜欢的不少，眼窄不好说。

你是怎样判断和决定在什么语境下呈现你的哪些作品的？你是怎样看待作品呈现的语境和作品的关系的？

我目前不太考虑语境这个问题，个人的兴趣点几乎都是和这个社会、制度发生最直接的对应，是对这个大语境个人编造的寓言或哑谜。

如何在创作上形成了现在的面貌，描述一下最近年来作品的发展和变化？

创作面貌都是在时间的轨迹中慢慢浮现，开始时或过程中都很模糊，只是把几件作品放在一起看似乎有那么一条线索。就像未来的东西，自己也无法预测。随着阅历的增长和心志的成熟，有些东西会变，那些内心深处的东西是变不掉的。我个人对过去的总结是：前几年较多聚焦于个人身体内部，这几年更关注身体的外部，换句话来讲就是从医学的身体过渡到社会学的身体。我记得以前一个朋友谈到：其实每个人的第一件比较

剪纸，作者日常的素材准备
Paper cutting material

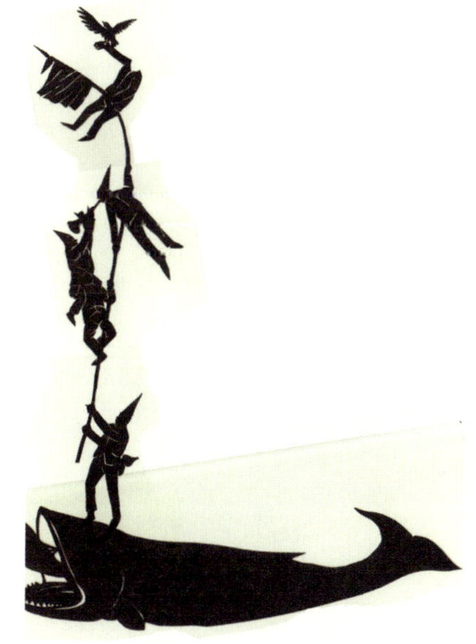

严肃的作品就是他全部作品的主题。我深有同感！

你会在什么情况下摧毁你自己的作品？

当一件作品让我觉得厌恶，我会把它藏起来，搁置一段时间。我几乎不摧毁我的作品，但总是试着找出更合理的解决办法。如果是一张完成的画，很可能已经被刮掉或覆盖过好几遍；如果是一件前几年的录像作品，只要觉得不满意我也会重复改。

你怎么看待艺术史和艺术家创作的关系？

艺术史影响艺术家，艺术家受惠于艺术史，艺术家创作植根于艺术史脉络的土壤。艺术史是个选择史，不考虑艺术史创作或针对艺术史创作的艺术家都有可能进入艺术史，艺术家是被动的。历史是现在对过去或未来对现在的筛选，没有现在对现在的判断。我的看法是艺术家创作属于那个时代的作品，并且能够做到和那个时代艺术家不一样多一点的作品就够了。
附：最近的案头创作之　《献给某某的礼物》就是和艺术史对应的作品，就是你在做某件作品过程中忽然觉得它和记忆中的某种作品气质上特别相近，像接上某种超越时空的信号波。

在你的工作中，理性和情感冲动各自扮演着什么样的角色？

在阅读或胡乱浏览互联网时，往往会蹦出一个觉得有戏的"图像"，如何在作品中保留住那个最初让你觉得有意思的感觉，有时很清晰有时又很模糊，如何捕捉，又如何把几个感觉串为一件作品，这时理性就得给这念头擦"屁股"，要费掉好几天或数月。
应该说在对作品质量控制的层面感觉的比较占优势，在作品制作的角度理性耗费比较大。

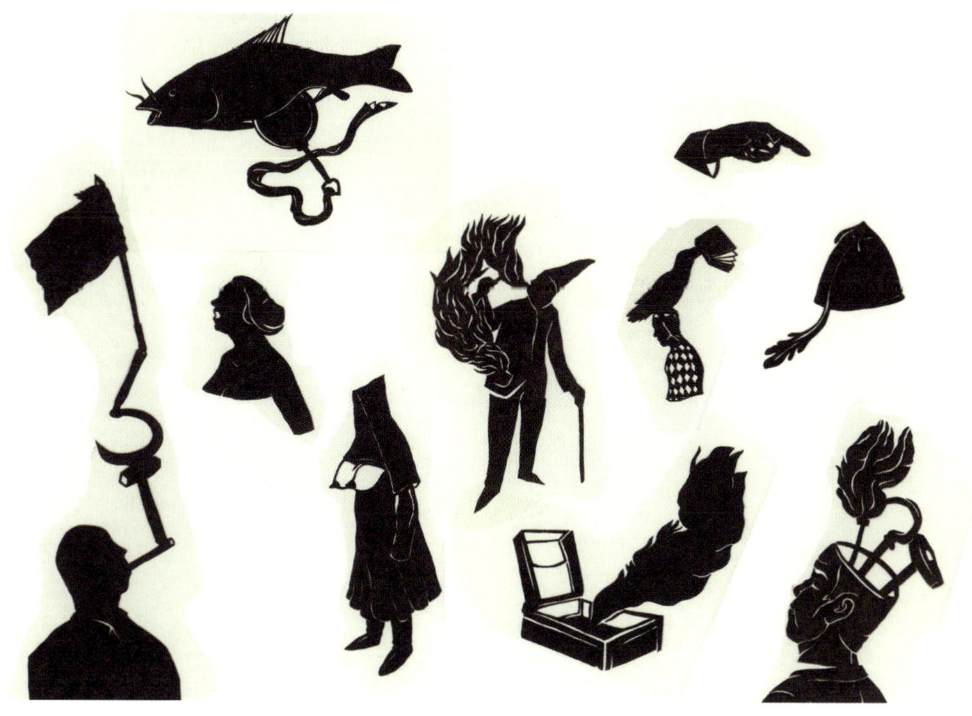

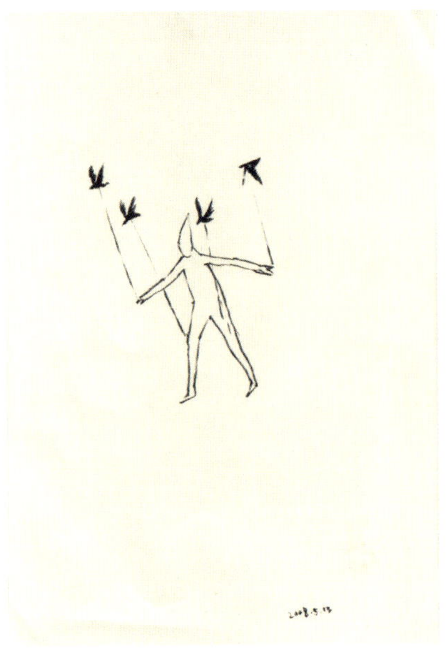
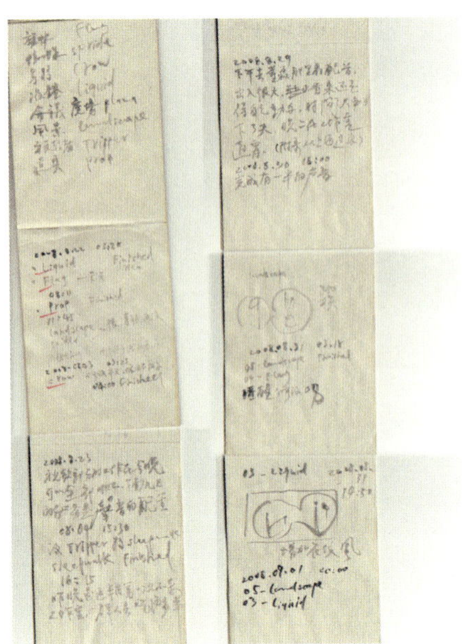
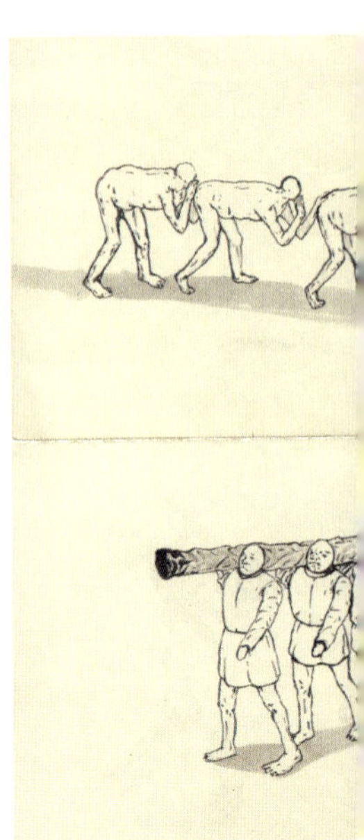

日常记录性手稿，为《蜘蛛的圆周》等作品准备
Manuscripts and notes, making preparations for *Circle of Spider*

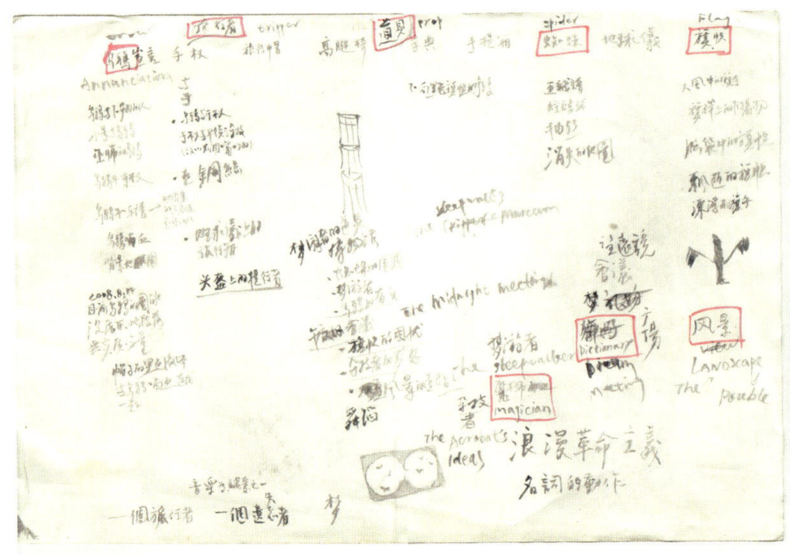
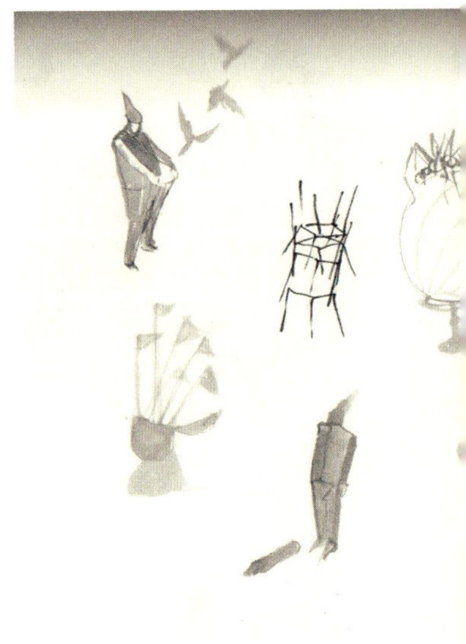

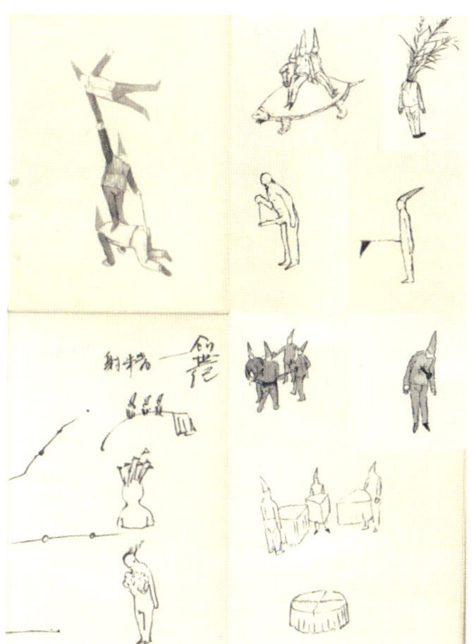

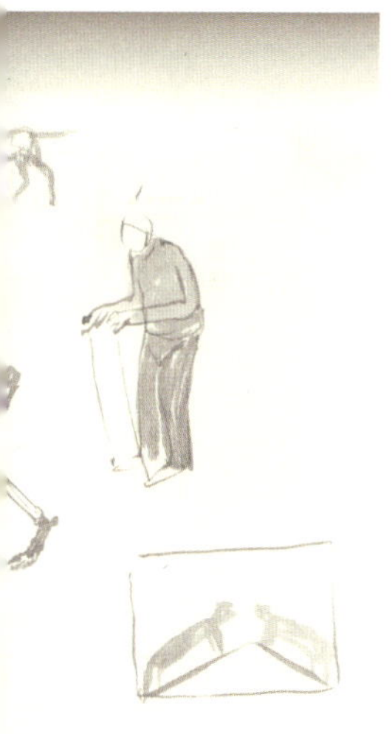

日常记录性手稿，为《蜘蛛的圆周》等作品准备
Manuscripts and notes, making preparations for *Circle of Spider*

As an artist, what do you care most during working? Could you please give an example to introduce the process of your work for us?

I become fairly interested in the absurd scene after a lie is covered up with high-sounding words. Take "to call a stag a horse" (to confuse right and wrong) as an example. To me, it is not important what one says when he calls a stag a horse, but the new "species" that derives from the called—a horse with deer horns becomes a public view, or "grotesque public scenery" independent of reason. I tend to "go to the bottom while gilding the lily" these days.

Again, if "special feature" (special color in Chinese literally) is a color, then what color is it in the color spectrum? It's something puzzling, fascinating and also frustrating.

Suppose you are a critic, from what perspective would you explain and comment on your works?

I will choose Critical Realism if it is possible.

What books and which artists have had, or are having an influence on your way of thinking and working?

I'm an omnivorous reader of fragments. It's neither profound nor systematic. Lots of things can influence me. Some might be integrated into my works immediately and some into deep consciousness and will surface unexpectedly some time in the future. What influences me is generally those neglected details, such as a word, part of a picture, a stage property, and many other things. Personal taste is also at work when we choose our interest. I prefer classical intellectuals or those with craftsmanship. They are precise and graceful, serious and absurd.

Among the artists, I prefer those types like Margaret and Bruegel. As to books, I like them quite a lot. It's hard to draw a conclusion now.

How do you make judgment and decision as to in what context you'd like to present your works? According to you, in what way is the context created by the work related to the work itself?

At present I don't think much about context. Personal interest invariably and directly corresponds to the society and the system. It is a fable or a riddle made up by individuals in a broad context.

How does your work take the present shape? And please give a few words about the latest development and changes in your work.

The style forms gradually as time goes. It's something vague both in the initial stage and in its development. A clue seems to surface when we compare several works. It's like something in the future. I can make no prediction. As I get more experiences and become more mature psychologically, some things may change, but what is buried in the recesses of my mind will not. I can conclude that more focus had been given to the inner part of human body before I came to concentrate more on the human exteriors. In other words, it is a change form medicine to sociology. I remember a friend of mine once said that everyone's first serious work covered all the

山中公园，2009
影像装置
效果图1

Shanzhong Park, 2009
Video Installation
Drawing 1

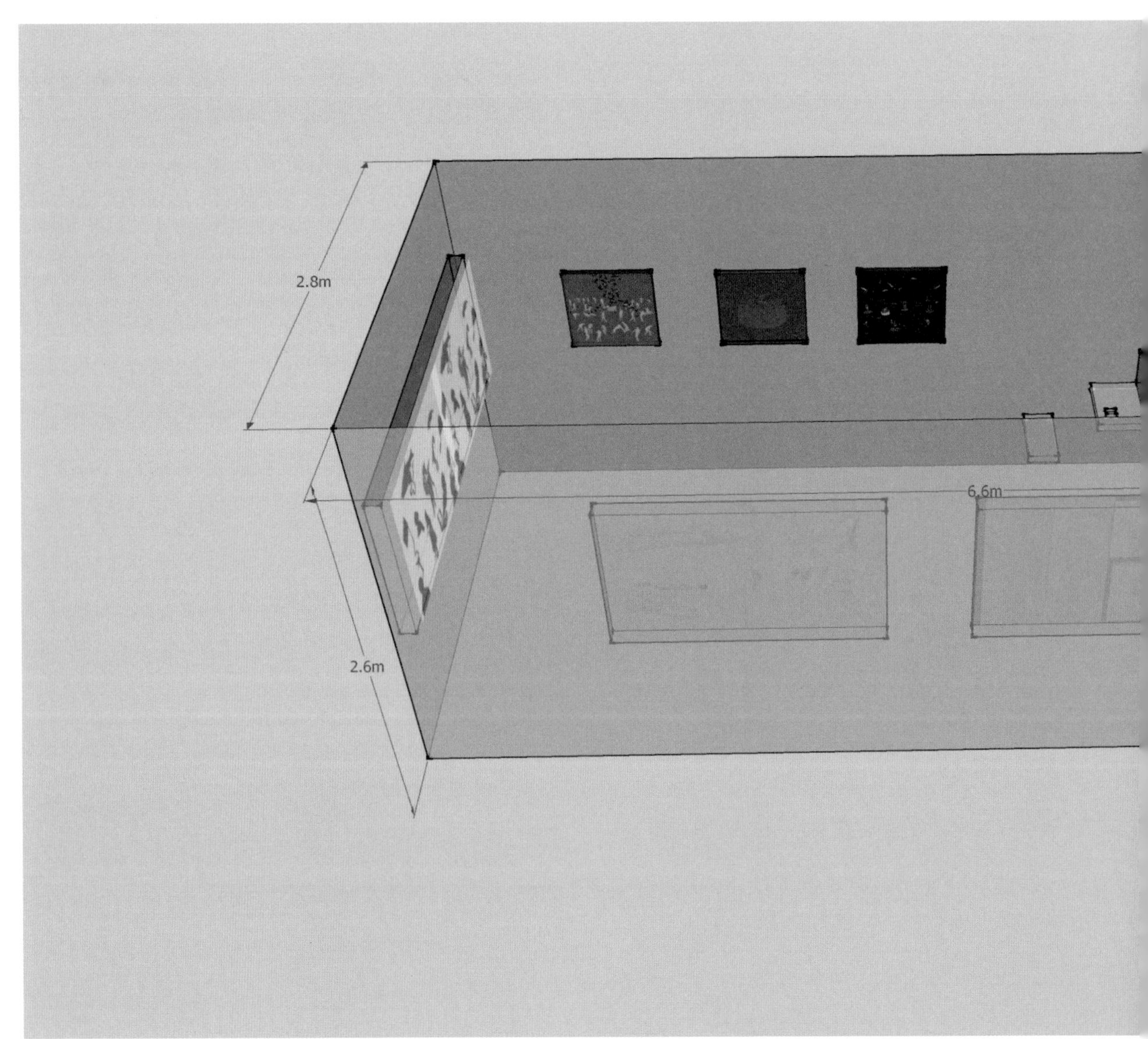

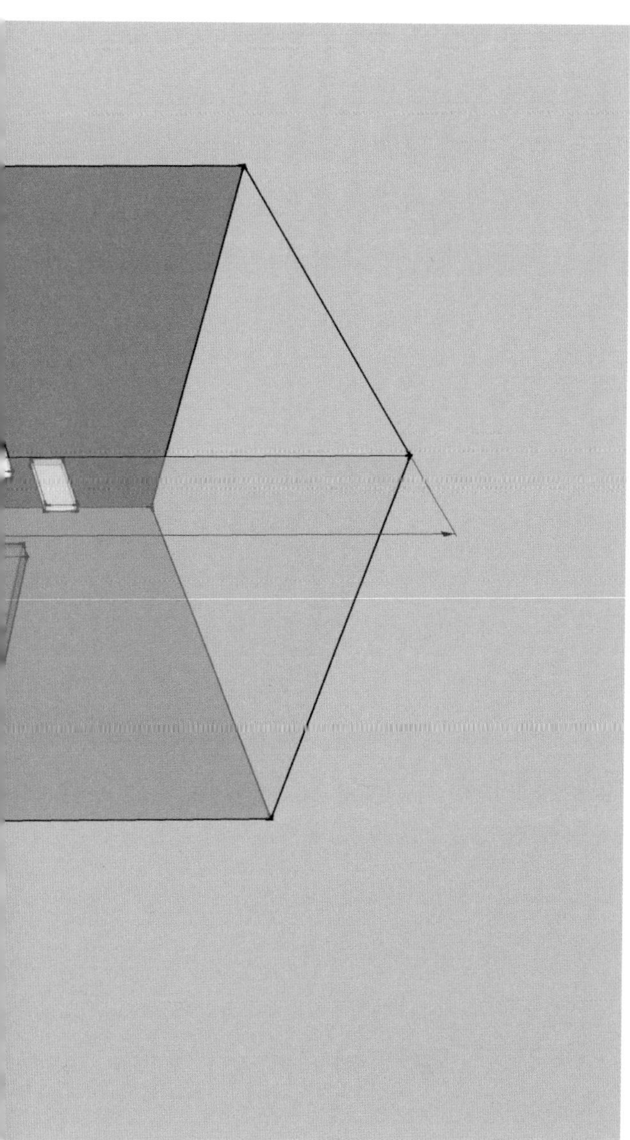

themes to come. I can't agree more.

In what circumstances would you want to destroy your own creation?

I would put my work in a secret place and keep it there for some time if it bothers me. I rarely destroy my own works, but I do try to find more reasonable ways to improve it. If it is a finished one, it might be scraped or covered again and again. If it is a video shot several years ago, I will keep on making modifications until I am satisfied.

What do you think about the relation between the art history and artist's work?

History of art influences artists and the latter benefit from and root their works in the former. History o f art is a history of selection. Both artists who are independent of history of art and those who are reliant on it will be remembered. Artists are passive.

History is the present selection of the past or the future selection of the present. In history there is no judgment of the present. I think it's enough if an artist can offer works that belong to his age and differ greatly from his peers.

Note: *A gift to Somebody*, a recent work of mine, corresponds in some way to history of art. During my creation, it occurred to me that the work I was engaged in at that moment shared something with certain works in my memory. It's like you are getting connected with some signal wave beyond time and space.

What kind of roles would rational thinking and emotional impulse respectively play in your work?

An "image" that seems to be leading to inspiration will come out when I read or search the Internet with no particular aim. How to retain this feeling that interests you in the beginning? How to catch this feeling that is sometimes clear and sometimes vague? How to include several feelings of this kind into a work? Here reason is needed to "clear up the messy situation". It takes days or even months.

Feelings reign when it comes to a work's essence; reason weighs more when the work needs to be brought to the public.

我的兴趣点一直聚焦于"身体和政治的混杂体",几乎所有的图像都衍生和游离在生理学和社会学的交界地带。

现实的荒诞,我更愿选择一种寓言象征的黑色叙述。在现实和幻想的两个世界间编织个人视角的社会肖像。

如果要打个比方的话,我的工作更像是在摆弄一个图像符号的魔方,在器官、肢体、俚语、记忆、符号等漂浮的染色体中发现和拼凑出某种不确切的"图像链接"。

它们可能是一场狂欢的夜宴,是沉默的黑暗对聚光灯的戏谑和嘲讽;或者,仅仅是个人恍惚中视网膜上漂浮的幻象世界。

"Melange of human body and politics" is always my focus of interest. Almost all the images derive from and drift where physiology and sociology border each other.

The absurdity of reality leads me all the more to allegorical black narration, portraying the world as an individual commuting between reality and imagination.

If we need an analogy, my job is no more than playing with a Rubik's cube of images—from such drifting chromosomes as organs, bodies, slang, memory and symbols, I identify and piece together certain indefinite "image links" that might be a noisy night party, silent darkness's amusement and sarcasm of the spotlights, or just a world of illusion floating on the retina of a soul in trance.

我的兴趣点一直聚焦于"身体和政治的混杂体",几乎所有的图像都衍生和游离在生理学和社会学的交界地带。

现实的荒诞,我更愿选择一种寓言象征的黑色叙述。在现实和幻想的两个世界间编织个人视角的社会肖像。

如果要打个比方的话,我的工作更像是在摆弄一个图像符号的魔方,在器官、肢体、俚语、记忆、符号等漂浮的染色体中发现和拼凑出某种不确切的"图像链接"。

它们可能是一场狂欢的夜宴,是沉默的黑暗对聚光灯的戏谑和嘲讽;或者,仅仅是个人恍惚中视网膜上漂浮的幻象世界。

"Melange of human body and politics" is always my focus of interest. Almost all the images derive from and drift where physiology and sociology border each other.

The absurdity of reality leads me all the more to allegorical black narration, portraying the world as an individual commuting between reality and imagination.

If we need an analogy, my job is no more than playing with a Rubik's cube of images—from such drifting chromosomes as organs, bodies, slang, memory and symbols, I identify and piece together certain indefinite "image links" that might be a noisy night party, silent darkness's amusement and sarcasm of the spotlights, or just a world of illusion floating on the retina of a soul in trance.

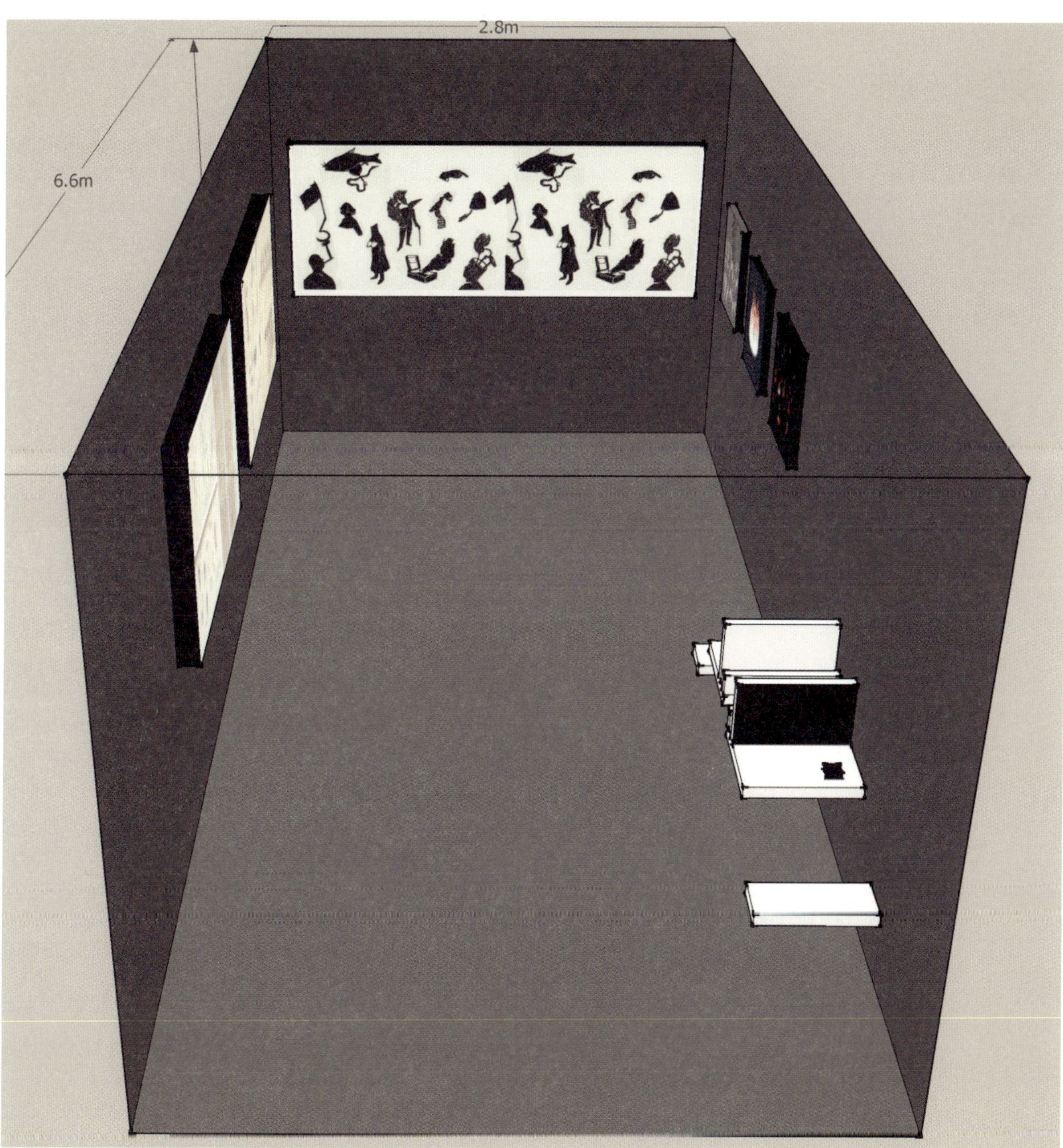

山中公园，2009
影像装置
效果图2

Shanzhong Park, 2009
Video Installation
Drawing 2

吴小军

WU XIAOJUN

作为艺术家，你在创作中所关心的是什么？以一件作品为例，分享你的创作过程。

作为艺术家在创作中所关心的是对公众、对社会、对艺术的价值判断。

通常情况下每件作品的创作过程都是不同的，就如《2025计划》这个作品，主要灵感来自于一本书和相关的事件及其一些历史文献。尤其是这些历史文献启发了我重新审视"劳动使人自由"这句"纳粹"口号在今天的回响。另外，我采集了200多个（近年矿难每月平均数）黑色矿工灯，用它设计、制作了一个装饰吊灯，并且安装了一个计时器，用以控制矿灯闪烁的次数，恰好是我的心跳的平均数值——每秒70次。最后通过阅读杰弗里·萨克斯的《贫困的终结》我总结了一个公式，就是2025年等于每人、每天、一美元，根据这个公式全球的极端贫困在2025年即将终结，这就像是我们的一个未来，同样还是用霓虹闪耀。这件作品本身的"阅读"特点也再次呈现出历史、现在、未来以及我们的"现实"。

如果你是一个批评家，你会从什么角度来阐释和讨论你自己的创作？

这种假设也是"问责"自己的常用方法之一，如果可能，我会从对抗主义和忧郁的马克思主义以及关系美学的角度来阐释和讨论自己的创作。

在你的创作和思考中，什么书籍和艺术家曾经或正在影响着你？

影响我的书籍和艺术家并不是很多，主要的书籍是《历史的观念》、《资本论》、《开放的作品》、《偶然性、霸权和普遍性》、《权利的眼睛》，艺术家是杜桑、Jennifer Allora & Guillermo Calzadilla、八大山人、圣地亚哥等。

你是怎样判断和决定在什么语境下呈现你的哪些作品的？你是怎样看待作品呈现的语境和作品的关系的？

首先我要强调的是"当代"语境下的艺术本质是什么？"当

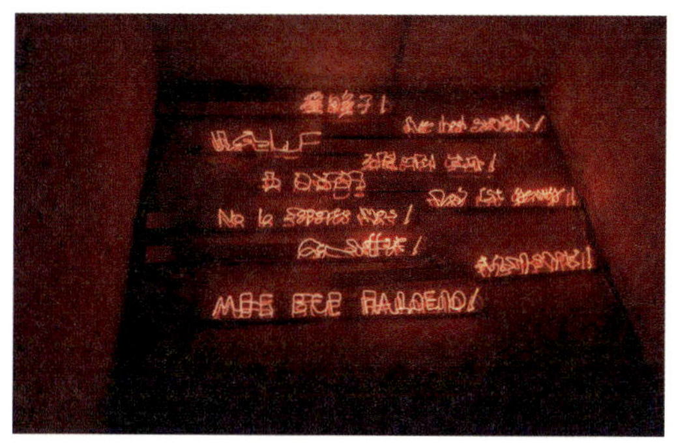

你伤了我的心、但伤不了我的灵魂，2007
装置
材料：木、霓虹灯
120 x 110 x 50cm

You Can Break My Heart But You Can't Touch My Soul, 2007
Installation
Materials: Wood, neon light
120 x 110 x 50 cm

劳动使人自由，2008
装置
材料：霓虹灯
200 x 300cm

Work Makes One Free, 2008
Installation
Materials: Neon light
200 x 300 cm

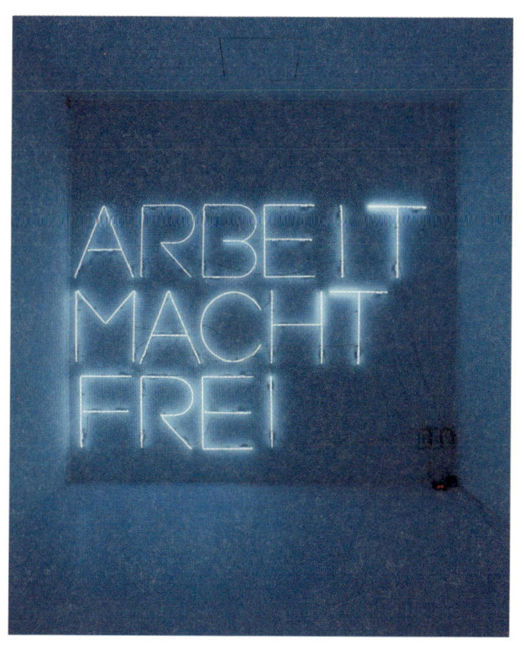

代"性的含义是什么？这既是历史性的假设，也是当今的世界图景以及全球危机中的低迷蔓延。我们要发现"当代"的最主要指标。因此在这个语境下，怎样了解当下的社会主张，也是当下社会内怎样创作艺术的主张，这对于艺术家而言尤为重要。所以《2025计划》正是在当下对新自由主义、超级政治的历史性自我反省。

如何在创作上形成了现在的面貌，描述一下近年来作品的发展和变化？

就目前而论，我的创作面貌还没形成，也许这是件好事，在不确定的各个面貌之间左右逢源，最先开始我是以社会、新闻事件为材料创作了一些作品，像《我没有太多的话要说》、《F1赛车》。而后慢慢地从"真实"的背景中抽离并转化成一种能量。像《礼物》、《2025年计划》这些做品，也为开启"真实界"空间的可能性提供例证。

你会在什么情况下摧毁你自己的作品？

其实每次作品的完成之时，就是它的毁灭之日，就物质而言我没有刻意摧毁它，但就意识而言它早就"消亡殆尽"。

你怎么看待艺术史和艺术家创作的关系？

如果还够幸运，那么艺术家的责任之一就是颠覆艺术史，在艺术史之外留下自己的一道划痕。

在你的工作中，理性和情感冲动各自扮演着什么样的角色？

这要视具体情况而定，通常情况下首先是感性先觉而后是理性，最终还原感性，用理性稀释情感冲动，因为我相信最彻底的反动和颠覆来白理性的力量。

你的创作有什么一致的倾向？

创作的一致性倾向正是我要努力清理的，这就是有关温度、有关情怀、有关记忆、有关诗意的内心"乌托邦"。

在最近观看和思考艺术家的创作时，技术性的层面、技法和过程越来越显得重要。情感和动机的叙述往往显得可疑。一个艺术家在向另外一个人描述自己的创作时，可否原原本本地把他的技法和创作过程讲述出来？

在这个技术垄断一切的"帝国时代"。的确，一切的情感和动机的叙述都显得即可疑又可怜，我们已经习惯了通过技艺的细枝末梢来感受观念、思维的存在。就像一场没有意外的"演讲"主题，叙述都可以忽略不计，而"演讲者"的一个姿态，一个手势确使人不能忘怀，对"就是这样"一个手势的能量，因此技艺的"手势"早已是艺术的重要部分之一，思想也好，观念也罢，都期待着这个创造性的"手势"来召唤来激活我们有限的想象力。对于大多数艺术家来说描述自己的创作就已经面临挑战和风险。还是最好在描述创作的过程中，迷茫一些、混沌一些并多留一些空间，为了想象力无限可能而保守秘密。

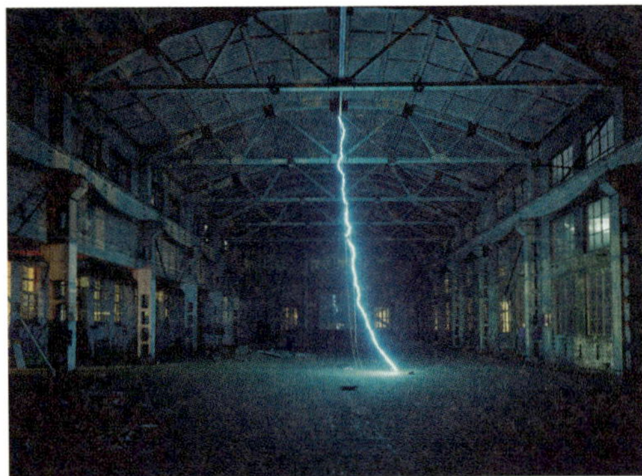

礼物2006，2006
装置
材料：霓虹灯
1500cm

Gift 2006, 2006
Installation
Materials: Neon light
1500 cm

心跳，2008
装置
材料：矿工灯、电缆、计时器
120x130cm

Heartbeat, 2008
Installation
Materials: Miner＇s lamp, wire, digital timer

As an artist, what do you care most during working?Could you please give an example to introduce the process of your work for us?

As an artist, what I'm concerned about in creating is the value judgment of art, the public, and society.

Usually, the creating process of each piece of work is different. For example, for *2025 Project*, my idea was mainly inspired by a book and its related events and some historical documents. In particular, these historical literatures evoked me to re-examine how the Nazi slogan "work brings freedom" resonates today. In addition, I collected more than 200 (the monthly average number of coalmine accident in recent years) black miner lamps, with which I designed and made a decorative chandelier, and installed a timer to control the number of miner's lamp flickering, which was exactly the average value of my heartbeat- 70 times per second. Finally, after reading *The End of Poverty* by Jeffrey Sachs, I summed up a formula - that is, the year of 2025 is equivalent to one dollar per person, per day. According to this formula, the extreme poverty around the world will end in 2025, which is just as one future of us as when neon light still shines. This piece of work itself once again features the history, the present and the future, as well as our "reality" in the sense of reading.

Suppose you are a critic, what perspective would you talk about and explain you work from?

This assumption is also one of the methods commonly used for the "accountability"; if it's possible, I would utilize antagonism and the depressing Marxism, as well as the relational aesthetics to illustrate and discuss my own creations.

What books and which artists have had, or is having an influence on your way of thinking and working?

There are not too many books or artists that influenced me - the books mainly are *The Idea of History*, *Das Kapital*, *Open Work*, *Contingency, Hegemony and Universality*, and the *Eye of Power*, and the artists are Duchamp, Jennifer Allora & Guillermo Calzadilla, Bada Shanren, Santiago and so on.

How do you decide the context in which your work is to be presented? How do you consider the relation of the context with your work?

First, I want to emphasize: in the "contemporary" context, what is the nature of art? And what "contemporary" mean? This is not only historical assumptions, but also today's world picture and spread of the downturn in the global crisis. We must find the most important indicators for "contemporary". Therefore, in this context, it is particularly important for the artist to figure out how to understand the contemporary social ideas; that's how does the contemporary society create arts. Therefore, the *2025 Project* is right historical self-examination in neo-liberalism and super politics nowadays.

How does your work take the present shape? And please give a few words about the latest development and changes in your work.

So far, my own creative outlook has not formed yet, and perhaps this

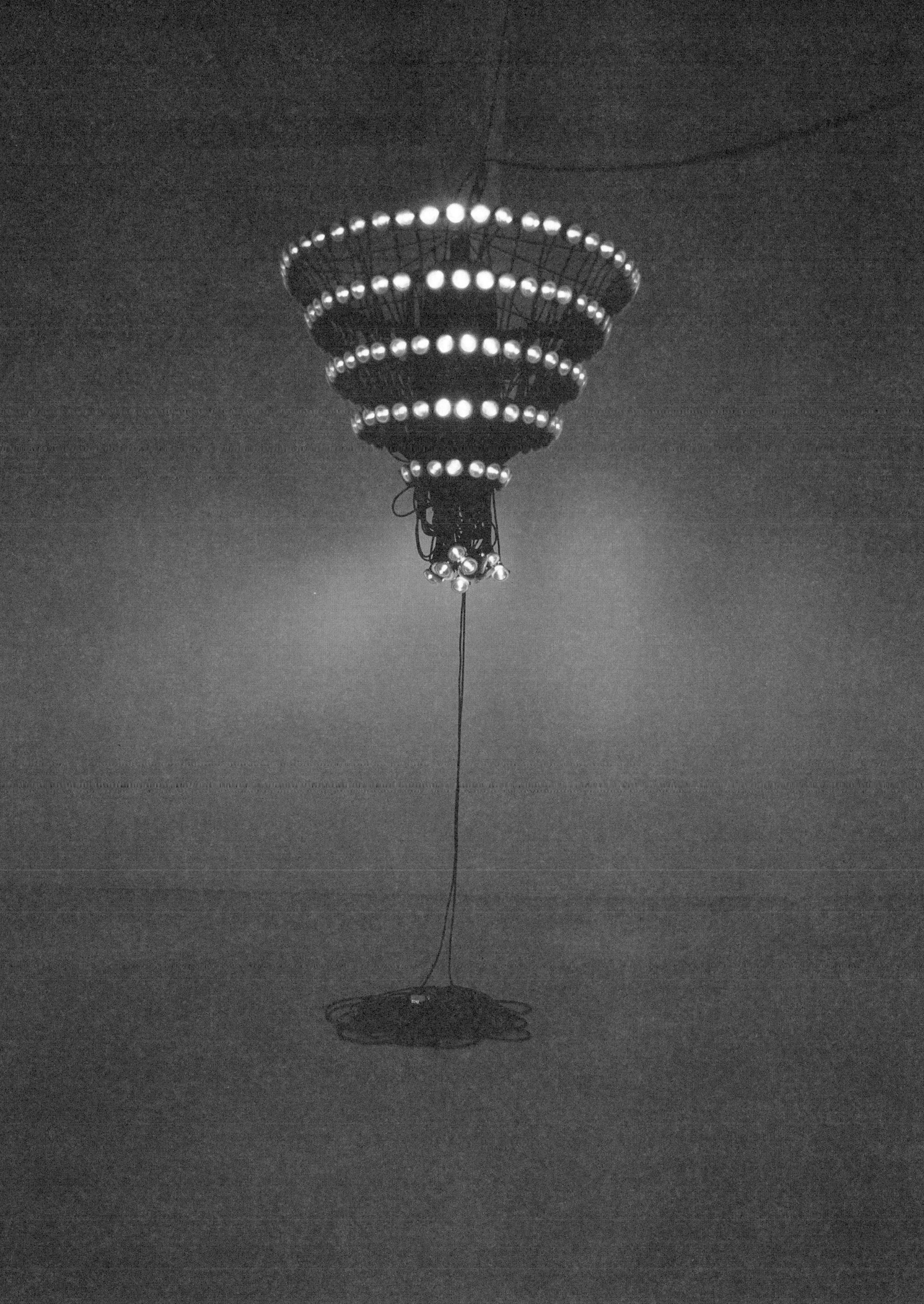

is a good thing, for I can try all directions and uncertainties best. At beginning, I created a number of works based on society and news and events, such as *I Have Not Too Much to Say* , *F1 Car*. And then slowly from the "real" backgrounds I detached and transformed them into a kind of energy, such as *Gift*, *2025 Project*, which also provided proofs for the possibilities to open a "real world" space.

In what circumstances would you want to destroy your own creation?
In fact, upon completion of each work, it's the day of its destruction; physically, it's not destroyed by myself intentionally, but consciously, it has long been "dead dreadfully".

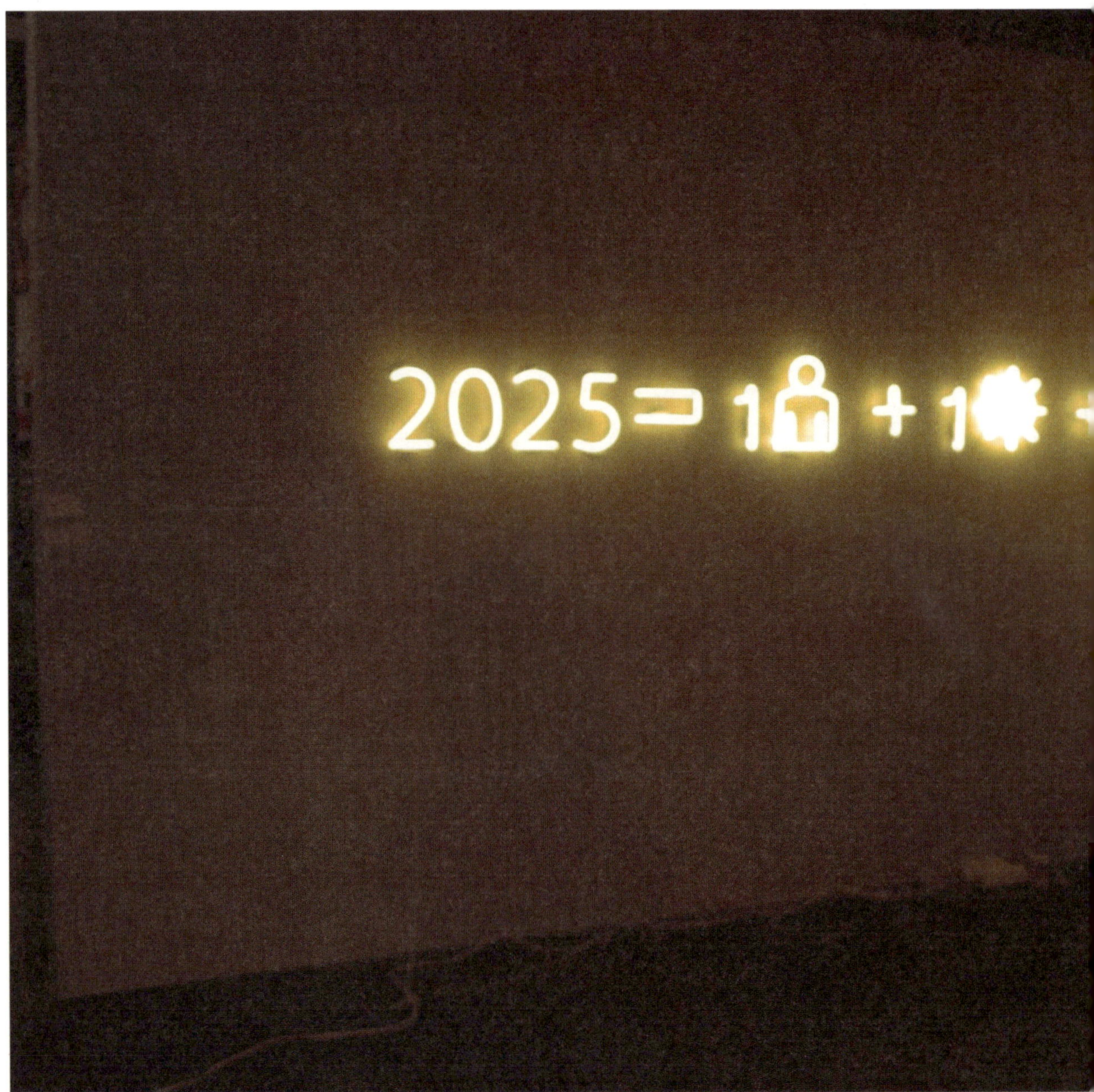

What do you think about the relation between the art history and artist's work?

If lucky enough, it is one of the artist's responsibilities to subvert the art history, to leave a track of own beyond it.

What kind of roles would rational thinking and emotional impulse respectively play during your work time?

It depends. Usually, first I'm emotional, then rational and eventually back to emotions. Sense can dilute emotional impulse, because I believe that the most radical reaction and subversion come from the force of sense.

Is there any consistent tendency in your work?

Consistent tendency in creating is exactly what I should work hard to clean up, which is inner "utopia" related to temperature, feelings, memories and poetry.

Recent studies and observations on artist's work show that technical devices, methods and the art-making process are more important parameters than we thought before. Narratives evolving from topics of sentiment and motive more often become unreliable. Is it possible for an artist to honestly describe to another person the techniques he/she has utilized in the working process?

In this "Age of Empires" when technology predominates everything, it seems suspect and poor indeed to narrate our feelings and motives, so we have become accustomed to through twigs and endings of art experiencing the existence of concept and thinking. Like a normal "lecture" speech, narrations can be negligible, but even a gesture can be unforgettable. That's it, the power of a gesture. So no mater for ideas or concepts, the "gesture" of techniques has long been an important part of art, through which they expect to activate our limited imaginations. For most artists, it's been already challenging and risk-taken to describe own creations. So when describing the creating process, it is better to be in certain confusion, chaos, and leave some more room, to keep secrecy for possibilities of endless imaginations.

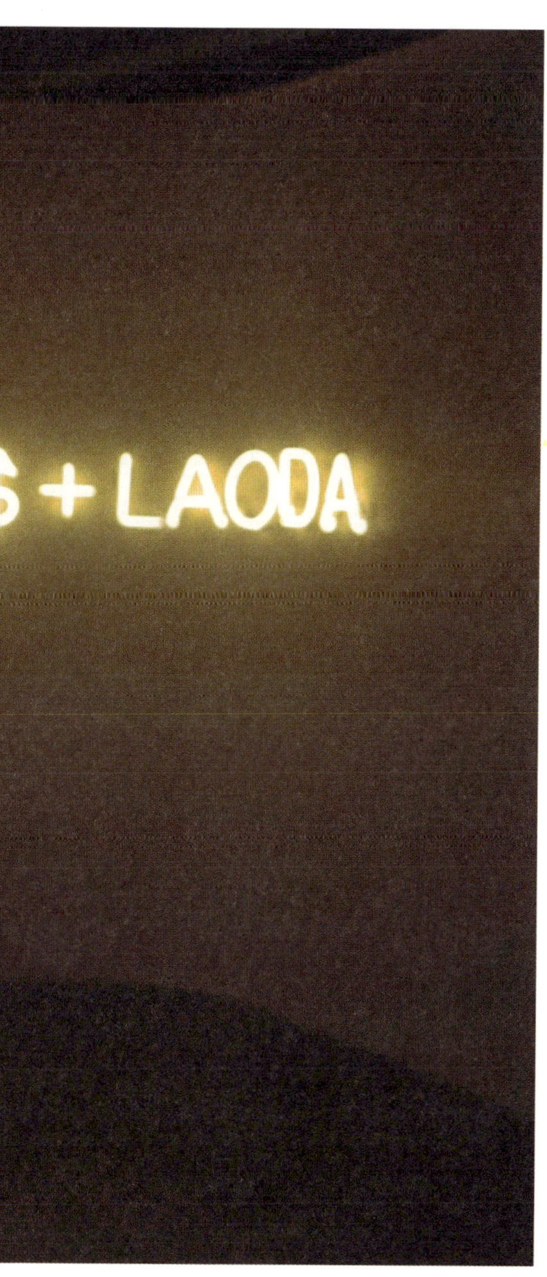

2025计划（No.3），2009
装置（霓虹灯）
400 × 40cm

2025 Project (No. 3), 2009
Installation (Neon light)
400 × 40cm

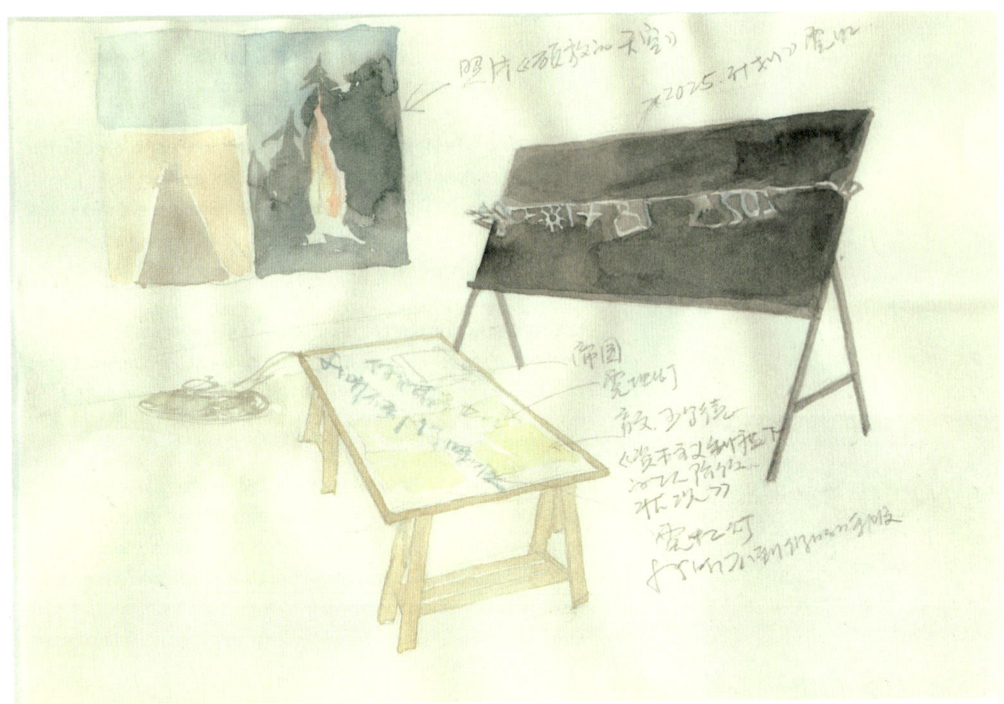

比如这样，2009
展览草图
综合材料

Such as This, 2009
Sketch
Mixed media

工作室一角
A corner in Wu Xiaojun's studio

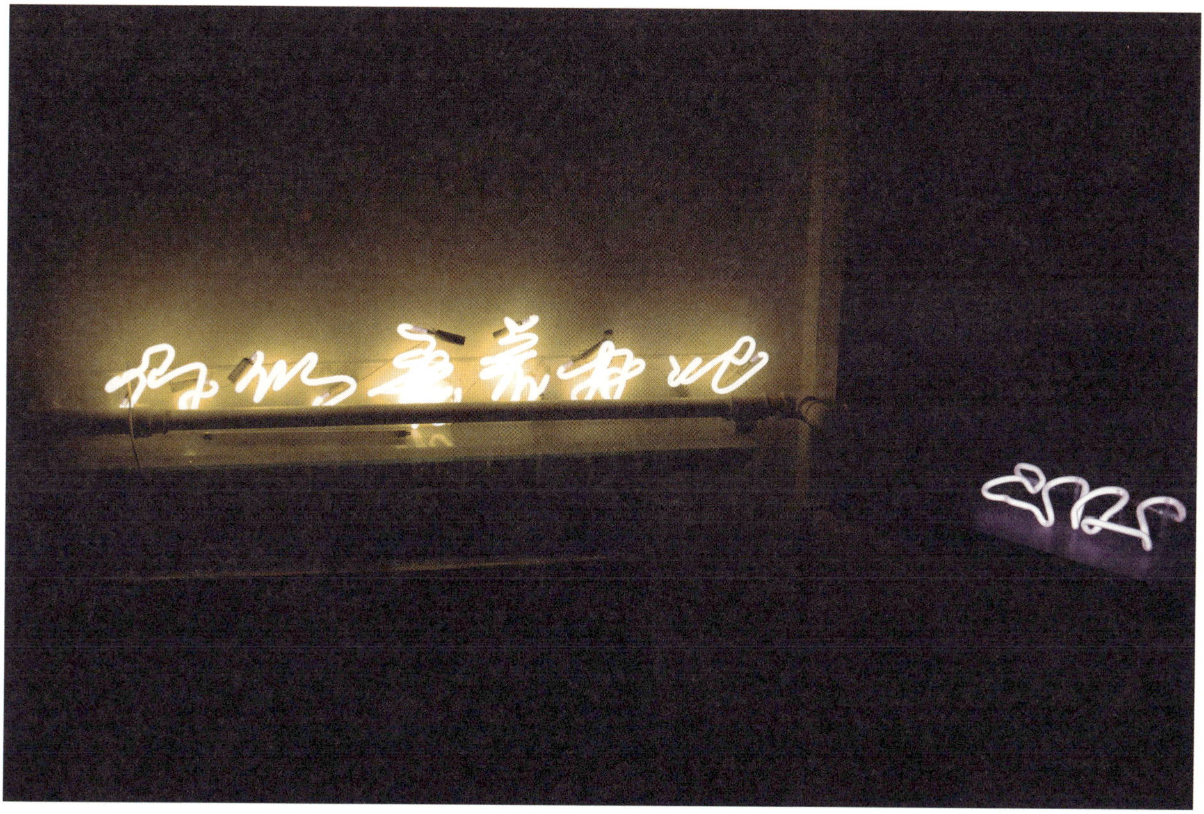

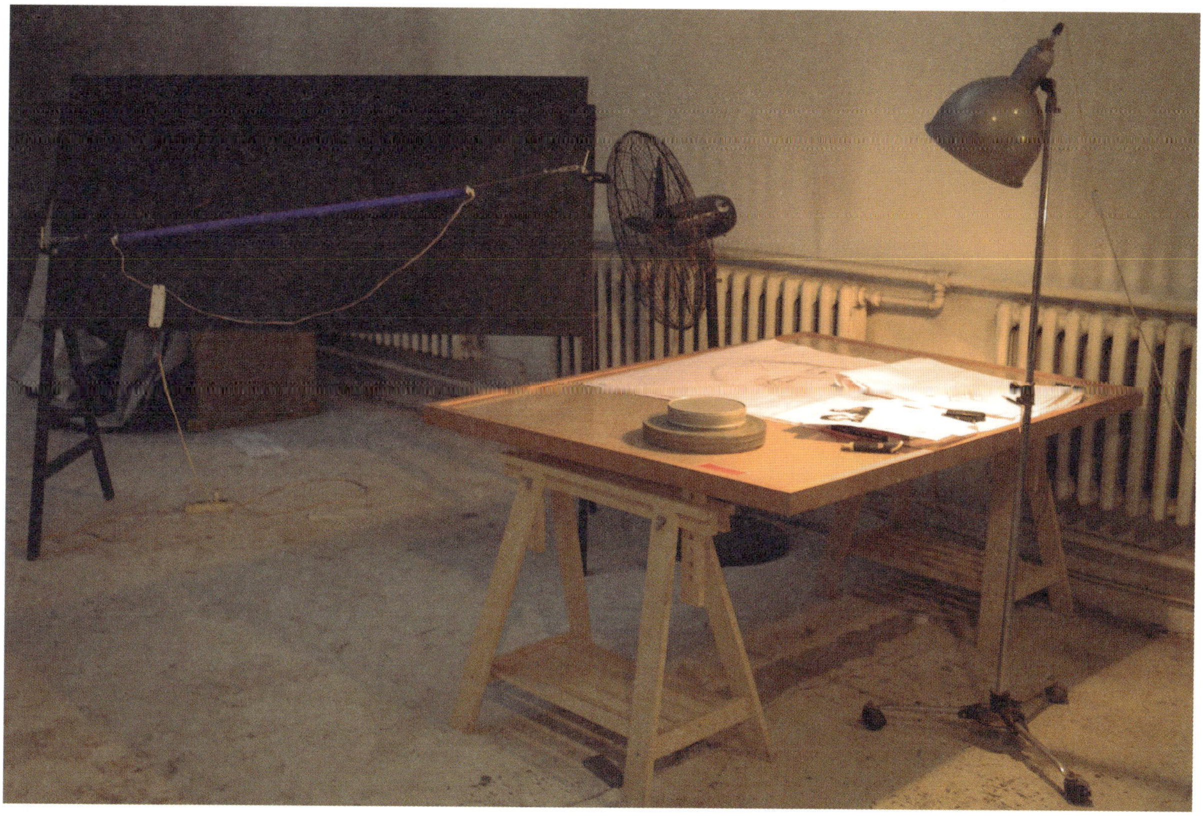

杨 俊

JUN YANG

作为艺术家，你在创作中所关心的是什么？以一件作品为例，分享你的创作过程。

创设一个能让我集中精神开展工作的情境。

这不仅仅指一个实在的物理空间，也包括为凝聚精力、对话以及创作时间制造一个可能的环境。

这个（讨论、质疑、斟酌、实验等等的）过程是极为重要的关键环节。

所以我的大部分作品最后可能是或者看上去会是十分简单，但它们实际都经过了长时间的准备和充分的讨论。

举例来说，我们今年夏天做了一个新的短片《幽灵岛》：实际拍摄时间只有两天，我们"只"用超16毫米胶片拍了三十分钟，可是整个的创作过程和准备工作却花费了超过半年……大部分时间都是在研究和思考什么是我真正想要的，来回地斟酌、选择……

同样，这次选择使用超16毫米拍摄的另一个用意在于想让整个团队做到真正地集中精力；因此特意压缩和限制了制作材料以及拍摄时间。我们需要问自己真正想要什么样的影像和作品，而不是生产大量的制片材料。这个展览中的另外两件作品也是如此（《回家》和《俊杨和军杨（树）》），都是视频作品，它们尝试去运用极为少而精的影像或文本；这里面绝对不存在任何多余或者任意的成分。

如果你是一个批评家，你会从什么角度来阐释和讨论你自己的创作？

在我看来作为艺术家的我同时也是批评家，其中的差异在于我同时还是生产者，这意味着我了解那些通常"被遮蔽"的全部信息，包括所有导致作品形成最终面貌的方方面面以及抉择的过程。我是我自己的评论人，但是我猜想，的确有时自己对自己的创作太熟悉了，因此需要倾听来自外部的意见。

一个旁观者、批评家或观者对各个方面进行剖析的角度是已完成的作品，进而去重构/构建或者思考潜在的阐释。

而作为艺术家或者生产者，我的出发点是某个特定的问题或者至少是一个关注点和创作愿望，从而思考生产某种东西 —— 这可能会生成最后的作品 —— 的"最佳"途径。一路走下去，最初的问题也许会隐入最终的结果中，变得不再清晰可见。

因而，这代表两个不同的方向：对于前者而言，分析的出发点是最终的产品；而对于后者，出发点是形成作品的关注点以及问题。

在你的创作和思考中，什么书籍和艺术家曾经或正在影响着你？

我现在所能想到的没有什么特别的。

我每次创作都会收集大量的研究资料，所以每个作品都有很多参考作品、著作、音乐、电影，基本什么都有，包括所有在我的创作语境中值得回顾和检视的有意思的事物以及瞬间。例如，制作《回家》一片时涉及到大量针对建筑物及其定义空间的方式的研究工作，尤其是鲁道夫·辛德勒（一位20世纪移民洛杉矶的奥地利建筑师）事实上，拍"回家"时，我正好住在辛德勒设计的一座房子里。因此，装置中的屋顶直接参照了他的建筑物，以及他如何运用屋顶的不同高度来定义特定空间的手法。

你是怎样判断和决定在什么语境下呈现你的哪些作品的？你是怎样看待作品呈现的语境和作品的关系的？

我希望能有人与我交流，一起工作。这也许听起来很老套，然而我需要去喜欢他们以及他们的立场和态度。因为我喜欢与策展人、艺术家、工程师和设计师进行双向的交流。

如果一个展览匮乏对话和交流（呈现作品的语境），那么我参与的必要性就不大了。

我不太在意是否是大型美术馆或"重要"展览。

如何在创作上形成了现在的面貌，描述一下最近年来作品的发展和变化？

我个人认为我的工作范围、创作意图以及创作方式的重心一直在变化着。

我觉得我对自身，对我自己身处的语境或自己愿意置身其中的语境 —— 换言之，即我希望借由艺术创作和当一名艺术家来投身其中并展开批评的语境和环境 —— 越来越有清醒的认识。

实际上，这个展览有意思的地方在于：对于"艺术家是如何工作的"这个问题的思考既指他或她的艺术创作模式的实际层面，同时也涉及艺术家一个时间段内围绕几件作品（新作和旧作）的工作方式。

在早期的大部分作品中，我特别喜欢使用"现成"影像，如在《回家》中我就采用了来自主流电影的画面和片段。这么做让我得以能够与观众分享和讨论这些影像，因为现有的图像对于他们而言也许可能曾经看过或者感觉似曾相识。而《俊杨和军

回家-日常生活结构，2000
录像装置
16分钟
洛杉矶
图片由维也纳Martin Janda画廊和维他命创意空间
（广州/北京）提供

Coming Home-Daily Structures of Life, 2000
Video installation
16'00"
Schindler House / Mackey Apartment - MAK, Los Angeles, USA
Courtesy Galerie Martin Janda, Vienna, Austria and Vitamin
Creative Space (Guangzhou and Beijing)

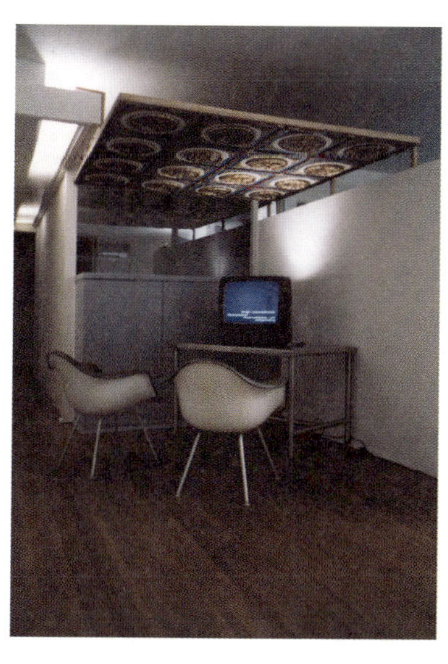

杨（树）》中的影像也许会让人联想到某个特定时代的特定话语或现象（比如上世纪八十年代的影星和流行文化等）

尽管我在许多较早的视频作品中对"现成"影像的话题更感兴趣，但是在最近的作品中我尝试自己再生产复制这些既定的影像瞬间。这就是为什么《幽灵岛》（参展作品）将会与一张"幽灵岛"的电影海报一起展出。

你会在什么情况下摧毁你自己的作品？

这个想法经常有 —— 但是也许"摧毁"这个词用得不对，更确切地说应该是"修订"。

这是创造过程的一个部分，对制作出来的东西一遍遍地重新审视。

我的每个作品都会有不同的版本，正如软件编程人员会制作测试版一样，甚至最后发布的版本也会在随后出现修订版或者升级版。

你怎么看待艺术史和艺术家创作的关系？

我认为事物以及艺术品所处的时空环境和语境很重要。我对艺术品的永恒普世价值持怀疑态度，然而我相信其中存在因果关系，但这并不表示历史和艺术生产之间必须是线性关系。

在你的工作中，理性和情感冲动各自扮演着什么样的角色？

我想这很难区分，情感冲动是我的经验的一部分，同时也是其结果。

很多时候我的理性和情感冲动相互关联。

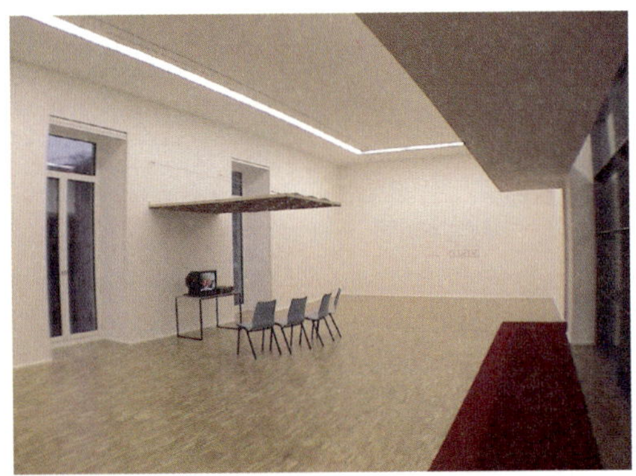

回家-日常生活结构，2001
录像装置
德国莱比锡当代美术馆
图片由维也纳Martin Janda画廊和维他命创
意空间（广州/北京）提供

Coming Home-Daily Structures of Life, 2001
Video installation
Gfzk - Museum of Contemporary Art Leipzig, Leipzig,
Germany
Courtesy Galerie Martin Janda, Vienna, Austria and
Vitamin Creative Space (Guangzhou and Beijing)

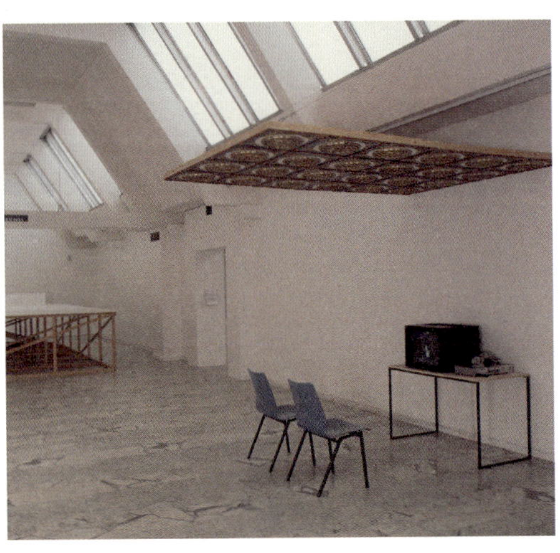

回家-日常生活结构，2002
录像装置
法国马塞当代艺术馆
图片由维也纳Martin Janda画廊和维他命创
意空间（广州/北京）提供

Coming Home-Daily Structures of Life, 2002
Video installation
MAC - Musée d'Art Contemporain Marseille ,France
Courtesy Galerie Martin Janda, Vienna, Austria and
Vitamin Creative Space (Guangzhou and Beijing)

上图
俊杨和军杨（树），英文版，2002
录像
图片由维也纳Martin Janda画廊和维他命创
意空间（广州/北京）提供

top
Jun Yang and Soldier Woods (english version), 2002
Video
Courtesy Galerie Martin Janda, Vienna, Austria and
Vitamin Creative Space(Guangzhou and Beijing)

下图
俊杨和军杨（树），法文版，2002
录像
9分钟33秒
法国尼斯阿尔松别墅
图片由维也纳Martin Janda画廊和维他命创
意空间（广州/北京）提供

bottom
Jun Yang et Soldat Dubois (french version), 2002
Video
9'33"
Villa Arson, Nice, France
Courtesy Galerie Martin Janda, Vienna, Austria and
Vitamin Creative Space(Guangzhou and Beijing)

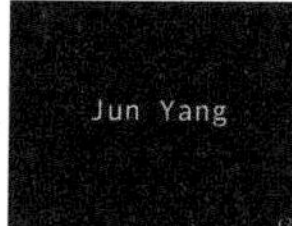

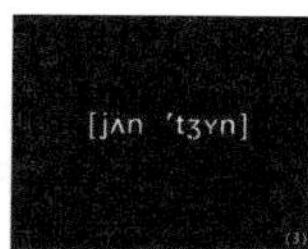

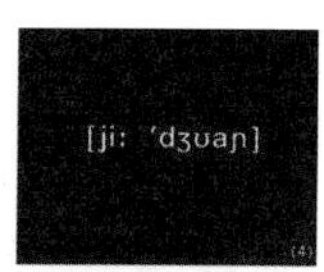

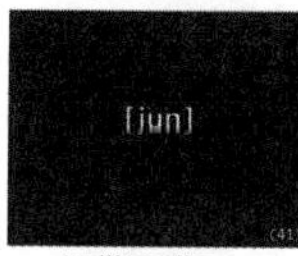

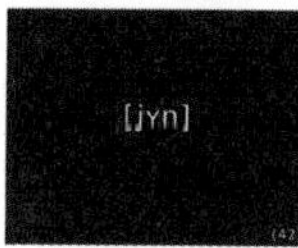

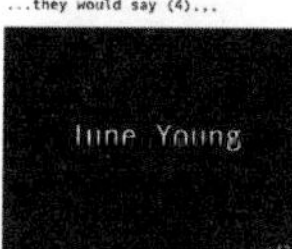

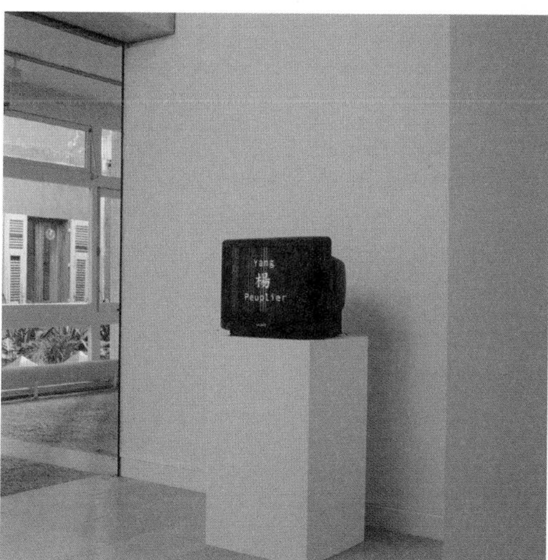

As an artist, what do you care most during working? Could you please give an example to introduce the process of your work for us?

To create a situation where I can focus and work.
That refers to a physical space but also an environment of concentration, dialogue and time.
This process (of discussions, doubts, re-considerations, experiments,...) is crucial and the most important part.
So most of the works I produce are or look very simple in the end; but they are connected to long preparations and discussions.
For instance we were working on a new short film this summer *(Phantom Island)*: the filming itself took only two days; we filmed "just" 30 minutes on Super 16mm; but the whole process and the preparations took more then half a year... Most of the time was spend researching and reflecting on what I really wanted; going back and forth with choices and decisions....
Also one of the reason to work on Super16 in this case was to get the whole team really focused; production material and time was therefore on purpose limited and concentrated. Instead of producing a lot of material we needed to ask what image and work we really want... The same goes for the other two works in the show *(Coming Home* and *Soldier Woods* both produced on video) each of them tries to use images or text very reduced but precise; there is absolutely nothing unnecessary or random.

Suppose you are a critic, what perspective would you talk about and explain you work from?

I believe as an artist I am a critic; with the difference that I am the producer as well in this case; which means I know all the aspects that are normally "hidden"; all the aspects and decisions that led to the final situation. I am my own critic, but I guess it is also true that sometimes one is to close to owns own work, and thus it is good to have an opinion from outside as well.
As an outsider, or the critic's or viewer's position we look first at the final work and try to analyze the different aspects, from there we try to re/construct or think possible interpretation.
As an artist or producer I start with certain question or at least a concern or desire; from there I try to think of the "best" way to produce something - which might become the final work. Along the road the initial question might not be that visible and clear in the end-result anymore.
So these are two different directions; the first we start with the end product; the second we start with the question and the concerns that result in the work...

What books and which artists have had, or is having an influence on your way of thinking and working?

There is not a single particular one; that I can now think of.
For every work i do, I collect a lot of material and research, so for every piece there are references works, books, music, movies; basically anything - things and moments that are interesting to re-look and examine in context of the things I am working on. For instance for *Coming Home* one aspect was researching a lot of architects and how they defined space; especially Rudolf Schindler (an Austrian architect who emigrated early 20th century to Los Angeles) In fact *Coming Home* was produced while I lived in one of Schindler's houses. So the celling in the installation is a direct reference to his architecture and how he uses different heights of celling to define certain spaces.

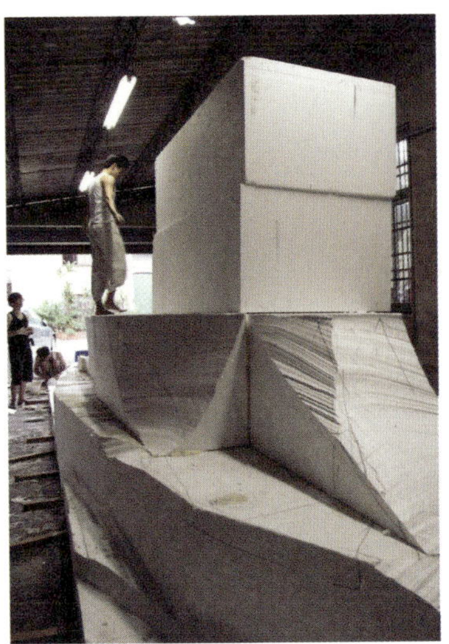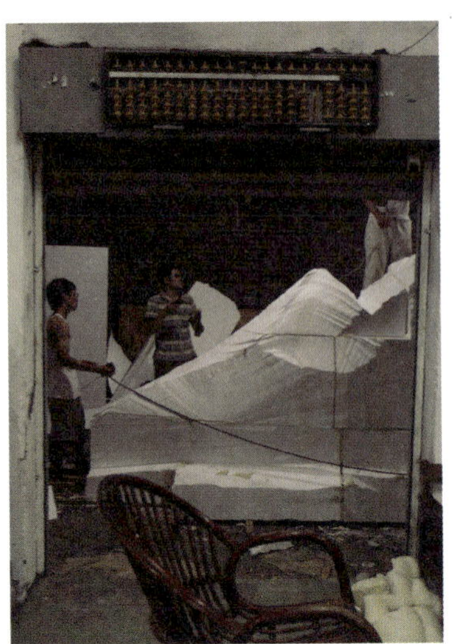

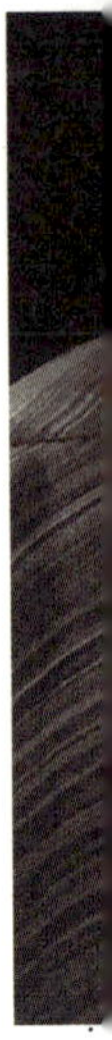

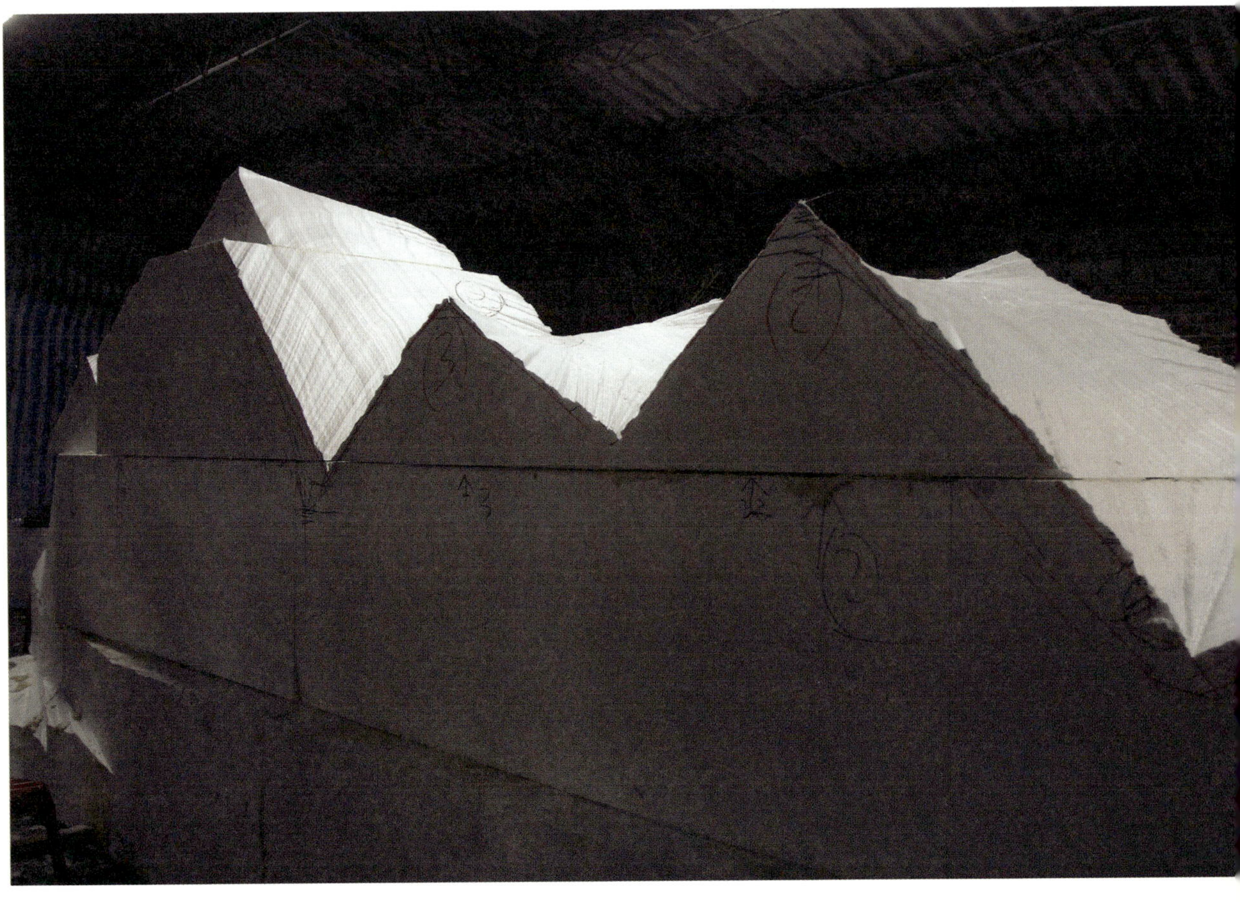

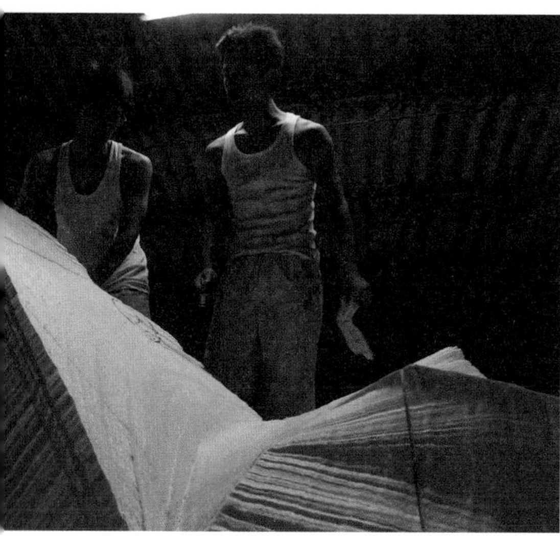

《幽灵岛》制作过程，2009
图片由维也纳Martin Janda画廊和维
他命创意空间（广州/北京）提供

Phantom Island in production process, 2009
Courtesy Galerie Martin Janda, Vienna,
Austria and Vitamin Creative Space
(Guangzhou and Beijing)

**How do you decide the context in which your work is to
be presented? How do you consider the relation of the
context with your work?**

I prefer working with certain people - it might sound banal, but I
have to like them and their positions. I refer to people since I am
interested in a dialogue between curator, fellow artist, constructor,
designers,...
If there is no dialogue in an exhibition (context of presentation),
there is no real need for me to engage.
I don't care much about whether it is a big museum or 'important' show.

**How does your work take the present shape? And please
give a few words about the latest development and
changes in your work.**

On a personal level I guess priorities change in what I can do, which
work I want to produce and how I want to produce them.
I guess I became more aware of myself and the context I am in
or want to be in; or the context and environment that I want to
contribute and criticize by making art works and being an artist.
Practically speaking for this exhibition it was interesting when
thinking of the question: "how do artists work" not only to refer to
his/her practical aspect of production mode but also how artist work
through out a period of time including several works (old and new).
In many of the earlier works I was particular interested in using
'existing' images; for instance in *Coming Home* I use images and
sequences taken from main stream movies. By doing so I was
interested to talk about the images that I would share with the
viewer; existing images the viewer might have seen or that look
familiar to them. In *Soldier Woods* images that one might associate
with certain words or certain popular phenomena at a certain period
of time (movie stars, pop culture in the 80's,...)
So where as I was more interested in many earlier video works to
talk about 'existing' images; in recent works I have been interested
to produce these images myself, images that reproduce filmic
moments. That is also why *Phantom Island* (in the exhibition) is
displayed alongside with a movie poster of *Phantom Island*.

**In what circumstances would you want to destroy your own
creation?**

Constantly - but perhaps 'destroy' is the wrong word, 'revised' is closer.
It is part of the process of producing something, to re-look at the
things again and again.
For every work I produce different versions, like within software
programming people produce beta versions, and then even with the
released version there are revisions or upgrades.

**What do you think about the relation between the art
history and artist's work?**

I think things, art works are important in the context of their
environment space and time wise. I am not convinced by the idea
of the universality of work, but i believe in the in a causality of
them; which does not mean that everything both history and the
production has to be something linear.

**What kind of roles would rational thinking and emotional
impulse respectively play during your work time?**

I guess it is difficult to differentiate, even my impulses are part and
the result of my experience.
And often my rational thinking are connected to certain impulses.

幽灵岛，2009
电影
8分钟
图片由维也纳Martin Janda画廊和维
他命创意空间（广州/北京）提供

Phantom Island, 2009
film
8'00"
Courtesy Galerie Martin Janda, Vienna,
Austria and Vitamin Creative Space
(Guangzhou and Beijing)

幽灵岛，2009
电影
8分钟
图片由维也纳Martin Janda画廊和维
他命创意空间（广州/北京）提供

Phantom Island, 2009
film
8'00"
Courtesy Galerie Martin Janda, Vienna,
Austria and Vitamin Creative Space
(Guangzhou and Beijing)

Phantom Island

a film by **Jun Yang**

Production: **Phoebe Huang**, **Yushin Wu**   Camera: **Wayne Lin**

Island production: **Chi-Bang Chen**, **Jun-Jie Ciou**, **Kai Chen**, **Chen-Yan Chen**, **Shao-Lan Fan**, **Chien-Wei Liu**, **Hsin-Ning Chang**, **En-Man Chang**, **Shao-Kang Wang**, **Jui-Tse Hsu**, **Pei-Chen Li**, **Fang-Chih Wu**

With the support of: **Open-Contemporary Art Center**, **Vitamin Creative Space**, **Galerie Martin Janda**

Thanks to: **Taipei Artist Village**, **Department of Cultural Affairs**, **Taipei City Government**, **Taipei Film Commission**, **Taiwan Area National Freeway Bureau**, **Traffic Engineering Office**, **Ministry of Education, Arts and Culture of Austria**, **Taiwan Coastal Guard**, **Arrow Film**, **Taipei Postproduction**, and **Huang Chien-Hung**, **Hsu Manray**, **Cheng Meiya**, **Kim Sunjung**, **Lin Mie**

Phantom Island was filmed in Taipei and the East China Sea, off Taiwan; in the territory between P.R. China, R.China (Taiwan) and Japan. 8 minutes. Super 16mm. ©2009

张耿豪华

CHANG KENGHAU&CHANG GENGHWA

作为艺术家，你在创作中所关心的是什么？以一件作品为例，分享你的创作过程。

生活中的感受。

以《1750东向坡》为例，这件作品是从一次旅行的经验所发生的，那是台湾中部山区标高1750公尺的东面山坡，我们在那片接近黄昏而幽暗的森林中寻找一种特有种的昆虫。在那里我们只能依靠听觉，听声辨位，随即出手捕捉。而各式样的昆虫飞舞其中，挑衅的飞近耳边，似乎在告诉着我们；我就在这呀！来捉我呀！我们在那昏黄又带点潮湿的空间中，挥舞手中的虫网。不久之后《1750东向坡》就完成了。

如果你是一个批评家，你会从什么角度来阐释和讨论你自己的创作？

观者的角度。

在你的创作和思考中，什么书籍和艺术家曾经或正在影响着你？

奈良美智、宫崎峻。

你是怎样判断和决定在什么语境下呈现你的哪些作品的？你是怎样看待作品呈现的语境和作品的关系的？

靠直觉。

如何在创作上形成了现在的面貌，描述一下最近年来作品的发展和变化？

从 2001年的《飞行器》为起点，耿华在创作的开始，所描述的是一个童年的梦想，一件童年时期幻想的大玩具，以粗重的钢铁支架搭配手工缝制的皮革翅膀，再以油压马达作为动力的来源，但硕大的体积仅能在原地拍动双翅，那似乎在暗示一个遥不可及的梦，2002年《呆头鹅》这件作品似乎带点戏谑及恶搞的态度，耿华亲手将鹅制作成标本，再与机械动力的身体结合，戏谑的是我们将这只机械鹅新放回它生长的鹅厂，造成了其他鹅群的惊吓，同时也形成了一种搞怪的幽默风格。

2003 年以 "飞天摇摇马/Flying Yoyo" 为主题的个展中依然延续着童年的记忆和飞行的幻想，展览中《双生仔》是运用我们两兄弟幼儿时期的照片作为创作的基调，透过电脑的复制以及再造来描写两兄弟的成长关系，《童年飞行计画》则是以卡漫的风格描写一个在课堂中无法专心的小孩，向往教室外无忧无虑游戏的童年。到了2004年的个展 "白日梦机场/Daydream" 以一系列的飞行机械装置在空间中，以原本笨重的机械结构轻轻的描写童话式的飞行情境幻想，《飞行器 2》从天花板悬吊下细细的挂点，简单的齿轮结构经由马达的减速后带动布质的双翼，加上齿轮缓慢的运转仿佛催眠一般，此展中的《风洞》、《云塔》、《摩天轮》、《童年飞行计画》…等等作品的比例尺寸都像小人国的世界一般，更加深了白日梦及幻想的特质。2004的下半年《班特1》以电线杆为空间的基础，上方伫立着双眼闭合看似安详沈睡的婴儿，却没有耳朵及翅膀，透露出拒绝启蒙拒绝沟通的一种状态，《班特2》就像被父母圈养在笼中的婴儿，安稳的睡着，却也被炫耀着。在 2006年台北当代馆的个展"瞎表感/Screw it"中，作品《啄木鸟》是将一只只的机械装置固定于玻璃窗上，像是啄木鸟一般辛勤的啄食，却无法成就任何事，犹如现代社会所制约的生活形态，充满无奈。《长腿叔叔我不要》极简的色彩与线条塑造初一只逃避现实的鸵鸟，藏匿进一台具有攻击性的浅水挺中，表达了当时沉溺于创作之中却被家人误认逃避现实的状态。《1750东向坡》则是转化一次旅游抓捕昆虫的经验，在一个有限的滑台空间中，精密的机械结构复杂的运转，吸引观者接近，却又瞬间逃离观者的视线，唯有保持一定距离，才能保有那微妙的关系。而《Shotgunblue》则是使用了人量的电脑计算观者与观者间的关系，硕大的银幕中一把漂浮的步枪，追踪着，冷不妨的开枪，观者完全失去了对作品的操控权，而反互动正是此作的精髓。

渐渐的我们从童年飞行的幻想中苏醒过来，意识到现实离我们越来越近，我们必须长大并开心的接受。

你会在什么情况下摧毁你自己的作品？
不可能。

你怎么看待艺术史和艺术家创作的关系？
就我们的个人经验来说，没太大关系。

在你的工作中，理性和情感冲动各自扮演着什么样的角色？
感性的发想，理性的制作。

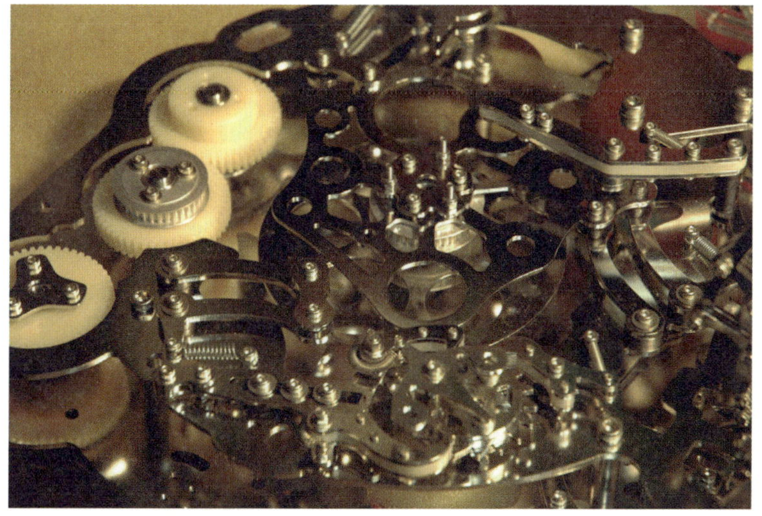

1750东向坡（局部），2006
装置

1750 East Mountainside (detail), 2006
Installation

As an artist, what do you care most during working? Could you please give an example to introduce the process of your work for us?

It's our feelings in life. Let's take *1750 East Mountainside* for example. It is based on one of my travels in the mountainous area in central Taiwan. The east-facing slope is elevated 1750 meters. We were searching the dim woods for a special species of insect in the dusk. There was only hearing for us to depend on to locate and catch them. In the meanwhile, insects of all sorts, mixing with the insect we wanted, flew by our ears, seeming to challenge us by whispering, "Catch me here!" Our insect nets danced in our hands in the woods, dim pale yellow and damp. It was not long before *1750 East Mountainside* was concluded.

Suppose you are a critic, from what perspective would you explain and comment on your works?

An observer's perspective.

What books and which artists have had, or are having an influence on your way of thinking and working?

Nara Yoshitomo and Miyazaki Hayo.

How do you make judgment and decision as to in what context you'd like to present your works? According to you, in what way is the context created by the work related to the work itself?

We depend on our intuition.

How does your work take the present shape? And please give a few words about the latest development and changes in your work.

It began with *Aerocraft* in 2001. Genghua started to describe a dream in childhood embodied in an imagined toy with big and heavy brackets of iron and metal, hand-sewn leather wings, and a hydraulic motor for power. Due to its great size, however, it can only flap its wings, unable to move. It seems to be a symbol of an unattainable dream. In *Goose* in 2002, we can find certain banter and kuso. First, Genghua made a goose specimen himself, and then gave it mechanical power. What is amusing is that when this goose specimen was sent back to the farm where it used to be, it put other geese into great panic. There is also a touch of wacky humor.
In the solo exhibition in 2003 under the title *Flying Yoyo*, memories of the childhood and the dream of flying recurred. *Twins* is based on a photo of ours in the childhood. It describes our growth by means of computer copy and recreation. *Flying Plan in the Childhood* features in the style of cartoon a child who fails to concentrate on study in class and dream of the free life outside the classroom.
In 2004 we had a solo under the title "Daydream airport". A series of flying machine equipment was suspended in midair, symbolizes the dream of flying by means of the heavy machines. In *Aerocraft* II we saw a lot of mount points from the ceiling, simple gears driving the cloth wings by going through the motor that slows down. The gears moved so slowly that is makes people drowsy.

1750东向坡（局部），2006
装置

1750 East Mountainside (detail), 2006
Installation

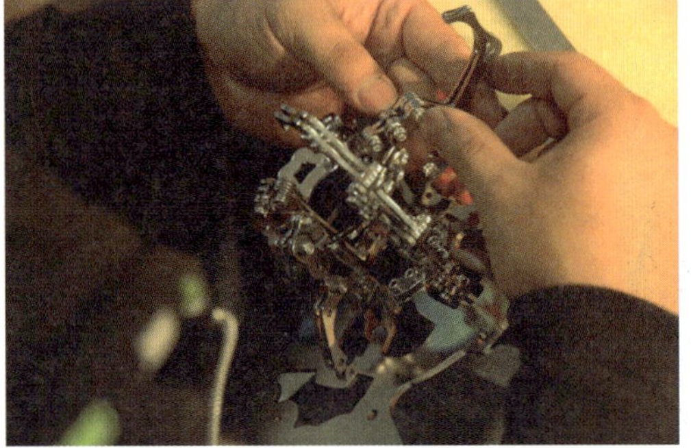

Other works in this solo, such as *Wind Tunnels*, *Tower*, *Riesenrad* and *Flying Plan in Childhood*, all in small scale, provides us a world for dwarfs, highlighting daydreaming and fancy. Benter I in the latter half of 2004 made use of the wire pole as spatial base with a baby above who, with eyes shut, seems to be in sound sleep, but with neither ears nor wings, appearing to rejecting initiation and communication; In Benter II, the baby looks like a sleeping baby who is encaged and shown off by his parents.

In Screw it, a solo at MOCA Taipei in 2006, some new works were presented. In *Woodpeckers* a collection of machinery are fixed on the window, like pecking woodpeckers, but they can reach nowhere. It is a metaphor of the helpless state of life handicapped by the modern world. With simple colors and lines *No Long-Legged Uncle* presents us an ostrich that avoids reality by hiding itself in a submarine that is ready for attack, sharing with the observers how someone engaged in his creation gets misunderstood for fleeing from reality. *1750 East Mountainside* converted one of our experiences in catching insects in a travel by arranging precision machines in a limited space with slipways. The observers are so curious that they keep approaching the machines that work in a complicated fashion, but the latter suddenly get out of sight. Certain distance is needed to keep the subtlety. *Shotgunblue* draws on a lot the relationship centered on computer. A floating gun in the center of the large screen is searching. An unexpected shot will deprive the observers of their power in relation to the work itself. Anti-interaction is the master card in this work.

Little by little we woke up from our childhood dream of flying and realized that reality keeps approaching, so we have to grow up and readily accept this fact.

In what circumstances would you want to destroy your own creation?
No, not likely.

What do you think about the relation between the art history and artist's work?
From our personal experience, we would say they are almost irrelevant.

What kind of roles would rational thinking and emotional impulse respectively play in your work?
I hunt for ideas with emotion and turn the ideas into works with reason.

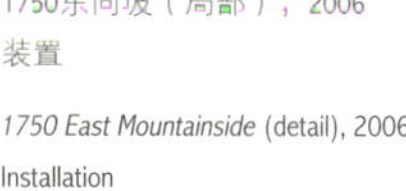

1750东向坡（局部），2006
装置

1750 East Mountainside (detail), 2006
Installation

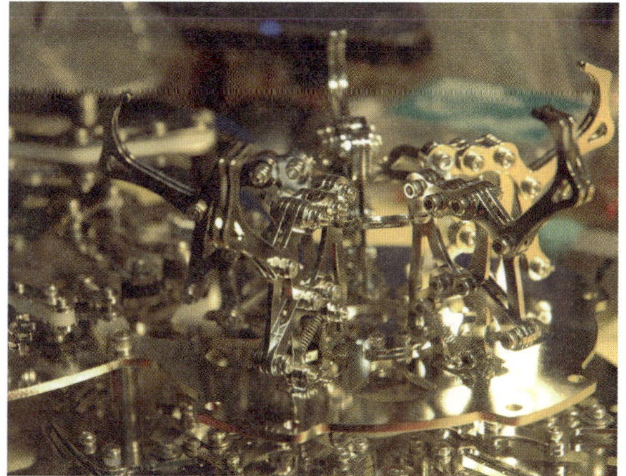

1750东向坡位于丛林野外，标高1750公尺，因面向东，因此称东向坡。风微微的吹动，枝叶摩擦，无数细微声响，无尽变化入侵体内，同时夹杂昆虫飞行于林间，翅膀高速振动，所产生的压力差，使得频率忽高忽低，快速的从身边呼啸而过，此时的身体只能依直觉反应，听声辨位。苍蝇、蚊子或是各类昆虫，在环境中，它以生物的本能四处的游窜，在它跟人类毫无接触的状况之下，拍动翅膀，飞行，那是一种惯性、一种本能，当它感测到热或发现气味时，振翅而飞，规律的振翅声，也许只是感觉到目标，所以飞行，

这件作品试着去营造一种听觉经验，这是一种听声音去判断种类、大小和位置的经验。此时以听觉感受到的无实体存在的声音比现实残影更迷人，更有引导性，但与其说那是虚影，不如看作是另一种存在的状态，你也许不容易看到它，但用另一感官却能感觉到另一种实际的存在，身体感知重心比例替换，"视觉降低、听觉替位"。

声音让人可以习惯性的测量、捕捉及掌控，由实际存在的平面向外延伸，发声主体无规律性的运动，也使得声音产生前后、上下、左右的距离感，以及空间感。如此声音装置便在三度空间产生流动、互动，试着引导出身体的存在，身体感知的重要性。

参与者在此件作品空间中游走，发声体吸引参与者趋前，当参与者靠近时，发声体便开始闪躲参与者，使得参与者需要去追踪音源，寻找音源，如此参与者与发声体便互相忙碌地追逐或者闪躲。倘若参与者接近放弃状态，或是静止不动时，发声体便缓慢的游走，或静止，甚至试探性的接近参与者，互存的好奇心，也是互动产生的动力。那也像是现代都市的写照，凡事都得保持一个巧妙的距离，维持一个平衡的关系。

Lying in the wildness, *1750 East Mountainside* gets its name from its elevation, 1750 meters, and its east-facing slope. Breezes come, leaves rustle, all kind of little sounds arise, and inexhaustible changes invade the body. In the meanwhile, insects brush by in the woods with wings vibrating at high speed, sending the frequency fluctuating due to the pressure difference. The body can rely on nothing other than instinct for orientation by sound.

It is instinct that enables flies, mosquitoes and other insects to move around. Inertia and instinct account for their flutter of wings and flight when there is no contact with human beings. They fly by flapping their wings, producing regular fluttering sounds when they sense heat or detect certain smell; or it maybe that they sense that there is a target, so they start to fly.

This work is intended for audio experience based on sound to determine the category, the size and the location. Here sounds without substantial content one get with the aid of hearing are more appealing and orienting than afterimages in real life. They can be viewed as a state of being, rather than ghosting, for you may not find it easily, but another sensory organ helps to sense their existence as reality in another form—change in the proportion of perception focuses, i.e., "vision reduced and replaced by hearing".

Sounds help people to get used to measuring, catching and taking control of the object and expanding the substantial plane. The irregular movements of the sound producer affect the sound by creating a sense of distance in all directions and a sense of space. With such arrangement sounds flow and interact in the three-dimensional space, trying to highlighting the existence of the body and the importance of body perception.

Participants can travel in this work. The sounding body attracts participants, but it dodges them as the participants come closer, so the latter have to follow the former and track it— it becomes a game in which they chase or dodge each other. If there is any sign of withdrawal or stop on the part of the participants, the sounding body will slow down or stop, or even make attempts to follow the participants. Interaction is also the source of mutual curiosity. It might be a portrait of modern cities as well in which it is preferable to keep neat distance from everything and keep the balance.

1750东向坡，2006
装置

1750 East Mountainside, 2006
Installation

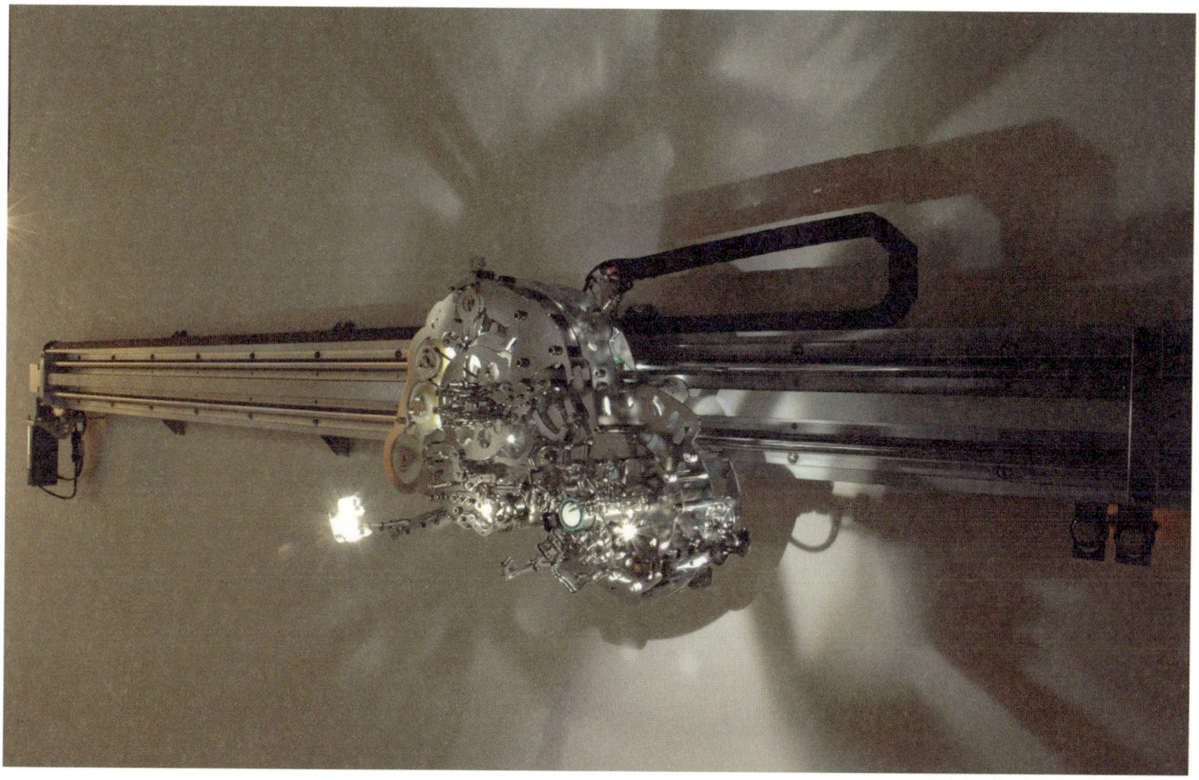

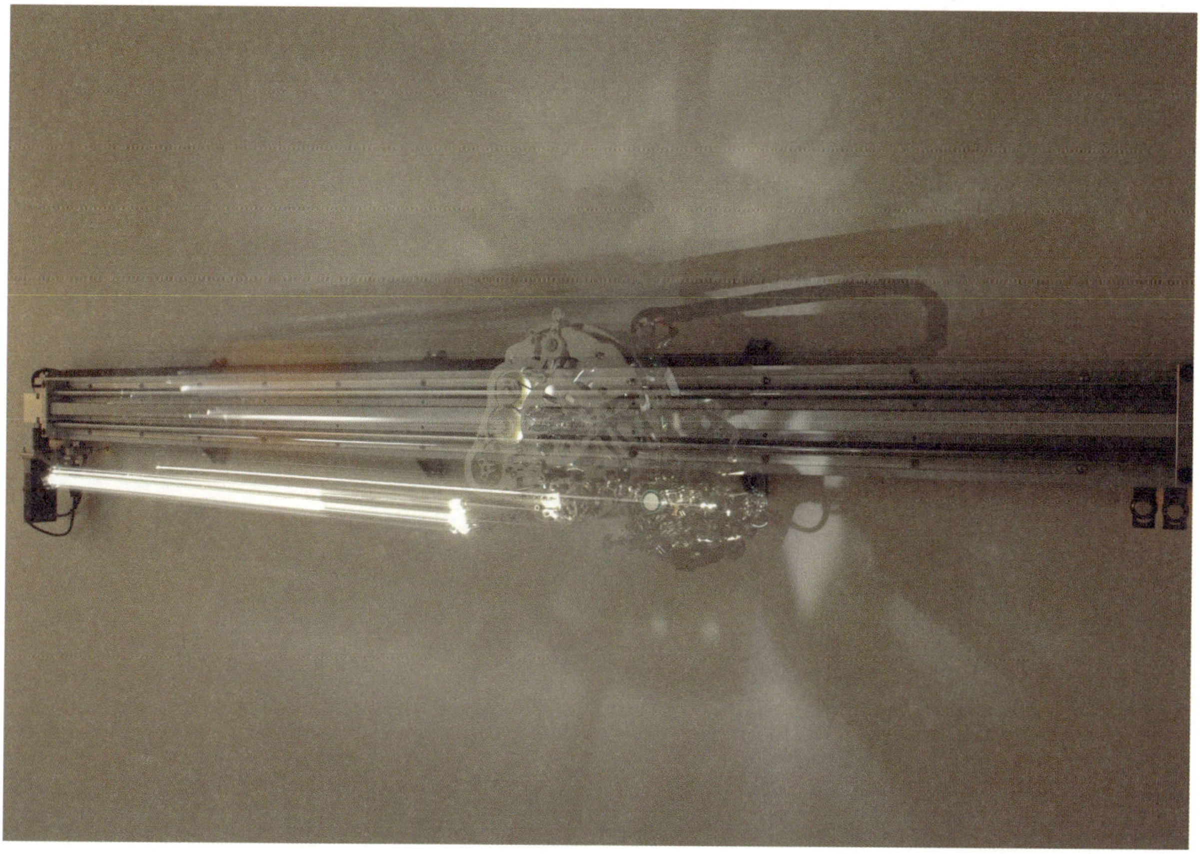

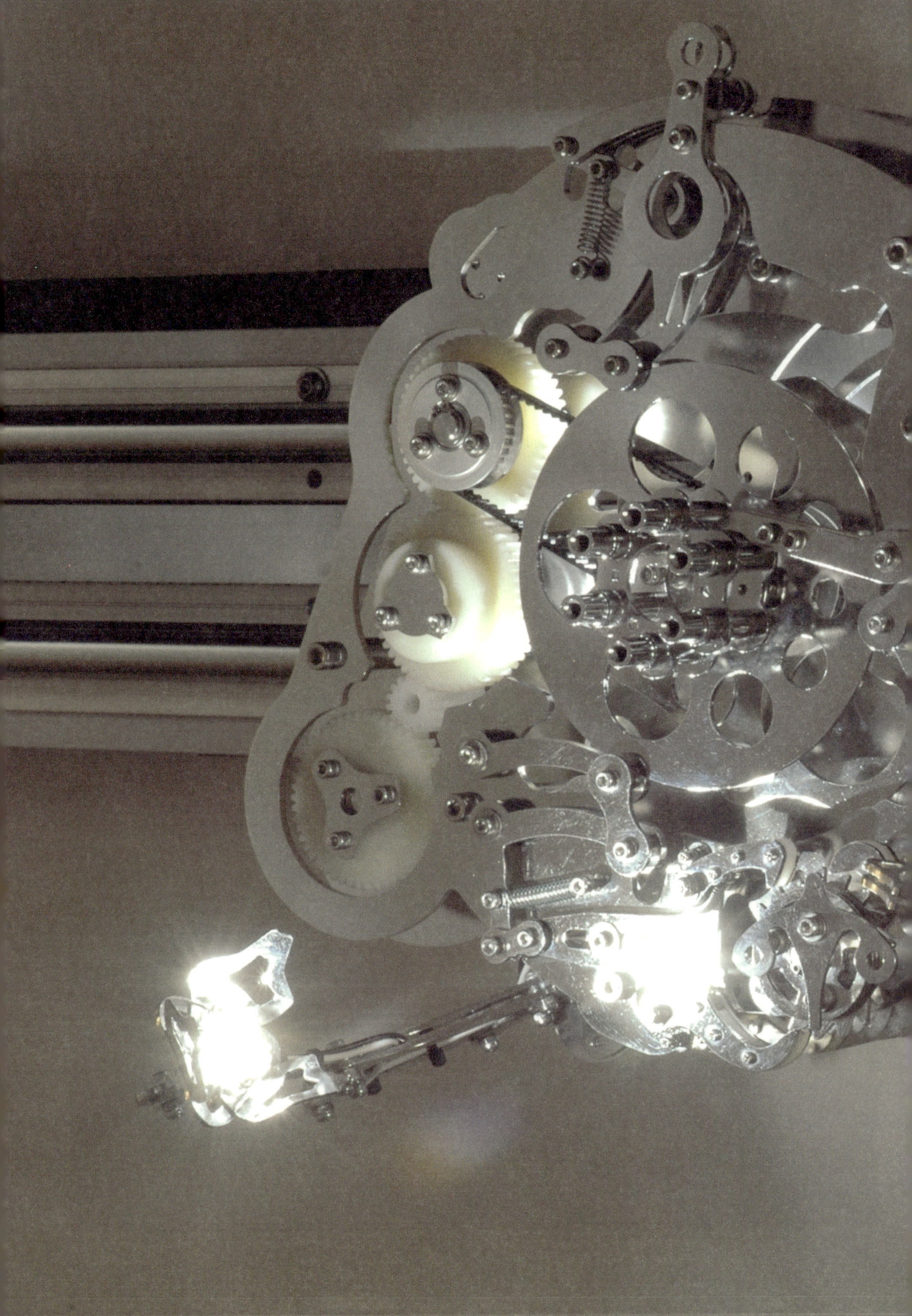

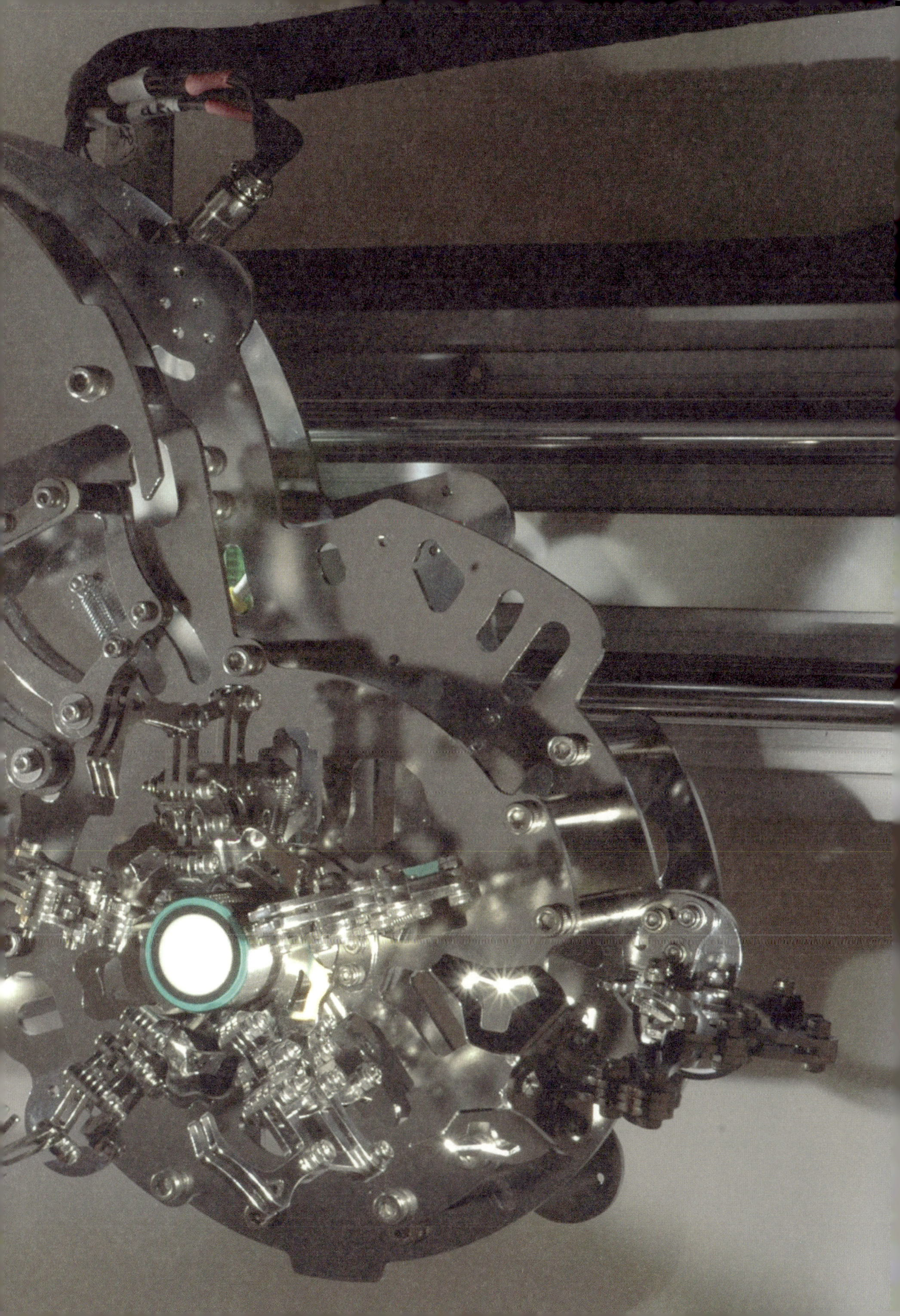

章 清

ZHANG QING

作为艺术家，你在创作中所关心的是什么？以一件作品为例，分享你的创作过程。

如果能在创作中产生更多的可能性，这更为重要。《603足球场》是在我家里的一场足球赛，用摄像头拍摄的，当在剪辑作品的过程中，摄像头拍摄的视觉感和摄像头材料特性，给了我一些很不一样的视频感受，从那时起就开始对这一工具的实验。这样的可能性会让我比较兴奋些，跳出了以前的经验去摸索。

如果你是一个批评家，你会从什么角度来阐释和讨论你自己的创作？

现在我的工作主要进行摄像头视频的拍摄。如果理想状态化，我希望批评家包括观众能先从摄像头本身材料特性上先有个概念，然后在思考我作品。

如：监视摄像视频所含的特质不同于用电影胶片机、DV和手机的拍摄。在日常生活中，它被用于窥视和揭示丑恶行为，录制的视频可以作为法律的证据；在政治上，政府通过操控录像监控系统，使民众的行为在有效范围内受到制约，及时地防止了各种损害政府利益的行为；在视觉语言上，它成像质量较低，略带模糊，并有着独特的观看角度，即避开人的直视有效视角，悬于肉眼水平观看的之上，有着很强的规避性，而这种以俯视为主的姿态，颇有小视大众与侵权的感觉。监视摄像这种成像角度、低视频质量、摆放空间和受众群体的特性，使它形成了一个自己独特的视觉系统。

在某些题材上拍摄，用摄像头比摄像机要更有深度，更能剖析事件和事物的本身。

在你的创作和思考中，什么书籍和艺术家曾经或正在影响着你？

这里很难说出哪一本书或哪一位艺术家，对我影响有多大。在大学时候周啸虎老师借我的一本《美术新解》，这本书对我认识当代艺术有着启蒙的力量。

你是怎样判断和决定在什么语境下呈现你的哪些作品的？你是怎样看待作品呈现的语境和作品的关系的？

个人不可改变一些判断力，或者说改变不了的那一些是我一直完成工作的力量，如果要陷入语境去呈现作品，会很累。当然，会有短期效应，但是会对个人的直接判断产生变形。个人直接判断是很重要的。所谓影响自己的语境只有做完作品以后，才能从中呈现出来。

如何在创作上形成了现在的面貌，描述一下最近年来作品的发展和变化？

从2004年开始就创作录像作品，先前做的行为艺术比较多。到2006年开始了摄像头视频制作，直到现在还在这个方向走。将来如果没多远的话还会在这个方向上继续。

你会在什么情况下摧毁你自己的作品？

为什么要摧毁？

你怎么看待艺术史和艺术家创作的关系？

艺术史肯定是不公平的，如果忘记有艺术史这档子事的艺术家，那他很有可能会进入艺术史。不了解艺术史也并不是很严重的问题。

在你的工作中，理性和情感冲动各自扮演着什么样的角色？

不兴奋的去寻找，这是很困难的事。如果有了好的开始，接下来工作和深入可能有些像六月里的天气，会变化无常。

的士桑芭，2003
行为表演/十辆出租车
南京

Taxi Samba, 2003
performance/Ten taxis
Nanjing

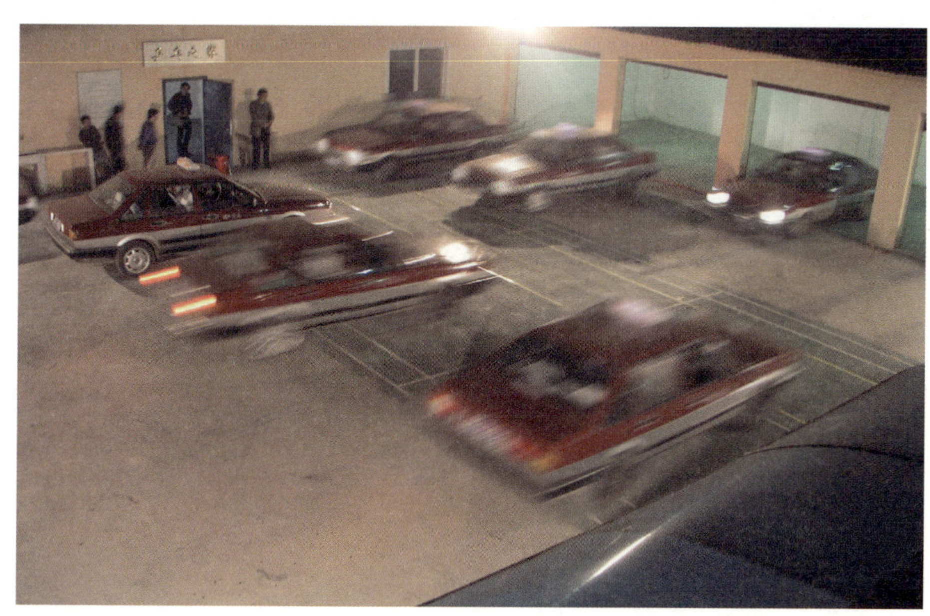

的士桑芭，2003
行为表演/十辆出租车
南京

Taxi Samba, 2003
performance/Ten taxis
Nanjing

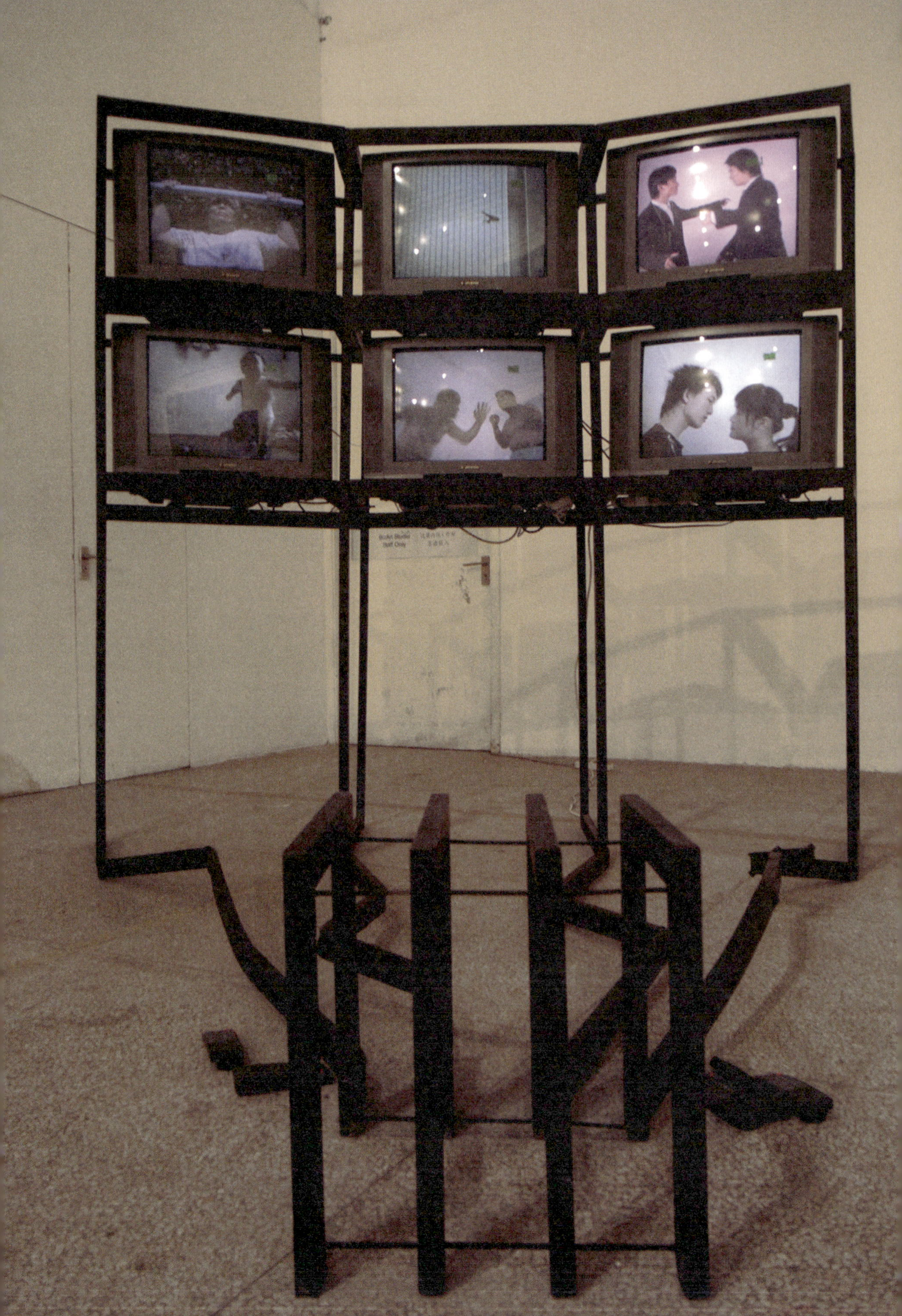

As an artist, what do you care most during working? Could you please give an example to introduce the process of your work for us?

It is more important if we can generate more possibilities during the creating process. *Football Field* No. *603* is a football game I shot with a camera at home. During the editing process, the visual sense of camera and its material properties gave me some different kind of video feelings, so since then I started the experiemtation with this tool. Such kind of possibility makes me more excited, to explore something out of the previous experience.

Suppose you are a critic, from what perspective would you explain and comment on your works?

Now I work mainly on shooting videos with the camera. Ideally, I hope critics, as well as audiences to know firstly about the material properties of the camera itself, and then think about my work.

For example, the nature of surveillance camera video is different from photography by film camera, DV and cell phone. In daily life, it is used to spy on and reveal the ugly behaviors, and its recorded video can be used as legal evidence; in politics, through the manipulation of video monitoring system, the government can ensure that people's behaviors are constrained within an effective framework, to prevent timely the actions that undermine the government's interest; in visual language, its image quality is low, slightly fuzzy, and has a unique viewing point - that is, it avoids the effective viewing angle that people look directly at objects, hanging above the level of eye viewing, thus has a strong characteristic of elusion, and such a gesture of mainly overlooking leads to the feeling of belittling the public and infringement. With its imaging angle, low video quality, display space and audience characteristics, surveillance camera has formed a unique visual system.

In shooting on certain themes, using a camera can be of deeper depth than using a camcorder, to give a better analysis to events and things themselves.

What books and which artists have had, or are having an influence on your way of thinking and working?

Here it is difficult to say which book or which artist has granted how much impact on me. But Teacher Zhou Xiaohu during my college years lent me a book *New Explanations to Art,* which has enlightened me to understand contemporary art.

How do you make judgment and decision as to in what context you'd like to present your works? According to you, in what way is the context created by the work related to the work itself?

An individual cannot alter some common sense, or let's say those that can not be changed have prompted me to complete my job; if you want to sink into a context to present a piece of work, it would be tiring. Of course, there can be short-term effect, but it would distort the direct judgment of an individual. Direct personal judgments are very important. As to the so-called context that influences the work, it won't show until the work is done.

How does your work take the present shape? And please give a few words about the latest development and changes in your work.

来不及，2007
六屏视频互动装置

It's Too Late, 2007
Video Installation

别太狠，2008
录像
5分18秒

Don't be bad, 2008
Video, 3 channels
5'18"

Since 2004 I had started to create video works, previously for more performance art though. Until 2006, I began camera video productions; so far I still go in this direction. In the future, if not so far, it would continue.

In what circumstances would you want to destroy your own creation?
Why should I destroy them?

What do you think about the relation between the art history and artist's work?
Art history is certainly unfair; if an artist has forgotten such sort of art history, then he is likely to enter it. It is not very serious problem even if we do not know about it.

What kind of roles would rational thinking and emotional impulse respectively play in your work?
It is very difficult to pursue (art) without passion. If you have a good start, it would be changeable like April weather for the following tasks and further doings.

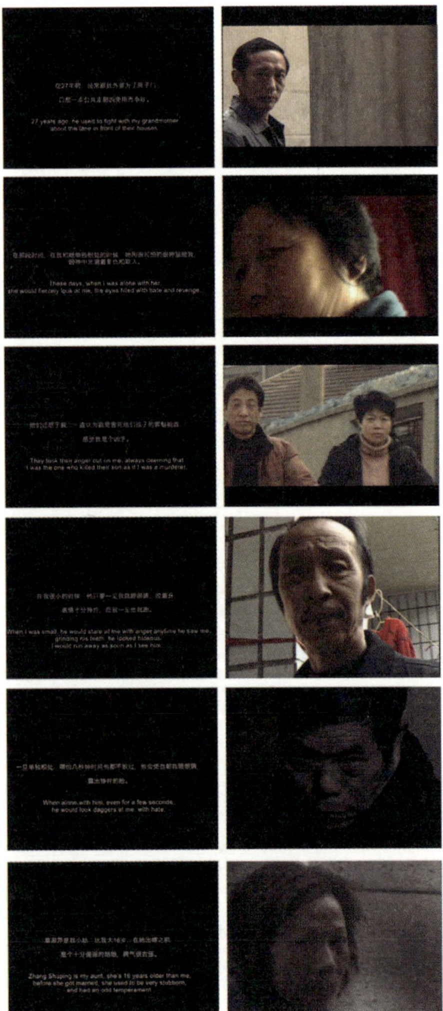

巴别塔，2008
装置（不锈钢，鸽子）
7.35 m (高) × 3.46m (宽)

Babel, 2008
Installation (Stainless Steel, Pigeons)
7.35 m (H) × 3.46 m (R)

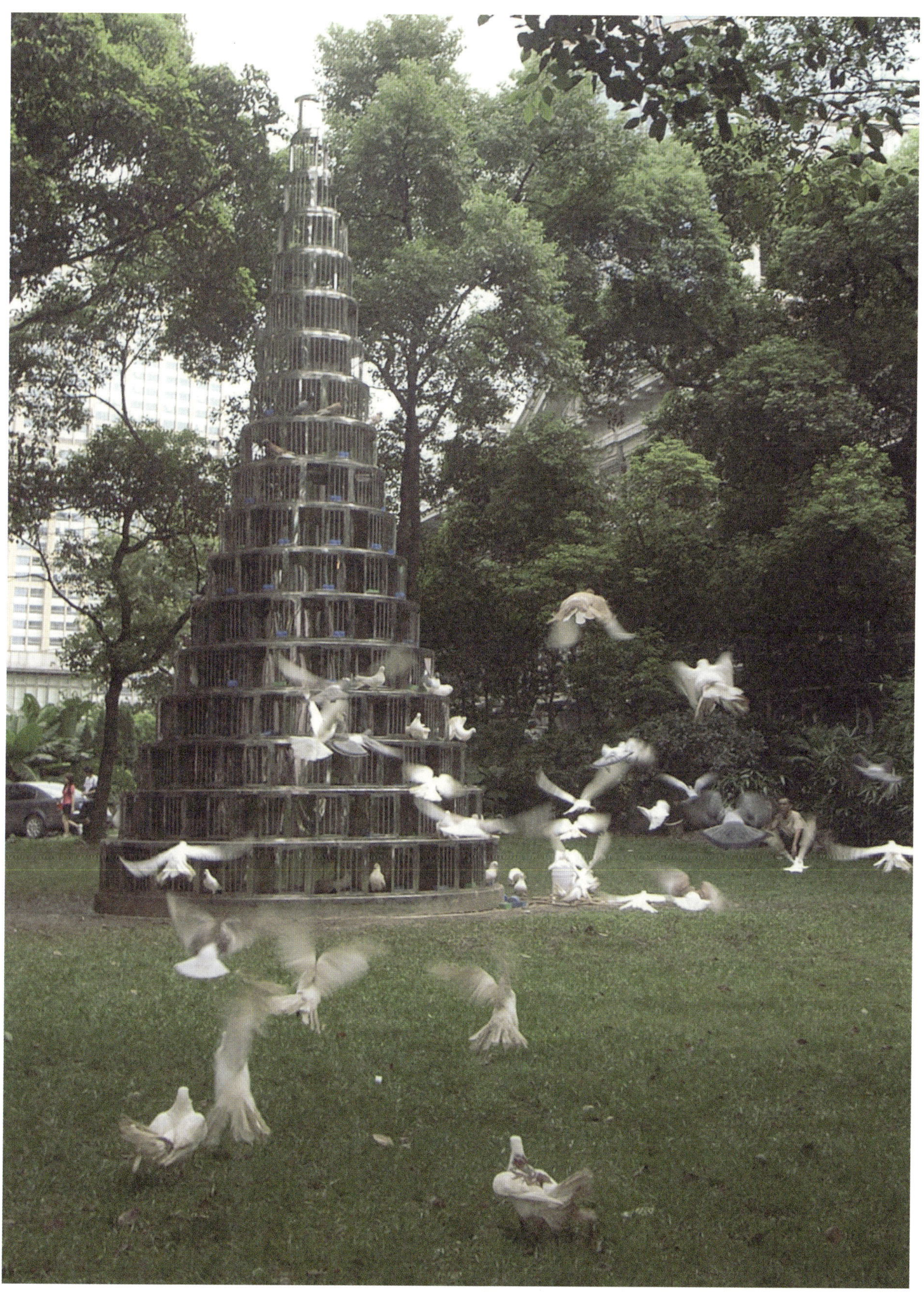

新中国成立6o周年后，经济好像复苏了，展览陆续的多了起来。手头的工作也开始活起来了， 6o周年像是个分水岭。

天安门广场上摄像头多的数不过来，但他们都挺安静的。至上而下记录广场的一针一线。摄像头至上而下的状态分两种。第一，拍摄角度是从上而下的镜头，这是物理上呈现。其二，政府管理层至上而下洞悉着群众一举一动，这是心理上。第二种至上而下的状态只是在两个对象之间产生心理差异，这个差异通过两者之间的主被动关系来确定。主动者对被动者产生一种至上而下的一种的观看方式。这种观看带着戏弄，好奇，盛气凌人，充满着等级的意识。而被动者是无奈的，不知的，甚至有被鱼肉的状态。

After the celebration of the 60 anniversary of the founding of PRC, economy seems to have rejuvenated and more exhibitions opened recently. Also I start to get busy for my work. All these changes make the 60th anniversary a watershed event to me.

On the Tiananmen Square, surveillance cameras there, though countless in number, seem to be so quite, recording everything to a hair's breadth from above. There are two layers of meaning regarding the cameras' high position: 1st is the downward shooting position speaking from the physical level; 2nd is the close surveillance over actions of the mass from the government's management agencies from psychological point of view. The second top-down situation only creates mental differences between the two subjects involved, which are defined by the initiative and passive relationship between the two. Here the initiative launched a dominant way of viewing towards the passive from above, which is characterized by mock, curiosity, arrogance and sense of hierarchy. The passive party is in a helpless, ignorant position and even being victimized.

603 足球场，2006
录像
8分钟

Football Field No. 603, 2006
video, 6 channels
8'00"

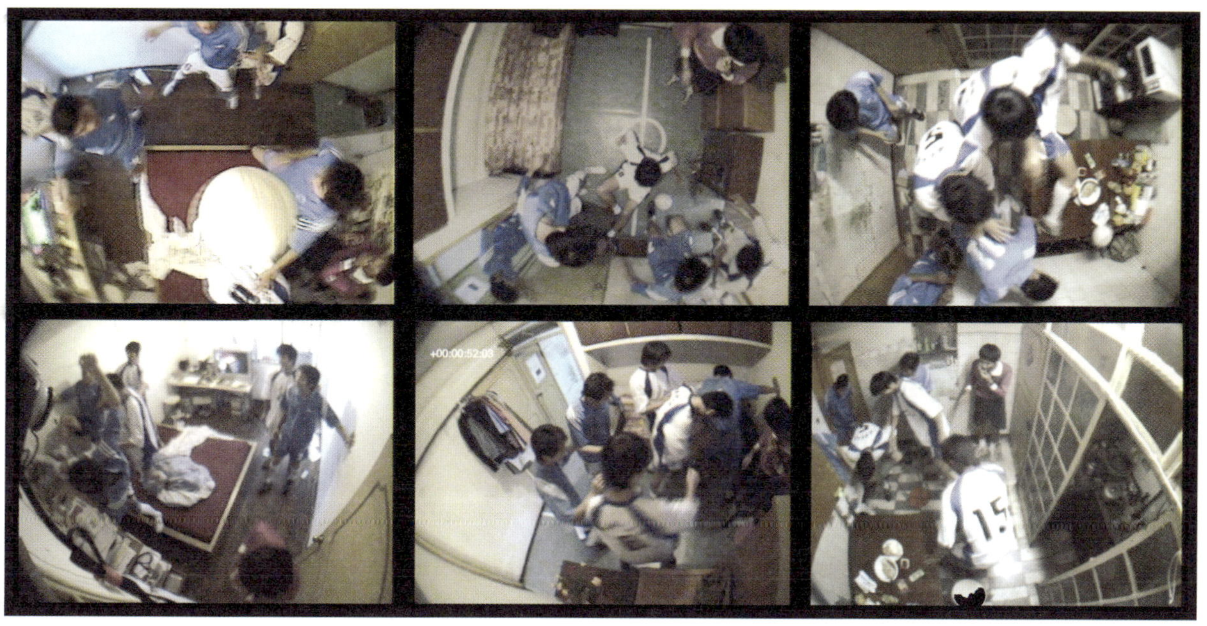

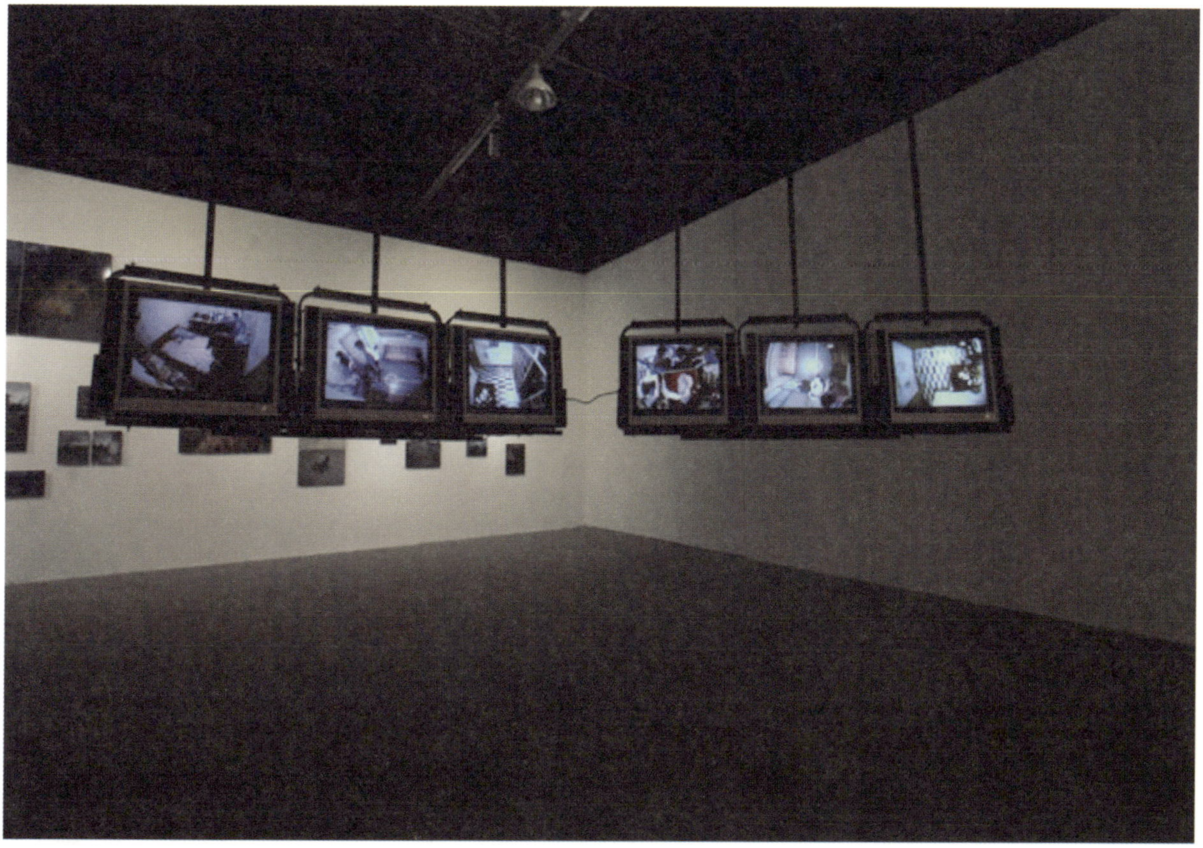

赵 要

ZHAO YAO

**作为艺术家，你在创作中所关心的是什么？以一件作品为例，
分享你的创作过程。**

就目前而言，我更看重作为艺术家个人在作品中有一个什么样
的位置。当然与此同时对于时间性，空间性的多种尝试也一直
关注。在创作上不是在为一个明确的结论而生，而是希望发现
创造一个"奇点"，让每个人各自满足。创作如中国画的笔
墨，着墨的地方只是工作，而"留白"的地方是重点。

《人口手，上中下》其实也就是英语里ABC的意思。在这由照
片组成的视频里面，我在持续的14个小时里，手持相机对准四
粒大米排放成的一个小十字使其与相机的聚焦"十字"重合并
且始终在画面中心。手把持着相机尽量保持在同一个位置连续
拍摄一万张照片。然后把这些照片以每秒24帧的速度按顺序播
放。即便是努力的保持在同一位置，从机械的角度说这本身就
不可能。但是随着时间和人的体力变化，这样的把持就会出现
更大的偏差。其实也就是这些偏差构成了这个作品的关键。

**如果你是一个批评家，你会从什么角度来阐释和讨论你自己的
创作？**

我更喜欢一个作品能让观众发现什么而不是给予什么。

在你的创作和思考中，什么书籍和艺术家曾经或正在影响着你？

具体的名字说不上来，存在哲学？语言哲学？福柯？时髦的
思想家我都看过，但是都没看进去都忘记了。我喜欢钱穆，
也喜欢苏东坡，陈鼓应的《庄子今注今释》系列我仔细读过
印象深刻。不过最近比较喜欢看IT科技新闻，淘宝，Google，
Web2.0……艺术家？毕加索、培根、Jeffe Wall、博伊斯，后来
我越来越发现我喜欢上了布鲁斯·瑙曼、科索斯这样的艺术家。

**你是怎样判断和决定在什么语境下呈现你的哪些作品的？你是
怎样看待作品呈现的语境和作品的关系的？**

就目前而言，我的作品都不为展览而生，没有什么特定的语境
而言。平常就好，只要不是时光倒流，战火纷飞，语境对于我

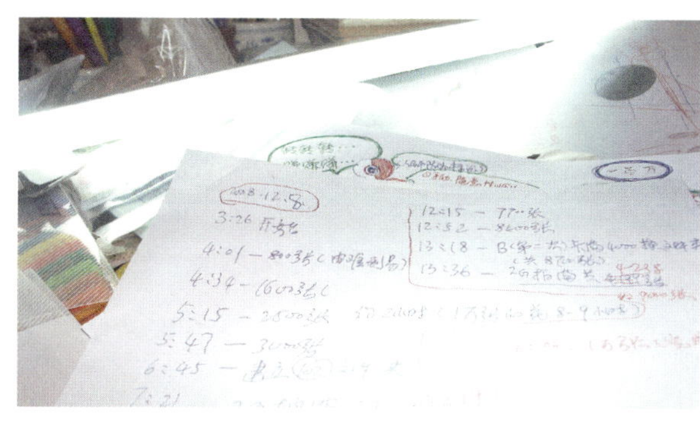

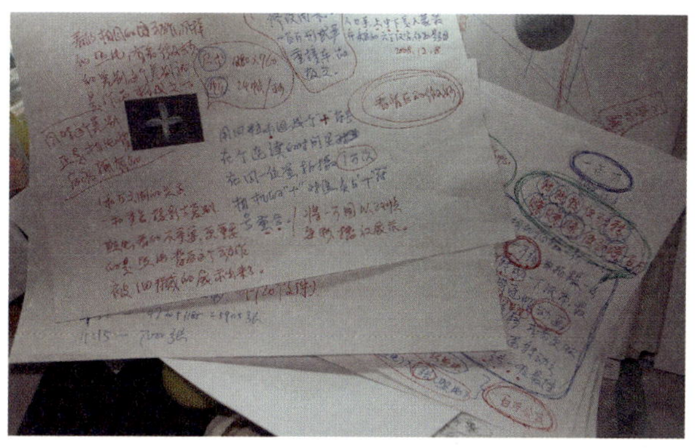

作品方案
Plan

来说不是重要。生活的当下足矣。

如何在创作上形成了现在的面貌，描述一下最近年来作品的发展和变化？

坦白的说，我以前一直想做一个摄影为主的艺术家，通过时间，空间的探索找到摄影的更多可能。结果差点卡死，后来发现摄影只是个情节，对事物始基元素的探索才是重点，于是我放弃摄影，然后才发现摄影还可以这样做。于是从一个井底之蛙，跳到了现在这个井里，虽然感觉大了一点，心情舒畅了点，估计这也只是现时的感觉罢了。

你会在什么情况下摧毁你自己的作品？

没成为作品以前毁掉。既然都出来了，就这样吧。不为一个好作品而生，不怕错误，当然也不怕平庸。既然是作品，你毁了它，它还是作品，除非毁掉这个行为也是作品。不然我觉得真没必要。

你怎么看待艺术史和艺术家创作的关系？

冰糖葫芦？艺术家是一个个的大红枣，艺术史是那根竹签？先有竹签还是先有大红枣？这个问题我没想清楚。批评家和画廊操盘手是不是就是那个卖糖葫芦的小贩？凑上几个相同大红枣都能穿成一串。就怕孤零零的一个……

在你的工作中，理性和情感冲动各自扮演着什么样的角色？

和结婚差不多。感性说这身材这脸蛋挺吸引我的，然后理性说这性格、这处世、这生活习惯也挺圆满的。综合综合，揉吧揉吧于是就凑合在一起结了婚。画个圈买鸭蛋的事情没干过。

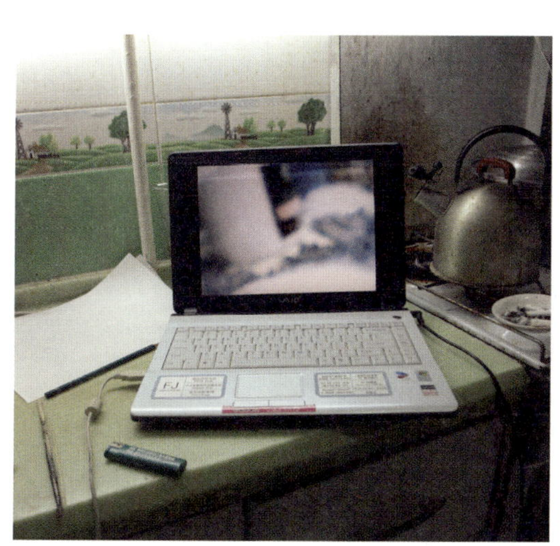

家中正在工作的电脑
The artist's laptop at home

As an artist, what do you care most during working? Could you please give an example to introduce the process of your work for us?

What is the artist's position in the work? It's my interest at present. Of course I have never stopped my exploration about time and space. We do not create for getting a definite conclusion, but for the discovery of a "wonder" that will bring satisfaction to everybody. Something about the use of ink in a Chinese painting applies to artistic creation— painting is the job to be done, but "the unpainted blank" is the focus.

People, mouth, hand, up, middle, and down, literally, is the Chinese version of ABC in English. It's a video work of photos. For fourteen consecutive hours, I aimed my camera at four rice grains that are arranged into the pattern of a small cross and is made to coincide with the cross of the camera focus. With my hands holding the camera in the fixed position, I took 10,000 photos at a stretch which would then be played in chronological order at a speed of 24 frames per second. Even if I made painstaking effort to keep the camera at the same position, it is mechanically impossible. As time went and I got tired, more obvious deviations were inevitable which constitutes the essence of this work.

Suppose you are a critic, from what perspective would you explain and comment on your works?

I prefer works that can lead to discoveries to those that only gives information.

What books and which artists have had, or are having an influence on your way of thinking and working?

It's hard to list the names. Existentialism? Philosophy of language? Foucault. I have read books by those popular thinkers, but I didn't remember much. I like Qian Mu and Su Dongpo, too. I have read Chen Guying's modern interpretation of Zhuangzi and was impressed greatly. Now I like It Science News, Taobao, Google, web 2.0... As to artists, I used to be interested in Picasso, Bacon, Jeffe Wall and Boyce. Later I found I came to like such artists as Bruce Naumen and Kosuth.

How do you make judgment and decision as to in what context you'd like to present your works? According to you, in what way is the context created by the work related to the work itself?

Until now I never design works for any exhibitions, so there is no specific context. I enjoy what is common. A war won't bother me if time doesn't go black. To live every minute when we are alive.

How does your work take the present shape? And please give a few words about the latest development and changes in your work.

Frankly speaking, I had been dreaming of becoming a photographer, thinking exploration in time and place would lead to more possibilities. I almost ended in complete failure when I found that photos can make up plot only and priority should be given to base elements. Therefore I gave photographs before I found that photos can be arranged in this way. I am still a frog at the bottom of a well (be a person with a very limited outlook), though now

独立项目《六张照片和一个小房间》现场，长征空间，2006年北京
Six Photos and a Small Room on view at The Long March Space, Beijing (2006)

the well seems bigger and I feel better. It won't be long before it changes, I guess.

In what circumstances would you want to destroy your own creation?
I won't destroy my work after they are finished. Since they are there, I will keep them. I don't want to be so fixed on one good work, neither am I afraid of making mistakes or being mediocre, of course. It is a work even if it is destroyed, unless we can destroy the action itself, otherwise it's unnecessary.

What do you think about the relation between the art history and artist's work?
Candied red dates on a stick (Chinese local delicacy)? Are the artists the red dates, history of art the stick? What comes first, the stick or the dates? I don't know. Are critics and traders at the gallery the candied fruit peddler? Similar dates can be put together on a stick. Nobody likes to stand alone.

What kind of roles would rational thinking and emotional impulse respectively play in your work?
It's like marriage. Emotion says that the figure and the face are appealing, and then reason points out that the character, the manners and habits are also satisfactory, so a marriage strikes on the basis of the overall qualities. I don't set particular standards before making a choice.

作品现场图
Installation view

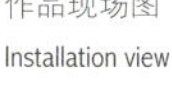

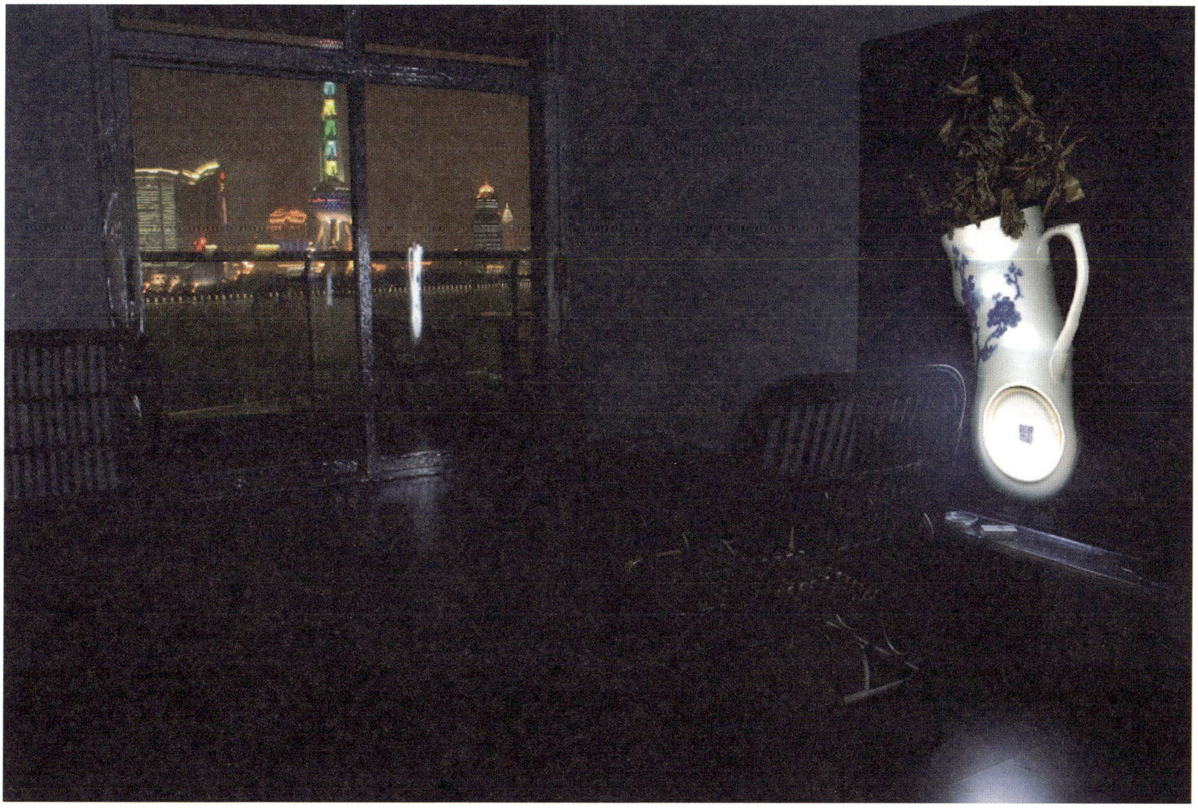

安静，2009
装置
尺寸可变

Stillness, 2009
Installation
Variable dimension

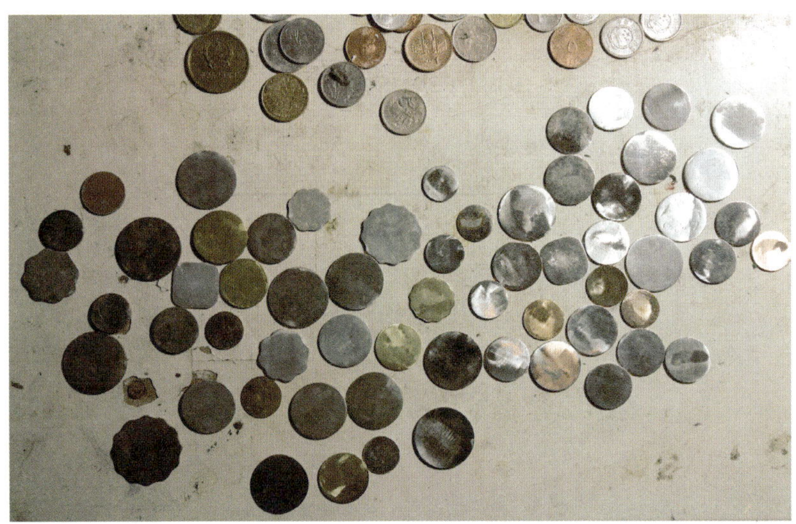

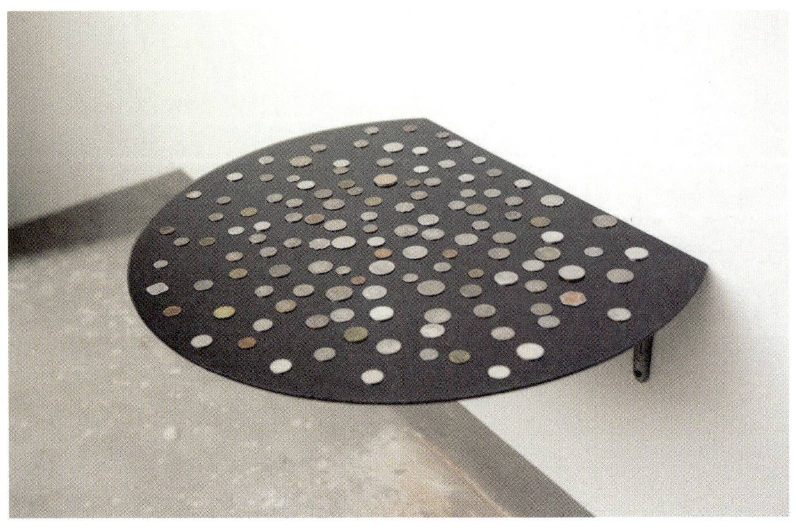

巴特福莱，2008
平板实物扫描
66×66cm

Hudie, 2008
Scan of object surface
66×66cm

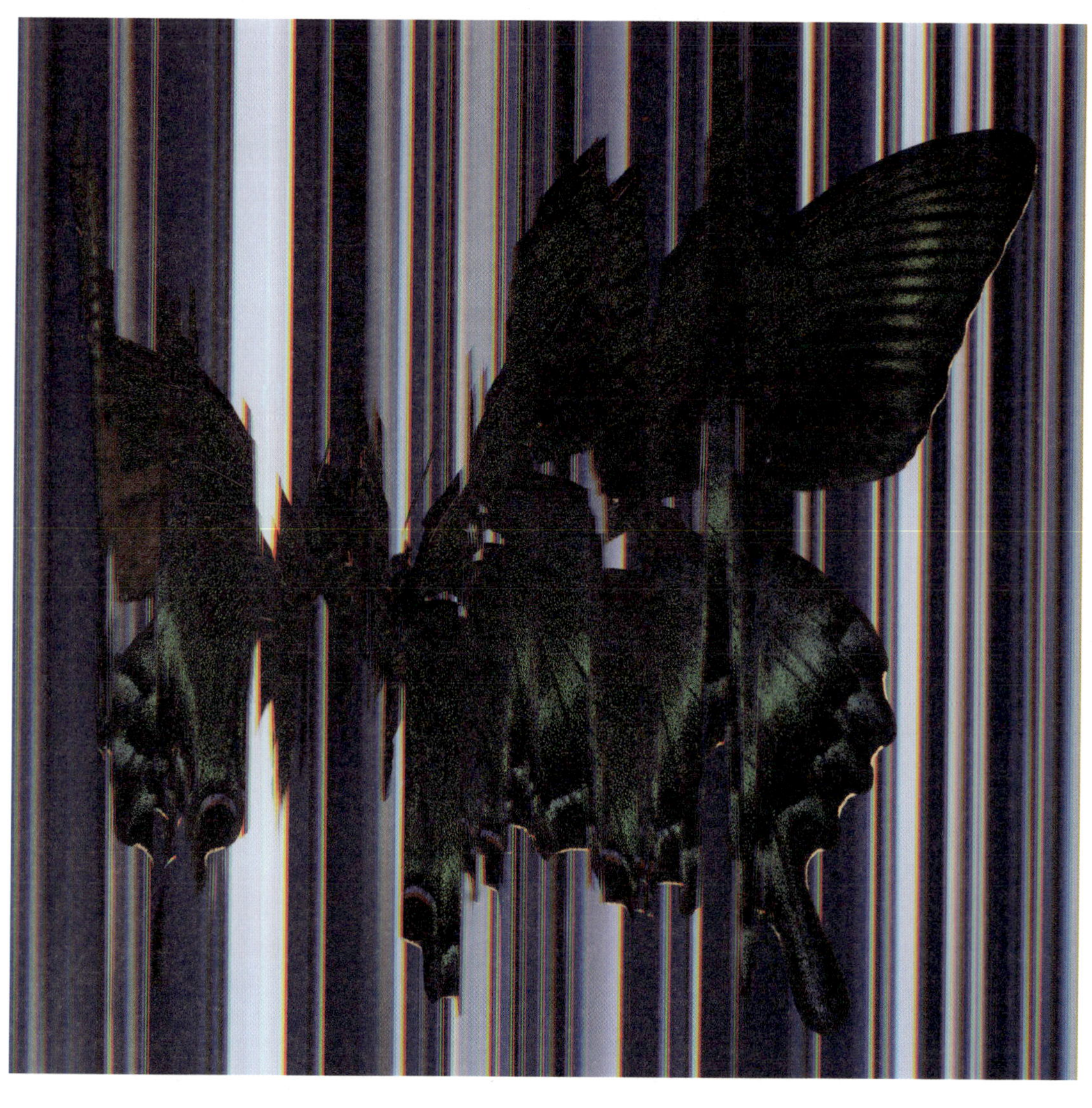

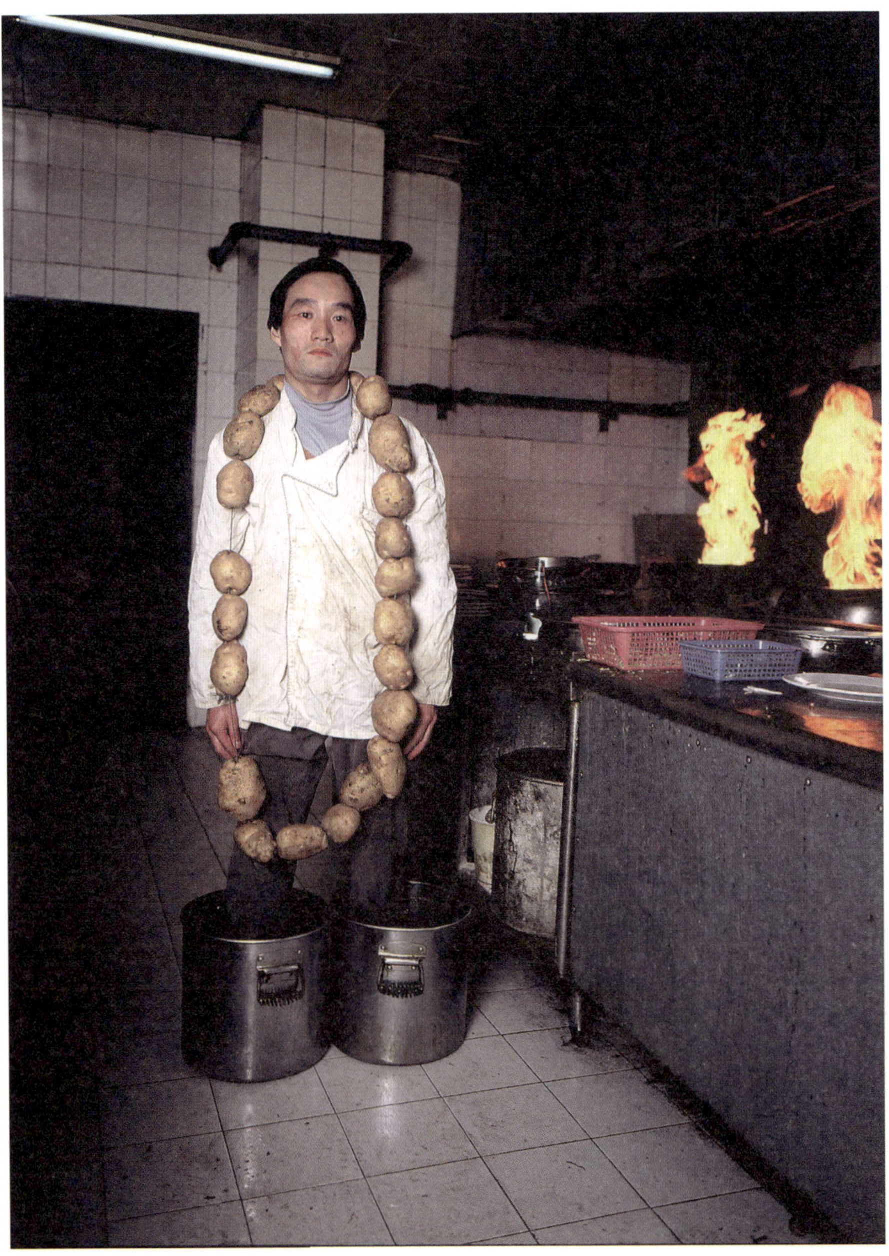

彭喜林，2007
摄影

Mr. Peng, 2007
Photography

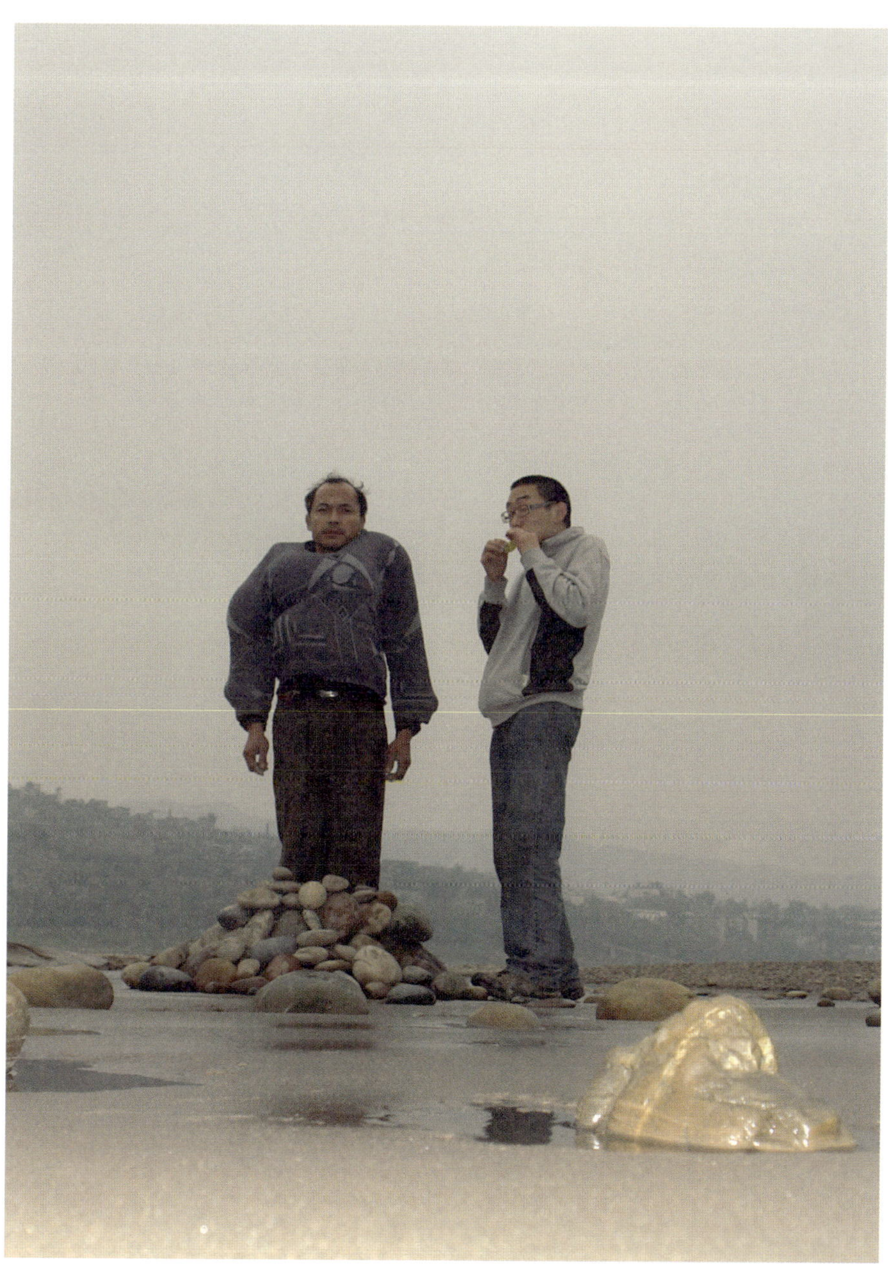

作品《周俊杰》拍摄现场。

Filming scene of *Mr. Zhou*

赵 赵

ZHAO ZHAO

作为艺术家，你在创作中所关心的是什么？以一件作品为例，
分享你的创作过程。
我要求把这个问题删掉。

如果你是一个批评家，你会从什么角度来阐释和讨论你自己的
创作？
我不认同假设。

在你的创作和思考中，什么书籍和艺术家曾经或正在影响着你？
哪跟哪啊。

你是怎样判断和决定在什么语境下呈现你的哪些作品的？你是
怎样看待作品呈现的语境和作品的关系的？
我强烈要求重新提问这个问题。

如何在创作上形成了现在的面貌，描述一下近年来作品的发展
和变化？
一步一步、勤勤恳恳。

你会在什么情况下摧毁你自己的作品？
你相信有鬼魂吗？

你怎么看待艺术史和艺术家创作的关系？
能拉屎的艺术家都是艺术屎。

在你的工作中，理性和情感冲动各自扮演着什么样的角色？
这八个大傻问题真让我冲动。

欧币，2008
80×120 cm
将安塞姆·基弗尔的作品《人口计划》（1991）上的铅皮撕
下一块做成八个一组的"欧元硬币"。
地点：汉堡火车站当代艺术博物馆，柏林，德国

EURO, 2008
80×120 cm
A set of eight "Euro coins" made of lead sheath taken from Anselm Kiefer's
art work *Volkszählung* (1991)
Hamburger Bahnhof – Museum for Contemporary Art, Berlin

**As an artist, what do you care most during working?
Could you please give an example to introduce the
process of your work for us?**
I ask you to delete this question.

**Suppose you are a critic, what perspective would you talk
about and explain you work from?**
I don't agree on hypothesis.

**What books and which artists have had, or is having an
influence on your way of thinking and working?**
What is this question about?

**How do you decide the context in which your work is to
be presented? How do you consider the relation of the
context with your work?**
I strongly ask you to re-consider this question.

**How does your work take the present shape? And please
give a few words about the latest development and
changes in your work.**
Step by step, diligently.

**In what circumstances would you want to destroy your
own creation?**
Do you believe in ghosts?

**What do you think about the relation between the art
history and artist's work?**
Any artist who can shit is art shit. (In Chinese, "shit" has the same
pronunciation as "history".)

**What kind of roles would rational thinking and emotional
impulse respectively play during your work time?**
These eight stupid questions really made me excited.

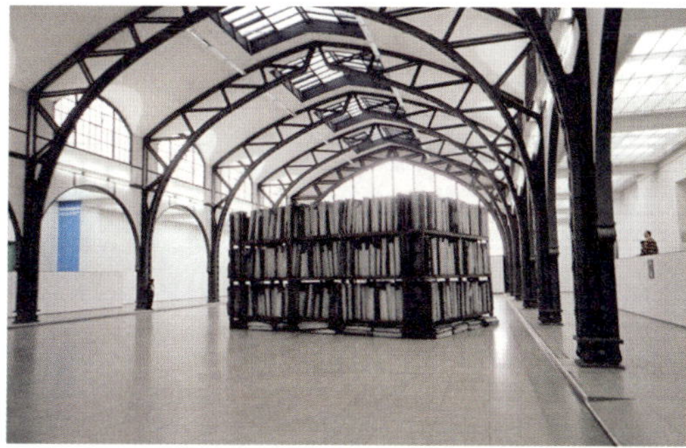

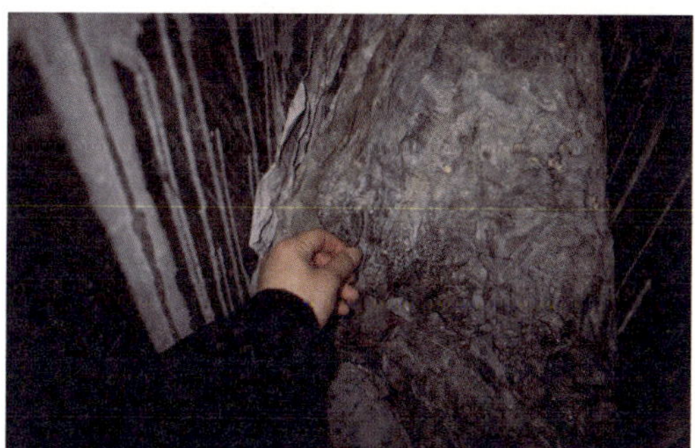

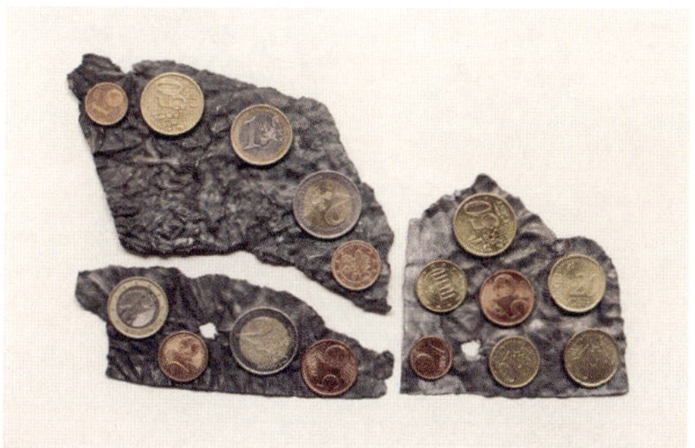

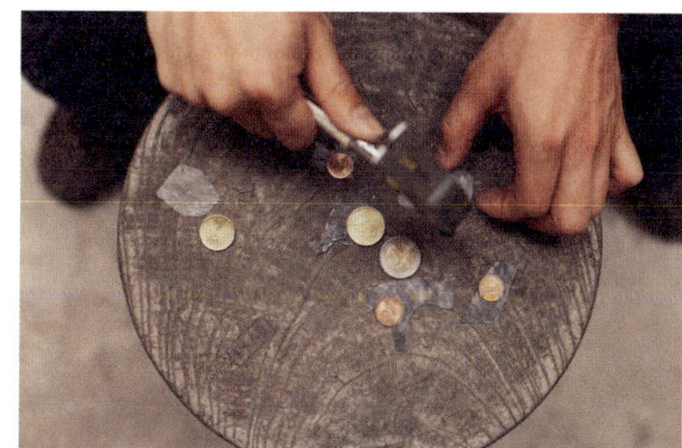

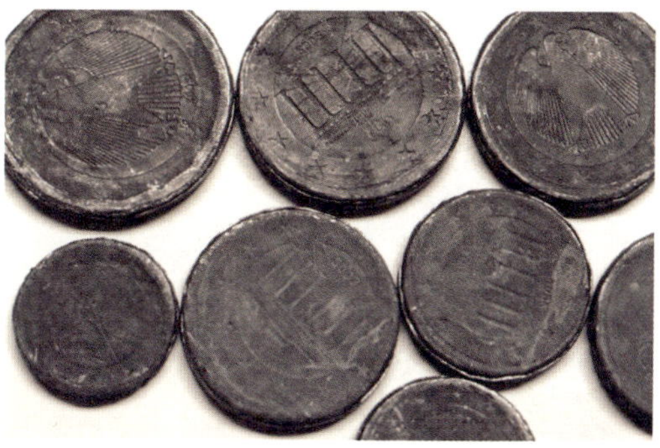

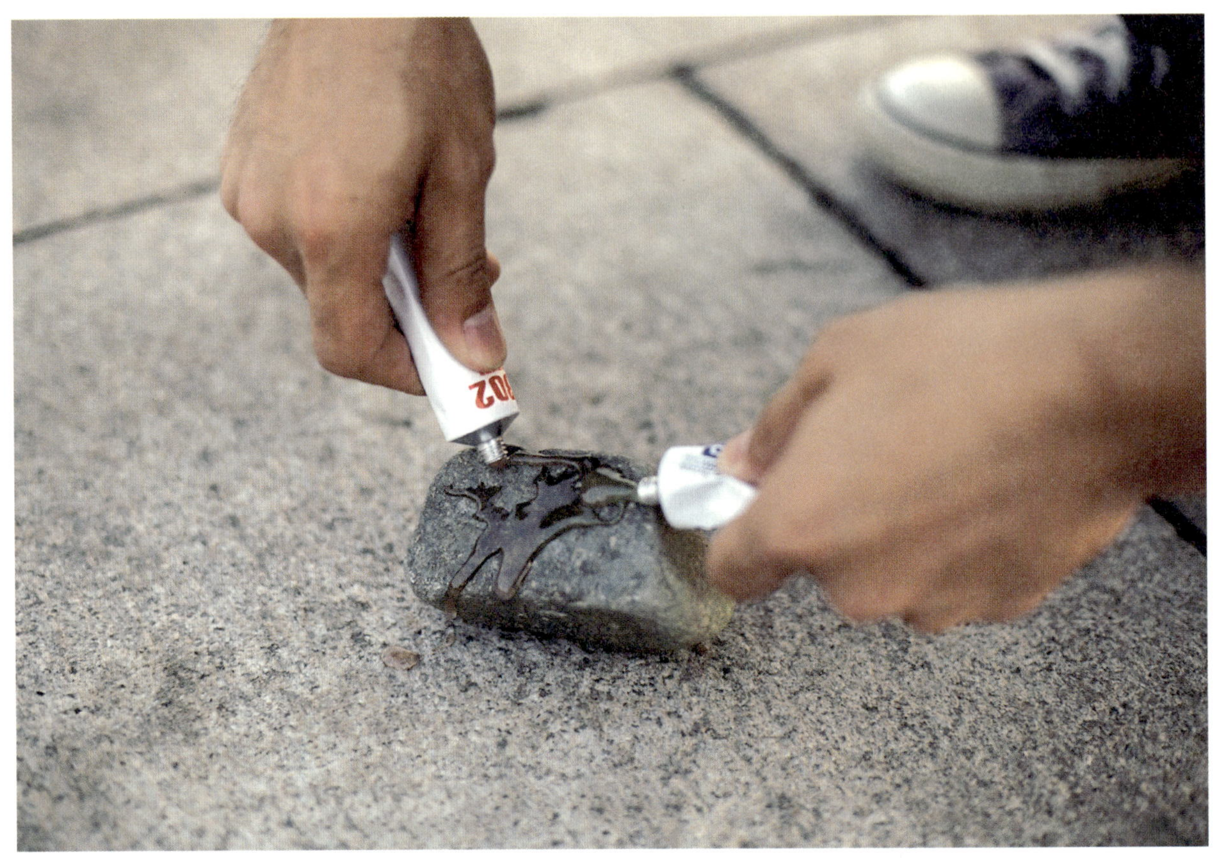

鹅卵石，2007
80 × 120 cm
将一块鹅卵石用强力胶粘在天安门广场的地上。
天安门广场，北京

Cobblestone, 2007
80 × 120 cm
The artist used strong adhesive to glue a cobblestone onto the
ground of Tiananmen Square.
Tiananmen Square, Beijing

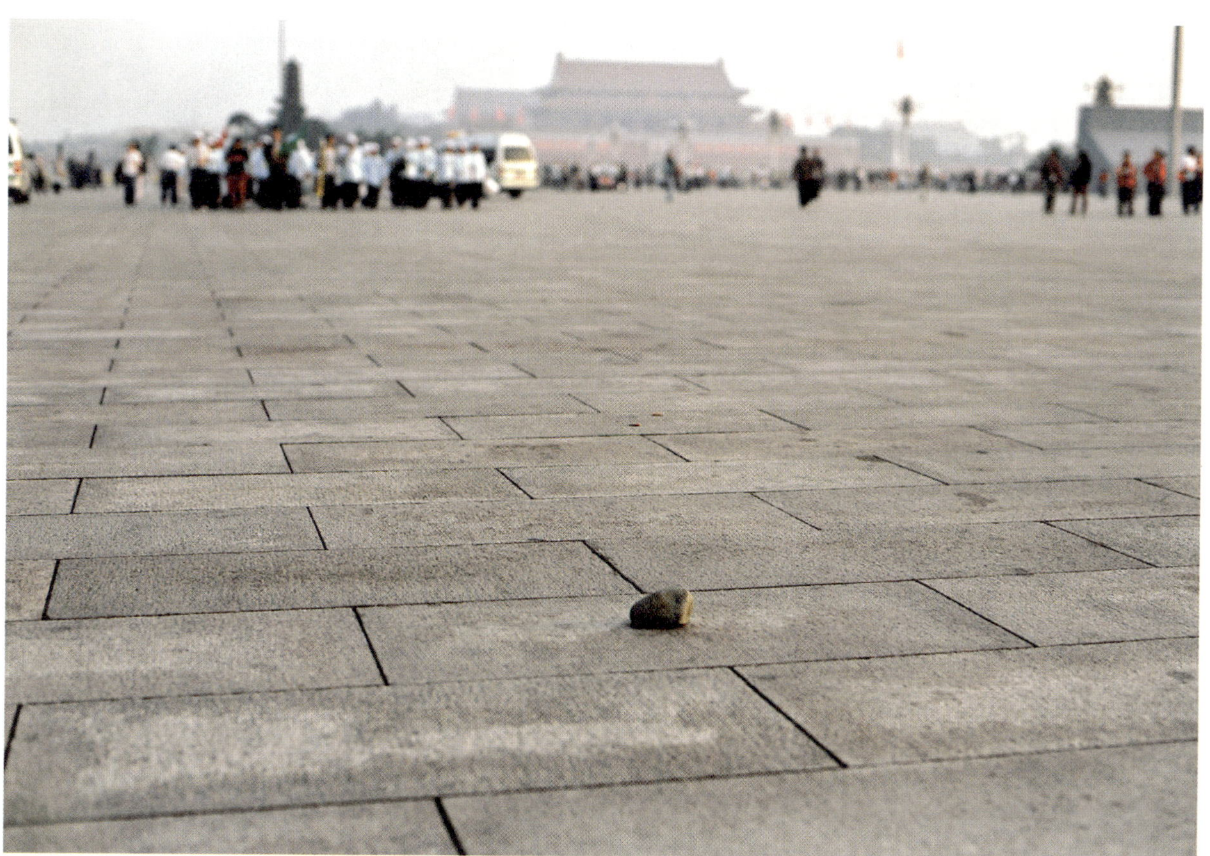

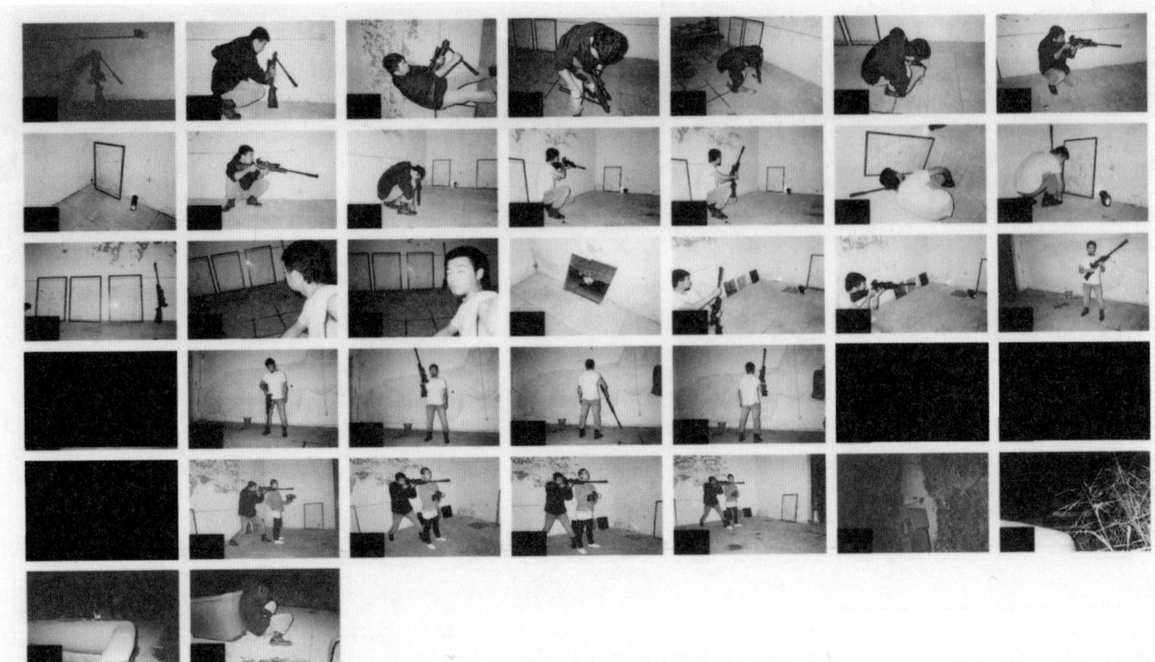

CSI, 2009
综合媒介

CSI, 2009
Mixed Media

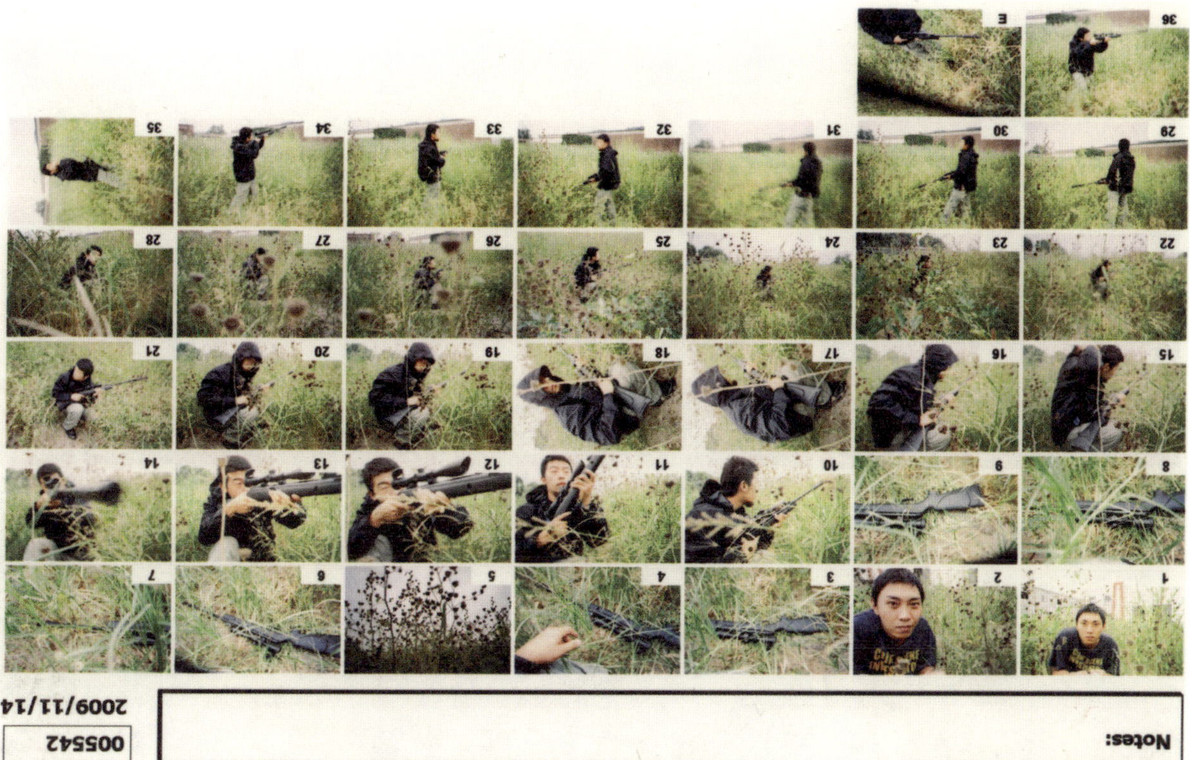

CSI, 2009
综合媒介

CSI, 2009
Mixed Media

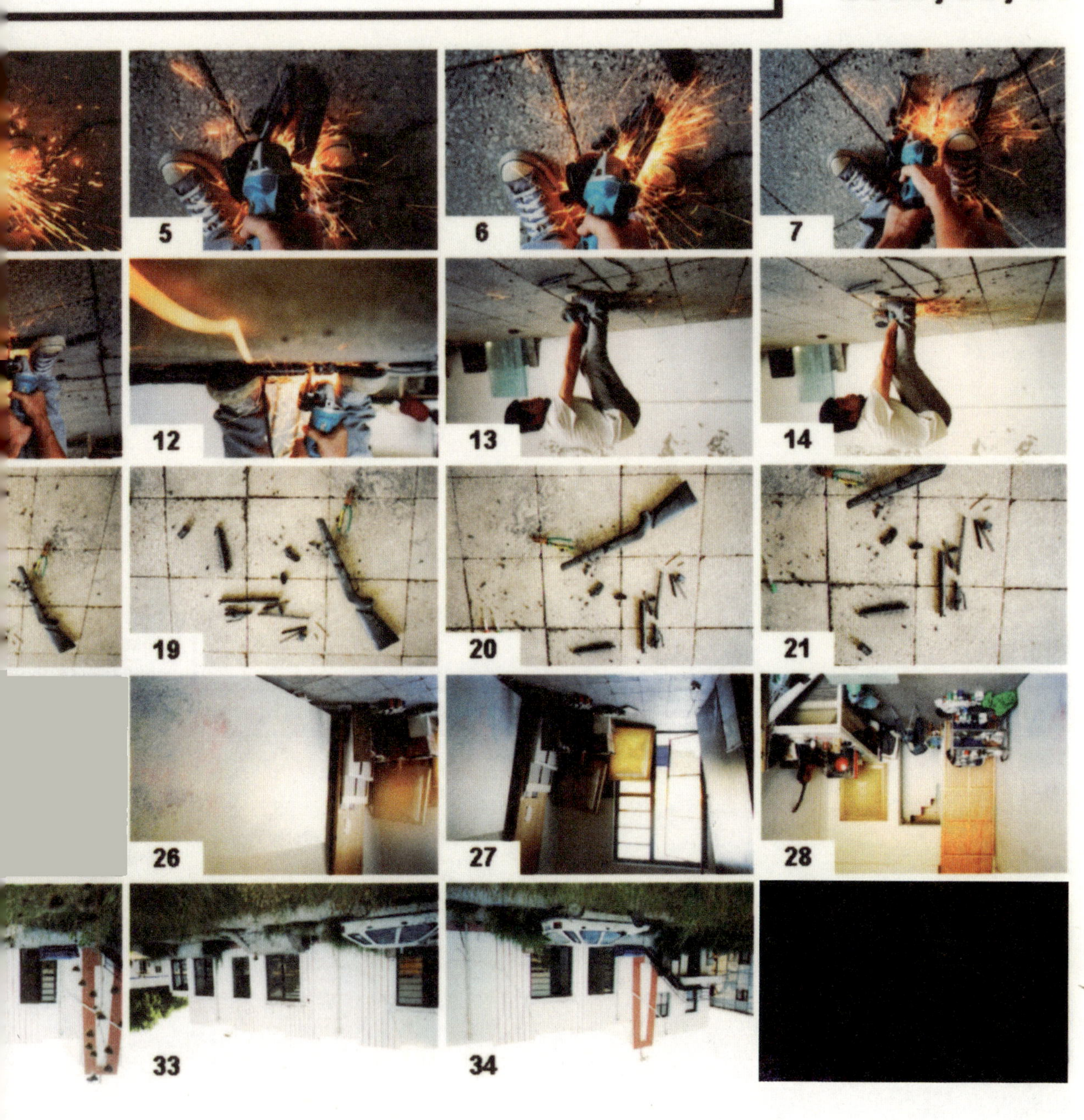

005537
2009/11/14
5
6
7
12
13
14
19
20
21
26
27
28
33
34

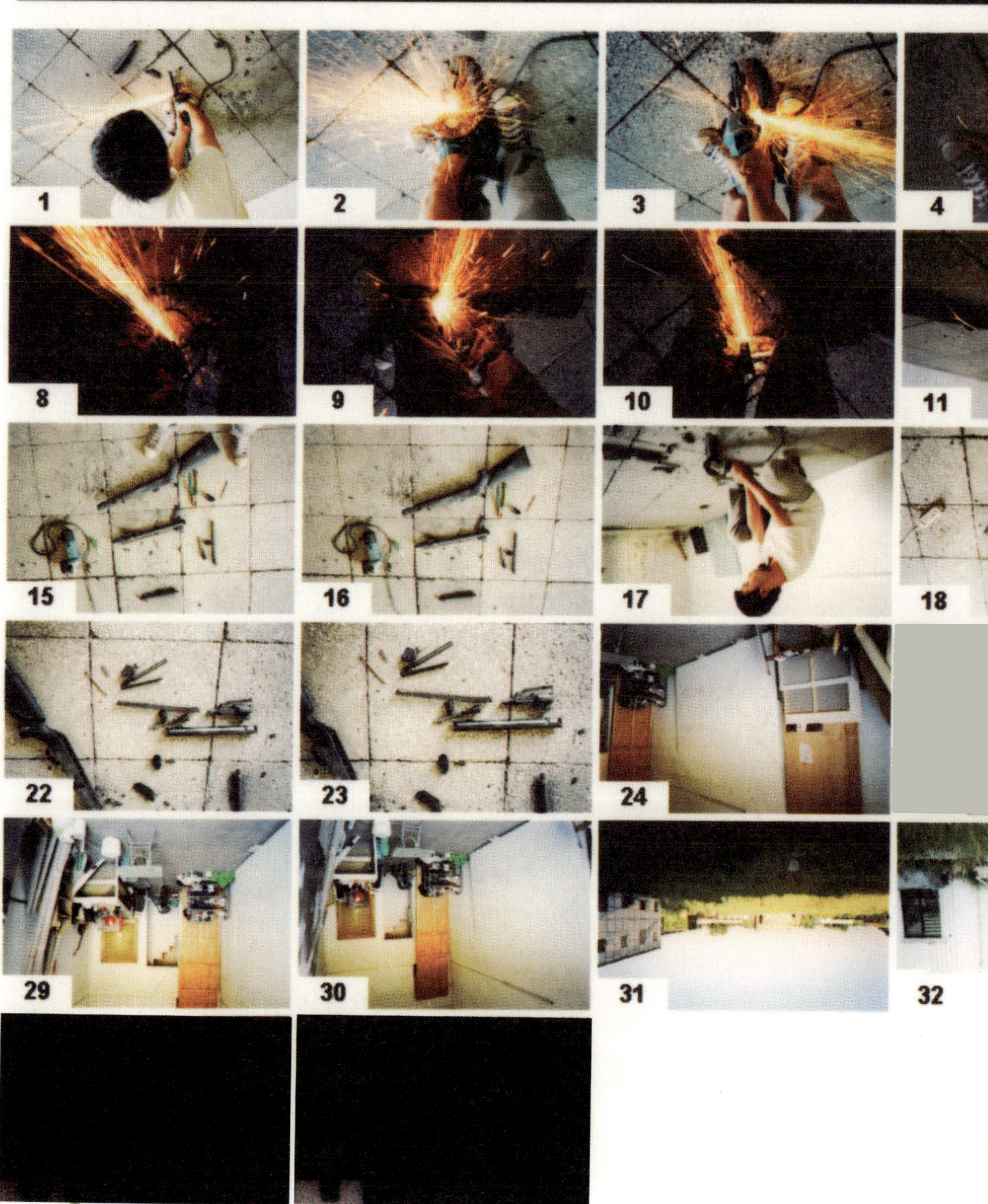

Notes:

周啸虎

ZHOU XIAOHU

作为艺术家，你在创作中所关心的是什么？以一件作品为例，分享你的创作过程。

2007年底开始实施拍摄录像作品《集训营》。内容是关于某跨国直销公司的培训项目，它显示出资本流向的同时，附带着强大的价值观影响力。在工作中我会去想的是，一种价值观和思想模式是如何被注射进入另一个民族的肌肉的。那么我又将怎么去处理这些被点燃的集体癫狂和激情，这个对我而言更具挑战性。我不是社会学家，我没有能力去评判人们该做什么。我能做的是寻找更有力的、更有意味的表达方式，制造出另一个平行于生活的、现在进行式的"可能世界"。我更愿意这样去想：那些看上去非常社会或者非常政治的东西，肯定会包含着更为疯狂的诗意，这需要一个动作，一个破坏性的动作才能够被打开，我认为艺术是一个动词。一些出乎意料的改变，是可以颠覆我们的审美惯性的。

素材是在上海某个影剧院的舞台上拍的，我事先搭好倒置的布景，舞台上的九根电动布景钢管将所有道具和演员全部吊起，悬在半空。表演者全部是杂技团的演员，因为是倒挂着表演，所以他们的表演是很艰苦的。拍摄之前必须排练得很充分，因为即使专业杂技演员也不可能倒吊着表演太久。在录像后期剪辑时，我再把画面再颠倒过来，让人看上去是一个"正常"的培训活动，但是他们已不再是一个习惯的视觉经验所能传递的内容和力度，我希望这些冒险的实验能带来某些出乎意料的逆转。

如果你是一个批评家，你会从什么角度来阐释和讨论你自己的创作？

你炮制出怎样的"不可能世界"？你制造了怎样的个人偏见系统？这个偏见改变了什么？它重要吗？它动摇了过往艺术价值观？

在你的创作和思考中，什么书籍和艺术家曾经或正在影响着你？

维特根斯坦的思想对我而言是有价值的——"词语的功能在于如何使用"。一个是如何使用工具，再一层是如何创造工具，还有是这个新工具制造出新经验。

你是怎样判断和决定在什么语境下呈现你的哪些作品的？你是怎样看待作品呈现的语境和作品的关系的？

在恰当和正当的时候做不恰当的事，在不恰当和不正当的时候做恰当的事。应该让人看到某个场景，闪现、惊呼自己的表象发现，这是直觉经验和思想的混合物；我期待第二次惊醒——
当你进入作品，发现一切不仅仅是惊呼或你以为的那样，会有
出乎意料的逆转，这是智性和精神的混合物。

**如何在创作上形成了现在的面貌，描述一下最近年来作品的发
展和变化？**

一个是个人精神历程的自然演进，另一个是社会生活的变化推
动着个人思考得变化。比如我原初利用动画的可操控性来实现
反操控，在意政治诗学的疯狂与荒诞呈现。再思考艺术呈现的
方式，需要更具颠覆性的动作去打开，动作本身即是意义，现
场应该的一个精神发动机。后来对训练的概念感兴趣，它代表
着特定的功利目的诉求而制造集体迷狂。而"社会自动写作"
的概念，是要依赖社会规则才能获得艺术颠覆要求。

你会在什么情况下摧毁你自己的作品？

摧毁一个概念的重要性远甚于摧毁一个作品。

你怎么看待艺术史和艺术家创作的关系？

艺术史是一个关系链，艺术家必须创造新的链接，才能不断扩
展它。艺术史是有营养的，但不能因袭，因袭任何的链接都将
是艺术史的赘肉。

在你的工作中，理性和情感冲动各自扮演着什么样的角色？

当你寻求解决某个问题的方式时会有情感冲动的动力，而实施
的过程多半是理性的。

传闻，2007
装置

Renown, 2007
Installation

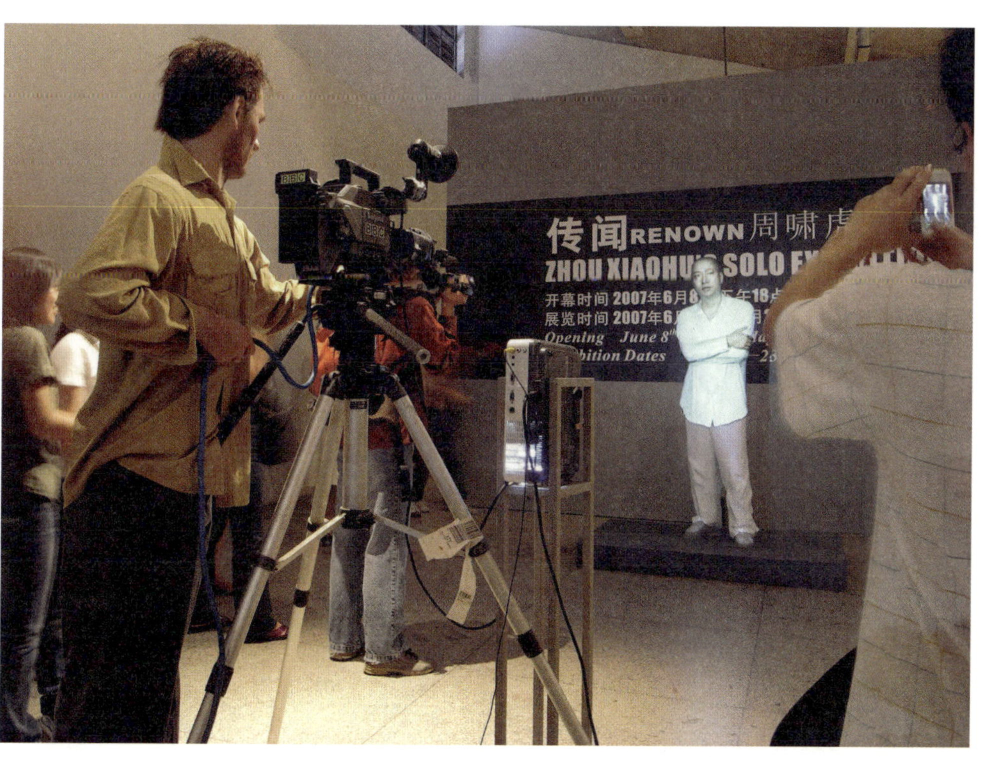

**As an artist, what do you care most during working?
Could you please give an example to introduce the
process of your work for us?**

I started *Concentration Traning Camp* at the end of 2007. It's a
video work about a multinational direct sales company's training
program. It shows not only where capital flows but also how
powerful the influence of values can be. While working, I wonder
how a type of values and ways of thinking get transplanted into
another people. In what way can I reflect the burning frenzy on a
collective scale? It's a challenge to me. I'm no sociologist, so I'm not
able to make judgment about what people ought to do. What I can
do is only to develop more powerful and more meaningful ways
to build a present continuous "possible world" in parallel with life.
In what appears too social and political there must be something
crazily poetic hidden. To start a destructive move, another move
is needed. Art is a verb, I believe. Some unexpected changes can
subvert our aesthetic habit.

The video was shot in a theatre in Shanghai. I first had the set
inverted. Then all the properties and actors were suspended in
midair by nine electric set pipes on the stage. All the actors were
acrobats. It was quite a job since they had to perform suspended.
They had to rehearse again and again as it was very difficult even
for a professional acrobat to perform upside down for a long time.
When I edited the video work, I turned the frame upside down
again, so that it might seem to be a "normal" training, but the
content and intensity was different from what the traditional visual
experience could transmit. I wish such adventurous experiment can
bring us some unexpected reversions.

**Suppose you are a critic, from what perspective would
you explain and comment on your works?
What is the "impossible world" you made? What kind of**

集训营，2008
长征空间展览现场

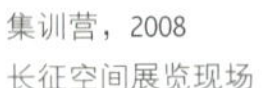

Concentration Training Camp, 2008
Long March Space

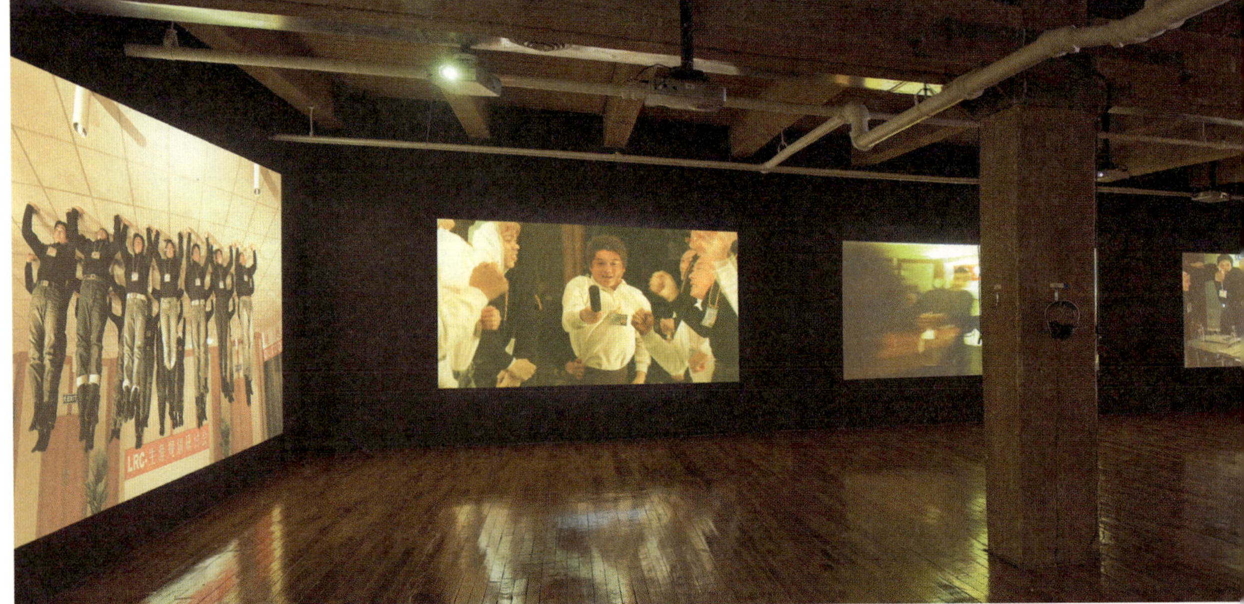

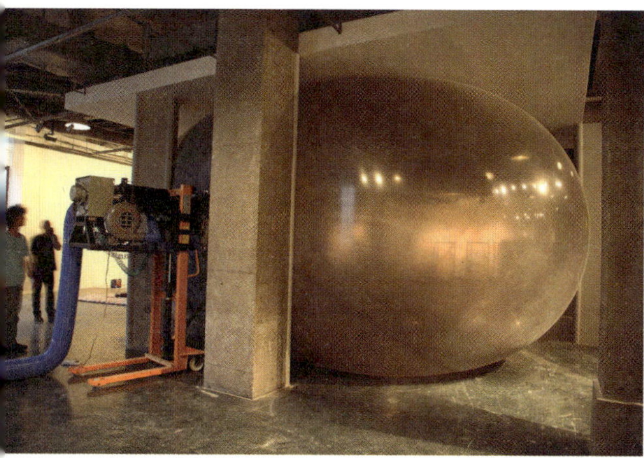

甚至怀有恐惧，2008
装置

Even in Fear, 2008
Installation

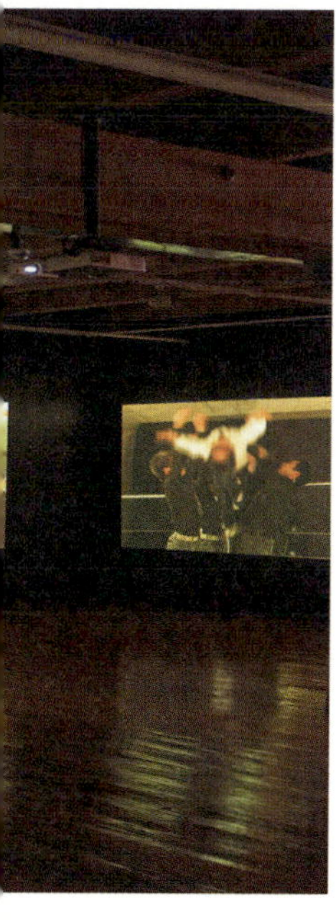

personal prejudice system have you developed? What has the prejudice changed? Is it important? Does it revolutionize the values of the existing art?
What books and which artists have had, or are having an influence on your way of thinking and working?

To me, Wittgenstein's comments on words prove to be meaningful that the function of a word is how it is used. One is about how to use the tool, another is how to create tools, and what experience one can get with the new tolls.

How do you make judgment and decision as to in what context you'd like to present your works? According to you, in what way is the context created by the work related to the work itself?

Do what is undesirable at certain and right time, and do what is right in the wrong time and place. We ought to reveal and enable people to watch every scene, even it is fleeing, and you will be surprised at the discovery of images. It's a mixture of intuition and idea; I wish to be awakened a second time. You read into a work, so you can discover that things are more than exclamations or the way you like them to be because there are unexpected turns, which reveals the mixture of intellect and psyche.

How does your work take the present shape? And please give a few words about the latest development and changes in your work.

One is the natural evolution of one's spirit; and the other is changes in one's thinking as a result of the changes in social life. I, for example, used to refer to manageable cartoons for the expression of anti-manipulation. What is important is the frenzy of politic poetics and the appearance of absurdity. Further, when we rethink about the way art presents itself, we find we needs a more subversive move to get it unlocked. An action itself is its meaning, and the scene is a spiritual engine. Later, I got interested in training, for it leads to collective craziness in answer to certain utilitarian demands. The concept of "social automatic writing" can subvert art only when it is based on social rules.

In what circumstances would you want to destroy your own creation?

It's far more important to destroy a concept than a work.

What do you think about the relation between the art history and artist's work?

History of art is a chain of relation and an artist has to keep creating new links and extend it. History of art is nutritious, but it can't be copied. Any copy of the chains in the art history would be superfluous.

What kind of roles would rational thinking and emotional impulse respectively play in your work?

Affective impulse may be at work when I look for ways to solve a problem, while the implementation mostly involves reason.

侦探计划-1，2008
文献

Detectives' Plan 1,2008
Document

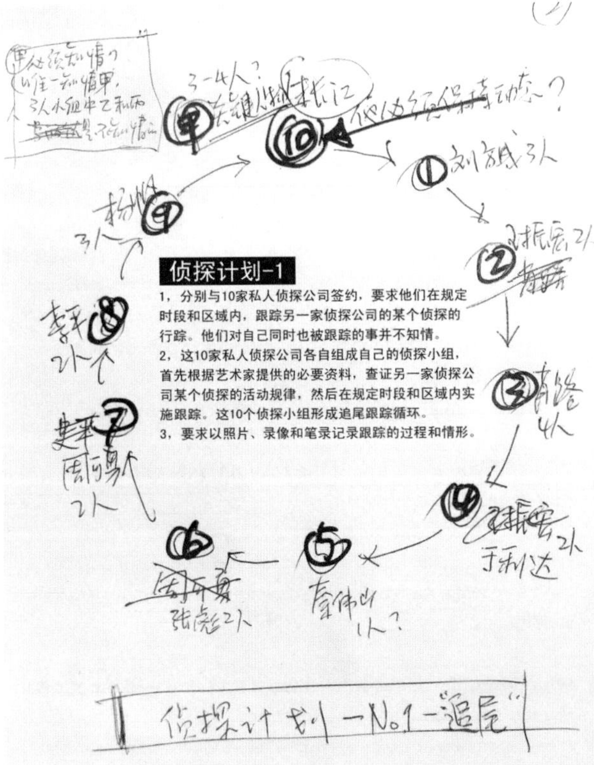

Detective Plan No.1

Sign contacts with ten private detective companies;
ask them to track some detective from another detective
company in the required periods and areas, making sure
that they themselves don't know that they have been tailed.

The ten private detective companies may form their
own detective groups. Based on what the artist provides,
they should first investigate some detective's activity
regularity from other detective company,
and then adopt the tracking in the required periods and areas.
The ten private detective companies form a cycle of tracking
one after another, photos, video tapes and note books are
required to record down the whole processes and occasions.

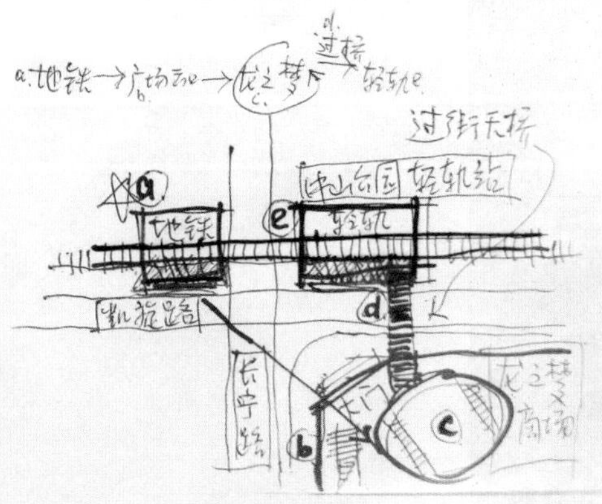

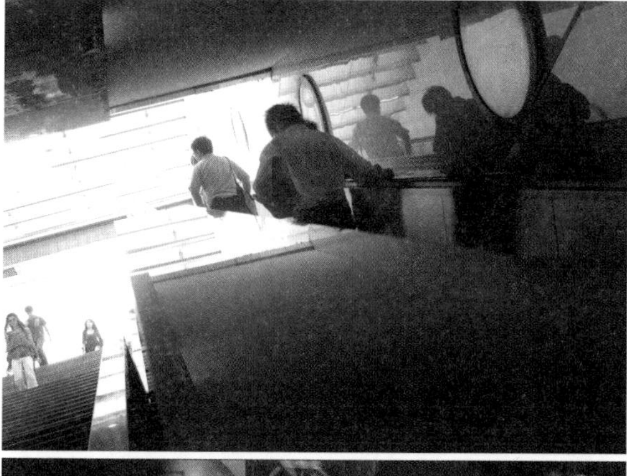
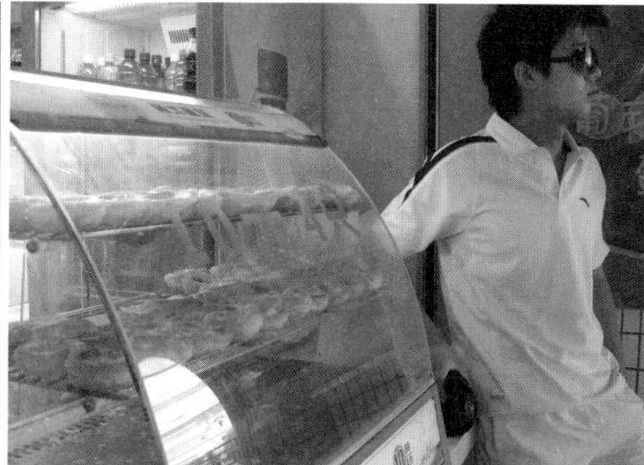
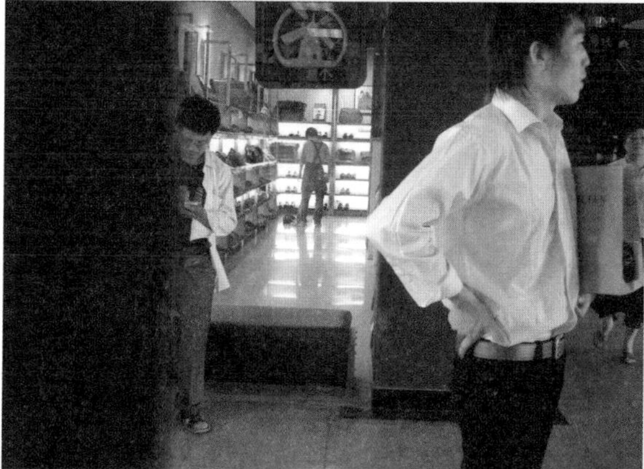
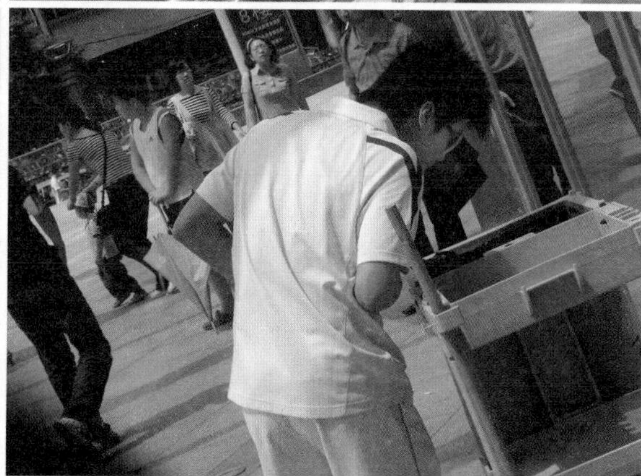
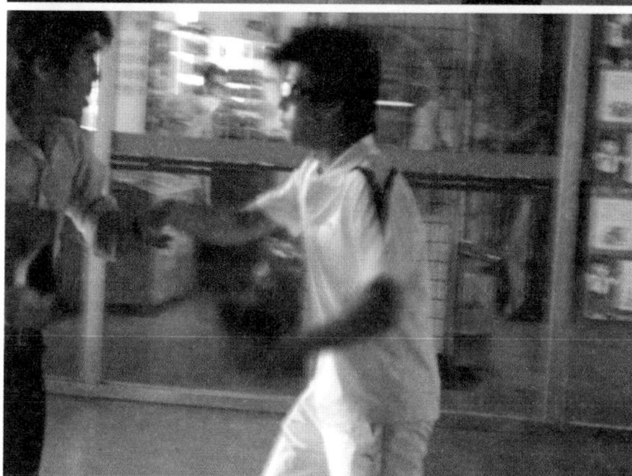
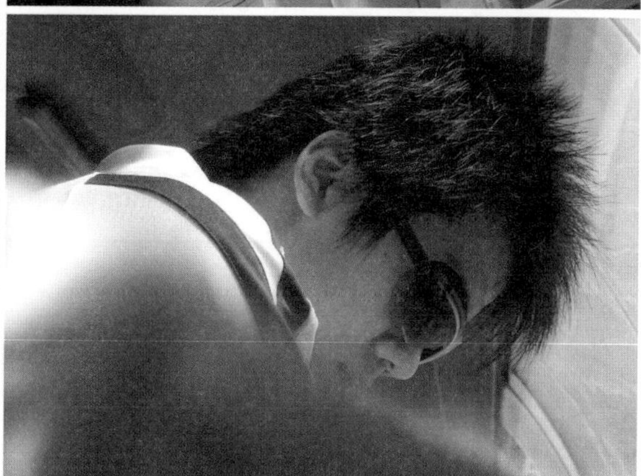

查证任务和说明　Direction of the verification

根据委托人所提供的目标人的相关资料，办案人员调查目标人的活动规律。
本记录只作为事务性查证备忘，不能作为有效的法律证词文本。不得将本记录用于任何胁迫行为，违者将自行承担一切法律责任。

Task and requirement of the verification: based on the materials about the target people provided by the clients, the relevant agents are supposed to investigate the target people's activity regularity.
The record is only used for the clients' transactional verification, memory or reference, which can not be regarded as effective legal parol evidence. The record can't be used for any coercing actions, and those offended will bear sole legal liability by themselves.

笔录5 Record Five

跟踪时间：2008年8月19日下午14点到15点　　　　跟踪地点：上海市中山公园地铁站和龙之梦购物中心
Tracking time: from 2pm to 3pm on August 19, 2008　　**Tracking places:** Shanghai Zhongshan Park metro station and Cloud Nine Shopping Mall
查证人：4——上海某商务调查有限公司。记录者：于利达　　　　　　5——上海某咨询公司，秦伟山
Agent: No.4 one from some Shanghai business research Co. Ltd　Recorder: Yu Lida　　　　Target person: No.5 one from some Shanghai consultant company , Qin Weishan

8月19日下午2点05。在中山公园地铁站2号线的走道，高个秦伟山出现，穿白衬衣，手提一只大纸袋。

2点10分进入麦当劳餐厅，出餐厅看手机短信并且发送短信。

2点15进入地铁商场闲逛。他腋下的大纸袋有破损，纸袋好象很重要，他不停地调整夹拿姿势。

2点25出地铁站，秦伟山是在跟着另一个微胖的男子向前走。从地铁站出来到龙之梦广场，在此停留等待着什么。

2点30秦进入龙之梦商场，乘电梯上二楼闲逛，很散漫，不象是有很明确的目标。

2点45米到通向轻轨的通道，在这里逗留很久，始终跟在胖男的后面，而且保持距离。

2点55秦突然快速跑到胖男的前方，并且把腋下的大纸袋掉转方向，远远地对着胖男，我断定那纸袋里一定是摄象机。

3点多钟秦下楼梯去出口。这时，前方的胖男突然回身向秦冲来，责问秦手里拿的是什么？双方发生激烈的争执，胖男动手抢夺纸袋。

此时有一个穿黑衣男子上来劝架，并且帮胖男夺纸袋，纸袋被两人夺走逃跑，秦在后面急追。目标跟丢。

At 2:05 pm, on August 19th, 2008. Qin Weishan, a tall man appeared in the passage to No.2 Zhongshan Park metro station. He was in a white shirt, with a big paper bag in his hand.
At 2:10pm, he entered into the McDonald restaurant, and then he went out, checking text messages and sending some text messages at the same time.
At 2:15pm, he strolled in the shopping mall. The big bag under his arm was a little broken. The paper bag seemed very important, because he constantly changed his posture of taking it.
At 2:25pm, he went out of the metro station, followed a fat man. After he walked out and came to Cloud Nine Shopping Center, he stayed there waiting.
At 2:30 pm, Qin Weishan entered into Cloud Nine Shopping Mall, went upstairs by elevator, randomly, and he seemed he was not purposed.
At 2:45 pm, he came to the passage to a light railway station, and dwelled here, all along behind the fat man, but they always kept distance.
At 2:55 pm, Qin Weishan suddenly ran to the front of the fat man, and turned the big paper bag under his arm to the fat man far away. I was sure that there must be a camera in the bag.
At around 3 pm, Qin Weishan walked downstairs and walked to the entrance. At the moment, the fat man in the front suddenly turned around and ran towards him, and angrily asked Qin what he took in his hand. A fierce quarrel burst between them. The fat man started to grab the bag. Then a man in black came up to hold them up, and tried to help the fat man to seize the bag. When the bag was grabbed away, Qin Weishan ran after them. But he lost the target finally.

查证任务和说明　Direction of the verification

根据委托人所提供的目标人的相关资料，办案人员调查目标人的活动规律。
本记录只作为事务性查证备忘，不能作为有效的法律证词文本。不得将本记录用于任何胁迫行为，违者将自行承担一切法律责任。

Task and requirement of the verification: based on the materials about the target people provided by the clients, the relevant agents are supposed to investigate the target people's activity regularity.
The record is only used for the clients' transactional verification, memory or reference, which can not be regarded as effective legal parol evidence. The record can't be used for any coercing actions, and those offended will bear sole legal liability by themselves.

笔录6 Record Six

跟踪时间：2008年8月19日下午14点到15点　　　　跟踪地点：上海市中山公园地铁站和龙之梦购物中心
Tracking time: from 2pm to 3pm on August 19, 2008　　**Tracking places:** Shanghai Zhongshan Park metro station and Cloud Nine Shopping Mall
查证人：5——上海某咨询公司。记录者：秦伟山　　　　　　目标人：6——上海某调查事务所，张彪
Agent: No.5 one from some Shanghai consultant company　Recorder: Qin Weishan　　　　Target person: No.6 one from some Shanghai research firm , Zhang Biao

8月19日，今天下午14点07分，上海某调查事务所张彪出现中山公园地铁站内。张彪身着一身白衣，戴墨镜，手持一只黑色小包。

张彪进入麦当劳餐厅，左顾右盼地转悠。出餐厅后行为诡秘、鬼鬼闪闪。出地铁，从龙之梦广场进入商场。乘电梯上二楼商场。

又从二楼商场晃到通往轻轨的通道。

张彪一直保持晃晃悠悠、漫无目标的样子。但是他始终对垃圾箱十分感兴趣，只要遇到垃圾箱，他都会向内仔细地观察。

而且他手持黑色小包的姿态也很可疑。

快要离开轻轨站时，张彪突然转身气势汹汹地向我走来。责问我纸袋是什么，张彪动手抢我的纸袋，他还有一个帮凶，我的东西被他们抢走。

On August 19th, at 14:07 pm, Zhang Biao, from some Shanghai research firm, appeared in Zhongshan Park metro station, who was in white, wearing a pair of sunglasses, with a small black bag in his hand.
Zhang Biao walked into the McDonald restaurant, strolled there, looking around. Outside the metro station, he went to the shopping mall through Cloud Nine Square. He went upstairs by lift and then he walked from the second floor to the passage to a light railway station.
Zhang Biao kept a figure of walking unsteadily and aimlessly. But he was always interested in the dustbins. Whenever he met a dustbin, he would observe it carefully. What's more, his holding the black bag was very doubtful.
When he was leaving the light railway station, Zhang Biao suddenly turned around and walked towards me angrily. He asked what was inside my paper bag, then he began grabbing my bag, unfortunately he had a partner to help him. Finally my bag was seized away by them.

2008实施的综合行动作品《侦探计划—追尾》，用电视媒体装置、摄影和文本呈现。这是我利用社会资源炮制的一个"实训项目"。在互联网中，可以搜索到成千上万条关于侦探公司的信息，好像我们的生活突然间需要大量这样的服务。我有了一个恶作剧的念头：可以借助于侦探公司这个社会奇观来设一个局。我希望这个作品不需要经过我的手去拍摄，消除个人过多的主观介入。拍摄工作的目的，变成为单纯的为了清晰记录实时的现场和过程情形、是为了完成雇主的提出的要求，当然不会有任何的美学标准的限制。我设计一个大的框架，接下来让它自由生长。这个作品完成以后，我获得一个有意思概念：可以称之为"社会自动写作"，更准确地说，是"社会发生学"式的创作手段。将会发生什么？将会得到怎样的结果？一切依赖社会自身的规则自然发生，没有确切的定数，带有很大的冒险成分。

我分别与10家私人侦探公司签约，雇用他们在规定时段和区域内，跟踪另一家侦探公司某个侦探的行踪。当然，他对自己同时也被跟踪的事是不知情的。在我指定的时段和区域内，10个侦探在中山公园的龙之梦商场开始相互跟踪，他们在跟踪别人的同时也被跟踪着，形成追尾跟踪循环。同时，他们必须根据我事先协议的要求，用照片、录像和笔录形式记录下各自跟踪对象的状态和情形。

2009年，在另一件双频道录像作品《我买单，我享有特权》中，我意图在"社会发生学"或"社会自动写作"概念上走的更远些。

Detectives' Plan : Tagging, completed in 2008, is a comprehensive action work including TV media installation, photographs and texts. It is a "training program" based on social resources. On Internet one can find more than plenty of information about detective agencies, so it seems as if, all of a sudden, we find ourselves in dire need of such service in such quantity. A practical joke struck me—to devise a game by means of such a social wonder as detective agencies. In order to keep subjective intervention to the minimum, I chose not to shoot the video by myself. The aim of the shooting therefore turned out to be no other than recording truthfully and clearly the setting and the plot to fulfill the task given by the client, there obviously being no aesthetical restrictions. What I did is to provide nothing but a framework for its free growth. The conclusion of this work led me to an interesting concept, "social automatic writing" as it might be called, or more precisely, a technique of social genological style. What will happen? How will it end? Everything runs its own course. Nothing is certain, and it involves great adventure.

Respectively I signed contracts with ten private detective agencies asking them to follow some detective from another agency in a specified place within specified time. Of course, this detective did not know that he was to be followed as well. Ten detectives began to track each other in Dragon's Dream Shopping Mall near Zhongshan Park in the time and place I specified. Tracking and getting tracked, they formed a tracking cycle. They had to, in the meanwhile, record what ever happened to their objects with photographs, video and a pen, as was required in the contract.

With I paid, so I have the privilege, another dual channel video work in 2009, I hope to go further along the line of "social genology" or "social automatic writing".

侦探计划—追尾，2008
录像装置

Detectives' Plan: Tagging, 2008
Video installation

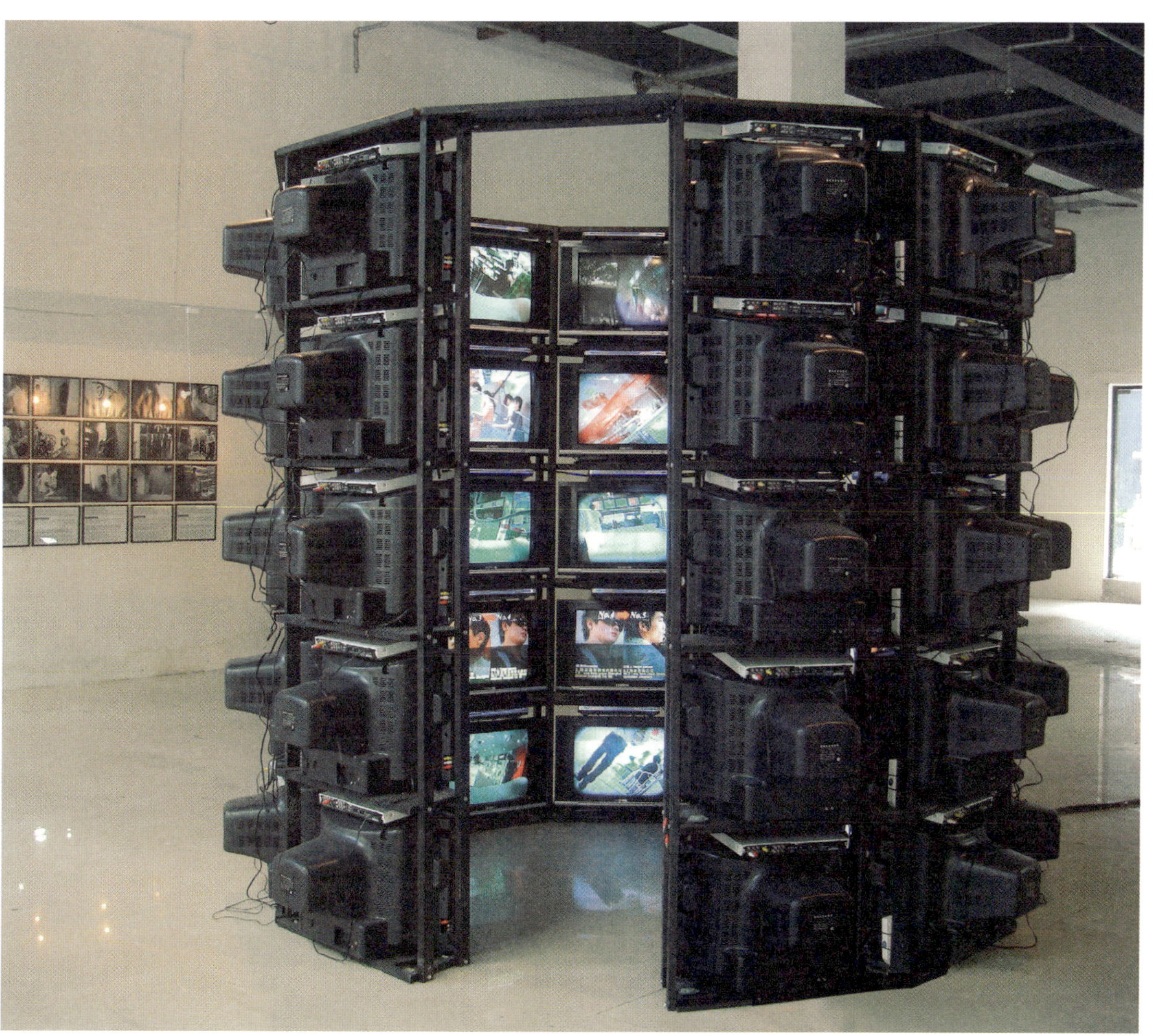

艺术家简历

BIOGRAPHY

董文胜

1970年出生于江苏赣榆。现工作生活于常州。

Dong Wensheng

1970 Born in Jiangsu Province, China. Currently works and lives in Changzhou, China

何云昌

1967年出生于云南。现生活和工作于北京。

He Yunchang (A Chang)

1967 Born in Yunnan, China. Currently lives and works in Beijing, China

蒋志

1971年生于湖南沅江。1995年毕业于中国美术学院。现居住和工作在深圳和北京。

Jiang Zhi

1971 Born in Yuanjiang, China. 1995 Graduated from China Academy of Fine Arts. Currently lives and works in Shenzhen and Beijing, China

金石

1976年生于中国河南。2005年毕业于中国美术学院雕塑系。现工作生活于中国杭州。

Jin Shi

1976 Born in Henan Province. 2005 MA Department of Sculpture,the China Academy of Fine Arts. Currently lives and works in Hangzhou.

李超

1983年出生于江苏南京。2007年毕业于中央美术学院壁画系。现生活于北京。

Li Chao

1983 Born in Nanjing, Jiangsu Province, China. 2007 Graduated from Department of Murals, Central Academy of Fine Arts, Beijing, China

李景湖

1972年生于广东东莞。1996年毕业于华南师范大学美术系。现工作生活于东莞长安。

Li Jinghu

1972 Born in Dongguan, Guangdong Province. 1996 Graduated from South China Normal University,
Fine Arts Department . Currently lives and works in Chang' an, Guangdong Province .

李明

1986年生于湖南。2008年毕业于中国美术学院新媒体系。

Li Ming

1986 Born in Hunan,China. 2008 Graduated from China Academy of Fine Arts, New Media Art Department.

李超

1983年出生于江苏南京。2007年毕业于中央美术学院壁画系。现生活于北京。

Li Chao

1983 Born in Nanjing, Jiangsu Province, China. 2007 Graduated from Department of Murals,
Central Academy of Fine Arts, Beijing, China

梁硕

1976年生于天津蓟县。2000年毕业于中央美术学院雕塑系。2002-2007年任教于清华大学美术学院雕塑系。
2009至今任教于中央美术学院雕塑系。现生活工作在北京。

Liang Shuo

1976 Born in Jixian of Tianjin Province. 2000 Graduated from the Central Academy of Fine Arts,
Sculpture Major. 2002-2007 Teacher of Tsinghua University - Academy of Arts and Design, Sculpture
Major. 2009 Teacher of Central Academy of Fine Arts, Sculpture Major. Currently lives and works in Beijing

李郁

1973年生于湖北武汉。1995年毕业于华中师范大学信息技术系。现工作生活于武汉。

Li Yu

1973 Born in Wuhan, Hubei, China. 1995 Graduated from Information Technology Department, Central China
Normal University. Currently works and lives in Wuhan, China.

刘波

1977年生于湖北石首。2001年毕业于湖北美术学院油画系。现工作生活于武汉。

Liu Bo

1977 Born in Shishou, Hubei, 2001 Graduated from Hubei Institute of Fine Arts,Oil Painting Department.

卢征远

1982年出生于辽宁大连。2001- 2006年中央美术学院雕塑系，获学士学位。
2009年获中央美术学院雕塑系硕士学位。现工作生活于北京。

Lu Zhengyuan

1982 Born in Dalian, Liaoning. 2001 - 2006 Bachelor in sculpture, Central Academy of Fine Arts.
2009 Postgraduated from Sculpture Department of CFFA. Currently works and lives in Beijing.

马秋莎

1982年生于中国北京。2005年毕业于中央美术学院数码媒体工作室。
2008年毕业于美国阿尔弗雷德大学电子综合艺术专业。现生活在北京。

Ma Qiusha

1982 Born in Beijing, China. 2001-2005 BFA Central Academy of Fine Arts, Beijing, China. 2008 MFA Electronic Integrated Art, Alfred University, NY, United States.

邱黯雄

1972 年生于四川。1994 年毕业于四川美术学院。2003 年毕业于德国卡塞尔大学艺术学院。
现工作生活于上海，任教于华东师范大学设计学院。

Qiu Anxiong

1972 Born in Sichuan, China. 1994 Graduated from the Sichuan Art Academy, China. 2003 Graduated from Kunsthochschule of University kassel, Germany. Currently works and lives in Shanghai.

石青

1969年生于内蒙古。现工作生活于北京。

Shi Qing

1969 Born in Inner Mongolia, China. Currenty works and lives in Beijing.

苏文祥

1979年生于安徽宣城。2002年毕业于蚌埠高等专科学校美术系。现工作生活于北京。

Su Wenxiang

1979 Born in Xuancheng, Anhui Province, China. 2002 Graduated from The Art & Design Department, Bengbu College, Anhui. Currently works and lives in Beijing.

孙建春

1970年生于中国江苏省南京市高淳县。1995年毕业于南京艺术学院美术系。现工作生活于北京。

Sun Jianchun

1970 Born in Gaochun County, Nanjing, Jiangsu Province, China.
1995 Graduated from the Fine Arts Department of Nanjing Arts Institute with BFA Degree.
Currently works and lives in Beijing.

汤艺

1982年生于重庆。2004年毕业于四川美术学院油画系。现工作生活于北京。

Tang Yi

1982 Born in Chongqing. 2004 BFA, Oil Painting Department, Sichuan Fine Arts Institute. Currently lives and works in Beijing

屠宏涛

1976年出生于中国四川成都。1999年毕业于中国美院油画系。现工作生活于成都、北京。

Tu Hongtao

1976 Born in Chengdu, Sichuan Province, China. 1999 Graduated from the Oil Painting Department, China Academy of Fine Arts. Currently lives and works in Chengdu, China

王光乐

1976年出生于福建。2000年毕业于中央美术学院油画系。现居北京。

Wang Guangle

1976 Born in Songxi, Fujian. 2000 Graduated from Oil Painting Department, Central Academy of Fine Arts, Beijing, China. Currently lives in Beijing, China

王宁德

1972年生于辽宁省宽甸县。1995年毕业于鲁迅美术学院摄影系。现工作生活于北京。

Wang Ningde

1972 Born in Kuandian county,China. 1995 Graduated from Photography Department, Luxun Academy of Fine Arts. Currently lives and works in Beijing

邬建安

1980年生于北京。2002年毕业于北京广播学院广告系，获学士学位。2005年毕业于中央美术学院，获硕士学位并留校任教。现工作生活于北京。

Wu Jian'an

1980 Born in Beijing, China. 2002 Graduated from Beijing Broadcasting Institute. 2005 Post-graduated from Central Academy of Fine Arts. Currently lives and works in Beijing.

吴俊勇

1978年生于福建莆田。1996-2000年中国美术学院版画系。2002-2005年中国美术学院新媒体。现工作生活于北京和杭州，任教于中国美术学院综合艺术系。

Wu Junyong

1978 Born in Fujian Province. 1996-2000 Printmaking Department, 2003-2005 MFA, New Madia Arts Department,China Academy Of Art. Currently works and lives in Beijing and Hangzhou

吴小军

1988年毕业于南京艺术学院。现工作生活于北京。

Wu Xiaojun

1988 Graduate form Nanjing Art Academy, Currently works and lives in Beijing

杨俊

1979年全家移民至澳大利亚。1994-1996 年，Gerrit Rietveld 学院，独立媒体系，阿姆斯特丹，荷兰。1996-2000年，维也纳美术学院，维也纳，奥地利。现工作生活于奥地利维也纳。

Jun Yang

1979 Moved to Australia.1994-1996 Gerrit Rietveld Akademie, Free media department, Amsterdam,Netherlands. 1996-2000 Akademie der Bildenden Künste, Vienna , Austria, Academy of Fine Arts, Vienna, Austria.Lives and works in Vienna ,Austria

张耿豪

1980年生于台湾台北。2003-2007年国立台北艺术大学科技艺术研究所。
1999-2003年国立台湾艺术大学雕塑学系学士。

Chang Kenghau

1980 Taipei Taiwan. 2003-2007 Graduate School of Arts and
Technology, Taipei National University of the Arts. 1999-2003 Sculpture
department,National Taiwan University of Arts.

张耿华

1980年生于台湾台北。1998 – 2002年国立台湾艺术大学雕塑学系学士。
2002年国立台湾艺术大学造形艺术研究所雕塑。

Chang Genghwa

1980 Born in Taipei, Taiwan. 1998-2002 Sculpture Department, National
Taiwan University of Arts. 2002 Graduate School of Arts and Sculpture.
National Taiwan University of Arts.

章清

1977年生于中国江苏省常州。1999年毕业于中国常州工学院。现生活工作于中国上海。

Zhang Qing

1977 Born in Changzhou, Jiangsu Province, China. 1999 Graduated from the Changzhou Institute
of Technology, Changzhou, China. Currently lives and works in Shanghai, China.

赵赵

1982年出生于新疆。2005年毕业于新疆艺术学院。现生活工作于北京。

Zhao Zhao

1982 Born in Xinjiang, China. 2005 Graduated from Xinjiang Fine Arts University.
Currently lives and works in Beijing.

赵要

1981年生于中国四川泸县。2004年毕业于四川美院设计艺术系。现生活工作于北京。

Zhao Yao

1981 Born in LUZHOU, Sichuan Province, China. 2004 Graduated from the Design Arts Department in
Sichuan Fine Arts Institute. Currently lives and works in Beijing.

周啸虎

1960年生于中国江苏省常州市。1989年毕业于中国四川美术学院。现生活工作于上海。

Zhou Xiaohu

1960 Born in Changzhou, Jiangsu Province, China. 1989 Graduated from the Sichuan Academy of Fine Arts, China.
Currently lives and Works in Shanghai.

工作坊：艺术家是如何工作的
Work in Progress: How Do Artists Work?

主办：西班牙国际文化艺术基金会 /《艺术与投资》&《当代艺术与投资》杂志社
Presented by: International Art & Culture Foundation of Spain
Art & Investment and *Contemporary Art & Investment* Magazines
协办：伊比利亚当代艺术中心
Co-organized by: Iberia Center for Contemporary Art

伊比利亚当代艺术中心
2009年12月5日 — 2010年1月9日
中国北京市朝阳区酒仙桥路4号798艺术区E06
Iberia Center for Contemporary Art | Beijing
2009/12/05 – 2010/01/09
E06, 798 Art Zone, No.4 Jiuxianqiao Rd., Chaoyang District, Beijing, China

www.iberiart.org / info@iberiart.org / Fax +86 (0) 10 5978 9537 / Phone +86 (0) 10 5978 9530

艺术家：
董文胜、何云昌、蒋志、金石、李超、李景湖、李明、梁硕、李郁/刘波、卢征远、马秋莎、邱黯雄、
石青、苏文祥、孙建春、汤艺、屠宏涛、王光乐、王宁德、邬建安、吴俊勇、吴小军、杨俊、张耿豪华、
章清、赵要、赵赵、周啸虎

Artists:
Chang Kenghau & Chang Genghwa, Dong Wensheng, He Yunchang, Jiang Zhi, Jin Shi, Li Chao, Li
Jinghu, Li Ming, Liang Shuo, Li Yu&Liu Bo, Lu Zhengyuan, Ma Qiusha, Qiu Anxiong, Shi Qing, Su
Wenxiang, Sun Jianchun, Tang Yi, Tu Hongtao, Wang Guangle, Wang Ningde, Wu Jian'an, Wu Junyong,
Wu Xiaojun, Jun Yang, Zhang Qing, Zhao Yao, Zhao Zhao, Zhou Xiaohu

总策展人：夏季风
Chief Curator: Xia Jifeng

策展人：左靖、卢迎华、董冰峰、苏文祥
Curators: Zuo Jing, Carol Yinghua Lu, Dong Bingfeng, Su Wenxiang

出品人：高平 / 总监：夏季风 / 艺术总监：左靖
Producer: Gao Ping / Director: Xia Jifeng / Art Director: Zuo Jing

项目负责：谷静
推广：谷静、戴伟平、戴佳芷、陈田
Project Coordinator: Gu Jing
Communications: Dai Weiping, Gu Jing, Dai Jiazhi, Chen Tian

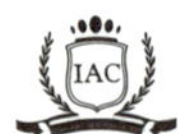 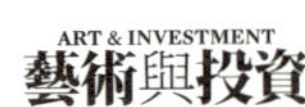 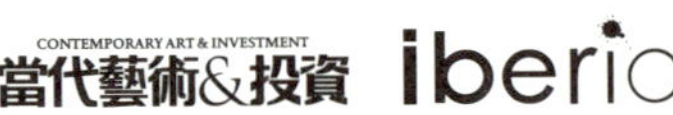 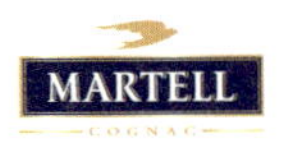

赞助 Sponsor

工作坊：艺术家是如何工作的
Work in Progress: How Do Artists Work?

编辑： 左靖、卢迎华、董冰峰、苏文祥
撰文： 夏季风、左靖、卢迎华、董冰峰、苏文祥
翻译： 陈雪茵、黄静远、戴伟平、吕静静、陈早、戴佳芷、李丙奎、胡争艳
校对： 戈登·劳林、常旭阳、严潇潇、刘品毓、玛吉·康诺利、欧拉·韦纳丽扬
设计： 王云冲

Editors: Zuo Jing, Carol Yinghua Lu, Dong Bingfeng, Su Wenxiang
Text by: Xia Jifeng, Zuo Jing, Carol Yinghua Lu, Dong Bingfeng, Su Wenxiang
Translations: Xueyin Chen, Coco Collins, Dai Weiping, Lv Jingjing, Nicole Chen, Dai Jiazhi, Li Bingkui, Hu Zhengyan
Proofreading: Gordon Laurin, Chang Xuyang, Yanxiaoxiao, Liu Pinyu, Maggie Connolly, Ola Winnerljung
Graphic Design: Wang Yunchong

鸣谢：麦勒画廊
Thanks to: Galerie Urs Meile

出版：
Catalogue published by:

东八时区书店
Timezone 8 Limited
info@timezone8.com
www.timezone8.com

伊比利亚当代艺术中心
Iberia Center for Contemporary Art
info@iberiart.org
www.iberiart.org

timezone 8

2009年印刷于中国北京
Printed in Beijing, China, 2009